Praise for *American Brutus*

"Booth's scheme, as this book intricately reconstructs it, involved much more careful, long-range calculation than has previously been acknowledged. . . . Mr. Kauffman seriously challenges conventional wisdom."
—JANET MASLIN, *The New York Times*

"Kauffman's often minute-by-minute account of the night of [Lincoln's assassination] and its confused aftermath is a wonder of modern scholarship, and his tracing of the histories and motivations of the oddball group of men who followed Booth down this path to destruction is first-rate. . . . [Booth] managed to weave a web of confusion that almost 150 years later has been fully unraveled only by Kauffman's patient scholarship."
—*San Francisco Chronicle*

"Kauffman tells his story with vigor and skill. . . . There can be no doubt that he has done a superb work of research and analysis."
—*The Boston Globe* (top ten nonfiction book of the year)

"[The book] is a well-told story of America's most famous tragedy, related in a manner that gives fresh meaning to each part of it. Along the way, Kauffman challenges a number of conspiracy theories, but his main purpose is to provide an accurate, compelling account of the assassination and its aftermath."
—*St. Louis Post-Dispatch*

"In this crisp work of narrative, Kauffman corrects the record. . . . Like many assassins, Booth led perhaps too rich an interior life. In *American Brutus*, Kauffman captures it perfectly."
—Bloomberg News Service

"[Kauffman] makes a good case for considering his book the last word on the nearly 140-year-old crime."
—*Los Angeles Times*

"[*American Brutus* should] settle all the arguments that have raged for nearly a century and a half about Lincoln's assassin and his cadre of pathetic lunatics and misfits. Kauffman has done incredibly detailed research and is able to trace Booth's movements almost minute by minute. We know how the story ends, but he still manages to keep the reader in suspense."   —JONATHAN YARDLEY, *The Washington Post*
(one of the best nonfiction books of the year)

"The great values of Kauffman's approach are dispassion and mastery of documented detail. Here is the best picture that today's Americans can expect as to what happened, how, and why."   —*Baltimore Sun*

"An exhaustive and well-written examination of Lincoln's killer and the years leading to that fateful night at Ford's Theatre."
—*San Jose Mercury News*

"Thoroughly researched . . . In Kauffman's vivid and often fresh telling, Booth was ruthless in pursuit of his goal. . . . What is so remarkable, as Kauffman amply demonstrates, is how close Booth actually came to killing the three leading executives of the United States."
—*The New York Times Book Review*

"The reconstruction of Lincoln's assassination is as spellbinding as a *Law & Order* episode. . . . Mr. Kauffman creates a gripping portrait of Booth, not as failed actor or Confederate agent, but as a glory-obsessed manipulator."   —*The Dallas Morning News*

"Michael W. Kauffman's *American Brutus* is several unlikely combinations rolled into one: a meticulous history with propulsive narrative power, a fresh take on one of the most examined events in American history, and the eminently rational and convincing product of a raging obsession."
—LAURA MILLER, *Salon.com*

AMERICAN BRUTUS

AMERICAN BRUTUS

JOHN WILKES BOOTH
AND THE LINCOLN CONSPIRACIES

MICHAEL W. KAUFFMAN

RANDOM HOUSE TRADE PAPERBACKS
NEW YORK

2005 Random House Trade Paperback Edition

Copyright © 2004 by Michael W. Kauffman

Published in the United States by Random House Trade Paperbacks,
an imprint of The Random House Publishing Group,
a division of Random House, Inc., New York.

RANDOM HOUSE TRADE PAPERBACKS and colophon are trademarks of Random House, Inc.

Originally published in hardcover in the United States by Random House,
an imprint of The Random House Publishing Group,
a division of Random House, Inc., in 2004.

LIBRARY OF CONGRESS CATALOGING-IN-PUBLICATION DATA
Kauffman, Michael W.
American Brutus: John Wilkes Booth and the Lincoln conspiracies / by Michael W. Kauffman.
p. cm.
Includes bibliographical references and index.
ISBN 0-375-75974-3
1. Lincoln, Abraham, 1809–1865—Assassination. 2. Booth, John Wilkes, 1838–1865. I. Title.
E457.5.K38 2004   364.152'4'097309034—dc22   2004049075

Printed in the United States of America

www.atrandom.com

246897531

Book design by Casey Hampton

For Mary, Emily, and Brian

and in memory of
Michael E. Patten and Lea Anne Brown

CONTENTS

INTRODUCTION

O N THE NIGHT OF APRIL 14, 1865, PRESIDENT ABRAHAM Lincoln was shot by an assassin as he sat in a Washington theater. At the same time, his secretary of state was savagely attacked in his home a few blocks away. Investigation revealed that other men had also been targeted: the vice president, secretary of war, and general in chief of the army. There were subsequent reports of germ warfare, of plans to burn ships and cities, and of a proposal to poison the New York City water supply. The prospect of further attacks kept the nation on edge, and every citizen was on the alert for any sign that terrorists were in their midst. Hundreds of suspects were rounded up on the vaguest suspicions, and some were arrested on looks alone. Of those, many were kept in isolation, bound and hooded, to await a trial by military tribunal. The reaction was unprecedented.

Who did this, and why? How large a conspiracy was behind these attacks? Is this the end, or will more follow? How far can we bend the rule of law to find and punish the conspirators? These were the questions on everyone's lips.

Investigations in 1865 were crude by modern standards. Detectives did not have electronic money transfers, telephone records, or e-mail traffic to track the conspiracy to its roots. Nor did they have the time. After the assassin, John Wilkes Booth, was killed and brought back to Washington, the government turned its attention to Confederate officials and the suspects they already had in custody.

Since then, little has been done to investigate the full extent of the plot, to sort out the conspirators' movements, or to explain the motives behind Lincoln's killing. While new versions of the story are regularly published, they are never based on the best sources, and often rely heavily on the worst. None have critiqued the conspiracy trial with 1860s criminal law in mind. None have examined Booth's mental state based exclusively on facts, as opposed to folklore. And none seem to have considered the key clues to the assassin's own world: the views he espoused, the profession in which he worked, the society in which he moved. They have lifted him out of his own time and surroundings, as if such things were irrelevant. Borrowing heavily from other sources, they then repeat their same mistakes.

The Lincoln conspiracy demands another look. Generations of readers have been fascinated by its drama, its intrigue, and especially by its leading character. John Wilkes Booth was a captivating person. Traveling in the highest social circles, with a roster of friends that included some of the most notable people of the era, he was remembered fondly even by Unionists. This, I think, is the real mystery of the case. How could this lover of nature, this gentle poet who touched so many hearts, who frolicked on the floor with his nieces and nephews, and who practiced sign language in order to converse with a deaf poetess—how could this man be the embodiment of evil, and the perpetrator of such a cold-blooded crime? This question lies at the heart of the story. Without examining it, we can never hope to understand the "one mad act" that played such a momentous role in the shaping of our nation.

Many writers contend that Booth was *not* the guiding spirit of the plot, that he was little more than a rabid Southerner whose mind lost its balance as both the Confederacy and his professional career collapsed, and that he acted merely as a pawn, following the orders of a larger cabal. And though some authors have taken pains to find (or fabricate) a connection between him and some sponsoring organization, they have all failed to take even the most basic steps to sort out the movements of this criminal conspiracy. Invariably, they oversimplify, and in doing so, rob the story of its essential interest.

Most pundits now agree that the conspiracy's original intent had been to capture the president. The public first assumed that Confederate officials had urged Booth to do so. Later accounts averred that a coup within the Lincoln administration, led by Secretary of War Edwin Stanton, had set the plan in motion. At various times the Catholic Church, the secret Knights of the Golden Circle, and unnamed Jewish bankers were also blamed for the killing. The literature has come full circle, and in recent years has implicated Confederate leaders once more. Each of these theories was constructed using dubious reasoning rather than hard evidence. None gave much weight to the temper of the times.

The shooting of Abraham Lincoln came at a critical juncture: millions in the North were rejoicing, and their brethren in the South had just begun to accept the inevitability of defeat. Win or lose, a sense of relief was finally setting in, and attention turned once more to a future that *had* to be brighter than the recent past. The assassination changed everything. Lincoln supporters were stunned and outraged at what seemed a senseless act of revenge. His opponents, put on the defensive, had to disavow the killing or maintain a respectful silence. Even those who understood Booth's motives dared not explain them, lest they appear to excuse his crime.

Newspapers were constrained by many factors. The press conference had not yet been invented, and ambush-style interviews were out of the question. Most journalists considered themselves passive observers, not detectives, and few thought to contact witnesses, investigators, or families of the accused. Leaked affidavits, government press releases, and unchecked rumors were their main sources. While these helped flesh out the story, they were often inaccurate and misleading.

Most of the evidence was in federal hands, and the government did relatively little to analyze it. In any event, its detectives might not have been up to the task. They were not experts in criminal profiling or the forensic sciences. None were trained investigators in any modern sense, and most had been farmers, sign hangers, tinners, or merchants just a few years before. They lacked the resources, the experience, and by some accounts even the ordinary brainpower needed to perform an in-depth study of this monumental crime. The most prominent investigators were not even in Washington at the time of the shooting, and in some cases it took the War Department more than a full day to locate them. Once on the case, each went his own way in a mad scramble to catch up. They ignored potential witnesses, took few notes, and lost some of the most important evidence in the case. They rarely consulted one another on what questions to ask, so their interrogations were disorganized and incomplete. Some even spread false rumors to throw others off course.

No single person was assigned to keep track of the leads, the witnesses, and the available resources. Cavalry raids and search patrols were almost never coordinated. The city was not sealed off for hours after the shooting. Booth's photograph was not distributed until more than a day had passed. The next best thing—a verbal description—caused hundreds of innocent men to be arrested simply because they fit the bill. Though today we would deem this a slapdash investigation, bear in mind that the world was a different place in 1865. Even after years of reflection, most investigators remained proud of their work. By their standards, they had done well.

The detectives' notes were not much more than a pile of scribbles, memos, and fragmentary statements. While prosecutors had a difficult chore in making sense of it all, they were in a better position than the historians who followed; later researchers would no longer have access to witnesses or evidence lost in the interim. Indeed, many of the documents used in the conspiracy trial have subsequently disappeared. Some were lent to the district attorney's office for the 1867 trial of John Surratt, and they never made it back. Others disappeared after a House committee borrowed them for the Andrew Johnson impeachment hearings. Thousands of useful items had never been given to prosecutors in the first place. They went instead to the Adjutant General's office, to the House committee of claims, or to the private collections of those who had found or produced them.

Most trial papers, however, remained in the War Department's possession. They were tucked away until the 1930s, unknown to all but a few, while researchers turned to aging witnesses for the "best" accounts of what had transpired in the spring of '65. Thousands of these recollections found their way into newspapers over the years, and no editor could resist passing them along as a genuine slice of history. While inconsistent with one another and often distorted by the failings of memory, these first-person accounts are still the most widely used sources of information on the Lincoln assassination.

It has become the custom in historical writing to assert that only the most reliable government documents have been used. This promise is an empty one, and in practice it has always been abandoned at the first opportunity. The truth is, even the best sources—those first-person sworn statements given just after the event—do not tell the whole story. The thoughts and concerns of ordinary people, the waves of terror that gripped the city, and the details of how a particular official heard the news are not the sorts of things one finds in official records. Even a detailed chronology of Booth's plot must be pieced together from scattered bits of information—not all of it reliable. Here, regrettably, intuition and guess-work become a necessary part of the process.

I have presented the case as it developed in 1865. Though I have occa-sionally resorted to more recent recollections to fill in the blanks, I have avoided using any quote, fact, or anecdote that is incompatible with the earliest sources. I've paid particular attention to the context in which a statement was written. To me, it matters a great deal whether someone provided information while defending himself, talking with a friend, specu-lating, or trying to shore up a claim for reward money. The words used by other writers have often turned out to be those of a third party—such as a detective or soldier—and not of the subject named in the document.

Even the best sources do not amount to much unless they are organized. For that, I turned to modern technology. Though I bought my first com-puter for its word processing capabilities, I soon began experimenting with a database program in hopes of storing and working with historical infor-mation. I used microfilm purchased from the National Archives, inputting synopses of each and every document found in the eleven-thousand-page Lincoln Assassination Suspects file. Through trial and error, I found ways to organize and sort this data by hundreds of different criteria. I could call up everything that happened in Surrattsville, in chronological order, dur-ing any time covered in the records. I could quickly find any event that in-volved, say, George Atzerodt, and I could sort those entries by date, by place, or by the names of other people mentioned in the same context. I could list all the arrests of suspects, all of Booth's arrests, all financial deal-ings, and all references to his horse, his health, or the quality of his voice. Without being sorted or analyzed, all these government records meant very little.

The event-based system I designed was far different from the statisti-cal models used by most historians, and it may actually be unique in the way it applies technology to the study of historical developments. Most important, it works. It brought to the fore new relationships among the plotters, unnoticed patterns in Booth's behavior, and a fresh significance to events I once considered unimportant. All this has given me a clearer pic-ture of the Booth conspiracy—including incidents no writer had previously noticed. I found recruiting trips, secret meetings, and a dozen visits by Booth to New York City—which suggest a Northern connection that, in light of this long neglect, may never be explained. By sorting events over time, I could see how one conspirator fades from the scene while another is shoved into his place. I got a sense of how much work and money went into the plot. I noticed how carefully choreographed the scheme really was. But most surprising of all, I learned how Booth managed to organize and run a dangerous plot—*undetected*—in the face of unprecedented government paranoia.

Misdirection was Booth's secret weapon. It was not only a form of life insurance, but it helped him place attention just where he wanted it. Through lies and false insinuations, he crafted the impression that his conspiracy against Lincoln was larger than it actually was. He did this to boost his credibility, to confuse potential witnesses, to prod his cohorts into action, and to entrap anyone who might potentially betray his trust.

It seems clever in retrospect, but it wasn't hard to do. He told friends he was heading for New York when he was actually going to Washington. He claimed to have struck it rich in the oil business, though he never made a cent. He implied he was working with Confederate agents, but his only contacts were personal. He stretched the facts at every phase of the plot. On stage or off, he was always an actor.

I once thought of Booth as a tragic figure, torn between competing ideals and led by hubris and emotion to commit one of history's greatest blunders. He was a traitor *and* a patriot; a villain to some and a hero to others. But there was more to Booth behind his carefully constructed wall of lies. He was more cunning and complex than I had ever imagined. He wasn't just caught in the middle; he worked his way there, playing one side against the other and taking full advantage of their mutual distrust. He was a manipulator, not a pawn.

The pattern of his lies calls into question almost everything Booth said about the plot, and about all those involved. It certainly puts a different spin on the case of Dr. Samuel A. Mudd. Much has been written about Mudd, and lately his detractors seem to have gotten the upper hand. But they have built their case on faulty assumptions. They assume the literal truth of every damaging statement, though it may be hearsay twice removed. They consider all proffered information accurate, even when it was recorded many years after the fact. They seem to think that Booth was reckless with sensitive information, that he was scrupulously honest, and that he was a monumentally poor judge of his cohorts. The facts simply don't support that view.

Nearly all the evidence pertaining to Dr. Mudd is ambiguous, but I cannot interrupt the narrative to explain every plot development in terms of his guilt, then again in terms of his innocence. For practical purposes, I must write from a single perspective all the way through. So I chose a particular view based on the totality of the evidence. My opinion on Dr. Mudd's case will rankle those who have always understood the facts to be different, but I ask them to suspend their disbelief, and in time, they will see how the story develops and why I made the choices I did. My arguments on reasoning and evidence are fully laid out in the notes.

A great many history buffs have given their lives to this subject, and they're always quick to point out factual errors. They howled at Jim Bishop's description, in *The Day Lincoln Was Shot,* of Corporal James Tanner *tiptoeing* quietly up to the president's deathbed, because in fact Tanner had lost both feet at Bull Run. They smirked at the frequent references to John Surratt's "acquittal" on murder charges, when in fact it was a hung jury. They cringe at the phrase "Lower Maryland"; down here it's *Southern* Maryland. Trivial though they are, such details often say a lot about the bigger picture. For example, whether Booth hobbled across the theater stage or deliberately strode is of little importance in itself. But the "stagey stride" described by eyewitnesses speaks of self-possession, not panic. And the fact that Booth lost his hat on the stage would hardly be worth mentioning, except that he had put a spare in his saddlebag. This demonstrates, as we shall see, an astonishing degree of premeditation.

I have tried to remain faithful to the original records. The only liberty I have taken is to arrange the order of events to make sense of them chronologically. The times and dates given in the original records were hopelessly confused, and their lack of consistency was a constant source of frustration. Rest assured that the timing I give for every event is corroborated by other evidence.

For me, the study of Lincoln's assassination was not merely an exercise in historical detection. It was an interactive affair, and required personal involvement. I've walked the same roads and alleys that Booth took; rowed the same waters on the Potomac; jumped to the stage of Ford's Theatre; and spent more than four hundred nights in the Booth family home. I've even burned down a tobacco barn like the one in which Booth was trapped. And as I drive home across the Navy Yard Bridge at night, I look for the moon that rises over the heights in the distance. On some nights it is enormous; it gives me chills to think that this same moon lighted the way for Lincoln's killer as he passed this spot in his first hour on the run.

This story will always have an element of mystery, but its solution may not be out of reach. Though many questions remain, many answers have been hidden for all these years in plain sight. It is time to take another look.

AMERICAN BRUTUS

ONE

"BY GOD, THEN, IS JOHN BOOTH CRAZY?"

GOOD FRIDAY HAD NEVER BEEN A WELL-ATTENDED NIGHT at the theater, but on that evening, the city of Washington was in a partying mood. On Palm Sunday, General Robert E. Lee had surrendered his Virginia troops to General Ulysses S. Grant at the village of Appomattox Court House. Though some forces remained in the field, Lee had been the greatest obstacle on the path to victory. Now that his troops were out of the way, the bloodiest war in America's history would soon be over, and the celebrations had already begun. Four years to the day after its surrender, Fort Sumter was again under the Stars and Stripes. The flag raising there that day was marked with speeches, music, and prayers of thanks. There were prayers in Washington as well, but a lighter, more carefree atmosphere prevailed. There, buildings were "illuminated" with gas jets configured in the shape of stars, eagles, or words such as "peace" and "victory." The city's population, which had ballooned to more than two hundred thousand during the war, had gone crazy. The streets were crawling with silly, drunken revelers—soldiers back from the war, tourists passing through, and all the usual odds and ends—staggering from one bar to another in search of a party and another toast to the military victors. All things considered, maybe this Good Friday 1865 was not such a bad night for the theater after all.

Ford's Theatre, on Tenth Street, was one of Washington's leading establishments. It had all the amenities of a first-rate playhouse. Its owner, John T. Ford, presented the finest talent the American stage had to offer. The audience that turned out this night made up a pretty fair cross section of Washington society: clerks, businessmen, politicians, tourists. And of course, there were soldiers. An ever-present part of life in the capital, they came to Ford's from every camp, fort, and hospital in the area, their dark blue uniforms scattered among the hoopskirts and crinolines. Some wore the light blue of the Veterans' Reserve Corps, whose members once served in the ranks but were no longer suited for combat or strenuous duty. Here, they mingled comfortably with socialites, power brokers, and people from all walks of life. It was a diverse crowd, but nearly everyone had something in common, which explained, in large measure, the *need* to be in a house of entertainment on such a holy day: these people had been through hell.

One could hardly name an event in recent history that someone in this audience had not witnessed. Here were the veterans of Bull Run, Shiloh, and Gettysburg; the political warriors who shaped the nation; and the commercial giants of the age. One man had survived the horrors of Andersonville prison, and others had just arrived from Appomattox. This was more than just a "large and fashionable audience"; the people who came to Ford's Theatre that night had already been eyewitnesses to history. No doubt they were eager to get back to an ordinary life.[1]

The play was *Our American Cousin,* a popular British comedy from the 1850s. Its humor was derived from the homespun "Yankeeisms" of Asa Trenchard, a backwoods Vermonter, and the physical eccentricities of Lord Dundreary, a self-important British nobleman. The star was Laura Keene, a London native, whose character, Florence Trenchard, believes that her cousin Asa (played by actor Harry Hawk) has just inherited the family fortune. Florence and her British relatives try to stay in Asa's good graces, but find it difficult to overlook his crass country-boy manners. It is this culture clash that carries the play.[2]

For most of the audience that night, however, *Our American Cousin* was not the main attraction. A notice in that day's *Evening Star* had announced that President Abraham Lincoln and his wife would attend the performance. Their guest would be Ulysses S. Grant, lieutenant general of the army, victor of the recent war, hero of the hour. Their surprise reservation had come in that morning, and it sent Harry Clay Ford, brother of the theater's owner, on a mad dash to organize a special program. A patriotic song called "Honor to Our Soldiers" was written for the occasion, and Ford sent notices of it to the *Evening Star*. He even redesigned the evening's playbill to reflect the new developments. By late afternoon, the reservations were rolling in. A normally dismal night was now showing some promise. By curtain time, at eight o'clock, Ford's Theatre had a fairly good house.[3]

Abraham Lincoln was famously fond of the theater, and had passed many an evening at Ford's or its competitor, the National. At Ford's, he always occupied the same box, on the right side, directly above the stage. It was an oddly shaped space with sharp angles and cramped, narrow corners, accessible only through a narrow passageway just off the balcony. It actually consisted of two boxes, numbered 7 and 8, which were normally divided by a partition. Stagehands set aside the divider and brought in more comfortable furniture to fill the space. For the president, a large walnut rocker, upholstered in burgundy damask, was placed in the corner nearest the door. A matching sofa went along the rear wall of the box, and the third piece, a large, comfortable armchair, was placed in the "upstage" corner, farthest from the door. The box had just enough space for those chairs, plus a small one for Mrs. Lincoln.

American flags were hung on either side, and two more were draped over the front balustrade. The blue standard of the Treasury Guards hung on a staff in the center, just above a gilt-framed portrait of George Washington. The flags added more than just a festive dash of color. They let everyone know where to look for the hero of Appomattox. Make no mistake about it: General Grant, and not Lincoln, was the evening's chief attraction.

James P. Ferguson was keeping an eye out for the general. Ferguson owned a saloon next door to the theater, and he always made a point of attending when the president was there. But he took a particular interest in Ulysses S. Grant, whom he claimed to have known since boyhood. When Harry Ford told him that Grant was coming, Ferguson bought two tickets for the dress circle, or first balcony, with a clear view into the box directly opposite. With the best seats in the house, "Fergy" brought along his young sweetheart so she could see the general as well.[4]

They were in for a disappointment. General Grant had taken an afternoon train home to Burlington, New Jersey. A young couple came to the theater in his place. The presidential party arrived late, and as they appeared in the dress circle, the audience burst into a long, spontaneous ovation. The president acknowledged the approbation with a smile, then took his seat, partly hidden behind a flag. Miss Clara Harris took a seat at the far side of the box, and her fiancé, Major Henry Rathbone, sat on the sofa just behind her. Though Grant's absence was a disappointment, many in the audience assumed he would appear later. Ferguson, for one, kept a lookout for him.

By ten-fifteen, *Our American Cousin* had progressed to the second scene of the third act. Asa Trenchard had just told a woman named Mrs. Mountchessington that he hadn't inherited a fortune after all, as everyone thought, and the character (played by Helen Muzzy) had a change of heart about the marriage she had hoped to arrange between Asa and her daughter Augusta.

ASA (to Augusta): You crave affection, you do. Now I've no fortune, but I'm biling over with affections, which I'm ready to pour out to all of you, like apple sass over roast pork.

MRS. MOUNTCHESSINGTON: Mr. Trenchard, you will please recollect you are addressing my daughter, and in my presence.

ASA: Yes, I'm offering her my heart and hand just as she wants them, with nothing in 'em.

The president's guests seemed to enjoy the play. Miss Harris had been the Lincolns' guest here before. Major Rathbone, of the 12th U.S. Infantry, was not quite so familiar to them. He had commanded a company under Burnside at Antietam and Fredericksburg. More recently, he had served as the head of disbursing for the Provost Marshal General's bureau. Henry and Clara had known each other since childhood, when her widowed father married his widowed mother.[5]

Mary Todd Lincoln seemed especially pleased to make a public appearance that night. Sitting next to the president, she looked radiant in her flowered dress. She seemed to be enjoying a rare moment of happiness, her mind unburdened, for now, by personal loss and suffering. One lady in the audience noticed that Mrs. Lincoln smiled a great deal, and often glanced over at her husband.

The years had weighed heavily on Abraham Lincoln, and an occasional night out gave him a much-needed diversion. But even the theater did not free him from the weight of his duties. Twice he was interrupted by the delivery of messages. Charles Forbes, the White House messenger, brought one dispatch, then took a seat outside the entrance to the box. A newspaper reporter named Hanscom brought the other. Neither message seemed to require an immediate response, and the president settled quietly back in his rocking chair, head propped in his hand, looking lost in thought.

Though Lincoln was hidden from view most of the time, he occasionally leaned over the box railing to look down into the audience. That is how Isaac Jacquette, in the dress circle, got his first look at him. It was halfway into the play, and a woman sitting nearby remarked that she had never seen the president before. A man whispered that she might see him now, as he was leaning forward. Every time he came into view, the president stole the show.[6]

On the far side of the dress circle, James Ferguson, still watching for General Grant, had borrowed his girlfriend's opera glasses for a closer view. He noticed a dark-haired man with a large black mustache walking toward the box from the rear of the dress circle. It was the actor John Wilkes Booth—as usual, immaculately dressed and groomed. Ferguson watched Booth inch his way past a clump of people who had moved their chairs against the wall for a better look at the stage. Booth then stopped near the entrance to Lincoln's box and stood there for a moment, hat in hand, looking around.[7]

On stage, Augusta Mountchessington realized she'd been wasting her time with the American cousin. She left the room in disgust, and her mother turned to Asa. "I am aware, Mr. Trenchard, you are not used to the manners of good society, and that, alone, will excuse the impertinence of which you have been guilty." She stormed off stage right, away from the president's box. Now alone on the stage, Trenchard said, half to himself, "Don't know the manners of good society, eh? Wal, I guess I know enough to turn you inside out, old gal—you sockdologizing old man-trap!"[8]

The actor Harry Hawk had turned to follow the lady off stage when he was startled by a loud pop. Spinning around, he saw a commotion up in the president's box. A man in black made a quick jerking movement, then stepped out of the shadows, his face glowing eerily from the stage lights below. The man stood there, wrapped in a veil of smoke, and hissed out the words *"Sic semper tyrannis!"* Then he suddenly vaulted over the balustrade and dropped to the stage more than twelve feet below. Landing slightly off balance, he rose to his full height, then raised a gleaming dagger triumphantly over his head. "The South shall be free!" he cried. With that he dashed straight toward Hawk, who turned and fled in terror. The man disappeared into the wings.[9]

In the box office next to the lobby, Harry Ford was tallying receipts while ticket agents Joseph Sessford and Thomas Raybold talked with Laura Keene's manager. They all heard the gunshot, and Ford looked up from his tally. "That was not in the piece," he said. The men exchanged puzzled glances, then made a dash for the window that looked out toward the stage. Ford reached it just in time to see a man rising to his feet with a knife in his hand. He looked familiar, but before Harry Ford could even form the words, Joe Sessford spoke for him. "By God, then, is John Booth crazy?"

John Booth. To those who knew him, this dramatic interruption did not make sense. Booth's late father had been known for his antics on stage and off, but his son had always tried to live that down. He had led a decent life, traveled in good society, and made a respectable name for himself. He was a longtime friend of the Fords, and disrupting one of their productions was entirely out of character for him. To Sessford, it smelled like a cheap stunt, nothing more serious than that.

Nearly everyone was slow to catch on. People in the audience thought something new had been added for the president's appearance. Some wondered if a piece of the set had collapsed, and one audience member even thought a pistol shot had been incorporated into the script. John F. Sleichman, a scene shifter, was standing backstage with James L. Maddox, the property man, when they heard the shot. Sleichman figured a part of the president's box must have collapsed. But when he told Maddox, the property man stepped into position for a look. What he saw instead was John Wilkes Booth darting across the stage with a knife.[10]

A piercing scream came from the president's box, and in an instant everyone knew. To Isaac Jacquette, in the dress circle, that scream was like a slap in the face. A murder had been committed right in front of him, and neither he nor anyone else had done a thing about it. Edwin Bates, a businessman from Vermont, thought it was fear that froze everyone in their seats. "The actors seemed no more to comprehend the matter than the audience," he wrote that night. "Or they might perhaps [have] stopped the man as he ran right past them[.] If [only] they had not been intimidated by his dagger." In fact, the audience was full of men in uniform, and dozens of them were armed. One would have thought that after four years of war, *somebody* in the house would have recognized the sound of gunfire. But the element of surprise worked against them. A moment of hesitation was all the killer needed. As Charles Addison Sanford, a young student, put it: "Everybody was confounded & paralyzed . . . no one comprehended the moment. . . . Then all rose up trying to recover themselves—imagining anxiously what it meant & if the President had been assassinated. It was an awful moment."[11]

Major Joseph B. Stewart was the first to react. Stewart, sitting in the front row, had just turned to say something to his sister when he heard the shot. He couldn't tell where the sound had come from, but looking around, he caught a glimpse of a man in black dropping to the stage. The knife in his hand told the story. At six feet five, Stewart might easily have overpowered the assassin, but he never got the chance. By the time he bounded onto the stage, the killer had already vanished into the wings. Stewart followed, but his path to the back door was blocked by a couple of bewildered actors who had wandered into the dark passageway. By the time he got outside, all he saw was the faint silhouette of a man struggling with a horse. Stewart took a swipe at the reins, but the man gained control of the animal, then turned it around and galloped into the darkness.[12]

Like a slow-burning flame, awareness of the shooting built momentum as it swept through the house, and the audience, at first at a low simmer, started to boil. A murder had just been committed in front of them all, and the killer had strode right past them. He had taunted them, and had gotten away with it. In minutes, the stage swarmed with people—men leaping over the orchestra pit, kicking over chairs, and clambering over one another to reach the president's box. Shock and indignation were etched on every visage. Even the veterans had tears streaming down their faces. Some, looking into the box, could see a look of horror frozen on Mrs. Lincoln's face. She let out another shriek, then swooned and fell out of view. Other women in the audience fainted as well.[13]

Saloon owner James P. Ferguson, on the far side of the first balcony, had recognized the man in black as John Wilkes Booth. Ferguson was sure that Booth stared right at him as he ran across the stage. Was he to have been another victim? Not taking any chances, he pushed his female companion to the floor, shielding her behind the balcony railing. As Booth darted across the stage beneath them, they heard him whisper, "I have done it!"[14]

The assassin may have gotten away, but certainly not by intimidation. Many of those present had faced far greater dangers than a man with a knife. Lt. John J. Toffey of the 10th V.R.C., for example, was one of those who froze when Booth ran by. Once, while serving with the 33rd New Jersey Infantry, Toffey had launched a ferocious assault on the enemy that would earn him a gunshot wound in the hip and (eventually) a Medal of Honor. Yet in Ford's Theatre, all he could do was stare vacantly as the killer fled. Self-reproach ate at him. "I had a Revolver with me," he wrote, "and would to God I had presence of mind enough at the time the man jumped down to have shot him. Several other officers had revolvers but the thing was done so quick that there was hardly time to draw them and shoot."[15]

In fact, nobody even drew, and though a few men did make a rush for the back door, for a variety of reasons they went no farther. James S. Knox and E. D. Wray were among those who ran to the stage. Wray made a detour to pick something up off the stage, and others stopped when they heard a woman say, "They'll get him" or "They've got him"—nobody was sure which. Only a few actually went out the back door, and the only person they found there was a frightened young boy, who said that Mr. Booth had struck him on the head with something as he mounted his horse.[16]

In the president's box, Mrs. Lincoln clutched her husband, pleading with him to open his eyes, to say something, to let her know that he would be all right. Major Rathbone stood a few feet away, bleeding and in pain. Rathbone had not seen Booth enter the box. He heard the shot, and the next instant turned to see the assassin lunging at him with a knife. He sprang to his feet, but managed only to deflect the blow, taking a deep cut in the arm. He was the only man close enough to have prevented the assassination, but he didn't have the chance.

A pounding noise brought Rathbone to his senses. People were trying to reach the box, but could not even get into the passageway leading to it. Apparently the outer door was blocked. Rathbone rushed to help. Fumbling for the door handle, he discovered that one end of a wooden bar had been placed against the door and the other end jammed into the plaster of the opposite wall. The killer had barricaded himself in with the Lincolns and their guests—for how long, he did not know. A few blows dislodged the board, and the door flew inward, flooding the narrow space with people. One of them was Dr. Charles A. Leale, who pushed his way in to see the president.

In the dress circle, Isaac Jacquette went numb. All he remembered saying was "Oh, God! The President is murdered!" followed by pandemonium. A few seats to his right, Captain Theodore McGowan looked down and saw "a heaving, hoarse-sounding sea of men." Helen DuBarry said that even strong men were sobbing. Some were completely overcome, as much from frustration as grief. A rumor went around that Booth had been captured, and cries of "Hang him!" tore through the crowd. That was the first of many such false alarms, and each was followed by louder shouts for revenge. This time, one man stood on a chair and shouted, "Take out the ladies and hang him here on the spot!"[17]

Laura Keene tried to restore order. Stepping up to the footlights, the actress called, "Order, gentlemen!" But her words were swallowed up in the din of a thousand voices. Jim Maddox thought she was asking for water, and he ran to the green room to get some. When he returned with four tumblers and a pitcher, Miss Keene had disappeared into the crowd.

Some of the men talked of mounting a pursuit. Stewart and others were sure the assassin had gone down the alley, then turned north toward F Street. After that, his direction was anybody's guess. But even if they knew where he was headed, catching up with him would not be easy. Booth already had a long lead, and it would take some time for anyone to get a horse saddled and on the road.[18]

While the men felt embarrassed that Booth had gotten away, the women were simply terrified. "It was the coolest, most cold-blooded deed ever heard, read, or dreamed of," wrote Sarah Hamlin Batchelder. Hours after the shooting, Sarah was still trying to find the right words for what she had witnessed:

"It certainly unnerved me. My own shadow . . . would have startled me. . . . This is terrible, awful horrible, nothing can describe the intense feeling of fear & dread of more to come and none can judge in the least degree its depth save those who witnessed the horrible scenes."[19]

Lt. John T. Bolton, 7th V.R.C., managed to get into the president's box. As officer of the day for the provost guards, Bolton had come into town to check soldiers' passes. Ford's was to be his last stop for the night, and after looking around, he had settled in to watch the play. Booth's shot startled him back into action. Unable to push through the aisles, he vaulted over seats to get to the stage. By then the assassin was gone, so he turned his attention upward. The president's box was getting crowded, and nobody seemed to be in charge. With help from a couple of bystanders, Bolton pulled himself up and over the balustrade.[20]

The place was jammed to suffocation, and Henry Rathbone was beginning to panic. He recognized Captain McGowan in the crowd, and asked him to keep anyone else from entering—unless, of course, they were surgeons. Dr. Leale was already attending to the president. Only twenty-three years old, Charles Leale had earned his medical degree just six weeks before. Yet he never hesitated. He called for medicinal brandy and water, then began an examination of the patient. Mr. Lincoln still sat in his rocker, locked in the arms of his wife. Unresponsive, he appeared to be comatose. Mrs. Lincoln pleaded, "Oh, doctor, do what you can for my dear husband. Do what you can for him." Leale assured her he would do all he could, but at this point he wasn't even sure how or where the president had been wounded. He remembered the knife in the assailant's hand and assumed the president had been stabbed. At first glance, though, no cuts were apparent.[21]

Just down Tenth Street, Sergeant John F. Drill was in charge of the detective desk at police headquarters. So far, this Friday night had been relatively quiet. A thirty-five-year-old prostitute had been brought in for attacking a man. A forty-year-old man had been bailed out after assaulting another man with a pistol. Considering how dense, drunk, and noisy the celebrations had been, the level of violence had stayed remarkably low. Though drunken soldiers occasionally got out of hand, that was a problem for military authorities. Civilian police had had nothing to complain about. Until now.[22]

A rumbling sound wafted down from Ford's Theatre, but Drill paid little attention. He was used to strange noises at night. In this quiet neighborhood, the still night air carried all kinds of sounds from the theater half a block up the street. Martial music, the clash of arms, and the roar of an audience were nothing to get excited about, especially when the windows were open. Then suddenly A. C. Richards, superintendent of the force, burst through the front door. James Ferguson and James Maddox followed. They could hardly get a word out between gasps for air. Richards fired off questions. Who did it? How did he get out of the theater? With a quick enough response, they might still capture him. Messengers were sent out, and the entire force was put on alert.[23]

Back in the theater, the press of the crowd was getting out of hand as onlookers pushed toward the stage for a better view of the box. Looking down on them, Lieutenant Bolton now ordered everyone to disperse. But the audience had worked itself into a frenzy, and nobody paid much attention to the provost guards officer. Dr. Charles S. Taft, a surgeon for the Signal Corps, saw that his wife, Sarah, was in danger of being crushed against the wall of the orchestra pit. He managed to boost her onto the stage, where at least she would have room to breathe. Her friend Annie Wright was forced to improvise. Annie's husband, John, was the stage manager at Ford's, and she was anxious about his safety. She tried to pull herself up with a bass viol from the orchestra pit, but a couple of failed attempts left her straddling the instrument in a painful and awkward position.[24]

The crush had Lue Porterfield in a panic. A petite young woman, Lue lacked the size and strength needed to push her way through the crowd. She was about to fall underfoot when a large man appeared out of the audience and lifted her up over the footlights. Actor E. A. Emerson, seeing her on the stage, thought she was about to faint. He took her in his arms and fanned her with his Lord Dundreary wig. In less grim circumstances, the scene would have been comical.[25]

Dr. Charles Taft was torn by indecision. His distraught wife wanted desperately to go home, but he was a surgeon and someone in the box was calling for help. He couldn't just walk away. Taft found Annie Wright and asked her to look after Sarah. Then he looked up at the box, and a man asked, "Do you want to get up there?" Taft nodded, and Daniel Beekman offered him a boost.[26]

Far too many people were in the box already. Actress Laura Keene was there, and a young obstetrician named Albert Freeman Africanus King had also pushed his way in. Like young Dr. Leale, King had just received his medical degree. When Dr. Taft finally pulled himself up over the railing, he found that he was the senior man in attendance, although he was only thirty.

Dr. Leale was still searching for the wound. He knew he didn't have much time. The president was in a state of paralysis. His eyes were closed, and his breathing was labored. The doctor could find no pulse, and though he needed to examine the patient, he couldn't do so in such a tight space. So with the help of a few soldiers, he lifted Mr. Lincoln out of his rocking chair and laid him on the floor. As he did so, he noticed a small clot of blood on the president's coat near one of the shoulders. Leale thought he had found the area of the wound, but when he tried to look at the president's neck, he found that the tie was too tight. He struggled to loosen it, and one of the men huddling over him suggested he just cut it off. He handed Leale a penknife.

Leale pulled off the president's coat and peeled back his shirt. But even with the shoulders and chest exposed, he could find no knife wounds. Fanning his fingers through the president's hair, at last he found something. On the back of the head, a little to the left of center, was a bullet hole. The tissues around it had swelled, and a clot had formed in the opening. Leale pulled his hand away, and the wound bled. As it did, the president began to breathe more freely.

Lieutenant Bolton stood to the side, awaiting orders. The crowd showed no signs of calming down. Though they should probably leave the building, Bolton alone was powerless to make them do that. Curiosity outweighed their fear, and even with the threat of a stampede, many refused to leave unless someone forced them out.[27]

Dr. Charles Taft quickly took in the situation. From the look of things, a couple of soldiers were preparing to carry the president back to the White House. Taft didn't think Lincoln could survive such a trip, even in a carriage. He announced that he was an army surgeon, and in his professional opinion, the president should be taken someplace close by—perhaps the nearest house. Dr. Leale concurred, then briefed Taft on the patient's injury. Such a wound, Dr. Taft said, would have to be mortal. Though Leale had already said as much, the older man had paid little attention; he didn't realize that the man who spoke to him was also a doctor. Nevertheless, Leale still had the soldiers' attention. He gave the signal, and six men lifted the president's limp, unwieldy form. As they carried him out of the box, someone noticed Mr. Lincoln's coat lying in the corner. Some papers had fallen out of the pockets, and at Dr. Leale's suggestion, they were handed over to Captain Edwin Bedee, 12th New Hampshire Infantry, who happened to be standing in the box.[28]

Witnesses flooded into the police station faster than anyone could deal with them. A sense of urgency forced detectives to dispense with formalities, and consequently, little of what anybody said was put in writing. Still, it is not hard to imagine the drift of the investigation. Police asked the usual questions—What was he wearing? Which way did he go?—and witnesses bickered over the details. On stage, actor Harry Hawk had been in a better position than anyone else to have observed what happened; yet of all the eyewitnesses interviewed, nobody remembered the shooting quite the way he did. He was the only one who recalled hearing Booth say, *"Sic semper tyrannis!"* while still in the box; others thought Booth had first jumped to the stage. A few had also understood Booth to say, "Revenge for the South!" Hawk was the only eyewitness who heard "The South shall be free!"[29]

As they talked to police, and to one another, eyewitnesses found it difficult to make sense of their fragmented memories. Not everyone had heard a gunshot, but all agreed that Booth had flashed a knife. Everyone had seen him leap to the stage, and most remembered seeing him land slightly off balance. A few had heard the sound of tearing fabric, and assumed he had torn his clothes in the jump. But Ferguson, sitting across from the Lincolns' box, was sure Booth had caught his spur in the blue flag; he even saw it fall to the stage in tatters. Nobody else reported anything of the kind. These differences would not have surprised investigators. In cases such as this, confusion and contradiction are the rule, not the exception. But fortunately for police, the identity of the assassin was not in dispute. John Wilkes Booth was a well-known figure in Washington, especially at Ford's Theatre.

If any one person stood out among eyewitnesses, it was James P. Ferguson. A tall, wiry man of thirty-five, "Fergy" had an adventurous past and a thirst for notoriety. He relished the unique opportunity to tell this story. He swore out a statement for the police, repeated his story for the War Department, and sought out newspaper reporters, to whom he gave interviews. His chief claim was that he knew the assassin and was the only person looking at him when he fired the shot. Little wonder that Jim Ferguson was so much in demand.[30]

At police headquarters, Superintendent A. C. Richards tried to bring order to the maelstrom of witnesses. Nehemiah Miller, the police justice, came over to take their sworn statements while detectives listened and jotted down ideas. They took a special interest in Booth's movements around the theater that day. He had been in and out of Ford's all afternoon, they learned, and had made a few trips to the neighboring restaurants as well. Almost everyone on the crew knew him and enjoyed his company. He took them to lunch, bought them drinks, and generally made them feel at ease. He always treated the crew as equals, and not many stars did that.[31]

Jim Maddox said that Booth had not been around much until the previous Christmas. That's when he had started coming to Ford's regularly. Booth had said that he was in the oil business and wanted to hire a clerk. He also needed a stable for his horse. Maddox found him one in Baptist Alley, about sixty yards down from the back door of the theater. It was actually a shed, twenty by thirty feet, and Mary Ann Davis, a widow living on E Street, rented it to Booth for five dollars a month. Ned Spangler fixed it up to accommodate a buggy, and Booth had been using it ever since. Some of the theater people looked after the horse and ran other errands for Booth as well. Until Friday night, nobody thought anything of it.

Superintendent Richards wanted his men to keep a watch out for the horse Booth was riding, and fortunately a description was easy to get. "Peanuts" Borrows had been holding the mare at the time of the shooting. Though he was just a boy, he turned out to be an excellent observer. He described the horse as a light bay mare with a long, wavy tail and a heavy fetlock. She had a small, flat forehead; small nostrils; and a very small, thin neck that was rather arched. Her mane fell on the left side, her ears were small, and her rump sloped. Richards was delighted to have such a wealth of detail, right down to the "uneasy" temperament, which would prove to be important. Booth was a superb horseman and wasn't the least bothered by her nervous disposition. On Friday afternoon, he had been showing her off to Ferguson. "See how she will start off?" Booth said. And with that, he had darted up Tenth Street.[32]

Doctors, officers, and investigators needed to know what had occurred, yet the government had no general plan for notifying its people in the event of an emergency. Eyewitnesses took care of that on their own initiative. It was they who spread the news of the shooting. Captain Joseph Findley told his military supervisors about the assassination. Samuel J. Koontz of the Treasury Department hustled out to summon a doctor. Dr. George B. Todd, surgeon of the U.S.S. *Montauk,* ran dispatches to the nearest telegraph office.

At the National Theatre, three blocks to the west, the news brought an abrupt halt to a long-awaited event. Manager C. Dwight Hess had spent a fortune on an "illumination" of gaslights to commemorate the flag raising at Fort Sumter that day. Hess had invited the Lincolns, but they declined. Their twelve-year-old son, Tad, however, wanted to go in their place. He was there enjoying a spectacular performance of *Aladdin; or, The Wonderful Lamp* when a man burst in and cried, "The President is assassinated in his private box!" As spectators made a rush for the exits, a man in the audience called for order. "Sit down!" he yelled. "It is a ruse of the pickpockets!" Miraculously, that worked. The house quieted down, and the play resumed. A dangerous stampede was averted. But a few minutes later, the performance was halted once more. An actor stepped up to center stage and announced that the news about the president was true after all. This time, the audience filed out in an orderly way. Tad Lincoln, confused and shaken, was hustled off to the White House.[33]

Back on Tenth Street, two young clerks had been walking past Ford's Theatre when they heard the commotion inside. Joseph A. Sterling and

J. G. Johnson learned from some bystanders that a fight had broken out in the theater, and they rushed in to see for themselves. The place was in pandemonium, with everyone talking about the assassination and the man who had run across the stage. Sterling and Johnson got the impression that the secretary of war, Edwin M. Stanton, had not been notified, and they made up their minds to run to his house on foot. Stanton lived about a mile away.[34]

Meanwhile, two blocks to the south, attorney Seaton Munroe and a friend were walking along Pennsylvania Avenue when a man came running down Tenth Street yelling, "My God, the President is killed at Ford's Theatre!" Munroe sprinted up to Ford's, where a dense and agitated crowd surrounded the front entrances. He somehow managed to work his way into the auditorium. "I had never witnessed such a scene as was now presented," he later recalled. "The seats, aisles, galleries, and stage were filled with shouting, frenzied men and women, many running aimlessly over one another; a chaos of disorder beyond control. . . ." Some soldiers were about to take the president out of the building.[35]

Jacob Soles, Bill Sample, John Corry, and Jabes Griffiths hadn't come to Ford's Theatre that evening to make history. But they happened to be near the box when Dr. Leale asked for help carrying the president away. Lincoln had to be taken out of there. The theater was too crowded, and no doctor could do anything in such cramped quarters. It appeared the president could not survive, but at least they could let him die in more dignified surroundings. After all, how would it look if the great martyr should die in a playhouse—and on Good Friday, at that? Theaters still carried the stigma of immorality, and nobody wanted Abraham Lincoln to take his last breath in such a place.

The four had served together in Thompson's Independent Battery C of the Pennsylvania Light Artillery. Their unit had been assigned to the Defenses of Washington for more than a year now, and Soles, nineteen, had spent his entire military career on garrison duty. He had come into town for a little amusement, never imagining that he and his companions would play a role in a real-life historical drama. Now, joined by two strangers from another regiment, they carried the dying president out of the box, determined to make his final journey a solemn one.[36]

Laura Keene led the way. At the bottom of the stairs, she found Seaton Munroe standing in the lobby. Munroe thought Keene looked dreadful. Her hair and dress were in disorder, "and not only was her gown soaked in Lincoln's blood, but her hands, and even her cheeks where her fingers had strayed, were bedaubed with the sorry stains!" Asked if the president would survive, Keene didn't have an answer. "God only knows," she said, with a shrug. Munroe looked up. At the head of the staircase above, the soldiers were turning the president around to carry him feetfirst. They were having a hard time of it, having to make frequent stops to adjust their hold or to wait for a clearing in the crowd. Bystanders kept closing in on them, and soldiers even had to break up chairs to widen a path. Lieutenant Bolton did what he could to clear the way for them. He cursed and threatened and slapped at the crowd with the flat of his sword.[37]

Following the procession was Major John Potter, who led Mrs. Lincoln by the arm. Clara Harris and Henry Rathbone moved with them. Rathbone was bleeding profusely, but so far nobody had paid him any attention. The three doctors present were all focused on Mr. Lincoln. While at first Dr. Taft had thought he was the only surgeon on the scene, when he made a remark to that effect, Dr. Leale set him straight. From that point on, Leale's authority was never questioned. It was he who briefed the others, and he who decided where the soldiers should take the patient.[38]

Police had not yet arrived at the theater, but in a manner of speaking, the crime scene came to them. Witnesses flocked to their office, many with evidence in hand. One man brought a spur found on the stage. Another turned in the assassin's hat. Made of dark gray felt, it was a fashionable "slouch" hat, with a pleated band, low crown, and turned-up brim. E. D. Wray, of the Surgeon General's office, picked it up only seconds after the shooting, and others identified it as the one that fell from Booth's head when he hit the stage. As evidence and statements accumulated, Sergeant Drill carefully noted the name and address of each witness: "Capt. G. S. Shaw on Genl Augur's Staff . . . Jacob G. Larner, 441 F St . . . Anthony Lully. . . ." They talked to sixteen people in the first forty minutes. Some would take part in the "trial of the century," while others were never heard from again.[39]

The crime scene had not been sealed off to protect evidence, nor would detectives have seen any point in doing so. The forensic value of bloodstains, fingerprints, and fibers had yet to be imagined. In any event, witnesses had already begun stripping the president's box of mementoes. They carried off some of the best evidence, which seems not to have bothered police at all. When Detective John A. W. Clarvoe, the first officer at the scene, arrived, he may well have been looking for a souvenir of his own.

A few doors away, Clarvoe's colleagues held further interviews with Peanuts Borrows and Ford's property man James Maddox. Both talked about Booth's stable in Baptist Alley, but neither seemed to know what had happened to the horse he had been keeping there. They knew that Booth had a buggy, but just a few days ago, Peanuts had cleaned it up for him, and Ned Spangler had taken it to an auction house. There was a good chance that evidence might remain in the stable, so Police Sergeant James O. Johnson went to see what had been left behind.[40]

While police searched behind the theater, a slow procession inched along in front of it. The soldiers who carried the president had left the building, but were not sure where to go. As they made their way through a sea of people, some of the spectators jockeyed for a better look, and some even helped by taking hold of an arm or leg. They moved aimlessly into the street, heading toward a row of houses that in recent years had become jammed with boarders. Some of those people stood there now looking out their windows and wondering how they might be of help. An artist named Carl R. Bersch sketched the event from his balcony, while one of his neighbors took a more active part. Henry Safford, a young War Department clerk, stepped out the front door with a candle and called down from the landing: "Bring him in here!" Safford was living in a respectable middle-class house at 453 Tenth Street. It was owned by William Petersen, a German-born tailor, who lived there with his wife, Anna, and three of their children. They had always taken in boarders, and the place had been a favorite among actors, who liked the convenience of living across from Ford's.[41]

A FEW BLOCKS AWAY, Col. George A. Woodward and some friends were drawn by the sound of music to the corner of Fourteenth Street and Pennsylvania Avenue. An impromptu serenade was taking place near Willard's Hotel for a group of Treasury clerks who had missed the illumination the night before. Standing in front of the hotel, Woodward heard a voice from across the crowd. "Have you heard what has happened?" a man called. "The President has just been shot in Ford's Theatre."

The colonel was shaken. "Good heavens! Can that be possible?"

"Yes," said the man, "I saw him carried out; he wasn't dead, but the doctors say he can't live." Two officers stood with Woodward. Their instincts told them to run down to the theater, but they couldn't possibly navigate through the crowds already forming there. As they talked over their options, the colonel remembered something he had seen earlier in the day. Confederate prisoners had marched right past here en route to the Old Capitol Prison. There were more than four hundred of them, marching along in their torn and tarnished uniforms "with no semblance of bravado, and yet with no apparent sense of humiliation." At the time, Woodward had felt sorry for those men. Now they came back to mind in a different light.

Could those same prisoners have been set loose to avenge their lost cause? The question preyed on Woodward's mind, and he decided at once to alert the city garrison. He and his friends commandeered a battered old hack, drawn by an ancient and pitiful-looking horse. They piled into the carriage, shouting out directions for the headquarters of General Christopher Columbus Augur, commander of the 22nd Army Corps.[42]

THE NEWS WAS CIRCULATING HAPHAZARDLY. On Newspaper Row, across from Willard's, reporter Lawrence A. Gobright of the Associated Press was wrapping up a quiet evening at his office. He had just picked up a newspaper for a last-minute check of the news when a friend came running up the sidewalk and excitedly told him that the president had been shot. Gobright could hardly believe it, but the man assured him that he had just come from Ford's Theatre, having left there right after it happened.

They ran to the telegraph office together, and Gobright dictated a quick "special" to alert the press: "Washington, April 14: President Lincoln was shot to-night, and is mortally wounded." He promised more details would follow, and then hurried over to the scene of the crime. At Ford's Theatre, everyone was still in a state of intense excitement. The president had just been carried out of the building, and Gobright wanted to see the box before they closed the place down. Holding on to his friend, a valuable eyewitness, he inspected the actual site of the shooting. They walked right in and surveyed the box to fix the scene of the crime in their minds.[43]

Major Thomas T. Eckert, chief of the War Department's Military Telegraph Bureau, was getting ready for bed when he got the news. Some of Eckert's operators had been at Ford's Theatre that night, and after the shooting, they ran back to the office to get its eight cipher machines up and running. While George Colton Maynard went straight there, Thomas A.

Laird, who lived in Eckert's house, went home to give his boss the news. Fortunately, the house was right along the way. The major was shaving when Laird burst through the front door and shouted up the stairs. In a matter of minutes, the major was dressed and in the saddle, looking for Secretary Stanton.[44]

——————————

"IT ALL SEEMS A DREAM—A WILD DREAM"

THE NEWS FROM FORD'S THEATRE WOULD NOT BE THE ONLY shock in store. At the same moment that Booth entered the president's box in Ford's, another attack was about to begin six blocks away, at the home of Secretary of State William H. Seward. A tall man in a light overcoat knocked at Seward's door, insisting he be allowed to give some medicine to the secretary, who was recovering from injuries suffered in a recent carriage accident. A servant resisted, but the man pushed past him, trudging up the steps toward Mr. Seward's third-floor bedroom. Upstairs, Seward's son, Assistant Secretary Frederick Seward, heard the commotion. He confronted the man at the top of the stairs, and after a brief exchange of words, young Seward cracked open the door to his father's bedroom and pretended to look in. "He's asleep," he assured the stranger, and the man turned as if to leave.[1]

But unexpectedly, the door opened again, and Fanny Seward, age sixteen, looked out at her brother. Softly, she said, "Fred, Father is awake now." Fred glared at her in annoyance. He started to say something, but the intruder cut him off.

"Is the secretary asleep?" The man seemed rude and impatient.

Fanny sheepishly answered, "Almost."

Frederick Seward had sensed the danger, and he hurriedly shut the door, while Fanny went back to sit by her father's bedside. Fred assured the stranger that he would make sure the secretary got his medicine. The man again turned away, but as he did, he drew a revolver from his coat. Quick as a flash, he spun around, pressed it against Frederick Seward's temple, and pulled the trigger. It clicked. In a panic, the man then raised the gun and brought it crashing down on Frederick's head.

In the secretary's room was an army nurse, Private George Foster Robinson. Wounded in the war, he had been assigned to light duty, helping Seward recover from his accident. From his seat in the bedroom, Robinson heard a dull thud, and thought it sounded like a man being struck with a walking stick. Fanny heard it too, but she thought that someone was chasing another rat around the hall. Turning to Robinson, she asked, "What can be the matter? Do go and see." But as she spoke, they remembered the man in the hallway. They raced to the door, and the nurse opened it. Frederick stood in the hall, his expression blank. His face was ghostly pale, and blood streamed down his head. Next to him, glaring directly at Fanny, was the intruder.

He came straight at Robinson, slashing at him with a large knife. The nurse parried the blow upward, and the blade struck his forehead. A tremendous blow hit him full in the face, and he fell backward to the floor. To Fanny, everything was a blur. She screamed for help, and wondered if this were just an awful dream. The attacker rushed past her, heading in the dark toward her father's bed.

Immobilized by his injuries, Secretary Seward lay weak and helpless on his bed. He had been trying not to fall asleep for fear of waking up with lockjaw. Though the lights were down, Secretary Seward had no trouble figuring out what was happening; he just couldn't do anything about it. The assailant leaped upon him, and Seward saw only the flash of a knife and the pink-and-gray fabric of an overcoat sleeve. In his shock and horror, the only thought that came to him was "That is a handsome fabric."

The first blow missed him, striking the headboard with a violent thud. The man grunted and tried again. The next strike found its mark, slicing deep into Seward's cheek. The assailant slashed again and again, turning his victim's head to uncover the jugular vein. As he did so, Private Robinson struggled to pull him away. Jumping on the man's back, Robinson pulled the attacker to the floor, giving Seward a chance to roll off the bed and out of the way.[2]

Awakened by Fanny's screams, Augustus Seward, another of the secretary's sons, was jolted from sleep in a nearby bedroom and joined the scuffle. He and Robinson forced the madman toward the door. While the nurse pinned him down, Augustus ran to get his revolver. That was the assailant's chance to escape. He leaped to his feet, throwing Robinson to the side, and stumbled out of the room. He was barreling down the stairs when a State Department messenger unexpectedly blocked his way. Emrick Hansell was about to run for help, but the assassin was moving quickly, and he knocked Hansell to the floor, stabbing him in the back for good measure. Fleeing outside, bellowing "I'm mad! I'm mad!" the man ran to a waiting horse.

The news of this second attack was explosive. Coordinated assaults could mean only one thing: a conspiracy, and a well-developed one. Was this an insurrection, as Colonel Woodward feared—the last dying gasp of the Confederacy? Had other officials been slaughtered too? Would rebel cavalry descend on the city out of the darkness? In an instant, the shooting in Ford's Theatre took on a new, more frightening perspective. Grief and indignation turned to terror in the blink of an eye.

Near Fourteeth and K streets, J. G. Johnson and Joseph Sterling had run as fast as they could to the home of Secretary of War Edwin M. Stanton. They rang the bell, and Edwin L. Stanton, a son of the secretary, answered. Johnson, out of breath, broke the news. "We have come to tell your father that President Lincoln has been shot." The younger Stanton had known Joe Sterling back in Ohio, and knew that this was no joke. He invited both men to wait in the library. His father, who had already retired for the evening, would be down soon.

There was hardly a man alive in the United States who didn't have strong feelings about Edwin McMasters Stanton. Stanton had acquired a fierce reputation since taking charge of the War Department in 1862. Gruff and self-assured, he was an intimidating figure with his long, flowing beard and his gold-rimmed spectacles. He seemed to fear nothing. After only weeks in office, he had taken over the nation's telegraph lines and railroads, censored news reports, and summarily fired anyone he considered corrupt or inefficient. He had been especially hard on dissidents, whom he regarded as traitors. Thousands fell under his ambit when Congress took the control of political prisoners away from the State Department. Pleas for clemency were ignored. Stanton appeared ruthless and uncompromising, and a face-to-face encounter with him was something most people tried to avoid.

Entering the room, the secretary spoke with an unaccustomed softness. "Mr. Sterling, what news is this you bring?"

"The President was shot while at the theater, and, I was told, is dead."

Stanton's response was surprisingly calm. "Do you know who shot him?" he asked.

"Yes," came the reply. "They say it was a man named Booth, who sprang to the stage from the President's box with a large knife in his hand and escaped."

The questioning was cool and methodical. Threats and rumors were a part of everyday life in wartime Washington, and Stanton had probably heard more than his share of wild tales. Few proved to be true. So, no matter how sincere these breathless young messengers were, he had reason to suspect that the situation was not as dire as they presented it. After all, they hadn't actually witnessed the shooting, nor had they seen Mr. Lincoln. Perhaps this was just another overblown story. Certainly that was what Stanton wanted to believe.

Almost as an afterthought, Joseph Sterling imparted another bit of news. "As we were coming to your house," he said, "a man informed us that Secretary Seward also had been assassinated." Hesitantly, he added, "But that may be street rumor and untrue."

This time, Stanton reacted. "Oh, that can't be so. That can't be so!" Clearly agitated, he insisted on going to Seward's immediately. His wife had just come down the stairs, and he told her to order the carriage at once. Ellen Stanton had rarely seen her husband look so alarmed, and she pleaded with him not to leave the house. If these rumors were true, then anyone in the Cabinet was in danger—especially the secretary of war.

The bell rang again, and Stanton hurried toward the door. Johnson and Sterling feared another attack, and they tried to intercede, but the visitor was just a clerk from the Provost Marshal General's office. He had been sent with the news about the attack on Seward. "Go quickly to Colonel Ingraham's headquarters," the secretary told him, "and ask him to send a cavalry guard to my house at once."

As Stanton dressed to leave, Major Norton Chipman, from the Bureau of Military Justice, came to check on him. Chipman had heard about the Seward attack, but not about the president's shooting. He and Stanton talked over the situation and agreed that the ruckus in Ford's Theatre was probably just a row among drunken soldiers. They ought to go straight to the secretary of state's house.[3]

When Secretary of War Edwin Stanton arrived at the Seward house, he stepped into a nightmare. A trail of blood ran from the third floor to the entrance foyer. Augustus Seward had been cut three times, twice all the way to the bone. Private Robinson was cut on the forehead and back. He could still move about, and insisted the others be treated first. Emrick Hansell, the State Department's messenger, lay on the floor of the downstairs hallway. A massive wound, more than two and a half inches deep, ran down the length of his back. Frederick Seward remained on the hallway floor upstairs, with at least five fractures in his skull. In some places, the brain was exposed. His recovery was doubtful.

In the secretary's bedroom, Fanny Seward found what she thought was a bloody pile of bedclothes on the floor. On closer inspection, it proved to be her father, lying between the bed and the wall. He looked ghastly, with his face badly cut. His lower jaw, already broken in the carriage accident, hung loosely from the skull and made his mouth gape. Robinson checked for a pulse, then assured the distraught girl that her father was still alive. With help from the orderlies, he lifted the secretary back onto the bed. Seward, reviving slightly, gave his daughter a reassuring touch on the arm. "I am not dead," he whispered. "Send for the police and surgeon, and close the house."

His face had been cut along the jawline for several inches on the left side. The second and third blows had glanced off the bone on the other side, and the cheek hung in a loose flap. A metal brace, designed to ease the effects of his recent injuries, had been nicked in several places. It had also shielded his jugular vein, saving the secretary's life. Luckily, shock deadened the pain, and all Seward felt was the sensation of blood drops "slapping" him on the face.[4]

Witnesses described the assailant as a mass of contradictions. He was a large, powerful man with the smooth, pink face of a boy. His hands were small, but possessed of superhuman strength. Crude in manners but elegantly attired, he had dark hair and blue eyes that glared with an unforgettable intensity.

Three young soldiers had nearly caught him on his way out. Theodore Bailey, Samuel Lynn, and Martin Gorman were orderlies in the office of General Augur, which happened to be next door. Standing outside on a short break, they had noticed a horse hitched to the iron fence surrounding Lafayette Park, across the street. Nobody thought much about it, and they went back into the office. But a few minutes later, someone came run-

ning out of the Seward house screaming "Murder!" and that horse immediately came to mind. Running back outside, they saw the animal at the far
end of the block. The rider was having trouble getting it to gallop. For a
moment it looked as if they might actually overtake him, but they didn't
quite make it, as the man finally got his horse up to speed. When they last
saw him, he was on H Street, cursing and flailing at his stubborn animal.[5]

In the hour after the attack, Seward's parlor filled with dignitaries inquiring about the secretary's condition. Secretary of the Navy Gideon
Welles had arrived just ahead of Stanton and was trying to calm the
servants, who were still frightened out of their wits. Stanton and Welles
went upstairs together and found three doctors attending to the injured.
The war secretary immediately cornered one of them and started pepper-
ing him with questions. Welles bristled at his insensitivity, and he was
pleased when another doctor angrily told Stanton to do his questioning
elsewhere.

Welles asked Stanton if he had heard rumors of the president's assassination. Stanton said yes, and in fact, he was going over to Ford's now;
perhaps they should go together. On their way down the stairs, they encountered General Montgomery C. Meigs, Quartermaster General of the
Army, and invited Meigs to go with them. The general was horrified. He
would go himself, certainly, but he didn't think the secretary of war should
go anywhere near Ford's Theatre. His comments made Stanton hesitate,
and suddenly Welles became the impatient one. "We're wasting time," he
barked. General Meigs followed him out the door, with Chief Justice
David K. Cartter of the newly created Supreme Court of the District of
Columbia right behind. Stanton followed, but with some trepidation.

The excitement had unnerved their carriage driver. All those injured
people, and the blood—streaming down the walls and spattered across the
woodwork—was beyond belief. Worst of all, the people who had done this
were still at large. Nobody knew where they were, or how many more
might still be lurking in the darkness, waiting to attack. Such thoughts had
the poor carriage driver paralyzed with fear, and he just sat there, unable to
move. Exasperated, Chief Justice Cartter let out a sigh, then shoved the
man aside. He drove the carriage himself.[6]

PRESIDENT LINCOLN HAD FINALLY REACHED the house across the
street. The main floor was well above the sidewalk, and the soldiers had to
carry him up ten steps just to reach the front door. Inside, a long hallway

ran the length of the house, past a couple of rooms on the left and a stair-case on the right. The rooms made up a double parlor, then occupied by George Francis and his wife, Huldah, who had already gone to bed. Their doors were locked. At the end of the hall was another room, fully furnished with a bureau, a couple of chairs, a washstand, and a dark walnut spool bed. It had been rented out to William T. Clark, a War Department em-ployee, but Clark wasn't home. For Dr. Leale, the decision was an easy one: Willie Clark was giving up his room for the night.

There was just one problem. At six feet four, Abraham Lincoln was too tall for the bed. The doctors tried to take off the footboard, but it wouldn't budge. The soldiers still holding the president were getting tired, so the doctors pulled the bed away from the wall, and the patient was laid diagonally across it. The room began to fill up as surgeons, officials, and the merely curious filed in. The deathwatch had begun.[7]

A MILE TO THE NORTHWEST, Col. George Woodward and his friends continued to spread the alarm. In the last thirty minutes, they had sent an orderly to find General Augur; sounded the alarm at Martindale Barracks; notified General George W. Gile, in command of the city's gar-rison troops; and alerted the Fire Brigade at Nineteenth and I streets. Through their efforts, hundreds of soldiers were awake and ready for duty. When the sound of "To horse!" cut through the humid night air, cavalry patrols were ready to mount up. They just didn't know where to go.

Seventy-two forts surrounded the city, and many were connected to a telegraph system. The first orders went out before midnight: close off the city.

Head Quarters Department of Washington
22nd Army Corps, April 14, 1865

Lt. Paul Brodie
Signal Corps
 Telegraph to all your stations that nobody is to be allowed to pass out of the lines this evening. Have them all arrested. Communicate this order to all officers Commd along the lines.

       By command of Major Genl Augur
       Capt. and AAG[8]

. . .

RUMORS MADE A BAD SITUATION WORSE. According to one, the entire Cabinet had been killed, and the vice president as well. Abraham Lincoln was dead; prisoners had broken out of the Old Capitol; and General Grant, en route to New Jersey, had been slaughtered in his railroad car at Havre de Grace. Some of these stories were put down quickly, but others persisted for days, and many made it into the newspapers. They fed the paranoia of senior officials, who wondered if they too were to have been assassinated. Some were convinced of the danger. Secretary of the Interior John P. Usher reported that suspicious men had come to his door at about the time of the assassination. Attorney General James Speed had heard a man walking on his back porch at the same time. Another man, seen hiding near Stanton's house, had run off into the night.

Wild stories even spread through official channels. In an army camp across the Potomac, an orderly woke Private Richtmyer Hubbell, 1st Wisconsin Heavy Artillery, with the news that Lincoln had been killed and an insurrection was under way. While Hubbell and his unit awaited orders, a second courier arrived with a "correction": Mr. Lincoln had only been shot in the hand, but the vice president had been killed. Stories like these left the soldiers anxious and agitated, and it is a wonder that they controlled their anger as well as they did.[9]

AT THE PETERSEN HOUSE, across from Ford's, people began showing up in ever-growing numbers, pressing for a glimpse of their dying leader. Realizing how quickly things might get out of hand, Dr. Leale asked a captain to help him clear the bedroom. Then, when all but the doctors had left, they began a thorough examination of the patient. Leale carefully removed the president's garments and tossed them, with the half-Wellington boots, off to the side. He was surprised to see what a remarkably strong physique Mr. Lincoln had. At fifty-six, he still had the chest and arms of an athlete. The doctors marveled at his muscular development, and one observer noted that if Lincoln were not possessed of such vital power, he would have died within ten minutes of being shot.

The head wound was his only injury, but his circulation was poor and worsening. Leale ordered synapisms and bottles of hot water to stimulate circulation and warm his legs. A couple of Petersen's boarders volunteered to get water from the kitchen. In the meantime, doctors covered the president with blankets and sent a hospital steward out for mustard plasters.[10]

The signs were not encouraging. Lincoln's left pupil was slightly dilated, while his right was contracted. His right eyelid was discolored, and the bruising had spread beyond the socket. The eye itself had begun to swell. The wound oozed constantly now, spreading a deep red stain over the pillowcase. A towel placed under the head would quickly be saturated as well. But as the doctors soon realized, bleeding was a positive sign. As long as it continued, the president's condition remained stable. When the flow stopped, his vital signs weakened. The proper treatment, apparently, was to keep the wound free from blockage, and the only way to do that was to have someone hold the head up and away from the pillow. For now, Dr. Taft assumed that duty. In the meantime, more surgeons arrived at the house. They all agreed on the prognosis: the president would not survive the night.[11]

ANDREW JOHNSON, the vice president, had been living in the Kirkwood House, a hotel just a few blocks west of Ford's Theatre, since his inauguration in early March. Everyone in town knew where he lived, and his room was easily accessible from the street. When news of the Seward attack reached Leonard J. Farwell at Ford's Theatre, he thought of Johnson immediately. Farwell, a former governor of Wisconsin, also lived in the Kirkwood House, and he sometimes visited the vice president, a fellow former governor, in his first floor suite. He raced over and pounded on the door. "Governor Johnson," he yelled, "if you are in the room, I must see you." The vice president, who had already gone to bed, was slow to respond.

Johnson wept at hearing the news. Farwell offered words of support, but there was no getting around the awesome responsibilities that were about to fall on Johnson's shoulders. They talked about how to handle the emergency, and Farwell suggested they make security their first priority. He offered to check on the president's condition and that of the Sewards. While the vice president locked himself in his room, Farwell arranged for a watchman to stand outside.[12]

Back at the Petersen house, Governor Farwell found Washington's provost marshal, Major James R. O'Beirne. Major O'Beirne wasn't a criminal detective in the usual sense; his job was to track down deserters and enforce the draft laws. But when Farwell pointed out how vulnerable the vice president was, O'Beirne hastily arranged for his security. He went straight to the Kirkwood House, and sent for his chief of detectives, John Lee, to meet him there.

Before working for the provost marshal, Lee had had no experience as a detective. He was a sign hanger by trade, but he had enlisted early in the war and found that military life agreed with him. At fifty, he was the oldest man on O'Beirne's staff, and his good, practical sense put him in good stead with the major. He arrived at the Kirkwood House just after his boss, and immediately assessed the hotel's security. It was a large place, and a recent addition had more than doubled its former size. Posting men on the ground level, Lee checked the building from top to bottom, eventually ending up in the bar.

Michael Henry, the bartender, did not know John Lee personally, but he knew what his job was. He approached the detective and told him of a suspicious man—a grubby-looking German fellow—who had checked in Friday morning. He was a villainous-looking fellow, and Henry felt he didn't belong in such an elegant hotel. Henry did not know the man's name, but he suggested Lee talk to Lyman Sprague, the manager. At the hotel desk, Sprague took out the register and looked at the entries for April 14. Running his finger down the list, he tried to imagine which of the guests might be that suspicious man: "Wm. W. Snow . . . Thos. Clark . . . J. T. Hauser . . ." *There it was.* Near the bottom of the page, in a crude and spidery scrawl, was the German name they were looking for: G. A. Atzerodt, from Charles County, Maryland. He had paid for a full day in advance, and was assigned to Room 126, on the second floor.[13]

Lee and his men nearly tripped over one another looking for the room. It was up the stairs and all the way to the back of the new section. The door was locked, and no one answered their knocks. Back at the desk, Mr. Sprague confirmed that Atzerodt had taken the room's only key. Nonetheless, Lee took a full set of keys back and tried them all. When nothing worked, he forced the door open and his men rushed in. They found the room unoccupied.

The first thing Lee noticed was a black coat hanging against the wall to the left of the door. He looked all around the room, then began a detailed search, checking under the rug, in and around the washstand, under the bureau, and in all the drawers. He even took the ashes out of the woodstove, sifting through them carefully. Nothing suspicious. Moving to the bed, Lee took up the covers one by one, feeling the quilt to see if anything had been sewn inside it. He soon found something of interest. Under the pillow was a pistol, loaded and capped. A Bowie knife was under the sheets in the middle of the bed. John Lee headed back down to tell Major O'Beirne what they had found.

O'Beirne had already left, so Lee made a list of the items. Some things were unremarkable: a piece of licorice, a toothbrush, a pair of gray socks, and a colored handkerchief, along with a mutilated copy of the *Evening Star* from April 11. But Lee also found three boxes of .44-caliber cartridges, and a pair of gauntlets. That coat on the wall turned out to be the best find of all. In its pockets were two handkerchiefs—marked "Mary A. H. Booth" and "F. M. Nelson"—and two small books. One was a copy of *Perrine's Map of the Southern States;* the other, an account book from the Bank of Ontario. The account holder was John Wilkes Booth.[14]

GEORGE COLTON MAYNARD, of the War Department's telegraph office, was not supposed to transmit messages without orders. Though such orders had not come in, he still took the initiative in alerting his counterparts at the Washington Navy Yard. He told Henry H. Atwater, an operator there, that the president had been shot at Ford's, and suggested he pass the news on to the commandant of the yard. Though Atwater found the news incredible, he knew that when something came over that line, it was to be taken seriously. He ran over to headquarters, arriving at the same time as the commandant. Commodore John B. Montgomery was skeptical at first. He had just come from uptown, and had heard nothing of it there. Atwater assured him the story was true; the shooting had occurred just a short while ago. Taking no chances, the commodore put his entire staff on full alert.[15]

THE POLICE WERE INUNDATED with eyewitnesses. Lyman Bunnell, who had been sitting in the dress circle, told officers about three suspicious men who had taken seats near the president's box. They had all disappeared when the shot rang out. William Somersett Burch, an inventor who lived around the corner from Ford's, told police he had heard a strange, shrill whistle in the alley behind the theater. That had been just before the shooting. John B. Pettit had heard the whistle too. Pettit had been reading a book in his room on F Street. His window was open, and he had heard low whistles, like signals, coming from a vacant lot near the theater. The last was loud, and it came just before the commotion started. There were other suspicious circumstances. A. Q. Stebbins saw a horse on F Street, hitched and waiting next to the alley. It looked out of place there, and he didn't see it when he looked again after the assassination. Taken together, these details painted a disquieting picture of a neighborhood in-habited by conspirators.[16]

What of Booth's own neighborhood? Not long into the investigation, A. C. Richards began to wonder if the assassin had planned to hide among his hometown friends. It was common knowledge that Booth was from Baltimore, but the police did not have a telegraph system with which to alert anyone there. Superintendent Richards ran over to the American Line telegraph office, where he sent a message to Maryland authorities let-ting them know that Lincoln's attacker might be heading their way.[17]

William Heiss had been thinking of the Baltimore connection in a dif-ferent way. Manager of another telegraph service, the People's Line, Heiss controlled a commercial wire that led directly to Booth's hometown. His brother, Courtland V. Hess, was in the Ford's Theatre stock company, so Heiss already knew something of the Booths and their Maryland roots. He was less concerned with the assassin's escape, though, than with the violence that might still be in store. If this were indeed the opening spark of a general uprising, news of the shooting in Ford's would undoubtedly be the signal to set it all in motion. Heiss was determined not to let his own company help the conspirators. So he shorted out his line, making it un-usable until he or someone else reestablished the proper connections.[18]

In the middle of all the turmoil, James R. "Dick" Ford arrived to find his place of business under siege. Ford was the treasurer of his brother's theater, but had spent the day in Baltimore looking after the Holliday Street Theatre. He returned just in time to see a crowd of men carrying the president across the street. By then, a swarm of bystanders had begun making threats against the theater. Bent on revenge, they blamed the build-ing for what had happened there. Many were still inside, vandalizing the place and carrying off decorations for souvenirs. There was nothing Ford could do but watch in despair. Afraid even to identify himself, he walked through the crowd, staying until soldiers forced everyone out.[19]

President Lincoln never regained consciousness, and doctors could do little more than check his vital signs, which had remained relatively stable. Before midnight, his pulse rate settled at around 45, but the heart seemed weaker with every beat. The number of doctors in attendance grew, as Sur-geon General Joseph K. Barnes and others arrived. Dr. Robert King Stone, the Lincolns' family doctor, was there by then, and at Dr. Leale's request, Stone took charge of the case.

Soon afterward, Edwin M. Stanton arrived, and thereafter nobody could doubt who was really in charge. Gideon Welles, Justice Cartter, General Meigs, and Major Eckert accompanied Stanton. Their presence transformed the home of William Petersen from a simple boardinghouse to the seat of government, as each officer began putting the federal behemoth back in working order. Major Eckert took immediate steps to get his telegraph lines working. He called in Stanton's messenger, Sgt. John C. Hatter, and instructed him to set up a relay between the Petersen house and the department's telegraph office on Seventeeth Street. Soldiers were to be posted on every block, ready to pass along messages as fast as humanly possible.[20]

After consoling Mrs. Lincoln, Secretary Stanton was briefed on the overall situation. Then, bracing himself, he went to the back bedroom. As he looked down at the president, Surgeon General Barnes whispered the obvious: *Mr. Lincoln cannot recover.* Acknowledging with a faint nod, Stanton lowered himself into a chair next to the bed. All eyes turned to him in anticipation of some pronouncement, but instead he burst into loud, convulsive sobs.

Nobody was prepared for that. It had not occurred to anyone that a close personal relationship had developed between the war secretary and the president—or anyone else, for that matter. To one and all, Stanton was a man of steel, unmoved by events or personal feelings. But in fact, the war had forged a bond between him and the president. Beneath that hard exterior, this god of war felt a deep and abiding respect for Lincoln. For several minutes, he sat with his face buried in his hands, shaking and quivering and weeping aloud. It was an awkward sight, and those around him busied themselves checking pulses, wiping up blood, and the like. In time, Stanton composed himself and got back to business.[21]

A FEW BLOCKS TO THE NORTH, an eighteen-year-old delegate from the U.S. Christian Commission was relaxing in his cot. C. C. Bangs had spent a long, tiring day at his job, delivering hospital supplies, and he was looking forward to a quiet evening alone. But one of the commission's drivers rushed in with the stunning news. Bangs quickly threw on some clothes and ran down to Ford's Theatre. He threaded his way through the crowd and bounded up the steps of the Petersen house. Someone had just opened the front door, and Bangs could see Mrs. Lincoln standing a few feet inside the hallway. She was asking if someone could go to the White

House and get her son. Surely, she said, her husband would revive at the sight of his son. Bangs saw an opportunity to help.

"I'll go, madam!" he blurted out.

The intrusion startled a colonel standing by the door. "And who are you?" he demanded.

"A member of the Christian Commission," said Bangs, showing a silver insignia on his lapel. That was always a welcome sign to army officers, whose wartime fatigue was often relieved by organizations like the commission.

"Well, Christian Commission, do you know the way to the White House?"

"Yes, sir, and anywhere else in Washington," came the reply.

"Well, fire away, then." With that, C. C. Bangs ran down the stairs and hurried to Willard's, four blocks away. Bangs needed a carriage, and he knew that he could always find one, day or night, in front of this grand establishment. From there he rode to the White House at full speed, telling the driver to turn the carriage around for a return trip. News of the assassination had not yet reached the staff, and Bangs had to take an usher aside to explain why he was there. The man led him upstairs, to the bedroom of the president's oldest son. Captain Robert Todd Lincoln was almost ready for bed. Stunned at the news, he hurriedly dressed himself and followed Bangs down to the waiting carriage. The mansion staff had gathered at the bottom of the stairs, anxious to hear more about the president's condition. Senator Charles Sumner had just come in, and he, too, was eager for information. Sumner was one of Lincoln's close friends, and Robert suggested he ride along to the house on Tenth Street.[22]

THERE WAS A COMMOTION on Tenth Street as the crowd rushed toward police headquarters, just below Ford's, shouting "Hang him!" From the look of it, Booth or one of his accomplices had been captured and was being hustled into the building. The excitement continued to build, but the police refused to confirm or deny anything, and eventually it became apparent that the man in custody was a witness, not a suspect. The crowd settled down, and their attention turned once more to the tailor's house just up the street. This manhunt was not over yet.

That would not be the last false alarm of the night. Time and again, police ushered some hapless witness into their offices, and each time the mob grew more impatient to tear the poor man apart. Many of these witnesses were employees at Ford's Theatre, and they knew that people already blamed them for the president's murder. Some in the crowd called for setting the theater on fire—with them inside it. Stagehand Edman Spangler was terrified. Spangler was one of those who normally slept at Ford's, but now that soldiers were taking over the place, he had nowhere to go.

Actor Harry Hawk's predicament was slightly different. He had been staying at the Kirkwood House, not the theater. But since he was one of the stars, he might be recognized and set upon by the mob. Afraid to go back to his room, he roamed the streets for hours, then eventually spent the night with a friend. The actress Laura Keene, meanwhile, took a room at the Metropolitan Hotel, on Pennsylvania Avenue. Her husband's family owned a house in Georgetown, but she seemed eager to avoid the place.[23]

Dick Ford, the treasurer, never managed to find a room. He was afraid to go back to his apartment, which adjoined the theater. The last train had already left for Baltimore, and his Washington friends, who might have given him a room, spent the night in and out of police custody. So Ford wandered around until daylight. His older brother, John, happened to be in Richmond, checking on elderly relatives. He was spared the indignity of being taken into custody, at least for now.

Midnight approached, and none of the conspirators were in custody. Frustration added to fear and anger made for a combustible mix, and in every gathering there were at least a few who wanted to take out their frustrations on the nearest Confederate. It was no secret where the rebels could be found. The Old Capitol Prison had been Washington's most notable repository for spies, traitors, and political prisoners since early in the war. It also housed prisoners of war, and, with its Carroll Annex, it could hold nearly a thousand at a time. The main building had once served as a temporary home to Congress and the Supreme Court after the original Capitol was burned by the British in 1814. It was later converted to a boardinghouse, and some of Washington's most prominent men had lived there. But in 1861, it began to house a different clientèle. The State Department took it over as a pen for political prisoners, and dissidents came to refer to it as an "American Bastille."

The Old Capitol was filled to capacity, and this night, an angry mob wanted to get at those prisoners. Someone suggested they storm the building and usher those "damn Rebels" into eternity. Congressman Green Clay Smith of Kentucky heard what was going on, and he gathered together some friends to try to cool down the crowd. Standing on a crate, Smith delivered a rousing patriotic speech that he hoped would distract the mob from violence. When he finished, one of his friends stepped up and held forth with another rousing oration. And then another. Meanwhile, Smith slipped away unnoticed and alerted Secretary Stanton to the volatile situation. The secretary dispatched troops to the scene, and in a short while, two thousand men formed a battle line around the Old Capitol. No mob, drunken or otherwise, dared challenge them.[24]

Most of Washington had been secured by then. Guards were already in place at the White House and the homes of leading officials. The Petersen house, to which almost everyone of importance had gone, was protected by twenty-five soldiers from the 9th V.R.C., who cordoned off the entire block. In fact, troops were deployed all over the city. Twenty-six thousand men were stationed in Washington, and almost all were put on duty in the course of the night. Southeast of the Capitol, a detachment from the 13th New York Cavalry reinforced the guard at the Navy Yard Bridge. Other units covered the roads in every direction. Garrisons arranged their pickets in a line to connect all of Washington's forts. Their orders were often specific: "Detail an officer and ten Enlisted Men to accompany each train which leaves this City for Baltimore . . . the Officer in charge will search every Car in the train and arrest if found John Wilkes Booth and other parties whom you deem it for the interest of the service to apprehend." The chief engineer of the Fire Brigade was ordered to watch out for an incendiary strike. Similar messages went to commanders in Baltimore, Philadelphia, and New York. Authorities had done everything in their power to guard against further attack, but much time had gone by since the shooting, and no one could say whether their net would capture anyone of interest.[25]

CLARA HARRIS WAS A WRETCHED SIGHT. Her eyes were swollen, her hands and face smeared with blood. She was worried sick about Henry Rathbone, whose wound was more serious than anyone initially thought. Booth's knife had severed an artery just above the elbow and nearly struck the bone. For more than an hour, Clara had cradled Henry in her arms and watched him grow faint while doctors hovered over the president, who couldn't be helped in any event. A surgeon finally took the major home, while Clara stayed at the Petersen house. She thought that Mary Lincoln needed her company, but soon realized that the first lady could hardly stand the sight of her. "Poor Mrs. Lincoln," she told a friend, "all through that dreadful night would look at me with horror & scream, oh! my husband's blood, my dear husband's blood. . . ." It was Henry's blood, not the president's, but explanations were pointless.[26]

It is no accident that Mary Todd Lincoln found herself alone for much of the night. When Assistant Treasury Secretary Maunsell B. Field arrived at the Petersen house, Clara Harris met him at the front door with a warning. "Oh, Mr. Field," she whispered, "the president is dying! But for heaven's sake do not tell Mrs. Lincoln!" Field was surprised to find the first lady standing all by herself in the front parlor. His first impulse, naturally, was to offer words of solace, but as soon as their eyes met, she latched onto him. "Why didn't he shoot me?" she shrieked. "Why didn't he shoot me? Why didn't he shoot me?" Field fumbled for words. He asked if there was anything he could do, and she said yes, he could go and get Dr. Stone. Major Eckert, standing nearby, came to the rescue. He pointed out that Dr. Stone was already there, and he suggested that the assistant secretary send for Dr. James C. Hall instead. The grateful secretary nodded and backed away slowly, an expression of concern frozen on his face. He was gone in a flash.

Mary Todd Lincoln could not understand why she was still alive. She seemed to think that because she had been sitting next to her husband, she should have seen and stopped Booth. But it had all happened too quickly. She never even heard the shot. When a man in black tumbled over the rail in front of her, she thought for an instant that the president had fallen out of the box. The assassin was gone before she even realized what had actually occurred.[27]

She may have been surprised when her son Robert arrived with Senator Sumner. It was actually Tad she had wanted to see. But Robert was here, and after a word with his mother, he went to be near his father. He stood near the head of the bed, staring vacantly and occasionally weeping on Sumner's shoulder. He stayed there the rest of the night.

EYEWITNESSES WERE STILL REHASHING the night's events, but by now their accounts were purely redundant. What really mattered were the physical clues left at the scene: the spur, the hat, the board used to jam the box door. They spoke of nerve, premeditation, and prior access to the site. At Seward's, the evidence presented more of a puzzle. Here the crime scene had been ransacked. Rugs, walls, and bedsheets were stained with blood, and many things in the secretary's bedroom had been broken in the scuffle. One of those was a bowl on a washstand. On the floor beneath it was an old navy revolver made by Whitney. A plain lead ball was chambered and ready to fire. Others were loaded as well, but the rounds were too small for the weapon, and their paper cartridges barely kept them from falling out. The gun might have been operational when the assault began, but at some point its steel plunger link, just under the barrel, had been broken—apparently over Frederick Seward's head.[28]

On the inside of the bedroom door was the bloody imprint of a hand. Fanny Seward had wanted to preserve it, but before anything was said, the maid washed it away. In searching over her father's room, Fanny picked up a fawn-colored hat that had fallen on the floor. It was an expensive and fashionable beaver hat, size 7, with a wide brim, low crown, and silk lining. On the sweatband inside was the inscription "Exposition Universelle. Médaille de 1ère Classe. Paris. New York. London." A man of wealth and taste would wear such a hat, yet this one had been dropped by a cold-blooded killer. It was saturated with blood.[29]

No matter how they looked at it, the evidence on Seward's assailant was contradictory. He was well-dressed, but not well-armed or -mounted. He was strong and silent, like a cool professional, but he bungled the attack through panic. Was he a hired killer? A rebel acting on official orders? As the authorities sorted through the mess at the crime scene, they were unsure whether they would ever be able to make sense of this crime.

As the hours went by, some measure of reason settled over the city. An uprising now seemed unlikely, and a massive conspiracy, if one existed, failed to wreak any further havoc. Would their assumptions that this was a Confederate plot prove true? Would the assailants be caught? The uncertainty was as unsettling as the fear. As Dr. William A. Child, of the 5th New Hampshire Infantry, wrote to his wife that night: "Are we living in the days of the French Revolution? Will peace ever come again to our dear land? Are we to rush on to wild ruin? It all seems a dream—a wild dream. I cannot realize it though I know I saw it only an hour since."

The nation's fortunes had turned on a heartbeat. As Col. George Woodward observed, "What a change a few hours had wrought! From a scene of rejoicing the capital would in a brief space of time be filled with mourning . . . the nation's chief had been stricken down by the bullet of an assassin, and hearts that had been elated with joyful anticipation of peace and reunion and the re-establishment of fraternal amity would be sickened with dread forebodings of evils yet to come."[30]

THREE

"THE PRESIDENT'S CASE IS HOPELESS"

W HEN ASKED WHETHER HE THOUGHT THE ASSASSI-
nation was an act of insanity, Major Henry Rathbone said he
had serious doubts. The crime had been carefully planned. The box had
been prepared, a wooden bar had been laid in place for a barricade, and the
strike was timed to leave the stage clear for Booth's flight across it. "These
preparations were neither conceived by a maddened brain, designed by a
fool, nor executed by a drunkard," Rathbone said. "They bear most unmistakable evidence of genius, industry, and perseverance in the perfect accomplishment of a deliberate murder." Odds were, an escape had been laid
out just as carefully. Capturing all those responsible would be a formidable
challenge.[1]

In the days and weeks that followed, many theories emerged about the
conspirators and the people who might have backed them. Finding them
was crucial, not only as a matter of justice, but for national security as well.
It was natural that the task should fall to the War Department. It was the
only government agency whose facilities embraced all the transportation,
communications, and manpower resources of the nation. Every mile of
railroad track, fifteen thousand miles of telegraph lines, and more than six
hundred thousand armed soldiers fell under the department's control. Its
provost marshals held police power over the entire North and much of the

South. Its military commissions could try anyone in the United States. Its $516 million budget was more than adequate to absorb the cost of a man-hunt.[2]

With the right help, Booth might remain hidden indefinitely, even inside the city. Outside, he had more options, though the risks were there as well. He might seek refuge in the South, but much of the former Confederacy was now in federal hands. He might escape by boat on the Chesapeake, but the bay was heavily patrolled, especially at its mouth. He could have headed for Baltimore, but his haunts there were well known. In truth, however, authorities had no idea where to look.

One incident was very much on Stanton's mind, though, as he directed the pursuit in those early hours. In the wide plain east of the Capitol stood a complex of tents that made up Lincoln Hospital. Near this place a couple of pickets on patrol had heard two horses galloping toward them in the darkness. They called for the countersign, but the riders ignored them and kept coming. When the pickets called again, more riders darted out of the woods and joined the first two. The guards, in a full panic, shouldered their weapons and called once more for the countersign. The answer this time was a fusillade of small arms fire. The pickets scattered for cover, and when the dust settled, they found that one of their own had been wounded. The riders, meanwhile, galloped into the darkness, toward the road that leads to Baltimore. To the soldiers, that confirmed what they had already begun to suspect: that these men—presumably the conspirators—were Baltimoreans, headed back home.[3]

Edwin Stanton was still a little unsteady. News of the assassination had unhinged him, and the horrors of the Seward house had left him shaken and distracted. He feared for his own life, and for good reason. The attacks were presumed to be a Confederate war measure, yet they had missed the most logical targets—Generals Grant, Halleck, Augur, and Hancock, or any telegraph operator in Washington. Stanton himself should have headed the list. But indeed, he and the entire chain of command beneath him were untouched. It remained to be seen whether the conspirators would correct that oversight.[4]

A court of inquiry was convened in the rear parlor of the Petersen house, as three of the city's most experienced lawyers examined witnesses to the crime. Chief Justice David K. Cartter had appointed himself chief investigator. Cartter, an enormous man with a pockmarked face, was an intimidating figure. His fellow panelists, attorney Britten A. Hill and Justice Abram B. Olin, were seasoned attorneys with a good sense of the relevant. Hill was a law partner in the firm of his cousin, General Thomas Ewing, Jr., and Olin, a former New York congressman, was a sitting justice on the Supreme Court of the District of Columbia. Together, their interviews would put some crucial facts on record in those early hours.[5]

The process of taking down testimony was agonizingly slow, and General Halleck suggested it might go faster if they could find a shorthand reporter. There were many such people in Washington, and as it happened, one of Petersen's boarders knew a "phonographer" who lived right next door. James A. Tanner, lately of the War Department, was eager to help. Though not quite twenty-one, Tanner had already seen more in his brief life than most people could imagine. As a private in the 87th New York Infantry, he had fought on the Virginia Peninsula under George McClellan. Then, as a corporal at the Second Battle of Bull Run, Tanner was nearly killed when a cannonball shattered both feet. He often described the experience of being carried from the field of battle face-down on a stretcher made from a blanket and two rifles. "The blanket was short," he recalled, "and lying on it on my face, I looked under and saw my feet dangling by the skin as they hung off the other end. Some kind-hearted soul gently lifted them and laid them on the edge of the blanket." Discharged from the service, Tanner moved to Syracuse and took a course in shorthand. His new skill got him a job in Washington, and brought him to the deathbed of Abraham Lincoln.[6]

Surrounded by generals, Cabinet members, and dignitaries, Tanner must have been awed as he scribbled down his notes. The president lay dying in the next room, and the secretary of war was depending on him to take an important role in ferreting out the killers. He would do so in a home that could just as well be the next target for attack, should another come. That was a heady thought for a man so young.

The sudden and dramatic revival of his department left Edwin Stanton with his greatest challenge since Lee's surrender five days before. The federal war machine had been winding down, and the demobilization had left hundreds of officers, including General Grant himself, in transit and out of contact with Washington. Fortunately, though, the men from Stanton's inner circle were still in the capital, and they performed flawlessly in the crisis. Major Eckert expedited the sending of telegrams. Quartermaster

General Meigs dispatched horses, supplies, and even ships on short notice. The Army Chief of Staff, Henry W. Halleck, moved personnel where they were needed. All stayed within shouting distance of Stanton, and their presence had a steadying effect on him. Within hours, his dispatches were more focused, his orders more forceful, and his priorities more effectively arranged. Though his press dispatches were not as quick, complete, and accurate as they could have been, that may have been his only failing. He performed remarkably well, even if it took a while for him to catch his stride.[7]

Parallel investigations were under way in different parts of the city. While the Petersen house lawyers questioned those who came to them, the Metropolitan Police were collecting evidence and actively tracking down witnesses. Their work centered on the crime scene and those immediately involved with Booth. Near Lafayette Park, General Augur had been busy as well. He had secured the Seward house, posted guards at critical sites, put thousands of soldiers on alert, and sent cavalry detachments to patrol the city. Augur set up a command post of his own, and interviewed several witnesses who appeared there with information. Meanwhile, Washington's provost marshal, Major James R. O'Beirne, gave most of his attention to the vice president. At the Kirkwood House, O'Beirne's detectives uncovered evidence of a planned attack on Johnson, and they subsequently took measures to keep him protected. Thus, at four separate locations, information was being gathered on the Booth conspiracy. So far, very little of it had found its way to the man in charge of the pursuit.

The assumption was that John Wilkes Booth had shot the president. Booth was well known to theater patrons, and he had made no effort to disguise himself. He had also known his way around the stage. As Laura Keene noted, "A person not familiar with the theater could not have possibly made his escape so well and quickly."[8]

Some eyewitnesses, such as Jim Ferguson and Laura Keene, positively recognized Booth. Their identification was confirmed by William H. Bennett, a restaurateur who had known Booth for two years. "I recognized him distinctly," said Bennett, and "I exclaimed on the stage that it was Wilkes Booth." Henry B. Phillips, of the Ford's Theatre stock company, saw Harry Hawk just after the shooting, and Hawk told him, "That was Wilkes Booth who rushed past me . . . I could swear to it if I was on my death bed." (Phillips, who had known Booth "almost from infancy," had not seen the man himself.) For a while, this was the general drift of the testimony, and James Tanner was convinced that "in fifteen minutes I had testimony enough down to hang Wilkes Booth."[9]

But that was hindsight. An hour after the assassination, there was still room for doubt. Harry Hawk, who could swear on his deathbed, refused to swear to it right away. He actually waffled on the identification, saying, "Still I am not positive. . . ." Major Rathbone could not identify the killer, despite his close encounter, and some people who knew Booth claimed he was *not* the man they saw on stage. As Sarah Hamlin Batchelder noted, certainty developed over time. "Geo[rge] said to me then, it is a man . . . *who looks just like Wilkes Booth*—he did not however know it was really he, but a few hours & it seemed beyond doubt it was indeed."[10]

No matter who had done the shooting, investigators continued to believe the assassin had had accomplices in the theater. Everyone who worked there came under suspicion, and police repeatedly interviewed the stage crew in the early morning hours. They asked Peanuts Borrows how he came to be holding Booth's horse at the back door of the theater. According to the boy, Booth had actually asked for the stagehand Ned Spangler, but Spangler was busy, and Booth turned the reins over to Borrows instead. Asked why nobody caught up with Booth in the alley, Ford's employee Jake Rittersback said that someone had slammed the door shut just after the assassin went through it. Rittersback also said he knew right away that the assassin was Booth, but when he said something to that effect on the stage, Ned Spangler told him to shut up.[11]

Police were hearing the name of Edman "Ned" Spangler a lot, and detectives didn't take long to decide that he was a suspect. Spangler had often run errands for Booth, and he had been seen talking with him several times on the day of the assassination. He had been among those who fed Booth's horse from time to time, and had sold the assassin's buggy for him earlier that week. As stagehand Joe Simms put it, "They were always very much together." Though Booth was friendly with all the stagehands, Spangler had been closer to him than most. And he disappeared for a short time after the shooting.[12]

While police focused on the theater staff, General Christopher C. Augur directed most of his energy to preventing further attacks. Commander of the 22nd Army Corps, Augur was a distinctive figure about town—extravagantly coifed, with graying hair and a pair of side whiskers that nearly touched his shoulders. He had spent years in command of garrison troops, and was once the commandant of cadets at West Point. He had fought valiantly in the war, but after receiving a serious wound at Cedar Mountain, he had been reassigned to head the Defenses of Washington. In the Booth investigation, his detective force took an active role, and was always at Stanton's disposal.[13]

One of the most important eyewitnesses happened to be Augur's subordinate. Captain Theodore S. McGowan had been sitting just outside the door to the president's box when he saw a man show Charles Forbes, the president's messenger, a large, official-looking envelope with a printed heading and some bold writing on it. McGowan paid little attention, but soon observed another man who wanted to get by as well. This second man stopped at the door to the passageway and stood there for a moment looking around. He drew a number of visiting cards from his coat pocket, and as McGowan put it:

"With some attention [he] selected one, returning the remainder. Then, stepping down upon the next level & to the messenger's right side, he stooped & exhibited the card. I do not know whether the card was carried in by the messenger or his assent given to the entrance of the man who presented it. The latter is more probable, for, in a few moments, I saw the man enter the door of the lobby leading to the box & close it behind him."[14]

McGowan was the only witness who saw how Booth got into the box. Forbes, the messenger, apparently did not give his side of the story. That was one of many puzzling gaps in the investigation.

The theater had already been cleared out before William T. Kent realized that he was missing the key to his house. Kent had gone into the president's box sometime after the shooting, and had lent Dr. Leale his pocketknife to cut off the president's collar. Now halfway home, he wondered if his keys had fallen on the floor when he pulled out the knife. So he turned around, and in the company of Lt. Newton Ferree, went back to look for the keys. The crime scene was dimly lit by the time they arrived, as the gas had been lowered to a faint sepia glow. Reporter L. A. Gobright had been allowed in, and a few others milled around in search of souvenirs. By then the place had nearly been picked clean. Actor E. A. Emerson had taken a playbill from under the president's rocker, and another man had picked up a "Reserved" tag that had fallen nearby. Detective John Clarvoe had acquired the president's bloodstained cravat, and Isaac Jacquette had made off with the bloodstained wooden bar that Booth had used to jam the door shut. That board was a coveted relic, and even though it was only Rathbone's blood, Jacquette had to fight off others just to keep it in one piece.[15]

Looking around in the box, Newton Ferree found a valuable souvenir: the president's collar. Right next to him, in a dark corner, Will Kent kicked a small object on the floor. He felt around on his hands and knees. He thought he might have found his keys, but instead, he came up with a single-shot .44-caliber pistol. It was a so-called gentleman's pistol, with an ornately carved stock, a silver lock plate, and the name "Deringer" engraved on the side. This, apparently, was the murder weapon. In his excitement, Will Kent looked around for someone in authority. Finding no one, he handed the gun over to Gobright, the reporter.[16]

A few hours after the shooting, Lt. John J. Toffey, 10th V.R.C., reported a discovery of his own. After witnessing the assassination, Toffey ran back to his quarters at the Lincoln Hospital to tell the officer of the day what had happened. While they were talking, a riderless horse galloped by. It was a large, heavy-legged horse, saddled and bridled, but with no rider in sight. Suspicious, Toffey and a guard chased the animal down and took it under control. It was exhausted, and had obviously been pushed too hard. Sweat poured off it. And it was blind in one eye. Thinking it must have something to do with the assassination, Toffey took the horse to General Augur's headquarters at once.[17]

BY MIDNIGHT, almost every major official in Washington had paid a visit to the Petersen house. The entire Cabinet showed up within an hour, joining such luminaries as Speaker of the House Schuyler Colfax and Senator Charles Sumner. Dozens of military officers filed through, but only Generals Halleck and Meigs stayed for the duration; most had come for a specific purpose. Captain James McCamly, for example, returned Mrs. Lincoln's opera glasses, which were found when his detachment secured the theater. Captain William Greer brought in the president's shawl. Thus a silent and steady traffic kept up throughout the night. Given the dismal prognosis, these deathbed visits must have seemed something like a wake in advance of death.[18]

Some of the city's best-known doctors joined those attending the president. Among them was John Frederick May, who once made medical history with the world's first leg amputation at the hip. Charles Liebermann, past president of the city's medical association, was another. In all, as many as fourteen doctors were in attendance during the night.[19]

Though the house was crowded, its owner was nowhere in sight. William Petersen, distraught over what was taking place there, refused to watch his property be torn apart. His objections were personal, not political. Two of Petersen's daughters had died in that same bedroom, and he had come to regard it as a shrine to their memory. But on this night, strange men had trudged through in muddy boots, pushing him aside and taking over his home without so much as a nod of recognition. Souvenir hunters had already gone to work, chipping away at the threshold of his front door to recover bloodstained bits of wood. Finally fed up, Petersen stormed off to an upstairs room, and didn't emerge until everyone had left the following day.[20]

The president's vital signs remained steady, and doctors followed his every heartbeat. This was not just medicine, it was history, and every development in the patient's condition was meticulously recorded. The wound opening was kept clear by positioning Lincoln's head off the edge of the bed, then monitoring the amount of discharge. On a few occasions, coagula would build, and, as Dr. Leale reported, the effects were immediately noticeable: "[It] would produce signs of increased compression: the breathing becoming profoundly stertorous and intermittent and the pulse to be more feeble and irregular." Before midnight the pulse rate ranged from 40 to 48 beats per minute, with 24 loud, labored breaths per minute. At 12:30, the pulse began a slow rise upward, and half an hour later, it shot up to 80 beats. That is when Dr. Ezra Abbott, sitting on the bed, noticed a struggling motion of the arms, as if the president were trying to regain consciousness. But Lincoln never opened his eyes, and in a moment, the pulse rate settled back down. It was a false alarm—one of many that kept the doctors alert and on edge.[21]

The ubiquitous C. C. Bangs, of the Christian Commission, was not yet through for the night. When Bangs returned from his last errand, Robert Lincoln, whom he had fetched from the White House, now asked him to get his mother's friend Elizabeth Dixon. The wife of a Connecticut senator, Mrs. Dixon had once been very close to Mrs. Lincoln. In time, Bangs returned with her and a small entourage, who remained with the first lady well into the next day.[22]

Edwin Stanton was still calling in reinforcements to help investigate the attacks. At 1:00 A.M. he handed a message to Major Eckert for transmittal to New York:

WAR DEPARTMENT,
April 15, 1865 — 1 a.m.

John A. Kennedy,
Chief of Police, New York:
     Send here immediately three or four of your best detectives to investigate the facts as to the assassination of the President and Secretary Seward. They are still alive, but the President's case is hopeless, and that of Mr. Seward nearly the same.

Edwin M. Stanton,
Secretary of War.[23]

The New York Police Department had the most experienced detective force in the country. When most cities were just beginning to establish detective corps, some New Yorkers had been solving mysteries for more than a dozen years. Stanton's telegraphic summons was also a sign of the times. After four years of war, the government had become accustomed to using any and all forms of communication at its disposal. Couriers, mounted patrols, and signal torches were all used routinely in emergencies, and even boats were pressed into service, carrying large placards as they patrolled close to shore. But the magnetic telegraph had become the eyes and ears of the War Department. Military necessity had expanded the telegraph's reach up to a thousand miles from Washington. And on the night of April 14, those connections were put to good use. Within just a few hours, Union commanders in Richmond knew all about the attacks; troops in Harpers Ferry were on the alert; the mouth of the Potomac was secured; and the nation's newspapers had all the "particulars" of the case in hand. Over civilian lines, Washington police alerted their counterparts in Baltimore, New York papers filled their morning editions, and detectives everywhere transmitted leads and instructions to where they could do the most good. The telegraph allowed Stanton to order roadblocks on the most likely avenues of escape.[24]

     It was a telegraphic message that brought the news to General Grant that night. Grant was in Philadelphia, sitting with his wife in Bloodgood's

Restaurant, when a one-legged veteran hobbled in on crutches and handed him a message from Washington.

War Department, Washington
April 14, 1865, midnight [sent 12:20 A.M.]

Lieut. Gen. U. S. GRANT
On the night train to Burlington:
　　The President was assassinated at Ford's Theatre at 10 30 tonight & cannot live. The wound is a Pistol shot through the head. Secretary Seward & his son Frederick, were also assassinated at their residence & are in a dangerous condition. The Secretary of War desires that you return to Washington immediately. Please answer on receipt of this.
　　　　　　　　　　　　　　　　　　　THOS. T. ECKERT

Assistant Secretary Charles A. Dana sent Grant another telegram moments later. "Permit me to suggest to you to keep a close watch on all persons who come near you in the cars or otherwise, also that an Engine be sent in front of the train to guard against anything being on the track." Grant did not want to create a stir, so he kept the news to himself. In a few minutes he handed the telegrams to his wife, and with hardly a word, they left for the Philadelphia-Camden ferry. From there, they continued to Burlington that night, and arrangements were put in place for the general's immediate return from there.[25]

A LIGHT RAIN FELL in the early morning hours, but a crowd still waited on Tenth Street for word of the president's condition. Soldiers of the V.R.C. had herded everyone out of the theater and had put the street itself under heavy guard. Dr. George Saylor, an army assistant surgeon, saw that his brother John was posted near one of the theater doors. He complained of having missed an opportunity to visit the scene of the crime. Capt. James R. Stone, standing nearby, offered a solution. Stone had been ordered to inspect the building's interior for signs of arson, and he would be glad to have the Saylors accompany him. They went inside for an unforgettable tour. Even by the light of a camp lantern, the signs of injury and panic were plainly evident. Bloodstains, broken chairs, playbills left in a hasty exit—these things told the story better than words. On the stage, they saw the green baize carpet, torn on the spot where Booth had landed. Above them was the flag that threw off his balance on the way down. The rocking chair still sat in the president's box. Looking around, Dr. Saylor noticed a cane lying on the floor under the sofa. He picked it up and quietly tucked it under his arm.[26]

Gradually, investigators filled in the details of the night's events. It was Alfred Cloughly who described the aftermath of the Seward attack. Cloughly told Justice A. B. Olin that he had been taking a stroll with a lady when they heard the cries of "Thief! Murder! Stop that man!" coming from nearby Lafayette Park. Rushing toward the park gate, he saw a man on horseback just outside the Seward house, frantically trying to get his horse in motion. Cloughly ran toward him, but the horse started off, and he disappeared toward H Street. It occurred to Cloughly that soldiers might still have a chance to catch the assailant, so he ran over to the White House, where a company of infantry had been camping on the south lawn. The officer of the guard said he would do what he could.[27]

As Alfred Cloughly finished this interview, another front in the investigation opened a few blocks to the west. In his office at Nineteeth and I streets, Col. Timothy Ingraham was informed that Lincoln's assassin could probably be identified through his private papers. Ingraham was provost marshal of the Defenses North of the Potomac, with jurisdiction over the area north and east of the city. A balding man with a graying beard and steel-gray eyes, he was much hardened by the war. Once a merchant and customs official, he had commanded the 38th Massachusetts Infantry before taking on his present duties. As provost marshal, his work was directed at draft evaders and such, but as a father, he carried a special grudge against practitioners of "irregular warfare." The year before, his son was almost killed by bushwhackers who shot him far from the field of battle in Louisiana. Since then, underground warfare had become a deeply personal matter. He needed no prompting to pursue the Lincoln conspirators.[28]

Lt. William H. Tyrrell was one of Ingraham's best men. Tyrrell was on duty when General George V. Rutherford reported that Booth had been staying at the National Hotel. The word was passed along to Ingraham, who ordered Tyrrell to take some men over there to see what might have been left behind. The National was a major landmark at Sixth Street and Pennsylvania Avenue. It was one of Washington's more upscale establishments, and was known for its political clientèle, especially New Englanders. Tyrrell and his men wasted no time getting there. They questioned the desk clerk, George W. Bunker, and learned that Booth had been staying in Room 228, on the fourth floor. He had left at about seven o'clock in the evening, and Bunker had not seen him since.

Lieutenant Tyrrell had learned to be especially careful in situations like this. Once, last June, he was making an arrest, and let his guard down for a moment. The suspect had surprised him and bolted. Tyrrell chased the man down, but in the scuffle, he had taken a bullet in the side of the neck. Already wounded five times during the war, he had nearly been finished off for good by that last shot. He had no intention of letting down his guard again.[29]

Room 228 was furnished with only the bare necessities. On a small table in the center of the room were some envelopes and a few sheets of paper. On the dresser were a clothes brush, a broken comb, and a pair of slippers. Next to them, in a brown paper wrapping, was a half-pound plug of Killikinick tobacco. In the bureau drawers were a few items of clothing and half a bottle of hair oil. On the floor were a black leather valise and a pair of scuffed boots. Taken together, the room had the look, as one reporter said, of "a hasty exit." What interested Tyrrell, though, was a large wardrobe trunk by the wall. On its lid were marked the name "J. Wilkes Booth" and the word "theatre." Inside was a wealth of evidence: some pistol cartridges, two pairs of handcuffs, a gimlet, a large quantity of papers, and the dress coat of a full colonel in the Union army. Tyrrell bundled up the papers and took them, along with the coat and handcuffs, back to Colonel Ingraham's office. He turned the trunk and valise over to George Bunker, who took them to the hotel's baggage room. They would remain unopened and forgotten there for years.[30]

Out at the Navy Yard, telegrapher Henry H. Atwater finally got official confirmation of the tragic news. It wasn't even directed to him, but came in the form of a pass-through message. General Halleck wanted to put the prison camp at Point Lookout, in the far reaches of Southern Maryland, on alert. Rumors predicted an uprising there, and the camp could be reached only through Atwater's line.

War Department, April 15.

To Brig. Gen. Barnes, Point Lookout, Md.
  Stop all vessels going down the river and hold all persons in them till further orders.

An attempt has been made tonight to assassinate the President and the Secretary of State. Hold all persons leaving Washington.

> (Signed) H. W. HALLECK
> Major General Chief of Staff
> Navy Yard, Washington

To this army order, another was appended for the navy:

April 15, 1 10 a.m.

To S. Nickerson, Acting Vol. Lieut.

Send the fastest vessel you have with the following message to Comdr Parker.

> (Signed) T. H. EASTMAN
> Lieut. Comdr. Potomac Flotilla.
> Navy Yard, Washington

April 15, 1865 1 15 a.m.

To Comdr. [Foxhall A.] Parker:

An attempt has this evening been made to assassinate the President and Secretary Seward. The President was shot through the head and Secretary Seward had his throat cut in his own house. Both are in a very dangerous condition. No further particulars. There is great excitement here.

> (Signed) T. H. EASTMAN
> Lieut. Comdr. U. S. Potomac Flotilla[31]

At the Petersen house, James Tanner had finished taking down testimony and was rewriting his notes in longhand. He had recorded only six brief interviews, and of those, only James Ferguson, Harry Hawk, H. B. Phillips, and Alexander Crawford had actually witnessed the shooting at Ford's Theatre; Alfred Cloughly and General Rutherford had been elsewhere.[32]

While Tanner transcribed, Secretary Stanton composed a dispatch for the newspapers. He always sent these messages through General John A. Dix in New York, who (because of better telegraph connections) could disseminate them to the nation more effectively than anyone in Washington. Operators would clean up Stanton's copy, removing all signs of confusion that were present in the original.

War Department
April 15.1 30 AM

Maj. General Dix. New York

Last evening about 10.30 PM at Ford's Theater the President while sitting in his private Box with Mrs. Lincoln, Miss Harris and Major Rathbun was shot by an assassin who suddenly entered the box and approached behind the President. The assassin then leaped upon the Stage brandishing a large dagger or knife and made his escape in the rear of the theater. The Pistol ball entered the back of the President's head and penetrated nearly through the head. The wound is mortal. The President has been insensible ever since it was inflicted and is now dying.

About the same hour an assassin (whether the same or another) entered Mr. Seward's house and under pretense of having a prescription, was shown to the Secretary's sick chamber, the Secretary was in bed a nurse and Miss Seward with him. The assassin immediately rushed to the bed inflicted two or three stabs on the throat and two on the face. It is hoped the wounds may not be mortal my apprehension is that they will prove fatal. The noise alarmed Mr. Frederick Seward who was in an adjoining room & hastened to the door of his father's room, where he met the assassin who inflicted upon him one or more dangerous wounds. The recovery of Frederick Seward is doubtful. It is not probable that the President will live through the night. General Grant & wife were advertised to be at the theater this evening, but he started to Burlington at 6 o'clock this evening.

At a Cabinet meeting yesterday at which General Grant was present, the subject of the State of the Country & the prospect of speedy peace was discussed. The President was very cheerful & hopeful spoke very kindly of General Lee and others of the Confederacy, ~~The assassin when he proceeded upon the~~ and the prospect of establishment of government in Virginia.

~~The assassin when he jump~~

The members of the Cabinet except Mr. Seward are now in attendance upon the President. I have seen Mr. Seward but he & Frederick
were both unconscious.

Edwin M. Stanton
Sec of War[33]

Sergeant Hatter, the messenger, had his relay team run this over to the
War Department, seven blocks away. The operators there had been busy
this night, but this was the first one from Stanton, and it would be the first
official description of what had occurred in Washington that night.

Vice President Andrew Johnson arrived at the Petersen house without
fanfare. One can only guess what he must have been thinking. He was
keenly aware that he had few friends in Washington. Many in this city, and
some in this very room, did not want to see him become president. They
regarded him as a lowlife—an uneducated man unworthy of the honor.
Rumors of drunkenness at his inauguration only compounded the problem, and now, before he had even redeemed himself in the eyes of the
public, he had been elevated to the presidency in the most regrettable circumstances. But Johnson did not share his thoughts that night. After a
short visit to the deathbed, he returned to the parlor and assembled the
Cabinet for a brief meeting.[34]

Outside, the crowd erupted once more, and a few people rushed to
the front windows to see what had caused all the fuss. It was another false
alarm, and another dangerous passage for some unfortunate witness. These
flare-ups were becoming routine, and the crowd grew more agitated whenever they occurred. Their excesses might be overlooked after all they had
endured. Having started their day in a state of euphoria, they had been
plunged into the deepest grief. Now, with every false alarm and every
dashed hope, they became more volatile and prone to violence.

The police took two separate approaches. Superintendent Richards
prohibited the sale of liquor for the rest of the night, while Detective James
A. McDevitt appealed to the crowd's sense of reason. After one too many
false alarms, McDevitt went out onto the front steps of police headquarters and asked the crowd for their attention. "You are the friends of the
president," he told them, "and so are we. You are anxious to see justice done
to the perpetrators of this crime, but your anxiety is no greater than ours.
If you will help instead of hindering us, we shall be able to do our work.
These people who are coming to headquarters with us are not crimi-

nals. They are friends of the president, too. They are coming here to tell us what they know, so that we can use the information in capturing the assassin." That seemed to work. Thereafter, witnesses were allowed to pass unmolested.[35]

Reporter Lawrence A. Gobright had been fighting off souvenir hunters ever since Will Kent handed him the murder weapon. At least now he didn't have to brave the mob. As he turned the derringer over to Sergeant Drill, they both noticed there were three extra caps in the stock. Drill took the gun and put it with the other items already booked in. The morning's blotter would list them all: "One Pistol one Slouch hat. One Opera Glass Case, one Spur and two buttons one a brass and the other an india rubber button, also a hat supposed to be the President's were brought to Office by Supt. Richards and A[cting] A[ssistant] S[uperintendent] [Bushrod] Reed." Drill noted that everything but the president's hat was supposed to be connected in some way to the assassination.[36]

Ford's orchestra leader, William Withers, came in to swear out a statement before Justice Miller. The justice asked Withers to describe what he was doing at the moment he heard the shot, and the answer caused a minor stir. "I was in the act of going under the stage to reach the orchestra when I heard the report of a pistol it excited my surprise as I had never heard of a pistol being fired in this play 'The American Cousin.' Just at that time a man came running by me and gave me a severe blow. I turned round he then cut me twice inflicting a rent in my coat vest and shirt which you can now see. I am satisfied that this man was J. Wilkes Booth for I had a good side view of him and heard him say do let me pass." Other eyewitnesses had talked among themselves, and some felt that Withers had changed his story, giving different versions of the shooting every time he told it. The bickering had begun.[37]

Investigators were not always sure what to make of the information that came streaming in. Some would prove valuable only in hindsight. Such was the case with the testimony of John Fletcher, who presented himself at police headquarters in the middle of the night. Fletcher was the foreman of Thompson Nailor's livery stable, on E Street near Fourteenth. At about the time of the assassination, he had chased a man out of the city for failing to return a rented horse. When a cavalry sergeant suggested the animal might have been turned over to the police, Fletcher went to speak with them. Though police had not seen any horses, they knew that somebody had brought one in to General Augur's headquarters a short while ago. They sent Fletcher up there, and thus began a chain of events that would grow in importance over the coming days.[38]

Detectives John Clarvoe and James McDevitt hoped that some clues would lead to the discovery of Booth's accomplices. When someone dropped a name, they made a note. Within the policemen's circle was John Claggett Proctor, a reporter who worked for the *Daily Morning Chronicle* and until recently had worked for the *Evening Star.* On this night, Proctor slipped in to police headquarters to learn what he could about the investigation. Clarvoe and McDevitt had found an important lead, but they didn't want it published. Proctor gave his word. According to the detectives, several parties were rumored to be close associates of John Wilkes Booth. One of them was a young man named John H. Surratt, who may have been the assailant of Secretary Seward. Surratt lived on H Street, and police were getting up a search party to go there now.[39]

That Surratt clue remains one of the great mysteries of the Lincoln assassination story. The original tip was probably not recorded, and accounts written long after the event are incompatible with the known facts. McDevitt later claimed his informant was the actor John McCullough, but McCullough had left town the month before. A. C. Richards insisted it was *he* who first went to the Surratt house, following leads he had developed himself. That version is at odds with the records. Nevertheless, only four hours after the assassination, a party of detectives headed for the house at 541 H Street. It was a three-story brick town house built close to the street. The place was actually the home of John Surratt's mother, Mary. Her late husband, John Sr., had owned it for years, but Mrs. Surratt had only recently moved there from her other place in the country. Soon afterward, she started taking in boarders.[40]

The Surratt boardinghouse was just a few blocks from Ford's Theatre, but that quiet neighborhood seemed worlds away from the Tenth Street turmoil. When police arrived, they found the shades down and the house dark. Light rain beat steadily on its tin roof. Two detectives stayed outside to cover the exits. David Bigley stood on the sidewalk, by the staircase that led to the front door. John Kelly kept an eye on the kitchen entrance; he could see the back yard from there as well. When all the exits were covered, Detectives Clarvoe, Charles Skippon, and McDevitt crept up the wooden steps to the front door.

Louis J. Weichmann, a boarder, had just gone to bed when he heard a violent tug on the doorbell. Hastily pulling on his pants, Weichmann shuffled down to the front door in his bare feet. "Who is there?" he asked.

"Detectives," a man replied. "Is John Surratt in?"

Weichmann cracked the door open and braced himself against the chilly night air. "No, sir. He is not in the city."

Though Mrs. Surratt had gone to bed, Clarvoe said he needed to speak with her, *now*. Weichmann said he would talk to her first, but as he turned to go toward her room, the detectives shoved the front door open and stepped inside. Clarvoe strained to see as someone cracked a door open at the far end of the hall and softly engaged Weichmann in conversation. The detective could not hear what passed between them.[41]

Detective Clarvoe approached them and asked if the lady was Mrs. Surratt. He wanted to speak with her son, John.

"John is not in the city, sir." Mary Surratt said she had not seen her son in almost two weeks.

The detectives hastily searched the house, waking and questioning everyone they found—thirteen people in all. All residents were accounted for: Anna Surratt, Honora Fitzpatrick, Olivia Jenkins, Mary Apollonia Dean, and Louis Weichmann. John T. Holohan, an old friend of Clarvoe's, lived on the third floor with his wife and children. A couple of servants slept downstairs, in the kitchen.

Weichmann showed the detectives around, but he hesitated outside his own room. "Will you be kind enough to tell me the meaning of all this?" he asked.

Clarvoe eyed him suspiciously. "That is a pretty question for you to ask me. Where have you been tonight?"

Weichmann answered, "I have been here in the house."

"Have you been here all evening?" asked the detective.

"No. I have been down in the country with Mrs. Surratt." His voice trailed off. He knew this was building to something, but he couldn't imagine what the detectives were getting at.

"Do you pretend to tell me you have not heard the President has been murdered?"

Lou Weichmann was stunned. "Great God!" he said. "I see it all now." Was it really true? Of course it was, Clarvoe assured him. He reached into the pocket of his coat and pulled out a black bow tie, stained with blood.

"Do you see the blood on that?" Clarvoe said. "That is the blood of

Abraham Lincoln. John Wilkes Booth did that, and I suppose John Surratt has assassinated the Secretary of State." Many suspicious things had happened in the Surratt house, and Louis Weichmann probably thought he had figured out what was going on. But this was unbelievable. Dazed and frightened, Weichmann followed the police downstairs, where his fellow boarders had gathered in the front parlor.

"Mrs. Surratt, what do you think, Booth has murdered the President," he said.

"My God, Mr. Weichmann, you do not tell me so." The other boarders all talked among themselves for a while, but with Mary Surratt sitting right in the room, nobody brought up her son's name.

Downstairs, police talked to Susan Mahoney, a recently hired servant described as "very tall and very black." Her fiancé, Sam Jackson, had been asleep in the house as well. Neither seemed to have any useful information.[42]

In the front parlor, John Clarvoe took Mrs. Surratt aside and told her he wanted to ask a few questions. "Be very particular how you answer them," he warned, "for there is a great deal depends upon them." They talked about Booth, and she admitted seeing him at about two o'clock on Friday afternoon. She was less forthcoming about her son, of whose whereabouts she claimed to have no idea. She had received a letter from him the day before, postmarked in Canada. If the detectives suspected him of doing something in Washington, they had to be mistaken. Though Clarvoe was skeptical, Mrs. Surratt held firm. "There are a great many mothers," she assured him, "who do not know where their sons are."[43]

AT GENERAL AUGUR'S OFFICE, John Fletcher, the stableman, came in to ask about a horse. With him was Charles Stowell, of Provost Marshal O'Beirne's office, who had insisted on escorting Fletcher. Stowell could hardly wait to make an inflated announcement as they walked into the office. "Here, General, is a man that knows all about the party!" He had gotten Augur's attention, and the general began asking questions at once. Slowly, laboriously, John Fletcher repeated his story about the stolen roan horse.

While they talked, Augur noticed how Fletcher kept staring at a saddle and bridle on the floor, next to the general's desk. "Do you know that saddle and bridle?" he asked. The stableman certainly did. They belonged to a regular customer at Nailor's. He often came in with a large brown pac-

ing horse, blind in one eye. Fletcher couldn't remember the man's name—
it was something German—but on his first visit, nearly two weeks ago, he
had written it down. General Augur knew that Fletcher had just described
the horse Lieutenant Toffey had turned in a short while ago. If he could
identify the owner, it could be an important break in the case. So he sent
Stowell down to Nailor's, and he returned with a small card. There was a
name childishly scrawled across the back: "George A. Atzerodt."[44]

Augur had already sent his men out to look for suspicious characters.
Their orders were all the same: "Deploy your troops between the forts of
your command and form a continuous line of pickets. Stop every one from
going out of the line. . . . Leave sufficient guard at each post. It is supposed
one of the assassins is still in town." These instructions were repeated every
few hours to ensure a renewed vigilance. General Martin Hardin, commanding one of Augur's divisions, issued an order of his own, and followed
it with a stunning announcement: "J. Wilkes Booth has been apprehended."
Once again, rumors of Booth's capture had wormed their way into official
channels, and in this case, even the generals passed them along. The troops
must have been demoralized every time someone was forced to set the
record straight.[45]

The city's garrison stood at full alert, and pickets were especially vigilant on every road leading to Baltimore. Samuel B. Lawrence, Assistant
Adjutant General of the Middle Department, extended his coverage even
farther with an order to General Kenly at Wilmington, Delaware: "In consequence of the assassination of the President and Secretary of State the
most vigorous measures will be taken in this department to suppress any
outbreak. . . . No trains will be permitted to leave this city. Do your utmost
to preserve order and keep a sharp lookout for Booth. Report your action."
Rail service had been halted long before this, but if Booth had already
boarded a train by then, they might still catch up to him. In any event, he
couldn't get out of the country. The Provost Marshal General, James B.
Fry, had already posted guards along the Canadian border.[46]

What should happen to Booth if he should be caught? Little thought
was given to the matter until Stanton was given a report that proved to be
false. In the early morning hours of April 15, a man was arrested on the
road to Baltimore. He so closely fit the description of Booth that authorities were certain they had captured the assassin. They informed their superiors in Washington. In minutes, Secretaries Stanton and Welles devised
a plan for his secure detention. Welles sent an order to Commodore Mont-

gomery at the navy yard: "If the military authorities arrest the murderer of the President and take him to the Yard, put him on a Monitor and anchor her in the stream with a strong guard on vessel, wharf and in Yard. Call upon Comdt. Marine Corps for guard. Have vessel immediately prepared ready to receive him at any hour day or night with necessary instructions. He will be heavily ironed and so guarded as to prevent escape or injury to himself."

The man in custody proved to be someone else, and the unfortunate look-alike was set free. But Welles's detention plan was a good one. It was put into effect later, when the real culprits were caught.[47]

FOUR

"ARREST EVERY MAN, WOMAN, OR CHILD ATTEMPTING TO PASS"

A BRAHAM LINCOLN'S CONDITION HAD CHANGED LITTLE
since midnight. His pulse was stable at about 48, and his respiration held at 30. In the early morning hours, Mrs. Lincoln came in to see her husband. He was, to all appearances, dead. The face was drained of color. The bedclothes were stained a deep crimson. One look, and Mary Lincoln burst into sobs. She had already lost two sons, and their deaths had left her devastated. But the sight of her dying husband would test her sanity. She seemed to be the only one who could not accept the hopelessness of the case. Kneeling by the bed, she pleaded with her husband to open his eyes and to speak to her. The Reverend Dr. Phineas Gurley, of the New York Avenue Presbyterian Church, knelt and prayed beside her. Then he gently suggested that she leave her husband to the doctors and the hands of God.

In the next room, Andrew Johnson was talking with Secretary Stanton when Provost Marshal O'Beirne brought in some of the items his men had found at the Kirkwood House. As O'Beirne saw it, this evidence proved that Johnson was indeed also a target of the conspirators. Evidently, this man Atzerodt had been supposed to kill him. Though nobody knew where Atzerodt had gone, O'Beirne assured the vice president that he and his men had neutralized the threat. From then on, a guard would stay with Johnson at all times.[1]

Every so often, Edwin Stanton went to the back room. Each time, he came and went without a word. After one such visit, he returned to the parlor and sat down to write another dispatch for the press:

Washington City,
No. 458 Tenth Street, Apl 15, 1865 — 3 am

Major-General Dix:
New York.

The President still breathes, but is quite insensible, as he has been ever since he was shot. He evidently did not see the person who shot him but was looking on the stage as he was approached behind.

Mr. Seward has rallied, and it is hoped he may live. Frederick Seward's condition is very critical. The attendant who was present was stabbed through the lungs, and is not expected to live. The wounds of Major Seward are not serious. Investigation strongly indicates J. Wilkes Booth as the assassin of the President. Whether it was the same or a different person that attempted to murder Mr. Seward remains in doubt. Chief Justice Cartter is engaged in taking the evidence. Every exertion has been made to prevent the escape of the murderer. His horse has been found on the road, near Washington.

Edwin M. Stanton
Sec. of War[2]

That last sentence was telling. Evidently, Stanton regarded the discovery of that one-eyed horse as a major development in the manhunt. Investigators in the War Department assumed it was the assassin's horse, unaware of what Peanuts Borrows and Jim Ferguson had told police: that Booth had ridden a small mare. But since this horse was found east of the Capitol, General Gustavus DeRussy sealed off the eastern part of the city. His orders were emphatic: "Arrest every man, woman, or child attempting to pass any Bridge or through the lines." DeRussy and General Hardin were now confident that Booth had not made it past the pickets, and Hardin even ordered the commander of Fort Baker to close off the rivers as well. "The horse and saddle of [the] supposed murderer have been found near Lincoln Hospital," he wrote. "Check all boats on the Eastern Branch and Potomac River to guard against crossing between bridges. Continue doing so throughout the night." Authorities felt they were closing in on Booth, and that one-eyed horse was keeping their hopes alive. General Augur even sent Lieutenant Toffey back to scour the neighborhood where he found it. From Lincoln Hospital to Glenwood Cemetery, Toffey would check every building in sight.[3]

The more he thought about it, the more General Augur was convinced that the stableman, John Fletcher, was an important witness. Augur questioned Fletcher again, and learned the names of a few more of Booth's associates. But getting to their names was not easy. Fletcher felt no sense of urgency, and insisted on covering every detail in a long and torturous narrative. The story, as he saw it, began on April 3, when two men came to Nailor's Stable with two horses—one a brown and the other a bay. One of the men, who proved to be Booth, told Fletcher that he was going to Philadelphia, and would like the other man—Atzerodt—to sell the brown horse while he was gone. That horse was blind in one eye. Atzerodt did not return until the day of the assassination, and when Fletcher saw him, he asked what became of that horse his friend wanted him to sell. Atzerodt said that a man in Montgomery County, Maryland, had bought it.

George Atzerodt stopped at the stable a couple of times that day. He still had the bay mare, and he asked Fletcher if he could leave her there that evening. He would need to pick her up at ten o'clock that night, and wondered if the stableman would mind keeping the place open until then. He came back right on schedule, but instead of leaving with the horse, he invited Fletcher to have a drink with him. The stableman went along reluctantly; another horse was long overdue, and Fletcher had begun to think he would never see it again. Mr. Nailor, the stable owner, would probably hold him responsible for that.

That horse was called Charley. Light roan in color, he had a black tail and black mane. He was especially valuable for his gentle gait and mild disposition. The renter, who gave his name as Herold, had asked for him specifically. He picked the horse up at four, and paid in advance. Fletcher insisted he bring it back no later than nine o'clock. Both horse and rider were still gone at ten.

John Fletcher and Atzerodt had a warm glass of ale, then walked back to the stable together. On the way Atzerodt remarked, "If this thing happens tonight, you will hear of a present." The comment made no sense, and it seemed to come out of nowhere. Fletcher figured the man was drunk, so when Atzerodt mounted up, a few minutes later, the stableman asked if he ought to be riding a horse in his condition. "I would not like to ride that animal through the streets at night," he warned. "She looks too skittish." But Atzerodt just shrugged it off. "She is good upon a retreat."

A retreat? Fletcher suddenly recalled that this man Atzerodt knew Herold, who was still out with Charley, the roan. They sometimes came to the stable together. So he voiced his concern, and Atzerodt reassured him, "Oh, he will be back after a while." There was something in his manner that made John Fletcher wonder if those two were up to no good. On a hunch, he followed Atzerodt as far as the Kirkwood House. Then he headed back to the stable. And that's when he heard Charley.

To an expert, each type of horse has its own signature sound. Charley was a racking horse, or, as Fletcher called him, a single-footed pacer. His gait had a distinctive sound, which Fletcher recognized as he walked back to the stable. The horse was coming toward him from the direction of the Treasury building, and when the stableman saw Herold in the saddle, he was livid. "You get off that horse now!" he shouted. "You have had him long enough!" Hearing that, Herold put his spurs to the animal and galloped away.

Fletcher ran back to the stable and saddled another horse. The assassination had not yet occurred, and the stableman knew nothing about Booth's conspiracy. But he was convinced that Herold and Atzerodt were tied together in some kind of scheme, and knowing that Atzerodt came from Southern Maryland, he figured that either he or Herold—or both of them—would be heading in that direction. Fletcher started after them, but he didn't get far. At the Navy Yard Bridge, a sergeant confirmed that two men had indeed crossed out of the city. The first one might have been Herold, but the second rider looked nothing like Atzerodt. Though the sergeant was willing to let Fletcher cross after them, there was one hitch: he was not willing to bend the rules and let him return to the city before morning. So John Fletcher gave up. He rode back into town, and heard about the assassination shortly afterward. Presumably, the police had more important things to do than look for his horse.[4]

THE RAIN HAD FAILED to disperse the crowd on Tenth Street. At the Petersen house, Cartter, Olin, and Hill completed their interviews and joined the bedroom vigil. Though no doctor expected to save the president, proper medical procedures demanded a full exploration of the wound. So at about two A.M. the surgeons began to assess the full extent of the damage. Surgeon General Barnes led the examination. Crouching on the floor, Dr. Barnes inserted a silver probe into the track of the ball. It struck something hard about two and a half inches in—probably a plug of bone forced inward by the shot. Barnes gave a gentle push, and the probe went past it, though not by very much. The instrument, it appeared, was too small to do anything more, and Dr. Taft suggested they send out for a Nelaton probe. Not only was it longer, but it had an unglazed porcelain tip that would come away discolored from any contact with lead. A steward was sent to the Judiciary Square Hospital to get one.[5]

Meanwhile, Stanton placed the security of the capital in the hands of General Grant. Since the general was still on his way back from Burlington, he wired back instructions every time his train stopped. First, he wanted his route back to Washington secured. The ferryboat that would carry his train car over the Susquehanna should be thoroughly searched. Pickets and patrols should be placed along the tracks, with everyone on full alert. From Newark, Delaware, Grant directed that an officer and ten men meet him at the President Street Station in Baltimore. They were to ride with him the rest of the way. In all, hundreds of people were involved in the process of getting General Grant back to Washington unharmed. They were in for a long, tense night.[6]

At the office of the Provost Marshal, Colonel Ingraham and his officers pored over the papers Tyrrell had found in Booth's trunk. Among them were a crudely drawn map of the Southern states, some personal correspondence, and a sheet with letters and numerals on a hand-drawn grid—obviously the key to some sort of cipher code. There was some printed matter pertaining to oil company investments, and a series of letters on the same topic from one Joseph H. Simonds. A letter from Junius Booth mentioned oil as well, and another from Orlando Tompkins asked about the "ile"—obviously some kind of inside joke.

There was also a letter from an actor named Young, who was being drafted and wanted Booth to appear in a play for his benefit. There were notes on theatrical engagements, and a bill from Tiffany's in New York for braiding hair into a ring. One envelope bore a New York address, along with some cryptic lines scribbled on it like roads on a map. Many of the papers were about family matters: a letter from Booth's mother; a playbill announcing a benefit for Booth's niece Blanche; and a note from Ben DeBar enclosing a favorable review of Blanche's performance.[7]

Taken together, they gave a superficial but wide-ranging glimpse of the man's life. They touched upon his professional business, family concerns, investment dealings, and personal gossip. They even suggest something of his legendary sex life. A note from "E. S." urgently implores her "darling Boy" to pay her a visit. On another slip of paper was a New York address, with a fragment of a woman's note on the reverse: "I am about your age, possibly a few months younger, and you will probably wonder that a woman——" The rest was torn off.[8]

Colonel Ingraham was looking for clues to the conspiracy, and this bundle of papers would not disappoint him. One item in particular caught his attention: a letter dated at "Hookstown" on March 27—less than a month earlier—from a man named Sam. In a neat and flowing script, this man refers to an unspecified arrangement and pleads with Booth to delay any further action, at least until they could see what "Richmond" thought of their plans. Now, this was explosive. If Ingraham was reading this correctly, Confederate authorities had some kind of interest in John Wilkes Booth's plot. It was right there in the letter!

Hookstown, Balto Co.
March 27th, 1865.

Dear John:
    Was business so important that you could not remain in Balto. till I saw you. I came in as soon as I could, but found you had gone to W——n. I called also to see Mike, but learned from his mother he had gone out with you and had not returned. I concluded therefore he had gone with you. How inconsiderate you have been. When I left you, you stated we would not meet in a month or so. therefore I made application for employment, answer to which I shall receive during week. I told my parents I had ceased with you. Can I then under existing circumstances, come as you request. You know full well that the G——t. suspicions something is going on there. therefore, the undertaking is becoming more complicated. Why not for the present desist, for various reasons, which if you look into, you can readily see, without my making any mention thereof. You, nor any one can censure me for my present course. you have been its cause, for how can I now come after telling them I had left you. Suspicion rests upon me now from my whole family, and even parties in the county. I will be compelled to leave home any how, and how soon I care not. None, no not one, were

more in for the enterprise than myself, and to day would be there, had you not done as you have—by this I mean, manner of proceeding. I am, as you well know, in need. I am, you may say, in rags whereas to day I ought to be well clothed. I do not feel right stalking about with means, and more from appearances a beggar. I feel my dependence, but even all this would and was forgotten, for I was one with you. Time more propitious will arrive yet. do not act rashly or in haste. I would prefer your first query, "go and see how it will be taken at R——d, and ere long I shall be better prepared to again be with you. I dislike writing, would sooner verbally make known my views. Yet your non writing causes me thus to proceed. Do not in anger peruse this. weigh all I have said, and as a rational man and a *friend*, you can not censure or upbraid my conduct. I sincerely trust this nor aught else that shall or may occur, will ever be an obstacle to obliterate our former friendship and attachment. Write me to Balto. as I expect to be in about Wednesday or Thursday. Or if you can possibly come on, I will Tuesday meet you in Balto. at B——. Ever I subscribe myself,

> Your friend,
> Sam.[9]

The colonel congratulated Tyrrell on this important find, and he ordered him to report to Secretary Stanton immediately.

AT ABOUT THREE O'CLOCK, the hospital steward arrived with a Nelaton probe, and Dr. Barnes went right to work. Kneeling next to the bed, he carefully fed the probe into Lincoln's wound. This instrument went in deeper than the last one. It too struck something hard—something with a rough and jagged surface, but not lead. Dr. Taft suggested it might be the president's right eye socket. Barnes agreed, and he checked again. This time the probe went in to a depth of seven and a quarter inches. That seemed to be the extent of the damage.

The ball had been shot from just a few inches away. It had entered the back of Lincoln's head, not far from the base of the skull, about an inch and a half to the left of center. From the bruising and swelling of the right (opposite side) eye, it appeared that the bullet had crossed over the centerline, but not at a trajectory low enough to sever the brain stem and stop the heart and lungs. Dr. Crane and Dr. Stone each took a turn with the probe, and each concurred that Booth's bullet was behind and above the right eye.[10]

All of this occurred under the gaze of more than a dozen people. Secretary Welles kept watch from a rocking chair near the foot of the bed. Attorney General Speed, Treasury Secretary McCullogh, and Postmaster General Dennison joined Secretaries Stanton and Usher on one side of it, while the Reverend Dr. Gurley, John Blair Smith Todd, and Rufus Andrews stood at its head. Robert Lincoln remained by his father's side, always in the company of Senator Sumner. Eventually, his mother returned. Mary Lincoln knelt and wept, begging her husband to take her with him. Suddenly a change came over her. She straightened up and gasped. Her eyes widened, and after a slight pause, she fainted dead away. Mrs. Dixon, standing beside her, caught her and, with some help, dragged her over to an open window, where the cool air helped restore her to consciousness. She returned to the bedside, but one of the doctors suggested she might feel more comfortable in the parlor. Saying nothing, she answered with a faint nod. The weary, vacant look never left her face. Leaning over the bed, she tenderly kissed her husband for the last time, and stood up. Mrs. Dixon helped her from the room, and as she passed by the back parlor door, James Tanner heard her moan, "O, my God, and I have given my husband to die." As he told a friend, "I never heard so much agony in so few words."[11]

Secretary Stanton was too busy to grieve. Sitting at the marble-topped table in the rear parlor, he sent off another message to authorities in Baltimore:

WAR DEPARTMENT,
Washington, April 15, 1865 — 3 a.m. (Sent 3.55 a.m.)

Brigadier-General MORRIS,
Commanding District of Baltimore:
    Make immediate arrangements for guarding thoroughly every avenue leading into Baltimore, and if possible arrest J. Wilkes Booth, the murderer of President Lincoln. You will acknowledge the receipt of this telegram, giving time, &c.

EDWIN M. STANTON,
Secretary of War.[12]

The shooting of that picket near the Lincoln Hospital remained very much on Stanton's mind. If the horsemen who fired on those guards had indeed been conspirators, then the assassin was likely to be heading toward Baltimore. Maybe the criminals had exchanged horses, and that one-eyed horse was left there to distract pursuers. Perhaps the two men seen heading for the Navy Yard Bridge were decoys. After all, the bridge was southeast of the city, but all the other signs pointed northeast.[13]

In ordering acknowledgment of his messages "giving time, etc.," Stanton betrayed some frustration about the distribution of his orders. They simply weren't getting through quickly enough. In fact, the process of communicating was slow by nature. Though the secretary might finish a dispatch in a matter of minutes, he would have to give it to Major Eckert, who would hand it off to Sergeant Hatter, who would relay it, through five or six men, to the War Department, a mile away. Once there, an operator converted the message into a cipher code. When a line came open, he sent it out, one character at a time. Add receiving and deciphering delays at the other end of the line, and Stanton's message might finally reach its destination a full hour after he wrote it. In 1865, they called that "instantaneous."

Other forms of communication were no quicker. Court-martial testimony taken shortly after the assassination offers a glimpse of how orders traveled from commanding general to private on patrol. Just after midnight on April 15, General Martin Hardin commanded all troops in his division to take precautions and prevent the escape of the assassins. That message went out by flag signal. Colonel Charles H. Long, in charge of the forts northwest of the city, received the order and sent out cavalry patrols to detain or turn back anyone who looked suspicious. Long received another message to the same effect at 2:55 A.M., and he, in turn, reiterated the need for vigilance. Just like the first order, Long's second message passed to the smaller command of Captain Charles Dupont at Fort Reno. Dupont passed each order on to the officer of the day, Lt. Frederick Dean, who relayed them to the men on guard duty. Soon every soldier in the command knew what the general's orders were—with a delay of perhaps an hour.

But while that first message was in transit, General Hardin's headquarters also sent duplicate orders directly to Lieutenant Dean. This redundancy was meant to accelerate the process, but sometimes it lessened the sense of urgency along the regular channels. This may account for the tendency in some officers to reiterate orders ad nauseam—and for Stanton's insistence that his own messages be acknowledged and acted upon.[14]

Stanton's three o'clock telegram got on the line at about average speed, but the reply came back right away.

> BALTIMORE, MD., April 15, 1865 — 4.16 a.m.
> [Received 4:30 a.m.]
>
> Hon. E. M. STANTON,
> *Secretary of War:*
> Your dispatch received. The most vigorous measures will be taken. Every avenue is guarded. No trains or boats will be permitted to leave this department for the present.
>   W. W. MORRIS,
>   Brigadier-General.[15]

Like most senior officers, General Morris didn't wait to be told. When the first reports of the shooting had come in, he tightened security throughout his command.

PRESIDENT LINCOLN WAS SINKING RAPIDLY. At 2:54 his pulse had been barely perceptible. Since then, his breathing had grown more feeble and shallow. Dr. Barnes kept a finger on the president's carotid artery, while Drs. Taft and Liebermann took turns holding his head. They had kept it up for hours, and fatigue was taking its toll. All were amazed that the president had lived for so long. At 5:30 A.M. his wound stopped bleeding, and brain matter no longer oozed from the opening. The pulse by then was intermittent, with two or three beats followed by a long silence. From that point on, the patient's breathing increased in frequency but decreased in strength. Inhalations came in short bursts, and exhalations were drawn out. Each breath made a loud guttural sound that almost everyone in the house could hear.[16]

THE PACE SLOWED at police headquarters, so Bushrod Reed, acting assistant superintendent, went up to General Augur's headquarters office in search of a favor. Boarders at the Surratt house had suggested that Reed's detectives search for Booth in Southern Maryland. It sounded like good advice, but there was just one problem: the police department owned no horses. So Reed asked Augur's adjutant, Colonel John H. Taylor, if he might borrow some cavalry troops. Taylor wanted to be accommodating, but the cavalry had all gone out by then. The police were welcome to use whatever horses they could find.[17]

Though events were still pulling him in every direction, Edwin Stanton was finding the task more manageable. He also took on more duties. An aide reminded him that Jacob Thompson, the top Confederate State Department official working in Canada, had been spotted in Maine, allegedly on his way to Europe. Several other members of the so-called Canadian Cabinet were thought to have crossed the American border, but the federal government showed no interest in arresting them. Just the day before, President Lincoln was asked for guidance on the matter. "I should not be sorry to have them out of the country," said the president, "but I should be for following them up pretty closely to make sure of their going."

But things were different now, and the more Stanton thought about it, the more indignant he became. Abraham Lincoln had shown leniency to one of the very men who, Stanton believed, had been plotting Lincoln's death. So in the early hours of April 15, he countermanded the president and ordered the arrest of Jacob Thompson if found anywhere in the United States. Edwin Stanton was not in a forgiving mood.[18]

Much had happened since Stanton sent out his three o'clock dispatch, and an updated report was undoubtedly warranted. So at four o'clock, he checked again on the president's condition, then sat down to compose another message:

Washington City,
No. 458 Tenth Street, April 15, 1865 — 4.10 am

Major-General Dix:
The President continues insensible and is sinking. Secretary Seward remains without change. Frederick Seward's scull is fractured in two places besides a severe cut upon the head. The attendant is still alive, but hopeless. Major Seward's wounds are not dangerous.
It is now ascertained with reasonable certainty that two assassins were engaged in the horrible crime, ~~Booth~~ Wilkes Booth being the one that shot the President the other a companion of his whose name is not

known but whose description is so clear that he can hardly escape. ~~The in~~ It appears from a letter found in Booth's trunk that the murder was planned before the 4th of March but fell through then because the accomplice backed out until Richmond [illegible, crossed out] could be heard from. Booth and his accomplice ~~got their horse~~ were at the livery stable at 6 this evening, and left there with their horses about 10 o'clock, or shortly before that hour. It would seem that they had for several days been seeking their chance, but for some unknown reason it was not carried into effect until ~~tonight~~ last night. ~~They~~ One of them has evidently made his way to Baltimore, the other has not yet been traced.

> Edwin M. Stanton,
> Sec. of War[19]

This 4:10 update was far less frantic than the original 1:30 telegram. Its words and lines were drawn more carefully, its message laid out with more precision. Stanton was regaining his composure and had again become the commanding figure that people had come to expect. His press releases were said to prefigure an organizational style that would become standard among journalists in later years. The so-called inverted pyramid composition gave the most weighty facts at the top of the story, with information of lesser importance tapering toward the end, or bottom, of the piece. The secretary's dispatches followed that system closely. If this was intentional, it shows a remarkable ability to stay focused and to systematize his thoughts under pressure. It is more likely, though, that the organization of these telegrams was inadvertent. Stanton was pressured by other demands, and he simply began his missives with the assumption that he would have only a moment to finish them. Thus, he put the most important information down first. Then, lost in thought, he kept writing for as long as he had something to say.[20]

This new dispatch had some glaring inaccuracies. Stanton mangled the details of Atzerodt's livery stable visits, and he connected Booth to the horse at Nailor's, though Fletcher never mentioned Booth. More important, he draws from the "Sam" letter something that wasn't there— evidence of a plan to attack on inauguration day, March 4.

It is easy to imagine the source of the confusion. For months, the city had swirled with rumors of an attack at the inauguration, and this letter may have given Stanton a vague sense that the rumors were based on fact. He may have been given inaccurate reports, and he may have jumped to unwarranted conclusions. Whatever the cause, we should not assume Stanton was deliberately distorting the facts. Inaccuracies colored every dispatch, affidavit, and report on record that night, and in all likelihood, Edwin Stanton was just passing along what he had heard.

That last message gave a sense of Stanton's priorities. The discovery of the Sam letter, the recovery of that half-blind horse, and the picket shooting northeast of the city were uppermost in his mind. That skirmish was one of several incidents that focused attention on the road to Baltimore. Those horsemen had been in a hurry, and desperate enough to risk their lives in fleeing from Washington. And there were *six* of them. If they were indeed Booth's accomplices, then the attacks on Lincoln and Seward were part of a vast conspiracy, planned and executed by many people. It was a tentative theory, and a bit paranoid in hindsight. But even if it was wrong, the facts still pointed toward a Baltimore escape route.

The identity of Seward's assailant was still in doubt, but some investigators were confident that George Atzerodt was their man. His saddle and bridle were on the one-eyed horse. Booth's bankbook had been found in his room, and he had obviously been tracking the vice president with evil intent. Though the case against Atzerodt looked solid, an early morning incident threw the whole case into doubt.

Just after dawn, two privates from the 3rd Massachusetts Heavy Artillery encountered a suspicious horseman on a road near Glenwood Cemetery, northeast of the city. Herbert Staples and Charles Ramsell were riding back to their command from a night on the town, when they stopped to chat with their regimental courier. As the three men stood in the driving rain, a horseman and his servant approached them and struck up a conversation. The horseman seemed nonchalant, considering all that had happened, and the soldiers found it strange that the first thing he said was "What's the news?" He, after all, had just come from Washington. Ramsell told him that Secretary Seward had been assassinated. "By God, is that so!" the horseman said, slapping his thigh. There was more than a hint of mockery in the gesture.

The soldiers assured him it was so, and the president had been killed as well. But the rider was not interested. Without even asking for details, he went on to inquire how he might get outside the military lines. "Is there anything to hinder me?" he asked. A sentry stood along the road in the distance, and Ramsell told the man that he would likely be stopped when he got up there. The stranger thought it over, then spun his horse around, saying, "I shall venture it." He rode off, and as the soldiers stared incredulously, he went unchallenged past the man they had *assumed* was a sentry. Ramsell thought they ought to go chase him down, but it was too late.[21]

To General Augur's detectives, Ramsell and Staples's report seemed to confirm that Seward's assailant was still in Washington. Though the soldiers could not identify that horseman, their description sounded just like a composite of Surratt and Atzerodt. Mostly, he resembled Atzerodt: medium height and build; long gray coat, stained in the front; scruffy whiskers; and in Staples's words, "a good head of hair, tossed back behind his ears in southern style." But his horse was a medium-sized dark bay, like the one John Surratt owned. He even wore boots with red morocco facings, like those worn by the Sewards' attacker.

If this horseman was one of the conspirators, the fact that he was still close to the city was encouraging. Yet there was something about him that didn't add up. Staples said that he looked like Booth, not Surratt or Atzerodt, and his friend agreed. When shown a photograph of the assassin, Ramsell said, "If that man didn't have a mustache, I should swear it was him." The stains on the long gray coat looked more like tobacco spittle than like blood. And the man sounded educated, or at any rate, he did not speak with a German accent. This stranger had some of the right traits, but they didn't add up to George Atzerodt. Could he have been one of the others? Was he John Wilkes Booth, riding Surratt's horse? The possibility could not be dismissed. That skirmish had occurred nearby, and a sweaty horse belonging to a known conspirator was discovered just a little to the south of there. Many clues were cropping up in the same area.

ELAM M. HACK, a young typesetter for the Washington *Critic*, was rousted from bed by a pounding on the door. Some officers informed him that Secretary of War Stanton had authorized an offer of $10,000 for the capture of the assassins. General Augur wanted flyers printed up as quickly as possible, and since the *Critic* was conveniently located on Ninth Street, just around the block from Ford's Theatre, it seemed the logical place to go. Hack went right to work, selecting the largest type in the shop. The flyer was no work of art:

$10,000 REWARD!

HEADQUARTERS DEPARTMENT OF WASHINGTON,
APRIL 15TH, 1865.

A REWARD OF $10,000 WILL BE PAID TO THE PARTY
OR PARTIES ARRESTING THE MURDERER OF THE PRESIDENT,
MR. LINCOLN!
AND THE ASSASSIN OF THE SECRETARY OF STATE,
MR. SEWARD!

C. C. AUGUR, MAJ. GEN. COMD'G. DEP'T.[22]

STABLEMAN JOHN FLETCHER KEPT THINKING about George Atze-rodt, and he couldn't shake the feeling that Atzerodt was tied to the as-sassination. With Charlie Stowell's encouragement, he decided to pick up where he left off—chasing that roan horse into Southern Maryland. He had a fair idea where to look. He remembered that Atzerodt had once mentioned a little village called "T.B.," in the southern part of Prince George's County. He didn't dare ask Thompson Nailor to supply him with a new mount, since he had just lost one of Nailor's best horses. So, borrowing a couple of sickly "hospital" horses from the K Street corral, Fletcher and Stowell headed down to police headquarters, where Detec-tives McDevitt, David Bigley, and Clarvoe joined them for a trek into Southern Maryland.[23]

First Lieutenant David D. Dana, 3rd Massachusetts Heavy Artillery, was already on the same mission. Dana was stationed at Fort Baker, south-east of the city, and just before dawn he set out for Maryland with an es-cort from the 13th New York Cavalry. General Augur had ordered the expedition, based on his interview with John Fletcher, but he left the specifics up to Dana. Unfortunately, the lieutenant had not yet spoken to Sgt. Silas T. Cobb, of the Navy Yard Bridge detail. Cobb was the man Fletcher had spoken to the night before, and he also served in Dana's regi-ment. He was one of the few people in Washington who knew that two men had crossed out of the city on Friday night. One had given his name as Booth.[24]

. . .

AS THE GRAY MORNING LIGHT CREPT over the city, most Washingtonians were already on the move. Thousands in this town had not slept the night before, and those who had awoke to a different world. Outside the Petersen house, hundreds still waited in the rain for word of the president's condition. An announcement, they knew, would be a mere formality. Col. George Woodward arrived at dawn. Woodward had spent most of the night in the saddle, inspecting pickets to see that they were properly deployed and attentive. He closed out his rounds with a stop at the Petersen house. Though reluctant to go inside, he eventually did, and the memory of that visit stayed with him for the rest of his life. General Augur was sitting on the hallway steps, looking thoroughly exhausted. Muffled wailing sounds came from behind the parlor door. At the entrance to the back bedroom stood General Meigs, stiff and silent as a sentinel. Just beyond lay the president, who could be seen through the doorway, and Surgeon General Barnes, who knelt next to him, sopping up his blood.

The vigil still moved in fits and starts. "Every now and then," Woodward recalled, "the sounds would cease, and for a moment or two it would seem as if the end had come; then they would begin again, and the failing flame of life would feebly flicker on."[25]

NOT EVERYONE IN WASHINGTON KNEW what had happened the night before. To some, the terrible news came with the morning light. Benjamin B. French, the commissioner of public buildings, was one of those who missed the excitement. French had fallen asleep at around ten o'clock, and when he awoke at daylight, he was surprised to see that the street lamps were still lit. On the sidewalk below, a sentry paced in front of his house. Puzzled and concerned, he dressed hastily and ran down to the front door. "Are not the doings of last night dreadful?" someone called to him. French asked what the man was talking about. "Have you not heard?" came the reply. Staggered by the news, French threw on his overcoat and hurried over to close the Capitol building. He then headed for Tenth Street.[26]

POLICE WERE FIRMLY CONVINCED that some of Ford's employees had played some part in the murder, and they concentrated first on Ned Spangler. He was said to be especially cozy with Booth, and according to backstage gossip, he had spoken disparagingly of Lincoln on Friday afternoon. Someone quoted him as saying, "I hope the damned son of a bitch will be killed here tonight." The more police learned, the more suspicious Spangler, along with Jake Rittersback, looked. Both were backstage at the time of the shooting, and both had behaved suspiciously in the preceding hours. At dawn on Saturday, orders were drawn up for their arrest as material witnesses.[27]

Spangler told police he had known Booth for eleven or twelve years. Booth had come to the theater on Friday at about five or six o'clock with a little bay mare. He took off her saddle, but insisted the bridle be left on. "She is a bad little bitch," Booth said, and would not stand to be tied. Together, they locked the mare in the stable, then went for a drink. That was the last Spangler saw of Booth until the play was under way.

Spangler was posted on the same side of the stage as the president's box. His job was to shove flats, or background pieces, into place when the scenes changed. At some point during the performance, actor John L. Debonay came over and told him that John Wilkes Booth was asking to see him at the back door. Going out to the alley, Spangler found Booth standing outside the door with the same little mare he had put in the stable earlier. The actor asked him to hold the horse for ten or fifteen minutes. "I have no time," said Spangler, "but I could call Peanut John." Booth wasn't listening. He brushed past the stagehand and went inside, leaving Ned Spangler holding the reins. Impatiently, Spangler passed the horse off to Peanuts Borrows, then went back to his post. He was there when he heard the shot.

In another room down the hall, Jake Rittersback was putting a different spin on things. Rittersback had been employed at Ford's for only the past four weeks, and though he had seen Booth around, he had only recently learned his name. He knew that Spangler did favors for Booth, and on the day of the assassination he had seen them together in the alley talking about a bridle for a horse. Beyond that, he didn't know much. Though Rittersback disavowed involvement in the killing, he was not so sure about Peanuts. On his suggestion, police went looking for Borrows, who was milling around on Tenth Street. When they took him to the station house, they let Rittersback go.[28]

THE PRESIDENT TOOK A DEEP BREATH—so deep, in fact, that it brought everyone in the room to attention. His chest rose, and the doctors waited for it to drop. They kept waiting, as the room went silent and time itself seemed to freeze. Then the chest slowly fell with a ghastly wheezing sound. His muscles relaxed, and the doctors waited for another breath. Nothing. The surgeons exchanged glances. The president was perfectly motionless. To all appearances, this hopeless vigil had come to an end. Dr. Ezra Abbott, sitting on the bed, looked down at his pocket watch. Another moment passed in silence, and Dr. Barnes flipped open his watch as well. Six-fifty A.M., and the president of the United States . . . drew in another breath. This was another false alarm.

AT HOWARD'S LIVERY STABLE, near Sixth and G streets, foreman Brooke Stabler was mulling over the events of last night when a young man appeared at his office door. He looked like an educated man: well-dressed, soft, and mannerly. Stabler had seen the man before, but could not recall his name. They exchanged greetings and talked about the assassination. The fellow tried his best to appear casual, but he was shaking all over; he looked scared to death. In conversation, he mentioned that his friend John Surratt had gone to Europe. Surratt, he said, had been in trouble with detectives, but the reason for mentioning that was not really clear. In further conversation, he seemed to hope that Stabler would forget that he had even mentioned Surratt, but in fact this strange talk had the opposite effect. It reminded the foreman that John Surratt was a friend of John Wilkes Booth's.

Now Brooke Stabler began to wonder if Surratt had had anything to do with the assassination. Surratt and Booth were close friends, and they often came to the stable together. They shared horses and buggies. The more Stabler thought about it, the more he realized that he might be able to help the investigation. In the desk was a note given him by John Surratt a few months ago:

Mr. Howard
    Will please let the bearer Mr. Azworth have my horse whenever he wishes to ride also my leggins and gloves and oblige.

Yours &c.
J H Surratt

Feb. 22, 1865
541 H St Bet 6 & 7 Sts

Stabler had always regarded this man Azworth as a suspicious character, and though he was a friend of Surratt's, he still refused to rent him a horse. He was a German man, with dark hair, light mustache, and whiskers. Typically, he wore a gray "salt and pepper" suit, and he always stooped a little. Stabler tried to remember all he could about Surratt, Booth, and Azworth. He wrote down everything he considered relevant, and sent it over to Colonel Ingraham's office.[29]

THAT LAST FALSE ALARM had reawakened the president's weary doctors, and they stood over him now, convinced that death was imminent. In time, the chest sank, and the pulse trailed off. Again, the doctors braced themselves, and the seconds ticked along. Dr. Abbott, watch in hand, stared and waited for the next breath. It never came. Abbott looked at his colleagues, then back at his watch. He made note of the time. Twenty-two minutes past seven. The suffering was over.[30]

The Reverend Dr. Gurley cleared his throat and stepped up to the bed, saying, "Let us pray." As the minister began his prayer, James Tanner quietly reached into his pocket for a pencil. In his haste, he broke off the point. The prayer went unrecorded.

The news took Mary Todd Lincoln unawares. "Oh! Why did you not tell me that he was dying?" she asked her son. All through the night, she alone had refused to give up hope. Now, she clung to Robert and wept.

The earthly life and suffering of Abraham Lincoln were over. The sun rose on a new nation that morning, and attention would now turn from the president to his killer.

The hunt was on.

FIVE

"A SINGULAR COMBINATION
OF GRAVITY AND JOY"

T HERE WAS NO QUESTION THAT JOHN WILKES BOOTH WAS the assassin, but his whereabouts now could only be guessed. The natural assumption was that he would find a safe haven among those who sympathized with his act. Anti-Lincoln partisans had inspired him with their violent rhetoric, and some now openly approved of what he had done. But these people could be found anywhere. They were not all Southerners; indeed, Democrats in the loyal states could be just as strident as anyone in the South, and many observers blamed them directly for the assassination. Even as far away as San Francisco, editorials reflected this common belief:

> The deed of horror and infamy . . . is nothing more than the expression in action, of what secession politicians and journalists have been for years expressing in words. Wilkes Booth has simply carried out what the Copperhead journalists who have denounced the President as a "tyrant," a "despot," a "usurper," hinted at, and virtually recommended. His weapon was the pistol, theirs the pen; and though he surpassed them in ferocity, they equaled him in guilt. . . . Wilkes Booth has but acted out what Copperhead orators and the Copperhead press have been preaching for years.[1]

It was a valid point. John Wilkes Booth was not a Southerner, but a native of Maryland, where political heat was more intense, but often stifled by the threat of arrest under martial law. While Southerners fought openly on the battlefield, Marylanders often took their war underground, by spying or ferrying people and contraband across the lines. An informal network in the state's southern counties could easily have helped Booth escape. Though it was by no means certain that he had headed their way, it had to be considered a possibility.

In many ways, Maryland was the key to the assassination. It was between North and South, and, more to the point, between Northern soldiers and the Southern battlefields. Surrounding the capital on three sides, it was an obstruction to the war effort that could not be ignored or dealt with at a later time. A heavy military presence was required, and martial law was swiftly put into place after the onset of hostilities in 1861. That in itself became the overriding concern for Marylanders, regardless of how they felt about other issues. It made opposition to Abraham Lincoln as strong there as it was in any state below it. This atmosphere nurtured the Lincoln conspiracy.

JOHN WILKES BOOTH'S LIFE BEGAN among the rolling hills of Harford County, Maryland. The landscape there reminds one of Pennsylvania, just a few miles to the north, rather than the land of Dixie. Farms and woods spread over the countryside in a patchwork of earthen hues. It was there that John's father, Junius Booth, settled after his arrival from England in the early 1820s. In London, Junius had enjoyed a meteoric acting career and was considered a serious rival to the great Edmund Kean. But, abruptly, he left for America, where he toured for a while and eventually bought 150 acres of wilderness, three miles from the village of Bel Air, Maryland. His new surroundings offered an escape from the yellow fever epidemics then raging in the cities, and a pleasant refuge from life's troubles, of which he had more than a few. He resumed his work on the stage, and became an even bigger success in his adopted country.[2]

Junius and his wife, Mary Ann, lived in a rambling four-room log house that they had bought from a neighbor, then rolled on logs to their own land. The feat branded Junius a genius, though perhaps an eccentric one. His father, Richard, came over from England to live with them, and in time other London relatives joined them as well. Seven of Junius and Mary Ann's children would be born here.[3]

They had ten children in all. Junius Jr., Rosalie, and Henry Byron, named for the poet, came along in the first few years. Mary Ann, Frederick, and Elizabeth followed in succession, but an 1833 cholera epidemic would claim all three of them in a single month. Henry died of smallpox four years later on a visit to London. The loss of four children brought Mary Ann closer to those who survived, and to those born afterward. Edwin, Asia, John Wilkes, and Joseph Adrian were smothered with affection.[4]

They called their place The Farm, and though life here was spartan, it was never uncomfortable. The parlor walls, papered with the "family colors" of dark green and gold, were adorned with scenes of classical antiquity such as "Timon of Athens" and "The Roman matron showing her husband how to die." The place had a quiet, comfortable dignity about it. It was a home, but more than that, it was a sanctuary, where Junius Booth could put aside the habiliments of a make-believe world and return to a place where everything was real.[5]

For the children, Junius built a swimming pond with an island shaded by willow trees. For the servants, he built sturdy and comfortable quarters. As a matter of principle, the Booths never owned slaves, but rented them from their masters for a set period of time. Most servants enjoyed life with the family, and they always found Mr. Booth to be a kind and indulgent employer. Hagar, Nancy, Amenda, Henry, George Brown, and "Pomp" Williams were just a few of the African Americans who grew up as companions to the Booth children. Much of what we know of the Booths' life in Maryland comes from the fond recollections of the people who served them there.[6]

John Wilkes Booth was born at The Farm on May 10, 1838, and by all accounts he was his mother's favorite. Attractive and good-natured, "Johnny" was one of those children who always seemed able to win over friends. His personality inspired high hopes of success in life, but Mary Ann had fears as well. Tragedy and personal loss had taxed her ability to explain life's hardships in earthly terms, and superstition filled the void. Even the most enlightened people took Edwin's birth during the most spectacular meteor shower in history as a portent of a glorious future. But with Johnny, the signs were written in flames. When he was six months old, Mary Ann had a vision of the word "country" rising from a fire in the hearth. She took it as an omen and watched over him constantly, lest he should involve himself in some dangerous patriotic cause.[7]

Though John was his mother's darling, the dominant figure in his life was undoubtedly his father. Junius Booth was a larger-than-life figure. It is no exaggeration to say that he was more than a celebrity; he was an entertainment phenomenon. According to a recent biographer, he gave more than 2,800 performances in sixty-eight American cities. His habit of accepting almost any engagement, no matter how small or remote the venue, helped spread his fame, and the legitimate drama, to the far reaches of the American wilderness. Though he died when John Wilkes was only fourteen, his influence outlived him and guided the lives of all his sons. Three of the Booth boys followed him onto the stage, and were always conscious of having large shoes to fill.[8]

Walt Whitman called Junius "by far the greatest histrion I have ever seen in my life," and the *Spirit of the Times* said he was "undoubtedly the best tragedian in this country at the present day, and in the world, to our knowledge." A compact, muscular man with a forceful personality, Junius could electrify an audience with the power of his acting. He had a powerful intellect as well; he spoke many languages, studied disparate cultures, and had a lifelong passion for words. He studied Milton, Locke, and Plutarch. He read Dante and Alfieri in Italian, Racine in French, Leibniz in German, and Vasquez in Portuguese. In his library, one might find Sterne and Byron alongside the Bible, the Koran, and the Talmud. He preferred verse to prose; Shelley, Keats, and Coleridge were familiar to all in the Booth household.[9]

He was also eccentric. Critics called him "the mad tragedian" and delighted in telling stories of his eccentric behavior. Sometimes he would fail to appear for a performance and would be found hours later roaming the woods in costume, and not the least bit inclined to account for himself. Other times he would snap out of a part momentarily just to return a taunt from the audience. It was great fun to guess what he might do next, and the prospect of a "mad freak" was undoubtedly a major draw. A few people thought that perhaps his peculiarities resulted from his use of cigars, but then again, he was also fond of liquor.[10]

Was he faking it? Like the young Prince Hamlet, he leaves us to wonder. One hometown critic was sure he had figured Booth out, and he was not amused:

Is this man a maniac? or is he not more a fool than a madman? On Monday he was announced to appear at the Holliday street [Theatre] as Pescara; but when the hour of performance arrived, the little eccentric was returned non est. "Booth is a genius," is the cry, and he has heard it reiterated so often that he imagines his vagaries will be overlooked; [but] the trick has become stale; the "gaggery" won't do; this affectation of madness may be a "good point" sometimes, but to make a business of it is disgusting.[11]

If indeed it was an affectation, Junius Booth carried it to the extreme. Mary Ann once discovered him in the act of hanging himself, and cut him down just in time. Realizing what he had done, he burst into tears and exclaimed, "My God! My God! what could have come over me?" Whatever it was, it was compounded by physical illness and the rigors of life on the road.[12]

Booth abhorred killing, and counseled his children to avoid it. In his household, even the insects were spared. "You should never kill a fly," he told his children; "they are scavengers, and cleanse the air of many impurities which no doubt is the cause of sickness. There is some medicinal quality in flies, or animals would not eat them; also in spiders, for birds, particularly caged birds, seek to get them." His physician, Dr. James Rush, noted that even his own family found his views obnoxious. "This fellow I say in his mad humanity, will not eat meat forsooth because it encourages acts of *suffering* to animals," he wrote incredulously.[13]

This "mad humanity" extended throughout the human race. He regarded all people as equals, and would share his meals and his quarters with anyone in need. He even risked the life of his daughter Asia to grant the dying wish of a local slave girl who had asked to see her one last time. And this at a time when any deference at all to a slave was considered evidence of insanity.[14]

His philosophical outlook was a family legacy. Booth's forebears had always been radicals, and for that, some had been exiled from Portugal generations before. But even in London they had lived as outcasts. They claimed a family connection to John Wilkes, "the agitator," whose story is one of unflinching hostility to the power of government. In the 1770s John Wilkes waged a fearless war against George III. He was expelled from Parliament three times, outlawed once, imprisoned twice, and exiled to Paris for more than three years. When the House of Commons rebuffed his return to politics, supporters made "Wilkes and Liberty!" their rallying cry. They elected him Lord Mayor of London, and he used his office as a platform to support American independence. Prime Minister William Gladstone would later say that the name of John Wilkes "must be enrolled among the greatest champions of English freedom."[15]

By Junius Booth's time, that outlook translated to a form of populism. Once in America, he became a friend of Sam Houston's and Andrew Jackson's, and he occasionally visited "Old Hickory" at his home in Nashville. When critics began to see the once-popular Democrat as an autocrat—"King Andrew," they called him—Booth joined his opposition. In a private letter to the president, he wrote:

> Brown's Hotel, Philadelphia
> July 4th, 1835
>
> You damn'd old Scoundrel if you don't sign the pardon of your fellow men now under sentence of Death De Ruiz & De Soto, I will cut your throat whilst you are sleeping. I wrote to you repeated Cautions so look out or damn you I'll have you burnt at the Stake in the City of Washington.
>
> > Your Master
> > Junius Brutus Booth
>
> You know me! Look out![16]

Though Jackson undoubtedly took the letter as a joke, he did commute the death sentences of Francisco DeRuiz and Bernardo DeSoto in a famous case of piracy. For what it is worth, all five defendants *not* mentioned in Booth's letter were hanged.

Junius's father, Richard, was deeply committed to the fight against tyranny, but was held in check by family obligations. Still, there was no mistaking his commitment. He even named his sons in the republican tradition. Junius Brutus Booth was named for "Junius," a writer of political tracts who inspired generations of anti-monarchists, and for the Brutuses, who established, and later tried to save, the Roman republic. Algernon Sydney Booth was named for a man who died for conspiring to kill Charles II. In his declining years in America, when Richard was asked to name a grandson, he drew once more from political history. He named the child John Wilkes Booth.[17]

Life on The Farm was often difficult, especially when Junius was away on tour. So the Booths rented a house in the Old Town section of Baltimore, where they spent the cooler months of every year. For John Wilkes, urban life offered excitement and an education in itself. The city was then at the peak of its industrial might. The telegraph was revolutionizing the American way of life, and railroads had just brought half the continent suddenly within reach. The new, locally produced "family flour" was much in demand throughout the world, and it helped make this metropolis a hub of international trade. The 1840s were a prosperous time, and for a young boy growing up here, it must have seemed that Baltimore was the most important place on earth.[18]

In 1845, when John Wilkes was seven, Junius bought a house on Exeter Street, near Fayette Street. By all accounts, the neighborhood was heterogeneous but close-knit. Children added vitality to the place, and John Wilkes had plenty of friends his age. He was especially close to Billy and Mike O'Laughlen, who lived on High Street. They were the best of friends, and even when the Booths were out at The Farm, the O'Laughlens stayed in touch by mail or visits.[19]

Against their father's wishes, the Booth boys dreamed of a career on the stage, and insisted on making Junius's world a part of their own. They engaged in amateur theatricals with their friends, and charged an admission price of one cent. Patrons were usually other children, but they were invited to bring their parents, who were charged twice as much. Stage properties and costumes were "borrowed" from neighboring families, and local parents furnished animals—sometimes unknowingly—for the occasional equestrian scene.

Edwin and John Wilkes Booth ran the show, but local boys John Sleeper and Henry Stuart were fixtures in the company as well. Edwin preferred the comical parts, and could play the banjo. Sleeper would play the villain, lurking and leering and gliding about in a long black cloak and top hat. Theirs was a traveling company of sorts, and they had to make do wherever they could. They might play at the boardinghouse of Theodore Hamilton's mother, or in a stable on South Street, or the cellar of a house on Lovely Lane. Their enthusiasm for show business was already evident, and each of them would grow up to be a famous actor.[20]

Junius Jr. was the first to take up the call. After traveling as his father's dresser, "June" took an apprenticeship in Boston and became involved with a woman in the stock company. Though Clementina DeBar was thirteen years older than he, she followed him to New York, and they were married there. The elder Booth's first grandchild, Blanche, was born in April 1844.[21]

Junius and Mary Ann valued education, and for several years they sent

John Wilkes and his younger brother, Joseph, to the Bel Air Academy. Eventually John Wilkes moved on to the new Milton Academy, a college preparatory school north of Baltimore. The school's Quaker headmaster, John Emerson Lamb, taught the classics in a pastoral setting. Most students boarded there, and were expected to exhibit "a pleasant and obliging disposition" at all times. The schedule was demanding and required an almost constant attention to academic pursuits.[22]

Milton Academy students were expected to read and recite from the works of Herodotus, Cicero, Tacitus, Horace, and Livy. Though not specifically mentioned in their literature, one other writer must have figured largely in the curriculum as well: John Milton, the poet. Milton was an ardent opponent of tyranny, and wrote "A Defence of the People of England" when his countrymen were criticized for executing their king. He argued that tyrannical rulers might justly be put to death, and cited Luther, Zwingli, Calvin, Bucer, and Pareus, among others who shared that view. It would be surprising, indeed, if Headmaster Lamb had left him out of the program.[23]

John Wilkes approached his studies enthusiastically. As his sister Asia recalled, "He possessed a tenacious rather than an intuitive intelligence like his brothers. He had great power of concentration, and he never let go a subject once broached until he had mastered it or proved its barrenness." He took great pleasure in testing the powers of his mind. At an early age, he memorized Byron's *Giaour,* an epic poem that filled his head with stories of the classic hero: an alienated man, inheriting his love of freedom, and fighting against all odds to save his homeland from tyranny and oppression. Asia claimed that years later her brother could still recite all thirteen hundred lines from memory. One suspects its political lessons persisted as well.[24]

Milton Academy was an island of serenity in a turbulent world. The volcanic issue of slavery had the rest of the nation embroiled in debate. As Webster, Clay, and Calhoun reached the peak of their oratorical powers, a new voice was heard among them—a weak and raspy voice, to be sure, but one whose message would change the direction of American politics. It was the voice of William H. Seward, freshman Whig senator from New York. In March 1850, Seward came out against compromise in any form as "radically wrong and essentially vicious." Slavery, he said, was doomed. Though the Constitution was devoted "to union, to justice, to defence, to welfare, and to liberty," there was "a higher law than the Constitution, which regulates our authority over the domain, and devotes it to the same noble purposes."

A higher law. To many, the concept seemed to justify an open defiance of the new Fugitive Slave Law, which required the help of all citizens in returning escaped slaves to their masters. Though Seward did not mean to stoke the flames of abolition, his words emboldened anti-slavery partisans who put conscience above the law. As they saw it, they were casting off an evil system in obedience to the service of a moral ideal.[25]

The law met its first major test when John Wilkes Booth was still at Milton Academy. In September 1851, a Maryland farmer named Edward Gorsuch applied for federal help in arresting some slaves who had fled to the village of Christiana, Pennsylvania. Gorsuch believed they had stolen some of his grain, and with a U.S. marshal and others, he set out to bring them back to Maryland. Warned of their approach, abolitionists and former slaves met them with armed resistance. Gorsuch was killed, his son was wounded, and the others were sent fleeing for their lives.

The so-called Christiana Riot divided the nation along sectional lines. From the South came demands for the swift and severe punishment of those responsible. From the North came applause for the attack, and outrage that federal laws favored slave catchers and kidnappers of free blacks. *The New York Times* voiced a common opinion. "Our chief regret in this matter," said one editorial, "grows out of the fact that men who believe in the 'higher law' . . . are not more numerous than they are." Seward's phrase was becoming a rallying cry for abolition.

John Wilkes Booth found the Christiana story hard to ignore. The Gorsuch farm was just a short walk from Milton Academy, and one of the boys was a friend and schoolmate.[26]

ON NOVEMBER 16, 1846, the steamship *Great Western* arrived in New York from Liverpool. On board was Marie Christine Adelaide Delannoy, or, as she preferred to call herself, Mrs. Junius Brutus Booth. She had ostensibly come to America to see her son, Richard, who was teaching Greek and Latin in Baltimore. But it was really Junius that she intended to waylay, and he was playing in New York. As she wrote her sister, "I shall wait until he comes to Baltimore, and as soon as he arrives my lawyer will fall on his back like a bomb." Junius had deserted her and their son a quarter-century before, when he came to America with Mary Ann.[27]

Junius Booth should have expected this sooner or later. He had eloped with Mlle. Delannoy while boarding at her mother's house in Brussels back in 1815. They were married in London and had two children, one surviving infancy. But by 1821, a lovely dark-haired woman had caught his eye, and the rest of his world ceased to exist. Mary Ann Holmes sold flowers outside the Covent Garden Theatre in London. She was infatuated with the young actor, and they courted in secret. In January 1821 they disappeared in the night, bound for America. Friends said that Robert Holmes searched his daughter's room and found ninety-three letters from Booth and a dark lantern. The old man died of a broken heart.[28]

Adelaide had been living on payments from Junius, and that had seemed sufficient. But then her son came to America and learned of Booth's wealth and success. His letters home brought Adelaide to Baltimore in a fighting mood. Passing by the house on Exeter Street, she looked around for "any one of that set," and eventually she found them. Neighbors spoke of loud, drunken tirades directed at Mary Ann. It was a painful situation for the children, who could only stand by and watch their mother be publicly humiliated. They had seen a marriage certificate verifying that their parents had been wed on January 18, 1821. Apparently, though, that ceremony was a theatrical production.[29]

Adelaide established a residence in Maryland, then sought a divorce. Her petition, filed in 1851, read like a tabloid scandal sheet rendered in legalese. Junius contested nothing, and the court affixed its approval. On May 10—John Wilkes Booth's thirteenth birthday—Junius and Mary Ann Booth were finally legally married.[30]

For John Wilkes, this episode did more than stigmatize his family. It challenged his legacy as a Booth. He was proud of that name, and had come to define himself as the son of the great tragedian. Being an adolescent, he was especially keen to establish himself and his place in the world. The scandal made him determined to reclaim his legacy and put it beyond dispute. He would defend the family honor, follow his family profession, and adopt the family politics. As if to confirm his identity once and for all, he pricked his initials in permanent India ink onto the back of his hand.[31]

THE MARITAL SCANDAL must have weighed heavily on Junius's mind, and soon after his divorce became final, he turned his attention to plans for a quiet, simple life with Mary Ann. He decided to replace the old log house near Bel Air with a fine new home. From a book of designs he chose a charming two-story, eight-room cottage in a neo-Gothic style. Built on a cruciform plan, it had a massive central chimney, a full-width front portico, steeply pitched gables, and diamond-pane windows. They would call the place Tudor Hall, after Henry Tudor, the Earl of Richmond and slayer of King Richard III. James Johnson Gifford, architect of the Holliday Street Theatre, would supervise the construction.[32]

By that time, two of the boys were already on their own. Edwin had tried his hand at acting, but a disastrous start forced him off the stage to serve as his father's dresser. Gradually he earned a second chance, playing minor roles when he could get them. Junius Jr. had been successful as an actor, but showed more talent as a manager. After leaving his wife and daughter for another actress, he moved to San Francisco to manage the Jenny Lind Theatre. In the summer of 1851, he persuaded his father to commit himself to an engagement there.

Before Junius left, though, he had to arrange for the education of his other sons. John Wilkes and Joe had both completed the course of study at Milton Academy. They had learned the basics, the classics, and the social graces. But with their father going on tour, they needed to be under close supervision in a strict school. Junius enrolled them at St. Timothy's Hall, a prestigious military academy in Catonsville, near Baltimore.

With each application for enrollment, St. Timothy's sent a twenty-four-page book of warnings and exhortations about the importance of discipline. These regulations would make the school "an institution of strict discipline, of good morals, and, by the grace of God, a religious home for the young." Only the best boys would be admitted, and as soon as they arrived, they *belonged* to the school. Parents would just have to trust the rector in the exercise of his own "parental discretion."[33]

The rector was Rev. Libertus Van Bokkelen, an Episcopal priest and transplanted New Yorker who had observed and studied the best educational systems of Europe. Though his school operated under the auspices of the Protestant Episcopal Church, the dominant theme was military training. It was chartered in the midst of the Mexican War—the first conflict fought under the leadership of West Point graduates. Suddenly a military education was perceived as the road to social and political prominence, and military academies flourished. Some of Maryland's leading families sent their sons to St. Timothy's.[34]

Milton Academy had encouraged a love of poetry and an obliging disposition. What St. Timothy's required was a white-hot lust for order. Students were fitted out in the gray uniforms of infantry soldiers and drilled in accordance with the U.S. Army's infantry manual. Their days were long and strictly regimented, with only two breaks in the course of the week.[35]

There were plenty of hardships, but no matter what was thrown at him, John Wilkes Booth not only endured, but throve. He had charisma and an ingratiating manner that made him popular among his fellow cadets, who called him "Billy Bowlegs" after the celebrated Seminole chief.

An anonymous schoolmate, writing in 1878, described Booth as having "one of the most lively and cheerful dispositions; was kind, generous and affectionate in his nature, with an admiration of his father and his abilities that amounted almost to idolatry." Though Booth revered his father, few things mattered more now than the acceptance of his peers. That's why his placement at St. Timothy's had been so important to his parents. In Baltimore, street gangs like the Blood Tubs and the Plug-Uglies were giving the city a reputation for mob violence. At least St. Timothy's would place the Booth brothers with a better sort of people.

Among his new friends were Sam and Billy Arnold, sons of a Baltimore confectioner, and Jesse Wharton, whose father was a college professor. Jesse grew especially close to Booth, and often came home to Bel Air with him on holidays. Asia described Jesse as "a rarely endowed youth both physically and mentally." He seemed to have everything going for him.[36]

Cadets sometimes engaged in pursuits that would have horrified the elder Booth. A schoolmate later recalled their school breaks, when "it was our delight to spend our Wednesday and Saturday afternoon holidays in cooking chickens, eggs, and such things as a schoolboy could procure by 'ways that are dark.' We had cooking utensils, and a gun hooked from the armory of the school, and each of us had a five-barrel Colt's revolver, with which we killed rabbits and birds that were very abundant in the surrounding woods. We became very expert with the pistol, and either of us could kill a rabbit running, and about once in three times a partridge flying."[37]

Writers would someday use this anecdote to argue that Booth had always been a sadistic killer. But the anonymous source of this story, who admits to the same behavior, saw nothing cruel in Booth's conduct. In the nineteenth century, almost all boys hunted small animals. It was a normal part of growing up, and the best way to associate themselves with the power and status of grown men. In fact, Booth's friends remembered him as a happy, normal boy, and his teachers kept in touch years after he had left their care.[38]

. . .

THE CALIFORNIA TRIP had gone reasonably well for Junius. His sons June and Edwin had toured with him, and critics were more than kind. But a few months in the rough-hewn West were enough, and leaving his sons behind, Junius set out alone for the East. He never made it home. After a brief engagement in New Orleans, he boarded the steamer *J. S. Chenoweth,* bound for Cincinnati. He became ill and died before the ship reached Louisville.[39]

MARY ANN RENTED OUT the Exeter Street house and moved back to The Farm and their new home, Tudor Hall. Rosalie and Asia went along, but the boys remained in school until the end of the term. June and Edwin were still in California, and neither had any intention of returning home. There were no men to plant the crops, chop the wood, or protect the property. To make matters worse, Gifford, the architect, surprised Mary Ann with a bill for finishing Tudor Hall. It was her understanding that Junius had paid for the work in advance, but Gifford assured her that that was not the case. He threatened to sue, and ultimately the matter was settled in Mary Ann's favor. The architect, unable to collect, lost his own house to creditors. In a rage, he rode up to Bel Air and tore the tin roof off the Booths' new home.[40]

Hearing of his mother's difficulties, John Wilkes resolved to come home and assume his duties as the man of the house. The hardships were often overwhelming, but he found country life exhilarating. He loved to spend his time galloping on his favorite horse, named Cola di Rienzi for a tribune who had tried to restore popular government to the Roman Empire. To his sister, John was "a singular combination of gravity and joy." She was almost puzzled by her brother's cheerfulness. "Don't let us be sad," he told her. "Life is so short—and the world is so beautiful. Just to *breathe* is delicious."[41]

His disposition never failed to amaze. His sunny self-assurance comes through in his letters to Billy O'Laughlen. They are full of all the boyish interests: nature, hunting, drinking—and, of course, girls. The young ladies got more than their share of attention. "I have my eye on three girls out here," he once wrote. "I hope I'll get enough!" With a dash of bravado, he tells of knocking a man down for calling his sister a liar. The sheriff put the man off the property, and Booth was bound over to keep the peace.[42]

His only extravagances were his books—texts from school; a large volume of Shakespeare; Greek and Roman histories; Plutarch's *Lives and Morals;* and the works of Scott and Bulwer-Lytton. While he loved the small, but impossibly thick, Captain Marryatt novels, his real love was poetry. Whittier, Longfellow, Willis, Byron, and Poe occupied much of his leisure hours, such as they were. Books must have been vitally important to all the Booths. They were a favorite gift for birthdays and Christmas, and many inscribed copies still exist. From these we have a fair sense of the thoughts and ideas they absorbed.[43]

Extra hands came on board to work the land, but their presence brought out a new impulse in John Wilkes. A military education had instilled in him the notion of *rank*—something his father and grandfather abhorred. Richard and Junius thought nothing of sharing a meal with servants of any color, but when those "sons of the soil" came to John's table, he could hardly keep himself in the room. Though he made excuses, nobody was fooled. His aloofness made the Booths unpopular among working-class whites in Harford County. They would get their revenge in the stories they told later.[44]

The issue of slavery drew a new dividing line in politics, and with members in both North and South, neither the Democrats nor the Whigs could plant themselves firmly on one side or the other. Voters came to feel that their parties no longer answered their concerns, and politicians scrambled to carve out new constituencies. Out of the confusion came a new party, formed for the express purpose of stopping the spread of slavery. They called themselves Republicans, and Senator William H. Seward, of "higher law" fame, proposed to make himself their standard-bearer. If Seward's arithmetic was correct, this new party could gather enough anti-slavery votes to capture a national election without even running in the South. All the Republicans had to do was keep the issue of slavery alive.

Maryland voters wanted none of that. Life on the "fault line" made slavery an especially volatile subject for them, and they reacted to developments by looking for something else to focus on. They found it in the nativist movement. Immigration was surging to its highest levels in history, and with each wave of new arrivals came a resurgence of fear that "outsiders" would somehow threaten the American way of life. Since many of these immigrants were Catholics, fear of "papists" was added to the mix. An alliance was formed against the Pope and against all foreign influence. Its members first met in secret and were told to disavow all knowledge of their organization. But the Know-Nothings, as they were called, soon came into the open, and they made a quick success. Within a few years they controlled several state and city governments.[45]

More than anyone else, Marylanders developed a special contempt for those who curried favor with Catholics and immigrants. Senator William H. Seward was such a man. In Maryland, Seward was seen as an opportunist, eager to polarize the country just to throw more people out of the "undecided" ranks and into his own camp. The more prominent Seward became in national politics, the more he was hated in the Old Line State.[46]

It was in this atmosphere that John Wilkes Booth showed his first signs of political awareness. He and Asia attended Know-Nothing rallies, where they listened with rapt attention as Henry Winter Davis and others counseled resistance to the foreign threat. As later developments would prove, their interests were more social than political. After all, Asia herself became a Catholic. And, of course, their parents were immigrants.[47]

SIX

"HE WANTED TO BE LOVED OF
THE SOUTHERN PEOPLE"

ONE DAY IN MID-AUGUST 1855, JOHN WILKES BOOTH RODE up to Tudor Hall looking jubilant. He had just made his first professional stage appearance and was flushed with excitement. Without telling anyone, he had signed up with Henry C. Jarrett to act at the Charles Street Theatre in Baltimore. John Sleeper, in the stock company there, had recommended Booth, and Jarrett cast him as Richmond in a popular adaptation of *Richard III*.[1]

John's dreams of glory were fueled by letters from his brother June, who was doing well in San Francisco, and from Edwin, who had been touring in Australia with Laura Keene and falsely claimed to have made a fortune there.[2] His friends were all going into the business: Sam Knapp, Theodore Hamilton, and George L. Stout had already started their careers. And Sleeper, who had changed his name to John Sleeper Clarke, was firmly established as a comedian in Baltimore.

John's first performance was a big step, but hardly an auspicious beginning. He did not actually perform all of *Richard III*—just the battle scene. Moreover, the Charles Street Theatre was not Baltimore's finest playhouse. It kept no consistent stock company, and rarely featured exceptional talent. It was the last week of a slow summer season, and manager Jarrett was doing little more than keeping the place open. Jarrett seemed to be using his theater to audition new actors for the Baltimore Museum, which he also ran, one block away.[3]

Mary Ann was not happy. She thought her son had been rushed into the business by Clarke, who was eager to cash in on the Booth name. In fact, the *Baltimore Sun*'s announcement made it obvious:

MR. J. S. CLARKE'S FAREWELL BENEFIT!

MR. J. W. BOOTH, (SON OF THE LAMENTED
JUNIUS BRUTUS BOOTH,) WILL MAKE HIS FIRST
APPEARANCE ON ANY STAGE, IN THE CHARACTER
OF RICHMOND, IN RICHRD III.[*sic*][4]

As Asia recalled, John Wilkes's ambitions were fairly modest. "He could never hope to be as great as Father, [and] he never wanted to rival Edwin, but he wanted to be loved of the Southern people above all things. He would work to make himself essentially a Southern actor." If Booth really had such an idea, the notion faded quickly. Professional experience would broaden his goals and interests.

Booth knew that his apprentice years would be rough and sometimes embarrassing. He dared not stain his family name with the inevitable mistakes of a neophyte. And he also realized his name would bring extra pressure and scrutiny. A pseudonym would help him avoid that. So, all things considered, he decided to cut his teeth under a different name. He would begin his career as "J. B. Wilkes."

IN 1856, EDWIN RETURNED to Maryland after a five-year absence. He had accompanied a troupe to California, Australia, and the Sandwich Islands, and the trip enabled him to sharpen his acting skills outside the critical gaze of Eastern audiences. Not everyone appreciated his progress. Laura Keene, the star of the company, considered the tour a financial failure, and she blamed Edwin's "bad acting" for that. She was furious at Edwin for sending notices of their travels to a friend back in the States, including the information that Miss Keene and her husband/manager, John Lutz, were not really married—at least not to each other. She was actually the wife of one Henry Wellington Taylor, a convicted felon who had gone off to Australia some years before. In fact, she had organized the tour there with the specific intention of asking Taylor for a divorce, but she had been unable to find him. The truth of the matter would return to haunt her, and she never forgave the little snitch who let out her secret.[5]

IN THE PRESIDENTIAL ELECTION of 1856, Maryland was the only state to support the Know-Nothing candidate, former president Millard Fillmore. Democrat James Buchanan won handily, and second place went to John C. Frémont, the first Republican ever to enter a presidential race. Frémont got only 281 votes in Maryland, out of almost 87,000 cast. Republicans were hated in the Old Line State.

In the summer of 1857, John Wilkes Booth placed an ad in Bel Air's newspaper, the *Southern Aegis:*

> FOR RENT—The splendid and well known residence of the late J. B.
> Booth, in Harford County, about three miles from Bel Air on the road
> leading to Churchville. This place will be rented to a good tenant if im-
> mediate application be made. There is 180 acres of land, 80 of which is
> arable. Address. JOHN BOOTH Baltimore, Md.[6]

Booth had taken a job at the Arch Street Theatre in Philadelphia. The pay was barely adequate, but at eight dollars a week, it was twice as much as some of the others were getting. Mary Ann, Rosalie, and Asia would follow him to the Quaker City. Joseph would come along, too, at least for a while.

Philadelphia had a rich dramatic history. It was home to Edwin Forrest and Charlotte Cushman and to a host of up-and-coming new talents. As Booth began his work at the Arch, he struck up a friendship with John McCullough, a fellow neophyte from the so-called Boothenian Dramatic Society, the largest of the city's theatrical clubs. A native of Blakes, Londonderry, McCullough was five years older than Booth. A man of little education, he had emigrated to Philadelphia in 1849 to escape the famine in his native land. He was working in a chair factory when a fellow worker gave him a book of Shakespeare's plays. McCullough was hooked, and joined the Boothenians right away. When manager Wheatley offered him four dollars a week for the smallest of roles, he accepted without hesitation, giving up a job that paid more than twice that much.[7]

In those days, most theaters were still run as "stock houses," employing a full roster of actors who worked in a given "line of business." Each line corresponded to a certain character stereotype, and if every actor knew the standard roles in his line, any number of plays could be performed on short notice. The choicest roles went to the leading lady and leading man. Speaking parts were spread among several other "lines": the supporting man or woman; old man or woman; first, second, and third walking gentleman; singing chambermaid; and "heavy," or villain. As a utility actor, McCullough fell into the lowest classification, while Booth, as third walking gentleman, was one step higher. Though neither did anything of great importance, they learned together and rehearsed a full range of plays in the popular repertoire.

Twentieth-century writers would claim that Booth never achieved much success as an actor, and they blame his supposed lack of training for that. But in fact, Booth followed the standard path for all actors of his day: private study, apprenticeship, and stock experience. Formal training did not yet exist, and the best one could hope for was a bit of coaching and advice from seasoned professionals. Booth had three of them living right at home. Nor did John Wilkes neglect his voice, as most historians believe. Vocal technique was almost certainly the subject of many a discussion at the Arch. His friend McCullough consulted with the prominent elocutionist Lemuel White, and it is perfectly reasonable to assume he passed White's advice along to his fellow neophytes.[8]

Booth seems to have preserved some measure of anonymity at the Arch, though insiders surely knew who he was. It probably helped that he was billed as "Mr. Wilks," when there happened to be a stage family of that name working in the city. But years later, reporter George Alfred Townsend recorded some unflattering memories of Booth's acting at this time. Townsend told of an embarrassing incident during the play *Lucretia Borgia,* in which Booth was supposed to introduce himself by saying, "Madam, I am Petruchio Pandolfo." He forgot the line, and stumbled through it. "Madam, I am Pandolfio Pet—Pedolfio Pat—Pantuchio Ped—Dammit! What am I?" Everyone, including Booth himself, had a good laugh. But the following night he was supposed to play Dawson in *The Gamester,* and this time the audience turned on him. Chuckles and hisses threw him off his stride. Seized with stage fright, Booth could not remember his lines, and stage manager William Fredericks had to excuse him for the rest of the night. His embarrassment was made worse by the presence of a young lady he had invited to watch the performance.[9]

Townsend would later claim that this Arch Street apprenticeship was a disaster. Booth, he said, was "stumbling and worthless." He lacked the

drive and initiative necessary to learn his lines. He was judged to be careless and indifferent, and nobody in the company regarded him as a man of
promise. Though Fredericks complained, he could do nothing about him,
and in Townsend's view, Booth never did become a good actor. This is a
matter of some importance, because it bolsters the common argument that
this bitter Philadelphia experience turned John Wilkes Booth against the
North and created the "professional despair" that led him to assassinate the
president. Like all of Townsend's works, it was part history, part moral lecture. In fact, there is really no evidence that Booth did poorly there.[10]

Chances are that Townsend placed too much faith in a seven-year-old
memory. Booth's character in *Lucretia Borgia* was Ascanio Petrucci, not
Petruchio Pandolfo. And he appeared in *The Gamester* the night *before*
that, not the night after. But supposing Townsend was right, then how did
Booth manage to salvage his career? Certainly, a poor reputation did not
follow him for long. Careless, stumbling actors do not enjoy a continuing
success on the boards, nor do they escape the resentment and criticism of
their fellow actors. Yet his Arch Street colleagues had no public complaints. Audiences loved him. Managers were delighted to engage him for
as long as he would stay. Critics and actors alike regarded him as a gifted
actor, and nobody seems to have grumbled about the irony of his success.
Though Booth was supposedly loath to play in Philadelphia again, neither
his correspondence nor backstage gossip bears this allegation out.[11]

FAMILY SKELETONS WOULD NOT STAY BURIED. The death of Adelaide Booth in March 1858 revived the story of her abandonment by Junius.
Newspapers dredged up the whole affair in detail, as they would occasionally do again over the years. Later accounts claimed that Adelaide died in
poverty and squalor, which may not be true. Soon after his mother's death,
Richard Junius Booth purchased three rental properties in Baltimore. He
owned six in all, and the timing of his last purchase suggests an inheri-
tance, and a substantial one. Nevertheless, the story of Adelaide's suffering
would follow all the Booths to their own graves and beyond.[12]

THE SEASON CAME TO A CLOSE ON JUNE 19. Of 153 plays staged
that year, John Wilkes Booth had performed in 83. The themes of these
plays may be of some interest in light of Booth's place in history. Many
were historical plays highlighting the struggle against tyranny and oppression. *Jack Cade* and *Wallace, the Hero of Scotland,* for example, focused on

the leaders of popular movements. *Hamlet, Pizarro, Brutus,* and *Venice Preserved* presented the just killing or overthrow of a ruler. A few plays went even further, glorifying assassination as a triumph of freedom over oppression. This had always been one of the great themes of political melodrama. *Richard III, William Tell,* and *Julius Caesar* were the most famous examples in their day, and all were to have a fatal significance in 1865.[13]

According to Townsend, Booth was not invited to return to the Arch for a second season. Maybe so. But when the 1858–59 season began, he was employed at a better theater, working for a higher salary. He moved up to Virginia's leading playhouse, the Marshall Theatre, where critics rated the new stock company "fifty per cent better than that of last season." Good productions, talented colleagues, and high visibility made the Marshall a fine place for any young actor to work. The star system was in full use here, and the house offered a steady flow of "new" attractions. They put a tremendous burden on the actors who would have to present them. Booth had to learn eighteen new parts, all in a two-week span. But such was life in a stock company. If Booth were not up to the task, he would not have been hired.[14]

Richmond was a comfortable place for Booth, in part because he was surrounded there by hometown people. All the managers—John T. Ford, Thomas L. Moxley, and George Kunkel—were Baltimoreans, and Ford always made a point of staffing his houses with people from back home. Sam Knapp (now Samuel Knapp Chester) was the Marshall's "first heavy," and leading man Harry Langdon was an old favorite at the Holliday Street Theatre. Richmond and Baltimore were sister cities, in a manner of speaking, with a fairly extensive commerce between them. The newspapers of one city often copied local items from the papers of the other.[15]

John M. Barron was in the stock company. He remembered Booth as a jovial and happy man of great natural talent—"born with the divine spark":

"He was the mold of form, delicately organized physically, with beautiful hands and small feet, graceful by nature, and in all a most effective actor. His eyes, like all the Booths [*sic*], were exceedingly brilliant and expressive of all the phases of his character."[16]

The Booths understood they were going to be compared to one another. In fact, it began early in John Wilkes's career. Edward Alfriend, an actor who knew both Edwin and John Wilkes, remembered them both from those Marshall Theatre appearances:

"It is saying a great deal, but [John Wilkes] was a much handsomer man than his brother Edwin. He possessed a voice very like his brother's, melodious, sweet, full and strong, and was like him, a consummate elocutionist."[17]

Looks figured prominently in every description. John Wilkes Booth had grown into a fine-looking man, with an athletic frame, dark, wavy hair, and the dark, lustrous eyes that were a Booth trademark. And, of course, there was raw talent. Alfriend thought that although John Wilkes was still in training, his natural ability was beyond question. Booth, as he recalled, had a knack for making friends. He knew "all the best men and many of the finest women." He had inherited an air of confidence and an easy faculty for social success. He always left a warm and pleasing impression. With men he was dignified and bore himself with "insouciant care and grace." To women he was "a man of irresistible fascination," with "a peculiar halo of romance with which he invested himself, and which the ardent imagination of women amplified."[18]

John Wilkes's sex appeal has, for some reason, drawn far more attention than it deserves. Certainly many women sought his companionship. They threw themselves foolishly at him, and we have no reason to suspect that he made a habit of turning them away. But in a breathtaking stretch of logic, George Alfred Townsend tied Booth's "worthless moral nature" to his poor acting. This in turn, he opined, gave rise to a professional despair that led him to kill the president. Booth, said Townsend, was distracted by that "careless class of women who are always looking out for acquaintance with actors," and he indulged too much in frivolous escapades at the expense of his studies. A more recent author went a step further, suggesting that Booth shot the president while suffering from the mental effects of tertiary syphilis.[19]

Both are speculations. Townsend concedes that his information was based on "intuition and hearsay," and little is really known about Booth's personal affairs. He was discreet and never divulged the details of his love life. When women sent him "mash" letters, he cut off the signatures lest they should fall into the wrong hands.[20]

Edwin, on the other hand, had been careless at times. He became engaged to the actress Mary Devlin, whom he regarded as the purest woman he had ever known. But before he would marry her, he insisted she go off to Hoboken, New Jersey, for a nine-month period of study to improve her mind. Mary never questioned the idea. "I know . . . that it is for me, for me alone, that your bounty gives so much," she wrote. Edwin's motives were not so altruistic, though. Just the year before, he had written June about "a little sweetheart of mine" who wanted to advance her theatrical career. Edwin had given her an audition, but not on the stage. She left him with a medical problem that would take the better part of a year to treat. Of course, none of this reached the ears of Miss Devlin, but the brothers knew all about it.[21]

Edwin and Mary had met at the Marshall, and his return in 1858 was regarded as a milestone in his career. He made it one for John Wilkes as well, asking that he be cast in higher parts. The papers called this run the most successful in the theater's history. One critic said of Edwin, "We are clearly of the opinion that, all-in-all, he is superior to any man of his day on the stage." Though John Wilkes was barely noticed, Edwin undoubtedly reminded him that reviews were sometimes nonsensical, often contradictory, and always a matter of opinion. There was simply no way to account for them. John Wilkes could take comfort in knowing that at least he was steadily improving and working his way up in the bills. His time was coming.[22]

THIS WAS A MID-TERM ELECTION YEAR, and William H. Seward was stumping for fellow Republicans in New York. As he saw it, America had always been two separate entities, one with slavery and one without. He spoke about the collision he saw in America's future.

"They who think that it is accidental, unnecessary, the work of interest or fanatical agitators, and therefore ephemeral, mistake the case altogether. *It is an irrepressible conflict between opposing and enduring forces,* and it means that the United States must and will, sooner or later, become either entirely a slave-holding nation or entirely a free-labor nation. . . ."[23]

To Southerners, that speech was threatening and offensive, and it seemed to plot a new course for Republicans everywhere. In Illinois, a lawyer named Lincoln had recently said that "a house divided against itself cannot stand." Together with Seward's speech, it seemed to form a clear and aggressive strategy by Republicans to keep the issue of slavery alive. William Seward was taken to task for it. The *New York Herald* called him an "arch agitator" and said he was more dangerous than the most strident abolitionists. *The New York Times* believed he had advocated federal intervention in the slavery issue, "and it is this, more than anything else, which has made his name an object of so much terror to the South." The most strenuous objections came from those who still believed in the compromises that, until now, had prolonged the peace and stability of the Union. To those people, the real message of Lincoln and Seward was simple: give up, and accept that this nation cannot last.[24]

John Wilkes Booth, in the meantime, was too busy to take an active role in politics. New scripts created a constant demand for study, and in February 1859, William Wheatley and John Sleeper Clarke brought in a sensational new comedy called *Our American Cousin*. This play, written by the Englishman Tom Taylor, had become an instant success when Laura Keene brought it to the United States in October. Miss Keene had paid the author for exclusive rights to the show, but Wheatley and Clarke managed to obtain a copy of the script, and mounted their own production at the Arch in November. They even persuaded their friend Joe Jefferson to jot down some of the gags he had ad-libbed as the original Asa Trenchard. Theirs was a splendid imitation—so good, in fact, that Laura Keene sued them. She was awarded $500, but not the exclusive rights to the play. Wheatley and Clarke breezed into Richmond for a twelve-night run, and *Our American Cousin* was on the bill for eleven of them.[25]

In April 1859, John Sleeper Clarke married Booth's sister Asia. Though Clarke had done much to help John Wilkes's career get started, Booth did not approve of this marriage. The *Our American Cousin* episode and a season together at the Arch had convinced Booth that his new brother-in-law was a shameless opportunist. He warned his sister, but Asia was not dissuaded. From then on, relations between Clarke and John Wilkes would always be strained.[26]

John Wilkes was in his second season at the Marshall when a dramatic incident changed the nation forever. On the night of October 16, 1859, eighteen men slipped quietly into the town of Harpers Ferry, Virginia, and seized control of the federal arsenal there. Their leader was John Brown, an abolitionist leader and fugitive from the Kansas border wars. Upon capturing some night watchmen, Brown's followers made a startling announcement: they intended to free all the slaves in Virginia, and any interference would lead to a bloodbath.

The reaction was instantaneous. Troops were put on the alert, and a heavy guard was posted as far away as the Washington Arsenal, just in case the riot should spread that far. Virginia governor Henry A. Wise boarded an evening train for Harpers Ferry, along with one hundred men from Richmond's home guard units. More city troops were ordered to follow in the morning.[27]

The men traveling with Governor Wise were from the 1st Virginia Volunteers. The regiment was the pride of the Commonwealth, well drilled and magnificently turned out. Other troops were to join them in response to the raid, but a standoff at the arsenal ended before most arrived at the scene. A detachment of marines, under orders from Col. Robert E. Lee of the U.S. Army, captured Brown and some of his followers. They were to be taken to the county jail for trial.[28]

Authorities believed that Brown wanted the slaves to rise up and exterminate all Southern whites. They knew he was capable of such butchery himself, as he was already known to have killed innocent people in Kansas. Now he had stockpiled a thousand pikes for distribution among the slaves, and his capture of the arsenal put a hundred thousand firearms within his reach. But Brown's plan was too extreme to be practical, and as even the moderates agreed, he was less dangerous than those who inspired him. To the *New York Herald*, that meant William H. Seward. The *Herald* claimed that Seward and other abolitionist senators had known of the raid in advance. Along with Sumner, Hale, and others, he had "suffered the project to ripen and bear the disastrous fruit that it has borne. They—not the crazy fanatic John Brown—are the real culprits; and it is they, not he, who . . . would have to grace the gallows." The *Richmond Whig* seconded that thought:

"The 'irrepressible conflict' foreshadowed by a distinguished Senator from New York has had a practical commencement earlier than he perhaps foresaw, and more tragical, as well as short-lived and abortive, than even his theory contemplated. It was, nevertheless, the first fruits and effect of his bloody instruction. . . ."[29]

William H. Seward had nothing to do with Brown's raid, but most people would have agreed with *The New York Times*, which thought that "Sewardism" and Harpers Ferry would be inseparable terms from this point on. The *Richmond Whig* called the senator an "atrocious assassin," and soon-to-be governor John Letcher of Virginia said that if Seward were elected president, his state ought to secede.

Many Northerners refused to condemn Brown, and some openly hailed him as a hero. To Southerners, that was an endorsement of terrorism, and it proved that sectional hatred was far more serious than anyone had imagined. Talk of disunion and war were in the air.[30]

John Brown was tried in the county seat of Charlestown, and after four days of testimony, he stood convicted of murder, inciting slaves to insurrection, and treason. Judge Richard Parker sentenced him to hang, and an execution date was set for December 2.[31]

Two weeks before the scheduled hanging, John Wilkes Booth was in Richmond preparing for *The Filibuster* when the bell tower on Capitol Square sounded an alarm. The governor had been informed that abolitionists planned to rescue Brown at Charlestown, and he called out the city militia for a second time. Virginia's capital was electrified. As it happened, the Richmond Grays were set to deploy on a Richmond, Fredericksburg, and Potomac train. The railroad tracks ran straight down Broad Street, and the end cars, assigned to the First Virginia, were parked in front of the Marshall Theater. Looking down from a window, Booth decided it was time to get involved. He dropped everything and headed for the train.

George W. Libby and Louis F. Bossieux encountered Booth at the door of the baggage car, and they told him that the train was reserved for militia members only. Booth persisted, and when he offered to buy a uniform, Libby and Bossieux gave in. They came up with trousers and a jacket, and soon the train pulled out with Booth aboard.[32]

A writer for the Richmond *Enquirer* followed the regiment on the trip to Charlestown and noted how professional the men looked:

"The Richmond Grays and Company F, which seems [*sic*] to vie with each other in the handsome appearance they present, remind one of uncaged birds, so wild and gleesome they appear. . . . Amongst them I notice Mr. J. Wilkes Booth, a son of Junius Brutus Booth, who, though not a member, as soon as he heard the tap of the drum, threw down the sock and buskin, and shouldered his musket with the Grays to the scene of deadly conflict."

The "deadly conflict" never came to pass, and the Grays only headed to the courthouse to provide security. That was a distinction that Booth himself didn't mind blurring.

Eleven hundred troops already occupied Charlestown, taking up every available space. Being among the last to arrive, the Grays had to settle for quarters in an old tin factory, with straw pallets on a bare floor. Brown himself remained in the county jail, treated as a sideshow curiosity. Activists, politicians, and spectators filed in to see him, and one paper noted that the prisoners "are worn out by these incessant visits. . . . [John E.] Cook and Brown both complain that during the week, they have not had an hour to call their own." Even the occupying troops were ushered in by turns to have a look at him.[33]

On the day of the hanging, sharpshooters were perched in the trees, and sentinels paced silently through the town. In front of the gallows were cadets from the Virginia Military Institute, under the command of Major Thomas J. Jackson. Forming oblique angles on either side were the Richmond Grays and Company F, 1st Virginia. Seven regiments were posted there, and before long many of those men would immortalize themselves on the field of battle. John Wilkes Booth stood in front of the gallows, just a few yards from the man who would be known to history as Stonewall.

The prisoner was escorted to the scaffold, where the sheriff and jailer stood on either side of him. They placed a hood over his head and a noose around his neck. A long, dead silence followed, as soldiers adjusted their positions in the field. When at last the troops were ready, the trap was sprung, and John Brown slowly strangled.

Philip Whitlock noticed how the blood ran out of Booth's face when the drop fell. "I called attention to it," said Whitlock, "and he said he felt very faint—and would then give anything for a good drink of whiskey." Booth would always remember this experience in the most solemn terms. He was moved by John Brown's courage in the face of death. "He was a brave old man," Booth told his sister.

Whether in fear or admiration, the public saw Brown as a pivotal figure in history—a prophet or a madman, willing to kill and die for his cause. He had an audacity that even Governor Wise admired, and that no man could ignore. While others merely talked about change, Brown had taken action. His dream was Booth's nightmare, but somehow that mattered little. His martyrdom was transcendent. "John Brown was a man inspired," Booth later said, "the grandest character of the century!"[34]

In the subsequent investigation, authorities learned that some of New England's most prominent men had supplied money for the raid, and many others were suspected of involvement. It was eventually conceded that most of Brown's backers were ignorant of his true goals and probably would have been horrified at the scale of violence he had planned. All they knew was that Brown would get something done, and the abolitionists' cause would somehow be the better for it. So even the most respectable citizens played along without asking for specifics. Only in hindsight would they realize how cleverly they had been used.

Brown had drawn them in with altruism, but kept his true aims hidden. In this way, he built the *appearance* of a large conspiracy—one that created panic in the public mind, wrought havoc with investigators, and gave his followers a false sense of support. It was a brilliant move, and something John Wilkes Booth would keep in mind when forming his own plot years later.[35]

BOOTH LOST HIS JOB at the Marshall, but on hearing the news, a contingent of the Grays marched on the theater and pleaded to have him reinstated. Though George Kunkel gave him his job back, Booth had lost his enthusiasm for acting. The excitement of recent events had made him think once more of a career in uniform. The idea terrified his mother, but as Asia said, military service was probably her brother's dearest ambition. His good friend Jesse Wharton had been commissioned in the army, and now John Wilkes pondered the idea of following him into the ranks. In the end, though, he chose to continue acting. Audiences loved him, and critical notice was uniformly good. When the fall season opened, he would return to the stage with top billing.[36]

Fallout from the Harpers Ferry controversy cost William H. Seward the presidency. Seward seemed too radical to be elected, and as he fell out of the public's favor, a new man became the Republican front-runner. At New York's Cooper Union, Abraham Lincoln issued his own closing comments on the Harpers Ferry incident. He denied that any member of his party had been implicated in Brown's plot, and he told his listeners that the raid had always been doomed to failure. "That affair, in its philosophy, corresponds with the many attempts . . . at the assassination of kings and emperors," Lincoln said. "An enthusiast broods over the oppression of a people till he fancies himself commissioned by Heaven to liberate them. He ventures the attempt, which ends in little else than his own execution." The same might have been said of John Wilkes Booth in 1865.[37]

In May 1860, Lincoln was nominated to be the Republican candidate for president. Seward's opponents were relieved, but hardly in a mood to celebrate; the Democratic Party was badly splintered, and no single candidate appeared able to overcome the advantage of Republicans united under Lincoln. Though the Illinoisan was not as obnoxious to Southerners as

Seward was, he shared the same values and goals—and more important, the same power base.

That summer, when Booth was in New York to attend the wedding of Edwin and Mary Devlin, he got in touch with Matthew W. Canning, Jr., a Philadelphia lawyer and part owner of some playhouses in the South. Canning had put together a touring company for the coming season, and on Edwin's recommendation, he signed John Wilkes as its leading man. After three years of stock acting, John Wilkes Booth was about to become a star.

SEVEN

"*THE* MAN OF GENIUS
IN THE BOOTH FAMILY"

THE SEASON BEGAN IN COLUMBUS, GEORGIA, WHERE PAPERS announced that John Wilkes Booth and Mary Mitchell would appear in *Romeo and Juliet* at Temperance Hall. It was Booth's first performance as a leading man, and critics were favorably impressed. The *Daily Sun* found him "not so much experienced as Edwin, but bids fair soon to equal him. He has all the promise, and in personal appearance is handsome and prepossessing." Booth quickly became a sensation with the ladies. They fussed over him, primped for him, and pined for a few breathless words with him. As one actress later wrote, "as the sunflowers turn upon their stalks to follow the beloved sun, so old or young, our faces smiling, turned to him." Booth left many a fluttering heart in his wake.[1]

Even now, he had a confidence and assertiveness that had taken Edwin years to develop. Knowing how closely the critics would look, he still chose to open with Romeo, a part he had never played before, and to follow it with Kotzebue's *The Stranger,* also for the first time. Then, for his benefit performance, he played Richard III, a challenging role that would certainly invite comparisons to the elder Booth. Apparently he was up to the task; a critic for the *Daily Times* had no doubt that the son would do credit to his father's memory. And as he pointed out, Booth was a Southern patriot.

"When John Brown made his raid into Virginia, Mr. Wilkes was playing in Richmond. So soon as the tocsin of the alarm was sounded and call made for volunteers to defend Southern honor and Southern homes, he, among the first, doffed the sock and buskin, and donning the musket, and knapsack, did faithful service until peace and quiet were restored to the borders of the Old Dominion. For this, at least, to say nothing of his merits as an actor, he should receive a bumper. Let us give him one worthy alike of the actor in peace—the soldier in war."[2]

John Wilkes Booth would always be associated with the capture of John Brown, and for the rest of his life he would encourage the belief that he had taken part in that event. In fact, he missed it entirely.

Hamlet was announced on October 12, but things did not go as planned. An hour before curtain time, Booth was in manager Matt Canning's hotel room, going through his lines with actor Johnny Albaugh, when Canning came in looking exhausted. Booth was concerned. "Now, you must let me nurse you," he said. "You are fagged out." The manager replied that he only wanted to go to sleep. As he lay on the bed, Booth noticed a pistol jutting out of Canning's back pocket and saw an opportunity to show off. Sliding the weapon out, he carefully took aim at a mark on the opposite wall. The loud discharge brought the startled Canning instantly to his feet. Booth was a superb marksman, but this time he missed the mark, and he wanted to have another shot at it. Canning, on the other hand, just wanted to get his heart back out of his throat. He insisted on having his gun back, but Booth would not give it up. They fussed over it, and as they did, Booth noticed some rust on the barrel. He got the manager to hold the weapon while he scraped it off with his pocketknife. The pistol discharged, and the ball struck Booth in the thigh, barely missing the femoral artery. It was a serious wound, and one that might have ended his career, if not his life. Albaugh played the role of Hamlet that night and became the company's new star; Booth remained in the hotel for weeks of recuperation. He did not return to the stage until the end of the engagement, and then just long enough to recite Marc Antony's oration over the body of Caesar. It was a feeble effort, but he wanted to show the city of Columbus that he had not forgotten its kindness to him.[3]

Though only partially recovered, Booth swept into Montgomery, Alabama, where patrons turned out in record numbers to see him. He was the toast of the city, and one fan even named a racehorse in his honor. Everyone agreed that his Columbus opening had been no fluke. His career was off to a phenomenal start. He was the darling of society, the favorite of critics, and the idol of countless belles.[4]

He was still there on November 6, when Abraham Lincoln was elected president. In the four-way race, Lincoln had won only 39 percent of the popular vote, but a wide electoral majority. The divide was especially pronounced along the Mason-Dixon line. To the north, 56 percent of Pennsylvania voters supported Lincoln, while their immediate neighbors in Maryland ranked him dead last with barely 2.5 percent of the vote. So William Seward was right. The slavery issue gave Republicans all the votes they needed to carry the election. Since the party did not exist in the South, Abraham Lincoln won without even being a candidate in the Southern states. The Seward strategy had rendered those voters irrelevant.

Reaction was swift and predictable. The Montgomery *Advertiser* recommended that Alabama secede, telling its readers, "You can only sink to the condition of Ireland as members of this Union." Farther north, the Baltimore *Daily Republican* pointed out that only the North and East had elected Lincoln, so it was doubtful he would "ever be President of the *United* States." Even federal employees in Washington were incensed. According to the *New York Herald,* they "were for forming a Southern Confederacy at once, and some of the more resolute and determined donned the cockade, and indicated their willingness to shoulder their muskets and resist the inauguration of Lincoln." One editor in North Carolina advised a cautious approach, but added, "If Lincoln violates his oath, let us dethrone him."[5]

Booth's reaction to all this is unknown, but we may assume his views reflected his upbringing. Like all former Know-Nothings, he still put the Union first. They believed the culprits in this crisis were those who tore the nation apart with their attacks on slavery. *They* were the real disunionists, and if the South made the next move, they did so because it was the only option left to them. Lincoln's election had already effectively put them out of the Union.

Booth returned to Philadelphia, where he recuperated and watched the national drama unfold. On December 13, a "Grand Union assembly" was held at Independence Hall, under a large banner that read: "Concession Before Secession." One after another, city leaders took the podium to blame anti-slavery influence for the state of affairs. They suggested that Southern fears were perfectly reasonable, and called for an end to state laws that resisted the Fugitive Slave Act.[6]

These were not unusual sentiments. Northerners everywhere held abolitionists responsible for the crisis. In his annual message to Congress,

President James Buchanan insisted that anti-slavery agitation had given slaves a dangerous thirst for freedom. "Hence a sense of security . . . has given place to apprehensions of servile insurrection. Many a matron throughout the South retires at night in dread of what may befall herself and her children before the morning." Booth had been hearing such talk in all his travels. From Baltimore to Richmond to Montgomery to Philadelphia, the "noisy element" seemed to agree that there would be no crisis if only some people would leave the slavery issue alone. Hearing this, Booth had every reason to believe that this was a moderate view, and that those now coming into power were extremists on the far fringes of politics.[7]

Victorious Republicans were riding an enormous wave of support, and they weren't above taunting the opposition. It became fashionable to show Southerners how much their influence had waned. Texas senator Louis T. Wigfall warned his fellow senators in Washington that the South was indeed serious about secession. "It is well known," he said, "that before this day next week one of the States will cease to be a member of this Union." His words drew loud bursts of laughter.[8]

Booth could read countless opinions and solutions to the crisis in the columns of the Philadelphia papers. Indeed, it was the consuming topic of the day. Not one to watch from afar, he wrote down some of his own thoughts in the form of a speech. Perhaps he intended to have it published, as so many others were doing at the time, or maybe it was nothing more than a therapeutic exercise. But it was written to be heard, not read, with a tone and cadence like that of Marc Antony's funeral oration. It is self-effacing at times, and expresses the hope that the cause will be taken up by a more capable speaker. It is a rough draft, full of misspellings and incomplete thoughts.

His arguments are the same ones aired at the Grand Union meeting: that this was an issue of Northern aggression versus Southern rights; that abolitionists were responsible for the current mess; that they should be "hushed forever," and their treason "stamped to death." Those who have "laughed at, prayed [sic] upon and wronged" the South should be punished, Booth wrote. In some ways, he thought, these sectional politicians were worse than an infamous abolitionist who had been put to death the year before. "I may say I helped to hang John Brown," wrote Booth. "His treason was no more than theirs, for open *force* is *holier* than hidden *craft*. The Lion is more noble than the fox."[9]

On the issue of human bondage, Booth had adopted the paternalist argument that was then in vogue. "Instead of looking upon slavery as a sin (mearly because I have none) I hold it to be a happiness for themselves and a social & political blessing for us.... I have been through the whole South and have marked the happiness of master & of man." This was a point that he and others would continue to insist on: that even as slaves, African Americans were better off here than Africans anywhere else in the world.[10]

All attempts at reconciliation failed, and on the afternoon of December 20, a special convention in South Carolina passed an ordinance of secession. Within weeks, Mississippi, Florida, Alabama, and Georgia followed suit. The Union was breaking apart. Virginia awaited further developments, and common wisdom held that Virginia's actions would determine Maryland's course.

Booth had fully recovered from his bullet wound, but no sooner had he returned to the stage than he suffered another mishap, this time in Albany. While playing Pescara in *The Apostate,* he inflicted a slight cut on the head of his co-star. They continued the scene, and only later did the audience learn that Booth himself had also been injured. He had fallen on his dagger, and the blade had cut away three inches of muscle near the armpit. As one critic wrote, "It seemed as though the climax of the TRAGEDY had indeed been reached."

Though the injury was serious, Booth would not let it stop his engagement. He returned to the stage a few days later, playing Pescara with his right arm tied to his side. "Mr. Booth makes an impression on you by the mere force of intellect," said one review. Another said, "He throws his whole soul into his sword, giving to the contest a degree of earnestness never approached, even by his father.... [Three cheers] were given with a power that almost took the roof off." Critics hardly noticed the handicap.[11]

Abraham Lincoln was also in Albany that night, having dinner with the governor. Lincoln was on his way to Washington, and the trip was about to get interesting. His advisers learned of rumors that an assassination would be attempted in Baltimore, and they asked him to skip the meandering journey he had planned. They wanted him to head straight for the capital, passing through Baltimore without fanfare and ahead of schedule. Lincoln agreed, and on the night of February 22, he quietly boarded an early train from Philadelphia to Washington. That was a mistake.

Hostile newspapers made the most of the story, showing cartoons of a terrified president-elect sneaking out of a railroad car in a ridiculous Scotch cap. Lincoln regretted the course he had taken, but felt he had little choice. He knew the threat was real, even if some were denying it, and he was just acting prudently in hurrying past the danger. But to the public he looked scared and undignified. He had been publicly embarrassed.[12]

Abraham Lincoln was inaugurated on March 4, and he named William H. Seward to be his secretary of state. It was an appointment to which Seward felt entitled. Like much of the public, the senator from New York assumed that he, and not the inexperienced president, would actually run the government. He was mistaken. In the coming weeks, Lincoln quietly put Seward in his place, and from then on, the secretary acted the part of trusted friend and adviser. Though Abraham Lincoln was certainly in charge, the perception remained that William Seward was the actual guiding force of the administration.

On April 12, Confederate batteries opened fire on Fort Sumter, and the nation was at war. President Lincoln met the emergency head-on. He called up seventy-five thousand militia troops to repossess all property taken by the insurgents, and to quell "combinations too powerful to be suppressed by the ordinary course of judicial proceedings. . . ." He called for an emergency session of Congress, and declared a blockade of Southern ports. To Lincoln, these were commonsense measures, and no more drastic than the situation required.[13]

Not everyone agreed, and on the seventeenth, states of the Upper South began to react. On that day, the Virginia State Convention voted overwhelmingly to put secession up for a popular vote. No one doubted what the outcome would be, and the only question was whether Maryland should follow her sister state. A large gathering of citizens met in Baltimore to consider the question, but they agreed to await further developments. Everyone was aware of the state's geographical importance. If the Old Line State left the Union, the nation's capital would be surrounded by hostile territory.

Torn by a dual temperament, Maryland had a sizable abolitionist following in the western counties, and a dominant slave culture to the south and east. Slave owners were the more vocal of the two, and the more likely to sway the legislature. Baltimore, the state's largest city, leaned in their favor, and it was here that the crisis would most likely come to a head. The city had long been known as a "mob town," where politics and violence went hand in hand. Deadly riots had followed every election in recent memory, and local gangs had even roughed up president-elect James Buchanan on his way to Washington four years before. Outsiders were especially vulnerable because of the long, awkward stop required of rail passengers trying to pass through the city. No railroad line went straight through, and anyone coming from the North had to disembark at one station, then travel by foot, coach, or streetcar to another station a mile or two away. Thus, the citizens of Baltimore could act as gatekeepers in the race to join the war.[14]

That became an important issue on April 19, when the 6th Massachusetts Infantry passed down Pratt Street and were attacked by a frenzied mob. Four soldiers were killed by flying bricks and other objects, and a number of citizens died when troops fired back into the crowd. News of the riot was unnerving to Lincoln, and it drove home the point that at this critical time, just a few hotheads could obstruct his efforts to assemble a fighting force.[15]

General Ben Butler secured a new route to Washington by way of Annapolis, but Baltimore's hostility still had to be addressed. The U.S. Army's ancient commander, General Winfield Scott, began planning a four-pronged assault on the city. The president chose a less drastic measure, but one that drew battle lines for another conflict—a fight over civil rights. On April 27, Lincoln ordered General Scott to suspend the writ of habeas corpus along the line from Philadelphia to Washington. The writ guaranteed a prompt hearing in court to determine the legality of an arrest. By setting it aside, the army could confine anyone for any reason—or for no reason at all. Its suspension was only one of several controversial measures. In the coming months, Massachusetts troops would slip into Baltimore at night and occupy the city. Nine local newspapers would be suppressed, and the city's police department would be replaced by federally appointed officers. Baltimore's mayor, its police marshal, and some of its most prominent citizens would be thrown behind bars.

The arrests led to a legal showdown in June, when Chief Justice Roger B. Taney of the U.S. Supreme Court, sitting as a circuit judge in Baltimore, denied the president's authority to suspend the writ of habeas corpus. Taney's decision included a blistering rebuke:

"If the President of the United States may suspend the writ, then the Constitution of the United States has conferred upon him more regal and absolute power over the liberty of the citizen than the people of England have thought it safe to intrust to the Crown—a power which the Queen of England cannot exercise at this day and which could not have been lawfully exercised by the sovereign even in the reign of Charles the First." The decision changed nothing. Arrests continued, and the policy was even extended to the state legislature. In September, thirty-two lawmakers and their sergeant at arms were taken from their beds at night and carried off to prison. No charges were ever filed.[16]

War measures were extended incrementally to the rest of the nation, but their impact fell disproportionately on the Border States. Lincoln always maintained that he had done what was necessary to preserve the nation, and that his policy targeted only "traitors," who might have suffered even more under existing laws. Marylanders, however, did not regard their acts as treason, but merely as opposition to an overly harsh policy. The state legislature had never voted for secession, and many citizens supported the Union as vigorously as anyone in the North. They were being falsely accused, in their view, and that is what made Abraham Lincoln an issue unto himself, quite apart from slavery or union.[17]

The president did not take all the blame for this. There was a strong and lingering perception that William H. Seward was actually running the government—an impression he sometimes cultivated. Seward had taken the lead in implementing the war measures, and he was said to have relished his newfound power. "My Lord," he supposedly told a British diplomat, "I can touch a bell on my right hand, and order the arrest of a citizen of Ohio; I can touch a bell again, and order the imprisonment of a citizen of New York; and no power on earth, except that of the President, can release them. Can the Queen of England do so much?" The secretary showed little compassion, and sometimes he even ordered extra prison time for anyone who tried to engage the services of a lawyer. President Lincoln almost always deferred to Seward's judgment.[18]

The arrests stiffened resistance to the administration's war effort, and when Lincoln sent out his first call for volunteers, Maryland refused to provide any. Instead, hundreds of men fled to Harpers Ferry, where they enlisted in Virginia regiments. Over time, the opposition at home moved underground. From Baltimore to the southern counties, subversive networks began to form among farmers and ordinary citizens. Confederate couriers would find a safe haven among them, and would come to depend on their help in running people, mail, and supplies across the Potomac to Virginia. Without these associations, Booth's conspiracy would never have been feasible.[19]

Whether John Wilkes Booth took part in the events of 1861 is a matter of dispute. Later reports had him burning bridges, tearing up railroad tracks, and being arrested in the Pratt Street riot. But Booth himself claimed only to have been present when the 6th Massachusetts was attacked. In all likelihood, even that was an exaggeration. He was far too busy building his career to involve himself in the affairs of his home state.[20]

Maryland was a place of divided loyalties, where the phrase "brother against brother" was often literally true. Long after the war, an old veteran from Baltimore reflected on his own divided family, and on what had become of the boys in his neighborhood. Though most had leaned toward the South, not all had served her cause. In all, he wrote, eighteen of his friends had joined the Confederate forces, and a few others tried to do so. Three had joined the U.S. Navy, and two went into the Union army. The Booth brothers, who grew up with all these people, were among the few who never served.[21]

Though Booth may have wanted to get involved, he dared not do so openly. Too many of his relatives favored the North, and if John Wilkes had "gone South," as he might have wished, the family would have split in two, perhaps for good. He had promised his mother he would never let that happen. The vow of neutrality put Booth in limbo for the duration. He would not leave the country, as Edwin and Joseph did, nor would he enlist. And it was not likely that conscription would affect him one way or another. The draft was easily avoided, especially by a man on the move. It was managed at the state level, and since Booth had not lived in his home state for years, the provost marshal there would have no cause to put him on the enrollment list. Officially, he was a resident of Philadelphia, but he wasn't there much either, and no enrolling officer had the time, resources, or authority to track him down elsewhere. Thus, if all else failed, he could avoid the threat indefinitely merely by staying on the road.[22]

But staying out of the war did not keep Booth out of danger. During a return engagement in Albany, he was joined by Henrietta Irving, a pretty actress who had recently been cast opposite him in Rochester. Henrietta was infatuated with Booth, and for a while her affections were returned in kind. But on the night of April 26, they had a falling-out. Angry words passed between them, and Henrietta flew into a rage. She came at Booth with a knife, jabbing it straight at him. He parried the blow upward, and the blade glanced off his cheek, inflicting a bloody wound. Henrietta stormed out sobbing and a short time later was found to have stabbed herself. Both she and Booth recovered, but the incident made John Wilkes Booth appear jinxed. Only halfway into his first season as a star, he had been seriously wounded three times.[23]

Once, after seeing his brother act in Richmond, Edwin Booth wrote, "I don't think he will startle the world." But three years later, John Wilkes was doing just that. Houses were full, and critics gushed. He had achieved the highest level of stardom in record time. His acting was fresh and original, with an expressiveness many critics found hard to describe. A Buffalo review said, "We do not flatter him when we say he has extraordinary physiognomical power, almost electrical feeling and weird and startling elocutionary effects." He had a "trained power of intellect," and seemed to fit every movement, expression, or gesture perfectly to the part. Most of all, he had *intensity*, which one critic called "the lightning of the soul. . . . [It] cannot be taught to the mind." Booth seemed not to play a part, but to *become* it.[24]

The key to his success, undoubtedly, was his originality. There was something mysterious in the way he moved. After seeing him in *The Lady of Lyons*, a Boston critic said, "When he moves, he does so with that aptness of motion, which forbids the observer to define it; he was there, he is here—he was seen to pass—but how he went, with what step upon the stage, or if borne through the air, can scarcely be told. . . . He has a physique . . . which is equal to any demands which he need make upon it." The physique, in fact, was an important factor in his acting style. Matt Canning said, "He was the most remarkable actor we probably had on the stage for hardiness, endurance, and strength. We sometimes called him the cast-iron man. . . ." He restaged battle scenes to give them more energy, and he loved to add dramatic leaps—sometimes from *twelve feet above the stage*—for a startling effect when he entered a scene.[25]

The critical praise was overwhelming, but it was not unanimous. A review in Chicago called his performance "scarcely worthy of toleration," and "somewhat below the median standard." A Washington critic called him "little more than a second-rate actor." But negative reviews were rare, and often contradicted. One, for example, said he "needs the development of arduous study," while at the same time, another review insisted that "deep study has made him conversant with all he has undertaken." One paper reported that Booth lacked grace and dignity, while another said that, in general, Booth had grace and dignity in abundance, but was too young to play some of his chosen roles. Whatever their observations, all agreed on one thing: few actors had ever risen to prominence with such *éclat*. His achievement was stunning.[26]

His onstage passion was sometimes too real, and injuries resulted. Actor E. L. Tilton once broke his arm when Booth knocked him into the orchestra pit. And on another occasion, Booth himself was cut across the eyelid by the swordplay of James C. McCollom; he almost lost his sight. Even the tamer roles were dangerous; Booth was playing Pescara when he fell on his dagger that night in Albany, and Romeo when he supposedly broke his nose. Some would call him reckless, and say that he cared little for the safety of his fellow actors. But his contemporaries knew better. They knew that even the most careful players had accidents. Such things are impossible to avoid, if one wanted a scene to look real.[27]

John Wilkes Booth gave his audiences everything he had, and they repaid the enthusiasm in kind. In Brooklyn, patrons were "pushing, crowding, and jamming" to get tickets. Louisville saw an "unprecedented" rush on the box office. And in St. Louis, more than twenty-five hundred fans came to see him, even in spite of extraordinarily cold temperatures. They loved to see action above all else, and that is where Booth excelled. Twenty-five years after his death, a Boston producer still believed the best stage duel of his generation was one involving Booth.[28]

His New York début went exceedingly well, and on his return to Baltimore, Booth found that John T. Ford was advertising his Holliday Street Theatre engagement in the most obsequious terms. Phrases such as "Baltimore's favorite son," "the brother and artistic rival of Edwin," "the son of the noble sire," and the like did not meet the new star's approval. He found it annoying, and insisted that Ford replace them all with a simple phrase: "I am myself alone." That was a line from *Richard III,* and serious patrons would have known that the full passage began with "I have no brother, and am like no brother. . . ."

Richard was widely considered Booth's best part, and he capped off every performance with an elaborate dance of death that led some critics to name him the very best Richard on the American stage.[29]

Booth's style of acting was strenuous, and made all the more difficult by the rigors of travel. Getting from place to place was an uncomfortable business that could easily leave an actor too sick to perform. Dangerous coaches, rough terrain, and severe weather made any long trip stressful, yet for Booth there was no time to let up. His engagements took him to thirty-three cities, requiring trips totaling more than 24,600 miles—five thousand in the first six months of 1862 alone. The star rarely had time to shake off the effects of a long trip, and he sometimes arrived in town only hours before the first performance. Then, too, fatigue was often compounded by the stress of uncertainty about the upcoming venue. One week he might play the palatial St. Charles Theatre, and the next might find him at the Brooklyn Academy of Music, whose nine-man stock company rendered *Richard III* so ludicrous that one critic said, "The War of the Roses could not be carried on much longer without resort to a draft."[30]

Booth played in the occupied South, and was popular there, as historians have rightly claimed. But he was not "an essentially Southern actor," as often charged. He was a particular favorite in Boston, and his closest friends believed that this was where he intended to make his home. Unlike the frantic New York or the boisterous Baltimore, Boston had an elegance and culture all its own. It was a place where, in the words of Adam Badeau, "mind and education are better appreciated; here it is talent and tact, and, above all, success that sways." Certainly, the city opened its arms to this dark and handsome star. Indeed, that is where he had some of his best audiences. At the Boston Museum, playbills advised patrons to buy tickets early, "as the EXTRAORDINARY FURORE Excited by this Young Artist's histrionic efforts has never been equaled by any star. . . ." One paper even claimed that "the carpenter of the establishment has it in contemplation to put a row of hooks and pegs around the lobby and gallery, for the latecomers to hang from." John Wilkes felt so much at home here that he bought a lot at 115 Commonwealth Avenue, intending to build a house in Back Bay.[31]

DEMOCRATS CONTINUED TO SNIPE at the president's extraordinary war measures. But Lincoln was not running the war alone; when the government seized railroads and telegraph lines, confiscated property, and expanded the size of the armed forces, it did so under congressional mandate. In the last days of the Thirty-seventh Congress, forty-nine bills had been passed by voice vote or parliamentary maneuvering. One of the most important of these added a tenth justice to the U.S. Supreme Court. That gave the president five solid votes—and a deadlock—on all the most volatile issues.[32]

The Civil War was unlike anything known in modern times, and the nation came closer to collapse than most people realize today. Emancipation of slaves, confiscation of property, and the draft often led to deadly clashes between the public and civil authorities. The political storm threatened not only the federal government, but state governments as well. In Indiana, Republicans shut down the state legislature for two years, and Democrats, lacking a quorum, seized control of state troops from the governor. In Illinois, Governor Richard Yates refused to call the legislature for two years in order to prevent Democrats from hindering the administration's war measures.[33]

In the middle stood Abraham Lincoln, blamed for the war and fired upon from all sides. It was not just the fringe element who hated the president; judges, senators, editors, and otherwise respectable citizens left no doubt of their contempt for him as well. Even the normally staid floor of the Senate saw its share of invective. One senator compared Lincoln to the tyrants of history, saying, "They are all buried beneath the wave of oblivion in comparison to what this man of yesterday, this Abraham Lincoln, that neither you nor I ever heard of four years ago, has chosen to exercise. . . ." To that senator and countless citizens, Abraham Lincoln was the American Caesar, out to establish a new empire from the ashes of a republic.[34]

Even when traveling among Unionists, Booth could hardly have missed the criticism. Editorials from one paper were often reprinted in another, for the benefit of a new and incredulous readership. Thus, Booth could have picked up a Louisville paper and read this editorial from the *Richmond Dispatch:*

"Assassination in the abstract is a horrid crime . . . but to slay a tyrant is no more assassination than war is murder. Who speaks of Brutus as an assassin? What Yankee ever condemned the Roundhead crew who brought Charles I to the block, although it would be a cruel libel to compare him politically or personally to the tyrants who are now lording it over the South?"[35]

And though Booth probably never read the London *Times,* he could have seen it quoted in the Indianapolis *Daily Sentinel:*

"Mr. Lincoln and his party have been dominant as no set of men ever were before in a land peopled by the English race. They have governed twenty millions of their countrymen with a revolutionary freedom from the trammels of law."[36]

It may belabor the point, but such editorials were part of the atmosphere that engulfed Booth's life no matter where he went, and they certainly influenced his thinking.

. . .

IN THE SPRING OF 1863, Booth played his first engagement in the nation's capital. Washington was a Southern city then, and even though the war had dramatically expanded its population, the place was still much like a small town. The roads were unpaved, and livestock wandered the streets. The city's main thoroughfare, Pennsylvania Avenue, was either dust or mud, depending on the weather. Here stood the Executive Mansion, where the president, his family, and a couple of secretaries lived. The household staff were still paid out of the president's own pocket, and since the mansion was open to everyone, they all had to endure life in a very public setting. A steady flow of riffraff had taken its toll on the curtains, drapes, and silverware, and the president was occasionally vexed to find tourists tramping through his private rooms. He moved out to the Soldiers' Home whenever the opportunity presented itself.

War conditions made Washington "a Sodom beyond redemption," with more than a hundred bawdy houses and thirty-seven hundred saloons. Some would have argued that playhouses belonged in that same class. The city had only two major theaters. Ford's, on Tenth Street, had once been a Baptist church, but was converted just before the war, after its congregation moved elsewhere. Three blocks to the west was the National Theatre, on E Street near Thirteenth. Both enjoyed a lively business in spite of the conflict, or perhaps because of it. Soldiers made up a large part of every audience. They seemed to regard theatrical entertainment as an escape from the boredom and occasional terror of a military life.

As a friend of the Fords, Booth might have been expected to play their theater whenever he was in Washington. But in late December 1862, Ford's Theatre was destroyed by fire, and it would take almost nine months to rebuild. In the meantime, Booth played at the National and his two-week engagement there drew the largest audiences of the 1862–63 season. It was during this run that Matt Canning, in Washington at the time, noticed a large growth on Booth's neck, and became alarmed. On April 13, he took Booth down to the office of Dr. John Frederick May, who diagnosed the growth as a tumor and recommended its removal. Always in a hurry, Booth suggested it be done right then and there. "Young man," said the doctor, "this is no trifling matter. You will have to come when we are ready for you, when I have an assistant here."

Nevertheless, Booth was insistent. "You can cut it out right now. Here is Canning, who will be your assistant." Wasting no time with argument, he seated himself on a chair and draped his head over the back of it. "Now cut away!" he said. The doctor gave Canning some instructions, and the operation began. It was unexpectedly gruesome. "The first swipe he made with his knife nearly made me fall on the floor fainting," Canning recalled. The dark blood gushed out, and he actually wondered for a moment if his friend had been decapitated. Booth hardly even twitched, but as the work proceeded, his skin grew deathly pale. It was all too much for Canning, who finally passed out. Booth reeled and collapsed on top of him.[37]

In spite of his doctor's orders, Booth returned to the stage that night. But he should have listened. Within days his stitches had been torn open, and he returned to May's office in agony. There was not much that the doctor could do. The wound had not healed properly. It was jagged, and looked more like a burn than a surgical scar.

Booth had always wanted to be a man of action, and that mark of the scalpel at least gave him a chance to act the part. To a friend in Boston, he wrote, "[I] . . . am far from well. I have a hole in my neck you could run your fist in. The doctor had a hunt for my bullet." Booth told the same story to anyone who would listen, and he asked Dr. May to confirm it if anyone should ask. He even convinced Matt Canning that the alleged bullet was the same one Canning had fired at him by accident several years before. "Do you know," Canning later said, "that that ball which I shot into his side came out of that tumor? It was in his body, and there it had worked up from somewhere in the muscles to the throat, and worked out at the throat." Booth must have been the consummate storyteller. He could make even the most ridiculous story seem plausible.[38]

HOURS AFTER THAT OPERATION, Booth was introduced backstage to a short, dark-haired young man with pouchy cheeks and a wisp of facial hair that barely qualified as a mustache. His name was David E. Herold, and the experienced eye of the actor sized him up instantly: fidgety, clownish, and more than a little insecure. At twenty, Herold still wasn't sure what he wanted to do with his life. He had attended the best schools, including Georgetown College, and had learned the pharmacy trade. But years as a drugstore clerk had left him wanting more. He craved excitement and an opportunity to prove his manliness. Talk to him for five minutes, and he was sure to mention his sexual prowess and hunting skills.

Herold lived near the Washington Navy Yard, where his father was the chief clerk of the naval store. Adam George Herold had eight children, and he would have given anything to start his only son on a respectable ca-

reer. But David was indifferent to everything that came along. He preferred to spend his time hunting or swapping lies with friends in the service. Indeed, he was so resistant to growing up that some musicians in the
Marine Band seemed to think of him as a mascot. They let him tag along
to their concerts and nighttime jobs in the city's theaters. That was probably how he met Booth in the first place.

Dave Herold was instantly charmed. Though Booth was rich and famous, he never seemed to look down on anyone. For Herold, that was a
novel experience. He was amazed that a star who had such a wide circle of
friends would even take the time to converse with an insignificant pharmacy clerk. Booth made him feel at ease, and Herold quickly came to consider himself a friend.[39]

During his run at the National, Booth learned that the old Washington
Theatre was available. Being free himself for almost a month, he arranged
to rent the place in the interim. He hired some of the stagehands left un-
employed by the Ford's Theatre fire, and brought in some of his best
friends to fill the stock company. In a matter of days, Booth had assembled
a respectable lineup, with Sam Chester, Effie Germon, and Alice Gray in
the cast. They worked together, made some money, and after a few weeks,
quit. Then, right on schedule, Booth headed to his next engagement in
Chicago.[40]

BY MID-1863, the tide of the war was beginning to shift in the North's
favor. Their military victories were more conspicuous, and even the political opposition seemed to be losing ground. Intense as his feelings were,
Booth managed to get through the first years with only a few outbursts. In
St. Louis, he was briefly detained for saying that "the whole damn government can go to hell." In New Orleans, he sang the forbidden tune "The
Bonnie Blue Flag" on a dare, and had to talk himself out of an arrest. In
New York, he railed at some fellow actors about the imprisonment of Baltimore's police marshal, George P. Kane. "He is my friend," Booth said,
"and the man who could drag him from the bosom of his family for no
crime whatever, but a mere suspicion that he may commit one sometime,
deserves a dog's death!" Kane's arrest took place at a time when William
Seward was overseeing such matters.

By and large, though, he kept his feelings in check. One fellow actor
said that Booth was known as a rebel, but "not the noisy kind." Even the
most staunch Unionists considered him a friend. He got along well with

Julia Ward Howe, whose husband had been one of John Brown's backers, and with Edwin's friend Adam Badeau, who would soon be an aide to General Ulysses S. Grant. During the bloody New York draft riots, John Wilkes and Badeau were both staying at Edwin's house in Manhattan. As a racist mob moved closer to the neighborhood, Badeau, who had recently been wounded, grew concerned for the safety of his African American servant. John Wilkes allayed his fears, vowing to protect the man at the peril of his own life. Touched by the gallant gesture, Badeau later admitted he would never have guessed that John Wilkes was an ardent rebel. Booth was proud of the deception. "Imagine me," he told his sister, "helping that wounded soldier with my rebel sinews!"[41]

Booth kept those "sinews" in check on November 9, 1863, when President and Mrs. Lincoln came to see him perform in the newly rebuilt Ford's Theatre. The play was *The Marble Heart,* and in light of the star's reputation, the Lincolns probably expected to see a gripping demonstration of true blood-and-thunder showmanship. But Booth showed little interest in gratifying the president. He merely walked through the part, giving an uncharacteristically flat rendition of a role that was often regarded as one of his best. Later accounts would mention angry glares and insulting comments, but there was none of that. Booth just slogged through the performance, and made it, in the words of Lincoln's secretary, "more tame than otherwise." The president did not come to see him again.[42]

TRAVEL AND TURMOIL WERE SAPPING Booth of the vigor and enthusiasm that had made him a star. No one doubted that he could still fill the houses, but in the estimation of critics, he was slowly sinking. Reviews now spoke more of promise than proven ability. "We do not pretend that Mr. Booth is the greatest actor on the stage," said the New Orleans *True Delta,* "but we have yet to find any . . . who give promise of such excellence." Booth seems to have put more stock in receipts than reviews. There is certainly no reason to believe what has been charged in the twentieth century: that critical comments about his acting "finally drove him to the assassination of Abraham Lincoln." In fact, the comments were quite good, even to the end. Booth's reviews were more consistently positive than those of any other actor of his day, Edwin included.[43]

Later writers have placed a strong emphasis on Booth's rivalry with his older brother. They claimed that John Wilkes was losing his voice and his career while Edwin's star was on the rise. Seething at his brother's good fortune, he could only watch his chance for fame slip by. This theory rests largely on reports of hoarseness that John Wilkes occasionally suffered on stage. An 1862 review in the Boston *Advertiser* ascribed the problem to vocal abuse:

"In what does he fail? Principally, in knowledge of himself,—of his resources, how to husband and how to use them. He is, apparently, entirely ignorant of the main principles of elocution . . . [and] the nature and proper treatment of the voice as well."[44]

Historians have given this review a great deal of weight while ignoring the rest of the evidence. Another critic, watching the same performances, noted only that John Wilkes had a voice much like Edwin's, with "the same smooth, silvery tones." Though Booth was hoarse from time to time, the problem was not chronic. It always cropped up after a long journey, and usually in severe weather. One of the worst episodes occurred in 1862, when a Chicago engagement began right after an exhausting fifty-one-hour train ride from Boston. Knowledgeable critics took such things into account. Knowing what Booth's life as an actor was like, they passed his hoarseness off as a temporary problem, or as a deliberate vocal effect. They did the same for his brothers, who were plagued by the same affliction. His brother June, for example, lost his voice completely during an 1864 engagement in Baltimore, and remained hoarse for a week.[45]

Harsh reviews tended to focus on Booth's spontaneity rather than on any lack of ability. Manager John Ellsler once noted the "unstudied effects" that cropped up in Booth's performances, and asked him, "Did you rehearse that business today, John?" "No," said Booth, "I didn't rehearse it, it just came to me in the scene, and I couldn't help doing it; but it went all right, didn't it?" Those ad-libs didn't always go over well. Older patrons and critics knew these plays down to the subtlest inflection. They knew what they liked, and any young actor who casually threw aside the old ways for something new risked a poor review for the "incorrect" reading. Booth's many plaudits for freshness and originality can be taken as evidence that, at least sometimes, his improvisations worked. More important, they show him to be a confident and uninhibited man—hardly the type to be tormented by insecurities.[46]

As for the sibling rivalry, there was none. Edwin and John Wilkes were often at odds, but their differences were political, not professional. In theatrical matters, they were mutually supportive. Actress Clara Morris once overheard John Wilkes telling someone, "No! No, no! There's but one

Hamlet to my mind, that's my brother Edwin. You see, between ourselves, he *is* Hamlet, melancholy and all!" And Edwin returned the compliment, telling actor Edward M. Alfriend, "John Wilkes had the genius of my father, and was far more gifted than I." A letter written by Edwin in 1863 confirms that high opinion:

"I am happy to say that [John Wilkes] is full of the true grit—he has stuff enough in him to make good suits for a dozen such player-folk as we are cursed with. . . . I am delighted with him & feel the name of Booth to be more of a hydra than snakes and things ever was."[47]

Critics often compared the brothers, and more often than not, they considered John Wilkes the better of the two. Family friends agreed. John T. Raymond once said, "[John Wilkes] was always looked upon as *the* man of genius in the Booth family," and Sir Charles Wyndham agreed. "His original gift," said Wyndham, "was greater than that of his wonderful brother, Edwin." Kate Reignolds Winslow, of the Boston Museum, hated John Wilkes, but admitted he "had more of the native fire and fury of his great father than any of his family."[48]

In early 1864, Edwin played a lengthy engagement at the National Theatre in Washington. Abraham Lincoln came to see him seven times, and on a couple of occasions he brought Secretary of State Seward with him. On March 11, Seward even hosted a dinner party in Edwin's honor. The secretary's daughter Fanny was especially pleased to meet her longtime idol, and his daughter-in-law Anna was positively giddy. As they sat and talked in the parlor of Seward's house, the secretary couldn't resist giving Edwin some unsolicited advice: *Don't make Cardinal Richelieu look so old.* Edwin graciously thanked him for the suggestion.[49]

John Wilkes Booth might have sneered at that visit, had he known about it, but he was on tour at the time. In late May he finished the season in Boston, then went to western Pennsylvania, where he was starting up a new business venture. John Ellsler and Thomas Y. Mears had formed a partnership with Booth in the Dramatic Oil Company. They purchased three acres along the Allegheny River just south of Franklin. Oil wells were springing up all over the region, and Booth felt he had a good shot at success with one of his own. But he never expected it to come easily. As he wrote to Ellsler, "This might be a big thing for us or it may be nothing, the last sure if we do not give it our attention. Throw things overboard and come as soon as possible." Ellsler came as directed, and his friend Joe Simonds came down from Boston to serve as a manager and consultant. On

Simonds's advice, Booth purchased a one-thirtieth interest in a second property, and for much of the summer he gave the oil business his full attention.[50]

Victory was slipping further away from the Confederates, who were now on the defensive in every theater of the war. All eyes seemed to be on Virginia, where General Robert E. Lee was trying desperately to keep his troops between the Union army and his own seat of government. General Grant, traveling with General Meade's Army of the Potomac, pushed relentlessly toward Richmond. He might have ended the war that summer but for a stunning upset at Cold Harbor, ten miles east of the rebel capital. Though downplayed in the Northern press, this costly battle gave Grant his worst defeat, while providing new and fleeting hope to those who argued that the Confederacy might yet survive.

War came directly to Washington in mid-July, when ten thousand soldiers under Confederate General Jubal Early engaged Union troops on the outskirts of the city. Col. Bradley Tyler Johnson, who served under Early, had planned to capture the president in the course of the fight and take him to Richmond as a prisoner of war. It seemed like a glorious idea, and Johnson's commander, General Wade Hampton, thought it feasible enough to give it his approval. But hearing of the plan, General Early wanted that mission for himself, and he reassigned Johnson to a prisoner rescue mission in Southern Maryland. By the new orders, Johnson would swing around Baltimore, then head south and liberate twelve thousand men from the Point Lookout prison, at the extreme southern tip of St. Mary's County. Early would capture Washington and hold it until the others could come up to join him.[51]

The plan was overly ambitious. Untrained Union forces had left their posts in Baltimore and met Early at the Monocacy River, north of Washington. Though Early pushed them back, they had delayed his progress long enough for Grant to send additional troops to defend the capital. By the time the Confederates reached the city, a full-scale assault was no longer practical, and Early was turned back within sight of the Capitol dome.

Bradley Johnson was foiled as well. Though his men did manage to cut telegraph lines around Baltimore, they never made it to Point Lookout. Word of the prison raid was leaked to the press, and the mission had to be called off. The Confederate plan to capture Abraham Lincoln ended in failure.[52]

It was becoming obvious that Cold Harbor had been a fluke. Military setbacks, food and manpower shortages, and the slow stranglehold of the blockade told the real story of 1864, and they seemed to put Confederate success further out of reach. Seeing their last chance at victory fade, Southern leaders planted the suggestion that subjugating them would cost the North more blood and money than anyone was willing to expend. In mid-July, they tried to pressure President Lincoln with a very public offer of peace. They knew that Lincoln had the upper hand and had nothing to gain from a peaceful settlement. But by proposing negotiations, they hoped to portray him as stubborn and indifferent to further bloodshed. Lincoln, however, refused to take the bait. In a letter to Confederate commissioners, he restated his long-held position on peace: return to the Union, recognize emancipation, and we'll offer liberal terms. Benign as that sounds, the commissioners took it as a slap at their dream of diplomatic recognition. And that was no accident on Lincoln's part. He had addressed his letter "To whom it may concern" to avoid even a *personal* recognition of the Confederacy's existence.[53]

So Abraham Lincoln stood firm, and the South slowly crumbled. Confederate momentum was gone, and the only thing that could save them now was a bold and daring move.

John Wilkes Booth had come up with a plan.

EIGHT

"MY PROFESSION, MY NAME,
IS MY PASSPORT"

CONFEDERATE COLONEL BRADLEY JOHNSON'S PLAN TO CAP-
ture Lincoln was anything but a secret. All over Southern Maryland, people had a sense that something big was about to happen, and
some knew exactly what it was. Johnson had arranged for local citizens to
have fresh horses ready and waiting on the roads leading out of Point
Lookout. A Marylander himself, Colonel Johnson trusted these volunteers. As he later wrote, "They were unanimously my friends."[1]

JOHN WILKES BOOTH SPENT much of the summer on the road. His
last acting engagement had been in Boston, and from there he went to
western Pennsylvania, then back to Boston, then down to New York. He
traveled more now than when he had been acting, even though he suffered
from painful boils on his neck and erysipelas on his arm. As he told his sister Asia, he had to keep moving; it was the only way he could help the
Cause. "I have only an arm to give," he said, but "my brains are worth
twenty men, my money worth a hundred. I have free pass everywhere, my
profession, my name, is my passport; my knowledge of drugs is valuable,
my beloved precious money—oh, never beloved until now!—is the means,
one of the means, by which I serve the South." He told her that he was involved in the underground, and the work demanded travel. The unexplained trips, the strange visitors at all hours, the callused hands "from

nights of rowing"—to Asia, it suddenly all made sense. When someone had recently shown up at her house asking for Doctor Booth, she thought he had meant Joseph, who had once studied medicine in Philadelphia. But John Wilkes then confessed. "I am he, if to be a doctor means a dealer in quinine." The South desperately needed this all-purpose drug, and Booth claimed to be providing them with it.[2]

If Booth were really smuggling quinine, there is no evidence of it beyond his own word. Asia did not actually see him do anything, and before the fall of 1864, he had almost no opportunity. Theatrical business occupied his time through the end of May, and for months afterward, his travels were confined to the North. His movements are well documented. They cover more than 2,400 miles, and are so far removed from the South as to admit few opportunities to cross the lines.[3]

THIS WAS AN ELECTION YEAR, and at midsummer, Abraham Lincoln seemed like a long shot to win a second term. His war measures still energized the opposition, and the split grew deeper as the fighting wore on. The lack of a clear victory would always play into the hands of Democrats, and many of them would have settled for a cease-fire under any terms. But there were two ways to end the war: let the South go in peace, or push more vigorously for a decisive win. By early March 1864, Lincoln's choice was clear. He called for a draft of half a million more men, and appointed "Unconditional Surrender" Grant to their overall command. The army targeted food supplies, burned the houses of suspected rebels, and brought a "hard war" policy straight to the homes of Southern civilians. This stepped-up strategy began with the boldest stroke of all—a cavalry raid designed to "destroy and burn the hateful city" of Richmond and kill Jefferson Davis and his cabinet. The raid failed, but the strategy remained.[4]

One of the most volatile issues of the campaign was a product of this policy. A cartel had once been in place for the exchange of prisoners of war, and the arrangement helped relieve the suffering of prisoners by trading them for captives held by the other side. But the process hit a snag when the South refused to exchange black soldiers, and as the North gained momentum, its leaders saw no need to resurrect the old agreement. General Grant was especially hostile to the idea. "It is hard on our men held in Southern prisons not to exchange them," he said, "but it is humanity to those left in the ranks to fight our battles. Every man we hold, when released on parole or otherwise, becomes an active soldier against us at once either directly or indirectly. If we commence a system of exchange which liberates all prisoners taken, we will have to fight on until the whole South is exterminated."

Lincoln supported his generals on the exchange issue. It was not a comfortable decision, but whenever he felt his resolve begin to slip, he would take out his wallet and read the editorials he had clipped and saved. They supported the need to get tough.[5]

Confederates responded to hard war with a new strategy of their own. Through political subversion, small unit raids, and incendiary strikes, they tried to undermine support for the war by targeting and demoralizing civilians in the North. This "irregular warfare" was meant to keep up pressure on the administration to end the war quickly by a negotiated settlement. Other raids, aimed at prisoner-of-war camps, were intended to relieve the Confederates' manpower shortage by freeing soldiers from captivity in the North. All of these operations would be planned and run from offices set up in Canada.

In May 1864, the Confederate government sought to defuse the escalating crisis by releasing hundreds of sick prisoners, even without an exchange. Though ostensibly a goodwill gesture, this move backfired. The men were emaciated, and many were near death. Seeing their condition, Secretary of War Stanton launched a vigorous campaign calling attention to the rebels' treatment of prisoners. "There appears to have been a deliberate system of savage and barbarous treatment and starvation," Stanton told a congressional committee, "the result of which will be that few, if any, of the prisoners that have been in their hands during the past winter will ever again be in a condition to render any service or even to enjoy life."[6]

Stanton's charges escalated the prisoner issue. All through the summer, newspapers told of abuse, starvation, and the use of prisoners as human shields. Each side blamed the other, and while they pointed fingers, prisoners continued to die on both sides in staggering numbers. Northerners claimed that Southerners were deliberately cruel, and Confederates blamed Grant and others for refusing to swap prisoners. The lack of an exchange, they said, forced them to feed and shelter an increasing number of prisoners when they could not even feed their own troops. Their prison camps, such as Andersonville and Belle Isle, consisted of little more than tents, and the soldiers who returned from such places were mere skeletons. After months of emotional debate, Stanton issued orders to cut prisoner rations in retaliation. His measure met with widespread public support.[7]

· · ·

SOMETIME IN AUGUST, Booth stopped at the Holliday Street Theatre and recognized an old friend from St. Timothy's Hall. William Stockton Arnold had not seen Booth in years, and they had a lot to talk about. The subject turned to Billy's brother Sam, who had also known Booth from school days. Sam Arnold was back from the war and was now living at his uncle's farm, five miles north of town. At that moment, he was in the city, and if Booth would like, Billy could send him over for a visit.[8]

Samuel Bland Arnold came from a respected Baltimore family. Six feet tall, with dark hair and complexion, he had a genteel look and an assertive air. His father, George, owned one of the city's largest bakeries, and had used his wealth to give his sons a good education. The Arnolds were a Southern family, and when the war broke out, Sam enlisted in Company C of the 1st Maryland Infantry, C.S.A. Discharged for medical reasons, he found work as a paymaster's clerk, and then with his brother George in the Nitre and Mining Bureau at Augusta, Georgia. On hearing that his mother was ill, Arnold returned home in early 1864, and found that Baltimore was a different place. He was distressed to see old friends who wouldn't even shake his hand. Feeling restless and out of place, he tried to join a U.S. Army expedition in the Northwest, but lacked the funds to make the trip.[9]

Sam Arnold had not seen Booth in eleven years, and he could hardly believe the changes in his old friend. "Instead of gazing upon the countenance of the mild and timid schoolmate of former years," he recalled, "I beheld a deep thinking man of the world before me, with highly distinguishing marks of beauty, intelligence, and gentlemanly refinement, different from the common order of man. . . ." Booth had arranged a meeting at Barnum's Hotel, in the center of town. He was a marvelous host, and regaled his boyhood friend with tales of the stage and wartime travels. In a few minutes, there was a knock on the door, and a small, dark-haired man joined the conversation. This was Mike O'Laughlen, Booth's friend and neighbor from Exeter Street. Arnold and O'Laughlen had never met, but both had served in the same Confederate regiment early in the war. A few glasses of wine made them as chummy as lifelong companions.[10]

Talk turned to the war, and Booth found that they all supported the Confederacy. It was hard to be optimistic these days. The North was pressing its advantages, grinding the South into a slow and agonizing submission. Provisions were scarce, and Confederate desertion rates were high. Under the circumstances, Lee could hold out for only so long. The South was in a quandary, but the war was not over yet. Booth believed that some drastic measure might force the Lincoln administration to resume the prisoner exchange—thus giving the Confederacy a resurgence of strength in the ranks.

He had an idea. Mr. Lincoln was known to make frequent trips to the Soldiers' Home, just outside Washington, and he often rode alone, over isolated country roads. A group of men could overtake his carriage, put the president in handcuffs, and transport him through Southern Maryland and into Virginia. They could have him in Richmond before a day had passed. With Abraham Lincoln as a hostage, his government would have to resume the prisoner exchange. Though abducting him would not be easy, it was certainly possible. And if the plan succeeded, Lincoln's captors would have saved thousands of prisoners' lives—not to mention the life of the Confederacy itself. Their names would live forever.

Arnold and O'Laughlen agreed to take part in the scheme, and they pledged themselves to secrecy and good faith. They parted company and went back home to await further developments. Booth went to New York, as he had planned, and would begin work on the plot after his return.[11]

Whether or not Booth claimed credit for the idea, plans to capture Lincoln had been discussed in the newspapers for years, and one editor later said that "such a plan was regarded at that time as fair game . . . there was very little blame attached to the idea, even in the North." Thomas Nelson Conrad, of the Confederate Signal Service, believed that only one of these schemes ever reached Jefferson Davis, and he firmly rejected the idea. Though someone might have pulled it off, it seemed foolhardy to make the attempt.

Daring captures had been tried in the past, sometimes with stunning results. On the night of March 9, 1863, Confederate Major John Singleton Mosby escorted Union General Edwin Stoughton right out of his headquarters in Fairfax Court House, Virginia. Mosby had been harassing Union operations in Northern Virginia for some time, and capturing the "Gray Ghost" had become Stoughton's top priority. But hunter and prey traded places when Mosby walked into the general's bedroom in full Confederate uniform. He yanked the covers off Stoughton and announced that he was taking him prisoner. His plan succeeded precisely because it was so improbable, and the incident made the name of John S. Mosby legendary in the South.[12]

Had Colonel Johnson succeeded in capturing Lincoln, he too would have covered himself in glory. But when Johnson was reassigned to the prison break, his abduction plan was left untried. Still, his idea spread. Thomas Nelson Conrad, the spy, had heard about this proposed abduction scheme in Richmond, and he decided to try it himself. He came up with a similar plan, and he even got the Confederate War Department's approval to go through with it. In the fall of 1864, Conrad went to Washington to study the movements and habits of his intended victim. He worked out the details, and in time put a team in place, ready to take action. When the time arrived, they took up positions along Seventh Street, north of the city, and waited for the president's carriage. When it finally appeared, it was surrounded by cavalry.[13]

That was a stunning development. The president had never been so closely guarded before. He had often received threatening letters, but few around him believed he was in any real danger. Even Secretary of State Seward, who should have known better, passed the threats off as "no grounds for anxiety." Seward explained his views in a letter to the consul in Paris:

> Assassination is not an American practice or habit, and one so vicious and so desperate cannot be engrafted into our political system. . . . This conviction of mine has steadily gained strength since the Civil War began. Every day's experience confirms it. The President, during the heated season, occupies a country house near the Soldiers' Home, two or three miles from the city. He goes to and fro from that place on horseback, night and morning, unguarded. I go there unattended at all hours, by daylight and moonlight, by starlight and without any light. . . .[14]

The president was always accessible, even in wartime. It came with the job. It was common knowledge that a person could see him almost any time by going to the White House. One could shake his hand at any public reception, or have a personal interview by merely waiting in line. His home was a public building, and its open-door policy was considered unavoidable.

He was not entirely unprotected, though. Washington had been heavily occupied since early in the war, and a couple of regiments camped at or near the White House. The Bucktails of Company K, 150th Pennsylvania Infantry, were posted on the south lawn, and they came to regard themselves as a "bodyguard" unit for the president. In fact, they were nothing of the kind, at least in the modern sense. People still came and went as they pleased. Even Cabinet meetings were fair game. A "fair, plump lady" from Dubuque interrupted one just to get a look at Mr. Lincoln. Such things happened, and Lincoln simply took it in stride.[15]

It is not hard to imagine where Booth got the idea of capturing Lincoln. Hundreds of Confederate soldiers had served under Bradley Johnson, and any one of them could have given up the details of his mission on a trip home. Four men from Booth's Exeter Street neighborhood had served in the Baltimore Light Artillery, which took part in the abortive raid on Washington. All had grown up with O'Laughlen, and if they had seen Booth during one of his occasional visits, they might well have mentioned their near brush with history.[16]

BOOTH SPENT MOST OF SEPTEMBER in the Pennsylvania oil region, where he closed out the business he had started only months before. He put up half the cost of a permanent lease on his riverfront property. Then, having secured his ownership rights, he signed them all away. He had a good reason for doing so. The government was confiscating the property of supposed rebels, and Booth knew that if he were caught in a conspiracy, they would take everything he owned. So he divested himself of all his property. He signed two-thirds of his Dramatic Oil stock over to his brother Junius, and the remainder went to Joe Simonds. He gave the Pithole Creek stock to his sister Rosalie, and after one final payment, his Boston property would go to Mary Ann.[17]

Booth never saw a penny from his investments. The Dramatic Oil well, nicknamed "the Wilhelmina," pumped hardly more than a trickle, and the driller's attempt to blast it did more harm than good. In all, the venture cost Booth six thousand dollars and depleted much of his savings. Drilling was suspended, and all his accounts settled. The theatrical season was already under way, and Booth told Simonds that he had no more time for oil. He wanted to get back to the stage.[18]

In fact, he wanted nothing of the sort. Writing from the oil region, he asked Sam Arnold to pick out a good saddle horse. He enclosed twenty dollars and said he would return as soon as he got the chance. Arnold was helping a neighbor thresh wheat when a messenger handed him Booth's letter. A man named Littleton Newman saw the look on his face when he read it, and asked what was wrong. Arnold showed him the note, but

Newman could make no sense of it. Arnold assured him that he would understand someday. It would be in all the newspapers.[19]

MARYLAND VOTERS WENT to the polls in October to determine the future of their state. They were voting on a new constitution, which outlawed slavery. The institution had survived thus far because emancipation touched only those states in rebellion, and Maryland had never seceded. Still, there could be no doubt that its days were numbered. Appraisers in Hagerstown had recently valued a group of slaves at just five dollars each, regardless of age or physical condition.[20]

Voters were required to affirm their allegiance to the Union, and Senator Reverdy Johnson complained that as written, the loyalty oath kept all Democrats away from the polls. In earlier times, that controversy would have torn the state in half, but by the fall of 1864, Democrats had lost much of their fighting spirit. Major General Lew Wallace, in command since the spring, had softened his approach to the occupation of Baltimore. He allowed civilian police officers to take their jobs back, and he guaranteed a speedy hearing for anyone arrested in his command. He even declined to interfere in the October election, except on the written request of Governor Bradford. With conditions thus improved, Democrats lost the issues that had once united Marylanders against the administration.

This was only the second election to allow the use of absentee ballots, and as it happened, those "soldier votes" made all the difference. In the initial count, citizens rejected the new constitution by a margin of two thousand votes. But when the absentee ballots came in, the measure narrowly passed. Critics cried foul. An editorial in the New York *World* said "soldiers' votes were 'needed' to secure the adoption of [the constitution] and they were cooked up to an exactly sufficient amount." The New York *Daily News* put it in even stronger terms:

> The last refuge and hope of law, order, and constitutional government, trampled under foot, it becomes the bounden duty of every man among us who would be free, to look, like our revolutionary fathers, to the remedy of his own right hand; and, standing on his constitutional rights, to declare in the face of bastille or banishment, or still better, in front of hurtling battle, that "resistance to tyranny is obedience to God."[21]

Democrats charged the president with vote tampering, and said that there was nothing to stop him from "re-electing himself" the following month.

UNTIL THE ELECTION, Booth seems to have done little work on his plot. On the fourth of September, Dave Herold, the pharmacy clerk, quit his job, and may have joined the conspiracy. But otherwise it remained dormant. Enlisting help was a delicate matter, and Booth had to feel his way carefully. For practical purposes, he could have sold himself in one of two ways: as the leader of a daring plot whose success would startle the world, or as an officer specially selected to lead a critically important operation. To most people, that first option would have sounded quixotic and perhaps suicidal. The second had some real advantages. It suggested that Booth had obtained the approval and support of intelligent, responsible authorities in Richmond—people who would not cut him adrift in the event of capture. Realistically, this was Booth's only choice. But since it required official sponsorship, he either had to enlist the support of Confederate officials, or had to find a way to fake it.

Sooner or later, Booth would have to pass along the idea to authorities in Richmond. After all, he could not just show up unannounced with Abraham Lincoln in handcuffs. A meeting shouldn't have been hard to arrange, considering the friendships Booth had made in Richmond before the war. Nor would it have been hard for him to get there, since many agents—including some familiar to Herold—went to the rebel capital on a regular basis. But instead of pursuing that course, Booth took a roundabout route that, on the surface, made no sense at all: he went to Canada.

The Confederate operation in Canada was run by Jacob Thompson, of the State Department, and Clement C. Clay, of the War Department. Together, they devised schemes to "give the Abolitionists trouble in the rear" while regular troops occupied their attention on the battlefront. Canada's strict neutrality laws prohibited them from waging war across the border, but those laws did not keep them from encouraging private citizens to act on their own. And indeed, transplanted Southerners showed no lack of inventiveness in helping the cause. John Porterfield, a former banker from Nashville, had a plan to destabilize United States currency with a buyout of greenbacks. George P. Kane, of Maryland, wanted to free prisoners of war from Johnson's Island in Lake Erie. Dr. Luke P. Blackburn, of Kentucky, proposed spreading yellow fever to the North through infected clothing. There were undoubtedly other schemes as well, but few details have come to light. We know that Kane, the former police marshal of Baltimore, had some other plan that was to be implemented in his home state, but whatever it was, General Lee refused to endorse it. Rev. Kensey Johns Stewart suggested something as well, and Lee nixed his proposal outright.[22]

Along with the schemers came a class of entrepreneurs who flocked to Montreal just to cash in on Lincoln's blockade of Southern ports. Confederates in Canada could not travel directly to the South, but for an exorbitant fee they could hire someone to take them and their goods to a third-party location, such as Bermuda, then arrange passage from there to the Southern states on a British ship. For anyone in a hurry, the direct route was still available, and the more greedy and adventurous were not deterred by the risks involved.

Nearly every scheme that was hatched in Canada failed, and according to Jacob Thompson, it was not hard to see why. "The bane and curse of carrying out anything in this country," he wrote, "is the surveillance under which we act. Detectives, or those ready to give information, stand at every street corner. Two or three cannot interchange ideas without a reporter." Yet this was the place to which Booth took his hostage idea.[23]

It would have been safer and simpler to present his plan in Richmond. Though the Confederate capital had its share of Union spies, they were hardly as pervasive as those in the free and open streets of Montreal. And if Booth were planning to take Lincoln to Richmond, he would have to have the cooperation of agents who knew the way, and who went there routinely. However, there is a good chance he saw that as a drawback. After all, he had no credentials as a covert operative, and more plausible schemes than his were rejected by the rebel government. What if they refused to sanction his plan? What if they approved of the idea, but assigned the job to an experienced agent? Nearly every one of those people on the route to Richmond would have known that, and Booth's claims of official backing would have fallen on deaf ears. He would have lost his last chance to do something glorious for the Cause.

Booth could always claim his plot had been approved in Canada, and nobody could challenge him on that. Because of neutrality laws, Confederate commissioners in Canada *had to disapprove,* and anyone checking on Booth's story would get the obligatory denial. What lent credibility to his approach was the fact that some of the officials in Montreal took a strong interest in prisoners of war. Since Booth's plot emphasized the exchange, he could have argued that a common aim led him to seek help from north of the border.

If Booth wanted to look like an insider, it would not have been hard to arrange. Confederate officials moved around freely in Montreal, and federal agents followed them at every step. It would be a simple matter to approach one of the commissioners in a hotel lobby and engage him in conversation. Spies and bystanders could hardly miss the fact that John Wilkes Booth, a noted celebrity, was talking to the Confederacy's senior men. Their actual words were irrelevant; appearances alone would boost his claims of official support, and no amount of later checking in Richmond was likely to get at the truth.

IN EARLY OCTOBER, Confederate Lt. Walter "Wat" Bowie led a small cavalry detachment to within a few miles of Annapolis, intending to capture Maryland governor Augustus Bradford. Bowie called off the attempt at the last minute, when he discovered that the governor had increased his security. Retreating through Montgomery County, his men tried to rob a country store, and local citizens fought back. The men escaped, but Bowie himself was fatally wounded in the skirmish.

On October 19, Confederates tried another raid fifteen miles below the Canadian border, in St. Albans, Vermont. A party of twenty-two men rode into town and robbed three banks, taking two hundred thousand dollars and mortally wounding one citizen. A U.S. provost marshal chased them across the border, capturing fourteen of them in Canada and sparking an international outcry. The men were eventually surrendered to Canadian authorities, who charged them only with a violation of neutrality laws. All were acquitted. What saved the raiders was their status, under international law, as belligerents. They carried no official papers at the time of the raid, but authorities in Richmond sent blank commissions to Montreal, to be filled in for the defendants as needed.

John Wilkes Booth arrived in Montreal just before the St. Albans raid and checked in to the St. Lawrence Hall on St. James Street. "The Hall" was probably the city's finest hotel, and had come to be regarded as the local center of Confederate activities.[24]

What he did there is still a matter of dispute. Witnesses in 1865 told of seeing Booth with various officials, talking openly about their plot against Lincoln. Not everyone has taken this testimony at face value; after all, it described a level of recklessness that defied common sense. But we know that Booth spent at least ten days in the city, and if he spoke with these men at all, they were probably not discussing anything so sensitive. Booth was supposedly seeking an interview with Marshal George P. Kane, but Kane was out of town. Instead, he spoke with Patrick C. Martin, a blockade-runner from Baltimore, whom Confederate officials regarded as a "slippery" character. Booth spent a great deal of time with Martin's family, and made particular friends with his little girl, Margaret.

When eventually he decided to return to the States, Booth persuaded Martin to write a letter of introduction to Kane, should he ever catch up with him, and another to Dr. William Queen, whom he had known in Charles County, Maryland. The letter to Kane was destroyed, and we do not have any idea of its contents. But we do know something about the letter to Queen; the doctor's son-in-law testified that it mentioned only real estate. It was vague, as such things had to be. After all, Booth was a stranger in a city full of detectives, and Martin was no fool.[25]

On October 27, Booth and Martin went to the Bank of Ontario to exchange some currency. Booth traded three hundred dollars in gold coins for sixty pounds sterling, and bought an exchange receipt for $455. After getting assurances that no one else could have access to his money, Booth left the bank and prepared for a trip back to the States. He left his wardrobe with Martin, and instructed him to ship it south by way of Nassau.[26]

HARD WAR POLICIES and a general sense of desperation brought the November election to an unprecedented level of intensity. Much of the hatred, of course, was focused on Abraham Lincoln. As *The New York Times* said, "No living man was ever charged with political crimes of such multiplicity and such enormity as Abraham Lincoln. He has been denounced without end as a perjurer, a usurper, a tyrant, a subverter of the Constitution, and destroyer of the liberties of his country. . . ." And that was the short list. The president was assailed from all sides, and not just in the Border States. In Syracuse, New York, Democrats marched through town carrying signs with some less than amiable sentiments: "A despot has his parasites, and liberty hath her avengers"; "Free ballots or free bullets. Crush the tyrant Lincoln before he crushes you"; and "If Seward 'touches' his bell again, the people will stretch his neck." No electoral contest before or since has matched the level of abuse seen in 1864.[27]

When it was over, Lincoln had carried more than 55 percent of the popular vote. Eleven states allowed absentee balloting, and those votes fell heavily in the president's favor. This was quite a turnaround from the previous summer, when his opponent, General George McClellan, seemed assured of victory. The reversal of fortune came on September 2, when General William T. Sherman captured Atlanta. Sherman's victory was seen as a possible turning point in the war, and it weakened the Democrats' most potent argument: that Lincoln's war measures, oppressive as they were, had not brought the nation any closer to military success.

This election made Abraham Lincoln the first president in thirty-two years to win a second term. His lopsided victory in the face of such vocal opposition left many to assume he had simply rigged the process, and there was nothing anyone could do to get him out of office.[28]

Actually, there was one way. Government sources reported that after the election, newspapers in Richmond began to discuss the idea of assassination. Editorials pointed out how vulnerable the president would be on inauguration day. The Richmond *Enquirer* cited some examples of tyrannicide, casting it in a positive light and asking, rhetorically, whether anyone in the South had the courage to risk his own life in the interests of his country.[29]

ON A VISIT TO PHILADELPHIA, John Wilkes Booth ranted about the election. "That sectional candidate should never have been president," he insisted. "He was smuggled through Maryland to the White House. Maryland is true to the core—every mother's son. Look at the cannon on the heights of Baltimore. It needed just that to keep her quiet...." Asia listened patiently to her brother's tirade. She knew he needed to let off steam, but his views might get him arrested anywhere else. Even here, he didn't dare raise his voice. He paced the room and jabbed at the air, spitting out his thoughts in a forced whisper. "He is walking in the footprints of old John Brown, but no more fit to stand with that rugged old hero," he said. "Great God, no!... *He* is Bonaparte in one great move, that is, by overturning this blind Republic and making himself a king. This man's re-election which will follow his success, I tell you—will be a reign!... You'll see—you'll see—that *re-election* means *succession*."[30]

As shrill as it sounded, Booth's opinion was hardly unique. Democrats had always bristled at the administration's hard-fisted approach. If this nation can be saved only by oppression, they wondered, then what is the point of saving it? The boundaries and symbols may remain, but what really mattered—the freedom of expression, and the permanence of constitutional guarantees—would still have been lost. It would take years for Southerners to appreciate the position in which Lincoln found himself. For every person who wanted him to back off, at least one other argued that he did not go far enough. John W. Forney, of the Philadelphia *Press*, actually criticized him for failing to encourage slave insurrections. General David Hunter urged a policy of "arming all the negroes and burning the house and other property of every slave holder." Radicals in Congress argued for the extermination of all Southerners, or at the very least, dire punishments for them. All across the North, editors and politicians clamored for a harder, more vigorous prosecution of the war, and to them, Abraham Lincoln seemed *too weak* for the job. Masterfully, he threaded his way through both camps, taking a moderate stand that looked extreme only from either end.[31]

That people could see Lincoln in such wildly varying ways is perhaps the key to our fascination with him. Everything about him blended one characteristic with its polar opposite—a trait that carried over even to his personal appearance. Sylvanus Cadwallader captured Lincoln's essential irony when he described him as "a long, gaunt, bony looking man with a queer admixture of the comical and the doleful . . . that reminded one of a professional undertaker cracking a dry joke. . . ." The president's politics and personal traits were no less mixed: he liberated millions, but was reviled as an oppressor; he was a gentle, fun-loving man with a brutal approach to war.[32]

Even his most rabid opponent would have had to admit, in hindsight, that Lincoln handled his dilemma with consummate skill. He sought and won congressional approval for all his emergency measures, and he never made a move without bipartisan involvement. In fact, his most controversial measures were implemented by prewar Democratic politicians. Secretary Stanton himself was a Democrat.

BOOTH DID NOT RETURN to the stage that fall, but spent his time planning the president's abduction. He must have had serious concerns about transporting Lincoln to the Confederate capital. Richmond was more than 120 miles away, and it would not be easy to get there safely with a high-profile hostage. Northern Virginia was heavily occupied, so a direct route was out of the question. A detour through the Shenandoah Valley would add days to the trip. By default, then, the only viable option was to go through Southern Maryland. Booth would have to use a Confederate courier route.

Common wisdom said that everyone along that path was a rebel. In all five counties of Southern Maryland, only twelve people had voted for Lincoln in 1860. Of these, half came from Charles County, where a citizens' committee asked one Nathan Burnham, a "black Republican emissary," to leave the area by January 1 or be escorted out. Allegedly, the only Republican in St. Mary's County was hanged. Because it was so close to Washington, the region was of special concern to the federal government. They flooded the area with spies and cavalry. Hostility and paranoia followed them at every step.

Politics and geography led almost naturally to the growth of a smuggling industry there. Farther south were millions of people who had been deprived by the war of everyday items that only Northern suppliers could provide. One had to run the blockade to meet those needs, and often made a huge profit doing it. Those who crossed the Potomac carried on their trade to an extent that one general found "simply incredible." The business was conducted by ordinary citizens and had little to do with the official operation of the Confederate Signal Service, which sent mail and agents across the lines. But their routes overlapped. One ran north and south, through an area called Nanjemoy in central Charles County. Another ran parallel to it, following the Zekiah Swamp south, to a little hamlet called Allen's Fresh. Though the Federals knew about these lines, they deliberately left them open so that their own operatives could infiltrate the other side.[33]

There were many places in Charles County for smugglers to hide. High bluffs and deep ravines alternated on the riverbanks, and shallow streams snaked across the flats west of the Port Tobacco River. A boat could be hidden anywhere in the marshes, or even on the open water. Some were fitted with plugs so they could be sunk, temporarily, just out of sight. The Potomac Flotilla, created to stem the problem, did little more than slow it down, and as many as sixty people crossed in a single night. At fifty dollars per passenger, the money was too good for smugglers to refuse.

The army once sent an entire division to clean out the area, but the raids and arrests only stiffened the farmers' will to resist. In 1862, after six months of frustration, the Federals brought in someone who knew how to fight dirty: Col. Lafayette C. Baker, provost marshal of the War Department. Baker took a hard-fisted approach to disloyalty. His spies quickly spread out over the county, breaking up boats, pillaging houses, threatening citizens, and frightening slaves into betraying their masters. They showed little regard for civil rights or the rules of evidence, and were almost universally hated for it. Their unseen presence made life unsettling for everyone, and clannishness became a way of life—not only on the underground network, but everywhere around it. Outsiders were looked upon with a great deal of suspicion.[34]

Such was the character of life in Southern Maryland by November 1864. On the eleventh of that month, John Wilkes Booth took the Leonardtown stage from Washington to the village of Bryantown, in Charles County. Stopping at Burch's Tavern, he asked how he might get in touch with Dr. William H. Queen. Dr. Queen was an elderly man who lived about six miles to the south. Since Booth had not made arrangements to get there, he checked in to the tavern, and the next morning, Dr. Queen's son Joseph came through town and picked Booth up.

Patrick Martin's letter of introduction got Booth in the door. Though the letter mentioned only real estate, it was all Booth needed to familiarize himself with the region and its people. Indeed, real estate was the perfect cover story. It helped Booth obtain the names of landowners, as well as all the factors that affected property values: proximity to roads, traffic flow, and access to the rivers. Any prospective farmer would want to know such things. But so would a smuggler.

There was no need for Booth to divulge his real intentions. Being an outsider, he knew that these people would be suspicious of him. Perhaps when he got to know them better he could gently make inquiries about getting across the river. Though crossings were commonplace, they were still illegal, and people spoke of them with a certain level of discretion. The tacit understanding was that people went to Virginia for the usual reasons: to deliver mail, messages, or minor forms of contraband. A guarded inquiry might draw out all the information Booth needed, and he wouldn't have to be specific about his own plans. To do otherwise would have been absurd.

Booth spent that Saturday with the Queens, and the night as well. He talked with the doctor and his family about casual subjects, and about his oil speculations. He claimed he had made a good deal of money from them, and now he hoped to do the same in land. He asked Queen's son-in-law, John C. Thompson, about roads in the area, but Thompson was from Georgia and knew little about Charles County. He knew that, in general, the best land might sell for fifty dollars an acre, while unimproved tracts could go for as little as five. Beyond that, he had no answers.

Two days after Booth returned to Washington, he realized that something was missing. He always kept a pistol in his carpetbag, but on his way to Bryantown, he had given it to the stage driver for safekeeping. The driver was supposed to take it back to the city and leave it with someone Booth knew. Apparently, he forgot. So on Tuesday, Booth wrote to the tavern keeper in Bryantown, hoping to find the stage driver:

Washington, Nov. 14th
J. D. Burch, Esq.

Dear sir.

Hope I shall see you again ere long. Our *friend* of the stage last Friday never left what I gave to his charge. You know what I had to take from my carpet-bag. Its not worth more than $15, but I will give him $20 rather than lose it, as it has saved my life two or three times. He has left the city. If you would be kind enough to get it from him and send it to me I will reimburse you for any outlay. And will never forget you. If you should ever recover it, either send, or give it to our friend, co. Fayette st. Where if you wish you can write me.

Remember me to all the friends I met while in your country.

I am yours truly
J. Wilkes Booth

That Booth had been in a few life-and-death scrapes would be news indeed—if it had actually happened. But even those he confided in, such as Junius and Asia, never mentioned anything of the sort. He seemed to be crafting an image as a man of mystery—perhaps a Confederate agent. Like his boasts of success in oil, it was a charade, but one he would find useful in the coming months.[35]

Booth deposited fifteen hundred dollars in Jay Cooke's Washington bank, then headed for New York. Conspiracy theorists have suggested he got the money from Confederates in Canada. But after making twenty-five to thirty thousand dollars a year as an actor, he could easily have funded the plot on his own. He probably kept his money in Philadelphia and drew from that account while passing through on the way back from

Canada. In light of subsequent developments, it made perfect sense that he would transfer his money to a Washington bank.[36]

EVEN AS THE PLOT against Lincoln took shape, presidential security remained of no more than passing interest to those in power. When the new federal budget was passed in the fall, it included funds to pay for a security force at the Executive Mansion. The idea had come from Benjamin B. French, commissioner of public buildings, who was fed up with vandalism in the White House. Visitors had peeled wallpaper from the walls, drapes had been cut to pieces, and an entire lace curtain had vanished, no doubt into the carpetbag of some tourist. Losses of this kind made the place unsightly and had cost the government more than anyone was willing to pay, especially in wartime. So in November, Police Superintendent William B. Webb assigned four of his most intimidating men to work as plainclothes officers in the mansion. Their forty-dollar-a-month salaries were to be reimbursed by the Interior Department.[37]

NINE

"I HAVE A GREATER SPECULATION . . .
THEY WON'T LAUGH AT"

AFTER A QUICK TRIP TO NEW YORK, BOOTH VISITED THE Clarkes at their new home in Philadelphia. He took Asia aside and gave her a large envelope, asking her to put it away for safekeeping. "I may come back for it," he told her, "but if anything should happen—to me— open the packet alone and send the letters as directed, and the money and papers give to the owners." The life of a touring star was hazardous by nature, and Asia thought nothing of his request. She just assumed he was taking care of loose ends. She promised to lock his package away, and was surprised when he said that that wasn't good enough. "Let me *see* you lock up the packet," he insisted. So with her brother looking on, she placed the envelope in an iron safe and locked it. He thanked her and left.[1]

Like countless other families, the Booths were torn apart by the war. Edwin and Sleeper Clarke were now committed supporters of the Lincoln administration, while John Wilkes and Joseph sided with the Confederates. Junius tried to appear neutral. He disagreed with John Wilkes, but as the eldest male, he felt an obligation to hear his brother out. He said that the war was like a family quarrel, in which both sides would eventually make up. For the sake of his own family, he urged John Wilkes to keep himself out of the struggle.

June and Asia had always listened to John's opinions, even if they didn't agree with them. But Edwin and Clarke took a dismissive attitude. That was insulting, and it only made Booth more determined to be taken seriously. Relations with those two had been deteriorating steadily for years, and in August 1864, an argument with them threatened to split the family for good. "If it were not for mother, I would not enter Edwin's house," John Wilkes told his sister. "But she will leave there if we cannot be welcomed, and I do not want her to be unhappy for me. As for Clarke . . . I would never darken his door, but for you." Mary Ann had apparently threatened to move to neutral ground, and a truce was called for her sake. Thereafter, political discussions were banned in her presence.[2]

All things considered, it was no small feat to bring Junius, Edwin, and John Wilkes together on stage, but it happened for the first and only time on November 25. The event took place at the Winter Garden, an aging Broadway landmark named for a playhouse and conservatory in Paris. It was filled to capacity that night, and Mary Ann proudly watched her sons from a box above the stage. The play was Shakespeare's *Julius Caesar,* one of those rare works that feature three roles for leading men. Junius played Cassius, Edwin played Brutus, and John Wilkes took the part of Marc Antony in the reenactment of an event the Booths knew so well from the lessons of history.

> *Liberty! Freedom! Tyranny is dead!*
> *Run hence, proclaim, cry it about the streets.*

By these words, the death of Caesar was declared an act of heroism, inspired by the most patriotic motives.

The play's themes of civil war, oppression, conspiracy, and tyrannicide were hauntingly relevant to Booth's own day. It cannot have gone unnoticed that it was presented now by the sons of a man named Brutus. Six months in the future, patrons would look back on this night and wonder what had gone through the mind of John Wilkes Booth as he stood in the wings, listening to the prophecy of Cassius:

> *How many ages hence*
> *Shall this our lofty scene be acted over*
> *In states unborn and accents yet unknown!*[3]

The sculptor J.Q.A. Ward had designed a magnificent bronze of the Bard to be placed in Central Park, and this performance was arranged to help pay for it. Actors all over the country were contributing as well, and as a member of the statue committee, Edwin did not want to be outdone. The production finally came off after two delays, and was a tremendous success. The Booths collected $3,500 for the statue fund.

This theatrical milestone did not go without a hitch. An alarm was sounded midway through the second scene. The prospect of a theater fire sent a panic through the audience, and patrons began a rush for the exits. They seemed on the verge of a stampede when Edwin stepped up to the footlights and assured everyone that there was no cause for concern; the building was not on fire. Nervously, the audience settled back into their seats, and the play resumed. But there really was a fire. It was at the LaFarge House, next door. That was one of a dozen buildings set ablaze that night by Confederate agents in an attempt to spread fear and panic throughout the city. But like everything else planned in Canada, it failed. The insurgents had used a concoction made of turpentine and phosphorus—something called "Greek fire." It was ineffective, and no serious damage resulted.[4]

The Booths' performance was a critical success, but it did nothing to smooth over relations between John Wilkes and Edwin. William Stuart, a partner and publicist for the latter, played up the event as a personal triumph for Edwin, to the exclusion of everyone else. And to make matters worse, he threw a post-performance reception and inadvertently forgot to invite the brothers. Junius wouldn't have gone in any event; he had to escort his mother home. But John Wilkes discovered the oversight, and, feeling slighted, went off in a huff.

The following night, Edwin Booth embarked on a series of "Grand Revivals" he hoped would reinvigorate the legitimate drama. He planned to present three Shakespeare plays over the next year or two, with historically accurate costumes, restored scripts, and details that most performers had long since put aside. The bill for November 26 was *Hamlet,* and little did anyone suspect that it would run for one hundred consecutive nights— a feat that would seal Edwin's place in American theater history. *His* star was clearly on the rise.[5]

This New York visit gave John Wilkes a chance to work with his old friend Sam Chester, who was a member of the Winter Garden stock company. Sam was a passive man, and his refusal to argue politics gave Booth the impression that they agreed on all the major issues. It was a critical misunderstanding.

One day in December, Chester was walking down Broadway when he saw Booth and some actor friends talking about the oil business. Booth insisted that his investments would make him rich, but the others just laughed. To them, oil sounded like a "humbug" speculation, and Booth's glowing picture of success hadn't changed their minds. So Booth gave up on them, and seeing Chester, he broke off the conversation and walked over to greet him.

"They are laughing at me about a speculation," he said, "but I have a greater speculation than they know that they won't laugh at." Chester didn't take the bait, and Booth said nothing more about it.

Booth returned to New York frequently in the next month, and he always made a point of looking up Sam Chester. Each time, Booth said a little more about that mysterious speculation, but he never said what it was. He even wrote to Chester between visits, in an effort to get him interested. But Sam's responses were as vague as Booth's entreaties. After weeks of playing cat-and-mouse, Booth finally told Chester that he was investing in Virginia and Maryland farmlands. He laid out a case for real estate, and said that if Chester wanted to join him, he would put up the funds to start him off. Chester was skeptical, and declined the offer.[6]

BOOTH RETURNED to the home of Dr. Queen on December 17, and again he spent the night. But this time, he attended church with the family the following morning. St. Mary's Catholic Church was a mile below Bryantown, on the road to Queen's place. They arrived a few minutes early, and the doctor's son-in-law, John C. Thompson, took the opportunity to show his guest around. By chance, he happened to notice Dr. Samuel Mudd standing with some other men in front of the church, and he introduced him to Booth. The Mudds owned a good many acres, and Thompson suggested that Booth might want to see if the doctor himself had any to sell. They talked for a few minutes, then everyone filed into church for the beginning of mass.[7]

The following day, Booth paid a surprise visit to Dr. Mudd's farm, four miles north of town. The Mudds found him polite, charming, and a good conversationalist. Booth told them a little about himself and his family. Junius was a good Republican, and had joined him in the oil business. Joe, his youngest brother, was living in San Francisco, and seemed to like it out there. After such small talk, he finally got to the point of his visit: land and horses. He had been exploring the surrounding area, he said, and he wondered whether anything around here might be for sale. Mudd said he had thought about selling his own place and moving to Benedict, but with the end of slavery, farm prices were much too low to get what he needed right now.

In better times, the Mudd place might have commanded a high price. The doctor had 218 acres, and they were as good as any around—fertile, well-drained, and situated on the highest elevation in the county. A freshwater spring ran nearby. He lived in a modest two-story white frame house with three bedrooms and an office. A new section joined the kitchen to the main house, and a few outbuildings clustered over the hills in the back. Two hundred yards behind the house were the headwaters of Zekiah Swamp, a tangle of wooded streams and freshets that led to the lower Potomac, twelve miles to the south.

It is not hard to imagine how the conversation moved along. Mudd would have described his own property, and Booth would have asked for the broader picture—about neighbors, roads, and anything else that might interest a prospective buyer. They would certainly have talked about the recent demise of slavery, and how the farmers of Charles County intended to get by without a labor force. These were necessary questions, because they touched on the value of the land. Though it is only speculation, it seems likely, in light of later events, that Booth got a little too aggressive in his questioning. He may have hinted at his need to get something across the river, or he may have said it outright. Either way, he did not get the information he wanted. Dr. Mudd had a distrustful nature, and he had too much at stake if Booth should prove to be one of Baker's spies. So he talked guardedly. By early evening, Booth realized that he had missed the Washington stage, and he asked if he could spend the night.[8]

Booth wanted to buy a horse, and he hoped to find one in Charles County so he could ride it back to Washington. Dr. Mudd suggested he talk with his neighbor, George H. "Squire" Gardiner, and the next morning, they walked across the field to see him. Booth chose a brown saddle horse with heavy fetlocks and a defect in its right eye. It was a large animal, about twelve years old, but it was a good pacer. Gardiner wanted eighty dollars, and Booth paid it. He still needed a saddle and bridle, and Dr. Mudd recommended he get them at Henry Turner's shop in Bryantown. They went into town together.

Booth offered to buy the doctor a drink at Montgomery's Tavern, and that is where they met Thomas Harbin, the former postmaster of Bryantown. Harbin, thirty-one, hated the Yankees. In 1861, they had arrested his brother-in-law, Thomas A. Jones, for blockade-running. Jones, who lived just below Pope's Creek, had frequently gone to Virginia and had helped establish a system of getting mail across the river, then hiding it at designated places a few miles inland. Anyone who knew the hiding places—and that included a sizable number of local citizens—could check those mail drops and deposit anything they found at the local post office. The federal government would do the rest.

For many people, that was the extent of their involvement, but Jones did not stop at carrying mail. "Scarcely a night passed," he later admitted, "that I did not take or send someone to Virginia." He often made the journey twice a night, and sometimes more than that. As he told his captors in 1861, "There are not twenty men in my county or the adjoining counties that would not have done the same as myself."

But Jones's case was different from most. In 1862, a special commission recommended he be released, but William Seward intervened personally, and Jones was denied clemency. By the time he was allowed to return home, his wife, Jane—Harbin's sister—had given birth to another child and lapsed into serious illness. She died soon after, and since that time, Harbin and Jones had been committed enemies of the Lincoln administration.

Booth had spent enough time in the county to know that Tom Harbin could help him find his way to Richmond. When Dr. Mudd introduced them, Booth asked if he might have a private word. The two went upstairs to talk, and as Harbin remembered it, Booth looked around with a dramatic air, and checked the hall and windows for eavesdroppers. Then he laid out his plan to abduct the president. He said that Harbin would be perfect to guide the party to Virginia, and he hoped to enlist his help. Harbin was taken aback. Certainly, it was an audacious plan, if not really original. It was risky, but so was his work with the Signal Service. After thinking it over, he agreed to join.[9]

Booth returned to Washington and left his horse at Cleaver's Stable, at Sixth and C streets, Southwest. His scheme would require a second horse, and a buggy as well, so he instructed Sam Arnold to find something suitable in Baltimore. Since he expected to spend a lot of his time around Ford's Theatre, he asked the staff there if they knew of a stable he might rent in the neighborhood. Jim Maddox, the property man, told him about a shed that opened onto Baptist Alley. It was about forty yards behind the theater, and Booth thought it sounded perfect. At his suggestion, Maddox worked out a deal with the owner, and got the shed for five dollars a month.

The chief carpenter at Ford's Theatre was James J. Gifford, the same man who had once torn the roof off Tudor Hall. Now, twelve years later, he and Ned Spangler, who had also worked on the Booth home, began working for Booth in their spare time. They partitioned the shed in the alley and raised its roof to accommodate a buggy. Booth promised to pay for their help, but somehow, he never got around to it.[10]

ON DECEMBER 23, Dr. Samuel Mudd came to Washington to do some Christmas shopping with his brother Jeremiah. Mudd had been planning to buy his wife a new cooking stove, and he had arranged to have a man in Bryantown take it back to the country for him on Christmas Eve. They registered at the Pennsylvania House, just across from the National Hotel, and took a good supper. Their hotel was not the finest in town, but it was the terminus of the Port Tobacco stage line, and popular with visitors from Charles County. The Mudds looked around to see if they might know some of the other guests, then headed over to Brown's Metropolitan Hotel to check for acquaintances there. The place was crowded, and the men became separated. Dr. Mudd started up Seventh, and had gone barely a block when he heard someone call his name. It was John Wilkes Booth.

Meeting Dr. Mudd at this time, and in this place, was an apparent stroke of luck for Booth. He had been seeking an introduction to John Surratt, whom he planned to ask for advice about finding a home in Southern Maryland. Dr. Mudd knew Surratt, as most people in the area did, but he had no idea where to find him. He tried to beg off, saying that some relatives from Baltimore were expecting to meet him at the Pennsylvania House. Booth promised not to take more than a few minutes. He already had Surratt's address written on a card.

It wasn't hard to figure out why Booth wanted this introduction. John Surratt had connections to the underground, and, as Mudd must have guessed by now, Booth was determined to work his way in. In that case, the Surratts were good people to know. They were one of the better-known families of southern Prince George's County. John's father once ran the tavern and post office at Surrattsville, ten miles south of Washington. The stagecoach made a stop there on every run, and passengers generally got out while the driver made a side trip to pick up mail. The elder Surratt passed away in 1862, and John left his studies at St. Charles College to come back and run the family business. But there was more to the job than most people knew. Surratt's Tavern was a Confederate safe house, and couriers often stopped there on their way to or from Richmond.

In time, John Surratt himself became a courier, with ambitions to be a spy. In the fall of 1863, he applied for a position in the U.S. War Department, hoping, no doubt, for access to sensitive information. But his plan backfired. His application called up rumors of rebel connections, and instead of moving Surratt into a better job, it cost him the one he already had. He was dismissed as postmaster of Surrattsville, and for the next year, he gave his time exclusively to the Confederate government.[11]

Dr. Mudd may have been wary of introducing Booth, as he later claimed, but he had no chance to back out of it. As they walked up Seventh Street, Booth pointed out a tall, fashionably dressed young man approaching them on the sidewalk with a companion. Booth recognized him as Surratt, and he insisted on being introduced.

John Surratt did not look like a secret agent. He was just twenty years old, and his smooth, pale skin made him look even younger. He had fine, sandy hair, deep-set eyes, and a prominent forehead that gave him the look of a genteel schoolboy. With him was a tidy-looking man with dark hair and rosy cheeks. He was Louis J. Weichmann, a former schoolmate of Surratt's and now a boarder in the home of his mother. Weichmann was also well dressed, but there was something distinctive about his trousers. They were blue, with stripes up the sides—from the uniform of the War Department Rifles. Lou Weichmann worked for General William Hoffman, the Commissary General of Prisoners.

For John Wilkes Booth, this meeting was too good to be true. Not only did he meet John Surratt, who could point the way to Richmond, but he also met a man who dealt every day with the central inspiration of Booth's conspiracy—prisoners of war. As he sized up this new acquaintance, Booth must have wondered if this meeting with Louis Weichmann would prove as fortunate for himself as it now seemed.[12]

Booth led the others back to the National Hotel and suggested they all go up to his room for a drink. Mudd said that his friends were probably waiting for him, but since Surratt was disposed to take Booth up on the offer, Mudd soon changed his mind. Again, the actor played the perfect host. He ordered refreshments and invited everyone to make himself comfortable. He pointed out that the room had recently been occupied by a member of Congress, who had left some of his papers behind. Pulling them off a shelf, he remarked, "What a good read I shall have when I am left to myself!" Weichmann, intrigued, took some of them over to the sofa to examine.

Dr. Mudd excused himself and pulled Surratt out into the hall. Mudd felt he ought to apologize to Surratt for introducing him to Booth. He knew very little about the man, he said, and did not want Surratt to think he was vouching for him. Booth had insisted on being introduced, and without being rude, there just hadn't seemed to be a way to avoid it. Surratt took it under advisement, and the two rejoined the others for drinks.

Booth looked tired. He said that he had not yet recovered from his trip to Charles County, on which he had been to Dr. Mudd's house, and had offered to buy the place. Mudd confirmed that with a nod, but added nothing more. Booth said that he had gotten lost on the way back and ridden several miles out of his way. As he talked, he took an envelope from his pocket and started tracing his route in the hope that Surratt could help him identify the roads and areas he had traveled. Weichmann, sitting on the sofa, paid little attention. All he remembered later was glancing up and seeing Booth drawing some lines on an envelope.[13]

At Dr. Mudd's suggestion, they all headed to the Pennsylvania House, across C Street. Sitting in the lobby there, Mudd talked with Weichmann about the war, and said that recent events had painted a gloomy picture for the South. Hood had been defeated in Tennessee, and nine thousand of his men had been captured. The rest of the army was demoralized, and the South was now at the mercy of Sherman. But Weichmann didn't think the situation was that bad. For one thing, only four thousand of Hood's men had been captured—or at least that was the count from his office. From the tone of the conversation, Mudd got the impression that Weichmann actually wanted the South to succeed. It struck him as a strange attitude for a man in a federal uniform.[14]

Booth left for New York on the morning train. He had kept up a correspondence with actor Sam Chester, and in several letters, had reminded Chester of that mysterious "speculation" he wanted him to join. So far, Booth's efforts had come to nothing, so on Christmas night, he paid a visit to Chester's house on Grove Street in Greenwich Village. They went for a walk, ending up at a pub called the House of Lords on Houston Street near Broadway. They talked over drinks and oysters, and eventually Chester said that he had better be going home.

"Hold on," said Booth. "I want to tell you what this speculation is."

"Yes," replied Chester. "I wish you would, because you have worried me enough about it." Booth asked him to take a walk up the street with him. This was private.

They headed up Broadway to Fourth, and after going a block or two, Booth stopped and turned to his friend. "This is the speculation that I am concerned in. There is," he said, "an immense party connected with it—fifty to one hundred people." He took a few more steps, his eyes scanning the darkness for hidden listeners. "It is a conspiracy against the government."

Booth said they had planned for some time to capture the administration's top officials—Lincoln included—and carry them off to Richmond. "It's nearly made up now," he said, "and we want you in." All Chester had to do, Booth said, was hold open the back door of Ford's Theatre so he and his conspirators could escape with the president.

Chester was stunned. "No, John," he said. "I can't have anything to do with anything of that kind." He said that it would ruin him, and especially his family.

"If it is money you require, I have three or four thousand dollars that I can leave them."

"It is no compensation for my loss."

They talked some more, but Booth could see that it was no use. Chester had always thought of him as a braggart, and this scheme of his sounded like more of Booth's patriotic posturing. It was simply too far-fetched to be believed. So they walked a bit farther, and Booth broke the silence. "At any rate," he said, a little hesitantly, "you won't betray me, because you can't; for I have facts in my possession that will ruin you for life."

Chester felt his heart sink. "It is very wrong, John, because I have always looked upon you as a friend, and have never done you any wrong."

Booth said that everyone in the party had sworn an oath to hunt down and punish anyone who betrayed their plan. "I carry a derringer loaded to shoot everyone that betrays us," he warned. Chester stood his ground. He insisted he could never involve himself in such a foolish scheme, and he was astonished to know that Booth would. Ending the discussion, he stormed off.

This was something Chester could not put out of his mind. The conspiracy was bad enough, but that threat—*that* must have preyed upon him for weeks. It was unlike Booth to test their friendship that way. And what

of those "facts" that could ruin him? His letters had mentioned that speculation, but only in vague terms. Did Booth have anything more than that?

Booth's revelation took Sam Chester by surprise, and it would have
been equally shocking to his own conspirators. They had always planned
to capture the president on the road to the Soldiers' Home, and nothing
had ever been said about an abduction anywhere else. If Booth was really
contemplating an attempt in the theater, it is strange that he told no one
except Chester, whom he had no reason to trust with the information.
Most likely, the theater plan was a ruse that, if reported to authorities,
would seem too far-fetched to be taken seriously.

On his way back to Washington, Booth stopped in Philadelphia and
spoke to his old manager, Matt Canning, at the Continental Hotel. Canning was still angry with Booth for canceling engagements that he had
gone out of his way to arrange. That he should ask for a favor now seemed
a little brash even for Booth. But the favor wasn't really for him; it was for
a friend.

"You know Sam Chester," he said. "He is a particular friend of mine.
He is dissatisfied in New York, and wants to go back to Ford [for whom he
had worked many years before], and if I interfere they might get angry
with me."

"But they might get angry with me," said Canning.

"Oh, no," said Booth. "There's no danger of that. I will give you anything if you see Ford."

Matt Canning gave in, and in due course he persuaded John T. Ford to
let Chester join his Ford's Theatre stock company. Neither Canning nor
Ford knew that this was Booth's idea, and that Chester himself wanted
nothing to do with it.

Canning sent Booth a telegram to confirm the transaction, and got a
puzzling response: "Don't fail to hush that matter at once." Booth later explained that he actually wrote "*push* that matter," but the telegraph operator misread his handwriting. Nevertheless, the telegram would someday
cast suspicion on Canning as a possible conspirator.

Before he left Philadelphia, Booth had one more thing to do. He went
back to Asia's house and asked if he could put something else in her safe.
It was an envelope marked "S. K. Chester." No doubt, he had saved Sam's
letters about the "speculation."[15]

Joe Simonds stayed in Pennsylvania and continued to look after his
own share of Booth's former business. He knew that Booth had been too

quick to give up on the Dramatic Oil Company, and his haste had cost him dearly. "I had hoped you were acting somewhere," he wrote, "for I had no track of you and [hoped] that you were taking in Greenbacks at the rate of $1,000 per week." He enclosed a check for five hundred dollars, saying that although it might not be much, it would help Booth stay on his feet. Coming from Booth's financial adviser, his letter said a lot. The boasts of success, the lavish entertainment, and the promises of financial support were all a show. At the end of 1864, John Wilkes Booth was getting by on borrowed money.

ON DECEMBER 30, John Surratt found employment with the Adams Express Company on Pennsylvania Avenue. Most of Adams's business consisted of delivering packages to soldiers in the field, so anyone working for them would have to know where the troops were. That would make him a valuable asset to the South, even if it wasn't his job to spy for them.

Booth knew the risks Surratt was taking when he joined the plot, so he gave him advice on how to avoid confiscation. On January 3, Surratt signed a quitclaim deed that relinquished all claims to property he now owned or would own in the future. If he were ever charged with treason, nobody could take his mother's houses in the belief that they were his. It was a protective measure Surratt's Confederate handlers had apparently never mentioned.[16]

THE WAR WAS GOING BADLY for the Confederacy. Their armies had not achieved a significant victory for some time, and the winter would make things even more difficult. Attrition was eating into their ranks at an alarming rate. Soldiers were weakened by starvation, and hard war was eroding public morale. And increasingly, the Yankees were bringing another weapon to bear on the political front: the military commission.

The idea of trying civilian dissidents before a military board had been a novelty before the war. Commissions were devised during the Mexican War by General Winfield Scott when judicial authorities fled Mexico City, leaving chaos and lawlessness to fill the void. When there was no one around to enforce the laws, military and civilians alike became the targets of thieves. So Scott improvised a system to restore order, using his own officers as jurors. It was an altruistic move, designed to bring civil stability back to the Mexican people.

Now, however, commissions had become a weapon. Their chief function was to expose and quell political dissent, and they were becoming very effective at it. Recent trials at Indianapolis had led to imprisonment and even death sentences for high-profile politicians. Along with another in Cincinnati, they helped expose the treasonous motives of anti-administration activists.

BY THE SECOND WEEK of January 1865, Booth had refined his capture plan and had a fair idea of the duties he would assign to his conspirators. Dave Herold, the pharmacy clerk, would be his all-purpose utility man. Arnold and O'Laughlen would provide muscle for the abduction itself. Harbin and Surratt would cover the route to Richmond, which they knew quite well. For security reasons, Booth kept his thoughts to himself and his conspirators in separate groups. They were unknown to one another.

That business with Sam Chester still preyed on Booth's mind, and he wrote Chester again in January. "You must come to Washington. We cannot do without you." When Chester refused again, he wrote by return mail, "You *must* come. Enclosed you will find $50 to pay your expenses and more money when you get here. If you can't come keep the money." Having compromised, bullied, framed, and threatened his former friend, he realized that nothing would sway him. Finally, he employed his most potent resource: charm. Returning to New York on January 11, he apologized to Sam for trying to involve him in the plot. He was sorry he had put him in such a difficult position, and he promised not to keep after him about it. He wanted Chester to know that he truly respected him, as well as his wife and mother. Sam was touched by Booth's sincerity, and he looked forward to putting all of this behind him.

While in New York, Booth purchased supplies for his conspiracy, and he probably used Joe Simonds's money to pay for them. He bought two Spencer carbines, six Colt revolvers, and three Bowie knives, plus caps, cartridges, belts, and two pairs of handcuffs. Since a heavy trunk was likely to arouse suspicions in the wartime capital, Booth chose not to accompany these items all the way there. He stopped in Baltimore and asked Arnold and O'Laughlen to take them the rest of the way. Arnold had bought a horse and buggy, as instructed, and Booth suggested he use them to take the carbines and revolvers to Washington. The rest of the items could be packed for shipment by express. That night, when Arnold and O'Laughlen arrived at the capital, they checked in to Rullman's Hotel, near the National, to await further orders.[17]

Booth needed someone to oversee the Potomac River crossing, and John Surratt was just the man. Surratt had barely started his new job at Adams Express, but he applied for a leave of absence anyway. His request was denied. The following day, his mother appeared at the office to plead her son's case. Mary Surratt said that her son needed to escort her on a drive to the country. Charles Dunn, the supervisor, was unmoved. He told her that John was free to go, but he could not come back. Surratt walked out.

On Saturday, January 14, Surratt rode with Tom Harbin down to Port Tobacco. They wanted to buy three boats, each large enough for fifteen men. The primary boat was to be kept in Goose Creek, south of town. Presumably, the others would be kept at alternate sites, in case something diverted them during their flight. Richard M. Smoot and James A. Brawner had only one boat, and it was still earning them good money. But eventually, they agreed to sell it to Surratt for $250, half in advance. There is no indication that Surratt ever found more than one boat to buy.

They still needed an oarsman, and Surratt found a willing recruit at Port Tobacco. George Andrew Atzerodt, twenty-nine, was a seedy but inoffensive character who had been running the blockade since early in the war. He was born in Prussia, but moved to Virginia at an early age. He and his brother John had come to Charles County in 1857 to set up a carriage shop. The partnership lasted until 1861, when sectional tensions split the family. John and his brother-in-law, John L. Smith, became detectives on the Union side, while George and his brother Henry supported the South.[18]

Andrew Atzerodt, as he preferred to be called, seemed to come right out of a Dickens novel. Grimy and consumptive, he looked like a man who might go for years without a change of clothing, then boast of the fact. A spinal curvature gave him a stooped appearance, and he walked with his head tilted a little to one side. Though Port Tobacco was a small town, few there even knew him, and those who did paid no attention to him. They all thought of him as an insignificant man whose most laudable quality was that he never took offense at an insult. The one thing he cared about was money, but he never seemed to have any of that. The bills were paid by Rose Wheeler, a thirty-five-year-old widow and seamstress with four children, the youngest being Atzerodt's two-year old daughter. She and Atzerodt lived together as man and wife, resisting all pressure to formalize their union.

Atzerodt's carriage shop was just off the courthouse square, and that is where Surratt and Harbin found him. They said that sometime soon, they would need to run the blockade, and indicated that this would be no ordinary mission. Though they declined to be specific, they did make it clear that the job involved prisoners of war and horse relays. Timing would be critical, so if he chose to work with them, he would have to keep himself ready to go at a moment's notice. If everything went well, the mission would make them all a lot of money.

In all likelihood, the last word Atzerodt heard was "money," and it was all he needed to hear. He joined the plot at once, and dropped all prior commitments. For one Eddy Martin, Atzerodt's change of plans was bad news. An agent of the Confederate Treasury Department, Martin was trying to arrange a $700,000 tobacco deal in Fredericksburg, and Atzerodt had just promised to smuggle him across the river. But now, without explanation, his ferryman lost interest. He offered nothing but excuses, and after a week of frustration, Martin found someone else to row him to Virginia.[19]

SOMETIME IN MID-JANUARY, Booth abruptly changed his mind about abducting the president en route to the Soldiers' Home. Over dinner one evening, Booth told Sam Arnold and Mike O'Laughlen that Lincoln was no longer making regular trips to the country, so he had devised a new plan. Everyone knew that the president was fond of the theater, and one of his favorite actors, Edwin Forrest, happened to be playing an engagement at Ford's. If Lincoln came to see Forrest, perhaps they could capture him right there in the theater. It was just a thought.

Arnold and O'Laughlen were taken aback. An isolated setting had always been crucial to the plan, and indeed, it was one of the few details that made the scheme plausible. Booth had planned meticulously for an abduction in the country. He often rode out Seventh Street to familiarize himself with the area, and he seemed to know every avenue of escape from there. But if they changed the plan now, they would have to start from scratch. Abducting Lincoln in a theater sounded completely impractical, and worse, it made Arnold and O'Laughlen wonder just how much Booth was improvising or leaving up to chance. Sensing their skepticism, Booth took them to Ford's Theatre and argued that the layout, the exits, and the alleys were ideal for a quick getaway.

ON JANUARY 20, Booth returned to the stage to play Romeo for the benefit of his dear friend, the actress Avonia Jones. This would be Booth's first performance since *Julius Caesar* two months earlier, and only his second since the end of May, but he seemed to have lost none of the old fire. A critic for the *Daily National Intelligencer* gushed: "As earned by his Romeo, we hasten to add our laurel to the wreath which the young actor deservedly wears; to offer him our congratulations, and to say to him that he is of the blood royal—a very prince of the blood—a lineal descendant of the true monarch, his sire, who ranks with the Napoleons of the stage. . . . We have never seen a Romeo bearing any near comparison with the acting of Booth on Friday night."[20]

THE HARD WAR POLICY WAS HAVING a devastating effect on food supplies in the South, and even the most basic staples were now beyond the reach of thousands. A small loaf of bread that had sold for fifty cents the year before was now hard to find at any price. Subsistence stores could not keep the troops fed, and starving soldiers deserted in large numbers. To alleviate the problem, Confederate officials began surreptitiously working their way into the cotton and tobacco trade that had been going on with the Lincoln administration's blessing. Such commerce was supposed to help stimulate the Northern economy while encouraging Southern planters and merchants to reestablish their ties to the Union.

For Northern cotton speculators this became a multimillion-dollar business. But it could also benefit the Confederacy, filling its coffers and bringing in some of the resources needed to stave off defeat, for at least a while longer. Southern leaders were determined to make the most of the opportunity, and they often set up illicit deals that looked very much like those sanctioned by the administration. They seem to have found highly placed friends in Washington to help with the ruse.

All of this made "cotton speculations" an excellent cover for John Surratt. An exchange of commodities would, in theory, have to be set up just like any other river crossing. Thus, Surratt's work for Booth would look perfectly legitimate. If anyone should ask, Surratt could just explain that *his* speculation was the legal kind, though, of course, he could not produce any proof. That is exactly what Eddy Martin said when detectives caught up with him that spring. And for him, it almost worked.[21]

ON SATURDAY, JANUARY 21, John Surratt told Lou Weichmann that he had some business in Baltimore, and he invited him to come along. Weichmann knew of Surratt's ties to the underground, and he had always been intrigued by his friend's cloak-and-dagger world. Perhaps he saw this as a chance to see Surratt in action. So that evening, Surratt and Weichmann went to the Maltby House, on West Pratt Street. They both signed the register and headed up to Room 127 for the night. When Weichmann woke up the next morning, he was surprised to see that Surratt had risen early and was about to leave without him. Surratt claimed to have three hundred dollars in his possession and said that he needed to see some gentlemen alone.

Confused and annoyed, Weichmann went to see some friends in town, then took the evening train home. He did not realize that Surratt had tricked him into signing the Maltby House register. If necessary, that signature could be used as evidence that Weichmann himself was tied up in Confederate intrigues. This was an important point, because a suspect could not testify against his cohorts.

John Surratt had gone to a china store at 210 West Baltimore Street. The shop's owner, David Preston Parr, had summoned him over to meet a young man who had stopped in to look for work. He was Lewis Thornton Powell, the twenty-year-old son of a Baptist minister and an ardent Southerner. Powell was a large man with a strong, silent manner that inspired curiosity and even awe. He also had an impressive history. He had served in the 2nd Florida Infantry at Antietam, the Peninsula, and Chancellorsville. Wounded in the wrist at Gettysburg, he was captured and sent to a makeshift hospital, where he met Maggie Branson, a young Baltimore woman who was working there as a nurse. Transferred to another hospital in Baltimore, Powell saw Miss Branson again, and she probably helped him escape from there. After serving briefly with Harry Gilmor's raiders, he joined the famed 43rd Virginia Cavalry—Mosby's Rangers—as a private. He served with Mosby for more than a year, and took part in some of the "Gray Ghost's" most notable exploits.

Life under Mosby was a little like life in the underground. The Rangers didn't fight the way ordinary soldiers did. They lived as ordinary citizens among the families of Northern Virginia, and would come together only for a raid. They had little in the way of military training; beyond a few basic commands, their most useful maneuver was the "skedaddle." As one Ranger explained:

"You see when the Yankees broke they would always run in a bunch, and all we had to do was to follow and pick them up. . . . But when we found it necessary to leave the scene of action, each man worked out his own salvation and 'struck for home and fireside' by his own particular path. We dissolved like the mist 'before their wery eyes wisibly' and left them nothing to follow."

For more than a year, Powell lived near Warrenton, Virginia, with relatives of General William H. Payne. He was a fierce warrior, but one with a softer side; years later, the general remembered him as "a chivalrous, generous, gallant fellow, particularly fond of children."

Daring raids and crippling attacks had made the Rangers' defeat a leading priority in Washington, and eventually the Federals called in Dick Blazer, a noted Indian fighter, to take Mosby out of the picture. It didn't work out that way. In mid-November 1864, Blazer led his Ohio troops against a group of Rangers near Kabletown, Virginia. His men were turned around in short order, and in the rout, Powell and three of his comrades captured the old scout. They were given the privilege of escorting him to Libby Prison.

While in Richmond, Powell happened to see an acquaintance from Baltimore. His thoughts turned back to the kindness he had received there, and perhaps to his brief flirtation with Mary Branson, Maggie's twenty-eight-year-old sister. He returned to his command sullen and reflective. As a young friend remembered, he was a changed man. "He often spoke of his visit to Richmond and his intention soon to go to Baltimore to meet friends he had met in Richmond. . . . After his return . . . he never went on any raid, but was continually talking about a visit or a raid into Maryland. . . ."[22]

Powell finally followed his heart. In the second week of January, he left the Rangers and went to Fairfax Court House, where he changed into civilian clothes. He sold his horse in Alexandria, then took an oath of allegiance, calling himself a civilian refugee. Being an escaped prisoner *and* one of Mosby's Rangers, he dared not give his real name. So he borrowed the name of his Virginia hosts, and from that time forward he was known by the alias given on his oath of allegiance: Lewis Paine.

Powell headed straight for Baltimore and the Eutaw Street boardinghouse of the Branson family. They had a lot of catching up to do. The war occupied much of their attention, and they undoubtedly talked about all the suffering it had wrought. Practically everyone had lost friends or relatives in the war, and Powell was no exception; two of his brothers had been killed at Murfreesboro—or so he thought. He talked about them, and about life in Mosby's area of operations. He seemed to idolize his former commander, and was proud to have taken part in the famous Greenback raid.[23]

For the past few years, the Bransons had belonged to a prisoner relief operation. It was an informal group, composed of women who either had relatives in prison or just considered it a good cause. Among them were Ada Egerton, who once lived in the Branson house, and Annie Parr, whose husband, Preston, was a china dealer. Mrs. Parr had a son at Point Lookout, and Mrs. Egerton ran supplies to the same camp. Their common interest may have linked them to each other, and indirectly to the Lincoln conspiracy. Indeed, prisoner relief was the issue that underlay the whole story of the plot. When Booth revealed his plan to Arnold and O'Laughlen, he had given the prisoner exchange as its goal. His feigned connection in Canada used men who planned prison raids. When Surratt set up the river crossing, he implied that prisoners were involved. In fact and rumor, the same laudable goal had always given Booth's scheme a certain humanitarian appeal. Of the thirty or more people who eventually learned that Booth was planning something, nearly all had a vague sense that prisoners of war were at its heart.[24]

The Baltimore relief network was about to give John Wilkes Booth his most trusted lieutenant. Lewis Powell had no job and no apparent means of support. He was staying at Miller's Hotel in Baltimore, but visited the Bransons several times. Then he met Preston Parr, the china dealer, who knew John Surratt. Parr contacted Surratt on the twenty-first of January and set up an introduction. Surratt had found a new recruit for Booth, and the arrangement worked out for all concerned: Powell resumed his fight for the South; Surratt found a new asset for Booth's plot; and Parr satisfied his debt to Surratt, who had once obtained information about his "exceedingly frail" son at Point Lookout. Soon Booth came over to assess Powell. He was powerful and silent, with nerves of steel. He was a good soldier— the kind of man who does what he is told. In a word, perfect. He moved into the Branson house to await Booth's orders.[25]

· · ·

THE BOARDINGHOUSE at 541 H Street was a busy place. Friends, family, and boarders came and went under the watchful eye of Mary Surratt, a forty-three-year-old widow and the matriarch of the house. As Mary Elizabeth Jenkins, she had been the belle of Prince George's County, but hard times and a difficult marriage had left their mark. Her late husband, John Harrison Surratt, Sr., was once wealthy and respectable. He had owned a mill and several tracts of land in the District of Columbia, and in the early 1850s, he had added a large farm in Prince George's County to his holdings. For a while, the Surratts seemed to have everything. Their house in Maryland was just off an important crossroad, and it quickly became a post office, a polling place, and a benchmark on the Port Tobacco stage route. But their prosperity was an illusion. Alcoholism and abusive behavior strained the marriage, and debts compelled John Surratt to open his home as a public house. His wife, a Catholic convert, grew more alienated from her husband and deeply involved in the church. In these circumstances she raised her three children: Isaac, Anna, and John Jr.[26]

When John Surratt, Sr., died in August 1862, his widow found herself in debt with little prospect of finding her way out. Her tavern was still the center of life in Surrattsville, but the income from it did not pay the bills, and in the fall of 1864, Mrs. Surratt decided to move into the city. On November 1, she took her family to a house that her husband had left her on H Street. She placed ads for several rooms "suitable for four gentlemen," and the following month found someone to move into the tavern. John M. Lloyd, a former police officer, began renting the place for five hundred dollars a year.

Mary Surratt's boarders were decent, ordinary people. Honora Fitzpatrick, eighteen, had been placed there by an elderly father who wanted to see that she stayed in good company. Lou Weichmann, the War Department clerk, was a former divinity student and friend of John Surratt. Ten-year-old Mary Apollonia Dean was attending school just around the corner, at St. Patrick's Institute, and John T. Holohan, who brokered draft exemption deals, took two rooms for his wife and children.

Though Mary Surratt had a great many friends, not everyone who stopped at her house was an acquaintance. Some came and went in secrecy: people with disguises; nameless associates of her son; agents of the Confederacy on their way south. Like the tavern at Surrattsville, the house on H Street became a safe haven for Southern spies and couriers. They passed through at all hours of the day and night.[27]

Among these nocturnal guests was Augustus Spencer Howell, a Marylander who had been spying and running Confederate dispatches for several years. Howell often traveled with a mysterious young woman named Sarah A. Slater. A North Carolinian by birth, Mrs. Slater was described as "spruce and neat," with black eyes and a fair complexion. She had been to Surratt's house several times, but none of the boarders ever got a good look at her, as she always wore a veil over her face. She was said to be a clever woman, and her fluency in French made her a natural for the Montreal route. The Confederacy trusted her with some of its most important missions.[28]

Mary Surratt went away for a few days in early February. In her absence, George Atzerodt appeared at her house for the first time. Atzerodt did not explain the nature of his business. He asked for John Surratt, who was not at home just then. Surratt arrived a few minutes later, and they greeted each other like old friends. Surratt offered Atzerodt a place for the night, suggesting he share a room with Spencer Howell, who was upstairs showing Weichmann how to use a Confederate decoding machine. Weichmann liked Atzerodt, whom he found to be a friendly, ingratiating man. Anna Surratt couldn't pronounce his name, and started calling him "Port Tobacco." The nickname stuck.

The following evening, a carriage appeared in front of the house. Lou Weichmann, looking out a front window, thought he saw Mrs. Slater in the carriage, but she did not come in. While she waited by the curb, Spencer Howell went out and joined her. They left together, and no one in the house said a word about it.[29]

Mary Surratt returned in a few days and met George Atzerodt for the first time. She was horrified to find such a pathetic specimen actually living in her house. Atzerodt, she said, would have to go. She did not care to have "such sticks" about the house. Though she did not want Atzerodt living there, she did not seem to mind that he visited. He came back often.[30]

Arnold and O'Laughlen had been staying at Rullman's Hotel, but when Booth unveiled his theater abduction plan, he told them to take a room at Mitchell's Hotel, near Grover's Theatre. They had not met any other conspirators, and had no idea there were any. But one morning in February they went to Booth's hotel room and found him in conversation with John Surratt. Booth introduced Surratt as "Mr. Cole," but later told them who he really was. After that, the name of Surratt often came up, and

Arnold got the impression that he was an important figure in the plot. Booth always seemed to have business with him.[31]

In early February, Booth told Arnold that his mother, Mary Ann, had had some kind of premonition and had asked June to come down and have a talk with him. The family had always taken such things seriously, or at least they pretended to for Mary Ann's sake. Junius wanted his brother to leave town for a while, and though John Wilkes was working on his theater abduction plan, he really couldn't offer that as an excuse. So on February 9, he left for New York, and the following evening, Abraham Lincoln and his wife went to see John Sleeper Clarke in *Everybody's Friend* at Ford's Theatre. Their guest was General Ulysses S. Grant.[32]

Booth traveled a great deal, and he usually made a point of stopping in Philadelphia on the way back to Washington. He was at Asia's house on Valentine's Day, and sat up all night to work on an acrostic poem for his fiancée.

Lucy Lambert Hale had been secretly dating Booth for some time. She was a daughter of John Parker Hale, an abolitionist senator from New Hampshire, and was one of the most intriguing young ladies of Washington society. She had a magnetic charm that was rumored to have piqued the interest of some highly placed young men, including Oliver Wendell Holmes, Jr., and Robert Todd Lincoln. She also had a free-thinking outlook that placed no shackles on the lifestyle of her husband-to-be. Booth still kept mistresses, and when Lucy traveled with him, they unabashedly checked into hotels as "J. W. Booth & Lady." They sometimes met for trysts in Baltimore, accompanied by Lucy's sister Elizabeth and John McCullough. Such things had to be kept secret; after all, Booth was an actor, and McCullough had a wife and two sons living in Philadelphia.[33]

ON FEBRUARY 20, Sam Arnold and Mike O'Laughlen began renting a room in the home of Mary Van Tyne, a widow and dressmaker who lived on D Street near Eighth. Mrs. Van Tyne was a gracious woman who tried not to be too nosy about her tenants. As far as she could tell, Arnold and O'Laughlen were decent fellows who lived quietly and kept to themselves. They went home to Baltimore every Saturday and usually stayed for a few days. Their only visitor, for the most part, was John Wilkes Booth, and Mrs. Van Tyne was pleased to see him. Booth was a gentleman, and he seemed to like her—maybe because she had come from London, like his mother. He stopped by four or five times a week, and he always asked for O'Laughlen. When Mike wasn't there, Booth would leave a message to meet him at a nearby stable.

BOOTH HAD ONCE BEEN a chronic optimist with a passion for life, but lately he seemed distracted and short-tempered. The transformation was so pronounced, Joe Simonds noticed it from three hundred miles away. At his office in Franklin, Pennsylvania, Simonds voiced his concerns in a letter. "I hardly know what to make of you this winter—so different from your usual self," he wrote. "Have you lost all your ambition or what is the matter[?]" He hated to see Booth growing idle and spending money he didn't have. "If you are not going to act this season come out here John where at least you can live prudently and where I really believe you can make money." Simonds was especially bothered by Booth's extravagant claims of success. Booth, he learned, had told Sam Chester that he had already made eighty to a hundred thousand dollars in oil profits, and would have made more but for Simonds's timidity. In reality, Booth hadn't made a penny, but he could hardly admit that. After all, it was the promise of money that had lured Atzerodt into the plot. But the deception did not sit well with Simonds. "We have not got rich yet John," he chided, "and when I do you will be the first one to know of it."[34]

Friends and family were puzzled by Booth's idleness, though he always had some excuse for doing nothing. He had left a string of broken engagements, and theater manager James H. McVicker was one of those trying to reschedule him for the spring. "There are plenty of little fish," said McVicker, "but I don't want them if I can help it." He knew that Booth was still a good draw, if he could only coax him back to the stage. Booth, however, showed no interest.[35]

That month he went back to New York a few times and to Southern Maryland more often. The trips were fast and frequent. He called on Sam Chester again, and the two went for their customary walk down Broadway. Booth said that he had approached John Mathews, of Ford's stock company, about joining the plot. Mathews had refused, and Booth hated him for it. In fact, he would have sacrificed him without a second thought. This callous attitude surprised Chester, and he told Booth that he shouldn't talk that way. "No," Booth replied. "He is a coward, and not fit to live." Then, in spite of his promise not to bring it up again, he repeated his cash offer to Chester and asked him to reconsider. There really wasn't much work in it; Booth and others would perform the actual abduction.

True to form, Chester refused to hear anything more about it. He returned the fifty dollars Booth had sent him, and Booth accepted it, saying that he was short of funds at the moment. The plot had already cost him four thousand dollars, he said, "for horses and such like." He would have to go to Richmond for more.[36]

THOUGH JOHN SURRATT HAD TIES to Booth and to the Confederacy, there was nothing in his movements to suggest he had linked the two. In February, though, both interests converged in New York City. Booth and Surratt happened to be in town at the same time, and on Booth's invitation, Surratt stopped at Edwin's house and was introduced to Mary Ann, Edwin, and Rosalie. It was a memorable experience for him, and he talked endlessly of how elegant the place was. Clearly, he enjoyed Booth's trust and confidence.

Not so with everyone in the plot. George Atzerodt was Surratt's hireling, and if Booth had had anything to say about it, he would never have been let into the loop. Atzerodt's problem was that he drank too much, and when he drank, he talked. He bragged of getting rich, and of doing something that everyone would read about in the papers. His worst mistake, though, was asking a local man, George Bateman, to help him hide John Surratt's boat. Bateman knew Surratt, and when he reported (or inquired about) what was going on, Surratt was shaken. He told Bateman to move the boat from Goose Creek, where Atzerodt wanted it, to King's Creek, ten miles out of town. Presumably, he also told him to keep quiet.[37]

ONE EVENING IN LATE FEBRUARY, a large, muscular, dark-haired man appeared at the H Street boardinghouse and asked for John Surratt. Lou Weichmann, who answered the door, informed him that Mr. Surratt was not at home, and asked if he wanted to meet the lady of the house. The stranger, who gave his name as Wood, stepped inside. He seemed to be a man of culture and breeding, polite and well dressed. He chatted with the ladies, and when Mrs. Surratt ushered him into the parlor, he noticed a piano and asked if she would favor him with a song. When John Surratt returned home that night, he invited Mr. Wood to spend the night. Mrs. Surratt offered him a room on the third floor and asked Weichmann to take his supper to him there. The next morning, the visitor was gone. Eventually, the boarders would learn that his real name was Lewis Powell, and his brief stay at the Surratt house would change their lives.[38]

THE CONFEDERATES MADE a last-ditch effort to negotiate an end to the war, but when their envoys at Hampton Roads made an offer, President Lincoln responded by saying that they could have peace when they stopped asserting their independence. Like everyone else, Lincoln knew that the South's days were numbered. Food, manpower, arms, and supplies had dwindled to almost nothing. Lee's army had been holed up near Petersburg for months. Now, this diplomatic failure demoralized them even more.

The war news was depressing to Booth, and sometimes even frightening. The government had cracked down on "irregular warfare," and in early 1865 they made an example of one of its more celebrated practitioners. John Yates Beall had been involved in a plan to capture a gunboat on Lake Erie, with the intention of using it in the rescue of prisoners on Johnson's Island. His scheme never got very far. The plot was discovered, and Beall was later captured, tried, and sentenced to death. A long list of prominent citizens pleaded with the president to commute his sentence, but Lincoln declined to intervene, and on February 25, Beall was put to death. His hanging was a clear sign that the administration would deal harshly with terrorists.

The lesson was not lost on Booth. He knew that Charles County was infested with government agents, and he also knew that Port Tobacco, the county seat, was awash in rumors about George Atzerodt and his big plans. Sooner or later, someone would get to the bottom of those stories. Something had to be done.

Booth had not been foolish enough to associate with Atzerodt; in fact, they had never met. But Atzerodt's behavior prompted Surratt to move him out of Port Tobacco, and in Washington, Booth reversed course and embraced his lowly cohort. They were introduced in Lou Weichmann's office, and as Booth studied the broad, greasy grin and the easygoing manner, he must have wondered how he could possibly control this man who showed so little control over himself. For now, all he could do was take Atzerodt by the lapels and offer a stern word of advice: *Don't drink so much.*

George Atzerodt wasn't the only security risk. Several people were in a position to figure out what was going on, and Booth needed a strategy for neutralizing potential witnesses before they had a chance to hurt him. For Sleeper Clarke, whose house he used at all hours; for Lou Weichmann, whose office he used for meetings; for Dr. Mudd, whose introductions had brought Booth into the underground; for Herold, Atzerodt, Arnold, O'Laughlen, and a growing list of acquaintances, Booth did all he could to create and preserve the evidence that would intertwine their fates with his own. This, more than anything else, ensured the survival of his conspiracy when the odds favored exposure.

This strategy could work on anyone, and the target did not have to be a member of the plot, as the case of Sam Chester illustrates. Booth did not tell Chester of his intentions right away. He brought up a mysterious "speculation," and mentioned it several times in subsequent correspondence. Naïvely, Chester responded in writing, and his letters must have seemed just as circumspect as Booth's. When Booth finally decided he had the kind of evidence he needed, he met Chester again and laid out the details of his plot. The disclosure came with a warning: *Betray me, and we'll hang together.* As he told Chester, "I have facts in my possession that will ruin you for life." And just in case he should call Booth's bluff, two witnesses—Canning and Ford—could tell detectives that Sam Chester did indeed try to get a job at Ford's Theatre, just as Booth requested.

As the conspiracy developed, Booth grew adept at this strategy. He even directed it at his good friend John McCullough. The two of them shared a room at the National Hotel, and one day in early March, McCullough burst in without knocking. Booth was sitting on the bed studying a map, with gauntlets, knife, and pistol spread out around him. The intrusion startled him, and he jumped to his feet in panic. McCullough managed to calm him down, but Booth realized he had nearly been discovered. So he came up with a plan.

Booth prodded McCullough into renting a couple of horses for a ride in the country. Though McCullough was no horseman, he knew it was pointless to argue. He followed Booth out to a wooded area north of Washington and down along the Eastern Branch of the Potomac. Every now and then they would stop, and Booth would point out some topographical feature, saying something like, "Now, Johnny, if a fellow was in a tight fix he could slip right out here, do you see?"

McCullough was not catching on. "Well," he said, "when I leave Washington I shall leave on the cars. I am all raw now with riding this old horse. For God's sake take me back to the hotel." McCullough never figured out that Booth had incriminated him. To all appearances, the two of them had gone scouting for a quick way out of Washington. And at least one man—the stableman—knew enough to infer what they were doing. Booth and McCullough had given their names, and Booth made a point of asking about Crystal Springs, a remote area on the way to the Soldiers' Home.[39]

ON FRIDAY, MARCH 3, Lou Weichmann happened upon Booth and Surratt at a Washington restaurant. They took some refreshments together, and Booth invited the others for a walk to the Capitol. The legislative session was in its final hours, and they all wanted to see what was sure to be a spirited debate. Climbing the gallery steps, they came upon a statuary bust in a corner of the landing. Booth asked Weichmann who it was.

"It is Lincoln," came the reply.

"What is *he* doing here before his time?" Booth sniffed. Nobody knew what to say.[40]

The following day, the careworn president renewed his oath of office in the old Senate chamber. After the ceremony, Lincoln walked to the Capitol's east front to address the public. As he stood up to speak, the sun broke through the clouds and bathed him in a ray of bright light. He then began what many consider to be his finest speech, full of hope and promise for a reunited nation.

"With malice toward none; with charity for all; with firmness in the right, as God gives us to see the right, let us strive on to finish the work we are in; to bind up the nation's wounds; to care for him who shall have borne the battle, and for his widow, and his orphan—to do all which may achieve and cherish a just and lasting peace among ourselves, and with all nations."

Many people were surprised that Lincoln had made it this far. He had beaten the odds, and he stood there now, in his moment of glory, to set a brighter tone for the nation's future. Little did he suspect that in six weeks he would die at the hands of a man he would have recognized—and who was even then standing just a few feet away.[41]

TEN

"YOU CAN BE THE LEADER . . .
BUT NOT MY EXECUTIONER"

M ARCH 5, THE MORNING AFTER THE INAUGURATION, WAS bleak and cheerless for Booth and Lucy Hale. They sat in Booth's room at the National Hotel commiserating on life's troubles and despairing of future happiness. They might not even have a life together; Lucy would soon accompany her father to Spain, where he was about to begin his duties as ambassador. The emptiness of the moment reminded Lucy of Whittier's "Maud Muller," and she jotted down some lines on an envelope:

> *For all sad words of tongue or pen,*
> *The saddest are these: It might have been!*

Booth added a few lines of his own:

> *Now, in this hour, that we part,*
> *I will ask to be forgotten, never*
> *But in thy pure and guileless heart*
> *Consider me thy friend, dear Ever*
> J. Wilkes Booth[1]

When the inauguration excitement died down, Booth once more turned his attention to abducting the president. He moved the carriage into the shed in Baptist Alley, and brought the small bay mare in as well. He began renting a horse from Pumphrey's Stable, just behind the National Hotel, on C Street. James Pumphrey had known John Surratt for years, and would only rent to Booth on his recommendation. Booth took out a high-spirited sorrel horse, and insisted on having the same one from then on.

Horses played a key role in Booth's plans, not only in the abduction itself, but in the shell game he had devised to confuse potential witnesses. He still owned that half-blind horse he had acquired in Charles County, in addition to the small bay mare Arnold had bought in Baltimore. But not everybody knew that. One stableman thought the mare was Arnold's, while another had the impression that John Surratt owned her. Adding to the confusion was another bay mare that looked like Booth's. She was supposedly owned by Surratt.

For Booth, the shuffling around had a more subtle purpose: to bind each man to the plot. Surratt, Arnold, Herold, and Atzerodt all used the public livery, and all shared their horses with Booth. Each transaction was witnessed by a stableman, and each helped establish the intimacy that existed among these men. Thus, public stables gave Booth something to hold over his conspirators. Knowing this, none could expose the plot without implicating himself.[2]

TO AN ACTOR, deception can become second nature, and for Booth, lies were a vital means to an end. He lied to friends, to his conspirators, and to potential witnesses. He came to depend on the confusion and the false impressions his words had wrought—especially about his success in the oil business. His illusory wealth was a large part of what made his conspiracy work, and though John Surratt seems to have known from the beginning that it was a sham, the others learned the truth only over time. Eventually, Booth admitted to Arnold that he was forced to borrow money and sometimes had trouble getting loans. O'Laughlen knew this because his brother Billy was among the creditors. Once Herold learned the secret, he had to sell his favorite horse to raise money for the plot. To the rest of the world Booth was a wealthy man, and even George Atzerodt, who spent much of his time with him, never suspected that the oil money was just a mirage.[3]

On the stage, Booth had earned more than enough money to finance the plot. But he wasn't acting anymore, and his charade was depleting funds at a rapid rate. Arnold and O'Laughlen lived reasonably at Mrs. Van Tyne's, but meals at the Franklin House and a hefty bar tab at Rullman's had to be factored in as well. Atzerodt's room at the Pennsylvania House was hardly a top-flight accommodation, but food and livery added to the cost. Booth's room at the National Hotel was expensive, and even when he stayed at the Herndon House, on Ninth Street, he had to maintain appearances. Travel may have been his greatest expenditure, with more than a dozen trips to New York alone. And then there was the cost of keeping several horses. All told, the conspiracy must have cost Booth a small fortune.[4]

It was vitally important that Booth's associates look as if they belonged in his company. Most were happy to go along with the dress code: Powell bought a fine double-breasted sack coat and a light beaver hat; Surratt and Herold dressed like a couple of dandies in expensive suits, while Arnold and O'Laughlen wore dark business suits. George Atzerodt was the odd one out. Though Booth had bought him a new salt-and-pepper coat with pocket flaps, even that failed to make him look respectable.

Atzerodt's lowly nature was always a concern. The manager of Howard's Stable, who knew Atzerodt as "Azworth," noted how different he and his companions were. "Booth was a pleasant man," said Brooke Stabler, "and we felt rather an attachment for the two men—not for Azworth, we never liked him—but for Booth and Surratt we had a friendly feeling. They were gentlemanly in their manners." Many people considered it strange in retrospect that Atzerodt, who was "in every respect . . . their inferior," could appear to be so close to such "men of refinement." A. F. Kimmel, former owner of the Pennsylvania House, wondered if Atzerodt might be a detective, but Stabler scoffed at the idea. "There was no detective in him," he said. And anyway, everyone knew that Azworth was an "arrant rebel."[5]

Kimmel was not the only one asking questions. At the house on H Street, Lou Weichmann asked Mary Surratt why her son brought such fellows as Atzerodt and Herold to the house. She said that John "wished to make use of them" for a cotton speculation. That was only one of John Surratt's cover stories. In another, he and Booth were going to open up a theater with Atzerodt as their ticket agent. When Surratt told Weichmann he wanted to pursue a career on the stage, Weichmann was surprised. "Would you be an actor?" he asked.

"Of course I would," said Surratt. "It is no disgrace." In fact, Booth had told him he was a pretty good actor.[6]

Most of the conspirators used false names in addition to cover stories. Surratt was John Harrison, James Sturdey, Harry Sherman, John

McCarthy, and Charley Armstrong; Atzerodt was Azworth and Atwood; Powell was Wood, Paine, Mosby, Kensler, and Hall.

It was the alias "Paine" that saved Powell from serious trouble in Baltimore. He had been living with the Bransons for about six weeks when, on March 6, he beat a servant girl, claiming she had been insolent to him. Arrested on orders from Col. John Woolley, he was taken to an old slave pen for interrogation. Woolley's chief of detectives, Lt. Henry Bascom Smith, found him to be a "sullen, dumb looking, overgrown young person." His oath certificate identified him as Lewis Paine of Fauquier County, Virginia, and Smith believed that that was who he was. He also thought he was extraordinarily stupid.

Asked whether he had ever been in the army, "Paine" said that he was only eighteen and a half years old. Asked why he wore gray clothes, he seemed unable to understand the question. Asked about his Baltimore connection, he said he was related to Miss Branson by marriage, but he didn't know her sentiments on the war. He didn't remember hearing any disloyal remarks at her house. Though he admitted whipping the servant, he gave up little else. When questioned about Mosby, he said he had heard of a few of the men who served with him. But the names he gave were false. Apparently, Lewis Powell wasn't such a bad actor either.

Though Lieutenant Smith was sure that Powell was a spy, he stood little chance of proving it. On March 14, "Lewis Paine" was released on taking the oath of allegiance. He was free to go, but only on the condition that he stay north of Philadelphia. Presumably, being that far north would separate him from the subversive element.[7]

Powell's associates anxiously awaited his release, and on the night of the fourteenth, John Surratt wired Preston Parr for an update. "Immediately telegraph if my friend is disengaged and can see me this evening in Washington. J. Surratt." The response was immediate: "She will be over on the six P.M. train. Parr."

Lewis Powell appeared at the Surratt boardinghouse that night and introduced himself as Reverend Paine, a Baptist preacher. His presence stirred up the boarders, who made fun of "Reverend Paine's" cover story and wondered out loud why a Baptist preacher should seek out the home of a Catholic lady in the first place. One of the women called attention to the wild look in his eyes and said that he was a queer-looking preacher who probably wouldn't convert many souls. Mary Surratt, however, thought he was "great looking," and she offered him a room upstairs with her son.

When one of the women referred to him as "Wood," it suddenly occurred to Lou Weichmann that this same man had been there before. He had spent the night then, too, but under a different name.

Powell's release was a relief to Booth, who was edgy about not having access to his people. Just the day before, on March 13, he learned that O'Laughlen had not come back from his usual weekend trip to Baltimore, and he wired a message to him: "Don't fear to neglect your business. You had better come at once." Now, with Powell's arrival, everyone was in reach.[8]

On the night of the fifteenth, Booth, Powell, and Surratt took Nora Fitzpatrick and ten-year-old Apollonia Dean out for an evening at Ford's Theatre. The play was Nicholas Rowe's *The Tragedy of Jane Shore*, but the real attraction was the theater itself. Booth wanted his people to familiarize themselves with the presidential box, so he gave them all tickets to watch the play from there while he milled around with the cast and crew. Near the end of the play, he went up to the box and called the men outside for a private discussion. It was almost midnight when they all returned to the Surratt boardinghouse. The men dropped the ladies off, then turned to leave. Lou Weichmann asked where they were going, and Surratt replied, "Mind your own business."

Later John Wilkes Booth went over to Gautier's Restaurant, near Twelfth Street and Pennsylvania Avenue, and paced nervously out front. Booth had rented a private room there and had it stocked with steamed oysters, liquors, and cigars to last the night. He was expecting some friends, and he asked a waiter, John Miles, to direct them upstairs when they arrived. Some of the men, he said, had made a fortune in the oil business, and he planned to win some of their money.[9]

Powell and Atzerodt arrived first, and they sat down with Booth for a game of cards. Herold had been sent to get Arnold and O'Laughlen, whom he had never met, and they came in a short while later. This was the first time that all these men had been in one place together, and for Sam Arnold and Mike O'Laughlen, it was a rude awakening. They had not been told in advance about the meeting, nor did they know the participants. The others, whom Booth introduced as Herold, "Mosby," Surratt, and "Port Tobacco," were complete strangers, save a brief encounter with Surratt. Indeed, Arnold and O'Laughlen had led a separate existence for months. They had never set foot in Southern Maryland after joining the plot. They had never heard of Mrs. Surratt. Their cover story was oil, not cotton. They met at Nailor's Stable, instead of Howard's, and their bar of choice was the one at their hotel, not the Star Saloon or the Greenback Saloon, on either side of Ford's Theatre. In fact, Booth may have sent them to Rullman's just to keep them away from Surratt. Adams Express had an office in the lobby there, and after Surratt's abrupt departure from the company, he wouldn't go near the place.[10]

Now it was clear that Booth had been keeping them in the dark as well. If they felt put off by that, they would just have to keep it to themselves. They drank and smoked and played cards with the rest until 1:30 A.M., when the last of the waiters left. Only then did Booth get down to business, and what he told them was incredible. He said that the Lincolns frequently attended plays at Ford's Theatre, and were always given an upper box above the stage. They had all been to that box by now, and they knew what it looked like. Booth believed that the president could be captured there and spirited out of Washington with little trouble.

The plan went like this: on Booth's cue, Sam Arnold would rush into the president's box and seize Mr. Lincoln. Booth and Atzerodt, or "Port Tobacco," would handcuff the president and lower him to the stage, where Powell, or "Mosby," would wait to catch him. All would gather around their hostage and hustle him out of the building. With a carriage waiting in the alley, they could make a quick dash out of the city, then meet up with Surratt and Herold on the other side of the Eastern Branch.

Booth sat back and waited for reaction. After a stunned silence, someone pointed out that the president was a strong man, and perhaps it ought to be "Mosby," not Arnold, who subdued him in the box. Someone else wondered how they were going to keep an entire audience at bay. There were understandably quite a few objections, but with each one, Booth merely adjusted the details; he still thought the plan was sound. They fought and argued, and over time a new script evolved. Now O'Laughlen and Herold were to put out the gaslights. Arnold would catch the president on the stage, and Surratt would join "Port Tobacco" as a guide outside the city.

The revisions did not placate Arnold. He had joined a plot to capture Lincoln in the country, not in a crowded theater, and he didn't see how this new scenario could possibly work. Even if they managed to get the president out of the building, he said, they were bound to run into a sentinel somewhere on their way out of the city.

"Shoot the sentinel," Booth snapped. But someone would surely send up an alarm, and the whole thing would collapse around them.

In fact, Arnold had a long list of complaints. They had been talking about doing this for months, and it seemed to be nothing but talk. Opportunities had come and gone, yet nothing ever happened. When the president had appeared in public, Arnold had called it to Booth's attention . . . and still nothing. Just this evening, in fact, the Lincolns had gone to Grover's National Theatre for a performance of *The Magic Flute*, but Booth took no notice. And what if they did abduct the president? What would they do with him? As Arnold recalled, the whole point of capturing Lincoln was to force a resumption in the prisoner exchange. Yet that had been accomplished without them. Though little had been said of it at the time, Grant had actually resumed the exchange in mid-January.

Arnold's revelation was explosive, and potentially fatal to Booth's plot. Indeed, his information was accurate. That very day, in fact, a thousand more prisoners had come home under the new arrangement. General Grant had testified on Capitol Hill about it, and the papers were filled with stories about the soldiers' return. So the question naturally arises: Why did Booth keep planning to abduct the president, knowing his goal had already been achieved?

Though he didn't dare say it, Arnold was getting uncomfortably close to the answer. The policy change on prisoners had come at about the same time that Booth had changed his plan. Was he really serious about capturing Lincoln in the theater? Did he adopt this ridiculous scenario hoping it would go awry and lead to the president's "accidental" death? Was this new scheme just a blind for assassination? Arnold's own account of the meeting—the only one ever written from the inside—skirts the issue completely. It was ridiculous to think that the president of the United States could be successfully carried off from among a thousand of his friends. Any such attempt would surely meet with armed resistance, and Arnold urged Booth to go about it in some other way. "I want a shadow of a chance," he said. O'Laughlen tried to second that, but Booth cut him off, saying sharply that Arnold found fault with all of his ideas. In reply, Arnold told Booth, "You can be the leader of the party, but not my executioner."

Subsequent events show clearly that Booth convinced his people that he had not given up on capturing Lincoln. The president would always be a viable hostage, for peace or Confederate independence if nothing else. He urged his people not to give up, and at least some of them were persuaded.[11]

Booth rarely failed at the art of persuasion. He had always been extremely effective at laying out his arguments. A keen intellect, forceful gestures, the graceful modulation of his voice, and those expressive, dark, and lustrous eyes served him in life as they had on the stage. But the conspirators were not a theater audience, and Booth sought more than their approval; he was asking them to risk their lives in a scheme that did not look feasible even with the best presentation.

Booth was angry with Arnold, and he reminded him of the oath they had taken last summer. "Do you know you are liable to be shot?" he said. Arnold's answer was that the plan had changed since then, and as far as he was concerned, it was Booth who broke the compact. "If you feel inclined to shoot me," he said, "you have no farther to go. I shall defend myself." Ultimately, Booth backed down and agreed to stay with the original plan. Arnold relented as well, but with an ultimatum. "Gentlemen," he said, "if this is not accomplished this week I forever withdraw from it." It was already Thursday morning.

Booth glared at Arnold, his eyes flashing and his jaw clenched. The whole plot seemed about to unravel, and he was speechless.

The meeting broke up at five A.M., and Manning, the watchman, locked the door behind them as they left. Nothing had gone as Booth anticipated. Sam Arnold had stirred things up, and he might undo the entire enterprise. He had to be dealt with.[12]

On Thursday afternoon, George Atzerodt stopped at the boardinghouse to see John Surratt. Lewis Powell joined them, and all three went up to Lou Weichmann's room for a discussion. An hour later, Atzerodt was gone, and Weichmann walked in to find Surratt and Powell sitting on his bed surrounded by Bowie knives, revolvers, and four pairs of spurs. They offered no explanation, but merely stared at him until he left. Suspicious, Weichmann came back later and looked around. He noticed that "Reverend Paine" had left a false mustache on a table by the bed. Weichmann tucked it away in his lockbox, then played dumb when Powell returned to look for it.

The lady in the veil slipped into the boardinghouse that same afternoon. Sarah Slater kept to herself all evening, and left for Canada early the next day.[13]

. . .

BOOTH COULD NOT GET that incident with Sam Arnold out of his mind. Arnold was a threat, but not in the way that Sam Chester or John Mathews was. He knew a great deal more than either of them, and would require special handling. Fortunately for Booth, he found a way to compromise Arnold, using Mathews to do it. He learned that Mathews was going to Baltimore and asked if he would mind dropping something off with a friend there. It was a trunk filled with canned meats, sardines, crackers, brandy, and toilet items to be kept for the president's use in the event they captured him. Mathews didn't know what the items were for, but obligingly he took the trunk as requested. The addressee—most likely, Sam Arnold—was not home, so Mathews left a note:

My Dear Sir:—
     Please deliver this trunk to Mr.——, who will see that it is delivered to Mr.——, who will have it safely shipped to its destination of which he is informed. Be careful.

Very truly,
John Mathews.

That note, in Mathews's own hand, might have been used as evidence of his complicity in the plot. His account of the incident did not reveal the identities of the people involved—it used dashes in place of their names— but his later account referred to the intended recipient of the abduction supplies as Booth's "friend on Fayette street." The Arnolds lived at Park and Fayette. Though Sam Arnold was trying to leave the plot, Booth was, in effect, planting evidence against him where it might easily be discovered.

John Mathews had been staying in the house of William Petersen, across the street from Ford's, and Booth sometimes visited him there. So it came as no great surprise when he came home on March 16 and found Booth stretched out on his bed, waiting to see him. (This was the same bed in which Abraham Lincoln later died.) James Wallack and E. L. Davenport were with Mathews at the time. Both actors who were then appearing at the Washington Theatre, they were scheduled to perform the following afternoon at the Campbell Hospital, not far from the Soldiers' Home. The hospital had a five-hundred-seat theater, and every Friday, real professionals would give a matinée performance there as an act of charity. Tom Taylor's *Still Waters Run Deep* was on the bill for the following day, and that is what Wallack and Davenport talked about in the back bedroom of the Petersen house. Booth sat to the side, saying little. An idea had just come to him. As he left the house, he told Mathews that he might stop by the next day to watch the play.[14]

That afternoon, Booth went to Rullman's and apologized to Arnold for the harsh words that had passed between them. Obviously, he said, Arnold had been drinking too much.

"No!" Arnold shot back. "It was you and your friends who were drunk. I was never more sober in my life." He assured Booth that he had meant everything he said, and he repeated his ultimatum: If nothing happened by the end of the week, he would sever his connection to the plot. Booth probably suspected Arnold would say that, but wanted to be sure. Though his Baltimore friends were no longer vital to the plot, they could not just walk away. They had more than just secrets; they knew where the weapons and handcuffs were, and Booth did not. Two weeks before, he had packed carbines, a monkey wrench, ammunition, and rope into a black box and sent them, by way of a hotel porter, to Mrs. Van Tyne's. Fearing discovery, Arnold and O'Laughlen had passed them off to an unidentified friend in town, and that man still had them. Now Booth had to get them back, and he had to do it quickly; Arnold's deadline was only a day off.

At about two o'clock the following afternoon, Booth sent Arnold and O'Laughlen an urgent message: *Get those things together; something is about to happen.* They joined up with Booth, Surratt, Powell, Herold, and Atzerodt on H Street, in front of Mrs. Surratt's boardinghouse, and Booth told them all that the moment had arrived. The president, he said, was supposed to be watching a play out at Campbell Hospital. That was practically on the way to the Soldiers' Home, so their first abduction scheme could be carried into effect.[15]

They had already discussed the plan, and knew it by heart. Herold would take the carbines down to Southern Maryland, where he would stand ready to escort the party to the lower Potomac. The others would wait in a remote area along Seventh Street, and when the president returned from the hospital, they would ride up alongside his carriage and overpower the driver. John Surratt would mount the box and take over from there. They would ride across the Benning Bridge, switch carriages in Southern Maryland, and, with Herold joining them, make for the lower Potomac. Going through Surrattsville, they would stop for fresh horses in the little village called "T.B.," then zigzag through some of the more deserted roads of Charles County. They would ditch their horses and carriage at the Lock II farm, near Nanjemoy, and take the boat from there to Virginia. If everything went as planned, they could be on Confederate soil in a few hours.

While Herold took the carbines out to Maryland, Booth led Arnold and O'Laughlen to a staging area in a restaurant near Seventh and Boundary streets. They waited for the others, and when no one else appeared, all three rode out Seventh Street toward the hospital. After riding about a mile, Arnold and O'Laughlen turned back, and Booth continued by himself. Eventually, all but Herold returned to the restaurant, and when Booth rejoined them, he announced that the plan was off. He said he had learned at the hospital that the president had not shown up and the play had gone on without him. He would keep the supplies, but the men were free to go. Perhaps they could try again some time, but for the next month or so, they ought to keep a low profile.[16]

This incident has gone down in history as a failed attempt to kidnap Abraham Lincoln. To Booth, however, it was anything but a failure. Going into that day, some of his people were about to quit the plot. They had Booth's weapons, and they knew what he intended to do with them. But when it was all over, Booth had his guns back, and more important, he had something more to hold over each of the defectors. By lying in wait for the president, they had each committed a crime, and arguably an act of treason. And since Booth had deliberately assembled them in a public place, rather than a deserted stretch of road, their "kidnap attempt" had been witnessed by many people. At Rullman's Hotel, Howard's Stable, the H Street rendezvous, and the Seventh Street restaurant were plenty of witnesses who could place each of Booth's men together in a criminal conspiracy. Now each was responsible for anything that resulted from that plot, *even if he quit.*

Booth knew something about the law, and in all likelihood, he staged this event to make it work for him. He really had no reason to think that Lincoln was planning to go to Campbell Hospital; in fact, the president was scheduled to be in the National Hotel that afternoon, presenting a captured battle flag to the governor of Indiana. There are some indications that Booth himself may even have attended that ceremony. Still, he needed everyone in position for the abduction, even if he knew it would never come off. The conspirators did as they were told, and Booth got some measure of security in the bargain. Once more, deception was a useful tool.[17]

Lou Weichmann sat in his room, burning with curiosity about Surratt and his friends. Dan Hawkins, the servant, had told him that "Massa John" had ridden off with six other men that afternoon, including Booth, Port Tobacco, and that big dark-haired man who was staying at the house. The story piqued Weichmann's interest, but when he went downstairs to ask Mrs. Surratt about it, he found her sobbing. "John is gone away," she said. "Go down to dinner, and make the best of your dinner you can." She went to her room.

About two hours later, John Surratt burst into Weichmann's room, very much excited. He paced the room like a caged wolf. "I will shoot anyone that comes into this room," he said. "My prospects are gone, my hopes are blighted. I want something to do. Can you get me a clerkship?" He wouldn't explain, but kept walking around nervously. Minutes later, Powell came in, also armed and agitated. Like Surratt, he had no intention of sharing anything. The two paced in silence, and soon Booth too stormed into the room, whip in hand, to join them. He seemed startled when Weichmann spoke. "I did not see you," Booth said. They all exchanged glances, and then without a word, the three went upstairs to Powell's room and shut the door. In thirty minutes they were gone. This strange and unexplained incident left Weichmann feeling unsettled.[18]

Somebody forgot to call David Herold back to the city. Posted with the buggy in Maryland, Herold waited around until sunset, then headed south along the planned route, just in case the others had gotten past him by a different route. Along the way he encountered his friend Walter Griffin, and they continued to Surrattsville together. John Lloyd, the tavern keeper, was there when they arrived. He was a huge man who didn't care much for strenuous activities, such as standing up. He settled himself into a barroom chair, then invited the others to join him in a game of cards. Herold said he would like to, but had to keep an eye on the road. He couldn't do that and play cards at the same time—that is, unless he could leave the door propped open. It was a bitter cold night, and Lloyd would have none of that. So Herold solved the dilemma by giving Lloyd's young nephew a quarter to sit outside and watch for traffic.

At ten o'clock, Herold suddenly remembered some pressing business he had to take care of. He ventured into the cold, bound for the crossroads village of T.B., five miles to the south. He checked in to the T.B. Tavern and asked the bartender, William Norton, if he might bring in some weapons. By "some weapons," he meant two shotguns, two carbines, a revolver, and a dirk knife. Norton was surprised, but he let Herold take the smaller weapons to his room, while he left the larger ones hidden behind the bar. As Herold went to his room, he said that he wanted to be awakened if John Surratt and another man came by.[19]

EARLY THE NEXT MORNING, John Surratt and George Atzerodt set out to look for Herold. They found him just beyond Surrattsville, coming toward them on the road from T.B. He had all the weapons with him. Surratt explained that the abduction attempt had failed and suggested they keep the guns hidden somewhere, ready for another try. Herold said that he wanted to leave them hidden in T.B., but nobody down there would let him. Under the circumstances, Surratt said, they would have to take them back to the tavern. He knew of a good hiding place there.

Lloyd's Tavern was always a busy place, but when Surratt, Atzerodt, and Herold walked into the barroom on the morning of March 18, they found one traveler they didn't expect to see. He was John C. Atzerodt, brother of George, and now a detective for the state provost marshal. John was just passing through on the way to Charlotte Hall in search of deserters. He saw his brother, and they sat down for a drink together.

It was a close call. Had the conspirators been in a hurry, they might have taken those guns out of the carriage right away and been caught in the act of hiding them. A few reckless words on the way in, and John Atzerodt might have discovered their purpose. As it happened, they saw the detective before he saw them, and they moved cautiously. He never guessed what they were doing. He took his drink, then left without having any idea how close he had come to disrupting the plot against Abraham Lincoln.

Surratt put the guns, a box of cartridges, and a twenty-foot coil of rope on a sofa in the front parlor. The rifles were completely strange to Lloyd, and Surratt explained that they were Spencer carbines, "something like those that the cavalry use." The Spencer was a repeating rifle with a short barrel that made it easier to shoot from horseback. Its cartridges could be spring-loaded, seven at a time, into the butt of the rifle for rapid firing. Surratt had two of these rifles, both with shoulder straps, and he knew where he wanted to hide them. He took Lloyd upstairs and showed him a space over the kitchen where the floor was about two feet lower than that of the adjoining room in the main house. From this unfinished area they could shove the rifles between the exposed joists over the dining room. If put far enough back, they would be completely out of sight. Lloyd had misgivings about hiding weapons in the house, but Surratt assured him he would be back to get them in a few days.[20]

THE SEVENTH STREET INCIDENT marked a turning point in the plot, and to all appearances, the conspirators were going their separate ways. David Herold accepted a clerkship at an Army of the James hospital, and was told to report for duty on April 1. Lewis Powell went to New York, and John Surratt resumed his courier runs for the Confederacy. Arnold and O'Laughlen gave notice to Mrs. Van Tyne on March 18. They said they were moving to Pennsylvania, but two days later, they returned to Baltimore. Atzerodt, meanwhile, not only remained in the plot, but moved up in the pecking order. He apparently still believed that Booth was going to make him rich, in spite of all evidence to the contrary. Indeed, Atzerodt had received nothing so far, and had actually lost money, having lent some to John Surratt. But he remained committed, and on the afternoon of the eighteenth, he checked in to the Pennsylvania House, just across C Street from the National Hotel. Logistics for the river crossing would now fall to Thomas Harbin and others.[21]

That same night, John Wilkes Booth appeared at Ford's Theatre in *The Apostate* for the benefit of John McCullough. It was a play that had special meaning for both of them. The lead role had always been associated with the elder Booth, and the play itself was the first that McCullough had ever seen. It was an old-fashioned melodrama set in Granada during the revolt of the Moors. *The Apostate* culminates in the killing of the tyrant Pescara and the suicide of Hemeya, his assassin. It was to be Booth's final performance, and it went extremely well. The full house included those conspirators who were still in town plus Lou Weichmann and John Holohan. Even Mrs. Van Tyne was there, on a complimentary pass given her by O'Laughlen.[22]

A COUPLE OF DAYS LATER, John Surratt asked Lou Weichmann to go with him to the post office. Surratt picked up a letter addressed to "James Sturdey," one of his aliases, and he showed it to his nosy friend. Weichmann found the letter a bit cryptic. All he got from it was that someone named Wood was stopping at the Revere House in New York City and would soon move to a boardinghouse on West Grand Street. That was one of two messages Surratt received from New York that day. Roderick D. Watson, the son of Thomas Jones's neighbor in Maryland, addressed a letter directly to Surratt at the boardinghouse. He claimed to have important business, and hoped Surratt would come up to see him right away.

From these letters, it appeared that something was happening in New York. Lewis Powell and Preston Parr were there, and on the twenty-first, Booth took an evening train up as well. The last performance of Edwin's "Hundred Nights of Hamlet" was to take place the following night, and John Wilkes apparently went to the Winter Garden to witness the event. It was touted as one of the great triumphs of theatrical history, but Edwin's accomplishment drew more attention to John Wilkes. Now more than ever, people turned to him and wondered why *he* did not return to the stage.[23]

With every trip to New York, Booth saw the widening contrast between North and South. In the South, people starved, suffered, and died in a struggle for existence. By comparison, New Yorkers were prosperous and carefree. They spent a fortune on mere entertainment, and people like Edwin and Clarke got wealthy in the process. To John Wilkes Booth, it didn't seem fair. Though Edwin was a Unionist, his support had been all talk, no action. At some level, John Wilkes must have known that his own situation was no different. Though he might still take an active part in the war, his chance to do so was quickly fading.

New York City was becoming a second home to the Lincoln conspiracy, and Lewis Powell's presence there underscores the importance of the place, as well as its mystery. Booth spent much of his time in the city. He tried to recruit Chester and other Broadway actors, and he probably met with rebel agents he had come to know through John Surratt. But it is hard to say with certainty. Though New York was an important hub in the Confederate underground, investigators seem to have missed the Booth connection almost entirely. They were slow to appreciate the number of sympathizers who could have given him aid and comfort. As one resident put it, "There is about as much Yankee in the city of New York as there is in South Carolina and about as much opposition to the party in power as there can be anywhere south." The place was a stronghold of anti-Lincoln sentiment, and it was where Confederates planned some of their "irregular warfare" operations.

It would be tempting to assume a connection between those Confederates and John Wilkes Booth. But in fact we just don't know. Indeed, New

York might be a red herring. Booth, Surratt, and Powell used it as a blind, and they often claimed to be going there when they really weren't. Though several conspirators referred to the city, they had clearly been misled as to its importance. George Atzerodt, for example, said that Booth had posted some of his people in New York and that he was getting money from there. But Atzerodt also thought that Powell had come from there; and according to Sam Arnold, all of the money Booth got in New York was borrowed.

New York City was never mentioned in any official report. Detectives were so fixated on Southern complicity that they ignored almost all leads that pointed elsewhere. Consequently, our knowledge is trivial. We know, for example, that Booth visited a club called the Lone Star, on Broadway; and we know that he consorted with prostitutes Annie Horton and Sally Andrews there. But looking for more substantive matters, we find only the visits with Sam Chester, and the fact that Booth ordered a pair of tall cavalry-style boots from Henry Lux, on Broadway. He wanted them made with pockets inside, for hiding papers.[24]

THE CONSPIRACY REMAINED ACTIVE, and to all appearances, Lou Weichmann was moving to the center of it. Weichmann had seen a lot recently: the meeting of Powell and Surratt in his bedroom, the note to Surratt from "Wood," and the comings and goings of Confederate spies. But on March 23, Booth gave him an actual assignment for the plot. He sent him a telegram with instructions to "tell John to telegraph number and street at once." The message, delivered to the Surratt house, was received by Eliza Holohan, who took it to Weichmann at his office. The "John" was John Surratt, and by the time he got the telegram, it had already been seen by government clerks, fellow boarders, and friends of Lou Weichmann. Only Surratt, however, knew what it meant.

Though Weichmann was thrilled to be entering Surratt's inner circle, he had no idea that much of what he was seeing had actually been gotten up just for his benefit. Take the "Wood" letter, for example. Its author, Lewis Powell, was not moving to Grand Street, as the letter indicated, but was coming back to Washington. Someone had recommended he check into the Herndon House, midway between Ford's Theatre and Surratt's. Powell needed to know how to find the place; hence the order to "telegraph number and street at once." The hotel was across from the post office, and Surratt got the address on his way back from there. He sent his girlfriend, Anna Ward, to inquire if a room would be available.[25]

The fact is, Lou Weichmann's conspirator status was an illusion. He was one of the last people Booth would have trusted to join the plot. Weichmann was too nosy, and he had already told his co-workers in the War Department about the strange goings-on at the Surratt house. He thought it was all about blockade-running, and that was relatively harmless. But he must have had doubts. At least once he had demanded to know what was really going on. Surratt could always placate him, but that might not always be the case. And he had been spending a lot of time lately with the drunken, unpredictable Atzerodt.

Weichmann had already forced some close calls—one of which nearly ended Booth's conspiracy. Surratt's March 17 ride out to Seventh Street, and the strange way that Surratt, Booth, and Powell had barged into his room afterward, left Weichmann disturbed and confused. On Monday the twentieth he reported his suspicions to his supervisor at the War Department. Major Daniel H. L. Gleason listened patiently, but with a bit of skepticism. He had often overheard his clerks trying to impress one another, and he knew that Weichmann could keep up with the best of them. On one occasion, in fact, Weichmann had boasted to his colleagues that he "could make thirty thousand dollars, easy as dirt." When asked how he could do that, he put on an air of secretiveness and said, "Never mind. I know how." So Gleason found it hard to take this report seriously. His intuition was confirmed a few days later when Weichmann recanted, saying that his friends were just having fun with him. John Surratt even came by the office, and they joked together about making huge sums of money.[26]

But Daniel Gleason was not the only person in whom Weichmann confided. On the evening of the seventeenth, he wrote to Father John B. Menu, his mentor at St. Charles College, and told him that something was not right with the Surratts. Father Menu thought highly of John Surratt, and this accusation bothered him. He replied by return mail. "Why do you not speak more fully?" he asked. "Could you not have said openly what is the [unintelligible] trip for which he is soon to depart? . . . Between us there should be no secret." Judging from that response, it seems that Weichmann had written "in an obscure way" that he thought Mrs. Surratt was a rebel. He probably never saw Father Menu's reply; somebody intercepted it, and after the assassination, it was found in John Wilkes Booth's trunk.[27]

Knowing that Weichmann was a security risk, the conspirators did all they could to compromise him. One day Booth sent him that "tell John" message, and the next, John Surratt asked him to write out "something flowery," in his own hand, about Booth's oil business. A few days later, Surratt had Weichmann write another note—one that made him seem deeply involved in the plot. James Brawner and Richard Smoot had never received payment for their boat. They had tried to contact him several times, but evidently Surratt could not get the money from Booth, so he had to look elsewhere. He asked Weichmann to write a note—again, in his own distinctive hand: "Tell _____ to have that money ready for me by the first of the week. I will call down and collect it."[28]

BOOTH RETURNED from New York on the morning of March 25. He had taken an overnight train, and Sarah Slater, the Confederate courier, probably traveled with him. For her, Washington was only a brief stop on a trip to Richmond. She was carrying letters from Confederate General Edwin G. Lee in Montreal to Secretary of State Judah Benjamin, and they needed to get through the lines quickly. Her movements were a study in efficiency. When the train arrived at seven-thirty, Booth went directly to his hotel. John Surratt picked Mrs. Slater up in a rented carriage and took her to H Street. As they pulled up to the curb, the front door opened and out came Mary Surratt. While her son steadied the horses, Mrs. Surratt stepped into the carriage. In just a minute or two, they were gone.[29]

Sarah Slater was supposed to go to Surrattsville, where Spencer Howell would escort her farther south. But detectives had arrested Howell the night before, and plans had to be adjusted accordingly. As it happened, they encountered a neighbor, David Barry, at the Surratt tavern. Barry had business in Port Tobacco, so he drove the carriage while Mrs. Surratt took the stage back home.[30]

John Surratt and Sarah Slater crossed the Potomac that night, and the next day, Barry brought their carriage back to Howard's Stable. He also delivered a note to Brooke Stabler:

March 26th, 1865

Mr. Brooks:
    As business will detain me for a few days in the country, I thought I would send your team back. Mr. Barry will deliver it safely and pay the hire on it. If Mr. Booth my friend should want my horses let him have them, but no one else. If you should want any money on them he

will let you have it. I should like to have kept the team for several days, but it is too expensive, especially as I have "woman on the brain" and may be away for a week or so.

Yours respectfully,
J. Harrison Surratt

John Surratt must have thought the conspiracy was finished. By letting Booth use his horses, "but no one else," he effectively rescinded the privilege from Atzerodt, who was still in need of transportation. He could hardly have done the same to Booth, since those horses actually belonged to him.[31]

ELEVEN

"THERE IS GOING TO BE SOME SPLENDID ACTING TONIGHT"

WAR AND POLITICS HAD MADE JOHN WILKES BOOTH an outcast. He was once a popular, beloved stage idol, but by 1865, people openly mocked him and taunted him for his convictions. Harry Ford and a friend named Abner Brady were talking one afternoon, and Booth joined the conversation. The talk turned to the war, and Booth grew defensive about the South and its chances of survival. He said that within two weeks, something would happen that would "astonish the world."

Brady had a quick retort: "What are you going to do—kill Jefferson Davis, take Richmond, or play Hamlet a hundred nights?"[1]

ON MONDAY, MARCH 27, a special announcement appeared in the *Evening Star:*

> FORD'S THEATRE — The Italian opera season about to be inaugurated at this popular theater, promises to be the most brilliant ever known in Washington. . . . The first of the series of six operas, La Forza Del Destino (the Force of Destiny) being selected for the debut of the troupe. . . . *The President and Mrs. Lincoln have secured boxes for several of the operas,* and the British and Italian Ministers for the entire series.

The wealth, beauty and fashion of the Capital will, we doubt not, be strongly represented during the opera season.

Now this was exciting news! Booth hurried over to Ford's, hoping to learn which of the operas the president planned to attend. In fact, Mrs. Lincoln had secured a box for *Ernani* on Wednesday, the twenty-ninth. She and her husband had gone off to visit Grant's headquarters at City Point, Virginia, but evidently they planned to be back soon. If Booth could reassemble his group in time, perhaps they could finally strike a blow.

He dashed off a telegram to O'Laughlen. "Get word to Sam. to come on with or without him Wednesday morning. We sell that day sure. Don't fail J Wilkes Booth." Then, impatient for a response, he took the first train to Baltimore. Finding neither Arnold nor O'Laughlen at home, he went to Barnum's Hotel and wrote out a couple of notes asking them to meet him there. By chance, Billy "Pomp" Williams was there. Pomp had once worked for the Booths, and John Wilkes asked if he would mind doing him a favor. He was going to New York, he said, and he needed someone to deliver a couple of letters. Williams agreed, and headed off to the Arnold Bakery on Fayette Street.[2]

Booth wasn't really going to New York. He headed back to Washington and went straight over to the National Theatre. He saw Thomas Wallace there, playing billiards in the parlor above the lobby. Wallace had met Booth some months before, and once agreed to rent out a theater box for him. Somehow, he had never gotten around to it. Now Booth renewed his request, and specified that it had to be Box 7, on the upper level, at Ford's Theatre. The ticket would cost ten dollars, but Booth wanted the arrangements made promptly, so he gave Wallace twenty.[3]

George Atzerodt must have been on alert. He went back to Port Tobacco that day and closed up his carriage shop. Handing the keys to his friend Nicholas B. Crangle, he said that he was going away; his customers could take their carriages if they needed them. That done, he picked up another friend, Henry Marcellus Bailey, and headed to Washington. Bailey, a Confederate veteran, had once tended bar in Brawner's Hotel, but quit his job abruptly in mid-January, at the same time that Atzerodt was recruited into the plot. He may have known what was going on, but perhaps not. Either way, he was another headache for John Wilkes Booth.[4]

Lewis Powell returned from New York that night and, using the name

Kensler, checked in to a third-floor room in the Herndon House. The hotel was just around the corner from Ford's, where Powell joined Booth for the Italian opera *La Forza del Destino,* then in progress. John Surratt was not with them, and in fact would never be back again. Though Arnold and O'Laughlen had received their notes too late, it was just as well. They also had given up on Booth.

It was not an easy break for Arnold. He had been out at his uncle's farm in Hookstown, near Pimlico, when he learned that Booth wanted to see him. By the time he got to Barnum's Hotel, Booth had already left. So Arnold went home to mull things over. He still wanted to be done with the plot, but he did not want to leave on such a harsh note. So that evening, he sat down to put his feelings in a letter. He wrote that Booth's summons had taken him by surprise, as he had not expected to hear anything more of their enterprise for a month or so, and that a revival of their plot now would raise suspicions among Arnold's family. He urged Booth to avoid any rash or hasty action, and suggested he "see how it will be taken in R——d" before doing anything at all. He hoped his position would not jeopardize his friendship with Booth, and offered to meet personally with him during the following week.

Arnold was not so sure he should have written this, but there was a lot he wanted to get off his chest. He finally mailed it, but only after thinking it over for a few days.[5]

AT SEVEN O'CLOCK on the morning of March 28, George Atzerodt and Marcellus Bailey walked into the Pennsylvania House, worn out and bedraggled. They had gone out the night before, after solemnly announcing to the manager, John Greenawalt, that they had to go away. Greenawalt figured he would never see them again. But here they were, looking half dead, and asking if Room 51 were still available. They took the key and dragged themselves up the stairs.

Later that day they went to Baltimore in the company of a mutual friend, Walter Barnes. Bailey and Barnes took a room on High Street, very close to Mike O'Laughlen's house. Their business there has never been discovered, and indeed the whole subject got lost in the post-assassination frenzy. But they stayed there until the assassination—long enough for the lady of the house to decide that they were a couple of drunken louts. Atzerodt checked in on them occasionally, but he couldn't stay for long; he didn't dare stray too far from Booth.[6]

George Atzerodt rarely left Washington after mid-March, but not because Booth considered him indispensable. More likely, he just wanted to watch him closely. Atzerodt was often drunk, and he was reckless when in his cups. Indeed, Booth probably never knew the worst of it. Atzerodt had boasted of having friends who could make him rich. He talked about Surratt's travels, and he even showed Brooke Stabler a letter Surratt had written him from New York. Several times he seemed on the verge of telling a secret, but each time, his face squeezed into a broad, sly grin, and he said that he was only joking. He even told his sister Katherine—the wife of a federal marshal—that he would soon get rich or die on the gallows. Neither Booth nor Surratt could control such a person, but they could neutralize the damage. They fed Atzerodt false information, and sometimes questioned his sanity.[7]

By the end of March, David Herold was coming regularly to the Pennsylvania House, often staying for three or four hours at a time. He and Atzerodt had known each other casually for years, and they got along well. They went to the circus together, to the "leg shows" at Canterbury Hall, and, of course, to bars. They were kindred souls—pranksters with a passion for fun and a gift for underachievement. Both had been teased as children and had used humor to disarm their tormentors. Neither had outgrown the habit, or the immaturity; a bout of flatulence might have them chuckling intermittently for half an hour.[8]

BOOTH OFTEN STOPPED at the Surratt boardinghouse, and he was always welcome there. The residents all liked him, and each visit was a special treat to the ladies, who brushed and primped whenever he was announced. Atzerodt was received less ceremoniously, but he was there just as often. Both had business with John Surratt, but frequently spoke with Mrs. Surratt when John was away.[9]

Contrary to the common understanding, though, Mary Surratt's house was not the conspirators' primary meeting place, nor did they all live there. Herold had been there only once, and Powell stayed there just twice. Arnold and O'Laughlen had never been inside the place. The conspirators typically met at stables, and Booth was known to show up at Howard's as often as six times a day. He checked in on Atzerodt at the Pennsylvania House, and Arnold and O'Laughlen at Rullman's Hotel, but he never called them together at Mrs. Surratt's.

John Surratt was seldom at his mother's house. He made his Richmond-to-Montreal run every thirty-five days or so, and he generally stayed in Southern Maryland the rest of the time. His mother claimed she wanted him to stay away from Washington. As she later told investigators, "I thought it better for him to be in Maryland than here, where there were restaurants and bad company. I thought it was not the place for a boy."[10]

MICHAEL O'LAUGHLEN WANTED OUT of the conspiracy, but he couldn't just walk out. Booth was a lifelong friend, and he would be devastated if any hard feelings came between them. So on March 30, he went up to Hookstown to seek advice from Sam Arnold. Both men had gone through the same inner struggle, and in fact Arnold had just taken three days to mail that heartfelt letter to Booth. But unlike O'Laughlen, he had an easy way out. John "Wickey" Wharton, a friend of his father's, needed a clerk for his sutler's store outside Fortress Monroe. If Arnold got the job, it would take him a long way from Washington. Then, should anything come of Booth's scheme, he might be in the clear—that is, as long as Booth destroyed that letter.

After talking with each other, Arnold and O'Laughlen were more anxious than ever about Booth's plans. O'Laughlen suggested they both go to Washington. Booth still owed him five hundred dollars, and it would be a little easier to ask for it if Arnold were there for moral support. So they took the next train out, and when they arrived in Washington, they saw George Atzerodt at the B&O station. Atzerodt told them that Booth wanted to resurrect his scheme. The president was expected to show up at Ford's Theatre that very night, he said, and they were planning to abduct him there.

That news sent Arnold and O'Laughlen hurrying to the National Hotel in a full panic. But Booth hastened to put their minds at ease. They were not going to capture Lincoln that night, or any other night, for that matter. The plot was finished. John Surratt had gone to Richmond, and the president was out of town. Booth was going back to the stage, and had no intention of reviving the conspiracy. Relieved, Arnold asked what they should do with the pistols, and Booth said they could keep them, sell them, or do whatever they wanted with them. He had made this easy for them, and almost as an afterthought, Arnold mentioned that letter, and said that he hoped Booth would destroy it. Booth assured him he had nothing to worry about.

Arnold knew better. The goal might be different, but the plot had not been abandoned. It would go on without him, and that was a frightening thought. His incriminating letter could still be used against him—by Booth on the one hand, or by the government on the other. Either way, he was in trouble. And though Booth promised to destroy that letter, Arnold could hardly have missed his unspoken message: *We're not going to hurt each other, are we?* He took the next available ship to Fortress Monroe.[11]

THE PRESIDENT AND MRS. LINCOLN had just been there the previous week. The Lincolns had stopped at Fortress Monroe on the way to visit General Grant at City Point. Grant had already begun a major thrust against the enemy, and he was optimistic that the war would be over soon. A series of assaults had dislodged Lee's army from its trenches near Petersburg, and by April 2, the Confederates would no longer be able to protect their capital. The Appomattox campaign was under way.

Booth was depressed over the news, and family visits had demoralized him even more. There was always a palpable tension between him and Edwin, who gloated over the North's success and taunted his brother with charges of false patriotism. Though they tried to avoid open warfare in the presence of their mother, Mary Ann was not fooled. The whole business saddened her, and she opened her heart in a letter to John Wilkes.

New York
March 28th

My dear boy
   I have just got yours. I was very glad to hear from you, & hope you will write often. I did part with you sadly—& I still feel sad, very much so. June has just left me. he staid as long as he could. I am now quite alone. Rose has not returned yet—I feel miserable enough. I never yet doubted your love & devotion to me—in fact I always gave you praise for being the fondest of all my boys—but since you leave me to grief, I must doubt it—I am no Roman Mother I love my dear ones, before Country or any thing else.
   Heaven guard you is my constant prayer.[12]

Mary Ann was resigned to an unhappy future. She knew that John Wilkes would throw himself, heart and soul, into a last-ditch effort to save the Confederacy. It would be a futile gesture, and possibly a fatal one. But she never imagined the enormity of his plans.

In hindsight, it should not have come as a surprise. Even as a child, John Wilkes had dreamed of glory. His role models were the heroes and martyrs of history, brought to life in the poems of Byron, the books of Plutarch, the plays of Shakespeare, Schiller, and Payne. They were no mere foot soldiers; they were giants, immortalized by the teachings of the elder Booth. With all the odds against them, they had fought to the death in a last-ditch effort to stave off tyranny.

There were Democrats now who called for the same kind of hero. Lincoln, to them, was Caesar in need of a Brutus. Indeed, the parallels were often noted. Caesar won his own civil war by the use of self-declared powers. He instituted martial law, and argued its necessity for as long as the war lasted. But when the fighting stopped, the tyranny did not, and thus ended the Roman republic.

The president's opponents did not mince words. "Let us also remind Lincoln," said one speaker at a New York rally, "that Caesar had his Brutus and Charles the First his Cromwell. Let us also remind the George the Third of the present day that he, too, may have his Cromwell or his Brutus." The same warning was sounded in public assemblies, on editorial pages, and in the halls of Congress. As one senator said, "Is this an American Congress or a Roman Senate in the most abject days of the Roman empire? . . . How much more are we to take?"

Booth believed it was pointless to take any more. He was convinced that most people wanted Lincoln out of office, yet the election process had failed to remove him. There was only one option left, and Booth must have hinted at it during the Gautier's meeting. When Arnold wrote, "I would prefer your first query 'go and see how it will be taken in R———d,'" "it" was the change of plans—a change that affected the whole nature of the conspiracy. Though Booth dared not say it, his plot to seize the president had become a conspiracy to kill him.[13]

It would not happen any time soon. The Lincolns were still at City Point, and the president himself had no immediate plans to return. The war was going extremely well, and when Richmond was finally taken, Abraham Lincoln wanted to see the fruits of victory with his own eyes.

FROM SOMEWHERE IN NEW YORK, John Surratt wrote to Atzerodt and instructed him to sell the horses he had been keeping at Howard's. Atzerodt was not the best person for the job, though. Too many stablemen had seen those horses before, and they had all been told that Booth or Surratt owned them. So eventually Booth had to get involved. At the beginning of April, he and Atzerodt took the horses to Nailor's Stable, at Fourteenth and E streets, across from Willard's, and asked to board them indefinitely. Booth told Fletcher, the stableman, that both horses belonged to him. He was going to Philadelphia, he said, and he wanted Atzerodt to sell them in his absence.[14]

ON THE MORNING OF APRIL 3, Confederate forces evacuated Richmond, fleeing to the south and west ahead of pursuing troops. They set tobacco warehouses and railroad bridges on fire as they left, and unexpectedly, a change in wind direction sent flames sweeping through the commercial district. By the time federal troops arrived, more than eight hundred buildings had been destroyed. The leading symbol of Southern culture and power had become a ruin.

Mrs. Surratt must have been frantic with worry. Her son spent a great deal of his time in Richmond, and indeed, he was on his way there the last time she saw him. But at about half past six on the evening of the third, John Surratt arrived at the boardinghouse unfazed and apparently unaware of recent developments. He was surprised to hear that the rebel capital had been abandoned. "I saw Benjamin and Davis in Richmond," he told Weichmann, "and they told me it would not be evacuated." Surratt went straight upstairs to change his clothes. He asked if anyone in the house could exchange some gold for greenbacks. John Holohan changed some of his money, but neither he nor anybody else could match the two hundred dollars Surratt was carrying. After taking a quick meal in his room, Surratt went downstairs to bid his mother goodbye. He said that he was going to Canada and had to leave right away. Mrs. Surratt pointed out that another draft had been called, and he had neglected to finish paying for an exemption. He said he wasn't worried about the draft, but would take care of it.[15]

THE FALL OF RICHMOND was just one part of a bleak picture in the final days of the Confederacy. The fight against hunger became a war in itself, and the Davis government pulled out all the stops to feed its armies, then in full retreat. There was said to be plenty of food in the direction of their march, but it was so far ahead of them that they might have to surrender before they could reach it. Crops were abundant in or near the occupied lands of Virginia, but foraging there was a dangerous business, and the Confederate government was compelled to offer enormous bounties to anyone willing to do it at the risk of capture. Nevertheless, people did what they could. Citizens poached from U.S. Army stores, and Mosby sent hundreds of Rangers down the Northern Neck in search of provisions.[16]

GEORGE ATZERODT FINALLY SOLD one of Booth's horses. Though John Greenawalt had misgivings, he bought the smaller animal for $140. Atzerodt, who once boasted of his rich friends, now admitted that poverty had forced him to let the horse go so cheaply. From now on, Booth would have to rent horses. Though he still owned the one-eyed horse, he apparently had no intention of riding it. As John Surratt said, it had a tendency to pull up and freeze in its tracks—not the kind of animal one would choose for a quick getaway.[17]

BOOTH WAS IN NEWPORT, Rhode Island, when Richmond fell. That morning, he and Lucy Hale checked in to the Aquidneck House on Pelham Street. After signing the register as "J. W. Booth and Lady, Boston," they went out for a walk, and were gone for hours. They returned in dismal spirits, and Booth told the desk clerk that the lady was not feeling well. He asked that a dinner be sent up to their room, but they were gone before it was delivered. Something had caused an abrupt change in their plans, and they left for Boston on the next available train.[18]

MARY LINCOLN HAD LEFT her husband in City Point and was back in Washington when two White House policemen came to her with a request. Joseph Shelton and John F. Parker were about to be drafted, and hoped that their service in the Executive Mansion would exempt them. Ideally, they would have liked to have a note from the president, but since he was out of town, they appealed to Mrs. Lincoln for help. She obligingly sent two notes to Provost Marshal O'Beirne.[19]

Though the White House was secure, not so the president. On hearing that Richmond had fallen, Lincoln insisted on having a look at the rebel capital. He and a small entourage, including his young son Tad, set out in Admiral Porter's flagship, the *Malvern*, on a journey that tested the nerves of everyone but, apparently, the president himself. Wrecked ships and dead horses often blocked their path, and several times they transferred to successively smaller boats in order to get past the obstructions. By the time Lincoln finally reached the city, he was in the admiral's launch—literally, a rowboat—with only Tad and a few naval officers. His marine detachment had been left behind, and six navy oarsmen formed his escort through the streets of the enemy capital. The place had never been swept for sharpshooters, and at six feet four inches, Abraham Lincoln was an easy target. But fate spared him, at least for now.[20]

ON APRIL 5, Secretary of State Seward met with a serious accident near his home in Washington. He and his family were going out for a drive when they stopped to pick up a friend of his daughter Fanny. When Henry, the driver, stepped down to open the door, the horses jumped and the carriage lurched forward. Frederick reached out to grab the reins, but missed and fell to the ground, injuring himself. Suddenly the team bolted and headed down Vermont Avenue at breakneck speed. Secretary Seward tried to jump out when the horses slowed for the turn onto H Street, but he misjudged the turn and was thrown violently to the pavement. Bystanders carried him home unconscious, his face bruised and swollen beyond recognition. His jaw was broken in two places, and his right arm had snapped just below the shoulder.[21]

JOHN SURRATT CHECKED IN to the St. Lawrence Hall in Montreal. He signed the hotel register as "John Harrison," though Confederates knew him as Charley Armstrong. By the time Surratt arrived on the morning of April 6, operatives here had heard all about Richmond's collapse. Neither Jefferson Davis nor his armies had surrendered, though, and until they did, the war was still on. Gen. Edwin Gray Lee, in charge of the Canadian operation, no longer had enough people to cover his assignments, so when Surratt came to him with some dispatches, Lee offered him a spying mission. The government was contemplating a raid on the Elmira prison in New York, and Lee needed someone to survey the place beforehand. Surratt jumped at the chance. He had tried to catch up with Booth on the way to Montreal, but when he stopped at Edwin's house in New York, John Wilkes was not there.[22]

Booth was still in Boston. After dropping Lucy off with friends, he went to see Edwin, who had just begun an engagement in the Boston Theatre. Rehearsals were under way for *Hamlet* when Booth went backstage and crept up behind actress Rachel Noah. "Hello, little girl!" he whispered. "They tell me you've been getting married since I saw you." He seemed in a playful mood, and Rachel chatted with him while she waited for her cue. She asked when he was going to act again, and he said that he had grown tired of all those months on the road. He might play again, but only in New York, Boston, and Philadelphia.

When the rehearsal was over, he went to his brother's dressing room for a talk. Edwin's dresser was a black man from Richmond, and John Wilkes addressed him first. "Well, Jim, Richmond has fallen at last. What do you think of it?"

"Yes," he said. "Poor Richmond!"

"Sorry, you rascal?" said Edwin. "You ought to be glad; it has been a great blessing to mankind that it has fallen." John Wilkes would not take the bait, and for once, he left without a fight. He had come all the way from Washington, and his business with Edwin was over in a few minutes. We have never learned what it was.

Booth could not leave Boston without seeing Orlando Tompkins. They had known each other for years, and Booth had often been a guest in the Tompkins home. He stopped there now, unannounced, and asked Orlando to take a walk with him. They went to a jewelry store, where Booth surprised his friend with a bloodstone ring inscribed "JWB to OT, April 6, 1865." Asked what the occasion was, he said, "I'll never see you again."[23]

Returning to New York, Booth ran into Sam Chester, and they sat down for a glass of ale. It seemed to Chester that Booth had already had enough to drink. He had spent the past few hours in bars, and was getting hard to control. At one point he spotted actor Harry Wall from across the room, and said, "I always wanted to like Harry Wall, but I don't like him for one thing." Wall had once revealed to Booth that he was a government detective, and since then, Booth couldn't bring himself to like the man, try as he might. Booth's surly, combative manner was embarrassing, and Chester said that perhaps they ought to go somewhere else. Maybe they should look for John McCullough, who was in town and hoping to meet up with him.

On Booth's suggestion, they went to the House of Lords instead. But as soon as they sat down, he started up with a man at the next table. Booth thought the man was eavesdropping, and voiced his objection loudly. "If there is one thing I despise more than another," he bellowed, "it is a damned scoundrel that will listen to what others are saying. Let us go away from him."

They moved to another table, and Booth calmed down. He brought up the abduction conspiracy, and assured Chester that he had completely abandoned the scheme. He had spent a fortune on the plot, he said, and was now forced to sell off horses to recover some of his losses. Chester tried to steer the conversation elsewhere, but that worked only for a moment. He was trying to say something when suddenly Booth slammed his hand down on the table. "What an excellent chance I had to kill the President, if I had wished, on Inauguration Day!" he said. "I was on the stand, as close to him nearly as I am to you."

Sam Chester was astonished. "You're crazy, John. What good would that do?" he asked.

"I could live in history," Booth replied. Sam said that there was glory enough in a successful stage career, if he would just attend to it.

Booth shook his head, mildly amused. "I could never reason with you. You're just like my brother Edwin," he said, which led to more talk of the family split. Chester noticed that as Booth talked, he kept kissing a ring on his little finger. He explained that he was engaged to be married, and despite what Chester thought, this was not just another crazy idea; he was deeply in love with the lady. She came from a good family, and in fact it was she who had given him a ticket to the inauguration. Her only objection to Booth, he said, was that he was an actor; his only objection to her was that she was an abolitionist.

Booth insisted on paying for their supper. He had already forgotten his candid admission, just moments earlier, that he was broke. Now, once again, he was faking success. "Petroleum pays for this," he said proudly.[24]

Booth stopped in Philadelphia on his way back to the capital, and dashed off a note to Chester. "Plead my excuses to John McCullough and tell him I am sorry that I could not see him that day. . . . Tell him I am going to Oil City." He saw William Sinn, an old friend and theater manager, on Chestnut Street, and started up a conversation. "You will hear from me in Washington," Booth said. "I am going to make a big hit."[25]

ON THE NIGHT OF APRIL 9, Booth returned to Washington and checked in to the National Hotel. He really hadn't given up on his plot, as he had told Chester, but by now only a few of his people were still involved. Time was running out.

The following day, newspapers carried the most sensational news in years.

SURRENDER OF LEE

AND

HIS WHOLE ARMY!

GRANT'S TERMS ACCEPTED!

Robert E. Lee surrendered his troops at Appomattox Court House, and a war that had cost the lives of 623,000 men would almost certainly be over soon. As the *Evening Star* said, "When Lee, the wisest and bravest of the confederate leaders, sees no ray of hope for the confederate cause, and voluntarily lays down his arms to prevent the further and futile effusion of blood, the most credulous optimist among his followers must accept his judgment as decisive."[26]

The city of Washington would fall into one long, loud, drunken jubilee. Mosby's Rangers were not quite ready to celebrate. Lee had surrendered his *regular* forces, but the Rangers were not so sure that they were included in the arrangement. They looked to Mosby himself for guidance, and late on April 9, they broke off their forage mission in the Northern Neck and headed north to consult with the colonel. But they left with a drove of cattle and a large number of wagons full of forage. Local farmers were enraged. They insisted the war was over, and they should no longer be forced to provide food to the army.

WHEN THE NEWS of Lee's surrender reached Washington, Abraham Lincoln was still on the *River Queen,* steaming back from his trip to Richmond and City Point. On his arrival he went straight to the home of Secretary Seward and talked with him for a while. He did not see Grant's telegram until after he retired to the White House—and that was two hours after it reached the War Department, right next door.[27]

Newspapers broke the story on Monday, and that's when the parties began. Thousands poured into the city, drinking, singing hymns, and setting bonfires. Everywhere the masses gathered, some aspiring orator would offer a few remarks; these words, mixed with alcohol, produced a euphoria unknown in Washington for years. A crowd of two thousand had worked its way from the navy yard to the Executive Mansion, and their cheers and whistles finally coaxed the president into making an appearance. Lincoln said he was "very much rejoiced" that people could finally give vent to their feelings, and he assumed there would be a formal celebration the following night. "Should such a demonstration take place, I of course will be expected to respond, if called upon, and if I permit you to dribble it out of me now, I will have nothing left to say on that occasion."

The band of the Quartermaster's Corps had come with the crowd, and they caught the president's eye. "I observe that you have a band of music with you," he said. "I have always thought that 'Dixie' was one of the best tunes I had ever heard. Our adversaries over the way, I know, have attempted to appropriate it, but I insist that on yesterday we fairly captured it. . . . I referred the question to the Attorney General and he gave it as his legal opinion that it is now our property. I now ask the band to favor us with a performance." He left the crowd cheering and clapping to the strains of the "captured" anthem.

Meanwhile, hundreds of revelers assembled at the War Department to cheer Secretary Stanton and his staff. Stanton was still preoccupied with the business of war, but a couple of lesser officials stood up to harangue the crowd. Somewhere among the masses were George Atzerodt and Lou Weichmann. Atzerodt seemed elated at the news—cheering wildly, and perhaps going overboard with glee. Weichmann thought he was acting crazy, and he told him so. His remark stopped Atzerodt cold. The smile left his face, and he turned to Weichmann in all seriousness, and said, "You will find out before long that I am not half as crazy as you imagine."[28]

A mile to the east, John Wilkes Booth would not even pretend to celebrate. Despondent over the surrender, Booth took out his frustrations at a pistol gallery on Pennsylvania Avenue. After shooting for a while, he walked up to the Surratt boardinghouse, where he encountered Lou Weichmann. They talked of Lee's surrender, and Weichmann said something about the Confederacy having "gone up."

"No!" Booth snapped. "It is not gone up yet." Excitedly, he pulled a map out of his pocket and pointed out how Joe Johnston might still escape from Sherman. He seemed to be getting himself worked up, and Weichmann became uncomfortable. He changed the topic, and asked Booth why he was not still acting. Booth said that he was done with the stage, and the only play he wanted to present now was *Venice Preserved*. That was a pointed message, but Weichmann didn't get it. That eighteenth-century play involved a plot to assassinate the leaders of Venice. The lead conspirator happens to be married to a senator's daughter.[29]

Wandering the streets again, Booth ran into Henry B. Phillips, of Ford's Theatre, who invited him to take a drink with a couple of friends. "Yes," said Booth, "anything to chase away the blues." When asked what he meant, Booth said that the news from Appomattox "was enough to give anyone the blues." Phillips's friends happened to be government employees, and he did not want to see Booth talk his way into trouble. So he changed the subject and led the way to Birch's Saloon.[30]

At eight o'clock, Booth appeared at Pumphrey's Stable and said he needed a horse he could keep overnight. He wanted to take a trip into the country, and he preferred the sorrel that he had been renting lately. Pumphrey said that that horse was out, and he suggested Booth check again later. Instead, Booth walked over to Ford's Theatre. There, he told Ned Spangler that he had no further use for his buggy, as he would soon be leaving town. He asked Ned to clean it up and sell it.

While they were talking, John Mathews walked by. Booth still held a grudge against Mathews for refusing to join his plot. Mathews had done all he could to smooth things over, even presenting Booth with a gift. Booth's response was cynical to the core. He reciprocated by giving Mathews a long black lacquer box he had once used for his theatrical swords. It seemed a touching gesture, but it came with a hitch: authorities would someday come looking for such a box, since Booth had been using one just like it to transport carbines.[31]

LOU WEICHMANN TOOK TUESDAY, April 11, off work. The night before, Mrs. Surratt had asked him to drive her to Surrattsville so she could settle some financial matters. An old land transaction had left her late husband indebted to the Calvert family since 1852, and the Calverts had already won two judgments against him in court. Now George H. Calvert was pressuring Mrs. Surratt to pay up so he could close the books on his late father's estate. But Mary Surratt did not have that kind of money on hand. In order to settle with Calvert, she had to call in a debt from John Nothey, who lived a mile or two from the tavern. Nothey had once bought seventy-five acres from the Surratts, and he still owed $479 on it.

The first thing in the morning, Mrs. Surratt asked Weichmann to go ask Booth if they could borrow his carriage. Booth said that he had sold it, but he gave Weichmann ten dollars to rent one, and by nine o'clock, Weichmann and Mrs. Surratt were on the road. They had just crossed the Navy Yard Bridge when they happened to recognize John M. Lloyd in another carriage, heading toward the city. Lloyd got down out of his carriage to speak with Mrs. Surratt. As he recalled later, she started right off talking about Gus Howell, the spy, who had been arrested a few weeks before in the Surrattsville tavern. She said that, if necessary, she would go personally to General Augur or Judge Levi Turner to secure his release. Then she said something that Lloyd did not quite understand. He asked what she meant, and she came right out with it: *Are those firearms still hidden at the tavern?* Lloyd said they were; he had shoved them back out of sight, and nobody had ever come to get them. She said he ought to get them ready, as they would be called for soon.[32]

Mrs. Surratt and Weichmann arrived in Surrattsville at midday, and right away she sent word to Nothey that she wanted to see him. They continued on to the home of Bennett F. Gwynn, a few miles farther south, where they took dinner and talked for a while. Gwynn had been involved in the original transaction with Nothey, and he returned to Surrattsville with Mrs. Surratt, just in case a dispute arose. They found Nothey waiting for them, and after a brief discussion, Mrs. Surratt went home empty-handed.

John Lloyd was on his way home as well. He had run into George Atzerodt in Uniontown, outside Washington, and asked him about those carbines. Lloyd said he was a little confused by Mrs. Surratt's instructions. What, exactly, should he do with those weapons? Atzerodt didn't know, but he ad-libbed a response: *Bury them.*[33]

Edman Spangler had spent the day at Tattersall's horse market, trying to sell Booth's carriage. As of late afternoon, though, nobody was willing to meet the $260 reserve. So Spangler brought it back to Baptist Alley, and he asked Booth what he should do next. Booth said he should try to sell it privately. "You will help me, won't you?" he asked.

Spangler said, "Of course."[34]

THE "GRAND ILLUMINATION" PLANNED for that evening was postponed, but President Lincoln did not put off the speech he had promised the day before. A crowd had gathered outside the White House, and at dusk, Lincoln appeared at a window in the north portico with a written address. His tone was serious. "We meet this evening not in sorrow, but in gladness of heart," he began. He promised a day of national thanksgiving, then went on to praise General Grant and all those who had contributed to the recent victory. The next great hurdle would be reconstruction. He suggested that the plan he had followed in Louisiana had worked well enough in the past few years, and despite some grumbling, it ought to serve as a benchmark for other states of the South. He acknowledged that everyone would be happier if the new government had a larger constituency of loyal men, but at least the states would have a new cooperative order.

Standing just below, at the front of the crowd, were John Wilkes Booth and Dave Herold. As the president delivered his speech, they listened closely for signs that he intended to pursue a radical course against the South. What caught Booth's attention in particular was Lincoln's suggestion on a subject that few had dared, so far, to touch: voting rights for African Americans. As the president put it: "It is also satisfactory to some that the elective franchise is not given to the colored man. I would myself prefer that it were now conferred on the very intelligent, and on those who serve our cause as soldiers."

That was all Booth needed to hear. "That means nigger citizenship," he fumed. "Now, by God, I'll put him through." He turned on his heels and pushed his way out of the crowd.[35]

NED SPANGLER FINALLY SOLD Booth's carriage, but he got only $250 for it. The buyer came to Ford's on Wednesday morning, but Booth wasn't around, so he asked Jim Gifford to close the deal on Booth's behalf. If Booth still entertained any notions of capturing the president, the disposal of that carriage would make it almost impossible; after all, an inconspicuous vehicle had always been a necessary component of the escape. Though a rented carriage might have served just as well, he could not count on finding a suitable one on short notice.

In time, Booth did stop at Ford's, but only to pick up his mail. Tom Raybold, Harry Ford, and Joseph Sessford were sitting in the box office when he came in. Booth greeted them with a sullen announcement: "We are all slaves now." Four years ago, abolitionists were the outcasts, almost universally condemned for stirring up war. But now the situation was reversed. "If a man were to go out and insult a nigger now," Booth said, "he would be knocked down by the nigger and nothing would be done to the nigger."

Tom Raybold replied, "You should not insult a nigger then."

Harry Ford smirked. Though he and Booth had once been close, politics had come between them. The breaking point had come a few months earlier, in an argument at Mr. Petersen's house across the street. Booth had launched into one of his tirades and quickly found himself outnumbered. Ford, Charles Warwick, and John Mathews all argued against him, and Ford threw a few jabs that could not be taken back. Since then, a coolness had existed among them. Of the other three, only Mathews felt compelled to make up.[36]

RICHARD SMOOT AND JAMES BRAWNER had still not received the rest of their money for the boat. Smoot had tried repeatedly to collect the balance, but John Surratt always managed to put him off in one way or another. Now he came looking for his money again. On Wednesday afternoon, he showed up at the H Street boardinghouse in search of John Surratt. The lady of the house, as he later recalled, gave him "a penetrating look" and curtly informed him that she did not know the whereabouts of her son. But when Smoot told her the nature of his business, Mrs. Surratt's demeanor changed. "Her face brightened up, and she extended me a most cordial greeting, and eagerly inquired if the boat was in its place and readily accessible, as it might be called into requisition that night." Then, as if suddenly reminded of something, she got an anxious expression and told Smoot he must leave at once. He might see her son and "the boys" on Friday night. They planned to be back in Washington by then.[37]

GENERAL ULYSSES S. GRANT ARRIVED with his wife and staff aboard the steamer *Mollie Martin* on Thursday morning, April 13. They took rooms at Willard's Hotel, and the general wasted no time demobilizing the army. He went straight to the War Department and recommended that Secretary Stanton take immediate steps to halt the draft and recruiting; curtail purchases of arms and supplies; reduce the number of officers and government personnel; and lift all trade restrictions with Richmond. The measures should begin saving money almost immediately.

The "grand illumination" had been rescheduled for that night, so Grant could witness the festivities. He had never been one for public appearances and, like the president, was content to keep a low profile that evening. Mrs. Lincoln had invited the general out for a drive around the city; otherwise, they had no plans.[38]

Not so with Booth. Much had changed since he formed his plot. The Confederate armies had either surrendered or were in full retreat, their capital taken, and all hope of independence lost. The president's abduction had been of questionable value for months, and it now seemed entirely pointless. Yet Booth had not given up. He continued to skulk around the theater, laying out schemes and keeping in touch with the few conspirators who remained. He was planning something, and very likely, Grant's arrival would make this a perfect night to strike.

Even the date seemed right. An assassination on April 13 would reemphasize how fate had driven Booth, and how history had guided him. Not only was it the birthday of Jefferson, but in the ancient Roman calendar it was a day of reckoning—the Ides. The symbolism was not lost on Booth. But in case anyone else should miss the point, he would script his own act in conscious imitation of the killing of Caesar. He would strike down the president in public, preferably in a theater. He would use a derringer made in a place called Northern Liberties. He would carry a dagger ornately etched with "America, Land of the Free" on its blade. He would commit the act in full view of an audience, with an accompanying message, in Latin, that would explain it all: *Thus always to tyrants.*

Booth knew that in the end, the Brutus conspiracy was foiled by Marc Antony, whose famous oration made outlaws of the assassins and a martyr of Caesar. The conspirators had always considered Antony an autocrat who cast aside the law, pandered to the masses, and reveled in unprecedented powers of his own making. They wanted to kill him along with the emperor, but Brutus would not allow it. That was a mistake that Booth had no intention of repeating. Lincoln had his own Antony, and the Booth conspiracy would target him as well. He was William H. Seward.[39]

For Booth, the need to kill Seward was a foregone conclusion. From his earliest days in the Senate to the present time, William Seward had consistently put himself on the opposite pole from any trend, law, or proposal favored by anyone in Booth's circle. His "higher law" doctrine set the Border States on edge. His appeal to immigrant Catholics infuriated Know-Nothings. His "irrepressible conflict" speech accelerated the march to war. Though a founder of the Republican party, Seward was considered too extreme to bear its standard. As secretary of state, he gave himself unprecedented powers, then boasted of having them. When "Seward's prisoners" appealed for mercy, he typically turned a deaf ear. For all his presumptions, William Seward made himself a target of Congress, the courts, and even his colleagues in the Cabinet, who considered him the most "meddlesome and intriguing" politician in memory. He was a man of insatiable ambition, and as a practical matter (though not a legal one), he was one of the few men capable of filling the power vacuum in the event of Lincoln's death.[40]

Preparations were soon under way. On Thursday morning, Lewis Powell strolled up to the Seward house and struck up a conversation with a male nurse who was having breakfast just inside the front window. Powell asked how the secretary was doing, and George F. Robinson said that his condition had improved. With a smile and a touch of the hat, Powell went on his way. Even then, he had his target in sight.

At the same time, Booth went to Baltimore in hopes of coaxing Mike O'Laughlen back into the conspiracy. O'Laughlen may have assumed that after Lee's surrender, Booth would have given up. But this visit dispelled all doubts. Though Booth returned to Washington without him, O'Laughlen could not rest easy knowing what kind of trouble might be heading his way. He had to talk Booth out of it.[41]

Back in Washington that afternoon, Booth barged into the manager's office at the National Theatre and interrupted a script reading. Manager C. Dwight Hess was startled by the intrusion; he had never known Booth to be so thoughtless. Booth seemed anxious to know what Hess had planned for the evening. Though he was going to illuminate, Hess said he had bigger plans for the night of the fourteenth. He was mounting a spectacular production that night to commemorate the fall of Fort Sumter exactly four years before.

"Are you going to invite the president?" Booth asked.

"Yes," was the reply. Hess had always dealt with Mrs. Lincoln on such matters, and Booth's visit reminded him to send her an invitation.[42]

MIKE O'LAUGHLEN DID NOT WANT to go to Washington alone, so he invited some friends to come along and see the illumination. They took the 3:30 train. Edward Murphy, James B. Henderson, and Bernard J. Early were more than just companions; they were witnesses who could vouch for O'Laughlen's movements throughout the day. All were men of unquestioned loyalty—especially Henderson, who was a naval officer traveling in full uniform. Their train arrived in Washington just past five, and after taking a few drinks at Rullman's, O'Laughlen and Early walked over to the National Hotel. Early waited in the lobby while O'Laughlen went upstairs to look for a friend.[43]

. . .

JOHN WILKES BOOTH SENT Herold and Atzerodt to the Kirkwood House, where Vice President Andrew Johnson was staying. He wanted Atzerodt to ask the vice president for a pass to go to Richmond. In the meantime, he went over to Ford's to reacquaint himself with the passageways and alleys, and he did the same at the National just in case the president should appear there. Sometime in the afternoon, he was back at Ford's yet again, sitting in the dress circle to watch Laura Keene and company rehearse for *Peggy the Actress*. Though he knew the place well, it was probably helpful to plan while actually on the premises.[44]

Thousands of people flooded into the city for the grand illumination. The human tide, which had been rising throughout the day, began to crest at sundown. It was a grand celebration, but not an organized one; it spread by its own momentum. At Willard's Hotel, gas jets formed the word "Union" in a large semicircle over the roof. The Patent Office had the most ambitious display, with five thousand candles lighting up the evening sky. A few blocks to the south, crowds surged onto Pennsylvania Avenue, forming swirls of confusion at every major intersection. Over this sea of life rose the dome of the Capitol, brilliantly lit as never before. An *Evening Star* correspondent could only describe it in otherworldly terms: "The very heavens seemed to have come down, and the stars twinkled in a sort of faded way, as if the solar system was out of order, and each had become the great luminary."

Mike O'Laughlen wandered the streets that night, looking at the displays, listening to the bands, and trying desperately to be noticed with someone other than John Wilkes Booth. He and his friends needed a place to stay, and though Rullman's was a great favorite, he didn't think it was a good idea to go there, or anyplace associated with the plot. So after dinner he took his friends down to Sixth and Pennsylvania, and they all checked in to the Metropolitan Hotel. The clerk assigned O'Laughlen to Room 45, and his friends took an adjoining room.[45]

HEROLD AND ATZERODT CAUGHT UP with Booth in Lewis Powell's room at the Herndon House. In contrast to the drunken revelry on the street below, the mood in Room 6 was deadly serious. The laughter, the cheers, the martial music were all in celebration of Southern defeat. Now Booth was going to shut those people up. He would take away their leader.

There was nothing elaborate about the plan. Booth would assassinate the president, and Powell would kill Secretary of State Seward. Herold and Atzerodt were to go back to the Kirkwood House and kill Vice President Johnson. The attacks would be timed to coincide, and they could all meet up afterward on the road to Nanjemoy. Powell, if he chose, could "skedaddle" in a different direction.

All of this was news to Atzerodt, and even soaked in alcohol, his mind could see the trap he had fallen into. He was not a killer, and he had no intention of becoming one. But by now he was in too deeply, and there was nothing he could do. He voiced his objections, but Booth shrugged them off. "Then we will do it," he said. "At least Herold has the courage. But what will become of you? You had better come along and *get your horse.*"

Those horses! Booth's subtle reminder struck terror in Atzerodt's heart. For six weeks he had swapped and shared animals with Booth, and had gone all over the city trying to sell them on his behalf. Every transaction had a witness, and every witness could tie him to the president's killer. So it didn't matter what he did now; he was already a dead man. He left the hotel and rented a horse. In a short while, he would check out of the Pennsylvania House. He had no plans to return.[46]

THE LINCOLNS DID NOT SEE the illumination with General Grant. The president stayed home with a severe headache, and the general and his wife ended up joining dozens of War Department employees for a party at Secretary Stanton's home. Four military bands serenaded from Franklin Square, and guests gathered on the front steps for a spectacular fireworks display.

Sgt. John C. Hatter was standing on the top doorstep when a man in a dark suit asked him if General Grant was in. "This is no occasion for you to see him," said the sergeant. "If you wish to see him, step out on the pavement, or on the stone where the carriage stops, and you can see him." Apparently, just getting a glimpse of the general wasn't what the man had in mind. He stepped off to the side and seemed to reflect on something. In a moment, he was gone.

After finishing his duties for the night, Major Kilburn Knox came over from the War Department and joined the party. The Stantons and the Grants had gone out on the steps by then to see the fireworks, and Knox took his place in front of them. He was standing there when a stranger asked, "Is Stanton in?"

"I suppose you mean the Secretary?" asked Knox.

"Yes," said the man. "I am a lawyer in town. I know him very well." Knox told the man he could not disturb Mr. Stanton. But as he said this, the stranger caught a glimpse of the secretary, and he walked over to him. He said nothing, but stood behind Stanton for a few moments, then, strangely, came back to Knox and asked once more, "Is Stanton in?"

Knox was convinced that the man was drunk, and he refused to answer or even look at him. "Excuse me," said the stranger. "I thought you were the officer on duty here."

"There is no officer on duty here," replied the major. The man stepped back, then walked into the house, where a few minutes later, he was asked to leave.

After the assassination, both Major Knox and Sergeant Hatter would identify that stranger as Mike O'Laughlen, and based on his odd behavior, prosecutors would charge him with attempting to kill Secretary Stanton. That was a stretch. In fact, O'Laughlen appeared to be unarmed that night, and he seemed far too nervous to carry off such a daring—not to mention suicidal—attack in the middle of a crowd. He had already separated himself from the plot by moving back to Baltimore; he had not attended the Herndon House meeting that night; and for some time, he seems to have wanted nothing more than to talk Booth out of his wild scheme. In truth, Mike O'Laughlen had no intention of killing anyone that night. It is far more likely that he stopped at Stanton's house to warn him of Booth's plot, but lost his nerve. He just couldn't bring himself to implicate a friend—even one who had put his life in jeopardy.[47]

SOMEWHERE IN THE CITY, John Wilkes Booth watched and waited, but never saw an opportunity to kill the president. Dejected, he went back to his room and wrote a letter to his mother.

April 14 2 A.M.

Dearest Mother:

I know you expect a letter from me, and am sure you will hardly forgive me. But indeed I have nothing to write about. Everything is dull; that is, has been till last night.

Everything was bright and splendid. More so in my eyes if it had been a display in a nobler cause.

But so goes the world. Might makes right. I only drop you these

few lines to let you know I am well, and to say I have not heard from
you [lately]. Had one from Rose. With best love to you all,

   I am your affectionate son ever.

                                                          John[48]

DAVE HEROLD MISSED the celebrations entirely. Anticipating another
attempt on the president, Herold had gone into Southern Maryland to
wait for Booth. The weather was chilly, and after getting caught in a
shower, he finally gave up. He found his way to the village of T.B., where
a man named Joseph E. Huntt, who had once planned to have fresh horses
ready for Booth, invited him in to spend the night. Herold slept by the
stove, and was gone before the Huntts awoke the next morning

   It was now Good Friday, April 14. Four years ago to the day, Major
Robert Anderson had lowered the flag in surrender at Fort Sumter; today,
General Anderson would raise the same flag in triumph. All across the
North, the event was marked by music, speeches, and unchecked drunk-
enness.

   The conspirators awoke early that day and made ready to carry out
Booth's contingency plan from the night before. Evidently, the idea was to
keep alert, then strike at the first opportunity. Lewis Powell took another
stroll past Lafayette Park, and he asked again how the secretary was doing.
At 7:30, George Atzerodt checked in to the Kirkwood Hotel and paid for
a full day in advance. Assigned to Room 126, on the second floor, he took
the key and walked out without even looking at the room.[49]

   O'Laughlen's friends also rose early, but it took a good many knocks on
his door to get O'Laughlen up and going. Against his better judgment, he
had decided to have another talk with Booth. He told his companions that
Booth owed him five hundred dollars, and he wanted to collect. So they
accompanied him across Sixth Street to the National Hotel. Henderson,
Early, and Murphy waited in the lobby as O'Laughlen went to Booth's
room alone. The day was wasting away, and after a while they sent a man
up to Room 228 with a note. The messenger came back saying there was
nobody in that room, so they all left. O'Laughlen caught up with them
later.[50]

   Booth was gone for much of the morning, and we cannot say whether
O'Laughlen actually spoke with him or not. Booth had breakfast at his
hotel, then walked over to Ford's Theatre to get his mail. Harry Ford and
Tom Raybold greeted him in the front lobby, and as Raybold handed

Booth a letter, Ford started in on him about the war. "Here is a man who does not like General Lee," he told Raybold. Booth did not care to argue this time. He calmly explained that he just didn't care for the way Lee had given up. He was getting a little defensive, and said that he was as brave a man as Lee. "Well," said Ford, "you have not got three stars yet to show it."

Ford said matter-of-factly that his fortunes had just turned around. They hadn't expected much of a house on Good Friday, but a short while ago, a messenger had come over from the White House to reserve a box. President and Mrs. Lincoln would like to attend the play, and they wanted to bring General Grant along. Booth showed no reaction. He just sat down on a step outside to read his mail.[51]

Dave Herold, now back in the city, stopped at Nailor's Stable and asked to rent a particular horse—a light roan pacing horse with black legs, mane, and tail. Herold had always found him easy to ride. John Fletcher, the stableman, said that he usually reserved that animal for the ladies, and Herold told him that as a matter of fact, a woman was going to be riding with him. He would pick up the horse at four o'clock.[52]

IN AN UPSTAIRS ROOM at the White House, President Lincoln brought his Cabinet together for their weekly meeting. Everyone was there except Seward, who was represented by his son Frederick. This week's topic was the surrender, and they would get to hear about that from General Grant himself, who was there at Lincoln's invitation. It raised two major issues: how to normalize relations with the South, and how to deal with their past transgressions. Lincoln's views were clear. He was in no hurry to punish Confederate leaders. In fact, he said that he should not be sorry to see them get away, but he was all in favor of watching closely to make sure they were gone.

Someone asked if the War Department had heard anything from General Sherman, who was still battling Joe Johnston's forces in North Carolina. Lincoln said he was sure that any news from Sherman would be favorable. He had had a strange dream the night before, in which he was on an indescribable vessel moving rapidly over the water. He didn't know what it meant, but he took it as a good omen; he had had the same dream just before receiving news of Sumter, Bull Run, Antietam, Gettysburg, Stone's River, Vicksburg, and Wilmington. General Grant reminded Lincoln that Stone's River was no victory. Maybe not, said the president, but that dream came before it just the same.[53]

. . .

RICHARD SMOOT CAME BACK once again for his money, but this time his reception at the Surratt boardinghouse was not so courteous. Mary Surratt rushed him out the door, assuring him that he would get the rest of his money soon. The boat was going to be used that night. Her manner was so alarming that Smoot took her advice and left the city as quickly as he could.

Government employees were given half a day off for Good Friday, and when Lou Weichmann came home at two-thirty, he found Booth in the doorway, on his way out. Mrs. Surratt didn't say what he wanted, but she asked Weichmann to go rent a carriage from Howard's. She needed to go back out to the country, and it was already getting late. Half an hour later, they were about to leave when Mrs. Surratt suddenly remembered a package she wanted to bring along. It was wrapped in paper, and Weichmann thought it looked like a stack of saucers.[54]

REHEARSALS FOR *OUR AMERICAN COUSIN* had finished at Ford's, and the stage crew prepared for the president's visit. There were four boxes on either side of the stage, and traditionally, Harry Ford gave the two upper ones at stage left (the audience's right) to the Lincolns. Ned Spangler, Jake Rittersback, and Peanuts Borrows unhooked the partition between them and leaned it against the back wall. They assumed that four people would be in the party, and though they didn't know it yet, General Grant was not going to be one of them. As it turned out, Mrs. Lincoln had reserved the box before inviting him. Since she and her husband had broken their engagement with Grant the night before, she wanted to make it up by hosting a theater party for him on Friday. Thinking it best to reserve the box early, she sent a note over to Ford's in the morning. But the president did not mention it to Grant until that afternoon, when the Cabinet meeting broke up. Grant offered his thanks, but said he just wanted to go home. By then, the *Evening Star* had already announced he would be there.[55]

AT THE HERNDON HOUSE, Lewis Powell told Martha Murray, the manager, that he was leaving for Baltimore and intended to check out soon. He asked her to send up an early supper. Booth, meanwhile, was just behind the hotel, rehearsing his escape in Baptist Alley. Margaret Rozier, a cleaning woman from Ford's, saw him ride a horse down from E Street, then pause, then ride out the other side, toward F. There was nothing unusual about that, except that Booth did it again a few minutes later. The second time, he came up to the back door of the theater, where Jim Maddox and Spangler soon came out to talk with him. In a few minutes, they all went to Jim Ferguson's Greenback Saloon, next door.

Booth was not riding his usual horse. The sorrel he preferred was not available at Pumphrey's, so instead he took out a small bay mare, about fourteen hands high, with a black mane and a long black tail. She had a white star on her forehead, and a spirited disposition that would have rattled a less experienced rider. But Booth seemed pleased to have her. He told James Pumphrey that he was going over to Grover's Theatre to write a letter, and he wanted a tie line for the horse. Pumphrey warned against it. She didn't like being tied, and was likely to break loose. Better to have someone hold her.[56]

THE PRESIDENT AND MRS. LINCOLN took some time in the afternoon for a leisurely carriage ride through the city. It was a rare opportunity to be alone, and Mrs. Lincoln remarked that she had never seen her husband so happy. "We must be more cheerful," he explained. "Between the war and the loss of our darling Willie—we have both been very miserable." He drove the carriage eastward on Pennsylvania Avenue, letting his mind wander while his wife chirped happily on about her plans for the days ahead.

They ended up at the navy yard, where the massive ironclad *Montauk* had become a popular attraction. The ship had been damaged in the battle for Fort Fisher and was undergoing repairs to the turret and machinery. It was one of the wonders of the modern navy, and the Lincolns were piped aboard for a firsthand look.

Just around Greenleaf's Point, to the west, the steamer *Cossack* brought in eight Confederate generals who were passing through Washington en route to prison in Boston. They joined 441 other rebels, most of them captured at Sayler's Creek, for a long march down the avenue. Thousands came out to watch the ragtag procession. It was a scene never to be forgotten.

John Wilkes Booth was in front of Grover's Theatre when they passed by. Booth had stopped in to ask Dwight Hess if Mrs. Lincoln had answered his invitation from the day before. Indeed, she had declined. Hearing this, Booth quickly changed gears, and asked for a piece of paper and an envelope. He wanted to write a letter.

Somehow, a rumor had gotten started that Robert E. Lee was one of those captured officers, and had checked in to Willard's Hotel. Scipiano Grillo, who owned the Star Saloon next to Ford's, ran into Dave Herold and suggested they go over and check it out. Lee wasn't there, of course, but on the way, Grillo noticed that Herold was limping. They stopped so he could adjust his boot, and when he lifted up the leg of his pants, Grillo saw a large knife stuffed down into the boot. "What do you want to carry that for?" he asked.

"I am going into the country tonight on horseback," said Herold. "It will be handy there."

Grillo was amused at the bravado. He had known Herold for years, and could not imagine him using such a dangerous weapon. Half jokingly, he asked, "You ain't going to kill anybody with that?" They went their separate ways—Herold to check on a horse, and Grillo to visit Geary's Billiard Room, above the lobby at Grover's. They both missed Booth as he came out of the theater.[57]

Booth was mounting up to leave when he happened to notice John Mathews hurrying toward him, waving. Mathews asked if he had seen the Confederate prisoners, and Booth looked over at the column kicking up dust in the distance. It was a depressing sight. With an agonized expression, he rubbed his forehead and said, "Great God, I no longer have a country." Mathews thought that Booth looked nervous, and he asked what was wrong. "Oh, it is nothing," Booth replied. He wondered if Mathews would do him a favor.

"Why, certainly, Johnny. What is it?"

"Perhaps I may leave town tonight, and I have a letter here which I desire to be published in the *National Intelligencer;* please attend to it for me, unless I see you before ten o'clock tomorrow; in that case I will see to it myself." Mathews put the envelope in his pocket. Then, glancing around, he called Booth's attention to a carriage that had just passed by. General and Mrs. Grant were in it, and judging from the baggage, they were leaving town. Abruptly, Booth excused himself and galloped up ahead to see them.[58]

Just across Pennsylvania Avenue, Dave Herold stopped at Nailor's to pick up that roan horse. Fletcher, the stableman, charged him five dollars, and insisted he return it by eight or nine o'clock. Herold promised. Booth, meanwhile, went into the Kirkwood House—not to see Atzerodt, but to leave a message for the vice president. Taking a blank card from the desk clerk, he wrote out in pencil: "Don't wish to disturb you. Are you at home? J. Wilkes Booth." The clerk placed it in Mr. Johnson's box, and Booth left.

George Atzerodt was supposed to be learning something of Johnson's habits, but he wasn't even sure what the vice president looked like. He saw a distinguished-looking man in the lobby and asked him where the vice president was staying. William R. Nevins said that Johnson was actually in the dining room having his supper. He pointed him out to Atzerodt, who looked, then walked away.[59]

DICK FORD HAD BORROWED two flags from the Treasury Guards, and his brother Harry arranged them, with some others, around the front of the president's box. Unknown to both of them, someone else had already been there preparing for the president's visit. In the passageway leading from the dress circle, a wooden board was hidden in the corner next to the door. A niche had been carved in the wall just opposite the door; the end of the board would fit snugly into it. A small peephole had been bored, about chest-high, in the left-hand door at the far end. One could hardly see anything through it—just the top of Mr. Lincoln's rocker.[60]

ON HER WAY TO SURRATTSVILLE, Mary Surratt noticed some pickets just off the road, and she asked one of the soldiers if they were going to be there all night. "No, ma'am," said the man. "We're being pulled in after eight o'clock." She thanked him, and said, "It is good to know that."

She and Weichmann arrived at the tavern around five, and Weichmann went into the bar for a drink. A few minutes later, John Lloyd drove up to the back door to unload some fish and oysters. Lloyd had just returned from Upper Marlboro, where he had gone to testify against the man who had stabbed him in a bar fight two months before. The case had been continued to the November term, but since the bar in Upper Marlboro was closer than the one in Surrattsville, Lloyd had stayed awhile. Though he came home staggering drunk, he would always maintain that he was sober enough to remember his conversation with Mrs. Surratt. She told him to have those "shooting irons" ready, and a couple of bottles of whiskey as well. They were going to be called for that night.[61]

Lloyd seemed to think that Mrs. Surratt had come out there just to deliver that message, but in fact she did have other business. She needed to speak with John Nothey again about his outstanding debt. She was furious at Nothey for telling her creditor, George Calvert, that she was in no hurry to settle her debts. Indignantly, Calvert had fired off a demand for immediate payment, and his letter had been received just that afternoon. But in spite of the urgency, Mrs. Surratt did not see Nothey, nor did she go to his house. She asked Weichmann to write him a note, care of Bennett Gwynn, threatening to sue if he did not pay up within ten days. Gwynn happened to be passing by the tavern, and he joined them for supper. They socialized for a while, and at about six-thirty, Mrs. Surratt said that she was supposed to meet someone in Washington and had to be going. After fixing a broken carriage spring, she and Weichmann started back to the city. Lloyd, alone at the tavern, took her package upstairs and unwrapped it. It was a large field glass, which he put on the bed. He laid the carbines alongside it.[62]

JIM FERGUSON SAW BOOTH in front of the Greenback Saloon, mounted on a bay mare. He seemed proud of the horse. Seeing how Ferguson looked at her, he said, "She is a very nice horse. She can gallop and can almost kick me in the back." With that, he took off down the street.

George W. Bunker and Henry Merrick were at the desk of the National Hotel when Booth came in. They both noticed how pale he looked, and Bunker asked if he was ill. Booth said he was fine. He asked for a piece of paper, and took it behind the desk to write. Merrick saw him still sitting there a few minutes later, with a confused look on his face.

"Is it 1864 or 1865?" he asked.

"Don't you know what year you live in?" Merrick replied.

Booth didn't answer. He just folded up the paper and dropped it into the mailbox. He asked Bunker if he was going to Ford's tonight. "You ought to go," he said. "There is going to be some splendid acting tonight."

George Atzerodt came into Nailor's Stable with a horse he had just rented from Keleher's Stable. She was a bay mare, much like the one Booth was riding, with a long, bushy tail. Atzerodt claimed she was his own horse, and he told Fletcher to keep her saddled and ready to go. He would be back for her at ten.[63]

ABRAHAM LINCOLN WAS always surrounded by people, and this night would be no exception. He couldn't even walk to his carriage without encountering someone in search of a favor. Such annoyances came with the job. So as he left the White House this evening, he was not at all surprised to see Speaker of the House Schuyler Colfax and a few others waiting outside the door. Colfax was about to take a business trip out West and wanted to bid the president goodbye. Mr. Lincoln said that he and his wife were going to the theater and asked if he would like to come along. Colfax declined, and went on his way. George Ashmun was not invited. Ashmun, a former member of Congress, had brought a friend with him, and hoped the president would speak to him. But since Lincoln was already late for the play, he told Ashmun to come back in the morning. He took a small card from his pocket and wrote: "Please allow Mr. Ashmun & friend to come at 9 A.M. to-morrow. A. Lincoln."

Finally breaking free, the Lincolns rode up to Fifteenth and H to pick up their last-minute guests, Clara Harris and Henry Rathbone. By the time they got to Ford's, *Our American Cousin* had been under way for twenty minutes. Seeing them enter, Harry Hawk, in the role of Asa Trenchard, ad-libbed: "This reminds me of a story, as Mr. Lincoln says . . ." A commotion rippled through the dress circle, and the band struck up "Hail to the Chief." All eyes turned to the president and his party as they worked their way through the audience. When they entered the box, Mr. Lincoln acknowledged their applause with a bow, then took his seat. The play resumed.

Francis Burke, the president's coachman, parked the carriage in front of the theater and waited for the Lincolns to return. A police officer walked by on his beat, and they started talking. In a few minutes, the two went next door to have a drink.[64]

A few blocks away, Mary Surratt returned from the country and found Booth waiting in her parlor. They talked in private, and in a few minutes, Booth left. He rode into Baptist Alley and dismounted by the back door of the theater. Looking inside, he called for Ned Spangler. Being at the far side of the stage, Spangler didn't hear him, so another stagehand relayed the message: "Mr. Booth wants you." Ned came over to the door, and Booth tossed him the reins of his horse, saying she needed to be held for a few minutes. Spangler protested, but Booth ignored him and went inside.

Ned Spangler had a job to do, which he couldn't do standing in the alley. He tried to pass Booth's horse off on someone else. John L. Debonay refused. Since Peanuts Borrows was assigned to watch the back door anyway, Spangler waved him over and handed him the reins. "Here," he said, "hold Mr. Booth's horse." With that, Spangler went back to work.

Lewis Powell and David Herold had already gone to Lafayette Park. The park superintendent always called out the time as he locked the

gate, and as soon as that happened, Powell would approach the Sewards'
house. He would knock on the door, then tell the servant that he had
medicine to give to the secretary. It seemed an excellent plan, but at the last
minute, a complication arose: one of Seward's doctors was still in the
house. Now Powell either had to come up with a new cover story or delay
his attack. Since nothing came to mind, he sent Herold galloping away to
tell the others to hold off.

Booth was inside the theater, walking in and out of the lobby, talking
with the doorman, John Buckingham, and asking for the time. He went
next door to the Star Saloon, slapped a few coins on the bar, and called for
whiskey and water. He checked on the time again, and paced some more.
In the alley out back, Peanuts was lying on a bench, holding his horse.[65]

Herold leaped out of the saddle and ran into the Kirkwood House. He
wanted to tell Atzerodt not to do anything yet, but the door to his room
was locked and nobody answered. A block away, Atzerodt was sitting
down to a glass of ale with John Fletcher. With an air of mystery, he told
the stableman, "You will soon hear of a present."

Booth walked up the stairs to the dress circle and edged his way along
the wall to the president's box. Charles Forbes, a White House messenger,
was seated outside the door, and Booth took out some kind of card and
showed it to him. Forbes, of course, let him pass. Stepping quietly into the
dark, narrow passageway, Booth closed the door behind him, then barred
it shut. The door ahead of him had been left open, and he could see Major
Rathbone watching the play.

HARRY HAWK, alone on the stage, said, "Don't know the manners of
good society, eh? . . ."

With his eyes fixed on Rathbone, Booth stepped up to the inner door.
In his left hand he clutched a hidden dagger. With his right, he slowly
drew a pistol from his pocket.

MARY SURRATT STOOD in her front parlor. In her hand was a rosary,
and as she nervously counted the beads, members of her household filed
past her on their way to bed. As Lou Weichmann walked by, she said to
him in a faint voice, "Please pray for my intentions."[66]

TWELVE

"SIC SEMPER TYRANNIS!"

NOBODY IN THE BOX KNEW BOOTH WAS THERE. HE STOOD in the passageway, derringer in hand, heart pounding, well aware that he had passed the point of no return. With his gaze fixed on Major Rathbone, he gripped the dagger in his pocket and took a deep breath. Stepping briskly into the box, he turned toward the president and thrust his pistol at the back of Lincoln's head.

The sound of the explosion jolted Rathbone, and he leaped to his feet. He started toward the dark figure in the box, but pulled up short when he saw the flash of a knife. The man lunged at him, and Rathbone reeled backward with a deep cut in his arm. The intruder quickly turned toward the stage and, stepping between the chairs, planted one hand on the railing and threw himself over it.

Booth landed in a crouching position twelve feet below and sprang to his feet, light-headed from the rush of adrenaline. He set himself, faced the audience, and raised his dagger.

"Sic semper tyrannis!"

Booth was out of sight before anyone could reach him. He rounded the turn at the far end of the stage and barreled into the unlit passageway leading to the back door. Throwing the door open, he bounded into the alley, grasping for the reins of the horse that Peanuts Borrows had been holding for him. The mare was startled and tried to pull away, but Booth flung himself over the saddle and gained control with barely a second to lose. As he spun the animal around, Joseph Stewart burst out the door and fumbled in the dark to catch him. Stewart just missed the reins, and the assassin galloped away.[1]

Confusion and human nature had played right into Booth's hands. He had entered the president's box, aimed and fired his pistol, disposed of the Rathbone threat, and leaped dramatically to the stage without hindrance. He had even passed in front of a large audience, and still managed to get out the back door. He had gambled with his life, and so far his instincts had not failed him. They would be put to the test again as he tried to flee the city.

A low wooden drawbridge spanned the Eastern Branch of the Potomac, southeast of the Capitol. It bordered the Washington Navy Yard, but was guarded at both ends by army personnel. At 11:40 P.M., the sergeant of the guard was called out to examine a man who asked permission to leave the city. Though the man seemed quite at ease, his horse looked as if it had been driven hard for a short burst. The rider gave his name as Booth, and for every question Sgt. Silas T. Cobb asked, he seemed to have a forthright response. Asked where he was going, he responded, "I am going down home, down in Charles." Asked to be more specific, he said, "I don't live in any town . . . I live close to Beantown." Sergeant Cobb said he didn't know the place, and Booth was surprised. "Good God, then you never were down there."

"Well, didn't you know, my friend, that it is against the laws to pass here after nine o'clock?"

"No," said Booth. "I haven't been in town for some time, and it is new to me."

The sergeant eyed him closely. He seemed genteel and well-bred. His skin was ivory white, his hair perfectly coifed, his nails recently manicured. Cobb couldn't help wondering what kept him out so late. "What is your object to be in town after nine o'clock when you have so long a road to travel?" he asked.

"It is a dark road, and I thought if I waited a spell I would have the moon."

Cobb looked over his shoulder. A huge moon, a few days past full, had just cleared the heights in the distance. He saw nothing suspicious about the man, and he let him cross. "I will pass you," he said, "but I don't know as I ought to."

"Hell!" said Booth, "I guess there'll be no trouble about that." It was all he could do to keep his horse under control. By the rules, he had to walk the animal to the other side.

Sergeant Cobb barely had time to get back to the guardhouse before another horseman came out of the darkness, riding a light roan. He was a smaller man, in his mid-to-late twenties, with pouchy cheeks and no whiskers. It was David Herold, but he gave his name as Smith.

"Where are you going?" asked the sergeant.

"Home to White Plains," said the rider, referring to a place in Charles County.

"You can't pass. It is after nine o'clock," said Cobb. "It is against the rules."

The man seemed incredulous. "How long have these rules been out?"

"Some time; ever since I have been here. Why weren't you out of the city before?"

"I couldn't very well. I stopped to see a woman on Capitol Hill, and couldn't get off before." His frank response seemed reasonable enough, given the number of parties taking place in the city. Besides, the war was almost over, and any danger to the government had surely passed. So Cobb let "Smith" cross out of the city.

This Good Friday was turning out to be a busy night at the Navy Yard Bridge. A short while after that small man crossed the bridge, a third rider approached. John Fletcher asked Cobb if he had seen anyone on a light roan horse. Cobb said yes, someone had just crossed over on such a horse. From the description Cobb gave, Fletcher felt certain he was on the track of David Herold. "God! I am after him," he said. The stableman then asked if he might pursue the man. Cobb said it would be all right with him, but the rules prohibited him from letting anyone back into the city until morning. Fletcher had no intention of waiting out in the country all night, so he turned back, and headed to police headquarters to report a stolen horse.[2]

AS THE EFFECTS OF ALCOHOL slowly wore off, George Atzerodt began to feel a sense of dread. He went to the Pennsylvania House, where he took a drink at the bar. The more he thought about it, though, the more he realized the authorities might come looking for him there. So he left the hotel and went for a ride. At Eighth Street, he dropped off his horse at Keleher's Stable, where he had rented it. He walked over to the Herndon

House, on Ninth Street. This was only a block away from Ford's Theatre, and Atzerodt found the whole neighborhood on the alert for conspirators. In a panic, he took a streetcar to the navy yard, at the far eastern end of the city.

An old acquaintance happened to be on the car. Washington Briscoe had met Atzerodt seven or eight years before, and was surprised that he did not recognize him. Briscoe asked if he had heard the news, and Atzerodt said yes, but left it at that. Then he asked if Briscoe would let him spend the night at his place. Though Briscoe turned him down, Atzerodt did not seem to regard that as the final word. He repeated his request a couple more times. When it was obvious that the answer would not improve, he gave up and decided to return to the Pennsylvania House.[3]

AT SURRATTSVILLE, tavern keeper John M. Lloyd was awakened by a sharp knock at his door. Lloyd had been drinking all afternoon and had been sprawled on a sofa, sound asleep, since about eight o'clock. Now it was midnight, and David Herold was standing on the porch, anxious and fidgety. "Make haste and get those things," Herold urged.

Lloyd knew exactly what Herold meant. After talking with Mrs. Surratt that afternoon, he had brought those guns down from their hiding place. He shuffled over to get them, while Herold came inside and helped himself to a bottle of whiskey. Another man waited on a horse outside, and while Herold handed him the bottle, Lloyd appeared in the door with a carbine, field glasses, and a box of cartridges. He said that he had to go back for the other carbine, but the second man told him not to bother; he had broken his leg, he said, and it was all he could do to keep himself in the saddle, even without carrying a rifle. He asked if there was a surgeon in the neighborhood, and Lloyd said he didn't know of one who still practiced.

The man on the horse seemed eager to let Lloyd in on something. "I will tell you some news if you want to hear it," he said.

Lloyd wasn't sure how to answer. "I am not particular," he replied. "You can tell me if you think proper."

The man straightened up in the saddle and announced, "We have assassinated the president and Secretary Seward." Lloyd was dumbfounded. He stood there in a drunken stupor as Herold handed him a dollar for the whiskey and said something about keeping the change.

"We must find a doctor somewhere," Herold said. Lloyd said that he couldn't think of one who still practiced, but as he was saying this, the two men turned to leave. Without waiting for him to finish talking, they galloped away.[4]

MIKE O'LAUGHLEN WAS IN A BAR with his friends when someone burst in and announced that Lincoln had been shot. The news hit O'Laughlen like a kick in the stomach. He couldn't believe that Booth had actually gone through with it. The thought sickened him, and he returned, pale and nervous, to the Metropolitan Hotel for the night.

John Mathews was also feeling sick. Soon after the shooting, Mathews remembered that Booth had given him a letter for the *National Intelligencer* the day before. With a growing sense of anxiety, he rushed back to his boardinghouse for a private look at Booth's letter. It was chilling. After beginning with a political statement, it closed with a veiled reference to this last, desperate act. It even named his fellow conspirators, thus sealing their fates—or, as Booth chose to see it, their place in history.

> For a long time I have devoted my energies, my time and money to the accomplishment of a certain end. I have been disappointed. The moment has now arrived when I must change my plans. Many will blame me for what I am about to do, but posterity, I am sure, will justify me.
>
> > Men who love their country better than gold or life.
> > John W. Booth, Paine, Herold, Atzerodt.

Mathews read the letter several times and committed it to memory. Then he burned it and resolved—for now—not to say a word about it.[5]

IT WAS FOUR O'CLOCK in the morning when Dr. Samuel Mudd was awakened by a knock on his door. Peering through a front window, Mudd saw two men waiting in the rain. One stood on the front porch, while the other sat on a horse some distance from the house. The man at the door said that they needed a surgeon for his friend, who had been hurt when his horse tripped. He and the doctor helped the injured man out of the saddle and into the house. While the patient waited on the parlor sofa, Mudd went to find a lamp. His farmhands got up to take care of the visitors' horses.

In the predawn darkness, Dr. Mudd did not recognize the injured man. He noticed that the patient seemed to suffer a great deal, and not just from the leg injury. His back was hurt, and he later said that he had been thrown against a rock when his horse tripped. He really needed to lie down for a proper examination, so Mudd and the other man helped him up the stairs and onto a bed in the front room. His left leg was swollen, and Mudd had to slit the boot up along the shin to remove it. The other man hovered over him the whole time, watching closely and urging him to hurry. They had gotten an early start, he said, and they still hoped to get back on the road before sunup. The patient himself said little.

After inspecting the injury, Mudd did not think it was all that serious. The fibula, or the smaller bone in the lower leg, had snapped straight across, about two inches above the ankle. It was not a weight-bearing bone, and since it did not break through the skin, Mudd did not foresee any major complications. He fashioned a splint from pieces of a bandbox, then had his English gardener, John Best, make a pair of crutches.

The patient was exhausted, and chose to remain in bed for a while. His companion, however, joined the doctor for breakfast. To Mudd, he seemed immature. He talked incessantly, and seemed eager to show off how much he knew of Charles County. Because of his friend's injury, he thought it best to look for a shortcut to the Potomac, where they might find a boat to take them to Washington. That would certainly be easier than riding a horse the whole way.

Mudd would later claim he had no idea who his visitors were. He had never met Herold and had not seen Booth since the previous November or December, four or five months before. And this time, Booth stayed in bed with his face to the wall, so Mudd never got a good look at him. Even Mrs. Mudd, who brought him food during the day, did not realize she had met him before. She said that this man was pale and haggard, and there was nothing in his appearance to remind her of the handsome, robust man she had spoken with on a previous visit. Both she and her husband claimed that the smaller man did all the talking, and that he gave his friend's name as Tyson. Only later did they suspect they had been duped.[6]

"EVIDENTLY CONSPIRATORS ARE AMONG US!" shrieked the *National Intelligencer*. The air was thick with rumors, and it was hard to know what to believe. Newspapers mixed fact and fiction, and even official reports were subject to error. Correspondence of the Signal Corps announced that Major Clarence Seward had died, and the *New York Herald* also named him among the casualties. But in fact none of the Sewards had been killed, and the secretary's son Clarence had not even been in Washington that night. To add to the confusion, the *Herald* reported that the president's assassin was rumored to be in custody.

Many people thought that Booth had been captured right away, and those who knew otherwise were busy chasing down false rumors of his whereabouts. General James A. Hardie, for example, wired the commander of the military railroad in Northern Virginia: "It is expected Booth has gone to Fairfax by way of Alexandria." Other troops were dispatched to Baltimore, and still more were sent on a house to house search in the city of Washington. All went about the job equally confident they were on the right track.[7]

Some serious obstacles slowed the initial pursuit. Rain, cold winds, and heavy fog impeded travel, and a lack of efficient communications handicapped the government's work from the beginning. Nevertheless, military authorities took all reasonable measures to seal off the capital. Trains were stopped in all directions. Bridges were blocked, and Baltimore police were notified that Booth might be heading their way, if he managed to get out of Washington.

Police Superintendent A. C. Richards was also moving forward. Just after midnight, Richards wired Provost Marshal McPhail in Baltimore about the assassination, and McPhail began looking for Booth's hometown associates. By mid-morning, his men had tracked down a local theater patron named Edwin Tuttle, who gave them photographs of Booth and told them that two Baltimore men, Sam Arnold and Mike O'Laughlen, had been working with him in the oil business. Tuttle had not seen either of them since they went to Washington. Both, ironically, were friends of McPhail's.[8]

Few could top General Henry W. Halleck for clear-headed, methodical thinking. As General Grant's chief of staff, Halleck had been privy to a wealth of information, and just after the assassination, he recalled seeing a diplomatic dispatch warning of rumors that a man in France was planning an attack on William T. Sherman. At the time, General Sherman paid no attention to the message. Like the president, he refused to be sidetracked by such threats. But the information from Europe was very specific, and Halleck urged Secretary Stanton to give it another look. He ferreted out the original dispatch and, showing it to Stanton, got the secretary to reiterate the danger. "I find evidence that an assassin is also on your track," wired Stanton to General Sherman, "and I beseech you to be more heedful than Mr. Lincoln was of such knowledge." In a separate message, Halleck added that the assassin's name was Clark and that he was a slender man, five feet nine inches tall, with dark brown hair and mustache, a long goatee, and high cheekbones. While in Paris the previous March, Clark wore dark gray clothes and a slouch hat, and had "a very determined look." General Sherman and staff were put on alert, but nothing ever came of it.[9]

There was a general belief that Booth had headed northeast toward Baltimore, and much of the search was directed accordingly. Only days later would authorities learn that he had gone south, into Southern Maryland, and a search of that area had been slow to develop. First Lieutenant David Dana was one of the first to go there. By sunrise on April 15, Dana had already embarked on a trek that, coincidentally, followed much of Booth's actual route. He intended to search at Port Tobacco, which the stableman John Fletcher had identified as the hometown of Booth's friend Atzerodt. Taking eighty-five men from the 13th New York Cavalry, Dana methodically searched all the roads and villages leading south. Though slowed by heavy fog, he was able to reach Piscataway, twelve miles below Washington, by seven o'clock.

A local hotel keeper named Nodley Anderson told Dana that the assailant of Secretary Seward must have been a man named John H. Boyle, a notorious guerrilla who had murdered an army captain on March 25. Anderson suggested that instead of going to Port Tobacco, Dana should make a detour to Surrattsville, a rebel hotbed just a few miles to the east, to question John Lloyd, the tavern keeper there. So Dana sent a messenger ahead to instruct Lt. William K. Lafferty at Port Tobacco to search for Atzerodt. He sent another courier back to Washington with a progress report. Then he and his men rode over to Surrattsville for a talk with John M. Lloyd.

Lloyd had sobered up since the previous night, but his judgment was still clouded. Asked whether anyone had ridden through there, he said no. Asked if he knew anything about Booth, he again said no. He promised that if anything came to his attention, he would report it. He said the same thing to John Fletcher when he brought the police through a short time later. For the next couple of days, Lloyd would continue to deny he knew anything at all about the assassination.[10]

AS THE INVESTIGATION DEVELOPED, the name of George Atzerodt was turning up a lot. Atzerodt's case was especially urgent because investigators believed it was he who had attacked the secretary of state. It was his saddle and bridle that had been found on the one-eyed horse; the stable-man Fletcher had identified them at General Augur's office. Booth's bankbook, found at the Kirkwood House, connected him to the assassin. He had shared horses with Booth and Herold, and he had hinted about important events and access to great wealth. By the morning of April 15, authorities were already referring to him as "G. A. Atzerodt, the assassin of Mr. Seward." Typical was a telegram by Assistant Secretary of War Charles A. Dana, who said: "The assailant of Mr. Seward has been known here by the name of G. A. Atzerodt. He is twenty-six or twenty-eight years old, five feet eight inches tall; light complexion, brown from exposure . . . rather round-shouldered and stooping. . . ."

Atzerodt's name was already familiar to authorities in Baltimore. He had reportedly been on the steamer *Harriet DeFord* just days before she was hijacked by Confederate agents on the Chesapeake. He had apparently boarded the ship at Fair Haven, and was seen showing off a roll of greenbacks to Walter Barnes and Henry M. Bailey, two friends from Charles County. All of this had been reported to Maryland's Provost Marshal McPhail in late March. Though McPhail thought little of it at the time, he now considered it worth a second look. Barnes and Bailey had been in Baltimore since the end of March, and Atzerodt had stopped in to see them a couple of times. They were staying in Booth's old neighborhood.[11]

Despite the attention, Atzerodt managed to avoid capture. But a search of his usual haunts turned up an interesting lead. John Greenawalt, of the Pennsylvania House, said that Atzerodt had checked in to the hotel at about two A.M. on the night of the assassination and left about three hours later. He came and went with a man who signed the register as "S. Thomas." This man Thomas looked every bit as filthy and disheveled as Atzerodt. He had a weather-beaten face and dark, matted hair. His suit was expensive but stained and threadbare, with frayed cuffs. Though nobody knew where he and Atzerodt had gone, they had left behind one incriminating item: a Bowie knife, found under the steps of a grocery store near the Herndon House. It was said to be Atzerodt's.[12]

AFTER HIS EARLY MORNING VISIT to Howard's Stable, Louis Weichmann returned to the Surratt boardinghouse for breakfast, then went out for a walk. He must have known that investigators would look closely at his connections to Booth and Surratt. The conspirators had never seemed to mind having him around, and indeed, they had treated him like one of them. Now he had to convince authorities that appearances were deceptive, and that he had never known the truth about Booth's intentions. Just as important, he had to show his willingness to help in the investigation. So when he learned, on the morning of the fifteenth, that Seward's attacker was wearing a long gray coat, he resolved to tell authorities immediately that George Atzerodt must have been that man.

Weichmann took his suspicions to police headquarters, and while there he also mentioned the large dark-haired man who had visited the Surratt boardinghouse. The man had used several names, but Weichmann remembered him as "Paine" and recalled that lately he had been staying at the Herndon House. Weichmann had once overheard Mrs. Surratt inquiring at the hotel desk about a "delicate gentleman" who needed to have his meals sent up to him. He assumed this was a cover story for "Paine," who was reluctant to leave his room for fear of being discovered south of Philadelphia, in violation of his oath of allegiance.

As he told this to police, someone nearby overheard the conversation and identified himself as a hotel waiter who had frequently taken meals up to Paine's room.

"Was he a delicate eater?" Weichmann asked the man.

"I should think not," he replied. "Why, if I had served a small pig to him, he would have eaten it, bones and all!"[13]

IN A POSH WASHINGTON TOWN HOUSE, a twenty-year-old prostitute named Ellen Starr pressed her face into a towel soaked in chloroform. She was in love with Booth, and for some months past had been his mistress. She was discovered and revived. Elsewhere, reactions varied. All across the country, public meetings were called and churches were opened for prayer services in memory of the late president. At Tiffany's in New York, stunned employees stopped the clock in front of their store at the time of Lincoln's death. The wave of indignation that followed the shooting threatened some Democrats with the possibility of retaliation. W. B. Lyndall sensed the danger. "I was a marked man from my well-known bitter opposition to the administration . . . ," he wrote, "and had I not had some friends who stood by me, my house would have been sacked. . . ."

Lyndall had had the good sense to avoid inflammatory remarks, but not everyone was as wise as he. In Fort Barrancas, Florida, Union Private

S. A. St. John said that the assassination ought to have happened four years before. He was immediately court-martialed. In Cleveland, J. J. Husband gloated over the president's death, saying, "You have had your day of rejoicing, now I have mine." A mob chased him up to the roof of his office, threw him through the skylight, then kicked him down the stairs. In Springfield, Massachusetts, a crowd of two hundred bowled over a sheriff's escort to get at a man who had rejoiced over the killing. They forced the man to kneel bareheaded and say, "I am sorry Abraham Lincoln was shot. So help me God."

Those people were lucky; the costs of their indiscretions were minor. For many others, though, rejoicing over Lincoln's death would have deadly consequences. A man at Hilton Head was shot dead the moment he said he "was glad of it." Another man in Estherville, Iowa, declared his satisfaction at the news, and was "hung without benefit of clergy." A soldier in the military prison at Fort Jefferson, Florida, cheered at the news and was "strung up" for so long that he died soon after being cut down. A soldier who witnessed this wrote, "I honestly confess that I have *very* little *sympathy* for him or any man who is punished for such expressions." It is not certain how many people died for their inappropriate reactions, but the number undoubtedly reached into the hundreds.[14]

Concerns about mob violence led Secretary Stanton to delay his announcement of the assassination to troops in the field. Safeguards had to be put into place before commanders could break the news. Guards were posted over Confederate prisoners, and paroled rebels were told to refrain from wearing their gray uniforms. Commanding officers were ordered to take "the most vigorous measures" to suppress any outbreak.[15]

Throughout most of the civilized world, foreign leaders expressed horror at the assassination and sympathy for the nation's loss. But in Montreal, reactions were mixed. Canadian officials offered condolences, and a great many citizens draped their buildings in mourning. But others celebrated openly, and their revelry caused the U.S. consul to remark that "treason has transformed them to brutes, and seems to have eradicated from their breasts all sense of moral right." He would have been deeply offended by an editorial in the London *Examiner* that said, "It must be remembered that atrocious as was Booth's deed, his 'sic semper tyrannis' was literally justified by the facts. The man he killed had murdered the Constitution of the United States, had contradicted and set at naught the principles under which the States came together, had practically denied the competence of the signatories of the Declaration of Independence, and overthrown all for which Washington fought and Patrick Henry spoke."

By and large, even Southerners greeted the news with sadness. Many recognized that Lincoln had favored a lenient approach to reconstruction and had probably been their best friend in the government. They were quick to disavow the assassination. In Richmond, civic leaders condemned the killing, while the editor of the *Whig* denounced Booth in unmeasured terms. They did not say it publicly, but many, in fact, were afraid of retaliation. Captain Joseph J. Westcoat, a Confederate prisoner of war, stated it plainly: "I am afraid that we poor devils will have to suffer for [Lincoln's] death." Like others in his situation, Westcoat could not imagine that anything good could come from the assassination. Confederate General Richard S. Ewell, on his way to prison in Boston, would have agreed. Ewell was visibly shocked, and he remarked that the loss of Mr. Lincoln was the worst thing that could have happened, for the South as well as the North. He hastened to assure General Grant that he and all good Southerners were appalled.

Some doubted the sincerity of these expressions. They saw the assassination as a natural extension of "irregular warfare," and they thought the only proper response to it was vengeance. General Sherman understood the public mood. "We have met every phase which this war has assumed, and must now be prepared for it in its last and worst shape, that of assassins and guerrillas," wrote Sherman. "But woe unto the people who seek to expend their wild passions in such a manner, for there is but one dread result."[16]

With public feelings running so high, critics of the Lincoln administration had to tread lightly or face dire consequences. Sidney Gay of the *New York Tribune* understood that. Gay's boss, Horace Greeley, had written a scathing editorial to be published on the fifteenth, and in the early morning hours, Gay pulled the offensive piece. Greeley was furious, but Gay stood his ground, insisting that if he had published that editorial, their building would have been torn to the ground—as it probably should have been. The *Tribune* was one of the few anti-administration papers not targeted for violence. In San Francisco, mobs destroyed the offices of the *American* and the *Union,* while a French-language paper, *L'Ecore du Pacifique,* was saved only by the timely arrival of guards. In Westminster,

Maryland, a citizen group ordered Joseph Shaw, editor of the *Democrat,* to leave town. He did so, but when he returned on the twenty-fourth, he was set upon and killed.

As Willie Clark observed, this was no time to be a rebel. Clark, in whose bed the president had died, wrote in a letter home, "The time has come when people cannot say what they please. . . . Leniency is no longer to be thought of."[17]

As Laura Keene learned, the threat of arrest was just as great as the fear of violence. Though cleared of suspicion, Keene and her co-stars were arrested several times en route to their next engagement in Cincinnati. After the third such incident, Edwin Stanton personally intervened to protect them from further detention. But the rest of the cast and crew—John T. Ford's permanent staff—did not fare so well. Detectives bore down on Spangler, Rittersback, Gifford, and Borrows, among others. Even Ford's Baltimore employees came under scrutiny when McPhail learned that the orchestra at the Holliday Street Theatre had played "Dixie" the previous week. Though none of the musicians was arrested, all were ordered to leave the state.

Theatrical people were especially vulnerable; as one Baltimore man said, "It wasn't safe for an actor to walk the streets." It was commonly assumed that someone in the theater had cleared a path for Booth's escape, and the whole profession was called to answer for that. Even their homes and workplaces were threatened. When Police Superintendent A. C. Richards learned that an anonymous group intended to burn down Ford's, he asked for reinforcements. "My force is entirely inadequate to protect the building and property in the neighborhood," he insisted. So Colonel Ingraham detailed an officer and twenty men to protect the place—but only after seven o'clock each night.[18]

Junius Booth was in Cincinnati, where he had just performed a farewell benefit in *The Merchant of Venice* at Wood's Theatre. Terrified of mob violence, he barricaded himself in his hotel room, pacing the floor and pulling at his hair "like a man deranged." He told a reporter that if John Wilkes were really the killer, then no Booth could ever appear on stage again. Indeed, he was not the only one to reach that conclusion. At Orlando Tompkins's house in Boston, Edwin learned the news when a servant tearfully handed him the morning paper. He anxiously scanned its columns, looking for some way to assure himself that his brother was not really the killer. Though friends suggested that the papers were mistaken, Edwin was not so sure. "If John didn't do it," he asked, "where is John?" Like most people who knew his brother, Edwin instinctively understood. The athletic leap to the stage; the flourish of the dagger; the cry of *"Sic semper tyrannis!"*—in style and spirit, it was all so much like John Wilkes Booth. He remembered, with some irony, the closing lines of *Don Cesar de Bazan:*

> *Long live the King! Long live the King! Long live the King!*
> *Who e'er repays out love with love again,*
> *Let peace be joined to length of days,*
> *Let peace be joined to bless his happy reign.*

Those were the lines Edwin had spoken just the night before, unaware that peace and happiness had already slipped beyond his reach. Now, the thought overwhelmed him. When he finally composed himself, he penned a note to Asia, offering some advice on how to cope: "Think no more of him as your brother; he is dead to us now, as he soon must be to all the world. . . ."

Edwin knew how the public would feel about his family. For his own part, he was compelled to reassert his loyalty. So when theater manager Henry C. Jarrett released him from all further obligations, he responded with a public note of thanks. "While mourning, in common with all other loyal hearts, the death of the President, I am oppressed by a private woe not to be expressed in words. But whatever calamity may befall me and mine, my country, one and indivisible, has my warmest devotion."

Mary Ann and Rosalie remained at Edwin's house in New York. Friends had rushed to comfort them, but the task was hopeless. John Wilkes had always been his mother's favorite, and the news of his act fell upon her with crushing force. Even worse than the hurt and shame was the prospect that her son would have to face a public execution. While she agonized over the thought, a newsboy passed the house, calling out, "The President's death, and the arrest of John Wilkes Booth!" Hearing that, Mary Ann moaned, "O God, if this be true, let him shoot himself, let him not live to be hung! Spare him, spare us, spare the name that dreadful disgrace!"[19]

Asia Booth Clarke bore the news stoically. Though in fragile health and pregnant with twins, she thought immediately of Mary Ann. She urged Clarke to invite her mother down from New York at once. She asked herself why John Wilkes would do such a thing, and searched her mind for warnings she might have missed. Mentally replaying her brother's conversations, she suddenly remembered that he had entrusted a packet of papers to her care. Quietly she slipped away and opened the safe. Inside the large envelope John Wilkes had left were several items. One was a smaller envelope, marked with the name of someone Asia knew. To protect him, she burned it, then scattered the ashes. The rest of the papers went back into the safe, to be rediscovered later.[20]

IN HIS THIRD-FLOOR OFFICE at the War Department, Edwin Stanton worked at his usual frantic pace, writing memoranda and dashing off orders to all parts of the country. Three years in charge had honed Stanton's leadership skills, and in theory he ought to have handled this crisis without a hitch. But, of course, this situation was unique. Civilians were taking part in the manhunt, and they were not so easy to control. They had never answered to the War Department, cared nothing about the chain of command, and had never learned how to deal with the dictatorial secretary and his idiosyncrasies. Their presence added an element of chaos to the task, and to someone who was used to having his own way, they must have been enormously frustrating.

MARY TODD LINCOLN WENT BACK to the White House an hour after the president's death. Elizabeth Dixon tried to find a comfortable place to leave her, but the first lady refused to go into any room that reminded her of her husband. The Cabinet, meanwhile, avoided her. They remained at the Petersen house, composing a formal announcement of the change in administration. They invited Andrew Johnson to designate a time and place to be sworn in as president. Johnson said that the ceremony could take place in his rooms at the Kirkwood Hotel, at eleven o'clock. The Cabinet adjourned to prepare.[21]

All of this occurred within sight of the president's body. It was not until after the Cabinet left that a detail of six men took charge of the remains, placing them in a rough wooden coffin and carrying them back out the narrow hallway and down the winding steps. An ambulance waited in front of the house. As the body was loaded into it, the crowd closed in for a final glimpse of their martyred leader. Then they embarked on a slow, mournful, rain-drenched procession to the White House.

A middle-aged African American woman stood in the rain and watched as the president's remains were carried up to the north portico. Hearing

Long after his death in 1852, Junius Brutus Booth, Sr., exerted an influence on the career and politics of his son, John Wilkes.
Library of Congress

Tudor Hall, home of the Booths, as it looked in 1865. Several of the men who built it later worked for John T. Ford, and were present when Lincoln was assassinated.
Author's collection

Handsome and captivating, John Wilkes Booth was hailed as one of America's most popular actors. This recently discovered photograph is one of dozens taken of him during his career.
Courtesy of Richard and Kellie Gutman

The Booth brothers appeared in *Julius Caesar* in November 1864. John Wilkes (as Mark Antony, left) remained on cordial terms with Junius (as Cassius, right), but his political sparring with Edwin (as Brutus, center) nearly split the family. Months after the assassination, three photos of Edwin were found among his younger brother's personal effects. All had been torn in half.
National Portrait Gallery, Smithsonian Institution

Mary Surratt, widowed mother of conspirator John H. Surratt, Jr., was suspected of being the plot's ringleader. This photograph, discovered by the author in 1988, is the only known wartime image of her. *New York Public Library*

David E. Herold had known Booth for years, and stayed with him throughout his flight from Washington. *Library of Congress*

Michael O'Laughlen (above) and Samuel Bland Arnold (right) were apparently the first to join Booth in his plot to capture the president. *Library of Congress*

George A. Atzerodt expected to be paid for his part in the plot, but on balance, he lost money when John Surratt borrowed from him. *Library of Congress*

Lewis Thornton Powell, shown in the hat and coat he had worn on the night of the assassination. Like much of the evidence, the clothes have since disappeared. *Library of Congress*

Rullman's Hotel (second building from left, with long awning) was the scene of daily meetings between Booth and some of his conspirators. *Author's collection*

This previously unpublished photograph shows the Herndon House (center) where Booth announced his plan of assassination at a meeting in Lewis Powell's third-floor room. Atzerodt said that the gathering took place on the night of April 14, but according to hotel manager Martha Murray, Powell had already checked out that afternoon. *Surratt House Museum*

Naming names: Years after the assassination, Richard M. Smoot (top left) admitted his complicity in the plot, and implied that Joseph Eli Huntt (top right) and Frederick Stone (right) were involved as well. Stone actually worked his way into the trial as defense counsel to Dr. Mudd and David Herold. *Smoot: courtesy of Barbara F. Plate; Huntt: courtesy of Elysebeth Huntt Mays and Laurie Verge; Stone: author's collection*

Booth's note to Andrew Johnson helped create the impression of intimacy between the vice president and the man whose act had put him in charge of the government. By the same kind of deception, Booth framed many unsuspecting people. *National Archives*

ABOVE: Ford's Theatre, with Ferguson's Greenback Saloon adjoining it to the north (left) and the Star Saloon on the right. *Author's collection*

RIGHT: Ford's interior as it looks today. It is an active theater once again, as well as a museum. *Photograph by the author*

Booth used this single-shot .44 caliber derringer to shoot the president. It was later found in the theater box and turned over to police. *Federal Bureau of Investigation*

Henry Rathbone (left) and Clara Harris (below) accompanied the Lincolns to Ford's Theatre and were later married. Henry died in a German asylum after he murdered Clara and tried to kill himself. These photos are previously unpublished. *Courtesy of Louise Randolph Hartley*

William H. Seward, Secretary of State, never fully healed from the grievous wounds to his face. *Courtesy of Dr. John K. Lattimer*

Edman Spangler was the only theater employee to be prosecuted for conspiracy. *Library of Congress*

The Seward house on Lafayette Square was the scene of unimaginable horror. The house no longer stands. *U.S. Naval Historical Center*

Booth escaped from Washington on a horse he rented from what was then Pumphrey's Stable (shown here circa 1907). The conspirators' habit of swapping horses with one another led to the identification of Booth's inner circle within hours after the assassination. *Courtesy of Jerry A. McCoy*

Though Secretary of War Edwin M. Stanton admired the slain president, twentieth-century writers would make the outlandish claim that Stanton had a hand in Lincoln's assassination. *National Archives*

General Christopher Augur posted a reward of $10,000 within hours after the assassination. This flyer, discovered by the author, is the only known advertisement for that offer. *Historical Society of Washington, D.C.*

$10,000 REWARD!

Headquarters Department of Washington,

APRIL 15th, 1865.

A Reward of $10,000 will be paid to the party or parties arresting the

Murderer of the President, Mr. Lincoln!

And the ASSASSIN of the

SECRETARY OF STATE, MR. SEWARD!

C. C. AUGUR, Maj. Gen. Comd'g Dep't.

ABOVE: Authorities ignored Booth's own escape plan, which they found in his hotel room just after the president's shooting. The assassin intended to flee toward Mexico. *National Archives* LEFT: Booth began his flight over the route he had laid out for the president's abduction, but his broken leg forced him to make a costly detour for medical aid. *Map by the author*

Six hours after the assassination, Booth showed up at the home of Dr. Samuel A. Mudd, thirty miles south of Washington. Though Mudd had not seen the actor since the previous winter, he was suspected of involvement in the conspiracy, and was later convicted. *Library of Congress*

The fugitives' first attempt to cross the Potomac ended near Nanjemoy Creek, where they took refuge in a slave cabin on the farm of John J. Hughes. Nearly every building associated with Booth's flight is still standing, and two (the Surratt Tavern and Dr. Mudd's farmhouse) are now museums. *Photograph by the author*

RIGHT: First Lieutenant Edward P. Doherty (right) led the cavalry detachment that caught up to Booth at Garrett's farm. Sgt. Boston Corbett (left) fired the shot that killed the fugitive. *National Archives*

BELOW: Booth died on the front porch of Richard H. Garrett's farmhouse, where some of Garrett's children are shown in this previously unpublished photo. *Courtesy of Annette Morriss*

The *Saugus* and *Montauk* (second and third from left) are shown anchored off the Washington Navy Yard, where they were used as floating prisons for suspects in the assassination. Previously unpublished photo. *U.S. Naval Historical Center*

LEFT: The star witness was Louis J. Weichmann, whom many suspected of being a conspirator himself. *Courtesy of Floyd E. Risvold*
BELOW: Judge Advocate General Joseph Holt (center), with John A. Bingham (left) and Lt. Col. Henry L. Burnett, prosecuted the alleged conspirators. *Library of Congress*

SURRATT TRIAL

The Surratt trial grew so acrimonious that defense attorney Joseph H. Bradley, Sr., was disbarred for allegedly challenging the judge to a duel. Previously unpublished photograph. *Courtesy of Thomas Bradley*

After nineteen months on the run, John H. Surratt was captured in Egypt, then photographed before his return to the United States for trial. *Lauinger Library, Georgetown University*

Photographer Jeremiah Gurney photographed the president's corpse in New York's City Hall. The plates were ordered destroyed, but one print survived. *Illinois State Historical Library*

LEFT: July 7, 1865: The trap was sprung on Mary Surratt, Lewis Powell, David Herold, and George Atzerodt. Powell slowly strangled to death. *Library of Congress*

BELOW: The convicted conspirators were imprisoned in a second-floor cell (center) of Fort Jefferson, a military prison seventy miles west of the Florida Keys. Michael O'Laughlen died here, and the others were pardoned in 1869. *Key West Public Library*

After being moved several times, Booth's remains were ultimately buried in the family plot at Baltimore's Green Mount Cemetery. *Photograph by the author*

her sobs, a sadistic man in the crowd taunted her by suggesting that with Abraham Lincoln gone, she would have to return to slavery. "Oh, no!" the woman wailed. "God ain't dead yet!"

The soldiers laid the president out on a table, then took the coffin back to the Quartermaster Department. They discovered later that Mr. Lincoln's shirt had been left in the box, and they cut it up for souvenirs. Each of the six men was allowed to keep a swatch of the sacred cloth, thanks to their commander, General Rucker.[22]

A GATHERING OF SENATORS and congressmen joined Andrew Johnson for a formal swearing-in at the Kirkwood House. Some of the guests made a few remarks, then Chief Justice Salmon P. Chase stepped up and administered the oath. The new president addressed the crowd. "I must be permitted to remark that I have been almost overwhelmed by the announcement of the solemn event that has occurred," he said, "and I feel the heavy responsibilities which I have just undertaken." From the powerful to the obscure, everyone expected Johnson to deal harshly with Southern leaders. Willie Clark, in whose bed Mr. Lincoln had died, expressed a near-universal opinion when he wrote: "We have a man now who will teach the south a lesson." Indeed, Johnson's record left little room for doubt. Just recently he had told some well-wishers, "When you ask me what I would do, my reply is, I would arrest them; I would try them; I would convict them, and I would hang them. . . . We have put down these traitors in arms; let us put them down in law, in public judgment, and in the morals of the world." Now he assured his listeners that he had not changed his mind, and he looked to all those present for their support and assistance.

Johnson's delivery was a relief to those who feared he might repeat his inaugural performance of March 4. His speech on that occasion had been, in the words of Gideon Welles, "a rambling and strange harangue, which was listened to with pain and mortification by all his friends." Johnson was not a drinker, but had apparently taken stimulants to relieve an illness. It was an embarrassment he would never live down.[23]

Johnson's first act as president was to call a Cabinet meeting at the Treasury building, three blocks away. The meeting was brief, and afterward Johnson went to the White House to observe the autopsy. He, General Augur, and a team of medical observers looked on as Drs. Joseph Janvier Woodward and Edward Curtis performed a postmortem examination of Mr. Lincoln's remains. The face was swollen, and the eyes were blackened and protruding slightly. Dr. Stone, the president's personal physician, suggested that both sockets were fractured when the shock of the bullet's impact momentarily distorted the shape of the head. All agreed.

When the skull was opened, a small leaden ball dropped with a clink into the pan placed beneath the body. The brain was dissected to determine the physical damage it had done. The track of the ball was filled with clotted blood and pulplike brain matter. Small skull fragments were scattered along it, and the largest of these had lodged about two inches into the brain. There was some disagreement on where the bullet came to rest. In his official report, Dr. Woodward said that it stayed on the left side of the brain, and stopped behind the president's left eye. Dr. Stone agreed with this observation, but others who were there did not. Surgeon General Barnes thought the path moved upward and to the right, with the ball lodging above the right eye socket. Dr. Charles Taft said it had crossed the midline to a point behind the right eye. A recent study sides with Dr. Barnes.

When the autopsy was complete, Drs. Stone and Taft took the ball and bone fragments to Secretary Stanton's office, where Dr. Stone used a penknife to inscribe the ball with the initials "A.L." He sealed it in an envelope, and marked it as evidence.[24]

There was now the matter of funeral arrangements. Some in the Lincolns' inner circle thought the president should be buried in Washington, but others favored interment in Chicago. Nobody, at this point, wanted to approach Mrs. Lincoln, and her wishes were not known. Mary Jane Welles, wife of the navy secretary, had been summoned to attend her, and she was the only one speaking with her just now. So tentative plans were set in motion for an elaborate state funeral in Washington. Such things took time to arrange, and already some of the army's finest units were being called to Washington to march in the procession.[25]

THIRTEEN

"I BELIEVE HE WOULD HAVE MURDERED US, EVERY ONE"

JOHN WILKES BOOTH WAS IN PAIN, WHICH WAS LIKELY TO worsen after more hours on horseback. So David Herold asked Dr. Mudd if he could supply a carriage for the trip to Washington. The doctor did not have one of his own, but just after midday, he took Herold down to Oak Hill, the home of Mudd's father, to see if there was an extra buggy there. Mudd's brother, Henry Mudd, Jr., said that only one carriage was in working order, and since the next day was Easter Sunday, the family would need it for church. So Dr. Mudd and his visitor left Oak Hill, heading for Bryantown. Mudd needed to buy a few items for his wife, and Herold, apparently, was just tagging along. They started out together, but after riding to within sight of the town, Herold changed his mind and rode back to the farm alone.

Bryantown was a small village, and the arrival of Lieutenant Dana and the cavalry, around midday, caused a stir among its citizens. Some had already heard rumors about the assassination, and though many of the stories were false, Dana's men did little to set the record straight. They made no formal announcement, but told anyone who asked that a man named Booth had shot the president, and the guerrilla John H. Boyle was probably the assailant of Seward. Since Boyle had threatened the lives of several Unionists in the neighborhood, he was notorious in and around the village.

Dr. Samuel Mudd mingled with the townspeople, and of course he heard the news that was on every tongue. Years after the fact, a friend of Mudd's suggested he had gone into town only to pick up contraband messages, but that was apparently a mistake. Confederate agents were no longer in Richmond, and a regular mail service from there was already in place, making smuggling unnecessary. In any case, Mudd took care of his errands and stopped to talk with some friends who were discussing the assassination; Mudd later claimed that nobody said anything that led him to suspect that the visitors back at his farm were involved. He took a leisurely ride home, even stopping off for a chat with a couple of farmers who lived along the way.

In conversation with his friends, Mudd said that the assassination was the worst thing that could have happened. As he understood it, the guerrilla Boyle was one of the assassins, and the other was a man named Booth. John F. Hardy asked if that was the same Booth who had been nosing around in Charles County the year before. Mudd said that he didn't know; there were several brothers in the family, but if it was the same person, he knew him. After chatting for another minute or two, Mudd left to go home.[1]

Evidently Hardy's question began to gnaw at Dr. Mudd, and he thought back to Booth's December visit, and perhaps to that encounter in Washington as well. He realized at some point that the injured man at his house must be Booth, and that he had been trying to conceal his identity. In hindsight, both of Mudd's visitors seemed more excited than they should have been. Such thoughts tormented him, and Dr. Mudd rode back home with a quickening pace and a deepening sense of dread.

As he approached the house, he saw his visitors leaving by a side road, and he galloped over to confront them. He upbraided Booth for having deceived him, and he threatened to give him up to the authorities. Booth admitted his identity and pleaded with Mudd, in a theatrical style, to keep quiet. The doctor relented, but insisted they leave at once. They rode off in the direction of Zekiah Swamp.

Mudd thought he knew where the fugitives were going. Herold had asked him for directions to the home of Rev. Lemuel Wilmer, on the opposite side of the swamp. He asked again as they left, and as far as Mudd could tell, they seemed to be heading that way. But the road they took led over a hill, then turned sharply to the right. Once they passed over that hill, they would be out of sight, and Dr. Mudd would have no way of knowing whether they stayed on the road or turned away somewhere off in the distance.

Back in the house, Mudd learned that his wife had had suspicions all along. She had spoken with the injured man during the daylight hours, when her husband was outside working the fields. He had worn a false beard, she said, and it slipped a bit as he came down the stairs later on. They both recalled that he had asked for a razor, and in hindsight, they found it odd that a man with full whiskers would want to shave them off during a trip through the country. After talking it over, they realized that Booth had made them accessories in his escape, and their only recourse was to report his whereabouts right away. That wouldn't be easy. It was already dusk, and Dr. Mudd could not go back to Bryantown without leaving his wife and young children alone in the house. For all they knew, the fugitives were still out there, hiding somewhere just over the hill. Though Mudd wanted to file a report anyway, his wife begged him to wait until morning, when they would all be in town anyway for Easter Sunday mass.[2]

THE AFTERNOON PAPERS were flooded with accounts of the assassination and manhunt. Almost all of them ran at least one of James P. Ferguson's interviews. Ferguson was so much in demand as a witness that he neglected his saloon, and eventually lost it. Somehow he managed to recount his experience in Ford's without saying a word about his companion. Mary Ellen Cecil had been sitting next to Ferguson in the dress circle, and probably saw just as much as he did. But she wanted to stay out of the limelight to avoid explaining her engagement to a thirty-year-old man when she was only fourteen. In fact, she was one of many eyewitnesses who, for various reasons, never spoke out on the subject. And no one was forcing her. The government made no systematic effort to interview those who had been present, or even to collect their names.

While many people assumed that hidden forces were behind the assassination, others speculated that Booth had acted on his own. The reason: he wanted to immortalize himself. Within days of the shooting, newspapers began to report that an anonymous source had once heard Booth talk about killing the president. Asked why he would do such a thing, he had quoted a couplet from the Colley Cibber version of *Richard III:*

> *The daring youth that fired the Ephesian dome*
> *Outlives in fame the pious fool that reared it.*

The story spread quickly, and it became the basis of the most popular explanation for Lincoln's killing. But it has the character of a modern urban legend. Though it sounded authoritative, its original source has never been identified.[3]

BY SATURDAY AFTERNOON, nearly a thousand soldiers were in the saddle, pursuing leads on Booth's whereabouts. Much of their search was now concentrated in Southern Maryland, a place that struck one reporter as "the most heaven-forsaken country within a hundred miles of Washington. . . . No fences anywhere, no green thing in sight, no trim farm houses, no people with white faces, save ever and anon a bankrupt and hopeless looking farmer stretched on a load of manure and cornstalks and gazing dejectedly at a team of palsied ponies." Through this supposed wasteland rode seven hundred men of the 8th Illinois Cavalry. Their commanding officer, Major John M. Waite, split them into three companies to cover all major routes and settlements in the area. When one detachment reached St. Peter's Church, near the home of Dr. Mudd, they asked if anyone there was familiar with Booth or his companion, "Harold." The jovial priest, Father Peter Lenaghan, assured them that the only Harold he ever knew was Byron's "Childe Harold."

While soldiers searched the countryside, detectives covered the city. At the Herold house, just outside the navy yard, Washington police officers borrowed a photograph of David from his sister Jane. They turned it over to Frank Van Benthuysen of General Augur's staff, and within hours, copies were being produced for distribution.[4]

AT HIS HOUSE on Lafayette Square, William H. Seward awoke to find his face covered in bandages and his wife trying to give him tea with a spoon. He could hear the murmur of low voices in the room, and he motioned for a tablet. When a doctor handed him one, he took it and wrote, "Give me some more tea. I shall get well." His family physician, Dr. Tullio S. Verdi, had already determined that the secretary's wounds were not life-threatening, but he knew that both Seward and his son would require constant care for months. Verdi would soon have the help of Dr. Thomas B. Gunning, a dentist who specialized in the treatment of jaw fractures. Dr. Gunning would fashion a splint for the secretary. Made of vulcanized rubber, it fit inside the mouth and was fastened by screws driven into the teeth. Eventually, saliva started to collect inside, and the cheek had to be lanced to relieve the problem. Thus did the suffering of William H. Seward continue for months on end.

Frederick Seward had been in a coma since shortly after the attack, and when he regained consciousness a few days later, his first thought was of a British diplomat whose credentials were to have been presented on April 15. He asked whether the ceremony had taken place as scheduled.[5]

GENERAL GRANT ARRIVED in Washington after a long and worrisome night in transit. He checked in to Willard's, as he always did. Only minutes later, he received a message from General Halleck advising him, as a matter of security, not to be so predictable. He went straight to the War Department for a conference with Secretary Stanton. That, too, was to be expected.

Attorney Britten A. Hill followed a busy night at the Petersen house with an even busier day of developing leads. In the morning, he spoke with Robinson and Bell, of the Seward household, and got a detailed description of the assailant. In the afternoon he went to Ford's Theatre to speak with witnesses about Booth's movements on the day of the murder. He even went inside the president's box, and discovered that the locks to both doors had been broken sometime before the shooting. Of all the investigators on this case, Hill was the first to take those commonsense measures. Still, his instincts were not perfect; he mistakenly concluded that Booth had ridden northeast, in the direction of Bladensburg, and was still bottled up in the city. "If not," he reported, "then I am wholly at fault."

Like Stanton, Hill read too much into the clues that Booth might be heading for Baltimore. It made sense that he would escape to his hometown, and even though they had not yet found him there, most authorities were convinced that they were on the right track. Only days later would they confirm that Booth had gone in another direction.

Many thought that Booth was probably still in Washington. The federal net could be drawn only so tight, though, and it would be difficult to keep him bottled up indefinitely. Soldiers had already blocked every road out of the city, and all forms of mass transportation were halted until further notice.

One of those caught in the traffic was George Atzerodt. On Saturday morning, Atzerodt borrowed ten dollars from a friend in Georgetown, putting his revolver down as collateral. He then walked up High Street to the home of Lucinda Metts, a family connection, and took a meal. He had apparently made up his mind to head north toward Montgomery County, where he might stay with relatives. He boarded the stage for Rockville, but outbound traffic had been stopped for hours and nobody could get past Tennallytown, on the northern edge of the city. So Atzerodt left the stage-coach and struck up a conversation with one of the men posted along the road. Before long, he and Sgt. Lewis F. Chubb, 13th Michigan Light Artillery, were sitting down together for a drink.[6]

Traffic jams and flaring tempers were paralyzing the city and putting the public safety at risk. By mid-afternoon, the problem had gotten so out of control that it had to be called to Stanton's attention. The secretary ordered the roadblocks removed at once, and he told General Morris, in Baltimore, that he never meant to stop all trains heading his way. From now on, Morris should let the trains pass, but watch the passengers carefully.

Once travel restrictions were eased, Mike O'Laughlen took a three o'clock train back home. He felt sick, and not just from a sense of dread; if his friend Edward Murphy was correct, O'Laughlen and his companions had spent their time in Washington visiting twenty-one bars, four bawdy houses, and one "leg show"—all in a period of thirty hours.

THE CAPITAL WAS quietly transforming itself from a party town to a city of death. Patriotic displays of red, white, and blue were replaced by the black crape of mourning. That, and a dreary sky, made Washington the picture of misery: weary, dull, lifeless, devoid of light and shadow. Charles H. Jones, of the navy, was ordered to hang rolls of crape on government office buildings. After draping the White House, he went to the War Department, next door, to size up the task there. He walked into a darkened office on the third floor and noticed a man sitting at a desk, head bowed as if asleep. "Pardon me," Jones said. The man looked up, and Jones was startled to see that it was General Grant. He looked haggard and utterly exhausted. "Don't mind me," sighed the general. "Carry out your orders."[7]

BOOTH AND HEROLD HAD NOT CROSSED Zekiah Swamp, as Dr. Mudd believed. They had gone away from Mudd's farm heading toward the swamp, but after disappearing over the hill, they turned around and rode in the opposite direction. A short while later, Herold was seen alone near the barn at Oak Hill, where he was confronted by Alexis Thomas, an elderly servant of Henry Mudd. Thomas and his wife thought that Herold seemed nervous. His conversation was disjointed, and he acted as if he had been caught at something he couldn't explain. He said he had lost his bearings, and asked if there was a "Dr. Sam" living nearby. Though Thomas gave him directions to Mudd's, Herold changed the subject, and asked, "Who lives here?" He wondered if he might spend the night at Oak Hill, but on second thought maybe he should just head for Bryantown. Instead of asking how to get there, though, he inquired whether there was a big swamp nearby. Thomas pointed toward the Zekiah in the distance, and Herold rode off in that direction. The Thomases were glad to be rid of him.

Booth was probably hiding nearby. Why they had gone to Oak Hill is anybody's guess, but quite possibly, Herold had gone back to steal the carriage he had tried unsuccessfully to borrow. Failing that, he rejoined Booth and they continued southward on horseback. They reached the present settlement of Hughesville, a few miles below Mudd's, long after dark. Somewhere west of there they got lost, and by nine o'clock in the evening, they decided to ask for directions.[8]

They could not have known it, but a company of Confederate cavalry passed within eight miles of their escape route that night. The federal government owned a farm along the Patuxent River where they raised food for the army, and some of Mosby's Rangers happened to be snooping around there to see how much they could divert for their own use. Assuming these men were in Southern Maryland to assist Booth, the commander of Union troops in the area sent a detachment to intercept them. The unit returned in a panic, and after sorting things out, Maj. John M. Waite concluded that the skirmish they reported was a "humbug," and the officer who made it up ought to be dismissed. In fact, the troops actually were fired upon— but by local citizens, not the Rangers. Three of those citizens were later arrested.

At about nine o'clock that evening, the fugitives spotted a small house off the Cracklintown road, southeast of Bryantown, and Herold knocked on the door. The man who answered was Oswald Swan, a so-called wesort— of white, African American, and Piscataway Indian descent—who lived there with his wife and eight children. Swan gave Herold whiskey and bread, as requested. For two dollars, he agreed to guide him and his friend to the home of William Bertles, who lived near St. Mary's Church. But as soon as they got on the road, Herold changed his mind and asked if Swan would take them across the swamp instead. For that, he offered an additional five dollars.[9]

The man they wanted to visit was Samuel Cox, one of Charles County's best-known citizens. Cox lived at Rich Hill, an 845-acre farm a few miles east of Port Tobacco. The Coxes had bought it from the family of Dr. Gustavus Brown, one of George Washington's physicians. The present owner was a humorless, domineering man with a commanding air and a social prominence that made the Yankees want desperately to catch him at something. Noting that he had once served as the captain of a militia company, the Federals once mounted an expedition to search for weapons Cox was said to have stashed away for his old comrades. He had none. The rumors were false, like most stories told about Cox. One, printed in the *New York Tribune,* accused the captain of murdering an escaped slave who had gone to the Federals for sanctuary but who was then returned to Rich Hill and killed. The story was a clumsy fabrication, and was exposed as such. But in time it reemerged, with different killers and different victims. For better or worse, these myths made Samuel Cox famous, and though Booth had never met the captain, he knew his reputation.[10]

The Cox home was a large white frame house on the crest of a hill just west of Zekiah Swamp. It was about one A.M. when the fugitives arrived there. Herold's loud knock on the front door awoke Mary Swann, a servant, who went to get the captain. Cox was leery of answering the door in the middle of the night. Looking out the window, he saw Herold standing back from the steps, calling out to Cox for a night's lodging and something to eat. He declined to identify himself, and the captain was inclined to turn him away. "I will not admit strangers who refuse to give me their names," he said. It was only then, as Herold turned to walk away, that Cox noticed another man waiting near the fence. They both approached the house and pleaded for help.

Samuel Cox told authorities that he turned Booth and Herold away, and his nephew, who heard the conversation, confirmed that. "If it is the last word I have to say on earth," said the captain, Booth "never entered my home, unless he came into the door and knocked before I got up." But as their guide Oswald Swan reported it, the fugitives *did* go into the house, and they stayed inside for several hours while Swan waited in the yard for the money promised him. Many years later, Cox's servant Mary Swann claimed to have served the fugitives a meal in the dining room. Whatever happened that night, it was almost dawn before Booth and Herold left the property. Swan and Herold helped Booth into the saddle, and Booth muttered, "I thought Cox was a man of Southern feeling." The fugitives left the yard with their guide, and a few minutes later, Herold gave Swan twelve dollars and a warning: "If you tell that you saw anybody you will not live long."[11]

A COLD FRONT SWEPT over the area that morning, with bone-chilling temperatures and a wind so strong it nearly tore the flag off its pole at the War Department. The change in weather concerned Samuel Cox, who probably worried that Booth and Herold would seek shelter among his neighbors, bringing danger to anyone who agreed to let them in. So after breakfast he went out to look for the fugitives. He found them shivering in a ditch, and promised to help them after all. The Potomac River was three miles away, and Cox said that a friend of his could get them across it. His overseer, Franklin A. Robey, would guide them to an old Confederate mail drop a mile or so west of Rich Hill. They should hide in the woods nearby, and someone would come to meet them. That man would identify himself by a certain whistle.[12]

THIS WAS EASTER SUNDAY, the day that Christians celebrate the martyrdom and resurrection of Christ. But Lincoln's death brought a new meaning to the idea of redemption and sacrifice, and ministers all across the North proclaimed a new national savior. Abraham Lincoln was now the "chief of martyrs," whose sacrifice would save the nation. The irony was inescapable: Booth had hoped to kill Lincoln on the Ides and highlight his resemblance to Caesar; but instead, he shot him on Good Friday, and the world compared him to Christ.

In Cincinnati, Rev. A. D. Mayo ran through a catalog of Southern atrocities and pointed out the irony of their last, brutal act. "Wicked men upon earth always go on to the last result," said the minister, "and that result is to slay their truest friends, and quench their blind rage in the blood of the noblest who would die to save them." From other pulpits came dire predictions and warnings for the South. As Rev. J. A. Thome told his congregation in Cleveland, "God is exalted among us; assassins cannot reach him, with pistol and dagger, and 'sic semper tyrannis'; but He can reach them, and He hath said, 'Vengeance is mine.' "[13]

EDWIN BOOTH HAD NOT BEEN in touch with his old friend Adam Badeau for some time, but he wrote him a letter before leaving Boston. He described his brother as one who "seemed so lovable and in whom all in the family found a source of joy in his boyish and fighting nature." What, he wondered, would now become of him and everyone who bore "the once honored and now despised name"? He needed Badeau's advice. "I was two days ago one of the happiest men alive," he wrote. "Now what am I? Oh, how little did I dream my boy when on Friday I was, as Sir Edward Mortimer, exclaiming, 'where is my honor now?' 'Mountains of shame are piled upon me' that I was not acting but uttering the fearful truth. I have a great deal to tell you of myself and the beautiful plans I had for the future, all blasted now but must wait until my mind is more settled. I am half crazy now." He was especially concerned about his mother, Mary Ann, saying, "I go to New York today expecting to find her either dead or dying."

Though Edwin wrote from the depths of despair, his glum outlook was not unrealistic; his fiancée, Blanche Hanel, would soon change her mind about marrying into the Booth family. But Mary Ann was not so frail as he imagined. She had taken a train to Philadelphia, and was with Asia by Sunday afternoon. In conversation, Asia mentioned the papers her brother had left with her. She said nothing about having looked at them already, but suggested they go through them now. So she, Mary Ann, and Sleeper Clarke went down to the safe and spent the rest of the afternoon poring over the items John Wilkes had left.

They found some bonds in the amount of $3,000; some city bonds for another $1,000; and a deed to Booth's oil property, signed over to Junius. They also found two letters, one of which was addressed to Mary Ann:

Dearest beloved Mother

Heaven knows how dearly I love you. And may our kind Father in Heaven (if only for the sake of my love) watch over, comfort & protect you, in my absence. May he soften the blow of my departure, granting you peace and happiness for many, many years to come. God ever bless you.

I have always endeavored to be a good and dutiful son, and even now would wish to die sooner than give you pain. But dearest Mother, though I owe you all, there is another duty, a noble duty for the sake of liberty and humanity due to my country—For four years I have lived (I may say) a slave in the north (a favored slave its [sic] true, but no less hateful to me on that account.) Not daring to express my thoughts or sentiments, even in my own home, constantly hearing every principle, dear to my heart, denounced as treasonable, and knowing the vile and savage acts committed on my countrymen their wives & helpless children, that I have cursed my wilful idleness, and begun to deem myself a coward and to despise my own existence. For four years I have borne it mostly for your dear sake, and for you alone, have I also struggled to fight off this desire to be gone, but it seems that uncontrollable fate, moving me for its ends, takes me from you, dear Mother, to do what work I can for a poor oppressed downtrodden people. May that same fate cause me to do that work well. I care not for the censure of the north, so I have your forgiveness, and I feel I may hope it, even though you differ with me in opinion. I may by the grace of God, live through this war dear Mother, if so, the rest of my life shall be more devoted to you, than has been my former. For I know it will take a long lifetime of tenderness and care, to atone for the pang this parting will give you. But I cannot longer resist the inclination to go and share the sufferings of my brave countrymen, holding an unequal strife (for every right human & divine) against the most ruthless enemy, the world has ever known. You can answer for me dearest Mother (although none of you think with me) that I have not a single selfish motive to spur me on to this, nothing save the sacred duty, I feel I owe the cause I love, the cause of the South. The cause of liberty & justice. So should I meet the worst, dear Mother, in struggling for such holy rights. I can say "Gods' [*sic*] will be done" and bless him in my heart for not permitting me to outlive our dear bought freedom. And for keeping me from being longer a hidden lie among my country's foes. Darling Mother I can not write you, you will understand the deep regret, the forsaking your dear side, will make me suffer, for you have been the best, the noblest, an example for all mothers. God bless you, as I shall ever pray him to do. And should the last bolt strike your son, dear Mother, bear it patiently and think at the best life is but short, and not at all times happy. My Brothers & Sisters (Heaven protect them) will add my love and duty to their own, and watch you with care and kindness, till we meet again. And if that happiness does not come to us on earth, then may, O may it be with God. So then dearest, dearest Mother, forgive and pray for me. I feel that I am right in the justness of my cause, and that we shall, ere long, meet again. Heaven grant it. Bless you, bless you. Your loving son will never cease to hope and pray for such a joy.

Come weal or woe, with never ending love and devotion you will find me ever your affectionate son

John.

To John Sleeper Clarke's way of thinking, the fact that Booth could not express himself at home was clear evidence that the family did not agree with him and would not have condoned or encouraged the assassination. He thought that in justice to the family, that letter ought to be published. Certainly, it would be more helpful than the second letter, which seemed to be addressed to Clarke himself. It was part manifesto, part explanation for Booth's plan to "make a prisoner of this man to whom the world owes so much misery." It rehashed the political arguments of the past, restated Booth's love for the Union as it once was, and expressed his certainty that Abraham Lincoln was wrong in making war against the South. "In a *foreign war*," Booth wrote, "I too could say 'country right or wrong,' But in a struggle *such as ours* (where the brother tries to pierce the brothers [*sic*] heart) for God's sake choose the right." Booth had always sought guidance from the past, and he was confident that his drastic action would help the United States avoid the failures of bygone civilizations.[14]

GEORGE C. COTTINGHAM AND JOSHUA LLOYD had spent most of Friday night standing guard outside Andrew Johnson's hotel room. Both were detectives on the force of Major James O'Beirne, and naturally both were eager to join the manhunt. They finally got their chance late on Saturday, when Lloyd realized that both David Herold and John Surratt, whose names had emerged in the investigation, were acquaintances of his. They reported this fact to O'Beirne, and the major reassigned them to find those men. At five A.M. on Sunday, the detectives saddled up and headed for Surrattsville.

By then, Booth and Herold were camping in a stand of pine trees forty miles south of Washington. Though Booth had brought an extra pistol in his saddlebags, he could hardly rest easy. He knew he was the most hunted man in American history, and pursuers might come at him from any direction. Though the fugitives were unaware of it, hundreds had already flooded into Charles County. Many of those who landed at Chapel Point were passing nearby on their way inland. So for hours they sat quiet and motionless, continuously scanning the woods for signs of danger. A subtle noise, and their eyes widened; a sudden move, and they gripped their revolvers. After hours of anxious waiting, they finally heard two whistles, a pause, then another whistle. It was the signal Captain Cox had told them to expect.

The man Cox had sent to them was slow-moving, dour, and gray-haired. Thomas A. Jones was forty-four, but could pass for sixty. The years had worn heavily on him. His imprisonment and the death of his wife had made him determined to do all he could in service to the Cause—or more to the point, against the administration. Jones had ferried countless people across the river near his old home, a few miles south of here. That place stood on an eighty-foot bluff, with dormer windows that had given him a clear view of the Potomac for seven miles to the north and nine to the south. But Jones had lost that home, and he now lived in a smaller house a few miles to the north. His new place was much farther from the Potomac, with nothing but dense woods and rough terrain between them. At its nearest point, the river was turbulent and far more dangerous to cross.[15]

ALL DAY SATURDAY, Secretary Stanton seemed to think that the manhunt would be over at any time, and that he could run the investigation using only the people at his immediate disposal. But by Sunday, Booth had still not been captured, and the flood of data had become unmanageable. It was clear that more brainpower would be needed to solve the case. So Stanton contacted local, state, and federal officials all over the country and asked them to send their best detectives to Washington. He freed up some of his own department's investigators, and he reassigned several provost marshals to concentrate on the case. In days he had assembled the largest investigative body in the nation's history.[16]

To make sense of the information they gathered, Stanton put three special commissioners in charge of the case. Lt. Col. John A. Foster, Col. Henry H. Wells, and Col. Henry Steel Olcott would run the investigation from their offices in General Augur's headquarters. Each was an experienced investigator with a distinct perspective. Foster, of New York City, was a thirty-two-year-old prodigy who had begun practicing law when he was barely out of his teens. Wells, forty-one, was a native New Yorker and a tough-minded prosecutor. He had once commanded the 26th Michigan Infantry, but served lately as the provost marshal of Washington's defenses south of the Potomac. Olcott, thirty-two, was an author, educator, and pioneer in scientific agriculture. When the department hired him as a detective, he was already famous as a debunker of psychic phenomena. Though

Secretary of the Navy Gideon Welles sized him up as "rash, reckless, at times regardless of the rights of others," Olcott would be the most conscientious member of the investigative team.[17]

On Sunday afternoon, Detectives George Cottingham and Joshua Lloyd set up their headquarters in the tavern at Surrattsville. They had been looking for John M. Lloyd as a possible informant, but Lloyd (who was not related to Joshua) had gone to Allen's Fresh, where he had sent his wife a few days before. The detectives talked about going after him, but before they could leave, something strange happened. A riderless horse, with a saddle and bridle, came trotting out of the woods just beyond the fence. A short distance from it was a man on foot. He noticed the detectives, and dashed back into the woods. A sergeant gave chase. He fired a couple of shots in his direction, but the man got away and apparently the horse fled as well. No trace of the stranger or the animal was found. Not knowing who else might be out there, Cottingham sent a messenger back to Washington for reinforcements. In the meantime, he and his partner would stay where they were and wait to see if the man reappeared.[18]

Meanwhile, Provost Marshal James L. McPhail continued looking for Booth's associates in Baltimore. Two of his men, Voltaire Randall and Eaton G. Horner, had already learned that Booth had been close to Sam Arnold and Mike O'Laughlen. They could not find either man in Baltimore, so they telegraphed their names and descriptions to authorities in Washington. Their search took on a new urgency when an item appeared in the papers about a letter Booth had received from someone named "Sam" in Hookstown. This had to be Arnold.

Hookstown was a small settlement about five miles northwest of the city. It was the kind of place where everyone knew everyone else and secrets were hard to keep. The Arnold family owned a 118-acre farm there, and it was left in the care of Mrs. Arnold's brother, William J. Bland. Sam Arnold had moved in with his uncle after leaving the plot in March, but his stay was short-lived. By the beginning of April, he had already gone away, and as McPhail's men learned, he had given the postmistress a forwarding address at Fortress Monroe, Virginia. Armed with that information, detectives took the 7:00 P.M. steamship to Old Point Comfort, next to the fort at the mouth of the Chesapeake.[19]

AT HIS HOME IN CAMDEN, New Jersey, Matthew Canning was taken into custody by Captain John H. Jack, 186th Pennsylvania. For Canning, his arrest was less of a surprise than the identity of the officer who made it. John Jack, a former actor himself, was an intimate friend of both Canning and the Booths. He trusted his prisoner, and spared him a traumatic ride to Washington in wrist irons. They traveled as companions.[20]

Harry A. Langdon was not so fortunate. As an actor, Langdon was also well acquainted with the Booths. He also bore a resemblance to them; for that reason, he was thrown in jail. He was just one of many look-alikes detained in the wake of the assassination. One such person, hustled off a train at Wilmington, was subsequently identified as Congressman Andrew Jackson Rogers of New Jersey. Others were less well known. By Monday, the jails were filling up with so many attractive dark-haired men that the Philadelphia *Inquirer* noted it was no longer safe to be good-looking. Authorities mistook one man for Booth and tried to seize him on a train in southeastern Pennsylvania. Unaware they were after him, the man traveled from Pottsville through Reading and into the Poconos with soldiers hot on his heels. They finally caught up to him after a sixty-mile chase, near Tamaqua. Records give no indication of his fate.[21]

Photographs of Booth would have spared these handsome men the agony, but not everyone had access to them. The War Department ordered plenty of copies, but the Surgeon General's office, which was printing them, could not keep up with the demand. Booth had been photographed more than forty times, and detectives were using at least two different images in their questioning of witnesses. One was selected for mass distribution. It showed Booth seated, with his left hand on his hip, cradling a small riding crop in his right hand. Apparently, it was not the best choice. Brooke Stabler and Sergeant Cobb both had trouble recognizing him from it, and Mary Ann Van Tyne noted how little resemblance it actually bore to Booth. "I think him a better looking man than that is," she said, "but I should think it is the man I saw. But it is a poor likeness of him." O'Laughlen's friend Dan Loughran agreed. Loughran had been shown a standing pose of Booth, and he said it looked a lot more like him than did the other one. The poor choice of photographs complicated matters for some suspects. Anyone who failed to identify Booth from the seated photograph was judged to be evasive, and all the more suspicious.[22]

WITH DETECTIVES SWARMING IN from many jurisdictions, some friction was bound to develop. The presence of Lafayette C. Baker, chief of the National Detective Police, would guarantee it. When Baker arrived in

Washington on Sunday, his first order of business was to offer a $30,000 reward—from funds he didn't have—to anyone who could find the conspirators. He copied Britten Hill's description of the Seward assailant onto the handbills he sent out. Then he happened upon two detectives from the police department and told them (falsely) that Stanton had put him in overall command of the investigation. The men shared some leads with Baker, and in exchange he offered the information that he already had Booth's horse in his possession. That, too, was a lie. In a matter of hours, Lafayette Baker had managed to alienate some of the best detectives around. And he was just getting started.[23]

PRIVATE THOMAS PRICE, 6th New York Heavy Artillery, was one of many soldiers assigned to look for Booth in Washington. At about three P.M., he was searching in a rural area near Glenwood Cemetery when he noticed an old path, now overgrown, leading into the woods between two forts. Lying next to it, in a gully, was a long gray coat with bloodstains on the right sleeve and breast. Price thought the garment might have something to do with the assassination, and excitedly he made note of the clues associated with it: a snail on the coat, the dampness of the fabric, and the nearby tracks of a large horse.

At about the same time, Justice Abram B. Olin accompanied Clara Harris, who had been the Lincolns' guest in their box, to the scene of the crime. Clara's father, Senator Ira Harris, was with them, as were Jim Ferguson and Chief Justice Cartter of the Supreme Court of the District of Columbia. On entering the box, Clara suddenly remembered a white-handled penknife she had seen lying open on the balustrade that Friday night. At the time, she had been distracted by the play, and forgot all about it. The knife had disappeared since then, but other important evidence remained. Justice Olin was particularly interested in the doors to the box. Olin had heard a rumor that Booth fired the shot through the closed door behind the president's rocker, and he wanted to resolve that issue. He asked Clara Harris to arrange the furniture just as she remembered it. Then, by the light of a candle, he and the others inspected the hole in the door. It did indeed line up with the back of the president's head, but it was smaller than a bullet, and had no powder burns around it. There were, however, fresh and distinct marks from a gimlet. Since there were no wood shavings on the carpet, it appeared that whoever had bored the hole had cleaned up after himself.[24]

. . .

AT THE LITTLE VILLAGE OF NEWPORT, in southern Charles County, Thomas Harbin and a Confederate boatman named Joseph N. Baden, Jr., left a local hotel and headed south toward a place on the Potomac called the Banks O'Dee. Harbin, who had enlisted in the plot when Booth spoke to him in Bryantown the previous winter, had not been seen with any of the conspirators in months, and may well have thought the abduction plan had been abandoned. Most likely, he and Baden had come over with Mosby's people in their quest for forage, but since Booth had drawn so much attention to the area, they no longer considered it prudent to remain. In light of subsequent events, it appears that someone in Maryland told them to recross the river, then wait on the other side, where a couple of men would join them later.

Meanwhile, Booth's mare had broken her bridle, and their slow-moving guide, Thomas Jones, found her grazing near the pine thicket. The fugitives could ill afford to have her running loose. Hundreds of people had been given a description of this horse, and if she were discovered, soldiers would intensify their search of the area. Jones advised the fugitives to get rid of her, and Herold's horse as well. Franklin Robey, Cox's overseer, and Herold led the animals down to the swamp. Pulling them into deep water, they shot both horses and watched their carcasses sink beneath the surface. Now even the vultures wouldn't find them.[25]

BY SUNDAY AFTERNOON, George Atzerodt had made his way to Germantown and the home of Hezekiah Metz, an old family friend whose daughter Elizabeth had caught his eye. Atzerodt—or Atwood, as his hosts knew him—was one of several guests who had joined the Metzes for supper, and around the table all anyone could talk about was the assassination. The news had come out in bits and pieces, and James Leamon was skeptical of what he had been hearing. He asked if it was true that General Grant had been murdered. Atzerodt said he did not think so, but added, "If it is so, someone must have got on the same train of cars that he did."[26]

FROM HIS HOTEL ROOM IN CINCINNATI, Junius Booth wrote to his brother Edwin. "Words of consolation are idle—we must use philosophy. 'Tis a mere matter of time the grief & shame of this blow will pass away. . . . But poor Mother who can console her, for a mother is a mother ever, and I am afraid she can never be brought to look calmly on this dreadful calamity." For decades, Mary Ann had been plagued by scandals, but at the present, rumormongers and blackmailers were the least of her worries. Now what she feared was violence, not exposure. Given the temper of the times, the worst of the threats might well be carried out.[27]

In New York, friends of Edwin Booth requested police protection at his house. At Asia's home in Philadelphia, police didn't have to be called. They searched her house, opened her mail, and followed her from room to room. If not for her difficult pregnancy, they would have carried her off in irons. But as it was, authorities allowed her to remain at home as long as she stayed in the company of a male guard. Friends shied away, and even her doctor refused to call on her. The sole visitor to the house was an actor named Claud Burroughs, who said that Edwin had sent him down to retrieve some papers. In fact, Burroughs was actually a detective. But no matter how difficult others made her life, the worst treatment came from her own husband. Within months, John Sleeper Clarke would decide that a Booth connection was no longer useful, and he asked his wife for a divorce. He said it would be *his* only salvation.[28]

AT SEVEN O'CLOCK MONDAY MORNING, detectives Randall and Horner of Provost Marshal McPhail's office entered John Wharton's store at Fortress Monroe and told Sam Arnold that he was under arrest. Arnold seemed more relieved than surprised. He gave the investigators everything he had brought with him. In return, Randall handed Arnold a note from his father urging him to tell authorities whatever he might know about the plot. This was more than just fatherly advice; it was damage control. George Arnold—born *Benedict* Arnold—was well aware of the stigma that crime could attach to a family name. On his father's advice, Sam began to talk, and soon the detectives had the information they sought. Randall wired back to McPhail: "You will arrest J. W. Booth, a Michael O'Laughlin [*sic*] of Baltimore; a G. W. Atzerodt, alias Port Tobacco, of Charles Co., Maryland, and John Surratt, residence not known, as all are implicated." Then, with the suspect in tow, the detectives boarded a steamship for Baltimore.[29]

GEORGE COTTINGHAM HAD REQUESTED reinforcements from Washington after seeing the stranger flee into the woods at Surrattsville. His message reached Major O'Beirne on Sunday night, but O'Beirne saw no point in sending out a party after dark. So just after daylight on Monday,

Detectives William Williams and Simon Gavacan left for Surrattsville with a detachment of ten soldiers under Lt. Alexander Lovett, 9th V.R.C. When they arrived at the tavern, Cottingham gave them a progress report and told them that they had been looking for the tavern keeper, John M. Lloyd. Lieutenant Lovett decided to take his detachment to Allen's Fresh in search of Lloyd. Joshua Lloyd joined them, and they left at midday.[30]

SECRETARY STANTON REMAINED at his desk, following up on some rumors and stamping out others. One source claimed that Booth was heading for the Mississippi River, and Stanton notified authorities along the way there. Another source reported seeing him near the Chesapeake, and more troops were dispatched in that direction. Sightings were commonplace, and one never knew where they might occur. In fact, some detectives were so sure they had seen him in London that week that the U.S. ambassador, Charles Francis Adams, requested a warrant to have him arrested there.[31]

SOME OF THE FORD'S THEATRE cast and crew were assembled on Monday to reenact *Our American Cousin* for the War Department. Investigators wanted to see if Booth had timed his shot for a moment in the play when the stage was supposed to be unobstructed. They found that of the twenty-nine people who occupied the stage at one point or another, only one would have been in Booth's path for that one scene in Act Two. The test confirmed once again that Booth had planned the shooting down to the smallest detail.

After the rehearsal, Edwin Stanton came in to look at the president's box. He examined the hole in the door, the broken locks, and the niche Booth had carved into the wall of the outer passage. His guide, James Gifford, knew all about the box—the way it was furnished and decorated, and the relative positions of everyone in the president's party. So when Mathew Brady, the photographer, came in a short while later, he was also told to consult Gifford. Together they re-created the original setting with borrowed flags and bunting in place of the originals, which had disappeared.[32]

DETECTIVE RANDALL'S TELEGRAM about the capture of Arnold specifically identified Mike O'Laughlen as a conspirator. Since Provost Marshal McPhail lacked the manpower to track O'Laughlen down, he asked the Baltimore city police to do it for him. They checked at O'Laughlen's house, and learned that the suspect was actually waiting to be arrested; he just didn't want his mother to see him being taken away. So, through an intermediary, he arranged to surrender at the home of his sister Kate.

Assistant Secretary of War Charles Dana sent instructions for getting O'Laughlen to Washington: "Have [him] in double irons, and use every precaution against escape, but as far as possible avoid everything which can lead to suspicion on the part of the people on the train and give rise to an attempt to lynch the prisoner. . . ."

O'Laughlen's escort, Officer William E. Wallis, described the prisoner as "not communicative," but he did learn something from talking with him. O'Laughlen admitted that he had joined a plot to capture—not kill—the president, but he insisted he had quit as soon as the government resumed the prisoner exchange. His only subsequent contacts with Booth were aimed at getting back the $500 he claimed Booth owed him.[33]

THE WAR DEPARTMENT WAS RECEIVING all manner of clues and offers in the mail. It was a mixed bag, with plenty of crank letters, but just as many solid leads. One man insisted that Booth was in Chicago, disguised as a woman in a house of ill repute. Another was signed by "Booth" himself, and challenged authorities to catch him. Still another announced his arrival in Canada. One crank—an especially poor researcher—addressed a note to "George Surratt, care of Mrs. Surratt" and began, "Dear Sir: You are to attempt the murder of Secretary Seward while I am to attempt the life of Mr. [Salmon] Chase. . . ." It was dated April 10, but postmarked a month later.

Psychic help seemed to come from all directions. One woman said that a reliable medium in Buffalo thought that Booth could be found in a "large, brown, Southern style house" situated "either north or south of Washington," and a Mrs. Van de Water said that her favorite clairvoyant sensed that a red-haired woman had Booth in her closet, but wanted him to leave.

On the whole, most mailed-in clues seemed entirely plausible. A prisoner in Fort Delaware advised the provost marshal to check for John Surratt at the home of Walter Griffin. A man signing himself "Loyalty" recommended searching for Herold at the Charles County home of his uncle, Horatio Nelson. Thomas Quinn, who grew up with the Booths, said that the assassin was "not a mile from here," in Baltimore. By using valid names and connections, these people commanded a top priority with

War Department investigators. They were honest people who wanted to help, even if they were usually wrong.[34]

Nevertheless, the War Department dared not ignore them. Sometimes their letters were a great help. Henry Clay Young, of Cincinnati, sent the department a list of scars and marks he had seen on Booth's body, and told them to look for a "J.W.B." tattoo on his left hand. A group of black men in Washington persisted in calling attention to an underground passage at the Van Ness mansion. When soldiers searched the house, they turned up some letters that tied John Surratt to Preston Parr. They also uncovered a tunnel-like sewer that ran very close to the White House.

For several days, investigators were ordered to keep their attention sharply focused on conveyances arriving in Philadelphia: a specific ship from Delaware City, a specific train from Baltimore. On Stanton's personal orders, rail and steamship passengers there were scrutinized closely, and the home of a man named William Mance was raided. These efforts yielded nothing, and they placed a burden on government resources that, in hindsight, would have been put to better use elsewhere.

It is not normally difficult to figure out what led to a given raid or other investigative action; one need only examine the telegrams and letters received at the War Department in the preceding hours. An exhaustive search of these records, however, has failed to turn up anything that might have pointed investigators toward specific targets in Philadelphia. Evidently, Stanton was acting on clues given to him orally, and not committed to writing. Only one high-ranking official had easy access to Stanton, his own network of witnesses, and familiarity with the city in question: Lafayette C. Baker. It is nothing more than a hunch, but if the flurry of activity in Philadelphia had been a ruse, Baker would have been just the sort of person to set it in motion. He had long been known as a competitive and unscrupulous man, and he had done everything in his power to neutralize his fellow investigators. He had diverted them, misled them, even arrested them to keep them out of his way. As Stanton would soon learn, Baker even sent some of Washington's best police detectives to Canada, where they could only get lost or scare off suspects they had no authority to arrest.[35]

THE CAPTURE of Arnold and O'Laughlen on April 17 was a major break in the case. But an even bigger break came later the same day. In Washington, an African American woman named Mary Ann Griffin learned from her niece, Susan Mahoney, that some suspicious men had stopped at the Surratt boardinghouse on the night of the shooting. Susan, who worked for Mrs. Surratt, had been present at the time. Mrs. Griffin thought the information was important, and she passed it on to Percival M. Clark, who worked for the War Department. Clark filed a report with Col. Henry Wells, and at 8:45 P.M., Wells ordered Major Henry W. Smith and two detectives to arrest Mrs. Surratt. Unfortunately, he sent them to the wrong address.

The mistake was soon corrected, and the party set out again with specific orders "to arrest Mrs. Surratt and all in the house; and to guard the place and arrest every person who might come to the house, to search the house, and to bring to [Colonel Wells] all papers, pictures, and other evidences." Apparently, the colonel still remembered how to draw up a search warrant.[36]

Smith took a couple of extra men with him this time, and as they rode over to 541 H Street, Lafayette Baker's men approached another boardinghouse only a block from Mrs. Surratt's. At the corner of Seventh and G streets, Ned Spangler was asleep in an upstairs room when his landlady's daughter came up and told him there were two gentlemen waiting to see him. Spangler knew what the men wanted. He had been in and out of jails since Friday night, and had come to expect visits like these. One of the men asked him to take a little walk down the street. Just as he suspected, they were taking him to the Carroll Prison.[37]

Meanwhile, Major Smith's men surrounded Mary Surratt's house. One stood by the basement door while another covered the gate leading to the backyard. Smith himself quietly ascended the steps leading to the front door and looked through the window. The parlor was well lit, and through the blinds he could see four women sitting on the sofa talking. When Detective Ely Devoe rang the bell, a woman came to the window and peered into the darkness. "Is that you, Mr. Kirby?" she asked.

"No," answered the major, "but open the door at once, if this is Mrs. Surratt's house."

The door opened, and Major Smith asked the woman if she was the widow of John H. Surratt and the mother of John H. Surratt, Jr. Mrs. Surratt replied, "I am." Smith announced that he had come to arrest her. A few men filed into the house, and Captain William Wermerskirch locked the door from the inside. Smith took Mrs. Surratt into the parlor, and he ordered Ely Devoe to go and get a carriage. Devoe suggested that the women could walk instead, but Smith wouldn't hear of it. Young Anna Surratt was crying and appeared to be sick. Besides, said the major, those ladies would be treated kindly as long as they were in his charge. He repeated his order.

Anna Surratt was shaken, and her mother tried to calm her. "Do not behave so, baby," she said. "You are already worn out with anxiety that you will make yourself sick. . . ."

"Oh, Mother!" said Anna. "To be taken for such a thing!"

Mrs. Surratt told her to hush, and get ready to go out into the chilly night. With the major's permission, she knelt in prayer.

Devoe had not yet returned with the carriage, and Smith was getting impatient. He was going to suggest that some of the officers go out and hurry things up, but just as he spoke, he heard footsteps coming up the outside staircase. Wermerskirch took up a position by the front door, and Colonel Olcott's clerk, Richard Morgan, stood next to him. The bell rang, and when Wermerskirch opened the door, a tall, dark-haired man stepped up to the threshold. He hesitated to come inside.

"I guess I have mistaken the house," said Lewis Powell.

"No, you have not," replied Major Smith. Morgan asked whose house he was looking for, and the man said, "Mrs. Surratt's." Smith slowly reached for his pistol, saying, "This is the house. Come in at once." The man took a step forward, and Wermerskirch slammed the door behind him.

The new arrival looked out of place. Powell wore a drab overcoat, black pants, and filthy boots. Wermerskirch thought he looked as if he had been marching on muddy roads. He carried a pickaxe over his shoulder, and on his head was a piece of fabric that appeared to be cut from an undershirt. The major questioned him closely.

"What do you want here?"

"I have come to dig a gutter for Mrs. Surratt."

"What do you come to a private house for at this hour of the night?"

"I came to get directions from Mrs. Surratt about digging a gutter tomorrow morning." Powell claimed that he had met Mrs. Surratt a few days before on Pennsylvania Avenue, and she hired him to do some digging behind her house. He noticed that the lights were still on, so he came up to ask if he might spend the night in her basement, then get an early start in the morning.

Skeptical, Major Smith stepped over to the parlor door and asked Mrs. Surratt if she knew this man. She swore she did not.

A certificate in the man's pocket identified him as "L. Paine." Something had been scratched off the paper, and even holding it up to the gaslight, Smith still couldn't make out what had been erased. He told the man, "I think you are a spy." Pointing to a chair in the hallway, he ordered Powell to sit down. "Your story does not hang together."

Ely Devoe eventually arrived with the carriage, and they took the ladies to General Augur's headquarters. There was no room in the buggy for "Paine," so the detectives kept him at the house, and they continued to ask him questions. Though the story he told was plausible enough, something didn't seem right. The pickaxe showed no signs of recent use, and some of the items in his pockets—newspaper clippings, for example—were not the kind of things a common laborer would have. From the mud on his pants and boots, it looked as if he had been crouching on the ground. And Mrs. Surratt did not support his story.[38]

Another carriage arrived, and Powell was driven away. The servants were ordered to follow on foot. When the house was cleared of its inhabitants, the rest of Major Smith's team gave the place a more thorough search.

AT GENERAL AUGUR'S HEADQUARTERS, Mary Surratt was taken before Colonel Wells for questioning. He wanted to know how her son came to know John Wilkes Booth. Mrs. Surratt had no direct answer, but said that she never saw anything suspicious in their friendship. "I never thought a great deal of his forming Mr. Booth's acquaintance," she said, "because he called very frequently when my son was not there; he called upon the rest of us sometimes." In her eyes, Booth was "very clear of politics," and neither she nor her boarders ever indulged in political discussions themselves.

To another question, she replied that she did not know where her son was, but supposed he was going to Canada. Wells responded bluntly: "No man on the round earth believes he went to Canada."

"I believe it," she shot back. As the questioning continued, Mrs. Surratt never became flustered, and indeed, she was amazingly cool. She answered questions about George Atzerodt ("I don't think [John] made an associate of him") and David Herold ("I assure you he is not a visitor to our house"). Though Weichmann had said that spies and other suspicious people had visited her home, Mrs. Surratt claimed to know nothing about them. That prompted the colonel to suggest that she knew more than she would admit.

"I assure you on the honor of a lady that I would not tell you an untruth," she said.

"I assure you, on the honor of a gentleman, I shall get this information from you. . . ."

Mrs. Surratt again denied knowing such people.

"Indeed you do," Wells insisted. "I pledge you my word you do, and you will admit it, and I should be very glad if you would do it at once."

"If I could, I would do so," she said. The more Mary Surratt stiffened, the more angry Wells became. *He* seemed to be the only one under pressure.

Wells finally asked about the man who had just been captured in her house. Did she arrange to have him do labor about the premises? Her answer was emphatic: "No, sir; the ruffian that was in my door when I came away? He was a tremendous hard fellow with a skull cap on, and my daughter commenced crying, and said these gentlemen came to save our lives. I hope they arrested him. . . . I believe he would have murdered us, every one, I assure you."[39]

So far, nobody in Augur's office had spoken to Powell. The detectives simply escorted him and a number of other men into a room full of people, then closed the door. William H. Bell, the servant of Secretary Seward, had been waiting to identify him, and detectives watched Bell closely as he looked at the men who had just walked in. Bell scanned the crowd slowly, looking back and forth, studying faces, returning glances. And then he froze. His eyes widened, his shoulders drew back, and he fixed his gaze on the tall, muscular, dark-haired man in the room. Powell stared back as Bell moved in close, never breaking eye contact, not saying a word. Then, standing face-to-face, he dramatically raised his hand and pointed a finger right at the face of that fearsome giant. Lewis Powell broke into a broad grin.

THE SEARCH of Mary Surratt's boardinghouse went on for hours, and it turned up some interesting evidence. Detectives found more than a hundred letters, a pair of spurs, a composite photograph of Confederate leaders, and a bullet mold. There were many *carte de visite* photographs scattered around, but one in particular caught their attention. It bore a patriotic shield and Confederate flags, along with the inscriptions, "Thus will it ever be with Tyrants," "Virginia the Mighty," and "*Sic Semper Tyrannis!*"[40]

FOURTEEN

"LET THE STAIN OF INNOCENT BLOOD BE REMOVED FROM THE LAND"

A S SOON AS LEWIS POWELL WAS IDENTIFIED AS THE SEW-ards' assailant, he was placed in shackles and transported to the ironclad *Saugus* at the navy yard. His capture, only three days after the assassination, capped a remarkably successful day for government investigators. Of the eight people put on trial that spring, five were arrested on April 17. Now only four of the prime suspects remained at large: Booth, Surratt, Herold, and Atzerodt.

After Powell's awkward entrance at Seward's, the revolver's malfunction, his panicked response, the unexpected resistance, and the uncooperative horse, he was lucky to have gotten away alive. He had intended to take his own route out of Washington, separate from Booth's. That "skedaddle" was something he had learned from Mosby. He had planned to take a right turn onto H Street at the top of Lafayette Park. That would have taken him across town to Benning Road, northeast of the Capitol, and to a bridge over the Eastern Branch. On the other side of the bridge, a fork in the road offered two options: turn right, and end up on Booth's escape route; turn left, and go to Baltimore.[1]

In his excitement, Powell forgot that the army had recently built a gate across the Benning Bridge and no one could cross it after nine P.M. Powell may actually have reached the bridge, but then been forced to turn around. It was an easy route heading out of the city, but coming the other way was more complicated. Inbound, Benning Road ended at an intersection where five streets converged like spokes on a wheel. Four of them looked about the same, and evidently Powell chose a wrong one. H Street would have led him back to familiar territory. But instead he took Boundary Street, then turned onto one of the roads that led north from there. He was lost.

Somewhere near Glenwood Cemetery, he found an abandoned coat and exchanged his own for it. After hiding in the cemetery for two days, he emerged cold and starving, carrying a pickaxe taken from a grave-digger's shed. Since he had lost his hat at Seward's, he improvised a sub-stitute by cutting a sleeve off his undershirt and wearing it as a skullcap.

John Wilkes Booth had been better prepared. He had spent a great deal of time thinking through the assassination and planning for every contin-gency. He knew that his own hat would probably fall off when he hit the stage, and indeed it did. Yet when he reached the Navy Yard Bridge, he was allowed to cross in part because there was nothing suspicious about him. He was wearing a new hat, which he had evidently packed in his saddle-bags before the shooting.[2]

NO ONE WAS ABLE to find or identify the man who ran into the woods near the Surratt Tavern. So on Tuesday morning, April 18, Lt. Alexander Lovett gave up trying and joined Detectives Cottingham and Lloyd on a search for the tavern keeper, John M. Lloyd. Along with a cavalry detach-ment, they headed south, toward Charles County, and ran into Lloyd on his way back to the tavern. They told him he was under arrest.

Lloyd was an emotional wreck. For the past three days, he had denied all knowledge of Booth's escape, but he knew that sooner or later he would be found out. As he saw it, his choice was between a government hanging and a neighborhood lynching. He was convinced that betraying Booth would cost him his life, and he was determined not to say a thing until ab-solutely necessary.

Detectives Simon Gavacan and William Williams escorted Lloyd to a makeshift guardhouse at Robey's post office and left him there. Then they joined Joshua Lloyd, Lieutenant Lovett, and three men from the 16th New York Cavalry on a foray back into Charles County. They reached Bryan-town at midday, and found Lieutenant Dana at a tavern. Though Dana had been there since Saturday, he had turned up little on Booth's move-ments. A local doctor had reported that two strangers stopped at the home of his cousin on Saturday morning, but Dana took no action. He was more interested in the fact that some of Mosby's Rangers had been spotted Saturday night near the government farm on the Patuxent, and had reportedly engaged Union troops in a skirmish. The way Dana saw it, Booth was almost surely with those men; his earlier movements were of little concern.[3]

Unlike David Dana, Lovett and the detectives thought that the sighting of the two strangers was worth investigating. They headed at once to the home of Dr. George D. Mudd, who had made the report, and questioned him at length about what he knew. Mudd said that he was attending church near Beantown on Sunday when his cousin, Dr. Samuel A. Mudd, told him about two strangers who had come to his house before sunrise the day before. One was suffering a great deal from a broken leg, and his companion said he had sustained the injury in a riding accident. He was treated, and spent most of the day recuperating in bed. His friend was a talkative little man who seemed to know his way around the area but was a stranger to Mudd. They left his farm Saturday afternoon, and Samuel Mudd had not seen them since.

George Mudd suggested that the detectives talk directly with his cousin, and he led their party out to the farm, four miles north of town. Dr. Samuel Mudd was out in a field when they arrived, and he came back in at once. They asked him about his Saturday morning visitors, and were particularly interested in learning where they went after they left his farm. Mudd said that the small man had asked how to get to the home of Rev. Lemuel Wilmer, who lived on the opposite (west) side of Zekiah Swamp. He had given them directions, and they appeared to be heading that way when they left. Armed with that information, the team headed for the home of Parson Wilmer. Dr. George Mudd led the way.[4]

In the meantime, hundreds of soldiers trudged over the countryside, searching every home for fugitives and, sometimes, for plunder. Even the hospital staff of Point Lookout was pressed into service. Fifty of them were sent out to search, and at least one of them enjoyed this temporary duty. As he wrote home: "A gay time we had of it. . . . Of course we met with all sorts of faces long, short, scared, indignant, and angry countenances, but little attention was paid to all remonstrations, and objections but particular attention was lavished on the many good things, with which the Pantry was, or happened to be stocked. . . . Objections were made on several occasions by some of the many southern sympathizer's [sic], with which this country is stocked, but they were soon convinced of the necessity of said proceedings just by showing and explaining to them the use for which handcuffs are intended."[5]

Many of these pursuers were closer to Booth than they imagined, and some passed within yards of his hiding place in the pines. He lay there quietly under the cover of the trees, aching to be on the move once more. Paranoid and impatient, he could hardly stand this forced inaction. He was eager to know what the world thought of his deed, and his first inkling came when Jones brought him some newspapers. The reactions were not good. "History," said the Washington *Evening Star*, "has on its record no suicidal act so terrible as that committed by the conquered South yesterday through its representative, the assassin of President Lincoln." They reported that in Baltimore, "all kindly feeling towards rebels and rebel sympathizers has, as it were, been obliterated, and one intense feeling of detestation and abhorrence for all connected with the rebellion takes its place." The Richmond *Whig* called Lincoln's assassination "the most appalling, the most deplorable calamity which has ever befallen the people of the United States."[6]

Booth was stunned. For years, the papers had assailed Lincoln as a tyrant who had no regard for laws or the rights of citizens. But now these same papers railed against *him* for his act of tyrannicide. Worse, the assassination changed Lincoln into something entirely unreal. The *Daily National Intelligencer*, once an anti-Lincoln paper, now said of him that "none has ever lived in all the tide of time who evinced more purity, and who was more trusted by a great nation in the issues of its life and death. He did not have, he could not have among those worthy of consideration, a single enemy." Booth was particularly offended by the suggestion, printed in several papers, that stepping up behind an unarmed middle-aged man and shooting him in the back of the head was somehow an act of cowardice. That was a charge he could not leave unanswered.

He still carried a pocket diary for tracking his professional engagements. He had it from the year before, and because he had not toured since May, most of the book remained unmarked. So he cut out the used pages and carefully composed a message he hoped would set the world straight:

Ti Amo
April 13–14 Friday the Ides[7]
  Until today nothing was ever *thought* of sacrificing to our country's wrongs. For six months we had worked to capture. But our cause being

almost lost, something decisive & great must be done. But its failure was owing to others, who did not strike for their country with a
heart.

To Booth, the important point was that he, the assassin, *did* strike with
a heart—and with courage. As he put it:

> I struck boldly and not as the papers say. I walked with a firm step
> through a thousand of his friends, was stopped, but pushed on. A Col.
> was at his side. I shouted Sic semper *before* I fired. In jumping broke my
> leg. I passed all his pickets, rode sixty miles that night, with the bone
> of my leg tearing the flesh at every jump. I can never repent it, though
> we hated to kill; Our country owed all her troubles to him, and God
> simply made me the instrument of his punishment. The country is not
> what it *was.* This forced union is not what *I* have loved. I care not what
> becomes of me. I have no desire to out-live my country. This night (be-
> fore the deed), I wrote a long article and left it for one of the Editors
> of the National Inteligencer, in which I fully set forth our reasons for
> our proceedings. He or the Govmt[8]

Undoubtedly, Booth was going to suggest that either the editor or the
government had suppressed his letter, and perhaps he intended to repeat
the gist of it here. But something cut him short.

In tone and substance, the writing in that diary was quintessential
Booth: posturing, defensive, and grossly inflated. Though he had certainly
walked among a thousand of Lincoln's friends, it was hardly a dangerous
move, since none suspected his motives at the time. Rathbone was a major,
not a colonel, and even though he was sitting near the president, he was
unarmed and unaware that Booth was in the box. Having fired the shot,
Booth rode thirty miles that night, not sixty, and subsequent information
proved that his broken leg was a simple fracture that could not have been
"tearing the flesh at every jump." These were all exaggerations, and all designed to show that Booth was not a coward but a hero who acted "boldly
and not as the papers say."

Of all the points Booth tried to make, only one has endured, and that
may have been unintentional on his part. When he wrote "In jumping
broke my leg," he left posterity with the image of himself breaking his leg
on stage after being caught in the folds of the national flag. "The revenge

of Old Glory" is one of history's most dramatic twists, but it may not be true. Assessment of the evidence actually substantiates the version that Booth himself later told. In the course of his escape into the countryside, he said, he broke his leg when his horse tripped and rolled over on him.

Booth's flight from the president's box to Baptist Alley had not been one fluid motion. Almost all eyewitnesses at Ford's reported seeing Booth crouch or stagger, and momentarily lose his footing when he landed. But they noticed no sign of pain, in movement or expression. What they saw was *dizziness,* such as one gets from a quick rush of adrenaline; that was to be expected under the circumstances.

If Booth had broken his leg in the theater, as history tells us, we should expect to find eyewitness accounts that describe him as limping across the stage. Yet within hours or days of the shooting, dozens of statements were taken, and every one of them described Booth's flight as a rush or a dead run. Many remarked on how quickly he made it into the wings. As one man said, "He ran with lightning speed across the Stage & disappeared beyond the scenes. . . . The whole occurrence, the shot, the leap, the escape— was done while you could count eight." An army lieutenant said that Booth "shot off like an arrow" in plain sight of armed soldiers like himself, who had had no time to react. Indeed, the way he "strode across the stage, in a real theatrical manner" was the key to his success.[9]

Flying through the door to Baptist Alley, Booth thrust his left foot into a stirrup and almost leaped into the saddle. His movement startled the mare, and she pulled out from under him, leaving him twisting with the full weight of his body on that (supposedly broken) left leg. Peanuts Borrows and Major Joseph Stewart both saw Booth's struggle to throw himself onto the horse, and neither reported anything that suggests he was in pain. Nor did Sergeant Cobb notice any discomfort when Booth approached him to cross the Navy Yard Bridge. Not until Booth reached the tavern in Surrattsville was he clearly suffering from a painful injury. He told John Lloyd that his horse had fallen on him, and he boasted of killing the president.[10]

Booth and Herold had switched horses by then. Sergeant Cobb and others were positive that Booth had ridden away on a bright bay mare, and everyone agreed that Herold was on a roan. But outside the city, everyone who encountered them remembered it the other way around. In light of Booth's broken leg, the switch made perfect sense. An injured man would certainly have preferred the gentle, steady gait of a horse like the one

Herold had rented. From Lloyd's to Mudd's, Booth stayed on that horse, and Herold rode the mare, who was now noticeably lame, with a bad cut on her left front leg. Clearly, she had been involved in an accident.[11]

For days on end, the fugitives lay in the pine thicket, pouring out their thoughts and their regrets over what had happened. Booth still clung to his lofty defense of tyrannicide, but the realities of the case had put everything in a different light. According to Herold, Booth was horrified by that bloodbath at Seward's, and he said that he was "very sorry for the sons," though he "wished to God that Seward was killed." He was especially pained to hear that he had caused so much trouble for Ford's employee Ned Spangler.

Booth could not understand how his own recollection of the shooting could differ so much from what the papers described. As Herold later described it, Booth's version was almost surrealistic:

"There was a soldier or officer trying to prevent him from going into the box, and the thought struck him to draw a letter from his pocket and show it to the man, which he did. The man let him pass. He was so agitated at the time, that he fastened the door, he thinks. He advanced toward the President, with the letter in one hand and the pistol in the other. He put the pistol to the back of the president's head, shoved it, and hollered 'Sic Semper tyrannis.' He says it was the President's secretary that caught him by the throat."

Booth was surprised to hear that Major Rathbone was wounded in the arm, since he had lunged straight at him, hitting him "in the stomach or belly."[12]

WHILE THE FUGITIVES HID in the pine woods, hundreds of troops crisscrossed Charles County looking for them. From Port Tobacco to Benedict, Chapel Point to Leonardtown, and all along the Potomac shore, soldiers covered every crossroads and settlement that Booth might have passed. The mission was unusually demanding, and some of the troops had been on constant duty from Friday night until Tuesday. A sleep rotation had been established, but only for those remaining in the city; those on patrol had to catch some rest when the opportunity arose. Their only compensation was an extra ration of coffee, sugar, and bread.

Weeks after the fact, George Alfred Townsend would describe the manhunt as a well-organized operation carried on with military precision. In fact, each unit had its own way of doing things. Some focused on the black residents, assuming they would incriminate their former masters. Secretary Stanton believed as much, and made a point of putting the 22nd U.S. Colored Troops into the search. But others, such as William P. Wood, banked on the goodwill of the white population. Wood treated them kindly and cultivated their trust. Officers and detectives employed all kinds of tricks and ruses to get people to talk. As for the actual search, there is no reason to believe that a systematic approach (such as a grid search) was ever even considered.[13]

Though the lead conspirator remained at large, the dragnet was productive nonetheless. Hundreds of people were detained, including Atzerodt's friend Walter M. Barnes, who was described as "one of the conspirators"; Adeline Adams, who had allegedly entertained Booth at her hotel in Newport; and Thomas Nelson Conrad, a "minister" who could not account for his presence in Charles County. Some of these people were seen as potential witnesses, but the large majority were just suspicious characters— blockade-runners, people who had threatened Union men, or those who had exulted in the president's death. Their numbers grew so large that on several occasions Edwin Stanton ordered a general purge to make room for legitimate suspects.

A few detainees got a great deal of attention even though nothing was proved against them. João Celestino, a Portuguese ship captain, was one such person. Celestino was known for his rabid political views, and government informants considered him perfectly capable of plotting against the president. But after his highly publicized arrest, detectives failed to connect him with Booth, and no charges were filed. The case of Benjamin Ficklin was similar. Ficklin, a blockade-runner, traded Southern cotton in the European markets. He was arrested after a man in Philadelphia reported him as a suspicious character "presenting the appearance of a refined pirate." It was subsequently discovered that he had once crossed the Potomac with Atzerodt, and that he had visited the Kirkwood House on April 14. He claimed that in both instances the timing was coincidental, and he insisted that he had traveled to the South with Lincoln's blessing. He suggested his captors confirm this with the president's friend Orville Hickman Browning. Apparently someone checked, and Ficklin was released.

Captain Edwin Bedee, 12th New Hampshire, presented a unique case. Bedee had been present at Ford's on the night of the assassination, and had made his way into the president's box immediately afterward. One of the doctors there handed him some papers that had been taken from Mr. Lincoln's pockets, and told him to deliver them to the White House. Apparently the papers disappeared, and Stanton ordered Bedee to stand trial for theft.[14]

Detention was always a harrowing experience, but occasionally it was physically hazardous as well. When Lieutenant Dana sent three men to Washington under heavy guard, word got out that two of them were Booth and Surratt. A crowd quickly formed around them, jeering and throwing stones. Their escorts managed to hold off the mob with muskets, but by the time they arrived at the Old Capitol, guards and prisoners alike were badly bruised and cut.

No suspect drew more attention than the tall, dark-haired man who had been arrested at the Surratt boardinghouse. Government investigators were burning to learn all they could about him, but without his cooperation, they didn't even know his name. All they had was a certificate found in his pocket verifying that "L. Paine" of Fauquier County, Virginia, had taken the oath of allegiance. Everyone assumed that this was an alias. So in the absence of solid information, speculation filled the void, and guessing his identity became a great sport. Some people claimed that the suspect himself didn't know who he was, that he had been stolen from his parents in infancy. He was reported to be a nephew of Robert E. Lee, and a former nanny of the Lee family almost identified him as such. Prosecutors believed he was related to the Paynes of Kentucky, three of whom were thought to have taken part in the St. Albans raid. An assistant U.S. marshal was assigned to look into the matter, but found no connection. Nonetheless, War Department investigators got into the habit of calling him "Payne," and he was eventually tried under that name. Strangely, nobody seems to have considered that he might be one of the Paynes of Fauquier County, Virginia.[15]

The morning after Powell's capture, Augustus Seward was brought on board the *Saugus* to identify him. The suspect was ordered to stand up, and Seward grabbed him by the clothes as he had done on the night of the assault. He had no trouble identifying him as the attacker. The size, the proportions, and the beardless face were a perfect match, and when the prisoner repeated the words, "I'm mad, I'm mad!" Seward recognized the same voice, "varying only in the intensity." When Seward was finished, Colonel Wells removed the prisoner's clothing and questioned him about the stains on his coat. Wells found his explanations unconvincing. Pointing out a bloodstain on the shirt, he asked, "What do you think now?" Powell had no response.[16]

EDWIN STANTON AND GENERAL GRANT were in conference at the War Department when a messenger interrupted with news that the Baltimore *American* had printed Sam Arnold's confession. Stanton was furious. Provost Marshal McPhail had said nothing about taking a confession, and he certainly hadn't admitted giving one to the press. So he fired off an angry letter to McPhail: "Your conduct in detaining Arnold and having an examination of him before reporting to this Department is strongly condemned and will be dealt with as it merits when I get the facts. You will stop all examination and publication and turn him (Arnold) over to General Wallace."

In fact, McPhail had forbidden the publication of sensitive information, but the papers had simply ignored him. Stanton would see that it didn't happen again, and he had General Augur's adjutant issue a warning that henceforth, anyone in the government who leaked information would be treated as a hindrance to the investigation. McPhail took it personally, and indignantly demanded a chance to clear his name. He spent the entire night composing a defense of his actions, and he supplemented it with a letter from C. C. Fulton, editor of the *American*, who denied that McPhail had been his source. Fulton said that Arnold's statement was "floating everywhere," and anyone in Baltimore could get it. Inexplicably, that seemed to placate the secretary.[17]

THE IDENTIFICATION of "Paine" as Seward's assailant did not let George Atzerodt or John Surratt off the hook. Arnold had implicated them both, and both were still eagerly sought as suspects in the conspiracy. Surratt had been in Elmira, New York, on April 14, and on hearing the news, he took the short route to Canada. George Atzerodt was still in the Washington area. Francis Curran, the driver of the Rockville stage, knew Atzerodt and saw him on the day after the shooting, riding in a buggy near Rockville with a man named William R. Gaither. Curran's report was the first hint of Atzerodt's whereabouts after he had left the capital. Subsequently, detectives learned that he had continued to stumble northward. After a brief ride with Gaither, he spent Saturday night at Clopper's Mill, near Seneca Creek. Then, on Sunday morning, he walked a few miles north to Germantown, where the trail grew cold for a time.[18]

. . .

WEDNESDAY, APRIL 19, began with the firing of guns. This was a national day of mourning, and hourly tributes were sounded in every place an artillery unit could be found. A funeral service would take place in the White House, followed by a trip to the Capitol, where the president's remains would lie on public display. Beyond that, plans were still uncertain. Mrs. Lincoln insisted her husband be interred in Illinois, but she had not selected a specific burial site. She would not do so until more than a week later, when the funeral train was already well on its way west.

Window shades were drawn in the Executive Mansion, and the gaslight was dimmed. Hundreds of officials and guests filed in, many of them tiptoeing, as if afraid to break the silence. All were ushered into the East Room, where a grand catafalque sat between the two massive chandeliers, now hung in black. It was an elaborate platform, with steps on all sides and an arched canopy of black velvet and crape above. Its four supporting posts were draped in black, with festoons and satin rosettes. Next to each post stood a soldier from the Guard of Honor, a special detachment of men selected from the Veterans' Reserve Corps. Along with nine generals, those chosen few would accompany the remains at all times from here to the grave.

Six hundred tickets had been issued, and by eleven A.M. the room was full. Upholsterers were not even finished tidying up for the service, and they had to drive in the last few nails on their way out. At front and center were the late president's relatives, or more correctly, those of his wife. Captain Robert Todd Lincoln sat among them, weeping quietly. His little brother, Tad, clung to him and sobbed. Their mother, prostrate with grief, did not attend.

On top of the bier lay three wreaths, and at its head stood a cross of white flowers. The coffin itself was made of mahogany, with eight silver handles, a lead lining, and a white satin interior. The outside was finished in black broadcloth, with a winding vein of silver tacks punctuated by silver stars. The upper part of the lid was open, and the head and shoulders of the deceased were open to full view. Below was a plate with this inscription:

ABRAHAM LINCOLN,
SIXTEENTH PRESIDENT OF THE UNITED STATES,
BORN FEBRUARY 12, 1809.
DIED APRIL 15, 1865.

Mr. Lincoln was dressed in his inaugural suit, and one observer thought he looked "quiet and natural, not like one who is sleeping, but one absent." He was "the perfect shell of the great man," whose empty expression was devoid of its customary lightheartedness. His face had a leaden pallor, and death had not smoothed his features. The right eye remained black and swollen—a reminder of Friday night's horrors.

The service was multidenominational, and the Reverend Dr. Phineas D. Gurley delivered the eulogy. "It was a cruel, cruel hand, that dark hand of the assassin, which smote our honored, wise, and noble President, and filled the land with sorrow," he said. "But above and beyond that hand, there is another which we must see and acknowledge. It is the chastening hand of a wise and a faithful Father." Dr. Gurley said that in human suffering there was a greater purpose, and that our national sorrow might be "a *sanctified* sorrow" that would someday bring joy through a better world.[19]

After the service, the coffin was placed in an elaborate hearse and drawn by six gray horses to the Capitol. Five thousand marchers accompanied it down Pennsylvania Avenue, and an immense crowd of spectators watched from every window, rooftop, and sidewalk along the route. They stood twelve deep on the avenue, and each had a good view of the coffin as it sat on the hearse, eight feet above the ground. A canopy of black crape adorned with a gilt eagle hung above it, and a lantern was mounted on each side. The Guard of Honor marched beside it, followed by the dead president's own horse and its two grooms. When the strains of the funeral dirge and the thump of muffled drums died away, one could actually hear the rustling of branches in the trees, so quiet and still did the crowd remain. Washington had never experienced anything like it.

Edwin Stanton had been planning this funeral since Sunday, and he had given a great deal of thought to the composition of the march to the Capitol. He was especially anxious that African Americans be given a prominent place in the procession, and one of the first steps he took was to order the 22nd United States Colored Troops in from Petersburg. They arrived shortly before the march began. Though all of the armed services took part, the cortège was predominantly civilian. Many organizations were represented, but one group—the Treasury employees—stood out above them all. They were marching behind their prized possession, the Treasury Guard flag torn by Booth as he leaped to the stage.

Apparently, anyone who could scrape together an organization could be included in the parade, and clubs such as the Sons of Temperance and the Fenian Brotherhood shared places of honor with the heads of departments and justices of the Supreme Court. Hundreds of marshals took part as well, and some participants, in retrospect, were offended by most of the appointments. When an investigation revealed that only sixteen of the two hundred marshals had supported the late president, the man who chose them was encouraged to resign from government service.

The procession was so enormous that a single formation of soldiers stretched down the avenue for two miles. All were supposed to begin marching at the boom of a signal cannon near St. John's Church, on the north side of Lafayette Park. But only minutes before the gun was to be fired, an officer of the Signal Corps realized how close they were to the home of Secretary Seward. He didn't want to frighten the household, after all they had been through, so he expressed his concerns to higher authority, and a new plan was hurriedly devised. A battery was thrown into place at City Hall, twelve blocks to the east, and soldiers posted at two-block intervals relayed its signal visually to army headquarters on Seventeenth Street. The impromptu system worked without a hitch.[20]

NEWS OF THE PRESIDENT'S DEATH was still trickling down through the military ranks, and everywhere it went, a wave of rumors followed. At Fortress Monroe, for example, word went around that Booth had sent Sam Arnold down to blow up the fort. Such stories enraged the soldiers and made them eager to seek vengeance. In Morehead City, North Carolina, Private John Walter Lee wrote that his fellow soldiers were ready to "wipe and exterminate every traitor from the United States." And that was fine with him. "If they have killed Abraham Lincoln," he wrote, "they have lost their best friend and I fear they will feel it too—for we are not yet through with them."

Soldiers typically assumed that the Confederates had killed Lincoln to reinvigorate their war effort. They knew better than anyone else that the war was not yet over. Though Robert E. Lee had surrendered his own men, the rebels still had four other generals and more than ninety-one thousand troops in the field. None were closer to Washington than the men under Joseph E. Johnston, and they were hundreds of miles away. Even as they retreated through North Carolina, their commanding general was trying to negotiate terms with the opposing commander, William Tecumseh Sherman.[21]

For his part, General Sherman expressed confidence that Confederate army officers had nothing to do with Lincoln's death. "I believe the assassination will do more harm to the South than any event of the war," he wrote. "I doubt if the Confederate military authorities had any more complicity with it than I had." But of the civilian authorities, he was not so sure. Stanton's early dispatches on the shooting had given Sherman the false impression that the attack had been set for Inauguration Day. That, he said, betrayed a political motive. He wouldn't put anything past Confederate civilians.

None of those closest to Jefferson Davis believed he would have approved of Lincoln's assassination. Davis had a grudging respect for Lincoln, and more important, a seething hatred for the man who would replace him. As everyone knew, Andrew Johnson was a Southerner who had remained loyal to the North, and for that, Jefferson Davis regarded him as a traitor to his own state. Johnson was known as a hard-liner on reconstruction, and was one of the last men Davis wanted to deal with in the days ahead. Moreover, state-sponsored assassination would have jeopardized the Southern president's fondest dream—recognition of the Confederacy as an independent nation.

Davis and his Cabinet had been on the run since fleeing from Richmond on April 3. On the nineteenth, his party reached Charlotte, North Carolina, and stopped at the home of Lewis Bates, a Massachusetts native living at Tryon and Fourth streets. News of Lincoln's death arrived in town just as they did, and telegrapher John C. Courtney rushed to the Bates house with the message. Davis had just addressed a crowd when Courtney handed him the note. He read it to himself, then handed it off to an aide, saying, "This contains very astounding intelligence." An aide read it to the crowd, but Davis himself said nothing. After shaking a few hands, he stepped inside the house to confer with his inner circle.

According to those present, Davis was skeptical of the news, but admitted that anything was possible. "I certainly have no special regard for Mr. Lincoln," he said, "but there are a great many men of whose end I would much rather [hear] than his. . . . I fear it will be disastrous to our people." He and his advisers assumed they would be blamed for the assassination, but had no illusions about changing public opinion.[22]

THAT SAME AFTERNOON, the tugboat *William Fisher* brought five of James O'Beirne's men to Chapel Point, below Port Tobacco. Two disembarked at the landing there, and the other three stayed on the ship until the next stop. They all hit the countryside, working their way into areas where a person might find passage to Virginia. In order to keep a low profile and gather better intelligence on their quarry, some pretended to be refugees, and others just claimed they needed a boat ride across the river. Officer Michael O'Callaghan went to Port Tobacco, where he kept an eye on some of Atzerodt's friends. Charles Bostwick and Lorenzo DeAngelis worked the same area, pretending to look for their horses—a bright bay and a roan—which had been stolen. They wanted to enlist the help of a local constable, but decided against it after hearing that he was tied up in the plot. On Wednesday evening, Officer Edward McHenry stopped at the home of a farmer named Claggett, near the Banks O'Dee. While having supper with the family, McHenry learned that two men had crossed to Virginia in a rowboat on Sunday morning, four days before. He had failed to mention that to anyone for a couple of days.[23]

DEVELOPMENTS IN THE INVESTIGATION left John L. Smith with a sinking feeling. As a deputy U.S. marshal, Smith was expected to make an all-out effort to track down Booth's conspirators. But one of those people was his own brother-in-law, George Atzerodt. To Smith's superiors, having a relative of Atzerodt's on staff was a mixed blessing. On the one hand, he possessed some valuable insights on the man's habits. But on the other, his personal feelings might cloud his judgment. Like John Atzerodt, who worked for Provost Marshal McPhail, Smith had no choice but to contribute all he could to the investigation. In the eyes of his colleagues, he had something to prove. So over the protests of his wife, Katherine, he decided to search for the suspect at the homes of relatives. He left for Montgomery County on the nineteenth, but his pursuit was stalled by a sudden downpour.

On the surface, it seems as if Atzerodt had a plausible escape strategy. While Booth and Herold disappeared into Southern Maryland, he went in the opposite direction, toward the northwest. They ended up in two different worlds. Along Booth's route, government informants feared for their lives. But the people Atzerodt encountered were eager to help authorities. Many had developed a good rapport with the Yankees and considered themselves strong allies in the Union war effort. James W. Purdom was one such person. When Purdom heard a disloyal remark, he reported it.

On April 19, Purdom learned that a man named Andrew Atwood had made suspicious remarks at the home of Hezekiah Metz. According to

Purdom's source, someone brought up the assassination while having supper, and Atwood stopped eating, threw down his knife and fork, and got up from the table, saying, "If the fellow that had promised to follow Grant had done his duty, we would have got General Grant, too." Nobody there knew that Atwood was really Atzerodt, but a few suspected that he was involved in Booth's plot.

Purdom thought the information demanded an urgent response, even though the story was three days old before it reached him. Now, with the sun hanging low in the sky, he set out to file a report with the 1st Delaware Cavalry, camped twenty miles away at Monocacy Junction. On the way he ran into Private Frank O'Daniel, whom he knew, and told him about this Andrew Atwood. O'Daniel notified his sergeant, George Lindsley, but hours went by before Lindsley was able to pass the report on to his superiors. Somehow he failed to convince his commanding officer that it ought to be taken seriously. Captain Solomon Townsend ordered a detachment to pursue Atwood, but not until morning.

Something must have happened to change Townsend's mind. Shortly after he issued that first order, he summoned Sgt. Zachariah W. Gemmill and told him to assemble a detail of six men right away. Their orders were to go and get Mr. Purdom and to take him in search of this man Atwood. The detachment left immediately, but even at a gallop, they did not reach Purdom's house until ten o'clock. Their informant joined them, and in a few minutes he was leading them to Germantown. According to rumors, Atwood was supposed to be staying there, at the home of his uncle, Frederick Richter.[24]

They arrived at about four o'clock in the morning. After posting some of his men around the house, Gemmill knocked on the front door. The man who answered it was Ernest Hartmann Richter, thirty-one, a son of the owner. On questioning, Richter said that his cousin, Atwood, had been there earlier in the week, but had gone to Frederick just the day before. When Gemmill announced that he was going to search the house anyway, Richter changed his story. Now he admitted that his cousin was in the house. The sergeant pushed him out of the way, and two men followed him inside. The front room had a "confused appearance," and seemed to be the living quarters of young Richter and his wife, Mary. Seeing nothing suspicious, the soldiers went upstairs, where they found Frederick Richter in one room and three other men in another. The three were sharing a bed, and two of them—Mary Richter's brothers—awoke right away. But their companion seemed to be sound asleep. Someone shook him and asked for his name. With some hesitation, he said it was Atwood.

"Get up and dress yourself," said the sergeant.

The soldiers and their prisoner were gone by sunrise. At Purdom's suggestion, they stopped at the home of Somerset Leaman, who identified Atwood as the maker of those suspicious remarks. As an afterthought, Gemmill then went back to the Richter house and placed the suspect's cousin Hartmann Richter under arrest as well. Richter asked why they were taking him away, and it suddenly occurred to Gemmill that it was a question Atwood had never asked.[25]

MOST OF THE PRINCIPAL SUSPECTS were now in custody, but Booth and Surratt were still at large. Edwin Stanton had been losing his patience, and now he was losing control of the investigation as well. On April 19 he called for Lou Weichmann and learned that both Weichmann and John Holohan had left the country. They had gone to Montreal with two of A. C. Richards's detectives.

Stanton could hardly believe what he was hearing. Two important witnesses had been spirited out of the country by the government's own agents? This was a huge embarrassment, and all the more so because Stanton had begun to think that Weichmann might be implicated in the plot. At least, that's what his fellow boarders were saying. They thought he was more intimate with the conspirators than at first supposed. Now he was in Canada, supposedly on a search for John Surratt. But if he chose to stay there, the government could do little to get him back. Relations with all the British provinces were poor, and Canada in particular had been reluctant to entertain requests for extradition. So Weichmann and Holohan were mingling among the Southerners in Montreal. They would soon leave for Ottawa, and officials in Washington would lose track of them for days.[26]

Lou Weichmann was not Stanton's only problem. Booth's brother-in-law, John Sleeper Clarke, had taken Booth's letters from the safe and turned them over to William Millward, a U.S. marshal in Philadelphia. The one addressed "To whom it may concern" had just appeared, with Millward's blessing, in *The Philadelphia Inquirer*. Again, Stanton objected: publishing the assassin's words could only help generate sympathy for him, and it might even telegraph his defense strategy to fellow conspirators. He angrily demanded an explanation, and the marshal defended his actions by saying that he thought the publication was appropriate, since the letter proved the existence of a conspiracy. It was ironic, then, that some newspaper editors thought it was concocted to help the conspirators by *denying* that there was ever a plot.[27]

THOUSANDS OF PEOPLE FILED into the new Capitol rotunda to view the remains of Abraham Lincoln. They lined up for more than a mile, standing quietly and respectfully for hours just to get one final, momentary glimpse of their fallen president. One observer was struck by the way "the refined and cultured walked by the side of poor untutored and lately emancipated slaves, each seemingly oblivious to the presence [of the] other." Many wept, and some left small tokens of their grief. A good many kissed the coffin as they passed. Nobody who witnessed the scene could help but be affected.[28]

AS EARLY AS APRIL 18, Lt. Alexander Lovett had made up his mind that it was Booth who had stopped at Dr. Mudd's for medical treatment. Yet he did not report this to his superiors until the twentieth. Since Lovett was one of the few people who had interviewed Mudd, his delay meant that almost a full week had gone by before authorities in Washington knew that Booth was traveling with another man, or that he had broken his leg. To Col. Henry H. Wells, those points were vital. If the cavalry was pursuing a *pair* of travelers, they needed to know that. And a broken leg would have slowed Booth down, making it more difficult for him to get across the Zekiah Swamp. In all likelihood, the fugitives were still near Dr. Mudd's. Stanton agreed and, on April 20, he ordered Wells to make his headquarters in Bryantown, a few miles from the Mudd farm. Wells would personally direct the search from there.

Stanton was sure that somebody had been sheltering Booth, and on the twentieth, he took steps to break the assassin's hold on the disloyal public. He issued a proclamation:

$100,000 REWARD
THE MURDERER OF OUR LATE BELOVED PRESIDENT
ABRAHAM LINCOLN IS STILL AT LARGE.

FIFTY THOUSAND DOLLARS REWARD WILL BE PAID BY THIS
DEPARTMENT FOR HIS APPREHENSION, IN ADDITION TO ANY REWARD
OFFERED BY MUNICIPAL AUTHORITIES OR STATE EXECUTIVES.

He said that $25,000 would be paid for the arrest of John Surratt and another $25,000 for the arrest of David Herold. Liberal rewards would also be paid for any information that led to the arrest of a conspirator.

Stanton's proclamation was a threat as well as an inducement. It said that any person found to be harboring or secreting said persons would be treated as accomplices and subject to trial by military commission. The punishment was death. "Let the stain of innocent blood be removed from the land by the arrest and punishment of the murderers," it said. "Every man should consider his own conscience charged with this solemn duty, and rest neither night nor day until it be accomplished."

The results of the proclamation were mixed. The promise of a reward made detectives guard their leads more jealously, but the threat of death made witnesses more cooperative. Certainly, the prospect of hanging was enough to shake a confession out of John M. Lloyd. Since his arrest two days before, Lloyd had been interviewed by Colonel Wells, Lieutenant Lovett, and Detective Cottingham, among others. They all offered the same advice: unburden yourself, and tell us what you know. Lloyd had resisted, but now seemed to weaken. George Cottingham had always treated Lloyd kindly. With the instincts of a good detective, Cottingham paid particular attention to the way Lloyd wept at the thought of leaving his wife. He would use that for leverage.

"*For the sake of your family,* make a clean breast of the whole matter," he said. "I have the proof against you." Cottingham left Lloyd alone to think it over. After a few minutes, he asked again if the prisoner was ready to talk.

"My God, they will kill me if I implicate them," Lloyd sobbed.

"Well," said Cottingham, "if you are afraid to be murdered yourself, and let these fellows get out of it, that is your business, not mine." He advised him once more to come clean. This time Lloyd gave in. He said there were guns hidden at the tavern, and Mary Surratt had come out on Friday to tell him that they would be needed that night. Booth and David Herold called for them at about midnight, and Herold came in to get them. Booth never got off his horse. He said he had broken his leg, and couldn't carry a gun, though he did take some whiskey. Booth said they had killed the president and Seward. Lloyd would have shot him right there, but he was afraid.

He now claimed to know where Booth was. "And if I had been taken there when I was arrested," he said, "I could have captured him." Cottingham pointed out that until just a minute ago he had denied knowing anything at all. Lloyd conceded the point, but said he supposed the fugitives were heading for Allen's Fresh.

This was the first time anyone had mentioned those hidden guns, and Cottingham was eager to find them. He went up to the tavern with Andrew Kaldenback, a friend of Lloyd's, in hopes of locating the rifle Booth and Herold had left behind. Lloyd said it was still there, between the studs of the dining room wall. When they failed to find it by prodding and searching, Kaldenback smashed through the plaster in what turned out to be just the right place. It was jammed tightly inside the wall.[29]

THOMAS JONES HAD HOPED to take the fugitives to Allen's Fresh, where the Zekiah Swamp empties into the vast tidal flats of the Wicomico River. The Potomac, just beyond, is six miles wide at that point, but gentle currents there made boat crossings relatively easy. There was just one problem: authorities had the place under constant surveillance. After several days of keeping his ear to the ground, Jones finally gave up on Allen's Fresh. On Wednesday, April 19, he told his servant, Henry Woodland, to bring back the rowboat he had been keeping there, and to leave it in the small creek near Jones's farm, known as Huckleberry.[30]

The following afternoon, Jones was in Allen's Fresh when a small cavalry unit rode up to Colton's store and dismounted. A couple of the soldiers came inside for a drink. Before long their guide rushed in with an announcement: "Boys, I have news that they have been seen in St. Mary's." In just a moment, the entire detachment had gone off to chase Booth and Herold somewhere to the east.

"Now or never," Jones thought. He rode at full speed to the fugitives' hiding place in the pine thicket. He arrived after dark, and approached with more than the usual caution. Booth and Herold were pleased to see him, and thrilled at the news he brought: that they would finally get a chance to cross the river. "The coast seems to be clear," said Jones, "and the darkness favors us. Let us make the attempt." While Booth rode on Jones's horse, Herold walked alongside. Jones himself walked fifty or sixty yards ahead of them, checking for signs of danger, then whistling for them to proceed. If they did not hear a signal, they were to slip quickly and quietly into the woods.

Thus did they make their way through the darkness for more than two miles to Huckleberry. They were there by ten o'clock, and Jones told the fugitives to wait outside. "Oh," said Booth, "can't I go in and get some of your hot coffee?" It was a pitiful request from one who had not been under a roof, tasted hot food, or felt the warmth of a fire in nearly a week. Jones hated to refuse it, but he had no choice.

"My friend," he said, "it wouldn't do. Indeed it would not be safe. There are servants in the house who would be sure to see you and then we would all be lost. Remember, this is your last chance to get away." Booth and Herold waited out by the stable while Jones went into the house. He found his own supper waiting on the table and Henry Woodland eating in the kitchen. Henry confirmed that the boat had been left in the creek. They talked awhile, and when everyone else had gone to bed, Jones slipped outside with some food.

Near the Huckleberry farm was a patch of dense woods with a winding stream cradled by steep hills and meadows. The bluffs rose sharply, then dropped fifty feet or more to the banks of the river. This is where the Potomac bends southward, turning toward Chesapeake Bay sixty miles downstream. The view from the heights is stunning, but otherwise it was a place to avoid. The river narrowed considerably from both directions, and the currents were unusually strong. It was said that anyone falling into the river here might never be found. Unfortunately for Booth and Herold, they had no other place to cross.

Jones guided the fugitives through the narrow gully to the mouth of the little stream. His boat was tucked under the weeds here, ready for immediate use. It was a flat-bottomed skiff, twelve feet long, equipped with only one oar and one paddle. Still, it was probably the best Booth could hope to get. Jones took Booth's pocket compass and, by the light of a candle, showed him how to steer a course of 190 degrees. "Keep to that," he said, "and it will bring you into Machodoc Creek. Mrs. Quesenberry lives near the mouth of this creek. If you tell her you come from me I think she will take care of you." He pulled the boat into the open water, then steadied it as Booth and Herold seated themselves inside. With the waves lapping at the sides of the skiff, Jones offered some last-minute advice. He reminded them to keep low and to keep their candle flame hidden. He took eighteen dollars for the boat, but nothing more. As he said later, "What I had done was not for money."

In a voice trembling with emotion, Booth bid him farewell. "God bless you, my dear friend, for all you have done for me," he said. "Good-bye, old fellow." Jones pushed the boat away from the shore and watched it glide out of sight.[31]

AT ABOUT THE SAME TIME, a special train pulled into the B&O station in Washington, and a cordon of soldiers surrounded it, blocking exits and keeping all passengers in place. Colonel Ingraham and Marshal Murray walked up to the last car and met Brigadier General Erastus B. Tyler there. As commander of all troops outside Baltimore, Tyler had personally supervised this important mission—to escort the prisoner George Atzerodt to Washington.

As General Tyler transferred custody of the prisoner, he insisted on getting his handcuffs back. Marshal Murray replaced them with a pair of his own. While changing them, Murray pinched the prisoner's wrist. "Don't pinch me," snarled Atzerodt.

The marshal snapped back: "I will pinch your neck before you are a week older." Murray delivered Atzerodt and Hartmann Richter to the navy yard, where they were placed in close confinement aboard the *Montauk*.

For nearly twelve hours, George Atzerodt had been sitting in General Tyler's headquarters chattering about Booth and the plot against Lincoln. Everything he said was recorded by a stenographer. But then, late in the day, a rather forceful message came over the wires from Secretary Stanton: allow no examination of the prisoner—*none whatever*. The order arrived too late, but Tyler passed it down the line, and for the time being, everyone on his staff pretended not to know anything about the prisoner or the stories he told. The transcripts have never been found.[32]

THE RIVER CROSSING WAS NOT GOING WELL for Booth and Herold. The weather was rough and visibility poor. They had almost reached the Northern Neck of Virginia when just off their path to the right, the faint glow of a ship's lantern cut through the fog. Seeing this, Herold pulled harder on the oars. The wind and current fought against him, and a gunboat rapidly closed in. They clearly couldn't outrun her, so Herold stopped rowing. He and Booth kept perfectly still, hoping the current would push them unnoticed past the point of danger. They were at nature's mercy, and all they could do was let the fog close in over them, hoping that the men on board the vessel would not hear the sound of their hearts pounding in fear.

Nothing was going according to plan. They were supposed to have rowed nine miles south, but a stiff breeze had forced them almost due west, toward Mathias Point, Virginia. The U.S.S. *Juniper* lay at anchor just south of there, and though the *Juniper* was stationary, the movement of the water and of Booth's own boat gave the impression that she was closing in on the fugitives. So they stopped rowing and rode the current north, then west where the river bends around Mathias Point. From there, they drifted across to the Maryland shore.

As the morning light broke over the distant bluffs, David Herold recognized the familiar sight of Nanjemoy Creek. On its bank was Indiantown Farm, owned by Perry Davis, a prominent politician and a man General Hooker once described as "one of the noisiest" rebels in the area. Davis's son-in-law, John J. Hughes, lived here. Reluctantly, Hughes allowed the fugitives to stay in an old slave shack near the water's edge.

In some ways their arrival was a lucky break. Herold had friends living nearby; in fact, some of them had been keeping an eye on the boat Surratt had bought for the abduction. But on the other hand, Nanjemoy Creek was in Maryland, and that is not where they wanted to be.[33]

FIFTEEN

"I MUST FIGHT THE COURSE"

AT 8:00 A.M. ON APRIL 21, A SPECIAL TRAIN PULLED OUT of the B&O station in Washington. On board were the mortal remains of Abraham Lincoln.

The train was heading for Baltimore on the first leg of a journey across seven states. It would travel nearly seventeen hundred miles and be seen by thirty million spectators. Its route had been laid out at the last minute. It would go from Baltimore to Harrisburg, then to Philadelphia, Trenton, New York, and Albany; thence westward, through Buffalo, Cleveland, Columbus, Indianapolis, and Chicago. Two weeks after its start, the journey would end at the president's hometown of Springfield, Illinois.

Its crew and attendants were to be governed by a long list of rules. The timetable had been calculated to the minute, with no room to dally. The train would consist of at least nine cars, with an engine supplied by whichever company owned the tracks. A pilot engine would ride ahead of the train to keep the path clear. The president's remains would be kept on one of the last cars: the *United States,* a luxury car designed in 1864 especially for Mr. Lincoln, but never used by him. Alongside his coffin was that of his son Willie, who had died in the White House three years before. The V.R.C. escort and members of the Lincoln family occupied the car behind it. Local dignitaries got on and off at different points along the way.[1]

. . .

BOOTH WAS DEJECTED over his failure to reach Virginia. His long hours on the river had been unnerving, and he was not looking forward to the prospect of setting out again. However, he could not stay in Maryland, though the only way out might cost him his life. In despair, he sat down once more with his pocket diary.

After being hunted like a dog through swamps, woods, and last night being chased by gun boats till I was forced to return [to Maryland] wet cold and starving, with every man's hand against me, I am here in despair. And why; For doing what Brutus was honored for, what made Tell a Hero. And yet I for striking down a greater tyrant than they ever knew am looked upon as a common cutthroat. My action was purer than either of theirs. One hoped to be great himself. The other had not only his country's but his own wrongs to avenge. I hoped for no gain. I knew no private wrong. I struck for my country and that alone. A country groaned beneath this tyranny and prayed for this end. Yet now behold the cold hand they extend to me. God *cannot* pardon me if I have done wrong. Yet I cannot see any wrong except in serving a degenerate people. The little, the very little I left behind to clear my name, the Govmt will not allow to be printed. So ends all. For my country I have given up all that makes life sweet and Holy, brought misery upon my family, and am sure there is no pardon in the Heaven for me since man condemns me so. I have only *heard* of what has been done (except what I did myself) and it fills me with horror. God try and forgive me, and bless my mother. To night I will once more try the river with the intent to cross; though I have a greater desire and almost a mind to return to Washington and in a measure clear my name, which I feel I can do. I do not repent the blow I struck. I may before my God but not to man.

I think I have done well, though I am abandoned, with the curse of Cain upon me, when if the world knew my heart, *that one* blow would have made me great, though I did desire no greatness.

To night I try to escape these blood hounds once more. Who, who can read his fate God's will be done.

I have too great a soul to die like a criminal. O may he, may he spare me that and let me die bravely.

I bless the entire world. Have never hated or wronged anyone. This last was not a wrong, unless God deems it so. And its [*sic*] with him to damn or bless me. And for this brave boy with me who often prays (yes, before and since) with a true and sincere heart. Was it crime in him, if so, why can he pray the same I do not wish to shed a drop of blood, but "I must fight the course." 'Tis all that's left me.[2]

In fact, Booth would have to wait another day for his chance to reach Virginia. For now, he had to be content with the reluctant hospitality of John J. Hughes.

FOR SEVERAL DAYS, detectives and cavalrymen had focused their attention on the east side of Zekiah Swamp, near Dr. Mudd's. They shared the impression that the Zekiah was impenetrable, and that Booth could not have crossed it en route to the Potomac. Apparently, local citizens had done all they could to discourage the soldiers from looking there. Their false hints of danger had the desired effect, and few Yankees ventured into the abyss even after being ordered to do so. They all seemed to share the impression that George Alfred Townsend, the reporter, had when he wrote of the place:

"Even a hunted murderer would shrink from hiding there. Serpents and slimy lizards are the only denizens; sometimes the coon takes refuge in this desert from the hounds . . . but not even the hunted negro dares to fathom the treacherous clay, nor make himself a fellow of the slimy reptiles which reign absolute in this terrible solitude. . . . The Shawnee, in his strong hold of despair in the heart of Okeefenokee, would scarcely have changed homes with Wilkes Booth and David Harold, hiding in this inhuman country."[3]

Lieutenant Lovett and Detectives Aquilla Allen and Washington Kirby were among those who believed the fugitives were holed up near Dr. Mudd's. For several days, they kept an eye on the place in hopes of seeing whether the doctor went out to visit them. Their surveillance turned up nothing, but after Stanton issued his reward offer they decided to get more aggressive. On Friday the twenty-first, they went back to speak with Dr. Mudd, and he handed them a break in the case.

Mudd was coming back from his father's house when he noticed a large number of cavalrymen milling around in his front yard. Lovett and the detectives were in the house, and when Mudd greeted them, he said that something had turned up since the last time they had spoken. Just that morning, as his wife was cleaning the front bedroom, she had found a boot left behind by the injured visitor on Saturday. It had been shoved under the bed and forgotten. Mudd's wife went upstairs and brought it down to Lieutenant Lovett. It was a tall brown leather boot, slit up the front about ten inches. Written faintly in pencil on the inside was: "H. Lux, maker. 445 Broadway. J. Wilkes."

Until now, the identity of Mudd's injured visitor had been a matter of speculation. But the inscription in that boot erased all doubt. Dr. Mudd was placed under arrest for harboring Lincoln's killer.[4]

This evidence of Booth's visit finally confirmed that Booth had gone to Southern Maryland, evidently because he regarded it as friendly territory. Secretary Stanton was sure that residents here were hiding him, and he issued a public declaration:

> The counties of Prince George's, Charles, and St. Mary's have, during the whole war, been noted for hostility to the government and their protection to rebel blockade-runners, rebel spies, and every species of public enemy. The murderers of the President harbored there before the murder, and Booth fled in that direction. If he escapes, it will be owing to rebel accomplices in that region. The military commander of the department will speedily take measures to bring these rebel sympathizers and accomplices in the murder to a sense of their criminal conduct.

William P. Wood and his men learned of Dr. Mudd's arrest when they saw him in Bryantown. Wood had spent a good deal of time in Southern Maryland, and he firmly believed the best way to deal with the people here was to seek their voluntary cooperation. He had already done some favors for Mrs. Surratt's brother, whom he had known for years. Now, with the consent of Colonel Wells, he secured the temporary release of Dr. Mudd. They went back to the farm together, and returned to Bryantown, as promised, in about three hours.

Wood picked up Detectives Allen and Kirby at the tavern there, and they all rode back to the Mudd farm. That interview with the doctor had given him some ideas, and he now took his men out to the stable to begin looking for horse tracks. From what they found, it appeared that the fugitives went out the swamp road, just as Dr. Mudd said, but after riding over the hill, they turned and went in the opposite direction. To Wood, that suggested that Booth and Herold had deceived the doctor. Evidently, they did not regard him as a friend.[5]

THE MANHUNT HAD BECOME SCHIZOPHRENIC. While detectives in Southern Maryland focused their search more narrowly, pursuers elsewhere were casting an even wider net. A week after the assassination, government officials were giving full credence to all conspirator sightings, no matter how far from the scene of the crime. In Chicago, they arrested actor James Nagle on the suspicion that he was Booth. In St. Louis, police went on full alert after "Herold" was spotted in a hotel there. In nearly every state of the Union, vigilant citizens were kept on edge by the thought that Booth was hiding among them.

The St. Louis report may have reminded authorities that Booth had a family connection there. The day after the Herold sighting, Assistant Secretary of War Dana ordered Missouri's Provost Marshal General, J. H. Baker, to search the premises of Junius Booth's daughter Blanche and her uncle, Ben DeBar, for correspondence that might shed light on the conspiracy. Such a step might have seemed pointless a week ago, but now anything was worth a try. Baker seemed to enjoy the visit. He reported that Miss DeBar, as she was called, was "possessed of considerable personal attractions, of a vigorous mind and marked histrionic ability." Judging from her papers, though, she was "an unmitigated rebel." As to John Wilkes, both she and her uncle Ben "never knew him to squander money in rioting or excesses of any kind—except possibly with women." Neither approved of the assassination, and Blanche's only correspondence with him was a personal note, signed from her "Nunkee John."[6]

NED SPANGLER HAD BEEN in Carroll Prison since Monday night, and had come to believe the authorities were holding him only as a witness. He had been called to the prison office several times, only to be identified or interrogated. So he thought nothing of it when called again on Saturday night. This time, however, he was in for a shock. "Come, Spangler," said a detective, "I've some jewelry for you." He was holding a pair of handcuffs, and an order to transfer the prisoner to the Washington Navy Yard.[7]

BOOTH AND HEROLD would set out for Virginia a second time that night. Their first try had taken them upstream from their objective, and to the west of Mathias Point. They were almost directly across from a Confederate signal camp at a place called Boyd's Hole, but for reasons never explained, they did not go there on their second trip. Perhaps their friends at Nanjemoy told them what the locals knew: that raiding parties had made some important arrests in the area, and that Union bluecoats were still over there in relatively large numbers. Whether Booth and Herold knew this or not, they avoided the short trip to Boyd's Hole. They rowed instead to the east side of Mathias Point, then down the Virginia shore more than ten miles to Machodoc Creek—a long trip, and all in plain sight of the Potomac Flotilla. They started at nightfall on April 22.

These days, the Potomac was alive with activity. The fugitives would have to slip past many government vessels on their way across. One would think that the number of ships alone would make the blockade impassable, but experienced watermen had no such illusions. Even the flotilla's commander knew better. On April 23, Commander Foxhall Parker wrote to his superiors that "twice the number of boats constituting this flotilla could not prevent a canoe from crossing at night from Maryland to Virginia." Locals were rumored to be crossing at will, and they got away with it in part because of loopholes that allowed legitimate maritime commerce to continue. Fishing boats, for example, were allowed on the Potomac, so long as they did not land below Alexandria. Local watermen knew this, and they took advantage of it.[8]

So even though the crossing of Booth and Herold was hazardous, it was hardly a miracle. By sunrise on April 23, they had succeeded in reaching the broad mouth of Machodoc Creek in Virginia. Along its northern bank was the home of Elizabeth Quesenberry, though finding it was a challenge. After hearing someone hail them from a gunboat, the fugitives ducked into Gambo Creek and got lost in its winding reaches. Eventually, Herold set out over land to find the Quesenberry house. Booth waited in the boat.

Elizabeth Rousby Quesenberry was an extraordinary woman in the most ordinary place. She was one of the Green family, born in Rosedale, near Georgetown, in the District of Columbia. Her grandfather was General Uriah Forrest, her great-grandfather was a governor of Maryland, and her mother was a cousin of Francis Scott Key. One of her sisters married a grandson of George Washington's sister, while another married the son of Mexico's last native emperor. Certainly, one wouldn't expect to find a woman of such circumstances living in a small frame house at the edge of an isolated swamp. Yet there she was, and the reason was simple: Mrs. Quesenberry was keeping a safe house for Confederate signal agents. On April 23, two of them waited there for Booth and Herold.

It was about one o'clock in the afternoon when Herold found her farm. The lady of the house was not at home, so her fifteen-year-old daughter, Lucy, sent for her. In the meantime, Herold struck up a conversation. He told Lucy that he had just left a nice little rowboat down by the creek, and she was welcome to take it if she wanted it. They had talked for only a moment when Lucy's mother arrived, and Herold got right to the point. He asked Mrs. Quesenberry if she could furnish him with a conveyance for a trip inland. She asked why he couldn't walk, and he said that he could, but his brother down by the river could not, as he had broken his leg. He asked if she would sell them a horse, and she said that if she were inclined to help them, she would just *give* them one—but she was not so inclined. In fact, she wanted them off her property.

Herold was dismayed at this treatment, and he walked away, much put out. But as he headed back to break the news to Booth, Mrs. Quesenberry called out, "Have you had anything to eat?" She offered to send some food.

Booth had trusted Herold when nobody else would, and his faith was repaid in times like this. Time and again, Herold had opportunities to go his own way, but he turned them aside. Now, instead of getting away from Booth, he rejoined him on the banks of Gambo Creek. The food arrived a short while later, and to their surprise, it was delivered by Tom Harbin— the same man who had agreed, the previous December, to join Booth's conspiracy.

Elizabeth Quesenberry did not speak with Booth, but had she done so, she might have discovered their common interest. In the coming days, Booth would make it clear that he was heading for Mexico, where the Emperor Maximilian was offering large bounties and a safe haven to unrepentant Confederates. The emperor was an Austrian by birth, and was now defending his throne against an indigenous uprising by the followers of Benito Juárez. To shore up support among native Mexicans, he had adopted Agustín de Yturbide, the grandson of the former emperor, as his own heir apparent. That child happened to be the nephew of Mrs. Quesenberry's.[9]

But in fact, there was no talk of Mexico on the banks of Gambo Creek. Mrs. Quesenberry kept her distance, sending Tom Harbin and Joseph

Baden to see Booth instead. Harbin was anxious to do his part and be gone. He and Baden gave the fugitives a quick meal, then dropped them off at the farm of William L. Bryant, about a mile away. Their parting advice was to seek out Dr. Richard H. Stuart, eight miles up the road. Stuart was a friend to the Cause.

Herold told Bryant that he needed a horse to get to the home of Dr. Stuart. He said that his brother John had been thrown by a horse down in Richmond, and had broken his leg. Bryant was not willing to part with either of his horses. The best he could do was give Booth and Herold a ride to Stuart's. For that, he accepted ten dollars.[10]

THE LINCOLN FUNERAL TRAIN was in Philadelphia that day. Its arrival the night before was announced by the report of a cannon. In the subsequent firing of minute guns, a soldier was killed—one of two fatalities associated with the president's obsequies. Many thousands had packed the streets to catch a glimpse of the coffin on its way from the train station to Independence Hall. An estimated 300,000 people lined up to see the body lying in state there, and some waited as much as five hours to get in. For a time, city leaders feared that the six-hundred-man police detail would be inadequate to keep the crowd under control.

This was the second Sunday following the assassination, and ministers took the opportunity to expand upon the hurriedly composed sermons they had given the week before. For some, the occasion would mark a high point in their careers. At the Church of the Holy Trinity, Rev. Phillips Brooks delivered a sermon on the deeper meaning of the president's death. Brooks eulogized Mr. Lincoln as a shepherd who led his flock from evil. The president's character was fundamentally in conflict with slavery. His assassination had been the final sacrifice necessary for the overthrow of that evil institution. Though still a young man, Brooks was establishing himself as a leading voice in the Episcopal Church, and some of his admirers would regard this particular sermon as one his finer efforts, rendered with the same dignity and eloquence with which he gave the world one of Christianity's most cherished hymns: "O Little Town of Bethlehem."[11]

THE ARRIVAL IN WASHINGTON of Col. Henry L. Burnett marked a milestone in the conspiracy investigation. Burnett, a star prosecutor for the Bureau of Military Justice, had just finished an assignment out West. He now joined Secretary Stanton in building criminal cases against the alleged conspirators. His first act, on the twenty-third, was to figure out what was missing in the investigation. Then he ordered a report on the fugitives' horses—what they looked like, where they had been seen, and how they tied the suspects to one another. In subsequent days he tried to track down the flags from Ford's Theatre, had handbills distributed up and down the Potomac, and ordered Colonels Foster and Wood to prepare memoranda on all the more viable suspects. He was bringing order to the investigation, and making great strides in the process.[12]

DR. RICHARD H. STUART LIVED about eight miles from William Bryant's farm. He called his house Cleydael, after a family owned château in Belgium. Stuart was one of the wealthiest men in Virginia, with a bloodline he traced to the House of Stuart and ties to the Lees and the Washingtons as well. His wife was descended from Lord Baltimore, Baron Henri Stier, and the painter Rubens. Oddly enough, Julia Calvert Stuart was also a sister of George H. Calvert, former mayor of Newport, Rhode Island, and the man whose threatening letter had drawn Mary Surratt to her tavern on the day of the assassination.

Dr. Stuart had come to Cleydael for safety's sake. His primary residence was Cedar Grove, a magnificent mansion on the Potomac, but since houses on the river were vulnerable to the danger of shelling by federal gunboats, Stuart had moved to this, his inland summer home. For the past four years, he and his family had been sharing the house with guests that once included the daughters of his cousin Robert E. Lee. Stuart's own daughters were here with their husbands and beaux on the evening of April 23. They had just finished their supper when two horses approached on the narrow lane through the woods. On one was William L. Bryant, and John L. Crismond was on the other. Each was doubled up with a stranger, and one of their passengers had already dismounted.

"We are Marylanders in want of accommodations for the night," said Herold.

Stuart looked him over closely. "It is impossible," he said. "I have no accommodations for anybody."

Herold said that his brother had broken his leg, and that Dr. Mudd had recommended they see him. Stuart did not know a Dr. Mudd, and had not authorized anyone to recommend him. Besides, he was a physician, not a surgeon. Herold continued to plead for help, and when the injured man spoke up to identify himself, Stuart cut him off. "I don't want to know anything about you," he snapped.

"But if you will listen to the circumstances of the case, you will be able to do it."

Dr. Stuart remained unsympathetic, and refused to budge on accommodations. He did not like the appearance of these men. They were too pushy, he thought, and when Herold said that they wanted to join up with Mosby, Stuart's suspicions intensified. He told them that Mosby had surrendered, and they would have to get their paroles.

Stuart was cautious for good reason. As a cousin of General Lee, he had been a special target of the Yankees. He had always opened his doors to strangers, but sometimes they had turned out to be spies. For his hospitality, Dr. Stuart had paid with months spent on a prison barge. These days, the most he would do for travelers was to give them a meal. But as Booth and Herold took their seats in his kitchen, Stuart suddenly realized that their transportation had gone away. Bryant and Crismond had taken their leave and were halfway down the lane before the doctor chased them down.

Meanwhile, Booth and Herold ate their supper with an audience. S. Turbeville Stuart, the doctor's son-in-law, was there, and so was Major Robert Waterman Hunter, from the staff of General John B. Gordon. Hunter, who was engaged to Stuart's daughter Margaret, apparently knew who the visitors were, and he talked with them about the assassination. Not much is known of their conversation, but Booth did say that the actual shooting was planned in a single day.[13]

Outside in the lane, Dr. Stuart asked William Bryant what he knew about these strangers. Bryant said he didn't even know their names; they had come out of the marsh, asking if he could take them to Dr. Stuart. They seemed to know what they wanted, and they paid him for the ride. The doctor was puzzled. "It is very strange," he said. "You will have to take them somewhere else." So Bryant and Crismond returned to the house to wait for the strangers.

When Stuart returned to the house, he found the men finishing up their meal. "The old man [Bryant] is waiting for you," he told them. "He is anxious to be off; it is cold; he is not well, and wants to get home." As Booth and Herold were hustled out the door, Herold asked if there was someone else around who might accommodate them. "I have a neighbor near here, a colored man who sometimes hires his wagons," said the doctor. "Probably he would do it if he is not very busy."

Stuart's brusque manner must have reminded Booth of how different his situation had become. He was in Virginia now, and Virginians did not see things as Booth did. For them, the war had ended on April 9, and anything that occurred after that date was beyond the bounds of civilized warfare. Clearly, they did not approve of the assassination. That is one reason why Booth and Herold were given such a hostile reception on this side of the Potomac. And it was not going to get any friendlier.

In a small cabin just across a field from Cleydael, William Lucas and his family were awakened by the barking of their dogs. Lucas heard the sound of a horse outside, and feared that someone might be trying to steal his farm animals. Cautiously, he stepped up to the door just as a man called his name. He asked who was there, and the man outside gave three names. Lucas did not recognize any of them, but when he heard the voice of William Bryant, he opened the door.

Before him stood two strangers, one of them on crutches. "We want to stay here tonight," said one of the men.

"You cannot do it," said Lucas. "I am a colored man, and have no right to take care of white people. I have only one room in the house, and my wife is sick."

It was already late at night, and Herold's patience was wearing thin. "We are Confederate soldiers," he said, his voice rising with anger. "We have been in service three years. We have been knocking about all night, and don't intend to any longer, but we *are* going to stay." As he said this, Booth forced his way into the house and took a seat inside.

"Gentlemen," said Lucas, "you have treated me very badly." He stopped short when Booth dramatically flourished a knife in his face.

"Old man, how do you like that?" he taunted.

Lucas was terrified. "I do not like that at all," he remembered saying.

Booth explained that they had been sent there; that they heard he had good horses, and they needed a good team. Lucas told him that he needed his horses; hired hands were coming to plant corn in the morning. He suggested that the strangers borrow an extra horse he was keeping out in the pasture. "Well, Dave," said Booth. "We will not go on any further, but will stay here and make this old man get us this horse in the morning." Lucas nervously gathered up his family and took them outside. They sat on the step until daylight.[14]

. . .

JUST AFTER MIDNIGHT, the search on the lower Potomac turned tragic when two ships collided. The *Black Diamond* was a small steamship carrying twenty volunteer firemen from Alexandria. She was lying at anchor near Blakistone Island when out of the darkness came the U.S.S. *Massachusetts*, a sidewheel steamer laden with three hundred men recently released from prison camps. The *Massachusetts* struck the smaller ship on her port side, and a hundred or more men were thrown from the larger vessel into the frigid water. Since damage to the *Black Diamond* appeared slight, nearly all of the men swam to her. It was a fatal mistake. Unknown to the soldiers, the vessel's boiler had ruptured, and she was taking on water. She went to the bottom in three minutes. Bodies would wash up on shore for weeks. At final count, eighty-seven men had lost their lives.[15]

ON MONDAY MORNING, April 24, Booth and Herold got into William Lucas's wagon. Lucas asked if they were going to take his horses without paying, and Herold asked how much he would charge for a ride to Port Conway. Lucas said that he usually got ten dollars in gold or twenty in greenbacks. He asked if his son Charley could go along, but Booth didn't like the idea. Herold disagreed. "Yes, he can go," said Herold. "You have a large family, and a crop on hand. You can have the team back again." Lucas was relieved, but couldn't resist making a comment about the Confederate collapse.

"I thought you would be done pressing teams in the Northern Neck since the fall of Richmond."

That raised Booth's ire. "Repeat that again," he said.

Lucas held his tongue, but his point was made: Confederates were no longer in power.

Herold counted out some greenbacks and handed them to Mrs. Lucas. In a moment they were on their way to Port Conway.[16]

NEW YORKERS WITNESSED an unusual sight that day as the president's funeral car was brought across the Hudson River—*sideways*—on the Jersey City ferry. The car had to be hoisted aboard the only way it would fit, and it was a precarious ride. The New York obsequies would be the most elaborate yet, and the hearse was so enormous that it had to be drawn by sixteen horses. It was the creation of Peter Relyea, a forty-nine-year-old undertaker who had been placed in charge of arrangements with only three days' notice. He had not slept since then, nor had the sixty employees working under him. Such toil and sacrifice were typical all along the funeral route.

The coffin was taken to the rotunda of City Hall and placed on a black velvet dais at the top of the stairs. A tasteful arch of black, white, and silver hung above it, and high-ranking officers of the army and navy stood guard at either end. More than half a million people lined up to view the remains, but most were unable to get in. Though mourners were herded in at a rate of nearly one hundred per minute, there was simply not enough time to get them all through. The funeral train was on a rigid timetable, and could not be delayed for any reason.

Scheduling was the responsibility of Stanton's right-hand man, Gen. Edward D. Townsend. General Townsend had been involved in planning the funeral from the start, and was invested with all the authority of the secretary himself when traveling with the cortège. He nearly lost that responsibility when Stanton learned what he had done in New York City that day. Townsend gave photographer Jeremiah Gurney thirty minutes to photograph the president's body as it lay in City Hall. Gurney recorded two images, both of which included the entire scene, not just the remains. They showed the coffin, with Townsend himself and Admiral Charles A. Davis standing at either end with their arms crossed. Though there was nothing unusual about postmortem photographs, Stanton thought the president's family should have been consulted first. With "surprise and disapproval," he ordered General Townsend to seize and dispose of the plates and all proofs made from them. After seeing the first plate destroyed, Gurney appealed the decision. He was sure the Lincolns would approve, and through General Dix, he got the order suspended until they could know the family's wishes. But Robert Lincoln concurred with Stanton, and the second plate was destroyed. Somehow one proof survived, which Stanton kept in his files.[17]

JAMES O'BEIRNE'S DETECTIVES put great stock in Richard Claggett's report that two men had crossed to Virginia on April 16. On the twenty-fourth, Officers Michael O'Callaghan and Lorenzo DeAngelis went to the Northern Neck in search of them. They went some distance inland, but found no trace of the fugitives. They did find the boat, though, and they brought it back to Chapel Point on their return.

Meanwhile, O'Beirne himself ran into Samuel H. Beckwith, General

Grant's cipher operator, at a house just below Port Tobacco. Beckwith and
a man named Cheney had gone there to help in the search, and when
O'Beirne saw them, he suggested they tap the wires and send a report back
to the War Department. He said that there were two theories about where
the fugitives had gone: one, that they were still holed up in the swamp; and
two, that they had crossed over to White's Point, Virginia, on the sixteenth. Beckwith got his field telegraph working, and at about ten o'clock
in the morning, he sent O'Beirne's message to Washington.[18]

THE DRAGNET CONTINUED without letup and, one might say, without
a clue. From a tavern in Bryantown, William P. Wood confidently asserted
that "all the tales about Booth being in Washington, Pennsylvania, or
Upper Marlboro are a hoax. We are on his track, *rely on it*." Wood and his
men still hovered around the Mudd farm. Manager Thomas A. Hall of the
Holliday Street Theatre persuaded authorities in Baltimore to let him lead
a cavalry expedition to the old Booth residence, Tudor Hall. They found
the place abandoned. No clever idea and no amount of effort seemed to
bear fruit. Secretary Stanton was feeling the pressure, and on the twenty-
fifth, he ordered Major General Winfield Scott Hancock to take personal
charge of security in the capital. Hancock set up his headquarters in the
tavern at Bryantown.[19]

IT WAS ALMOST MIDDAY on April 24 when Booth and Herold arrived
at Port Conway. In colonial times, this village had been a bustling port town
on the Rappahannock, but a century after its heyday, all that remained were
four houses and a church. Though one of these houses was the birthplace of
President James Madison, the village had little else to recommend it. Most
travelers considered it a brief stop on the way to somewhere else.

As soon as Charley Lucas stopped his wagon by the old ferry landing,
Booth handed him a note to give to Dr. Stuart. Herold jumped down and
took a look around. The place was almost deserted. A fisherman stood
nearby, and Herold asked if he could get a drink of water for his brother.
William Rollins handed him a dipperful, and Herold took it over to the
wagon. He then asked if Rollins knew where he might get a conveyance
to Orange Court House, on the way to the Shenandoah Valley. Rollins
didn't know, but with a little prodding, he agreed to consider taking them
at least part of the way himself—say, to Bowling Green. That was only fifteen miles, but there was a hotel there, and the railroad was only two and

a half miles beyond the town. They would have to wait in any event. The shad were running, and Rollins needed to get out on the river. The ferry-boat was across the river, at Port Royal, and he would summon it as soon as he got a chance.

As Rollins and his employee, Dick Wilson, headed toward the river, three young men rode up to the landing. Their Confederate uniforms put Herold at ease, and he struck up a conversation. "Gentlemen, what command do you belong to?"

One man spoke up. "Mosby's command." He was Mortimer Bain-bridge Ruggles, a lieutenant in the 43rd Virginia, and the son of a general. Standing next to Ruggles was his cousin and fellow Ranger, Absalom Ruggles Bainbridge.

"If I am not inquisitive, can I ask where you are going?" said Herold.

Ruggles started to answer, but one of the others cut him off. "That is a secret. Nobody knows where we are going because I never tell anybody." This was a younger man—a boy, really, with dark hair, and a soft, pink complexion that made him look even younger than his eighteen years. He was William Storke Jett, a former private whose brief service in the 9th Virginia Cavalry ended with a near-fatal wound in the abdomen. Jett had been sent to recuperate in the Star Hotel, at Bowling Green, and had fallen in love with the hotel owner's daughter, Izora Gouldman. He was on his way to see her now.

Recently, Jett had been serving as a civilian commissary agent, issuing draft exemptions to local farmers in exchange for crops or cattle. But after hearing of the fall of Richmond, he donned his uniform and tried to rejoin his old unit. He never found them, but he did manage to find Mosby's Rangers, with whom his brother served. Mosby apparently told him to go home. Now he and his companions were heading for Ashland, outside Richmond, to certify that they had laid down their arms. They would be issued a parole certificate, as required by the terms of surrender.

After an awkward silence, one of Jett's companions resumed the conversation. "What command do you belong to?"

"We belong to A. P. Hill's corps," replied Herold. "I have my wounded brother, a Marylander who was wounded in the fight below Petersburg." He said that his name was David E. Boyd, and that his brother was John W. Boyd. As he said this, Booth hobbled over on crutches. He stood near the group, but said nothing, and kept looking toward Port Royal. Jett thought he seemed anxious for the ferryboat to come over.

"I suppose you are all going to the Southern army," said Herold. "We are also anxious to get there ourselves and wish you to take us along with you." Jett was suspicious of strangers, and declined to speak with them. His demeanor bothered Herold. When he walked to a house nearby, Herold pulled him aside.

"I take it you are raising a command to go south to Mexico," he said in a trembling voice. "I want you to let us go with you."

Jett did not know what to say. Something about these men wasn't right; soldiers shouldn't be so desperate at the end of a war. So he just blurted out, "Who are you?" Jett was quite unprepared for the answer:

"We are the assassinators of the president."[20]

AT THE WAR DEPARTMENT telegraph office, Lafayette Baker noticed a message from Captain Beckwith at Port Tobacco. Baker was intrigued by the idea put forth in the telegram that Booth might have gone to Virginia. Few troops were looking in the Northern Neck, and Baker thought it might be a good time to expand the search into that area. He sent a request to General Augur's office for a detachment of cavalry.

An order went out for a "reliable and discreet commissioned officer" to command the mission, and Lt. Edward P. Doherty, twenty-five, answered the call. Doherty, a native of Canada, had enlisted as an infantry private, but he transferred to the cavalry in 1863 and had been serving in the 16th New York ever since. When he and Capt. Joseph Schneider, of the same regiment, reported to Colonel Baker's office, the colonel handed Doherty some circulars and photographs and told him to take twenty-five men to Virginia. He should divide his command and search everywhere between the Potomac and the Rappahannock. Everton Conger and Luther Byron Baker, who had both served in Colonel Baker's old unit, the 2nd District of Columbia Cavalry, would go along as civilian detectives.

The 16th New York Cavalry had been based in Vienna, Virginia, and had spent the last two years chasing after Mosby in that vicinity. But recently, much of the regiment had been transferred into the city. They had taken part in the president's funeral, and were now giving all their attention to the search for Booth. Some had just come back from a foray when the bugler blew "Boots and Saddles," announcing a call for volunteers. Though the request had gone out for twenty-five privates, Lieutenant Doherty took everyone who responded, regardless of rank.[21]

· · · ·

EVENTUALLY WILLIAM ROLLINS RETURNED from fishing, and he asked if Booth and Herold were ready to cross the river. By that time Herold had changed his mind. He had been talking to the soldiers, and they convinced him that he was better off without Rollins's help. "If you are in a hurry, go on," Herold said; "we are not going over now." So Rollins went about his business.

Unable to get over the fact that he was actually in the presence of Lincoln's killer, Jett couldn't help but stare. Every so often, he tried to sneak a furtive glance at the "J.W.B." tattoo on the back of Booth's hand, and he even asked the fugitives to sign something for him as a memento. Booth gratified his request with something less incriminating than an autograph; he wrote a poem.

There is no question that Booth had a lifelong passion for verse, and had occasionally written poems for friends by request. In this case, it was a good way to ingratiate himself with Jett, who might lead him to safety. And it offered one more opportunity—possibly his last—to express his thoughts on the assassination. His letter to the *Intelligencer* had not been published, and his diary might well be suppressed. But in the subtle phrasing of a poem, Booth could reassert the message he had failed to send in other ways: that his motives were pure, and his suffering great. He wrote:

> *He put aside the dainty bribe*
> *The little proffered hand*
> *Albeit he held it in his thought*
> *The dearest in the land*
> *Not sharply nor with sudden heart*
> *But with regretful grace*
> *Meanwhile the shadow of his pain*
> *Fell white upon his face*

Almost teasingly, these lines touched upon the feelings Booth would have known too well in the past ten days: premeditation, regret, and pain. If he did indeed refer to the assassination, his opening line suggested something that had never before come to light: that Booth may have turned down an offer for Lincoln's killing. Given his penchant for deception, one cannot help wondering if that "dainty bribe" was just an artful way of confounding authorities with a question they could never answer.

After writing those lines, Booth handed the paper to Herold, who wrote out a few of his own:

> *Dark daughter of the Sultry South*
> *Thy dangerous eyes & lips*
> *Essayed to win the prize and leave*
> *Dear honor we Eclipse*
> *She shyly clung upon his brow*
> *He stayed now at the door*
> *I could not love thee, dear, so much*
> *Loved I not Honor more.*
> *"Adieu, forever mine, my dear*
> *Adieu forever more!"*[22]

Booth sat on Ruggles's horse as the ferryman, Jim Thornton, took him and the others across the river. The Rappahannock was barely two hundred yards wide here, and beyond it was Port Royal, a charming old village that was home to some of Virginia's leading families—the Tayloes, the Fitzhughs, and the Lightfoots, to name a few. Washington and Jefferson had been intimately familiar with the place, and they had often stopped here in their travels. Now Booth was to inscribe his own name in the history of the village. While he waited at the landing, Jett went knocking on doors in search of a place for Booth to stay. A couple of blocks up the hill, Jett found Sarah Jane Peyton at home, and asked if she would mind taking care of a wounded soldier. Miss Peyton consented, and Jett went back to get Booth.

As soon as Booth entered her parlor, Sarah Jane had second thoughts. Maybe it was a simple change of heart, or maybe it was the assault on the senses that one gets from a man who has lived in the wild for more than a week. At any rate, she suggested to Jett that they take him elsewhere—perhaps to the Garrett place, two miles outside town. No one in the party thought to ask Miss Peyton if she could lend them a horse. Had they done so, John Wilkes Booth might have ridden away on the one extra mount in the Peyton stable: an old stallion named Brutus. Instead, he doubled up with Ruggles, while Herold rode with Bainbridge. Willie Jett rode by himself.

Booth had been rejected yet again. His spirit was broken, his optimism gone. Willie Jett was oblivious to Booth's low mood, and on the way out of

Port Royal, he tried to strike up a conversation about the assassination. Booth was reticent, saying it was "nothing to brag about." Life as a fugitive had taught him a new reality. Just days ago, he had drawn a calendar in his diary that would cover two full months on the run. Now, he didn't care how much time he had left. He took it for granted that authorities would catch up to him soon, and he had no intention of being taken alive. "If they don't kill me," he vowed, "I'll kill myself."[23]

LOU WEICHMANN AND JOHN HOLOHAN were still in Canada, and nobody had heard from them in days. Since they had left in the company of police detectives, Secretary of War Stanton called in their superintendent, A. C. Richards, to demand an explanation. He accused Richards of everything from gross stupidity to hindering the investigation, and he threatened to hold him personally responsible for losing those witnesses. Richards insisted it was not he who sent them away, but Colonel Baker. Still, that did not excuse his losing track of them. When the secretary asked where they were now, Richards admitted he did not know, but "supposed they were at Montreal, or Quebec, or somewhere." It was hardly the answer Stanton wanted to hear, and it didn't help to know that the detectives sent to search for them had not reported back yet either. Richards was ordered to find them all.[24]

THE LOCUST HILL FARM was a 517-acre spread that straddled a high ridge southwest of Port Royal. Its owner, Richard H. Garrett, lived here with his second wife and nine of his children. The two oldest, Jack and Will, had just returned from Confederate service, and were still in uniform when Willie Jett and four strangers rode up on the afternoon of the twenty-fourth. "Here is a wounded Confederate soldier that we want you to take care of for a day or so," said Jett. "Will you do it?" When Richard Garrett consented, Booth hobbled into the house.

Undoubtedly, Jett was relieved to be rid of Booth. He just wanted to get his parole and, on the way, to stop for a visit with his girlfriend Izora. But surprisingly, Herold also chose to leave Booth—perhaps a sign that those Mosby men had taught him the wisdom of a "skedaddle." Herold and the others headed for Bowling Green, and after pausing for drinks at a place called The Trap, they ran into Izora Gouldman's brother Jesse. Jett pulled Jesse aside and told him that their companion was Herold, the conspirator. They were bringing him along to the Star Hotel.

Jesse Gouldman was horrified. "My God, Jett, you can't do that," he said. "Why, the whole country is swimming with Yankee cavalry, and the hotel is the first place they will search. . . . If they find Herold there they will burn it down and hang every one of us!" Jesse's parents owned the hotel, and he was adamant that Herold could not stay there. The plan was changed. Jett and Ruggles still went to the Star Hotel, but Herold went with Bainbridge to the home of Virginia Clarke, three miles outside town. By coincidence, both knew her son James—Bainbridge from his service with Mosby, and Herold from an acquaintance made years before.[25]

FOUR HOURS OUT OF WASHINGTON, the steamship *John S. Ide* docked at Belle Plain, Virginia. On board were Lieutenant Doherty, Detectives Conger and Baker, and twenty-six enlisted men from the 16th New York Cavalry. Like nearly every unit that had fought in the war, this detachment was made up of ordinary men—mostly farmers and mechanics—uprooted by the call of duty from their homes in the Adirondacks, in Buffalo, or in New York City. The most colorful character among them was also its ranking enlisted man. Sgt. Boston Corbett, thirty-two, was a four-year veteran with an outstanding record for bravery. He was born Thomas H. Corbett in London, but moved to the United States at an early age and grew up in Troy, New York. He learned the trade of hatter, got married, and planned to start a family. But when death claimed his wife and newborn child, Corbett fell into a profound depression. He eventually drifted up to New England and underwent a spiritual awakening. Renaming himself Boston Corbett, for the city of his rebirth, he grew his hair and beard in the fashion of Jesus Christ and dedicated himself to a pious existence in the service of God. Of his sincerity, he left no room for doubt. He once encountered a couple of prostitutes, and resolved to put himself above their temptations. Returning to his room, he cut off his testicles with a pair of scissors, and spent two weeks recovering at Massachusetts General Hospital.

Though Corbett was only five feet four inches tall, he made up in confidence what he lacked in stature. He once upbraided an officer who took the Lord's name in vain, and was given a harsh confinement—which he actually enjoyed, because it gave him some time alone with his Bible. In early 1864 he was captured in a fight against Mosby and was sent to Andersonville. He nearly died there, but the Confederates released him, even without an exchange, and he recovered miraculously. When he returned to his unit, he held the rank of sergeant.[26]

Corbett was among those landing at Belle Plain. It was ten o'clock at night by then, and Lieutenant Doherty ordered Captain Henry Wilson, of the *Ide,* to wait there for two days before returning to Washington. Though all the men had been up since sunrise, their work was just beginning. From the landing at Belle Plain, they headed west three miles, then struck the main road that ran south out of Fredericksburg. There they split up the command and rode in two groups toward King George Court House. For the next twelve hours they pushed ahead, searching, foraging, and questioning anyone who might have encountered the fugitives. Detectives Conger and Baker preferred deception to coercion; they pretended to be looking for two friends—one of them lame—from whom they had become separated. The rest of the party, following another route, searched for doctors who might have treated a man with a broken leg.

ALL THE WHILE, Booth was asleep in a comfortable farmhouse in neighboring Caroline County. The Garretts had opened their home to him, and he was a great hit, especially with the youngest girls, Lillian, Cora, and Henrietta. They called him Mr. Boyd, and believed his story: that he had been wounded by an artillery shell while serving under A. P. Hill at Petersburg. For a time, he became a part of their household, and life was almost normal. Then the news arrived.

As the family sat down to dinner on Tuesday, Jack Garrett came in and announced that Lincoln had been killed. They had all heard rumors of an assassination, but nobody knew the details until Jack spoke to a friend in Port Royal. He said that a $140,000 reward had been offered for the killer, and one of his brothers remarked, "He better not come this way or he would be gobbled up."

Booth remained nonchalant through all of this. "How much did you say had been offered?" he asked. When Garrett repeated the amount, he said, "I would sooner suppose five hundred thousand."

Talk of the manhunt didn't seem to bother Booth, and even though he walked with crutches, nobody at the Garrett farm suspected he was actually the assassin. Indeed, they saw nothing suspicious about him until later that evening, when he took off his coat to go to bed. That's when Will and Jack noticed he had two revolvers and a knife tucked into his belt.[27]

· · · ·

A DAY AFTER they dropped Booth at the Garrett place, Herold and Bainbridge met up with Jett and Ruggles in Bowling Green. Herold had intended to keep moving west, toward Orange Court House, but someone had spotted a large cavalry unit on the way out there. Herold could not stay in town, so Bainbridge asked if he wanted to go back the way he came. "No," said Herold, "I am not anxious to do so, but the gentleman [Jett] left there yesterday will be anxious for me to come back, and I am almost afraid to stay away from him." So Bainbridge, Ruggles, and Herold went back to Garrett's, while Jett stayed in town with his girlfriend.

By then, Lieutenant Doherty and his men had come to the end of the line. After a long night of knocking on doors, they and the detectives converged at Port Conway on the afternoon of the twenty-fifth. They had fulfilled their orders to search the Northern Neck, and had found no trace of Booth. If they stayed on the road much longer, Captain Wilson might take his ship back to Washington without them. However, a chance encounter was soon to change their minds.

A group of soldiers were milling around the ferry landing, and they happened to notice Dick Wilson, a black man employed by William Rollins. They asked if any strangers had been around lately, and Wilson said that strangers came through all the time. But when someone showed him the photographs of Booth, Herold, and Surratt, he recognized two of them. Excitedly, Byron Baker took the photos and showed them to Rollins. He confirmed it: Booth and Herold had come through there just twenty-four hours before. They had wanted to go to Orange Court House, but whether they made it that far, he could not say. Perhaps Willie Jett could tell them. Jett was one of three Confederates who had crossed the river with them. He shouldn't be too hard to find; according to Rollins's wife, Bettie, he was probably in Bowling Green, where his girlfriend lived at the Star Hotel.

Finally, someone had found positive information on the fugitives' progress. Though Booth and Herold had a twenty-four-hour lead, they might still be within reach. The chase party sprang to life, and Lieutenant Doherty sent three men across the river to bring back the ferry.[28]

THAT WAS ABOUT FOUR-THIRTY on the afternoon of the twenty-fifth. At the same time, Booth was sitting on the front porch of the Garrett house jotting something down in his diary. He was still there an hour later when two horsemen went past the gate in the distance. Jack Garrett recognized them from the day before, and he said, "There goes some of your party now."

Booth wasn't expecting anyone, and the appearance of Bainbridge and Ruggles startled him. He jumped to his feet and shouted to Garrett, "You go get my pistols!" In a moment, he saw Dave Herold walking by himself toward the house, and he calmed down. Extending his hand, he asked his friend if he intended to stay.

"I would like to go home," Herold answered. "I am sick and tired of this way of living." But Booth welcomed him back, and asked Jack Garrett if Herold could spend the night.

Just then, Bainbridge and Ruggles came galloping up the lane. They had seen a column of Yankee cavalry on the road from Port Royal. "Marylanders, you had better watch out!" they warned. As Bainbridge and Ruggles "skedaddled" into the woods, Booth called for one of the Garrett boys to run and get his pistols. He hobbled into the woods, and Herold started to follow. But then he stopped in the yard and turned around. He was ready to give up.

What Bainbridge and Ruggles had seen, of course, was the 16th New York Cavalry, galloping past them in search of Willie Jett. Had the cavalry been more alert, they might have noticed the fugitives heading for the woods. Herold, at least, was fully visible from the road as they went by. But nobody in the detachment had had a moment's rest in the past thirty-six hours, and whatever energy they had left was focused ahead of the column, in the direction of Bowling Green. They stayed on track, and with William Rollins as their guide, they found their way to The Trap, where they made inquiries and continued on.

It was well after eleven o'clock at night before they arrived in Bowling Green. Doherty posted a few of his men on the roads outside town, then took the rest with him, along with the detectives. Just across from the courthouse, on a main thoroughfare, stood the Star Hotel, a large two-story building with a wraparound colonnade. The soldiers dismounted some distance away, then quietly crept up to the building. Byron Baker tiptoed onto the front porch while Conger and Doherty went around to the back. An old black man was walking down the alley, and he pointed out that there was a rear entrance to the place. Conger posted himself there and waited for the signal that all exits were covered. Then he rapped at the door.

After a long silence, someone inside walked up to the door and unlatched it. The door opened just a crack, and a woman asked who was there.

"Open the door, or we will break it down," said Conger. He and Doherty pushed their way inside, guns drawn, and confronted the petite middle-aged woman who had answered their knock. She was Julia Gouldman, wife of the owner, who had gone on a fishing trip. Mrs. Gouldman lit a lamp and, on Conger's orders, led the way to Willie Jett's room. They stormed in and found two men sharing a bed. One was Jesse Gouldman.

Conger turned his attention to the other man. "Is your name Jett?" he asked. "Get up. I want you!" As Jett pulled on his drawers, he stammered out some excuse for not having his parole. He said he was going to get it at the first opportunity. Conger said that this had nothing to do with his parole. He wanted to know where those two men had gone—the ones who came across the river with Jett at Port Royal. From the tone of voice, and a Colt revolver aimed at his temple, Jett knew that Conger meant business. He asked if they might speak alone.

When everyone else had cleared the room, Jett offered the detective a handshake, saying, "I know who you want, and I will tell you where they can be found." He asked for some assurance that he would not be blamed for aiding in Booth's escape. Conger agreed, and Jett got right to the point. "They are on the road to Port Royal, about three miles this side of that." Booth and Herold had both crossed the Rappahannock, he said, but Booth had gone no farther than Garrett's farm, where Herold had rejoined him. "I will go there with you, and show where they are now, and you can get them."

Conger thought that something didn't sound right. "You say they are on the road to Port Royal?" He said that they had just come from there.

"I thought you came from Richmond," said Jett. "If you have come that way, you have come past them." It occurred to Jett that Booth and Herold might not still be at Garrett's; the cavalry could have scared them off. Conger said they would just have to go back there and see.[29]

Jett got dressed, and the soldiers regrouped for the ride back to Garrett's. They would have to backtrack over twelve miles of rough country roads. With no moon, it was all they could do to stay on the road. They would have to go slowly, and after so many hours in the saddle, the trip must have seemed endless.

After two hours of riding, Willie Jett finally located the entrance to Garrett's farm. Doherty and the detectives asked about the layout of the place, and the best way to cover it. Jett said that there was another gate far-ther up, and when the soldiers gathered there, Lieutenant Doherty told them to have their weapons capped, loaded, and ready. "The assassin is in that house," he said. "I want you to surround it, and let no man out."

"Open file to the right and left— Gallop!" With that command, the soldiers split up and surrounded the house. There was a barn in the dis-tance, and when Doherty noticed it, he ordered Corporal Herman New-garten to take six or seven men to cover it.

Byron Baker looked for exits to the house. The front door opened onto a wide porch, and a kitchen wing, on the left side, had its own door that opened to the yard. Baker covered the kitchen door on horseback, and waited for the men to dismount and take up positions. The clamor awoke some dogs, and their barking aroused Richard Garrett from his sleep. He came to a window and asked what the trouble was.

"Strike a light immediately," Baker yelled. He dismounted and told Conger, who had just come from around the other side, that there was an old man in the house. They hitched their horses to a tree as Mr. Garrett stepped outside, without his clothes, candle in hand.

"Where are those parties who were at your house last night?" asked Baker. Garrett seemed befuddled, and had trouble getting out an answer. "Answer my question," said the detective, "or I'll blow your brains out!"

Richard Garrett couldn't help stammering; he always did that when nervous. He said that some strangers had stopped by earlier, but had gone into the woods.

"What?" said Baker. "A lame man go into the woods?"

"He went with his crutches."

Mr. Garrett was kept from going back into the house to get his clothes, but someone inside handed out a pair of pants and some boots. Everton Conger, watching this, asked where in the woods those men had gone. Garrett said that they had come without his consent, and he did not want them to stay, and—

"I do not want a long story out of you. I just want to know where these men have gone." He didn't think Mr. Garrett was getting to the point fast enough, and he ordered one of the men to bring out a rope. "I will put that man up to the top of one of those locust trees."

A man's voice came from out of the darkness. "Father, you had better tell him, for they have a whole regiment of cavalry here." It was Jack Gar-rett, striding toward the porch in his Confederate uniform. Garrett had

been sleeping in a corncrib with his brother Will. They had heard someone threaten their father, and Jack demanded to speak with the commanding officer. He said that two men had come there expecting to spend the
night, but something was not right about them, and he had refused to let
them sleep in the house. They were out in the barn.

About two hundred feet from the house stood a large shed, built with
wide, open slats for the curing of tobacco leaves. The shed had not been
used much, since tobacco was a labor-intensive crop and the older boys,
who would have done the planting, had been away in the war. In recent
years, the elder Garrett had been letting his neighbors store furniture and
other valuables there to protect them from the Yankees. That is why their
barn, unlike most tobacco barns, had a lock on the door.

Jack Garrett had kept a close eye on those men since yesterday afternoon, when the cavalry rode past the farm. He thought it strange that they
had taken to the woods even though the war was over. So when they returned to the house, Garrett and his brother Will questioned them again.
Herold said he had served in Captain Robinson's company of the 30th
Virginia—an unfortunate claim, since Jack Garrett knew there was no
such captain in that regiment. He confronted them and, brushing aside
their excuses, told them to leave at once.

But throwing them off the farm wasn't so simple. The sun was setting,
and the men were on foot. Throw them out now, and they would surely
come back in the night to steal a horse or two. So Garrett allowed them to
stay until morning, but told them to sleep in the barn. Will Garrett locked
them inside, and the two brothers kept watch over the barn from a nearby
corncrib. The two men could not have escaped.[30]

Lieutenant Doherty grabbed Jack Garrett by the collar and, shoving
him toward the barn, told him to go inside and bring out those men. Garrett protested, saying that they would shoot him if he went in there. Byron
Baker, walking up to the door, said, "They know you, and you can go in."
And besides, *he* would shoot him if he refused.[31]

Inside, Booth woke Herold and told him the barn was surrounded.
Herold suggested they give up, but Booth wouldn't hear of it. "I will suffer
death first," he said. Then Booth pulled Herold close, and said in a low
voice, "Don't make any noise. Maybe they will go off, thinking we are not
here."

As they whispered back and forth, the door opened, and by the light of
a candle outside they could see the silhouette of Jack Garrett as he stepped

inside. "Gentlemen, the cavalry are after you," he said, speaking into the darkness. "You are the ones. You had better give yourselves up." Booth remained perfectly still, but Herold made no effort to conceal his presence. Garrett repeated his advice, and pointed out that the barn was surrounded. As he said this, he thought he heard a man raise himself from a pile of hay. Then Booth spoke in a loud, angry tone. "You have implicated me!"[32]

Booth had just gotten the words out when Byron Baker, candle in hand, called out, "I want you to surrender. If you don't, I will burn the barn down in fifteen minutes." All of this was a surprise to Lieutenant Doherty. As commander of the detachment, Doherty had thought he was in charge of the whole expedition. But now, without a word of discussion, Baker had stepped in and taken over. And worse, he was threatening to flush out the fugitives in almost complete darkness. Conceivably, Booth and Herold might actually slip away, if the troops were somehow diverted. There was little Doherty could do; he was still positioning his men when Baker took charge.

Booth asked who was at the door and what he wanted. "This is a hard case," he said. "It may be I am to be taken by my friends." Baker declined to identify himself. He ordered Booth to turn his weapons over to Garrett, then give himself up. He could have ten minutes to consider it.

Herold was folding under the pressure, and he made up his mind to surrender. "You don't choose to give yourself up," he told Booth. "Let me go out and give myself up."

"No," snapped Booth, "you shall not do it." They argued in low, angry tones, and Garrett, fearing for his life, backed up to the door. He called out to Baker, who let him out.

Between angry whispers to Herold, Booth held Baker off by asking for other options. He pointed out that if he had been inclined to shoot his way out, it would not have been difficult; the candles outside made Baker an easy target. The detective hadn't thought of that. He looked around, then quickly backed up and placed the candle farther out in the yard. Going back to the door, he repeated his threat: *Give up your arms, or the building will be set on fire.* "Captain," Booth replied, "that's rather rough. I am nothing but a cripple. I have but one leg, and you ought to give me a chance for a fair fight."

"This is no child's play," Baker responded. "We are in earnest, and shall carry out our threats. We will give you five minutes to consider the matter."

Booth kept trying to draw him into conversation, but Baker insisted he should just think about his options and make up his mind.

"Well," said Booth, "you may prepare a stretcher for me. Throw open your door, draw up your men in line, and let's have a fair fight."

Everton Conger had had enough, and he decided to force the issue. He told Jack Garrett to get some pine twigs and pile them up against the side of the barn. Garrett came back with an armload, but Booth heard him placing it on the ground and warned him away. "You had better look out there. Put no more brush there or someone will get hurt." Garrett backed off, and Booth turned his attention back to Baker at the door. In the meantime, Conger picked up some hay and twisted it into a small rope. He put a match to it and pushed it through a wide crack onto a pile of hay inside.[33]

Slowly, almost imperceptibly, flames crept up the wall, licking at the planks, fanned by a light breeze. Herold panicked. "I am going," he told Booth. "I don't intend to be burnt alive." As he started for the door, Booth pulled him back and threatened to kill him if he went any farther. Then he said in a louder voice, "Go away from me, you damned coward." As Herold started to pull away, Booth yanked him back and whispered, "When you get out, don't tell them the arms I have."

Then he addressed Byron Baker. "Captain," he said, "there is a man in here who wants to surrender. He is innocent of any crime." When Baker instructed Herold to hand out his arms, Booth said, "He has no arms. I own and have all the arms that are here, and he cannot get them." Herold ran to the door and pounded on it, crying, "Let me out! Let me out!"[34]

With guns cocked, Lieutenant Doherty and a couple of his men moved in close. Baker pulled the door open, and the lieutenant told Herold to put his hands out, one at a time. He did as he was told, and Doherty grabbed him by the wrists, jerking him clear of the door. Corporal Newgarten took him away, to be searched and tied to a locust tree.

The flames had spread to the rafters, throwing strips of flickering light through the cracks of the barn and onto the faces of the soldiers. A few soldiers peered through those cracks, watching Booth's every move and waiting for him to make a quick break. He was the most hunted man in America, trapped like a wild animal, his eyes darting here and there, straining to see past the flames. In one hand, he gripped a Spencer carbine that he and Herold had picked up at the Surrattsville tavern. In the other, he steadied himself with a crutch. From the look of things, he seemed prepared to shoot his way out.

Booth appeared to be searching for something that would help put out the fire, but it was too late. As the flames swept through the barn, his expression suddenly changed from defiance to despair. He realized that his time had come. Taking one more look around, he dropped his crutch, turned on his heels, and shuffled quickly toward the door.

Barely ten feet away, Sgt. Boston Corbett watched closely through the slats of the barn. In his hand was a .44 Colt revolver, trained on the fugitive and ready to fire in an instant. As Booth turned toward the door, he also raised his carbine. Corbett fired.

Hearing the shot, Byron Baker threw the door open. Doherty, Jack Garrett, and some of the soldiers ran inside. Booth had fallen facedown, and was completely limp as they lifted him up by the arms and legs. Conger, who had heard the shot while running for the door, came in behind the others. "Is he dead?" he asked. "Did he shoot himself?"

Baker replied, "No," though he didn't know exactly what had happened. They checked Booth quickly and discovered a pistol wound on the right side of his neck. To all appearances, he was dead. They carried him outside and laid him on a soft patch of grass about thirty feet away. Conger went back inside to retrieve the carbine, and when he returned, he noticed that Booth was still alive. Though unable to move or speak clearly, he was trying to say something. The detective crouched over him and put his ear to Booth's lips.

"Tell my mother I die for my country." Conger repeated that, and asked if he had heard right. Booth signified yes.

While the soldiers scrambled to put out the fire, the detectives talked about what had happened. Conger was sure that Booth had shot himself, but each time he said so, Baker said it couldn't be; after all, he had been looking right at him when he heard the shot. Sergeant Corbett overheard the conversation, and immediately he reported to Lieutenant Doherty, telling him that it was he who shot Booth. As proof, he showed the lieutenant a spent cap and the empty chamber in his revolver. They walked over to see Conger, and Corbett gave the details. "I went to the barn," he said, "looked through a crack, saw Booth coming towards the door, sighted at his body, and fired." Corbett said that he had been afraid Booth would either shoot someone or get away. Since, in Conger's words, "they had no orders either to fire or not to fire," the matter ended there—at least for now.[35]

As the heat from the fire grew more intense, Booth was carried from the lawn to the front porch of the house. Mrs. Garrett had placed a mattress there, and Booth rallied as they laid him on it. He could make himself understood, though only in a feeble whisper, and he asked for water. He couldn't swallow. He asked to be turned facedown, then on his side, then his other side. Fluids accumulated in his throat, and he was powerless to clear it. Nothing anyone did for him eased his misery. Motioning for Conger, he whispered, "Kill me, kill me."

Everton Conger wouldn't hear of it. "We don't want to kill you," he said. "We want you to get well."

And so it went. For the next couple of hours, Booth kept asking to be turned, but every movement brought extreme pain. His throat swelled, and his lips turned purple. He would gasp, and his heartbeat would fade. But then he would revive, his heart would flutter, and his eyes would move. Byron Baker sat at his side, bathing his wound and waiting for the inevitable. He occasionally left the job to Mrs. Garrett's sister, Lucinda Holloway. When nobody was looking, Miss Holloway clipped a lock of Booth's hair as a memento.

Dr. Charles Urquhart had been summoned from Port Royal, and was apparently unnerved by the sight of so many blue coats. He at first indicated that Booth would recover, but when one of the soldiers pointed out that the ball had passed clean through the neck, his prognosis dimmed considerably. Booth had suffered a spinal cord injury, and his vital organs were shutting down. He was slowly suffocating.

Everton Conger did not wait for the end. Hearing the doctor's revised pronouncement, Conger headed back to Washington with the contents of Booth's pockets. Booth apparently wanted to be sure that someone would pass along his final message, so he indicated he wanted to say something else. Baker put his ear to Booth's lips, and the assassin repeated his declaration:

"Tell my mother—tell my mother that I did it for my country—that I die for my country."

The morning sun broke over the hills, and Booth winced at the bright, warm rays striking his face. A shirt draped over the back of a chair gave a small measure of relief. He looked toward his hands, and Byron Baker lifted them up, limp and nearly lifeless, above Booth's face. Baker leaned over as Booth made one last, feeble pronouncement:

"Useless. Useless."[36]

SIXTEEN

"THESE PEOPLE AROUND HERE CONTRADICT EACH OTHER SO MUCH"

T. J. HEMPHILL, OF THE WALNUT STREET THEATRE, KNOCKED on the door of Sleeper Clarke's mansion in Philadelphia. Pale and careworn, he could not raise his eyes to look at Asia Booth Clarke. She knew at once why he had come.

"Is it over?" she asked.

"Yes, madam."

"Taken?"

"Yes."

"Dead?"

"Yes, madam."

Booth's sister curled up in bed with her face to the wall, quietly thanking God that it was over. Mr. Hemphill turned to leave, choking on his sobs, and shut the door behind him.

Even as Lieutenant Doherty's detachment was heading back from Garrett's farm, James O'Beirne and Samuel H. Beckwith sent word to the War Department that they had traced Booth to a place about two miles north of Bryantown and they expected to capture him at any time. A similar report came from Colonel Wells, who also believed the fugitives were in Charles County. Yet at that very moment, Everton Conger and Boston Corbett were heading up the Potomac with evidence and "particulars" of the assassin's closing scene. They were carrying Booth's diary, and from it they erroneously deduced that Booth had broken his leg on the stage at Ford's Theatre. That story would reach the newspapers within hours.

They arrived in Washington late that afternoon and briefed Secretary Stanton at the War Department. Booth's revolvers, knives, keys, and compass were taken to the office of the *New York Tribune,* and reporters were invited to examine them. Some noted that a handkerchief taken from Booth's pocket had been folded up with wood shavings inside—collected, evidently, when the assassin bored that hole in the door to the president's box. A diamond stick pin taken from his undershirt was inscribed as a gift from his friend, the minstrel Dan Bryant. The display did not include Booth's diary and his Spencer carbine; they were locked away in Stanton's office. In a pocket of the diary were photographs of five women: four actresses, and Lucy Hale.[1]

The stunning news of Booth's death brought joy and relief to millions, and instant fame to Boston Corbett. The little sergeant was the talk of the nation, and he was already receiving monetary offers for his .44 Colt revolver. Within days, it would be stolen. For the moment, Corbett's fame outshone even that of General William T. Sherman, who had accepted the surrender of Joe Johnston's forces only hours after Booth's death. Since Johnston had commanded the largest body of Confederate troops still in the field, his capitulation signaled the end of major hostilities.[2]

Ten hours after Conger and Corbett's arrival, the *John S. Ide* steamed into the Washington Navy Yard. On board were Byron Baker, David Herold, the cavalrymen, and the body of Booth. Herold was hustled onto the *Montauk,* lying at anchor in the Eastern Branch, and confined in the ship's wardroom. Booth's remains were placed under a strong marine guard on the deck of the same vessel.

The War Department had already been flooded with advice on how to dispose of Booth's body. One man suggested they bury it beneath the threshold of Ford's Theatre, so everyone who entered could tread upon it. Another suggested "dissection and public display" with a sign that read *"Sic semper Percussorouibus."* Dozens of ideas were thrown around, and none of a very gentle nature. But no matter what choice Secretary Stanton made, he first had to verify that the remains were indeed those of Lincoln's killer. An inquest was arranged, and on the morning of April 27, some of the army's leading surgeons were ordered to report to the *Montauk.* They placed the remains on a makeshift table to be photographed and examined.

Surgeons Joseph Janvier Woodward and George Otis conducted a cursory examination. Removing a splint and bandage from the left leg, they found a fracture of the small bone, three inches above the ankle joint. It was swollen and badly discolored, but relatively minor as injuries go. Death was caused by a pistol ball, fired from several yards away, which passed through the neck from right to left. It punched through the fourth and fifth cervical vertebrae, driving bone fragments into the muscle and partially cutting the spinal cord. Surgeon General Barnes, who watched the examination, observed that "all the horrors of consciousness of suffering and death must have been present to the assassin during the two hours he lingered." Dr. Woodward removed the vertebrae and the tissues adjacent to the wound. They were preserved for the new Army Medical Museum, and remain in its collections today.[3]

Booth was a familiar figure in Washington, and ought to have been easy to identify. Even so, the War Department wanted to erase all possible doubt. At the Garrett farm, Lieutenant Doherty had compared the face of the corpse with a photo of Booth. They matched. But since then, the remains had been lying facedown, and blood had pooled under the skin, giving it a haggard and freckled appearance. Their identification would have to rest on something more positive than mere appearance.

Matt Canning must have told authorities about the tumor that Dr. John Frederick May had removed from Booth's neck. So they summoned Dr. May to the *Montauk* and questioned him about the operation. Though two years had passed, May still remembered the size and location of the incision he had made. Booth had torn it open before it had a chance to heal, and the scar looked more like a burn than the work of a surgeon, which made it distinctive. When Dr. May described the scar from memory, the other doctors checked the corpse and found the description to be accurate.

The remains had one other distinguishing feature: the initials "J.W.B." on the back of the left hand. Willie Jett noticed them at Port Conway, as did Jack Garrett at the end of the trail. Taken with the surgical scar, they put the identification beyond dispute.[4]

Because this inquest took place on a heavily guarded ship, modern researchers have assumed that the proceeding was cloaked in secrecy. But in fact, a crowd had gathered along the riverbank near the *Montauk*, and hundreds of people were able to see the corpse from a distance. From detailed accounts in the papers, it appears that reporters got a much closer look.

And they were not the only ones. Naval officers and guards from the Navy Yard Bridge brought their friends aboard the ship, and some took away souvenirs. One woman obtained a lock of Booth's hair, and when that came to Secretary of War Stanton's attention, he demanded to know why security was so lax. The *Montauk*'s commander, Edward E. Stone, explained that nobody had offered guidance in the matter. The corpse had been brought aboard without explanation or orders, he said, and no one from the War Department had bothered to brief anyone. Stone called the episode "a most informal and unmilitary proceeding," but he assured Stanton that at least the prisoner belowdecks was closely guarded.[5]

Among the people who came on deck that morning was Joseph Holt, Judge Advocate General of the Army, a man who would figure prominently in the events of the coming months. Holt, fifty-eight, was a tall, portly man with thick gray hair and the calm self-assurance of one whose orders are never questioned. He had served under President Buchanan, first as postmaster general, then as secretary of war. Though a strong supporter of states' rights, he had remained with the Union, and Lincoln had rewarded him with an appointment as head of the new Bureau of Military Justice. In that capacity, he reviewed the records of almost sixty-eight thousand courts-martial and military commissions.

Holt had come aboard to take down sworn statements from those who had witnessed Booth's death. The first was Byron Baker, who gave a minutely detailed account of the pursuit and events at the Garrett farm. Everton Conger added a few observations, and when they had finished, David Herold was brought up to help fill in the blanks. Herold's chief inquisitor was not Holt, but a slightly built man with a square jaw and hollow, deep-set eyes. He was John A. Bingham, congressman from Ohio and a long-time acquaintance of Edwin Stanton. Bingham had been defeated for reelection to Congress in 1862, and was commissioned a major in the Bureau of Military Justice. He had recently been voted back into office, but would continue as a prosecutor until the next session convened in December. This would be his last case.

The questioning of Herold yielded little. He denied knowing anything about a conspiracy, and said that his flight with Booth began innocently, after he encountered the assassin outside the city on the night of April 14. Booth talked him into taking a ride, he said, and it was only later that he learned of the president's assassination. Herold had wanted to get away from Booth, but assumed he would be prosecuted as a conspirator, since

Booth claimed to have implicated him in the plot. That is why he stayed with him to the end.

When the inquest had finished, a steam tug appeared alongside the *Montauk,* and a large covered object was transferred to it from the ironclad. The tug headed down the Potomac, and shortly afterward, a large rowboat cast off from the other side of the ship. A naval officer, two detectives, and four oarsmen were aboard. In sight of the shoreline crowd, this boat took a zigzag course out to deeper waters, where one of the men dumped a large weighted object into the river.

The incident was staged by Lafayette Baker. The detectives on the rowboat were his men, and instead of dumping Booth's body, as onlookers assumed, they took it around Greenleaf's Point to the western side of the Washington Arsenal. There, with an oarsman standing guard, they left it on the arsenal wharf, just a few yards from the old Washington penitentiary. Maj. Edward N. Stebbins, chief storekeeper, would take charge of the remains and have them buried in a gun box beneath the prison floor.[6]

THE INVESTIGATION DID NOT END with Booth's death, but from this point on, information came in fits and starts. In north-central Pennsylvania, the arrest of one Eugene T. Haines brought a momentary surge of excitement when the suspect was found to be carrying some of John Surratt's papers. He claimed to have found them. In Baltimore, authorities thought they were on to something when they learned that Joseph Thomas, who had once lived with Powell at the Branson house, had slit his own throat. News of his death did not reach Stanton until much later, and he angrily ordered General Wallace to have the corpse disinterred and embalmed for identification. Though Wallace's people had already looked into the incident, Stanton was quick to remind them that he was still in charge. He would not tolerate being kept in the dark.

Stanton felt that investigators were beginning to slack off. The spirit of cooperation had broken down, and most people now devoted their time exclusively to shoring up claims for the reward money. That in turn focused attention on the few suspects named in Stanton's offer, and as a result, others who once felt vulnerable to prosecution were growing confident and even defiant. Cooperation quickly went out of fashion, and informants like John Fletcher and James P. Ferguson began to fear for their lives.

Col. Henry H. Wells had never seen much cooperation in the first place. From his headquarters in Bryantown, Wells continued to forward prisoners to Washington, but he warned that it would not be easy to get information from them. Even when handcuffed and threatened with hanging, most continued to deny knowing anything at all about Booth. Though local citizens had banded together to offer Wells their support, they had produced nothing so far but frustration. "It is difficult to figure out fact from fiction," Wells complained, "as these people around here contradict each other so much."

Wells believed that the only way to learn about Booth's flight would be to have Herold retrace his steps. Stanton thought better of it, and he sent Byron Baker down to the Garrett farm with instructions to follow the fugitives' route from there back to the Potomac. The same method was employed by another party over Atzerodt's escape route, and by Lieutenant Dana over Booth's route in Maryland. These people were less aggressive and more successful than Wells, whose thumbscrew methods yielded nothing but bad blood.[7]

Aggressive methods were more productive in Washington, where Stanton and others used threats and imprisonment to pressure witnesses. The tactic worked especially well on the staff of Ford's Theatre. Though their connection to Booth made them all suspects, Ned Spangler was more vulnerable than the rest. Investigators found it suspicious that Spangler would fix up a stable, feed a horse, and sell a buggy on Booth's orders—all free of charge. His employer, John T. Ford, was also under suspicion, and as a result, he was going broke. He had not earned a penny since April 14, and was not likely to do so anytime soon. The public was venting its anger on the theater, and at least one person tried to burn it down. Stanton was determined to prevent Ford from reopening it, and brushing aside proposals to keep it intact, he confiscated the building for office use. Within months it would be gutted and completely remodeled.[8]

Most suspects were kept in the historic Old Capitol Prison. This former hall of government had once echoed with the voices of Clay, Calhoun, Jackson, and Webster. But to its present occupants, it was "one mass of dirt" where "spider webs hung in festoons from the ceiling, and vermin of all kinds ran over the floor." Conditions were no better where John T. Ford was confined, at the neighboring Carroll Annex. His garret room there was stark, and furnished with only a bag of straw, some blankets, and a slop bucket. "When I wrote," he recalled, "I did so on the floor & when I wished to sit down the straw was the only accommodation. . . . When I went to the barred dormer window the Sentry below threatened to shoot me. . . . I endured my confinement . . . with all the philosophy I could bring to bear."

Ford passed the hours by writing notes of his experience. His scribbles painted a dismal and sometimes horrifying picture of life in confinement. "Harry [Ford] released and rearrested and released again before Canning who was very despondent. . . . Festering wounds from Hand Cuffs Prisoners Shot by Sentry woman Shot. . . . Col. Luce Michigan acquitted 30 days ago not released The Prisoner handcuffed picking up his tobacco with his mouth."[9]

Government detectives were now tying up loose ends, gathering up all those who had helped Booth escape, and building criminal cases against those in custody. Among them were James A. Brawner and Richard M. Smoot, who confessed to selling a boat to Surratt; Charles Yates and George Bateman, who were suspected of keeping the boat hidden; and Walter Barnes and Henry M. Bailey, who had reportedly quit their jobs in mid-January, just as their friend Atzerodt was brought into the plot.

A few of Surratt's Confederate friends were also behind bars, but interrogating them was almost pointless. Preston Parr could not explain his exchange of telegrams with Surratt in March. Parr said he had no idea what Surratt meant when he asked if his friend was disengaged, and he didn't recall what he meant by saying "she" was on the way to Washington. Sarah Slater refused to say anything at all. With her in jail were Tom and Nannie Green, owners of the Van Ness mansion near the White House. A search of their house had turned up a note from Annie Parr and a letter of introduction for John Surratt. They, too, played dumb.[10]

The investigation moved abroad, as foreign service officers joined in the search for suspects and answers. The U.S. consul in Montreal obtained Booth's bank records and witnesses who claimed to know what the assassin was doing in that city. He also picked up clues on the whereabouts of Surratt, who was thought to be hiding nearby. Meanwhile, the consul in Frankfurt interviewed Baron August von Berlepsch, of Seebach, about the Atzerodt family. The baron had once hired George's father as a locksmith, and still remembered him as "a man of perfectly irreproachable character." He spoke highly of Frederick Richter as well.[11]

In spite of Booth's attempts to implicate his brother, Edwin managed to avoid the indignity of an arrest. But his other male relatives were not so fortunate. Junius, who had left Cincinnati to go to Philadelphia, found himself under suspicion after authorities intercepted a letter he had written to John Wilkes on the twelfth. In it, June had counseled his brother to tone down his politics and implored him to get out of the "oil business." Detectives learned from Sam Arnold that the "oil business" was a cover for the plot, and they arrested Junius soon after he arrived at Asia's house. John Sleeper Clarke was arrested with him. The assassin had left those letters at Clarke's house, and in the eyes of President Johnson, that made Clarke a suspect. He personally ordered the comedian's arrest. That left only Joseph Booth unaccounted for. Joe, who had been living in San Francisco, headed east as soon as he heard about Lee's surrender. His abrupt departure on April 13 struck the War Department as suspicious, and when his ship arrived in New York, detectives were waiting at the dock.

Ordinarily, the slimmest connection to Booth, or even the faintest word of praise for him, was enough to cause an arrest. But on one occasion, military authorities trod lightly. At a gathering in Georgetown, Delaware, U.S. senator Willard Saulsbury publicly rejoiced over the assassination, and supposedly even admitted knowing it was going to happen. The local provost marshal wanted to arrest the senator, but he could find only one witness who would admit to hearing the senator's remarks, and that man feared for his life. Nobody else was willing to testify.

Most of the people taken into custody were linked in some way to Booth or his inner circle, and hardly any had ties to the Confederate government. This was dismaying to Judge Advocate General Holt, who was convinced beyond a doubt that Jefferson Davis's agents were behind the plot. But his assistant, Col. Henry Burnett, had his own pet theory regarding the conspiracy. Burnett was sure that secret societies, such as the Knights of the Golden Circle, were involved. Both ideas were inspired by rumors of widespread subversion, and at Holt's urging, stories that had once been dismissed were now reexamined in light of recent developments. The first case reopened was that of Dr. Luke P. Blackburn. For almost a year, government informants had claimed that Dr. Blackburn was part of a Confederate plot to infect Northern cities with yellow fever. He was said to have gathered clothing from victims of the disease and sent them to various garment distributors in the United States. Supposedly, he even sent infected shirts to President Lincoln. Nothing was ever proven, but the State Department wanted to look again. They knew that Blackburn was living in Toronto, and they earnestly requested that he be sent to Washington for trial. Canadian officials declined to extradite the doctor, but they did arrest him for a breach of their nation's neutrality laws. He was tried and acquitted.[12]

DETECTIVE BYRON BAKER RETURNED to Washington on May 6 with some of the people he suspected of helping Booth escape. Jett, Rollins, and Bryant were among his prisoners, as were William Lucas and Elizabeth Quesenberry. Through Lucas, Baker located the note Booth had written to Dr. Stuart. Charley Lucas had taken it to Cleydael at the fugitive's request. It was written on a page torn from Booth's diary.

> Dear Sir:
>
> Forgive me, but I have some little pride. I hate to blame you for your want of hospitality; you know your own affairs. I was sick and tired, with a broken leg, in need of medical advice. I would not have turned a dog from my door in such a condition. However, you were kind enough to give me something to eat, for which I not only thank you, but on account of the reluctant manner in which it was bestowed, I feel bound to pay for it. It is not the substance, but the manner in which a kindness is extended, that makes one happy in the acceptance thereof. The sauce to meat is ceremony: meeting were bare without it. Be kind enough to accept the enclosed two dollars and a half (though hard to spare) for what we have received.
>
> > Yours respectfully,
> > Stranger.
>
> April 24, 1865.
> To Dr. Stewart[13]

HARSH AS CONDITIONS WERE at the Old Capitol, they were far worse on board the ironclads. Prisoners on the *Saugus* and the *Montauk* were entombed in small, dark recesses that would have made a prison cell luxurious by comparison. The air was noxious with the smell of pitch, paint, and much worse. Having no place to lie down, suspects were forced to remain seated and motionless twenty-four hours a day, under the constant watch of marine guards. Surprisingly, it was the stoic Lewis Powell who crumbled first. On April 22 (his twenty-first birthday), Powell tried to dash his brains out on the bulkhead of the *Saugus*. The incident led to even more stringent restrictions for all the shipbound prisoners. On April 24, orders were handed down for new standards of treatment:

"The Sec'y of War requests that the prisoners on board the iron clads belonging to this Dept. shall have for better security against conversation a canvas bag put over the head of each and tied around the neck with a hole for proper breathing and eating but not seeing, and that Payne be secured to prevent self destruction."

The hoods were heavy, and padded with wads of cotton over the eyes. An eight-inch triangle cut from the back was sewn over the front hole to make a cover for the nose. A cuff along the bottom held a drawstring that could be pulled tight around the neck. As Ned Spangler remembered, the hoods brought out a sadistic streak in some of the guards. One marine pulled the hood over Spangler's head and nearly strangled him with the drawstring. Though he loosened it somewhat, he made a point of telling his partner, "Don't let him go to sleep, as we will carry him out to hang him directly."

Each of the prisoners wore a peculiar kind of restraint. It was a medieval-looking device made of iron, with hinged wrist bands fixed and separated by metal bars. When the bars were folded over on one another, the bands clamped tightly over both wrists, and were then bolted in place. Thus, the prisoner could not move his hands. The restraints were called Lilly irons, and not surprisingly, the prisoners found them terrifying.

Modern writers sometimes give the impression that Secretary of War Stanton created these irons specially for suspects in this case. But in fact, Edwin Stanton had nothing to do with the design. They were said to have been invented by a Dr. Lilly, who worked with the mentally ill and used them on his most dangerous or self-destructive patients. Since the Government Asylum for the Insane, now known as St. Elizabeth's, was in plain sight of the ironclads, it is quite possible that the doctors there furnished the navy with the irons used on the suspects. They were certainly not an item one would expect to find on a ship.

The hoods and wrist irons made eating almost impossible. The hole in the hood did not line up with the mouth, and having no mobility of the hands, a prisoner couldn't possibly fix the problem. Knowing this, some of the guards took pity on Spangler. In violation of their orders, they teamed up to give him a hand. While one kept a lookout, the other fed him. It was a kindness the prisoner didn't dare acknowledge.[14]

· · ·

LOU WEICHMANN RETURNED from Canada on April 28, and the following day, Stanton committed him to the Carroll Annex. It was no secret that Weichmann was turning state's evidence, and his fellow prisoners hated him for it. There was something unseemly about a man who would testify against a woman, especially one who had shared her home with him and treated him like a son. But Weichmann was under tremendous pressure to cooperate, and the incentives often sounded like threats. To the amusement of his fellow inmates, he was terrified. One day, a prisoner said to him, "Weichmann, do you know that someone in Room thirty-seven is going to be taken out and hanged?"

Visibly shaken, Weichmann asked, "They don't hang bounty jumpers, do they?"

"I guess not," replied the inmate.

After a moment's reflection, Weichmann noted, "I am in thirty-seven," and, feeling his neck, said, "If it was me, I would rather be shot than hanged." If hanging was Lou Weichmann's worst fear, detectives who mingled among the prisoners made the most of it. Louis Carland, costumer of Ford's Theatre, overheard one of them threaten to do just that.[15]

SOONER OR LATER, the government would need to segregate the criminal defendants from the rest of the detainees, and to that end, Major Eckert suggested that Stanton reactivate the old penitentiary on the grounds of the Washington Arsenal. The building was ideally suited. It had 224 prison cells, and was almost entirely surrounded by water. No place in Washington was more secure. It even had a large room that could be used for the trial. So on April 28, Stanton ordered Major James Benton, commanding officer of the arsenal, to ready the prison building. Cells were cleaned and inspected, shuck mattresses were delivered, and a detail was assigned to guard the place. The transfer was made on April 29, when David Herold, Lewis Powell, Mike O'Laughlen, Sam Arnold, Ned Spangler, and João Celestino, the sea captain, were led, under cover of a late-night downpour, to the steamer *Keyport*. The ship took them to the old penitentiary. Some of them would not leave there alive.

Brevet Maj. Gen. John F. Hartranft was put in direct command of the prison. Hero of a recent battle outside Petersburg, Hartranft, thirty-four, performed the duties of a warden. Six officers were appointed to serve under him, including Dr. George Loring Porter, the arsenal's medical officer. The instructions issued to Porter undoubtedly applied to the entire staff: "While engaged on this duty you will be careful not to answer any questions addressed to you by the prisoners nor allow them to make any remarks not connected with your professional duties (to you)." Eventually Capt. Christian Rath joined the prison team. Rath, a former sheriff, had experience as a hangman.[16]

Nobody was sure who the defendants would be, and some papers speculated that as many as eighty people would be put on trial. Many of the prisoners were considered accessories after the fact, and in truth, Stanton had never shown much interest in their cases. His main focus was on those who had planned the assassination, and by the end of April his officers were hard at work sorting through evidence to see who should be tried for that offense.

The decision to file charges was not an easy one. In many cases the evidence was ambiguous, and it often turned on the word of an African American. Federal courts had just begun to admit their testimony, but social prejudices lagged far behind the law. In the summer of 1865, most juries were still reluctant to convict a white man on the word of anyone who might once have been his slave. Ultimately, prosecutors avoided the issue in this case, and that probably came as a relief to Samuel Cox, Thomas Jones, and Dr. Richard Stuart, who could have been prosecuted only on the word of a nonwhite witness.

Olcott, Foster, Wood, and Wells reviewed the evidence together, and one by one they dropped prisoners from the list of suspects. One of the first to be cleared was Junius Booth, whose letter to John Wilkes about the "oil business" looked much less incriminating in light of his brother's real oil venture. Most of the Ford's Theatre staff could breathe easier as well, and so could a few of the people who had helped Booth in his flight. The truth is, most were being held only as witnesses anyway, though they were never told as much. Stanton's threat to impose the death sentence was a bluff; their offense was only a misdemeanor.

In a few cases, the decision to prosecute would hinge on one specific, unbending rule of law: anyone indicted could not be a witness. While a suspect today might agree to testify in exchange for a lighter sentence, that practice was illegal in 1865. So if a prosecutor knew of evidence that a potential witness might have been involved in the crime, he had to weigh the value of his testimony against the public's interest in punishing him. It was an all-or-nothing proposition.[17]

This made George Atzerodt's case especially difficult. Though Atzerodt was clearly implicated in the conspiracy, his knowledge of the plot might make him indispensable as a witness. In fact, Colonel Wells specifically told him that his testimony could save him from the gallows. So Atzerodt made several attempts to demonstrate his usefulness to the government, and he got his brother and brother-in-law to help him write a proffer. But apparently he had nothing the prosecution could use. His various statements were confused, contradictory, and open to attack. At one time, he claimed that Herold had been assigned the job of killing the vice president, but everywhere else, he said that Booth had given him the task. In his proffer, Atzerodt claimed that Booth had never discussed assassination, but he had previously said that that was the whole point of the Herndon House meeting. And though he consistently maintained that the meeting took place in Powell's room, he could not make up his mind whether it had started at six-thirty, seven-thirty, or eight o'clock in the evening. Initially he claimed it happened on Thursday, but later said it took place on Friday night—not realizing that Powell had already checked out by then.

Atzerodt had no chance of taking the witness stand unless he could provide evidence against the others. Knowing that, he tried to implicate Dr. Mudd, but he made a weak case. As he said in the proffer, "Booth sent (as he told me) liquor & provisions for the trip with the President to Richmond, about two weeks before the murder to Dr. Mudd's." The operative phrase here was "as he told me." It confirmed that Atzerodt's information was secondhand. He did not really know whether Booth was telling him the truth about Mudd, or whether the doctor actually accepted those items, knowing how they were to be used. All he could offer was hearsay passed from a deceptive source through an unreliable witness.

Even when Atzerodt lied, as he often did, he could not implicate the Confederates that Joseph Holt had targeted. Indeed, he seemed to know nothing at all about a Southern connection to the conspiracy, in spite of having ties to the underground. All he knew is that Booth had been worried that someone in New York would kill the president before he got the chance. Atzerodt didn't know who these people were, but he spoke of them as rivals, not associates. "If he [Booth] did not get him [Lincoln] quick the N[ew] York crowd would," he said. Even with his life in the balance, Atzerodt could not be any more specific.[18]

The witness rule undoubtedly saved lives. Sam Chester and John M. Lloyd were good examples. Chester was privy to Booth's intentions, and he did not report the plot when he should have. Still, he was one of the few people who could testify that the conspiracy had existed for months. Colonel Olcott called him one of the most important witnesses he had seen, and he became one of the first to take the stand for the government. He shared that good fortune with John M. Lloyd. Though Lloyd could have been hanged for hiding Booth's guns, he was the only man who could link them to Mary Surratt, who was then thought to be the ringleader. Thus, he was a witness, not a defendant.

Of all the people spared by the witness rule, none was more controversial than Louis Weichmann. Though Weichmann seemed to be a member of Booth's inner circle, he was by far the best witness to tie Booth, Powell, Atzerodt, and Herold to the Surratts. He was also the only one who could testify about the failed capture attempt on March 17. Without the testimony of Louis Weichmann, the prosecutors would have a hard time building a case against any of their leading suspects. And it was he who tipped the balance against another prisoner.

During an interrogation in Stanton's office, Weichmann was asked if he knew Dr. Samuel A. Mudd. Yes, he said, he had met the doctor in Washington, when Mudd introduced Booth to John Surratt. To Stanton, that was a revelation. Mudd had specifically denied seeing Booth at any time after the assassin's fake real estate search through Charles County. If Weichmann were correct, Dr. Mudd had lied. After questioning Weichmann on the specifics of that meeting, Stanton turned to Colonel Burnett and snapped, "Write that down!" Soon Dr. Mudd was stricken from the list of prosecution witnesses and added to the list of defendants.

Detectives had always thought that Mary Surratt was deceiving them, but they had had trouble catching her in a specific lie. When interviewed a second time, though, Mrs. Surratt gave the government more to work with. She denied having any conversation with Lloyd about weapons in the tavern or even knowing they were there. When asked about relatives in the rebel army, she said, "I have no son in the Confederate army that I know of." But that wasn't true. Her oldest child, Isaac, was a sergeant in the 33rd Texas Cavalry.

After finishing with Mrs. Surratt, detectives talked again with some of her boarders. From Honora Fitzpatrick, they learned that Booth often came to the Surratt house, even when John Surratt was not home. Unidentified visitors stopped in at all hours, and occasionally they talked among themselves in Mrs. Surratt's bedroom. "Sometimes Mr. Booth would go up there and sometimes Port Tobacco [would]," she said, "and then Wood sometimes would." Apparently, meetings could take place without John Surratt, but not without his mother.[19]

It was Secretary Stanton who decided which prisoners would be put on trial. Ultimately, he indicted eight people. If he had had his way, the editor of the *New York Tribune* would have been the ninth. Stanton became convinced that by writing editorials critical of the administration, Horace Greeley was trying to have him killed. On May 12, he took action. He retained a New York attorney and told him that Greeley ought to be punished for inciting the assassins to "finish their work." Said Stanton: "I shall not allow them to have me murdered without a struggle for life on my part." Nothing ever came of his accusation.

CAPTAIN EDWIN BEDEE WAS NOT ACCUSED of conspiracy, but of stealing President Lincoln's papers on the night of the assassination. He had done nothing of the sort, but had delivered the papers to Stanton, as requested, on the morning of April 15. Now the date of his court-martial approached, and Bedee appealed to the secretary for help. Stanton responded at once and set the record straight. He insisted that all charges be dropped and ordered Bedee's accuser, Gen. James A. Hardie, to issue a full apology.[20]

THERE HAD NEVER BEEN any doubt that the defendants would be tried before a military commission. President Johnson confirmed it on May 1, when he ordered that a panel of officers be convened for that purpose. Though Johnson would always contend that his attorney general had endorsed the idea, James Speed did not actually write his opinion down until late June, when the defense had already given their closing arguments.

The Lincoln conspiracy trial would pit eight defendants against the federal government. Dr. Mudd and Mary Surratt were indicted for sheltering the conspirators and helping to plan the killing; Powell, Herold, Spangler, and Atzerodt for involvement in the attacks; Arnold and O'Laughlen for taking part in the plot. Had the government possessed an efficient means of sorting data, they might have tried many more. But as it was, the evidence lay piecemeal in War Department files, never effectively examined or organized. So many of Booth's cohorts were never caught, and people such as Sarah Slater, Preston Parr, Thomas Harbin, and Atzerodt's friends Walter Barnes and Henry Bailey were allowed to go free, taking their secrets with them.

Evidently, Judge Holt was still eager to indict Confederate officials, so on May 2, President Johnson took active measures to secure their arrests. He issued a proclamation:

> Whereas it appears, from evidence in the bureau of military justice, that the atrocious murder of the late President Abraham Lincoln, and the attempted assassination of the Honorable William H. Seward, Secretary of State, were incited, concerted, and procured by and between Jefferson Davis, late of Richmond, Virginia; and Jacob Thompson, Clement C. Clay, Beverly [*sic*] Tucker, George N. Saunders [*sic*], William C. Cleary, and other rebels and traitors against the government of the United States, harbored in Canada:
>
> Now, therefore, to the end that justice may be done, I . . . do offer and promise for the arrest of said persons, or either of them . . . so that they can be brought to trial, the following rewards. . . .

The sum of $100,000 was offered for the capture of Jefferson Davis, and $25,000 was set for most of the others.

Johnson's proclamation brought an immediate reaction from the newly accused. Beverley Tucker declared that he had never known or heard of any of those connected with the assassination and insisted that anyone who said otherwise "blackens his soul with perjury." Tucker pointed out that the Lincoln administration (and particularly William Seward) was known to favor the annexation of Canada, and by framing Confederates who lived and worked there, they hoped to incite a war that would achieve their ends.

Jacob Thompson was even more direct. "I aver upon honor that I have never known, or conversed, or held communication, either directly or indirectly, with Booth . . . or with any of his associates, so far as I have seen them named," he insisted. "I knew nothing of their plans. I defy the evidence in the Bureau of Military Justice. . . ." Thompson landed a solid punch on the administration when he referred to the card Booth had left for Andrew Johnson at the Kirkwood House. "I know there is not half the ground to suspect me," he said, "than there is to suspect President Johnson himself." Obviously, these men would not take the accusations lying down.[21]

THE LATE PRESIDENT'S FINAL JOURNEY came to an end on May 4, with a funeral service in Springfield. A large crowd braved the rain and chill to hear Bishop Mathew Simpson, of the Methodist Church, lead the graveside service at Oak Ridge Cemetery. There the bodies of Lincoln and his son Willie were placed in a public receiving vault to await a more permanent resting place.

ANDREW JOHNSON'S ORDER convening a military commission did not go into specifics, so when General E. D. Townsend returned from Springfield, he selected the nine officers who would serve on the panel. Major General David Hunter, who had just accompanied the president's remains to Illinois, was to preside over the trial. The others were men of respectable rank and service: Major General Lew Wallace, Brevet Major General August V. Kautz, Brigadier General Albion P. Howe, Brigadier General Robert S. Foster, Brigadier General Cyrus B. Comstock, Brigadier General Thomas M. Harris, Brevet Colonel Horace Porter, and Lieutenant Colonel David R. Clendenin. Brevet Brigadier General Frederick H. Collier was originally slated to serve as well. Collier, a former prosecutor from Pittsburgh, had known Stanton for years, and had served on many such commissions in the course of the war. But for unspecified reasons, his assignment to this case was canceled.

The commission met for the first time on the morning of May 8. Two members were absent, but the others moved ahead and got their first look at the defendants. All of the male prisoners were shackled, and of them, all but Dr. Mudd wore hoods. Powell and Atzerodt had chains riveted around their ankles, with a heavy iron ball attached; each was accompanied by a soldier who carried the ball. The accused took their places on a long raised platform, set apart from the room by a wooden rail. Soldiers sat between them. When all were seated, the hoods were removed.

General Cyrus Comstock was appalled at the treatment of the prisoners. Comstock was one of several officers who had tried to get himself excused from the commission. An early adjournment gave him one more opportunity to lobby for his release, and this time he was successful. When the members of the commission appeared the following day, Comstock and

Horace Porter had both been excused—ostensibly because they were senior aides to General Grant. Since Grant was thought to be a target of the conspiracy, their presence on the commission was deemed inappropriate. They were replaced by Brevet Brigadier General James A. Ekin and Brevet Colonel Charles H. Tompkins. General August Kautz, who had also tried to be excused, was forced to remain on the commission.[22]

When the full panel had assembled on the ninth, Judge Advocate General Holt introduced himself as the lead prosecutor. He would be assisted by two men with experience in high-profile military trials: Colonel Henry L. Burnett, who had served as a prosecutor in the Indianapolis and Cincinnati treason trials, and Congressman John Bingham, who had taken part in the court-martial of General Fitz-John Porter. They noted that some of the defendants were not represented by counsel, and they asked if they wished to have an attorney. Each answered in the affirmative. That said, the commission adjourned to allow the accused a little more time to find one. But with or without, the government would start presenting its witnesses the following day.

THE TRIAL TOOK PLACE in a heavily guarded part of the old penitentiary building, with grated windows and eighteen-inch-thick walls. Another wall, twenty feet high, surrounded the entire prison. The courtroom itself was on the eastern end of the cell block, on the third floor of what had once been the deputy warden's quarters. Workmen had altered the place, adding separate doors for prisoners and witnesses, new gas fixtures, and a raised platform for the accused. The room was divided by a line of three columns, on one side of which was a large green-baize-covered table for the commission. General David Hunter sat at one end of it, and Judge Holt and his assistants sat at the other. Law books and a few trial exhibits were placed in the center. A second large table was reserved for defense counsel and official reporters. A witness stand set up between the tables was arranged so that anyone giving testimony would have to face the commission when speaking. Reporters, sitting behind them, could not always hear what was said, but the rule was strictly enforced, and any witness who turned around drew a sharp rebuke from General Hunter.

Four reporters were borrowed from the Senate, and Benn Pitman, assistant to Henry Burnett, was appointed to supervise them. They worked in shifts, scribbling notes in the most common system of shorthand then in use—the one invented by Pitman's brother Isaac.

The May 10 session began with a reading of President Johnson's order calling for a trial by military commission. General David Hunter, president of the panel, announced that each defendant was charged with "maliciously, unlawfully, and traitorously, and in aid of the existing armed Rebellion," conspiring with Confederate leaders "and others unknown" to murder the president, vice president, secretary of state, and general in chief of the army. Their purpose, as alleged in the specification, was to deprive the army and navy of a constitutional commander in chief; to prevent a lawful election; and to deprive the army of its commanding general.

The prisoners had just been informed of the charges before the session began, and each was now asked if he or she objected to any member of the commission. It was an important question, but after sitting for weeks in pain and darkness, the defendants could hardly have known how to answer. In retrospect, they might have objected to General Hunter and General Howe, who had both just come from a two-week tour of mourning with the president's remains. They might have wondered why Hunter, whose troops had fought Mosby's Rangers in the Shenandoah Valley, could now sit in judgment of Powell, who was one of the very same men he had faced in the field. Colonel Clendenin had also fought against Mosby. Would he feel inclined to avenge the "irregular warfare" that Powell and his comrades had waged against him? And what about atonement? Hunter had been considerably embarrassed by General Early in 1864. Would he need to redeem himself in Secretary Stanton's eyes? Did Lew Wallace need to prove himself after a military blunder at Shiloh? None of these questions came to mind as the prisoners sat there, helpless and bewildered. It was just beginning to dawn on them that the trial had actually begun. At this point, only two of them even had lawyers.

It was almost impossible to get an attorney on short notice. Judge Advocate General Holt's staff helped advise the prisoners, and even sent couriers to inform prospective lawyers that their services had been requested. But some were unwilling to take any case before a military commission, especially this one. Some had obligations elsewhere, and a few were too pro-Southern to be admitted as counsel. At any rate, the commission had business of its own to attend to, so for the third time the prisoners were ushered back to their cells. At least they would have a few more hours to search for counsel.

Once the accused had left, the commission determined its rules of procedure. Not being a real court, they had a great deal of latitude in the way they could operate. Though Joseph Holt was the prosecutor, he was also the commission's legal adviser. He recommended they move forward with or without defense counsel. He also suggested they impose a five-minute limit on defense arguments. The commission agreed to move ahead, but rejected the time limit on arguments. They were more receptive to another, more controversial idea. Holt said that a few of the government's witnesses, fearing retaliation, preferred to keep their testimony secret. Others were expected to implicate people who were not yet in custody, and the War Department was afraid that an open proceeding might tip those people off. For both reasons, Holt recommended that the commission conduct its business behind closed doors. Only those persons officially engaged in the trial should be allowed in the courtroom, and all should be sworn to secrecy. The commission endorsed Holt's argument, and the following day, the Lincoln assassination conspiracy trial began in closed session.[23]

The defendants were still scrambling to find lawyers, and in a short time most of the accused had found someone. John Atzerodt hired William E. Doster, the former provost marshal of Washington, to represent his brother. Walter S. Cox, a law professor at Columbian College, agreed to defend O'Laughlen, and David Herold retained the services of Frederick Stone, from a distinguished Charles County family. Dr. Mudd and Sam Arnold would both be represented by General Thomas Ewing, Jr., former chief justice of the Kansas Supreme Court and a brother-in-law of General William T. Sherman. All were fine attorneys, but there were not enough to go around. Spangler and Powell were still unrepresented, and after several rejections, Mary Surratt could secure only the services of two neophytes, John W. Clampitt and Frederick A. Aiken. Neither had experience in a capital case, and Aiken was just completing his first year of practice.

The trial was just getting under way when Clement C. Clay, one of the Confederates accused in the president's proclamation, decided to give himself up. Clay was stung by the charges that he had conspired with Booth, and he insisted on fighting them head-on. He contacted the nearest federal authorities and promised to turn himself in. "Conscious of my innocence, unwilling even to seem to fly from justice, and confident of my entire vindication from so foul an imputation upon the full, fair, and impartial trial which I expect to receive, I shall go as soon as practicable to Macon to deliver myself up to your custody."

Clay's surrender was not the most startling news to arrive that day.

Jefferson Davis had been captured near the town of Irwinville, Georgia. Though Davis and Clay were both named as conspirators, they would not stand trial with the others. Both were taken to Fortress Monroe, where they were kept in legal limbo pending a decision by the president on what to do with them.

A couple of days into the trial, it appeared that Powell and Spangler would not be able to secure counsel. Colonel Burnett asked the other attorneys to take them on as well. Doster would take the case of Powell, and General Ewing, who already had two clients, agreed to add Spangler to his burden. At the same time, Frederick Stone asked to join in the defense of Dr. Mudd. Ewing, no doubt, was glad to have the help.

It was bad enough that these people had been hired at the last minute, without time to prepare. But Judge Holt compounded the difficulty by dispensing with an opening statement and keeping the details of the case to himself. Thus he made it plain from the outset that this was a military commission, not a court. Here the government made its own rules, shared them with no one, and changed them as it saw fit. As William Doster later recalled, it was as if "a few lawyers were on one side, and the whole United States on the other."[24]

SEVENTEEN

"NOTHING SHORT OF A MIRACLE
CAN SAVE THEIR LIVES"

N OT ALL THE DEFENSE ATTORNEYS HAD BEEN SWORN before the government presented its first witnesses on Friday, May 12. Eleven witnesses were heard on the first day alone. None of their testimony was even directed at the defendants. Joseph Holt wanted to begin the trial by showing that the Confederate government had repeatedly crossed the bounds of civilized warfare. The atrocities committed by Davis, Clay, Sanders, Thompson, and others formed a pattern that embraced many individual acts, including secession itself. Thus, the grand conspiracy that culminated in Lincoln's assassination was the same one that planned the burning of cities, the spreading of disease, and the starvation of prisoners. Any connection to the Confederacy, from mere sympathy to the Lincoln assassination itself, imparted an equal share of guilt. To Joseph Holt, it was all one enormous plot.

Richard R. Montgomery was one of Holt's first witnesses. Montgomery, a federal spy, claimed to know most of the rebel leaders in Canada. He said that in January 1865, Jacob Thompson, of the Confederate State Department, told him of a plan to kill Northern leaders. According to Montgomery, Thompson supported the idea, but was not allowed to set events in motion until Richmond gave its approval. Other witnesses testified that assassination was freely discussed by the rebels, and two of them claimed to have seen Booth talking with George N. Sanders, of the so-called Canadian Cabinet in Montreal.

Gen. Ulysses S. Grant also took the stand that day. He had been called to testify about his commission in the army and about Jacob Thompson's position in the rebel government. Before he even reached the courtroom, though, Grant was stopped by Private Alfred C. Gibson, a fifteen-year-old clerk to General Hartranft. Gibson pointed out that the general was smoking a cigar, and since new gas lines had been installed in the courtroom, he would have to leave the stogie downstairs. The hero of Appomattox was a bit taken aback. He paused for a moment and gave the nervous young boy a hard look. But he was right to follow orders, and Grant commended him for it. He put out the cigar and went upstairs, leaving young Private Gibson to boast that he once gave an order to a lieutenant general.[1]

Holt wrapped up the first day of testimony by calling Henry Von Steinacker to the stand. Von Steinacker claimed that he was actually present when Booth himself spoke with Confederate officers about the assassination. It was his testimony more than any other that connected those officials to the assassin and, through him, to the prisoners on the dock.

Though the following day was a Saturday, the trial resumed anyway. A Canadian doctor named James B. Merritt took the stand and testified that in February, he heard George N. Sanders lay out an assassination scheme that had the approval of Jefferson Davis. Sanders specifically mentioned Booth, and possibly Atzerodt, as players. According to Merritt, Booth had his own reasons for killing Lincoln: he wanted to avenge the hanging of his cousin, John Yates Beall.[2]

In the course of the trial, government witnesses exposed a stunning array of Confederate atrocities. They told of plots to kill Union prisoners; to launch raids on St. Albans and other cities; and to burn New York, destroy steamships on the Mississippi, and assassinate Northern leaders. They produced a letter, found in Confederate archives, proposing to "rid the country of some of her deadliest enemies." They claimed Confederates had confessed to spreading pestilence throughout the North—and even into the White House—by distributing clothing infected by disease. They laid open the bank accounts of Confederates in Canada, and showed an 1864 newspaper advertisement that offered to "cause the lives of Abraham Lincoln, William H. Seward, and Andrew Johnson to be taken by the first of March next." Interspersed with all this was the testimony of Sam Chester and others who told all about Booth and his travels during the same period. By alternating the acts of Booth and the Confederates, Joseph Holt was able to blend two subjects into one, even if only by implication.

Defense attorneys felt that such testimony only inflamed the commission without proving anything against their clients. Since it was all taken behind closed doors, none could be subjected to public exposure and scrutiny. But that would not be the case for long. After testifying on May 12, General Grant and General Comstock went to the White House to lodge a complaint with the president. Both were disgusted with the secrecy of the trial, and they urged the president to open all future proceedings to the public. Though Johnson made no promises, their appeal must have been effective; the following day, Judge Holt informed the commission that the most sensitive testimony had already been taken, and he saw no further need for secrecy. On Monday, May 15, the commission released some (but not all) of the prior testimony, and visitors were admitted to the courtroom for the first time.[3]

AS THE SESSION OPENED on Monday, counsel for Mary Surratt announced that Senator Reverdy Johnson, of Maryland, had agreed to join their team. Johnson was a formidable advocate, but his primary contribution would be to challenge the legality of the trial. That was a well-worn path. Almost everyone was by now familiar with the arguments pro and con. The government claimed that military necessity required a military trial. Since the president had declared martial law, *everyone* could be subject to trial by military commission. On the other hand, the defendants were not soldiers, and military necessity could not be demonstrated. Washington was not under threat of imminent attack. The city courts had continued to operate without interruption, and though troops were indeed "intrenched" in the capital, they were mostly invalid soldiers assigned to light garrison duty—not the combat-ready forces one would throw in the path of an enemy assault. Certainly, no battle would have been jeopardized, no ground would have been lost, no Union army would have been defeated if the trial had taken place in a civilian court.

Indeed, Lee's surrender seems to have removed the danger. Secretary Stanton conceded as much on April 13—the day before the assassination—when he issued orders to halt the draft, stop recruiting, curtail purchases, reduce the number of officers, and remove all travel restrictions imposed as a measure of war. On the fourteenth, brigade commanders in Washington were ordered to stop asking citizens for passes, and in one of his last writings, President Lincoln himself noted that "no pass is necessary now to authorize any one to go to & return from Petersburg & Richmond. People go & return just as they did before the war." If all those facts suggested that Washington was not a city under siege, Stanton's report to the president, prepared the following November, ended all discussion: "Since the surrender of Lee's army," the report said, "the danger to the national safety from combinations and conspiracies to aid the rebellion or resist the laws in the states not declared to be insurgent had passed away."

One final point might have been made on the question of jurisdiction: none of the offenses charged in the indictment were federal crimes. In 1865, the assassination of the president was like any other murder. It was a crime against local authority, and would continue to be treated as such until Congress federalized the offense more than a full century after Lincoln died.[4]

Reverdy Johnson might have been the first to address those issues, but before he could say a word, General Hunter, president of the commission, announced that one of its members had objected to Senator Johnson's participation in the trial. General Thomas M. Harris felt that the senator should not be sworn in because he did not "recognize the moral obligation of an oath that is designed as a test of loyalty." Johnson bristled at the challenge, but he knew exactly what inspired it. He explained that in October 1864, Marylanders were being turned away from a state election for refusing to swear allegiance to the federal administration. When some voters asked for his advice, Johnson said that Maryland had overstepped its authority when it required the oath in the first place. The only way that citizens could assert their rights, he said, would be to take the oath and vote regardless of their views.

After defending that stance before the commission, Johnson reminded them that his own oath of office was good enough for the United States Senate—a body that creates generals. Then he tried to put their minds at ease. "I am here," he said, "to do whatever the evidence will justify me in doing in protecting this lady [Mrs. Surratt] from the charge upon which she is now being tried for her life. I am here detesting from the very bottom of my heart every one concerned in this nefarious plot, carried out with such fiendish malice, as much as any member of this Court; and I am not here to protect any one whom, when the evidence is offered, I shall deem to have been guilty, *even her.*"

It was a strange speech for a lawyer—promising to leave his client if he became convinced of her guilt—and it may have been fatal to Mary Surratt. After listening to a few days of testimony, Johnson left the courtroom for good. Though he prepared an argument on the jurisdiction, he left it for a colleague to deliver. Otherwise he took no further interest in the fate of his client. He appeared to abandon her.

Reverdy Johnson had been challenged on the oath, but Augustus R. Cazauran, a newspaper reporter, was called to answer more serious charges. Cazauran was an ardent rebel who once spent three years in Sing Sing prison for forgery. After serving his sentence, he moved to Cincinnati, where he promptly stole a large sum of money from an orphans' fund. Authorities traced him to Memphis, where he had become a newspaper editor. He stayed there for the duration of the war. Benn Pitman knew all of this, and was incensed when he learned that Cazauran had been granted a courtroom pass. Pitman complained to Stanton, and told him that authorities in Ohio still held a fugitive warrant for Cazauran. The reporter was arrested, and his editor, John W. Forney, of the *Daily Constitutional Union,* apologized for having employed him. Apparently, courtroom security was not hard to breach.[5]

Each defendant was charged with conspiracy, and with particular acts laid out in the specifications. Their cases were fairly straightforward. Herold, according to prosecutors, had traveled willingly with Booth, and had been in the plot from the beginning. Almost exclusively, the witnesses against him were people who had met him and Booth on their flight.

Atzerodt had shared Booth's horses, and seemed to follow his script to the final hour. Prosecution witnesses told of suspicious behavior in and around the Kirkwood House. In rebuttal, the defense showed that Atzerodt was a coward who would never have agreed to kill anyone.

Sam Arnold was charged with giving Booth advice and support. The principal evidence against him was his own letter to Booth, which was found in the assassin's trunk. Testimony in his favor showed that he was nowhere near Washington after April 1.

Mike O'Laughlen had gone to Stanton's house on the night of the thirteenth, and prosecutors alleged he was lying in wait for the secretary's guest, General Grant. Government witnesses described his lifelong intimacy with Booth, and a few confidential meetings with him shortly before the shooting. The defense showed that O'Laughlen had his own reasons for going to Washington on April 13, and that he had spent almost all of his time celebrating there with friends.

Ned Spangler was charged with helping Booth arrange his escape. Prosecutors offered testimony to show his intimacy with Booth, and they wondered aloud if an eighty-foot length of rope found in Spangler's carpet-bag was intended for use in the assassin's flight through the country—perhaps to trip the horses of anyone who followed. The defense showed that Spangler was not the only one who did favors for Booth, and that he had done nothing suspicious at the time of the shooting.

Mary Surratt was said to be the prime mover in the conspiracy. She had met privately with Booth, had taken some of the conspirators into her home, and had delivered messages on Booth's behalf on the day of the assassination. Prosecutors made much of Lewis Powell's appearance at her house on the night of the seventeeth, and several witnesses recounted her false claim that she had never seen him before. The principal witnesses against her were Weichmann and Lloyd; those who appeared in her favor were friends, boarders, and priests who offered alternate explanations of her actions and testimony to her good character.

The simplest case was made against Lewis Powell. He had conspired with Booth, and was unquestionably the man who attacked Secretary of State Seward.

The most complex case was the one brought against Dr. Mudd. The prosecution claimed that there had been a series of meetings between Mudd and Booth: first, at his own home; second, at the National Hotel in January; and third, at the same hotel in March. That last meeting was inferred from the testimony of Marcus P. Norton, a patent attorney, who claimed that Mudd mistakenly barged into his hotel room looking for Booth. The doctor was also accused of delaying his report of Booth's whereabouts until long after the fugitives had left his farm.

Since John Bingham considered all rebel sympathizers to be guilty of conspiracy, he spent a good deal of time attacking Mudd on evidence of his pro-Southern leanings. Thus, he called the doctor's former slaves to testify about the way Mudd had treated them—he had once shot one in the leg—and about his sheltering of rebel soldiers in the woods. But other former slaves testified that Dr. Mudd was a gentle master, and one of the "rebel soldiers" in question tried to show (over Bingham's objections) that he was just a civilian, hiding there in fear of an unjustified arrest. Mudd's attorney also tried to show, over Bingham's objections, that Booth had first come to Bryantown in search of real estate, and that his meeting with the doctor came about *by chance* because John C. Thompson, who introduced them, thought that Mudd might have some land to sell.

The most damaging testimony against Dr. Mudd came from Louis Weichmann, who had already established himself as the government's most important witness. Weichmann described that December 23 meeting at the National Hotel, and said that Booth, Surratt, and Mudd were speaking confidentially among themselves. (He said the meeting took place in January.)

Though Weichmann's testimony seemed damning, he never actually claimed to know what the defendant was doing with Booth. This turned out to be the hallmark of all his testimony. Though it was Weichmann who tied Booth to almost everyone on the dock, he never claimed to see or hear what transpired among them. His testimony always *implied* that the defendant was engaged in guilty conduct, while asserting that his own presence there was innocent. Thus he walked a fine line: he made his points with the government, but left the onus of betrayal on others.

In the end, it was John M. Lloyd, not Weichmann, who incriminated Mary Surratt. Lloyd claimed that she had asked for those "shooting irons" at the tavern. More than all the shady visitors, more than Lewis Powell's arrest in her hallway, and more than her apparent intimacy with Booth, Lloyd's testimony showed direct participation in the plot *on the night of the shooting*. The testimony of Weichmann only brought her into Lloyd's presence.

THE COURTROOM WAS USUALLY PACKED to capacity, and reporters had to maneuver for a look at the defendants. A surprising number were reminded of wild animals. Jane G. Swisshelm, for example, wrote, "I think I could not have passed Harold on the street without mentally exclaiming, 'ape.' " She described Atzerodt as a panther, "who could only spring for prey when he felt assured of success," and said that "Payne" was like a buffalo, "who simply had a fierce delight in conflict, [and who] had been trained to believe that Mr. Seward was trespassing on his grazing lands. . . ." Of all the prisoners, it was "Payne" who inspired the most imaginative comments. Most observers seemed to think he was superhuman. "His name is a misnomer," said the *Sunday Mercury*. "He seems to have no comprehension of physical suffering. . . . His nerves appear to have gone into muscle."

It is almost impossible to find any description not tinged by a preconception of guilt. The Boston *Daily Advertiser* said, "Already such testimony has been taken as to assure the court and the world of the guilt of nearly all the accused; and nothing short of a miracle can save their lives from the doom, the justice of which every word from the witness stand makes more certain." In fact, this was published before a single word of testimony had been taken about any of the defendants.

The public loved reading about the "wretched accused," and they expected condemnation in the most colorful terms. The Washington press corps did not disappoint. They called Mary Surratt the "mother of conspirators," and observed, "We have seen cows and oxen with countenances very much like that of poor Spangler." They told of Atzerodt's lowness, Herold's stupidity, and Dr. Mudd's vanity, and their observations were often based on the configuration of bumps on the suspects' heads. One of the kindest remarks was reserved for Mike O'Laughlen, who, it was said, "must be young in crime, [as] the deformity of his soul has not pictured itself on his face."

Over the next six weeks, witnesses were questioned on Booth's movements, the shooting at Ford's, and various plots allegedly hatched by the Confederate government. Brooke Stabler and John Fletcher told how Herold, Atzerodt, and Booth shared their horses. John Greenawalt and Mary Van Tyne told of Booth's conferences with the defendants. Sgt. Silas Cobb and Willie Jett detailed Booth's escape, and Everton Conger told of the assassin's final moments. Thus did the trial move through the sweltering heat of summer in a room often packed to suffocation. Visitors shuffled in, defendants talked with their lawyers, and prosecutors lectured the commission on points of law.[6]

The proceedings often grew acrimonious. When that happened, prosecutor John A. Bingham was almost always involved in the fight. Bingham's style was anything but gentle; he scolded, mocked, and intimidated his adversaries, and never yielded an inch of ground. To him, an argument didn't simply have merit; it was so plain that anyone with a trace of common sense could perceive it. A legal authority wasn't simply on point; it was so precisely relevant to the argument that one would have thought the author had written it with this case especially in mind. While Holt and

Burnett were models of decorum, John A. Bingham was a scrapper. In law and politics, he gave no quarter.

Understandably, each side challenged the credibility of opposing witnesses, but in the eyes of the prosecutors, credibility often hinged on politics. They usually asked witnesses how they had voted in the last election, and they made a special point of asking those from Southern Maryland. Anyone who had supported Benjamin Gwynn Harris for Congress knew he was in trouble. Joseph Holt's office had just taught Mr. Harris a lesson in hardball politics. On April 23, two Confederate soldiers stopped at the congressman's home on their way back from the war. They spoke to Harris, and he supposedly counseled them not to take an oath of allegiance, but to let themselves be exchanged, then get back into the fight. Though he declined to give them a place to stay, he did give each a dollar to pay for a hotel room. For that, he was arrested and tried by a military commission. Convicted of harboring Confederates, he was expelled from Congress and sentenced to three years in prison. His case cast a long shadow over the conspiracy trial, which began just as the Harris trial ended.[7]

It was almost two weeks into the trial before Joseph Holt called his most important witness on the issue of Confederate involvement. This was Sandford Conover. As a correspondent for the *New York Tribune,* Conover had reported anonymously on plots against Lincoln in the spring of 1864. He said that he left the South in October of that year and, under the alias of James Watson Wallace, went to Montreal, where he got to know some Confederate officials. He said that they told him about various schemes to bring terror to the Northern public, and he claimed that Jacob Thompson even asked him to take part in one of these. Conover described it as a plot, led by Booth, to kill Lincoln and most senior officials in the federal government.

According to Conover, John Surratt came to Thompson's office sometime after April 6 with letters of approval for the scheme. After reading the letters, Thompson allegedly tapped on them and said, "This makes the thing all right." A few days later, Conover saw Thompson talking with his colleague William C. Cleary when they heard rejoicing over Lee's surrender. Cleary remarked that the Confederacy "would put the laugh on the other side of their mouth in a day or two." If prosecutors were looking for a smoking gun, they found it in the testimony of Sandford Conover.[8]

Considering how vigorously Judge Holt pursued a Confederate angle on the plot, it is strange that he ignored the undeniable link that existed between the rebel government and Lewis Powell. Though Powell had left the uniformed service in January, he fell in with a pro-Southern network almost immediately, and it was they who led him to John Surratt. Indeed, it is no stretch to say that Preston Parr, Maggie Branson, and Thomas Green were part of a spy network, and that they supplied Booth with his most trusted lieutenant. Yet Joseph Holt and associates did nothing with the information. Had they wanted to bring the real Southern connection to light, the man they called "Payne" should have been their way in.

The prisoner himself was hard to ignore. To Holt and almost everyone else, Lewis Powell was an object of wonder. He was a gladiator—a tall, cool killing machine who seemed utterly indifferent to his own fate. But that was the public image; in private, Powell was an emotional wreck. On the ship he had tried to kill himself. In his cell, he wept at the thought of what he had done. His confinement was such a jolt to his system that it left him constipated for weeks. Add the panicked behavior at Seward's and a racing pulse, and an entirely different picture of Lewis Powell emerges. He was not so much a heartless killer as a scared young man who just didn't show his feelings.

Much about him was still a mystery. His identity was yet unknown, and after a woodcut appeared in *Harper's Weekly*, guessing became a national pastime. Superintendent John A. Kennedy of the New York Police Department believed he was really William A. Johnson of New Bern, North Carolina. Others thought he was an illegitimate son of Jefferson Davis. By various accounts he was a Missourian, a Kentuckian, a Georgian, and a Canadian. Detectives spent a small fortune chasing down leads, but they missed one that might have proved helpful. Back on April 24, A. H. Windson suggested that the prisoner might be the same fellow who had captured Dick Blazer the year before. He urged authorities to have Blazer identify him, but no action was taken.

Powell himself did not break his silence for weeks. His own attorney, William E. Doster, could not decide whether to explain his conduct by "lunacy, unparalleled stupidity or fear of prejudicing his cause by communications with his counsel." But after the prosecution presented its case against him, Powell finally opened up. On May 20 he asked Doster to come back and talk to him the following day, a Sunday. They sat in the courtroom for hours, and Powell asked about the condition of Frederick Seward; he said he wished to apologize for the attack. Eventually he talked about his life. He spoke of growing up in a slave system, of enlisting at sixteen, and of losing two brothers in the war. As Powell told it, anyone in those circumstances would hate Yankees, and would have felt honored to be chosen for Booth's plot. Impressed with his sincerity, Doster made up his mind to put it all on the record. By the rules of evidence, though, he could do that only through an insanity defense.[9]

The general public had not really settled on a definition of insanity. Though everyone agreed that mental illness could result from organic brain disease, some also believed in such a thing as "moral insanity," which impaired only the "affective faculties." In lay terms, it was a lack of emotional control. This would form the basis for Lewis Powell's defense.

These days, insanity is strictly a legal term, but in 1865 it was an accepted medical diagnosis as well. Though relatively few specialized in the study of mental illness, the law allowed any physician to testify as an expert witness. And since the profession had not universally endorsed the concept of "moral insanity," an attorney could not be sure of finding a doctor whose views were favorable to the defendant. There were skeptics in the legal profession as well. Ironically, one of the nation's most visible proponents of the insanity defense was none other than William H. Seward. In 1846, Seward had defended two accused murderers on that basis, and had championed their cause at the risk of his own political career.

William E. Doster seemed to equate insanity with unreasonable behavior, and his client had certainly demonstrated enough of that. "In the first place," Doster said, "all the circumstances connected with the assassination show the work of insane men . . . look at the conduct of the prisoner, Payne, after he entered the house, without the slightest particle of disguise, speaking to the Negro [Bell] for five minutes—a person that he must know would be able to recognize him again thereafter; the ferocity of the crime, which is not indicative of human nature in its sane state; his leaving all the traces, which men usually close up, behind him. . . . He takes his knife and deliberately throws it down in front of Mr. Seward's door, as though anxious to be detected; and then, instead of riding off quickly as a sane man would under the circumstances, he moves off so slowly that the Negro tells you he followed him for a whole square on a walk; and afterwards [returns] to the very house . . . where he must have known, if he had been sane, that he would immediately walk into the arms of the military authorities. He goes to this house in a crazy disguise, because who in the world ever heard of a man disguising himself by using a piece of his drawers as a hat. . . . I ask you, is that the conduct of a sane man?"[10]

One is naturally tempted to ask whether John Wilkes Booth, son of the "Mad Tragedian," might have been found insane under existing laws. Privately, Junius Booth, Jr., believed that insanity ran "more or less thro' the male portion of our family," and his youngest brother, Joseph, admitted that he had become insane after hearing what John Wilkes had done. But both men were referring to *depression;* organic disease was another story. As a doctor well versed in mental health issues, Surgeon General Barnes testified that the "severest" test of sanity was the so-called Shakespearean test, in which the physician asks the patient a series of questions—usually about the patient himself—then repeats the questions later. If the answers match over time, the patient is considered sane. It was really a test of mental coherence. Since Booth had demonstrated the trait countless times on stage, such a test would have been superfluous.[11]

None of the prosecutors believed Powell was insane. They felt that his attack on Seward was carefully calculated, with the perfectly rational aim of throwing the government into confusion. The laws of presidential succession proved this. Though Seward would not have become president in the absence of Lincoln and Johnson, he would have been required, as secretary of state, to call electors to choose a new executive, should the president and vice president both die in office. If the secretary of state were taken out of the picture, prosecutors said, the whole system would shut down.

Their theory was interesting, but completely at odds with the assassin's own reasoning. Time and again, Booth had complained that the Lincoln administration had no regard for the Constitution, and that they had cast aside any law that interfered with their wishes. His sincerity in that belief is beyond question. So why would he think that another law—and an almost trifling one, compared to the First Amendment—could stop Lincoln's partisans dead in their tracks? Surely Booth knew about the long-settled practice of succession within departments. As early as 1803, subordinates had been assuming the duties of their absent superiors with no loss of authority. In fact, William Hunter, acting secretary of state, had moved seamlessly into the roles of the Sewards on April 15. He had done so before, and nobody questioned the legality of his work in that capacity.

It is worth noting that the law of succession provided only for the *death* of the president; it said nothing about a living executive who simply couldn't do his job. From a legal perspective, the capture of Lincoln would have been more disruptive than his death.[12]

. . .

ALMOST EVERY ACCOUNT of the trial has focused on the treatment of the prisoners while glossing over the specific testimony and points of law. But this was a landmark event that spoke volumes about the times and— since September 2001—about our own as well. The only way to put the Lincoln conspiracy trial in its proper context is to read the record closely, bearing two specific questions in mind: What might have happened to the defendants in a civilian court? and How different would the trial be under current laws? There are no simple answers.

It is not easy to put aside the barbarous image of people in hoods and chains. Prisoners had not been treated that way since 1696, and would not be again until 2001. But just as strange, in a way, was the fact that not all of the prisoners were forced to endure it. Mrs. Surratt and Dr. Mudd were never hooded, and Mudd, Arnold, and O'Laughlen were never weighted down with a heavy iron ball. Still, the treatment was shocking, and after some of the commission members objected to it, the hoods were no longer worn in the courtroom. They were removed altogether on June 10.

In his capacity as jailer, General Hartranft did all he could to alleviate the suffering. Though the cells measured only three and a half by seven feet, the general made sure they were kept "as comfortable as can be expected." Meals of coffee, soft bread, and salt meat were plentiful, and visitors to the prison could augment the fare. Of all the prisoners, Ned Spangler was the quickest to adapt to his conditions. Spangler surprised everyone with a voracious appetite and an upbeat disposition. He quickly learned to distinguish the voices of the different guards, and frequently tried to engage them in conversation to relieve the boredom. Mary Surratt, on the other hand, deteriorated steadily. She suffered from a gynecological disorder, possibly endometriosis, and as William Doster recalled, "Her cell by reason of her sickness was scarcely habitable." Twice, her illness forced an early adjournment, and Stanton ordered General Hancock to do whatever he could to make her comfortable. Eventually she was transferred from her cell to a large room next to the courtroom, where her daughter was allowed to join her.[13]

Contrary to his popular image, Judge Holt was not entirely heavy-handed. He used all the means at his disposal to track down witnesses for the defense. He agreed to delay the trial so doctors could assess Lewis Powell's state of mind. When two members of the commission objected to defense testimony by a former Confederate, Holt insisted they let the man be heard. Such things are taken for granted by defendants today; in 1865, they were purely discretionary. While Holt was always known as a stickler for rules, he was more flexible in this case than anyone had a reason to expect.

By modern standards, the trial was unmistakably slanted, but not because of the dictatorial whims of prosecutors. Criminal laws were different then, and they tended to favor the government. In 1865, a felony defendant was *allowed* a lawyer, but was not *entitled* to one, and the attorney was merely an adviser and could address the court only in a capital case. In a military trial, the rule was a little different. Here a defendant always had a lawyer, but sometimes the attorney was also the prosecutor. Strange as it sounds, judge advocates were required to represent both sides in any case where the defendant could not find a lawyer. Government officers were assumed to be impartial presenters of fact and were honor-bound to keep the process fair.[14]

Generally, military trials were less friendly to the defense than their civilian equivalents. For one thing, they did not require the rigid "technical structures" demanded in civilian courts. If a civilian prosecutor omitted the word "feloniously" in an indictment, for example, he could not call for the death penalty, no matter how serious the offense. Every word counted. But military courts were more lax about such things, and Judge Holt took advantage of that in the charges he drew up in this case. Here, each defendant was charged with a single offense that seemed to mix everything from murder to concealment to lying in wait—and all of it done "maliciously, unlawfully, and traitorously." In the words of Walter Cox, the charge "seems to have been intended . . . to fit every conceivable form of crime which the wickedness of man can devise." Cox observed that the prosecutors "seem to have tasked their ingenuity to invent a new species of crime— traitorous murder, traitorous conspiracy, murder which is something more than murder, yet something less than treason—a hybrid between them, partaking of both. On the same principle, stealing a percussion cap, with intent to use it against the government, would be traitorous larceny, instead of petty larceny."

Thomas Ewing complained that what appeared to be a single charge was actually four separate crimes, and some of them could not possibly apply to his clients. He pressed Holt repeatedly to define the actual charge, but the judge advocate refused to be pinned down. He said he could not point to a specific statute under which the defendants were accused, but their acts were clear.

What Holt did not say is that ambiguity made the military trial possible in the first place. Under the Habeas Corpus Act of 1863, Congress required the executive branch to turn all detainees over to civilian courts if their alleged offenses were covered under civilian law. Murder, conspiracy, and treason certainly fit that description, but a "traitorous conspiracy" did not.[15]

Judge Holt had drawn up the indictments, but the rest of the process was in the commission's hands. In a military trial, the judge advocate was only an adviser to the panel, and not "both judge and prosecutor," as often claimed. Nevertheless, Holt had a tremendous amount of leverage, and he used it both ways. He sometimes supported the defense over the more intransigent Bingham. More often than not, though, he threw his weight to the prosecution side. On one occasion he even argued that the commission need not vote on every point of law; if Bingham had objected to something, that should be enough.

The panel usually sided with Holt. Their leanings became apparent early in the trial, when the prosecutors asked to admit certain letters into evidence. One letter, said to have been written on April 15 by someone who identified himself only as "No. Five," urged "John" not to lose his nerve in carrying out his part of the plot. Attacks on Sherman and Grant had yet to take place, but the writer had just attended a meeting with his fellow conspirators, and "all were bent on carrying out the programme to the letter."

Though the "No. Five" note was supposed to have been found floating in the water off North Carolina, it looked, in the words of Walter Cox, "no more blurred, I think, than any paper on this table." Cox considered the letter a clumsy fabrication, and he could not see why anyone would consider it admissible. Thomas Ewing agreed. "In the first place," he argued, "I really believe the letter to be fictitious, and to bear upon its face the evidence that it is so. In the second place, it is testimony that is wholly inadmissible under the plainest rules of evidence. . . . It is a declaration of some person whose existence nobody knows anything of—a nameless man."

Ewing conceded that such a document could be admitted if written by a conspirator, and John Bingham said that that was his point exactly. Bingham argued that even though the author of that letter was unknown, he *must have been* tied to Booth's plot. His assertion brought a retort from

O'Laughlen's attorney. Walter Cox said, "The logic of my learned friend on the other side seems to be this: It is sufficiently established, at least by *prima facie* evidence before the Court, that Booth was engaged in a conspiracy with some unknown persons; this letter comes from an unknown person; ergo, it is a letter from somebody connected with Booth in this conspiracy. . . . I submit to the Court that this is chop logic."

Nevertheless, Bingham insisted that the author was a conspirator—"a fact clearly enough shown, I think, to hang him if he were found with that paper in his pocket, though no man knew his name, and no man ever testified about the writer. . . ." The defense put up a vigorous argument, but Holt sided with Bingham, and the letter was admitted.[16]

One might suppose that if the commission sided with Bingham on the letter controversy, they were probably disposed to support him in anything. Indeed, that was the conclusion of historian Otto Eisenschiml, who once counted up the objections raised, then tabulated the number decided in favor of each side. By that scorecard, the trial was manifestly one-sided. But in fact, such rulings make an especially poor measure of this trial. Many of the objections raised by Frederick Aiken, the attorney for Mary Surratt, would have been overruled in any court. Aiken was not an experienced lawyer. He did not understand the rules of evidence, and his frequent missteps played as heavily against his client as anything the commission decided. He rarely came prepared and often failed to anticipate what his own witnesses would say. For example, he insisted on defending the loyalty of Mary Surratt's brother, Zadock Jenkins, by showing that Jenkins had flown an American flag in defiance of his secessionist neighbors. But none of his own witnesses would confirm that. When he put Jenkins himself on the stand, he asked how much money he had spent in support of the Union. Jenkins said that he couldn't recall spending anything.

Aiken's strategy always seemed to backfire. He tried to get John Holohan to establish an alibi for Mary Surratt, but the witness wouldn't cooperate. Holohan testified that he saw Mrs. Surratt at home, and Aiken asked whether she might actually have been at church. "Mr. Aiken, you know me very well," said the witness. "Well enough to know that I am not a man to tell an untruth. . . . I have told you that I saw Mrs. Surratt there that morning, and she could not have been at church if she was there."

Perhaps Aiken's worst blunder was calling Augustus Howell to the stand. Howell was defiant, evasive, and inordinately proud of his opposition to the Yankees. His testimony was intended to cast suspicion on Weich-

mann, whom he had taught to use a Confederate cipher machine, but it
only called attention to the fact that Howell himself knew how to use the
device. The machine in question was identical to the one found in Judah
Benjamin's office after the evacuation of Richmond. Everyone in the room
knew that Howell was a Confederate spy, and the fact that he was captured
in Mary Surratt's tavern could not have done much good for her defense.

Frederick Aiken was painfully aware of his inexperience, and the prosecution would not let him forget it. Occasionally Joseph Holt offered him
advice, but John Bingham was brutal. He openly ridiculed Aiken, expressed contempt for him, and publicly lectured him on his inadequacies
as a lawyer. He even got Burnett to join in. Once, when Aiken asked for
leeway, he reminded the commission that he had not objected as often as
he could have. Burnett lashed out. "It is certainly a very weak argument for
counsel to say that he permitted illegitimate matter, and therefore that illegitimate matter should be permitted for him. It is his duty, under his
oath, to see that his client has the rights of law, and it is an admission that
I certainly would not make to this Court, that I had not maintained the
rights of my client. He is to blame, and no one else, if such has been the
case. . . ."

In an exchange with Lew Wallace, Aiken admitted that the process was
not at fault. The general said, "I understood the object of the counsel to be,
to impeach not only the witness for the government, but also the fairness
of the Court." To this, Aiken replied, "No, sir; only the witness; not the
fairness of the Court at all. I have no reason to complain of that. None of
us have had."[17]

Aiken knew enough to see how the odds were stacked against him. He
understood that the prosecution's real leverage came from its ability to
make its own rules. Because military commissions were not subject to judicial appeal, they were not legally bound to follow the common-law rules
of procedure. That gave Joseph Holt and associates the luxury of relying
instead on the "laws of war." They refused to define the term, but it probably referred to a common understanding of what constituted proper conduct in warfare. It was a new form of jurisprudence—fluid, unwritten, and
in short, anything Joseph Holt wanted it to be. Walter Cox could not resist giving it a verbal jab.

"What a convenient instrument for trampling upon every constitutional guaranty, every sacred right of the citizen!" said Cox. "There is no
invention too monstrous, no punishment too cruel to find authority and

sanction in such a common law. Is it possible that American citizens can be judged and punished by an unwritten code that has no definitions, no books, no judges or lawyers; which, if it has any existence, like the laws of the Roman Emperor, is hung up too high to be read?"

What Cox and the others did not know was that earlier in the year, the Bureau of Military Justice had published a set of guidelines based on the rules Holt himself had laid down for his subordinates. The *Digest of Opinions of the Judge Advocate General of the Army* was intended to serve as a guide for judge advocates in the field. Few people knew anything about it, and Holt appears to have wanted it that way. He did not want his own book to become a straitjacket.[18]

Any discussion of fairness would have to include mention of the rule on "defendant declarations." At common law, the words of a defendant were admissible only if he uttered them during the commission of the crime; anything said after the fact or later, in his own defense, was excluded. The rule benefited the prosecution exclusively, and in this case, it kept out some intriguing items: the interrogations of Mary Surratt, the confessions of Atzerodt and Herold, and the diary of John Wilkes Booth. Historians have often questioned the "suppression" of these items, but in fact, they would not have been allowed in *any* court at that time.

Formal statements made by the accused to government officials were not completely excluded, but they could be introduced only by the prosecution. Because those officials could hardly be expected to recite a defendant's full statement from memory, what the court actually heard was an edited or paraphrased version of it. This put defendants at the mercy of people who, generally, were hostile to their defense. As John A. Bingham explained, there was a reason for such a rule. "Those who are charged with crime," said Bingham, "are never permitted on their own motion to prove their random declarations to third persons, because if it were so, the greatest criminal that ever cursed the earth and disgraced our common humanity could make an abundant amount of testimony out of the mouth of the most truthful people on the planet."

The rule was as well known in 1865 as "You have the right to remain silent . . ." is today, and John Wilkes Booth had relied heavily on it to protect himself from eventual exposure. He knew that anything he said could someday be brought into court by a third party, and anyone incriminated by his words would probably be excluded from responding. Thus, if Booth considered someone a potential threat, he could neutralize him by making him look guilty and thus unable to testify against him. All he had to do was tell or show a third-party witness that the person in question had been on intimate terms with him. It was accusation by innuendo, and it had been Booth's most potent threat against those he needed to silence. He used it on conspirators, witnesses, and anyone else he didn't trust. This, more than anything else, allowed Booth to organize a plot in the most paranoid of times.[19]

Judge Holt knew how to use such rules to his advantage, and he did just that in the case against Dr. Mudd. Government witnesses claimed that Mudd had been uncooperative in the week following the assassination, and Detectives Lloyd, Lovett, and Gavacan all implied that the doctor's omissions were more incriminating than anything he actually said. This, in fact, was behind Stanton's decision to prosecute Mudd in the first place. But when General Ewing tried to address the issue, he ran into a road-block. Ewing tried to show that it was Mudd who reported Booth's visit to authorities in the first place, and that Lieutenant Dana, to whom the information was passed, simply ignored the report. Since Mudd was charged with concealment, he said, his "declaration" was made during the commission of that alleged crime. But at this point, Holt invoked the "defendant declaration" rule. He insisted that Mudd's crime ended when Booth left his farm on Saturday, and any report he made subsequent to that was considered to be after the fact, and hence inadmissible.

But much of what Dr. Mudd said during the week was entered into the record. It came through the testimony of Col. Henry H. Wells. According to Wells, Mudd admitted that he had recognized Booth while he was still at his farm, and yet he harbored him anyway. That was a damaging admission. But even though nothing of the sort appeared in Mudd's sworn statement, or in the one Wells had written for him, that was beside the point. Legally, only the colonel could tell the story. His unsupported memory went on the record, while the law excluded the words Mudd was actually known to have used. It was an especially hard pill to swallow because Wells was so careless; on important issues, he used equivocal expressions ("I think" or "if I am not mistaken") at least thirty-five times.[20]

By the laws of criminal procedure, the prosecutors set the limits of the case, and defense attorneys were strictly forbidden to venture outside those lines. Thus, when Sam Chester testified that Booth wanted "someone connected or acquainted with [Ford's] theater" to be in his plot, he bolstered suspicions against Spangler, the only defendant who was actually employed there. Spangler's attorney, Thomas Ewing, tried to respond by showing that Booth actually had no preference, having scoped out Grover's Theatre just as carefully as Ford's. But the point was not allowed. The prosecution had never mentioned Grover's Theatre, and the defense could not introduce it on their own.

The reactive role of the defense put all the cards—and the evidence—in the hands of prosecutors. Because the defense could introduce nothing, except in rebuttal, they could not argue that prosecutors got the wrong person, that their witnesses had been mistaken, or that detectives had failed to follow up on more promising leads. Information on such things would only be found in prosecutors' files, and in 1865, the government was not required to disclose anything of that nature. In fact, government agents actively thwarted Frederick Aiken when he tried to investigate on his own. George Cottingham told Aiken something in private, but something else under oath. On the stand, he openly admitted lying. As he explained, he did not think a defense attorney had any business talking to him in the first place.[21]

It is not hard to see how full disclosure might have hurt the government's case. Witnesses changed their stories, misquoted their sources, and gave details in their sworn testimony that were strangely missing in the pretrial investigation. In the case of Dr. Mudd, detectives' memoranda contradicted one another on key points, and an item in government files—an envelope with lines drawn on it—might have helped corroborate the defendant's story that Booth had drawn such a map as they talked together in his hotel room.

Government files could have been damaging to two of their most important witnesses, John M. Lloyd and Louis Weichmann. Everyone knew that Lloyd had hidden Booth's weapons, then retrieved them on the night of the shooting. But what the defense didn't know was that he had thwarted the pursuit for several days. Most detectives considered Lloyd a conspirator, and were outraged that he had not been prosecuted. Some even claimed a share in the reward money based on having arrested him.[22]

Lou Weichmann was even more vulnerable. Fellow clerks in the War Department had insisted that Weichmann was a Southern sympathizer, and Judge Holt had every reason to believe he was actively working for the other side. Augustus Howell said so explicitly. "Weichmann . . . gave me information and said it came from his Books in his office," Howell wrote. "Not only that—he obtained his office in the war department with the express understanding with Surratt that he W___ was to furnish Surratt with all information that came under his notice from time to time to be transmitted South—and he did furnish it."

Almost to a man, government investigators felt that Weichmann had played some part in the conspiracy. As Col. John A. Foster put it: "It seems extremely improbable that Weichmann was ignorant of the entire plot, if he was not an accomplice. . . ." Even though Stanton never wavered on his decision to spare Weichmann, he could not afford to let him get complacent. Weichmann was often reminded of how close the decision was, and those reminders sounded just like threats. In a pretrial letter to Burnett, Weichmann offered information that he had been unable to recall at his last interrogation. "You confused and terrified me so much yesterday," he said, "that I was almost unable to say anything." Yet the witness denied under oath that he had been influenced by fear, and the defense had no right to see this evidence to the contrary.

The common complaint about Weichmann was not that he lied outright, but that he bent the facts. He was challenged and contradicted often, but his testimony actually falls apart only once, when he claimed to have spoken with a colleague about an article he had just read in the *New York Tribune* of March 19, 1865. In fact, that article was published in 1864. It was written by the government witness Sandford Conover, and Weichmann's false recollection of reading it suggests that the information had come to him, directly or indirectly, through the author.[23]

One item might have compromised Weichmann beyond repair, had the War Department been required to let the defense see it. It was a letter dated February 15 from a woman who signed herself "Clara." This gushing and gossipy note refers to John Surratt's travels as if Weichmann knew all about them. The author asks Weichmann how he enjoyed his January trip to Baltimore—the one on which Surratt abandoned him at the Maltby House. Certainly, "Clara" was privy to some personal secrets, such as Weichmann's bisexuality and his unrequited love for Anna Surratt. More to the point, though, she was a Confederate insider, and her letter strongly implies that the prosecution's star witness was one as well. Had the defense known of it, they might have neutralized Lou Weichmann's effectiveness on the stand.[24]

Discovery laws could have made a world of difference in the trial. With access to the War Department files, defense attorneys might have uncovered the fact that at least once, Joseph Holt presented evidence he knew to be fraudulent. Specifically, it was a letter addressed to "J.W.B." and purportedly sent on April 6 to the National Hotel. It discussed the assassination, the "oil speculation," and an alternate plan of escape. When the letter was brought to Holt's attention, he noted the western Maryland postmark and sent detectives there to investigate. They quickly determined that the letter was a fraud; its author was a man named Robert Purdy, who had written it to implicate a neighbor, Leonidas McAleer. Other investigators reached the same conclusion, but the judge advocate endorsed the letter anyway, and allowed Purdy to validate it on the stand. At the same time, he had McAleer arrested and held without charges until the end of the trial.

HIGH-PROFILE CASES ALWAYS attract eccentrics, and this one had more than its share. Take, for example, Rev. William Evans. A Presbyterian minister and self-styled detective, the Reverend Mr. Evans said he felt a moral obligation to support the government. He claimed to have seen Dr. Mudd riding into Washington, and later going into the Surratt boardinghouse. But on cross-examination, Evans could only guess what the house looked like and where it was located. He guessed wrong. He offered conflicting stories to explain how he knew it was the right place, and though he had suggested his journals would help him fix the date, he retreated from that position instantly when the defense suggested he bring them in. Every material part of Evans's testimony was shown to be false. As General Ewing told the commission, "In his reckless zeal as a detective, he forgot the ninth commandment, and bore false witness against his neighbor."[25]

We may never know the extent to which people swore falsely in the conspiracy trial, but it happened often enough to throw the entire process into question. It was not a one-sided phenomenon. Though John Nothey testified that he owed money to Mary Surratt (thus supporting her reason for the April 14 trip to Surrattsville), a subsequent proceeding by the Prince George's County courts determined that the Surratts owed Nothey, and not the other way around. Did Nothey, a poor, illiterate farmer, succumb to local pressure in giving testimony, or did the courts get it wrong?[26]

It was not the process but the press that exposed the most egregious examples of perjury. Dr. James B. Merritt, Richard Montgomery, and Sandford Conover testified on the involvement of Confederate officials, and their secret testimony was not released to the public until Benn Pitman's wife gave it to the Cincinnati *Commercial* on June 2. Within days, Canadian newspapers reported that all their stories were "cooked to order." As it turned out, "Dr. Merritt" was not really a doctor, and his testimony was entirely false. Sandford Conover was really Charles A. Dunham, of New Jersey. When authorities searched Dunham's apartment in Montreal, they found evidence that he had been using many other aliases, and worse, that he had been a Confederate spy. Eventually, it developed that Dunham had concocted stories for a number of witnesses and had coached them on what to say. Though this was discovered before the trial ended, the commission heard nothing about it.[27]

William Doster wanted to close the case of Lewis Powell on a positive note. He decided to have Dr. Charles H. Nichols, superintendent of the government asylum, evaluate his client and explain his mental state in light of the "moral insanity" theory. But Doster planned to do this at the end of the trial so the commission would go into deliberations with Dr. Nichols's testimony fresh in their minds. His strategy backfired. On the day Nichols was slated to testify, word arrived that his wife had died. He rushed out, and Powell's defense left with him. Judge Holt offered to have someone else examine the prisoner, and Doster agreed. Three doctors visited the prisoner that day, and they all concluded that Powell was not insane. As Dr. James C. Hall said, what he found was "a very feeble, inert mind; a deficiency of mind rather than a derangement of it—a very low order of intellect." Though Hall had examined the prisoner for less than an hour, he felt confident that a person of normal intellect would at least be able to state his mother's maiden name. Powell was unable to do so.[28]

THE DEFENSE RESTED in mid-June, and began their closing arguments shortly afterward. They conceded that by the laws of conspiracy, the act of one participant transfers guilt to all. But that holds true only when it is the same act that they had conspired to do. Since the defendants had engaged in a conspiracy to *capture* the president, they could not be held responsible for Booth's last-minute change in the plan.[29]

Frederick Aiken argued that the evidence against Mary Surratt was purely circumstantial and showed nothing more than a social contact with Booth and various defendants. He said that none of the evidence pointed to her guilt in any conspiracy.

Frederick Stone pictured his client Herold as "a weak, cowardly, foolish miserable boy" who was fond of jokes and eager to please. "Such a boy," he said, "was only wax in the hands of a man like Booth." The evidence showed they were friends who spent time together, and nothing more. All Herold did for certain was aid and abet Booth in his escape, and that was only a misdemeanor. He was not guilty of the murder, and was not present at the time it was committed.

In defense of Ned Spangler, Thomas Ewing pointed out that his client was not the only stagehand who had done chores for the assassin, nor did Spangler prepare the president's box for Booth, as alleged. The fact that Booth used his own gimlet to bore the hole in the door must surely point to the innocence of his client, "for if Booth had a confidant and confederate in this rough carpenter, the work would have been done by Spangler, or at least, with Spangler's tools." He noted that Spangler's only contact with Booth was in and around the theater, and that he could not have helped the assassin escape, since he had remained at his post up to the moment of the shooting. Though Booth had told Sam Chester he needed "someone connected or familiar with Ford's Theatre," the only thing he wanted Chester to do was to hold open the back door, and in the end, Booth did that for himself.

Arguing for Dr. Mudd, General Ewing refuted Lou Weichmann's assertion that his client was on intimate terms with Booth. They had not seen each other since December, and Mudd had done nothing for Booth since then except dress his injured leg. He had reported Booth's visit at the earliest opportunity, and he should not be held accountable for the fact that Lieutenant Dana ignored the report.

In defense of George Atzerodt, William Doster showed that his client had never counseled Booth to kill anyone, nor had he lain in wait to kill the vice president. He had harmed no one, and had repeatedly tried to assist the government by offering a full confession. "He is guilty solely of what he confesses," said Doster, "—of conspiring to abduct the president—and of that [he] can be found guilty only under a new indictment." With the commission's assent, Doster finished his presentation by reading Atzerodt's last statement into the record.

Perhaps the ablest and most wide-ranging argument was that of Walter Cox, whose defense of Arnold and O'Laughlen was a masterpiece of reasoning and logic. After attacking the anomalous character of the charges, Cox dissected the evidence of Confederate involvement and showed that, as presented, the government's case made no sense. He argued that the only evidence against O'Laughlen was the Arnold confession, which would not be admissible in any real court, and which proved no involvement beyond O'Laughlen's presence at the Gautier's meeting. Their scheme, "though not innocent, might almost be called harmless, from its perfect absurdity and impracticality." Still, he said, capturing the president was "perfectly legitimate" under international law.

Doster's argument for Lewis Powell was as bizarre as it was eloquent. Since his insanity defense had crumbled, Doster began his summation by acknowledging that his client was "not within the medical definition of insanity," and that he believed his attack on the Sewards was justified. He argued that Powell was "the moral product of the war," which "made him an outcast and a fugitive on the face of the earth; took the bread out of his mouth; and gave him the alternative of dying obscurely by his own hand or notoriously by the death of a public officer." He was in desperate straits when Booth found him and molded him to his will.

Doster should have stopped there, but he continued, referring again to Powell's deep conviction that what he had done was right. He even went so far as to paint his client in heroic terms.

"What, then, has he done that every rebel soldier has not tried to do? Only this: He has shown a higher courage, a bitterer hate, and a more ready sacrifice; he has aimed at the head of a department, instead of the head of a corps; he has struck at the head of a nation, instead of at its limbs; he has struck in the day of his humiliation, when nothing was to be accomplished but revenge, and when he believed he was killing an oppressor."[30]

Doster said that many people played a role in shaping Powell's fate, from Southern slave owners to the brutal Union soldiers who burned homes and laid waste to civilian property. Yet even as he said this, he would surely have known that Gen. David Hunter, president of the commission, had been accused of such atrocities himself; that he had been declared an outlaw for arming slaves; and that Southerners considered him one of the most hated men in the U.S. Army. It was a serious miscalculation on Doster's part to spread the blame for Powell's crime to this man now sitting in judgment of him. He could not have harmed his client any more if he had stared General Hunter right in the eye and said, "You don't have the guts to hang that boy!"

If his closing argument did not guarantee a hanging, then surely a twist of fate did. On June 21, just as Doster was paying tribute to Powell, Frances Seward, wife and mother of Powell's victims, suffered a heart attack and died. Popular rumor said that the horrors of April 14 had hastened her death.[31]

After hearing the defense arguments, Lew Wallace wrote his wife, "I have passed a few words with my associate members, and think we can agree in a couple of hours at farthest. Three, if not four, of the eight will be acquitted—that is, if we voted today." But they did not vote that day, and the prosecution still had a few more cards to play. On June 27, Joseph Holt surprised the commission by calling more witnesses. They were there to explain their earlier testimony, and to refute the charges of perjury that were being thrown around in the press. This may not have been necessary, since the charges had never reached the commission, and indeed, the testimony of Conover was taken as truthful even by the defense. But apparently, Judge Holt wanted to give his witnesses the final word.

When they had finished, John A. Bingham presented a florid, two-day summation of the government's case. He said that the military trial was a necessary and proper step in the preservation of order. He said that the Constitution was sacred, but that it was "only the law of peace." In war, he said, it "must be, and is, to a great extent, inoperative and disregarded."[32]

Bingham summarized the evidence against Confederates, giving equal weight to hard facts, speculation, and outright fraud. He insisted that there had never been an abduction scheme, despite the testimony of his own witness, Sam Chester. And he ridiculed the notion of abducting the president in the theater, "much less to carry him through the city, through the lines of your army, and deliver him into the hands of the rebels. No such purpose was expressed or hinted by the conspirators in Canada, who commissioned Booth to let these assassinations on contract. I shall waste not a moment more in combating such an absurdity."

Bingham said that the letter from Sam Arnold found in Booth's trunk proved that Arnold had not abandoned the scheme; on the contrary, it expressed his willingness to return at a "time more propitious," and offered advice for the successful prosecution of the conspiracy. And because "the act or declaration of one conspirator . . . is the act or declaration of all the conspirators," the "Sam" letter spoke for O'Laughlen as much as it did for Arnold.

Since the law gave Bingham the final word, he was free to roam, as it were, without fear of contradiction. In the case of Dr. Mudd, he ran through the evidence, then insinuated that there was much more to the story. "What became of the horses which Booth and Herold rode to his house, and which were put into his stable, are facts nowhere disclosed by evidence. The owners testify that they have never seen the horses since. The accused give no explanation of the matter, and when Herold and Booth were captured they had not these horses in their possession."[33]

It was hardly a fair point to make, since the question had never come up. And even if it had, Dr. Mudd would not have been legally permitted to answer it. Bingham hit Mudd especially hard on the details of that encounter at the National Hotel. Though he had blocked every effort to show that it took place in December—not in January, as Weichmann claimed—he now argued that the date was immaterial because "the witness was not certain" about it. In fact, Weichmann *had* been certain, but as Bingham said, his subsequent wavering could help neither side, as "the burden of proof is upon the prisoner to prove that he was not in Washington in January last."

Peppered throughout his argument were ad hominem attacks on the defense counsel. Bingham criticized Reverdy Johnson for arguing "in behalf of an expiring and shattered rebellion," and he charged Thomas Ewing with hypocrisy for denying the need for martial law, when Ewing himself had instituted some of the most extreme measures on record. Bingham used the words of Lord Brougham to contrast himself with the other side: "A friend of liberty have I lived, and such will I die; nor care I how soon the latter event may happen, if I cannot be a friend of liberty without being a friend of traitors at the same time—a protector of criminals of the deepest dye—an accomplice of foul rebellion and its concomitant, civil war, with all its atrocities and its fearful consequences."[34]

John Bingham's summation justified his seat at the trial. Those who heard it would never forget the power of his presentation. "When referring to the rebellion or any of its leaders . . . ," said Lt. Col. Richard A. Watts, of the prison staff, "his invective burned and seared like a hot iron. But when he touched upon the great and lovable qualities of the martyred Lincoln his lips would quiver with emotion, and his voice became as tender and reverent as if he were repeating the Lord's Prayer."

On June 29, press, public, and prisoners were removed from the courtroom and deliberations began. As legal advisers, Holt, Bingham, and Burnett were allowed to sit in on the debate, answering questions on testimony, evidence, and the fine points of law. This was a privilege allowed by military law. They used it, apparently, to persuade the commission to adopt a last-minute rule: the nonunanimous verdict. Under this new rule, the accused could be convicted by a simple majority, while a two-thirds vote carried an automatic sentence of death.

After a day and a half of deliberations, the commission returned a verdict of guilty for each defendant. Arnold, Mudd, and O'Laughlen each received five votes for conviction, and each was sentenced to life in prison. Edman Spangler was acquitted of conspiracy, but was convicted of aiding and abetting in Booth's escape, "well knowing" what he had done. He received a six-year sentence. Mary Surratt, Lewis Powell, David Herold, and George Atzerodt were convicted by a two-thirds majority or more. Each was condemned to death.[35]

From May 8 to June 30, the commission had examined 371 witnesses, hearing testimony that filled 5,010 pages and took six weeks to brief and file. Witnesses, trial staff, and prisoners consumed 1,768 meals at government expense. One hundred twenty more witnesses were subpoenaed but did not appear.

Was the trial fair? John Bingham said it was "as fair as in any court," but the record left room for disagreement. Henry Kyd Douglas, a trial witness and author of *I Rode with Stonewall,* said, "If Justice ever sat with unbandaged, blood-shot eyes, she did on this occasion."[36]

The judge advocates have had more than their share of critics, especially in modern times. Even though history has denied them credit for following the rules of evidence, it rightly condemns them for the irregularities they brought to this trial: the disingenuous arguments, the subornation of perjury, the payment of witnesses, and the presentation of evidence they knew to be fabricated.

Their transgressions may not have been necessary. The laws in 1865 were already weighted in the government's favor, and a rigid adherence to the existing rules of evidence would probably have produced the same result. Given the temper of the times, a civilian jury was no more likely to acquit the defendants than the commission was—though they might have gone easier on Ned Spangler.

The commission itself was not above reproach. Its only attorney, Lew Wallace, spent much of the trial consumed with unrelated business. He wrote letters to his wife, Susan. He drew pencil sketches of the prisoners on the dock. He tried to instigate a war with Mexico. And all the while, he took pains to cozy up with the Judge Advocate General, an obsessively social man, to lobby for assignment to yet another military commission. Wallace would get that assignment, and Holt would present Wallace's wife with the gift of a sapphire ring while that trial was in progress.[37]

THE VERDICTS WERE SEALED on June 30, and the commission was released from further duty. Since President Johnson was ill at the time, he did not see the findings until Holt brought him the papers on Wednesday, July 5. They spent several hours going over the facts of each case, and at the end of the session, Johnson approved the sentences. The executions were set for Friday, July 7.

Few people doubted then that Mary Surratt was guilty as charged. Indeed, hardly anyone had suggested otherwise. But no woman had ever been executed by the federal government, and few thought they would actually go through with it in this case. Johnson, however, showed no inclination to commute her sentence. Frederick Aiken was desperate to save his client. He asked Thomas Ewing for help, and Ewing had his law partner, former senator Orville Hickman Browning, draw up a petition for a writ of habeas corpus. It would be Mary Surratt's last chance.[38]

THE CONDEMNED PRISONERS LEARNED of their sentences on July 6, the night before their execution. General Hartranft, accompanied by General Hancock, came to their cells and broke the news. Each prisoner reacted differently. Lewis Powell calmly thanked the officers for their fair treatment. He said that he was sorry for what he had done; at the time, he had thought he was avenging the wrongs committed against Confederate prisoners.

George Atzerodt quivered and his face turned pale, but he said nothing. Herold was unnerved by the news. He acknowledged getting into the plot, but pointed out that he had refused to kill anyone. Mary Surratt burst into tears, and asked if she might see her priests, her friend John P. Brophy, and her daughter Anna.

That night, Rev. Abram Dunn Gillette rode to the prison with Thomas Eckert, who had just been appointed assistant secretary of war. Powell had specifically asked for Gillette, having attended one of his services, and the minister was surprised to see how different the prisoner was from his public persona. Powell was candid, remorseful, and eager to talk about his crime. The moment he fled from Seward's house, he said, a sickening feeling came over him, and ever since, he had been living in horror of what he had done. His conduct was exemplary; not so with Atzerodt. When Gillette stopped to speak with him, he was greeted with a flurry of comments that "criminated Mrs. Surratt." That was not what the minister had come to hear, and he abruptly cut Atzerodt off. He said that a condemned man ought to prepare to meet his God. Atzerodt acquiesced, and expressed wonder that his soul could ever be saved after so many years of wicked habits.[39]

In these final hours before the executions, every legal maneuver had an air of urgency. A stay of execution was not automatic, and Mary Surratt might have been hanged with an appeal still in the works. So, in the middle of the night, Frederick Aiken hurried to the home of Justice Andrew Wylie with Browning's petition for Mrs. Surratt. In his capacity as a federal judge, Wylie could have commanded authorities to produce the prisoner in court, but no one supposed for a minute that the government would comply. As a matter of form, he granted the petition anyway, and ordered General Hancock to bring Mrs. Surratt to his courtroom later that morning.

The morning of July 7 brought pleas, cries, and frantic maneuvering to save the four condemned prisoners. Outside the White House, Anna Surratt waited for hours, hoping to speak with the president about her mother's execution, but Johnson would see no one, and by midday, Anna was wild with grief. Eventually she managed to contact Reuben D. Mussey, the president's private secretary, but the person who called Mussey down did not say who she was. Nor did Anna. She threw herself on her knees and, with loud sobs and streaming tears, begged for a chance to see the president. Mussey could hardly understand her. He went up to Mr. Johnson's room and reported that a crazy woman was downstairs begging to be let in. Anna Surratt was turned away.

A short time later, two of Herold's sisters appeared at the White House in full mourning dress. Mary Nelson and Jane Herold were David's only hope, since their mother refused to plead on his behalf. Denied an audience with the president, they addressed a note to his wife, and then to his daughter. The notes were not delivered.[40]

The writ for Mary Surratt was returnable at ten o'clock, but the hour came and went with no response from General Hancock. In the meantime, William Doster appeared on behalf of his own clients, and Wylie told him that a writ had already been issued for another party in the same case. Since the military authorities had chosen to ignore that one, he saw little point in issuing another. Then, just before noon, General Hancock entered the courtroom, accompanied by Attorney General James Speed. The general informed the court that the person of Mary Surratt was in his possession by virtue of a presidential order, which he presented:

Executive office, July 7, 1865.

To Major-Gen. W. S. Hancock, Commanding, &c.

I, Andrew Johnson, President of the United States, do hereby declare that the writ of habeas corpus has been heretofore suspended in such cases as this; and I do hereby suspend this writ, and direct that you proceed to execute the order heretofore given upon the judgment of the Military Commission; and you will give this order in return to this writ.

Andrew Johnson, President.[41]

FROM HIS CELL in the penitentiary, Sam Arnold could hear the sounds of hammering and sawing. It never occurred to him that a scaffold was being erected so soon after the trial. Like O'Laughlen, Mudd, and Spangler, Arnold would not be told of his own sentence until almost two weeks after deliberations had ended. In the meantime, he sat in his narrow cell, counting the bricks and insects and wondering what was to become of him.

The execution was set for one o'clock. By ten, reporters and spectators had begun to fill the enclosure on the south side of the prison. They stood in awe of that great machine of death, with its massive crossbeam, two trapdoors, and four nooses that hung knee-high above the platform. Just off to the right were four open graves with plain wooden boxes stacked alongside.

Captain Christian Rath, the executioner, had spent hours rehearsing for this. He had chosen four soldiers to help, and they all seemed to dread what they were about to do. General Hancock had prepared as well. Hancock posted the 60th Ohio outside the perimeter of the prison, and twenty men from the 16th New York Cavalry closer in. A relay had been established between the penitentiary and the White House, in case the president should have a last-minute change of heart about commuting the sentences. Everything was in place hours ahead of time, and all anyone could do was wait. Near the scaffold, a few soldiers amused themselves by hanging a rat, then tossing it into one of the open graves. Others passed the time by scavenging construction debris from the gallows, to be sold for souvenirs.[42]

The condemned prisoners had all been transferred to cells facing the prison yard. For the next few hours sobs and moans were heard through the grated windows of the building. Reporters strained and maneuvered for a better view, but all they could see was George Atzerodt, emaciated and barely resembling his former self, sitting on the floor of a cell with his lover, Rose Wheeler. Some reporters thought that Rose was his sister, but in fact, Katherine Henrietta Smith was too despondent to visit. Her brother would go to his death this afternoon under the supervision of a U.S. marshal. The marshal in this case was John L. Smith, Katherine's husband.

A hundred or more civilians waited under a blistering sun as General Hartranft and his staff emerged from the prison cell block. Following was Mary Surratt, dressed in black, with bonnet and veil. Too feeble to walk, she was supported at each arm by an army officer. George Atzerodt came next, also propped up by officers. David Herold, in light pants and a cloth hat, followed Atzerodt. Like the others, he appeared too weak to walk unassisted.[43]

The last prisoner was the most remarkable. Lewis Powell stepped through the prison door looking bold, erect, and confident in his blue navy crew shirt. A sudden gust took his hat, and Reverend Gillette, walking beside him, placed it back on his head. "Thank you, Doctor," the prisoner said with a faint smile. "I won't be needing it much longer." Powell walked to the gallows with an almost casual air, and bounded up the thirteen steps to the platform. Armchairs had been placed there for the condemned prisoners. In front of each, swaying in the breeze, was a noose of five-eighths manila.

The prisoners took their seats as soldiers knelt around them, binding their legs with strips of white cloth. As General Hartranft read the findings and sentences, Fathers Jacob Walter and Bernardin Wiget knelt beside Mary Surratt and whispered spiritual consolations in her ear. Their words alone seemed to keep her from fainting. When the general finished reading, Reverend Gillette stepped forward to address the crowd. He said that Powell had asked him to thank General Hartranft and his staff publicly for their kind treatment; not an unkind word, look, or gesture had been given him by anyone in the prison. Gillette then offered a prayer, which brought Powell to tears.

After prayers and speeches by the other ministers, the condemned were brought to their feet and led, tiptoeing, to the ropes that hung in front of them. Pairs of soldiers pinioned their arms behind them, and when they had finished, the prisoners were coaxed to the forward edge of the platform. Mrs. Surratt swooned. "Please don't let me fall," she said. Sgt. William Kinney removed her bonnet and veil, and she gave the spectators one last, determined look.

The nooses were adjusted, and Atzerodt, trembling, addressed the crowd. "Gentlemen, take warn—" Choked with emotion, he could hardly get the words out. "Good bye, gentlemen, who are before me now. May we all meet in the other world." A light cotton hood was pulled down over his head, and after a pause, he was heard to mutter something. A final adjustment was made to his noose, and he cried out, "Don't choke me!" The others stood silently, bracing themselves for the drop.

Captain Rath stood in front of the gallows and motioned for all attendants to step away from the trapdoors. When everything looked to be in order, he raised his hands and brought them together three times in a clapping motion. On the third clap, the four soldiers beneath the platform knocked the supports out from under the prisoners. The doors fell with a loud slam, and four bodies jerked violently at the ends of their ropes.

Spectators were aghast as Lewis Powell twisted and writhed and struggled for life. He kicked for a full five minutes, and those standing close by could see the rope cutting deeply into his dark purple skin. Herold twitched for a moment, and wet himself. Atzerodt's stomach heaved in a brief convulsion. For Mary Surratt, death appeared instantaneous. Twenty minutes after the drop, all four were pronounced dead.

The death of Abraham Lincoln had been avenged.[44]

CODA

RIGHT UP UNTIL THE MOMENT OF HER EXECUTION, FEW
people imagined that Mary Surratt would actually be hanged. No
woman had ever been put to death on federal authority, and many people
expected President Johnson to commute her sentence at the last minute.
His refusal to do so was called into question almost immediately.

Soon after the execution, the public learned that a majority of the military commission had not actually wanted Mrs. Surratt to die. Five of its
members had signed a petition asking President Johnson to spare her life
"in consideration of [her] sex and age." The petition, attached to the findings and sentences, was taken to the White House by Judge Holt. Johnson
later claimed he never saw it.

The clemency petition was just one of several issues that arose in the
wake of the hanging. On July 11, the Washington *Constitutional Union*
published a series of startling revelations by John P. Brophy, a friend of
the Surratt family. Hours before the execution, Brophy had sworn out a
sixteen-point affidavit that called into question some of the evidence that
convicted Surratt. He claimed that Louis Weichmann had repudiated
some of his testimony, and had conceded that he had only testified against
Mrs. Surratt to avoid being prosecuted himself. According to Brophy,
Weichmann believed that Mary Surratt was innocent, and he was willing
to write President Johnson a letter to that effect.

The Brophy statement was explosive. It came in the midst of other revelations that, taken together, seemed to undermine the government's entire case against Mrs. Surratt. It was reported that Lewis Powell also believed she was innocent, and had told General Hartranft as much on the day of his death. Father Jacob Walter, who had accompanied Mrs. Surratt to the gallows, said that he would have proclaimed her innocence as well, but General James A. Hardie, to whom he had applied for a pass, threatened to bar him from the execution if he said anything. General Hardie denied saying anything of the sort.[1]

Mary Surratt's surviving co-defendants knew nothing about this, nor indeed what their own sentences were. After the hanging, Mudd, Arnold, O'Laughlen, and Spangler were allowed out into the prison yard, where they got their first look at the gallows and the four fresh mounds of earth nearby. "Day after day," said Arnold, "we confronted this scene, the scaffold remaining in all its hideousness, involuntarily causing the eye to wander and gaze upon the small mounds, marking its feast of death." Their own fates would remain a mystery to them until July 15, when Edwin Stanton finally authorized General Hartranft to inform them that they had all been convicted. But even the general did not know the whole story. They were going to be sent to prison in the Dry Tortugas, a desolate island outpost in the Gulf of Mexico.[2]

Untried detainees were being released in droves, and before long, the only prisoner left in the Old Capitol was Confederate Admiral Raphael Semmes. Jack and Will Garrett had been confined in the brig of the Washington Navy Yard. They had missed the planting season, but with the help of a wealthy cousin, they returned home with new farming implements and a pocketful of cash. Neighbors suspected that that was blood money. Their fellow Virginians, Bainbridge and Ruggles, had been sent to Johnson's Island Prison on May 16. The commandant there was not expecting any new prisoners. When he asked why they were there, they said that they really didn't know; they had not been formally accused of anything. So he told them to go back home. They did.[3]

For some of the people touched by the assassination, life would now take a different course. Asia Booth Clarke, who gave birth to twins in August, refused to grant her husband a divorce. She moved with him to England, where he made a name for himself as one of London's leading theater managers. Unknown to Sleeper Clarke, his wife was composing a memoir of her younger brother, to be published at some distant time, when the world could be more forgiving.

Junius Booth resumed his career on the stage and eventually became a manager in Boston, where he settled with his new wife, Agnes Perry. They raised four children together. June developed a long association with the Boston Theatre, and in his last years he ran a resort for actors at Manchester-by-the-Sea, Massachusetts. He died there in 1886.

Like most other people in the business, Junius assumed that his brother's act would hang like a pall on their industry and the people in it. But contrary to all predictions, 1866 was the best year yet for the stage. Business was at an all-time high, and some Broadway productions brought in more than double the previous year's receipts. Booth's former manager, William Wheatley, set a new box office record that year with *The Black Crook*, a spectacular musical featuring women in body suits that made them appear naked.

Edwin Booth had expected to watch from afar. After the assassination, Edwin vowed he would never return to the stage, but it wasn't long before he changed his mind. He was in debt and had spent too many months "chewing my heart in solitude." So on January 3, 1866, he returned to the New York stage, appearing as Hamlet to an enthusiastic reception. He knew that after his brother's crime, he would have to be more serious, better focused, and ever mindful of the fact that the family name would always make him a target. Indeed, that was literally the case on April 23, 1879, when a man named Mark Gray fired a .22-caliber bullet at Edwin as he stood on the stage of McVicker's Theatre in Chicago. The shot barely missed.

Edwin continued to act for another twenty-five years, and his ownership of three major playhouses made him one of the most successful figures in the entertainment world. There were many people who knew him only as the brother of John Wilkes Booth, and he sometimes used that to his advantage. In late 1871 he staged a spectacular production of *Julius Caesar*, and toward the end of his career, he played Brutus with increasing frequency. When he toured the South, it was probably his most popular role. As a biographer later observed, John Wilkes had not ruined his brother after all; he just made him more famous.

Edwin rarely spoke of his brother, but the subject did occasionally come up. In the summer of 1865, an admiralty court in Canada auctioned off John Wilkes's trunks, which were salvaged from the wreck of Patrick

Martin's schooner, the *Marie Victoria*. The trunks were filled with costumes, play books, and family papers, and despite the water damage, they brought a good sum of money at auction. Edwin obtained them through a third party, and kept them in the Winter Garden Theatre. They were destroyed when the building burned on March 23, 1867.[4]

Through much of his post-assassination career, Edwin worked with his friend and occasional manager, John T. Ford. Cleared of suspicion in the conspiracy, Ford continued to take an active interest in all the Booths, and in the crime that haunted them. He frequently wrote articles about the Lincoln conspiracy, and he even acted as Edwin's agent in procuring the body of John Wilkes for burial in the family lot at Baltimore's Green Mount Cemetery. The War Department had confiscated his theater right after the shooting, but they eventually paid him for it. By the end of 1865, they had converted it to a government office building. The conversion was poorly done, and on June 9, 1893, all three floors of the old building collapsed, killing twenty-two people. On the same day, Edwin Booth was being laid to rest in Cambridge, Massachusetts.

With Edwin's death, Joseph became the last surviving child of the elder Booth. Joe had received his medical degree after the war, and became an ear, nose, and throat specialist in New York. He married twice, but died childless in 1902.

The old Ford's Theatre building was repaired, and was used by various agencies until the Lincoln Museum was established there in 1930. In the 1960s, the National Park Service restored it to its 1865 appearance, and it is now an active theater as well as a museum. Like the Surratt House Museum and the Dr. Mudd House, it is dedicated to preserving the story of Booth's conspiracy and his flight from Washington.[5]

FOR MUDD, SPANGLER, ARNOLD, AND O'LAUGHLEN, life in the Dry Tortugas was unbelievably harsh. But it was not without hope. Only months after the so-called conspirators arrived at the prison, the U.S. Supreme Court rendered a decision that seemed closely related to their own situation. In the case of Lambdin P. Milligan and others, the Court declared that a military commission could not try civilians so long as the civilian courts were open and functioning. The decision was especially heartening to Mudd and his co-defendants because it so forcefully slapped down the argument John A. Bingham had made at their own trial: that of military necessity. "Martial law," said the Court, "cannot arise from a *threatened* invasion. The necessity must be actual and present; the invasion real, such as effectually closes the courts and deposes the civil administration." In writing the opinion, Justice David Davis, a friend and appointee of the late president, could not have been more emphatic:

"No doctrine involving more pernicious consequences, was ever invented by the wit of man, than that any of [the Constitution's] provisions can be suspended during any of the great exigencies of government. Such a doctrine leads to anarchy or despotism, [and] the theory of necessity on which it is based is false; for the government, within the Constitution, has all the powers granted to it which are necessary to preserve its existence."[6]

As the prisoners' appeals moved through the system, Joseph Holt continued to pursue his theory that Jefferson Davis was behind the assassination. Now he was not alone. A committee of the House of Representatives was also investigating Davis, and its chairman urged the Johnson administration to take some sort of action in the case. Joseph Holt assured the committee that the evidence against Davis was solid, since he had obtained it through Sandford Conover and eight other witnesses. But Conover had already been exposed as a fraud; Holt knew that, and the rest of the country was about to find out. The committee subpoenaed Holt's witnesses, and one of them balked. He admitted the whole case against Davis was a lie. It was built on perjury, concocted by Conover, and fed by him to a group of coached witnesses. Hauled before Congress, Conover (whose real name was Charles A. Dunham) repeated the story he had told at the conspiracy trial. For that, he was tried and convicted of perjury. Incredibly, the Judge Advocate General supported him, even in prison. When Dunham applied to the president for a pardon, Holt endorsed his application and praised him for his valuable service to the government.

The committee's response to all this was mixed. The majority report, written by George S. Boutwell, glossed over the perjury, but Andrew Jackson Rogers, of the Democratic minority, believed there was a conspiracy to frame Davis, and that Joseph Holt, knowingly or otherwise, was shielding the plotters. Ultimately it was a moot point. Jefferson Davis was released on bail in 1867, and was never tried. He was included in President Johnson's sweeping Christmas pardons of 1868.

Leniency was the last thing anyone expected of Andrew Johnson. But after becoming president, Johnson softened his stance on reconstruction, and that did not sit well with Radical Republicans. They led a drive to impeach Johnson, and by 1867, hundreds of Washington insiders had been sucked into the maelstrom. The movement even involved the hapless prisoners in the Dry Tortugas, who were asked to provide incriminating evidence against the president. They had none to give.

Though the process failed to produce the "high crimes and misdemeanors" needed to remove Johnson, it did unearth some interesting revelations about the Lincoln assassination. In particular, it resurrected the long-forgotten fact that John Wilkes Booth had kept a diary during his flight from Washington. Members of Congress were dismayed at the War Department's "suppression" of the diary, and they were stunned to learn, when it was finally shown to the public, that some of its pages were missing. Lafayette Baker swore the pages were there when he saw the book two years before.

Congressman Ben Butler was livid. "Who spoliated that book?" he thundered. "Who suppressed that evidence?" Butler noted that Booth himself had described the assassination as a last-minute contingency, and he wondered who had coaxed him to change his plan from kidnapping to murder. He was sure that those missing pages would reveal "who it was that could profit by assassination [and] who it was expected by Booth to succeed to Lincoln if the knife made a vacancy."[7]

Lafayette Baker was among those questioned in the impeachment hearings. Baker was still miffed at having to plead, just like everyone else, for a share in the reward for Booth's capture. He wasted no time bolstering his claim with the publication of *History of the United States Secret Service*. This imaginative memoir gave a bloated and often fictional account of Baker's wartime service. In it, he claimed that he had been the first to issue a reward offer, the first to distribute Booth's photograph, and the first to organize a systematic search for the fugitives. He said that Mary Surratt had confessed her guilt to him personally, and he claimed his detectives had found Booth precisely where he had told them to look.

Reviewers were not fooled, and most agreed with the critic who wrote, "We presume that Baker told more falsehoods in the interest of the government than any man living, and he proposes to make double profit out of them by recounting his success, like other heroes. . . ."

Baker's book had described the midnight burial of Booth as a top-secret affair that only he and a few men from the prison staff knew anything about. But when questioned in the impeachment hearings, he was forced to admit that he wasn't actually present when the burial took place, and he didn't even know where it had occurred. And though the detective vouched for the overall accuracy of his book, he admitted it was ghostwritten, and he had not actually read it. The admission must have embarrassed his many patrons in Congress, and one member was moved to remark, "It is doubtful whether he [Baker] has in any one thing told the truth, even by accident." Nevertheless, the memoirs of Lafayette Baker are repeated as truth, even to this day.[8]

Baker was one of hundreds involved in the fight for a portion of the reward money, and the vast majority of claimants had no prayer of success. An entire company of cavalrymen applied for a share, and based their claim on a fruitless search in the neighborhood of Surrattsville. William M. Runkel sought payment for the capture of Atzerodt, though all he had done was transcribe the prisoner's interrogation.

When the War Department announced it would receive claims, battle lines were instantly drawn between the soldiers who were present at Booth's final standoff and the detectives who had gone to the scene with them. Byron Baker and Edward Doherty both professed to have shown the fisherman William Rollins the photographs that would put them on Booth's trail. But Rollins himself did not support either claim; he said that it was Everton Conger who first questioned him. In response, Doherty accused Conger of confusing the witness, and he produced affidavits from several of his soldiers, who said that Doherty had questioned the fisherman at a time when Conger was sound asleep.

The fight was no less acrimonious when it moved to Congress. Members had chosen sides, and partisans spread stories that further muddied the picture of what had happened on April 26.[9]

On April 18, 1866, an army panel recommended that Edward Doherty be awarded $7,500 for leading the pursuit of Booth. They recommended that Conger and Baker be given $4,000 each, with a little less to Lafayette Baker. The remainder, they said, should be divided among the cavalry soldiers in proportion to rank. But a congressional committee urged that the lion's share—$17,500 each—be given to Lafayette Baker and Everton Conger instead. They recommended giving $5,000 to Byron Baker and half that amount to Lieutenant Doherty. Partisans of both sides nearly came to blows, and after some tense negotiations, they finally reached a compromise. On July 28, 1866, Congress passed an appropriation bill that followed U.S. Navy guidelines for the distribution of war prizes. They gave $15,000 to Everton Conger and $5,250 to Lieutenant Doherty. Lafayette Baker got only $3,750, and his cousin, Luther Byron Baker, received an even $3,000. Each of the soldiers was awarded $1,654.

Byron Baker was furious, and he vented his anger on the humble, unassuming Sgt. Boston Corbett. He had always resented the public's adulation of Corbett, and after the reward fight, he began a deliberate campaign to knock the sergeant off his pedestal. Baker began by spreading the story that the cavalry had been instructed to take Booth alive, and that Corbett shot him in violation of those orders. The more Baker told the story, the more elaborate it became. He claimed that Everton Conger was so incensed, he had threatened to send Corbett back to Washington in irons (which, in any event, they didn't have). That seemed to have no effect on Corbett's reputation, so Baker changed tack, and insinuated that Booth might actually have shot himself. Even though the trajectory of the bullet ruled out suicide, many people believed Baker's revision, and it is even accepted to a large degree today. It survives in spite of Everton Conger's sworn statement, which said that Corbett had fired the shot. "[He] had no orders either to fire or not to fire," said Conger. "The sergeant told me 'I went to the barn, looked through a crack, saw Booth coming towards the door, sighted at his body, and fired.' He said he was afraid Booth would shoot somebody or get away."[10]

Lafayette Baker, disgraced and stripped of his power, died in 1868. Though he left a small estate, his real legacy was the cloud of disinformation that has perhaps forever confused what really happened in 1865. No other figure in this story came to so ignominious an end as the fabled National Detective chief.

Joseph Holt and David Hunter remained in government service for many years, and they both retired late in life. The Mary Surratt controversy never went away, and Judge Holt spent the rest of his life fending off criticism. In 1873, Andrew Johnson accused him of concealing the clemency petition from him, and Holt responded indignantly with a letter campaign and a published "vindication" in pamphlet form. He also assured the public that Mary Surratt had not been manacled, that her counsel had not been driven away, and that witnesses had not been intimidated.

As Father Walter said, Mary Surratt had become "a kind of martyr," and nobody wanted to appear insensitive to her family and defenders. But officially, the government conceded no wrongdoing in her prosecution. Joseph Holt would always consider her "the master spirit among them all," and detectives who had worked her case agreed with Andrew Johnson, who said that Mrs. Surratt had "kept the nest that hatched the egg." In fact, official animosity carried over to the next generation; when a young chemist married Anna Surratt in 1869, he was summarily dismissed from his job in the government.[11]

EDWIN STANTON WAS APPOINTED to the U.S. Supreme Court in 1869, but died before assuming office. Partisans of Mrs. Surratt would falsely claim that he had slit his own throat. Stanton's colleague in the Cabinet, William H. Seward, returned to work in October 1865, but his wounds never fully healed. He died in 1872, leaving the purchase of Alaska—"Seward's Folly"—as his most famous achievement. His son Frederick recovered from Powell's attack and lived productively for another fifty years minus one day. Private George Foster Robinson, the nurse who struggled to protect the Sewards, was commissioned an officer in the army. In 1871, the Treasury Department struck a medal to commemorate his heroic conduct on the night of April 14.

On July 5, 1865, President Johnson created the United States Secret Service, and he appointed William P. Wood as its first chief. The agency would one day be responsible for protecting the president, but not until 1901, after three of them had been assassinated.

Col. Henry H. Wells served a term as military governor of Virginia, then set up a private law practice in Washington. Col. Henry S. Olcott returned to New York and founded the Theosophical Society. By the time of his death in 1907, he was known as one of the world's great religious leaders.

While most members of the military commission returned to the field as professional soldiers, Lew Wallace remained in uniform for just one more assignment. He served as president of the military commission that tried and condemned Henry Wirz, the commandant of Andersonville prison. After practicing law for a number of years in Indiana, Wallace was appointed to serve as the territorial governor of New Mexico, and later as ambassador to Turkey. He was best known as a writer, and his most famous work is the novel *Ben-Hur*.

Thomas M. Harris was the only member of the Hunter commission to write a book about the case. By the time *The Assassination of Abraham Lincoln* was published in 1892, a large segment of the public had become convinced that Mary Surratt was a victim of "judicial murder," and Harris was quite unprepared for the wave of attacks that greeted his book. In response, he lashed out at Mrs. Surratt's partisans, and at Catholics in general. He claimed that Pope Pius IX had been responsible for Lincoln's death, and asserted the common belief that Booth and all of his conspirators were Roman Catholics. In truth, only Mudd and the Surratts were of the faith. But even with its false underpinnings, the theory of papal involvement persisted. The last of several books on the subject was published in 1963.[12]

Mary Todd Lincoln did not leave the White House until May 22, and her subsequent life is a tale of debts, tragedy, and personal estrangement. For a time she lived beyond her means, and sold off her old clothes to cover the costs of an extravagant lifestyle. She took her young son Tad to Germany for a few years, and not long after their return in 1871, Tad died of pleurisy. He was only sixteen. Consumed with grief and increasingly eccentric in her behavior, Mrs. Lincoln grew estranged from her surviving son, Robert. At his instigation, she was put on trial for insanity. Committed to a private sanitarium, she was released after a second trial, then moved to France. When she returned in 1881, she was broken in health and spirit. She died the following year in Springfield, Illinois.

Mrs. Lincoln was still abroad when a ghoulish attempt was made to steal her husband's remains. A couple of career criminals devised a plan to remove the president's coffin from the still-unfinished tomb in Springfield and leave behind a demand for $200,000 in ransom and the release of a friend from prison. They made their move on the night of November 7, 1876, unaware that an associate had tipped off the government. Federal agents swarmed the tomb, and shots were fired. In the confusion, the grave robbers escaped. Though they were eventually caught, they could be tried only for damaging the outer coffin, valued at $75. Each was convicted and sentenced to a year in jail.[13]

In 1878, a Chicago newspaper broke the startling news that Robert Todd Lincoln and John Wilkes Booth had competed for the affections of "Bessie" Hale. The paper offered the opinion that this rivalry assigned "a new motive for Booth's action in regard to President Lincoln." A subsequent issue of the paper printed a denial of the story by Robert himself—which was followed, in turn, by a disavowal of the denial. Though Robert had known Lucy Hale, there was nothing to suggest anything more serious than a friendship.

Robert later served as secretary of war under three presidents. He stood by the deathbed of President Garfield in 1881, and of President McKinley in 1901. Both had been assassinated.

Miss Hale eventually married William Eaton Chandler, who became a senator from New Hampshire and later secretary of the navy. He and Lucy had a son and, apparently, a dismal life together. She died in 1915.[14]

DR. LUKE PRYOR BLACKBURN, who had been accused of waging germ warfare, was elected governor of Kentucky in 1879. During his brief term in office, he created the state's university and reformed its prison system.

Most minor suspects in the assassination faded into obscurity, but Dr. Francis Tumblety, who had been arrested as a possible associate of David Herold's, resurfaced in London years later as a prime suspect in the Jack the Ripper killings. Press coverage of his case brought to light some chilling details, such as Tumblety's violent hatred for women and his gruesome collection of wombs that he kept in jars. Unfortunately, those stories could all be traced back to one Charles A. Dunham, the convicted perjurer who once went by the name of Sandford Conover.[15]

Boston Corbett was a more recognizable figure than Dunham. The little sergeant became a Methodist minister in New Jersey, then moved after a few years to Cloud County, Kansas. Death threats followed him wherever he went, and by the mid-1880s, Corbett had become increasingly paranoid and obsessed with protecting himself from "Booth's avengers." His neighbors eventually got rid of him by securing his appointment as assistant doorkeeper to the state legislature. His conduct in Topeka was no less erratic. On February 15, 1887, Corbett "adjourned" the House at gunpoint. He was taken into custody, tried, and committed to an institution for life. He escaped after only a few months, and seemingly vanished without a trace. Years later, someone tried to draw on Corbett's pension, but he proved to be an impostor and was prosecuted. The real Corbett never reappeared.

Of all those touched by the assassination, none had a more tragic story than Henry Rathbone and Clara Harris, the young couple who accompanied the Lincolns on that fateful night. Major Rathbone resigned from the army in 1867 and married Clara a few days later. Like Boston Corbett, he became increasingly erratic over the years, and eventually he moved with Clara and their three children to Hanover, Germany. On the night of December 23, 1883, Rathbone began acting strangely. He tried to enter his children's room, but Clara, sensing trouble, ordered their nurse to lock them in their bedroom. Henry followed his wife into their own room, pulled out a revolver, and shot her three times in the chest. He then stabbed her to death, and, turning the knife on himself, inflicted five chest wounds that nearly ended his own life. He was declared criminally insane, and spent the rest of his life at St. Michael's asylum in Hildesheim.[16]

IN 1867, YELLOW FEVER STRUCK the prison in the Dry Tortugas. Nearly everyone in the prison became infected. Dozens of guards perished, but the disease claimed only two prisoners. One of them was Mike O'Laughlen, who died on September 23. With so many officers laid up, Dr. Mudd might have escaped from the island. He had tried unsuccessfully to do just that in 1865, but declined to try it again. The prison doctor had died, and Mudd was the only physician left on the fort. In spite of his own illness, he cared for the sick and dying until another doctor could be sent from Key West. His actions were credited with slowing the spread of the disease and perhaps saving many lives. In gratitude, the surviving men of the garrison signed a petition urging the president to pardon him.

Unfortunately for Dr. Mudd, a pardon was out of the question. Andrew Johnson was still under siege in Washington. Mudd's only hope lay in the appeal process. In September 1868, his petition for a writ of habeas corpus reached the U.S. District Court at Key West, and Judge Thomas J. Boynton dismissed it out of hand. Mudd's attorney tried to argue that the Supreme Court's *Milligan* decision invalidated military trials of civilians. And even if it didn't, the prisoner was still entitled to clemency under one of President Johnson's amnesty proclamations.

Judge Boynton slapped down both arguments, claiming that neither *Milligan* nor the pardon applied in Mudd's case because the assassination was a military crime. "It was not Mr. Lincoln who was assassinated," said the judge, "but the commander-in-chief of the Army for military reasons. I find no difficulty therefore in classing the offense as a military one, and with this opinion arrive at the necessary conclusion that the proper tribunal for the trial of those engaged in it was a military one."

This decision was actually based on the Supreme Court's *minority* (and concurring) opinion in the *Milligan* case, and not on the opinion that became law. Had Boynton actually read the arguments in that case, he could not have missed the fact that it was Lambdin P. Milligan who had committed a military crime—namely, to raise an armed force for the purpose of opposing United States troops. But Booth's plot was altogether different. As Joseph Holt argued in the Lincoln conspiracy trial, "The murder of the President of the United States, as alleged and shown, *was pre-eminently a political assassination.* Disloyalty to the Government was its sole, its only inspiration."

So Judge Boynton got it backward. The Supreme Court could hardly have rendered its *Milligan* decision without considering how it would affect the more famous case of Dr. Mudd. They could easily have drawn a distinction between the two cases, but they pointedly chose not to do so.

Disheartened, Mudd and his family continued to press for a pardon, which finally came on February 8, 1869. Spangler and Arnold were pardoned a month later, on the last full day of Andrew Johnson's term.[17]

John Surratt had already been in and out of the system by then. While Mudd and the others sweltered in the Dry Tortugas, Surratt embarked on an odyssey that took him halfway around the world. On the night of the assassination, he was in Elmira, New York, to make a sketch of the prison camp there for Gen. Edwin G. Lee. The following morning, he learned of the president's death, and immediately headed north to Montreal. He hid for a couple of months in a Catholic rectory, then left for England and the Continent. Eventually he made his way to the Papal States, then at war with the Kingdom of Italy. He enlisted in Company C, 3rd Regiment of the Papal Zouaves, and ran into an old Maryland acquaintance who served in the same regiment. Henry B. Ste. Marie recognized Surratt and promptly reported his whereabouts to the State Department. They showed little interest, but the Pope ordered Surratt's arrest on his own authority. Before the prisoner could be transported to a secure jail, he escaped. Eventually, American officials traced his movements through Naples to a ship bound for Egypt. They followed the vessel to Alexandria, and when it arrived on November 23, 1866, Surratt was taken into custody.[18]

Returned to Washington, John Surratt was charged with the murder of Abraham Lincoln and was held over for trial in a civilian court. The first witnesses took the stand on June 17, 1867. To support the charge, prosecutors had to show that Surratt was actually at the scene of the crime, or was "constructively present" to render assistance when the shooting took place. For this, they offered the testimony of Sergeants Robert H. Cooper and Joseph H. Dye, who claimed they saw Surratt at Ford's Theatre, calling out the time, on the evening of April 14. The defense tried to show that Cooper and Dye were mistaken, and that Surratt could not have been there that night. He had been in Montreal when he sent his cousin a letter on the twelfth, and because of poor travel conditions, he couldn't possibly have made it to the capital two days later.

The trial had plenty of tense moments, especially when lawyers or witnesses referred to the case of Mary Surratt. Her name brought out powerful emotions from both sides, and her memory haunted every day of her son's trial. Defense attorneys made sure of that.

In some ways, John Surratt's trial echoed that of his mother. It was really the same case, with many of the same witnesses, but tried under different rules. Lou Weichmann was back, and this time, the defense brought a battery of witnesses to impeach his credibility. And he was not the only one under fire. Defense attorneys believed that some witnesses had been coerced by the threat of prosecution. Sgt. Joseph Dye, for example, had been indicted for passing counterfeit money, and somehow managed to get charges dropped just after he testified against Surratt. And William E. Cleaver had had an even greater threat hanging over him. Cleaver once owned a stable where Surratt kept his horse, and prosecutors wanted him to testify about incriminating statements he had heard the defendant make. But Cleaver had just been convicted of the rape and killing of a young Washington woman, and Judge George P. Fisher—the same man who presided over John Surratt's trial—had denied his motion for an appeal. But only two days before the Surratt trial was set to begin, Fisher changed his mind. He allowed Cleaver to appear as a witness, and he denied that the government had offered leniency in exchange for testimony. But that was untrue. It subsequently developed that Congressman James Ashley, a political ally of Joseph Holt, had personally told Cleaver that "if the evidence [he gave] was of value he [Cleaver] would undoubtedly be released." He was.[19]

Certainly, witnesses were paid, pressured, and otherwise induced to bend their testimony, and Judge Holt was responsible for at least some of that. But the jurors were not easily fooled, and Holt's behind-the-scenes maneuvering had little effect on the outcome of the trial. The rule of law predominated, and it brought about an interesting twist that would never have occurred in 1865.

In common law, a man could not be convicted solely on the word of a cohort. So defense attorney Richard Merrick tried to offer evidence that Louis Weichmann had confessed to spying for the Confederacy. Therefore, he argued, anything Weichmann said on the stand "was the testimony of an accomplice, seeking to save his own life by the betrayal of his associates." But Judge Fisher ruled against the defense—in a way. He said that Weichmann was not an accomplice in the assassination unless the defense could prove that the Confederacy, with whom he was allegedly involved, was a principal to that crime. He did not think they could prove any such thing.

Joseph Holt must have been aghast. Two years before, he had prosecuted Mary Surratt and seven others on the theory that their plot and the Confederate government were inseparable. But now, Judge Fisher spoke as if the whole idea were preposterous. He ruled that the Confederate link was irrelevant unless the *defense* could prove the Davis government was involved. They were not inclined to try.

Three hundred witnesses testified in all, but those who tipped the balance were the ones who placed Surratt in Elmira on the morning of April 15. If their testimony was correct, the prosecution would need to shore up its claim that the defendant could have been in upstate New York on Saturday morning when he had just been in Washington the night before. They were prepared to do that through the testimony of five witnesses who had seen Surratt at various stages of the journey. But just before the first of these was scheduled to appear, he lost his nerve and admitted that he and the other four had all been coached. The story was leaked to the *New York Herald,* and none of the witnesses ever appeared.

So the prosecution left much unexplained. After seventy-three hours of deliberation, the jury informed Judge Fisher that they were deadlocked at eight votes to four, with the majority favoring acquittal. The judge declared a mistrial, and the prisoner was taken back to his cell. As the lawyers gathered up their papers, Judge Fisher stunned them all by accusing the lead defense attorney of disreputable conduct. He said that Joseph H. Bradley, Sr., had recently handed him a note that seemed to be a challenge to a duel. Though Bradley denied doing anything of the sort, Fisher summarily disbarred him.

The jury's deadlock came as no surprise to prosecutors, who said that Washington jurors were too pro-Southern to convict Surratt. They lobbied for new laws that would allow a change of venue, but Congress failed to pass the necessary legislation. In truth, the government's real problem was not with the jury, but with the evidence. Even the district attorney himself didn't seem to believe that Surratt had been in Washington on the night of the shooting. In his summation, Edward Carrington told the jury that Surratt's whereabouts really didn't matter. Since the defendant had left

Montreal for the States when Booth summoned him, "his obedience to the order . . . to aid in the unlawful conspiracy" was enough to convict.

Carrington was not prepared to argue that again. On June 18, 1868, he presented another indictment against Surratt, charging him with "aiding the rebellion." To everyone's surprise, Judge Andrew Wylie (and not the attorneys) noticed that the statute of limitations had already run out on this particular crime. He dismissed the indictment, and the case was finished. The government's appeal was denied, and on November 5, 1868, Edward Carrington tried one last time to indict Surratt. The grand jury took no action, and the government gave up. A few days later the prisoner was released.[20]

IN THE SPRING OF 1869, Arnold, Mudd, and Spangler arrived back home in Maryland. Dr. Mudd returned to his farm, his family, and his medical practice. Sam Arnold moved into his father's house in Baltimore. Ned Spangler took a job at the Holliday Street Theatre. When the theater burned down in 1873, Spangler left Baltimore and headed for Charles County, where he went to work for Dr. Mudd. He died at the Mudd farm on February 7, 1875. Not long afterward, the doctor was looking for something in Spangler's tool chest, and he found a manuscript in Ned's own hand, detailing all he knew of the circumstances that had brought him so much trouble.

Many years later, a Boston newspaper inadvertently revealed the true source of Spangler's difficulty. It published an interview with Harry Hawk, the actor who was on stage when Booth fired the shot. Dazed and shaken, Hawk had frozen up in fear when the crowd pressed in on him. Someone demanded to know who had shot the president, and Hawk blurted out, "I won't tell. There'll be a terrible uproar, and I want to keep out of any trouble." Jake Rittersback heard those words, but in the confusion of the moment, he attributed them to his fellow stagehand. He repeated them to authorities, and Ned Spangler became a suspect in the conspiracy.

Dr. Mudd survived Spangler by eight years. He died in 1883 after going out on a house call and getting caught in a winter storm. He lies in the cemetery of St. Mary's Church, just a few paces from the spot where he and Booth first met in 1864.

Sam Arnold worked as a butcher in Baltimore, and in the 1880s he moved to the village of Friendship, Maryland, to manage the farm of an old friend. He wrote his life story, and in 1902 the Baltimore *American* published it in serial form. Arnold died on September 21, 1906, and was buried in Baltimore's Green Mount Cemetery. By then Mike O'Laughlen's remains had been transferred up from the Dry Tortugas, and had been buried there as well.[21]

THE OLD WASHINGTON PENITENTIARY was razed in 1867, and the remains of Powell, Atzerodt, Herold, and Mrs. Surratt were reburied under the floor of a warehouse at the Washington Arsenal. The bodies of Booth and Henry Wirz, the commandant of Andersonville prison, were placed beside them. In February 1869, Andrew Johnson released the bodies to their respective families for burial elsewhere.

Mary Surratt now lies in Mt. Olivet Cemetery, under a gravestone with the simple inscription "Mrs. Surratt." David Herold was removed to his family lot in Congressional Cemetery, and shares a grave with his sister Jane. George Atzerodt was buried under an assumed name in St. Paul's Lutheran Cemetery in Baltimore.

Booth's remains were taken to Baltimore, where they were identified by friends and family, then placed in a vault at Green Mount Cemetery. In June 1869, they were reinterred in the family lot, near a large monument to the elder Booth.

For 120 years Lewis Powell's final resting place was a mystery. In 1869, Powell's remains were taken up from the arsenal and buried in Washington's Holmead Cemetery. But the cemetery was disbanded a short time later, and no further record of their whereabouts survived. Then, in 1993, a government anthropologist located what appeared to be Powell's skull in the collections of the Smithsonian Institution. Within months the FBI laboratory confirmed the identification, and on November 11, 1994, Lewis Powell's remains were laid to rest in the town of Geneva, Florida. His biographer, Betty Ownsbey, gave a brief and dignified eulogy, and the present writer helped lower the remains into the grave.[22]

John Surratt was the last of Booth's cohorts. After his release in 1868, Surratt hurried off on a six-month vacation in South America. On his return, he worked as a commission merchant in Baltimore, then as a teacher in Rockville. In 1870, he began a series of lectures in which he admitted to criminal conduct. Worse yet, he criticized those who still had the power to reinstate the charges against him. "Never in my life did I come across a more stupid set of detectives than those generally employed by the U.S. Government," he told a Maryland audience. "They seemed to have no idea whatever how to search men." His cockiness caught up with him, and on December 29, 1870, Surratt was arrested in Richmond, accused of selling tobacco, the year before, without a license. He was never indicted, but his arrest ended his lecture tour.

From that time on, Surratt rarely spoke about the case. He married a relative of Francis Scott Key, raised a large family, and settled in Baltimore, where he worked as an auditor for the Old Bay Line. He died in April 1916.[23]

In time, eyewitnesses would look back on the case, recounting in vivid detail what had transpired in 1865. Their memories transformed the story, and over the years, Booth's rapid stride across the stage became a limp or a hop. The president became more visible in his rocking chair, and eyewitnesses themselves became more heroic and played a bigger role in the night's events.

Even the most conscientious witness could not help skewing the story with outlandish claims. Dr. Charles A. Leale recalled giving the president artificial respiration, years before the procedure had been invented. Samuel H. Beckwith said that his boss, General Grant, had declined the Lincolns' theater invitation because he had heard that the president was going to be kidnapped. Walt Whitman gave a richly detailed account of the shooting, as if he had been there himself. Even A. C. Richards got into the act. In the late 1870s, Richards, the former police superintendent, falsely claimed to have been present in Ford's Theatre when the shooting occurred.[24]

Eyewitness mistakes were compounded by deliberate falsehoods, and eventually it became almost impossible to separate fact from fiction. In 1928, a New Jersey woman recounted her own vivid recollection of the shooting, in which Booth's leg snapped on landing and protruded through his boot, sending a spray of blood across the audience. With stories such as hers in the air, it is not hard to understand why people came to believe the outrageous claims of Otto Eisenschiml. In 1937, Eisenschiml implied that Edwin Stanton was behind the murder. His book *Why Was Lincoln Murdered?* set forth one of the great conspiracy theories of the twentieth century, but it was built on a combination of spotty research, false assumptions, and leading questions. Nevertheless, some of his conclusions are still repeated as fact: for example, that all the bridges out of Washington were closed *but one;* that all of the city's telegraph lines mysteriously shut down that night; and that Stanton did all he could to see that the president would not be properly guarded.

More thorough research would have dispelled almost all of Eisenschiml's claims, but even the most exhaustive study leaves the question of security open to argument. The issue was never brought up in 1865, and at the time, nobody expressed surprise that Abraham Lincoln had gone out in public with no protection. But the assassination of James A. Garfield in 1881 brought a surge of interest in the subject of presidential security. For friends and associates of Mr. Lincoln, the interest became retroactive, and in time, several men came forward to tell their stories of life as a "bodyguard" and confidant of the late president. These accounts are no different from other long-ago memories—inaccurate, unlikely, and impossible to confirm—but they left the indelible impression that President Lincoln was betrayed by a lapse in the judgment of one of his guards.

In fact, Abraham Lincoln had no bodyguards in the modern sense. It was the messenger Charles Forbes who had allowed Booth into the box, and consequently Mrs. Lincoln held Forbes responsible for the president's death. To deflect the blame, Forbes filed a formal complaint against a White House guard, patrolman John F. Parker, and charged him with leaving his post outside the president's box to have a drink. Parker was tried and acquitted.

Though testimony at the hearing was not recorded, we can easily imagine why Parker was not found guilty. He had been assigned to the White House on detached service to the commissioner of public buildings, and was paid out of the Interior Department budget to protect the building and its furnishings—*not the president*. Mr. Lincoln had never been guarded in the theater before, and if anyone had suggested he be accompanied by guards on Good Friday, he undoubtedly would have rejected the idea.[25]

Eisenschiml may have been wrong, but at least he was honest. The same could not be said for a Memphis lawyer named Finis L. Bates. In 1907, Bates wrote a bestseller called *The Escape and Suicide of John Wilkes Booth* in which he claimed that Lincoln's assassin lived in Granbury, Texas, in the 1870s, and ultimately committed suicide, under the name of David E. George, at Enid, Oklahoma. This was one of many Booth escape legends, but it was the best known by far. Bates's story was featured in an episode of the *Unsolved Mysteries* television show, and it inspired a 1995 lawsuit aimed at digging up the remains in the Booth lot at Green Mount Cemetery.

Though Booth's relatives consented to the exhumation, the cemetery refused to permit it, and the matter ended up the Baltimore County Circuit Court. Green Mount presented five days of testimony about the shooting at Garrett's farm, and about the two separate identifications of the man who was killed there. Historians pointed out that the corpse examined on the *Montauk* had Booth's most distinctive features: a scar on the back of his neck and a "J.W.B." tattoo on his left hand. And the assassin's family had identified the remains to their own satisfaction in 1869.

Ultimately, what Judge Joseph H. H. Kaplan found most persuasive was the testimony showing that the whole dispute was rooted in the work of Finis Bates, and that *The Escape and Suicide* was filled with misquoted sources, doctored affidavits, retouched photographs, and appallingly poor research. And since the only test being sought (photographic superimposition) was not likely to resolve the issue, Kaplan ruled that the grave should not be disturbed.[26]

Worldwide coverage of the exhumation hearings demonstrated that John Wilkes Booth could still excite the public's interest 130 years after his death. There is something captivating about Booth as a historical character. He was a romantic villain—a strange mix that defies understanding but explains, in a way, why his story has inspired so many fanciful legends; why the ladies of Baltimore paid special attention to his grave on Decoration Day; and why his autograph is worth more today than that of his illustrious victim. More than anyone has recognized, the assassin of Abraham Lincoln reflected the complexities of a rapidly changing time. He was the Byronic hero, the tyrant-slayer of the past, resisting the advent of a new, uncertain time. In an age of sharply divided values, he was seen as both extraordinarily good and unspeakably evil.[27]

Booth lived in a violent time, when distrust was rampant and words alone could send a man to jail, or even to his death. Yet in the midst of unprecedented paranoia, he and his followers conspired against the government, undetected, for the better part of a year. Their survival, in spite of the odds, speaks more about its leader than any anecdote, memoir, or theatrical review. Booth shielded himself with a second conspiracy—one made of smoke and mirrors. Seen from within, it was an inducement to join and a hedge against breaking ranks. To the rest of the world, it was a genuine threat to free government, as real and as dangerous as one's own fears could make it. To Booth himself, it was a tool to cast suspicion on guilty and innocent alike.

It was this shadow conspiracy that made the real plot work. Booth wanted the world to believe that John Mathews, Sam Chester, John Sleeper Clarke, and others had a hand in plotting the president's death. But in truth, their guilt was a false impression created by the circumstances Booth orchestrated: the horseback ride that made Mathews seem to be scouting an escape route; the request to hire Sam Chester to work at Ford's Theatre; the letters left in Sleeper Clarke's safe.

Walter S. Cox, the attorney for Mike O'Laughlen, understood what Booth was doing, and he tried to call it to the attention of the military commission. In his closing argument, Cox urged the officers to look closely at Booth's methods, and to be sure they did not convict one man for something another man had done. If they allowed such a thing to happen, he said, "it would be in the power of any man to ruin another simply by sending him a telegram." Lou Weichmann knew that as well as anyone. It was Weichmann who received Booth's instructions to "tell John to telegraph number and street at once," and who innocently waved it around the office just to prove his friendship with a famous man. It was Weichmann who showed up at meetings, drove the carriage, and wrote incriminating notes in his own hand whenever Booth or the Surratts asked him to. Though all of these acts appeared to implicate him, John Surratt later admitted that Weichmann was not actually involved in the plot. Since Weichmann could neither ride nor shoot, they would not let him join.

The hurt of betraying Mrs. Surratt stayed with Weichmann for the rest of his days. Soon after the conspiracy trial, he moved to Philadelphia and was given a government job. He married, but then left his wife and moved to Anderson, Indiana, where he ran a business school. For many years he worked on his memoirs, but they were not published until 1975, seventy-three years after his death.

In the National Archives are two letters—both addressed to Weichmann—that sum up the nature of the evidence against him. One is the intimate and incriminating letter from "Clara," the apparent spy, and the other is from Father J. B. Menu, of St. Charles College. The Clara letter lays bare some of Weichmann's most intimate secrets, and implies he knew a great deal about Surratt's Confederate business. The letter from Father Menu came in response to an urgent and disturbing letter that Weichmann had written him on March 17, the day of the so-called kidnap attempt. Since Weichmann wrote of Mary Surratt "as if she were a rebel," Father Menu wanted to know what prompted his remarks.

Certainly, Weichmann would not have wanted to save these documents. If the conspirators had seen the priest's letter, they would have known how close Weichmann had come to reporting the plot. If detectives had found the other, they would surely have thought he was one of Booth's conspirators. So it is hard to imagine why Lou Weichmann even kept them in the first place. The answer is simple: he didn't. Those letters were found not among *his* papers, but among Booth's. They had been intercepted, and the addressee himself may never have known they existed.

Weichmann was not the only person who figured out that he was being manipulated. When Dr. Mudd introduced Booth to Surratt (with Weichmann, a stranger, standing by in a federal uniform), the event was carefully scripted. Indeed, Booth and Surratt probably knew each other already. But by the time Mudd realized it, he was on a ship bound for the Dry Tortugas. As he and his fellow prisoners talked over their plight, Mudd must have told them that Booth had arranged to run into him in Washington, as if by accident. But someone on the ship was listening, and however Mudd chose to describe the incident, his words came out a little differently by the time they reached Judge Holt. What was originally meant to describe a "setup" on Booth's part became a meeting "by appointment" on the part of all involved. On August 22, Captain George W. Dutton, who had escorted the prisoners to the Tortugas, told Holt that Mudd had made a full confession. Holt apparently believed it, and he forwarded Dutton's statement to Henry Burnett, who appended it to the official trial record. He did not print Mudd's heated denial.

Shortly after Dr. Mudd went off to prison, General David Hunter summed up his case this way: "The Court never believed that Dr. Mudd knew anything about Booth's designs. Booth made him a tool as he had done with others. Dr. Mudd was the victim of his own timidity. Had he acknowledged to the soldiers who he saw in search of Booth (the day after the assassination) that Booth had got his leg set at his house and went off, and had he, *like a man,* come out and said he knew Booth, instead of flatly denying it to the Court, he would have had little trouble."[28]

THERE WAS ONE MORE PERSON in Washington who knew from experience that with John Wilkes Booth, not everything was as it seemed. President Andrew Johnson had been compromised by a small card left in his hotel mailbox, and the false impression it gave of intimacy with Booth would haunt him for the rest of his career. So when Sarah Frances Mudd petitioned the president for her husband's release, Johnson could sympathize. He wrote out the text of Mudd's pardon, and made a special point of calling attention to the doubts he now had about the doctor's guilt.

For some of Mudd's descendants, a pardon was not good enough. In the 1920s, the doctor's grandson, Richard D. Mudd, began a seventy-five-year campaign to clear his family name. In 1992, he was granted a hearing by the Army Board for the Correction of Military Records. The five-judge panel reviewed the case and decided that Dr. Samuel A. Mudd's trial by military commission had indeed been illegal. But under intense lobbying, the secretary of the army refused to endorse the board's findings, and a long series of suits and motions followed. In 2001, a federal appellate court ruled that the army board had no jurisdiction in Mudd's case, since it could only correct "military records." An appeal was planned, but the attorney handling the case missed a filing deadline, and the last legal battle of the Lincoln conspiracy died in its sleep.

It was a cruel irony. Samuel Mudd had always argued that as a civilian, he should not have been tried in a military court. But his first appeal was rejected because the crime was military, and the last was rejected because the appellant was not.

Just after Dr. Mudd's death in 1883, one of his attorneys, Frederick Stone, granted an interview to George Alfred Townsend, and he supposedly said this of his former client:

"The court very nearly hanged Dr. Mudd. His prevarications were painful; he had given his whole case away by not trusting even his counsel or neighbors or kinfolks. . . . He denied knowing Booth when he knew him well. He was undoubtedly [an] accessory to the abduction plot [and] had even been intimate with Booth."

This was a shocking breach of ethics, and one cannot help wondering what possessed Stone to betray Dr. Mudd in this way. The answer may lie in the revelations of Richard M. Smoot, who, after the turn of the century, tried to set the record straight on the part he played in Booth's conspiracy. Smoot named others who were involved in the plot. Among those identified was one Judge Stone, who had secured the loan that allowed John Surratt to purchase a boat for the capture plan. Soon after the assassination, he said, Surratt defaulted on the payments, and Stone himself made good on the loan. This "Judge Stone" was the same man who jumped, uninvited, into Dr. Mudd's defense, and to whom the ungrateful doctor refused to admit his guilt. Did Stone join the defense to keep an eye on Mudd, lest

he should try to save himself by implicating his neighbors? Were those remarks to Townsend intended as a preemptive move just in case Mudd had
left behind a statement, the way Spangler did? It is intriguing to think that
the Bureau of Military Justice may have conducted a trial under the tight-
est security, unaware that another conspirator sat in the courtroom, free to
leave at any time.[29]

Like everything else in this case, it is hard to be certain where the truth
lies. Booth made certain of that. He spent months crafting the persona he
wanted the world to see—a heroic figure in the ancient mold. But his
boasts and posturing left him in a real bind: by April 14, all he could do was
sacrifice himself for the Cause, or accept the fact that his Unionist friends
had been right about him all along—that he was a hotheaded loser who
only talked while others gave their lives. Booth could not bear the thought
of life as a former actor, a failed investor, or a pale shadow of his brother
Edwin. His choice was made.

The list of Booth's victims is long and wide-ranging. It includes Frances
and Fanny Seward, whose horrific experience contributed to their early
deaths; Lucy Quesenberry, who was traumatized by her mother's arrest, and
died soon after; Henry Rathbone, who was tormented by self-reproach, and
his wife, Clara, whom he killed; the two soldiers who died in the president's funeral; the eighty-seven men who drowned while searching for
Booth; and the countless others who were killed for rejoicing or for looking a little too much like the assassin. To those, we should add the victims
of guilt by insinuation—the people Booth destroyed to keep his plot safe
from detection.

If Booth intended to make himself a modern Brutus, he succeeded too
well. Like the assassination of Julius Caesar, the killing of Lincoln did not
accomplish the conspirators' aims. It only martyred the victim, elevating
him to secular sainthood and leading ultimately to the disillusionment and
death of the assassin. Though some regarded Booth as a hero, the vast majority of people, both North and South, were horrified at what he had
done. It embarrassed the South and forced many of its leading citizens to
halt their support for continuing the war, lest they appear to endorse the
assassin's brand of warfare. Thus the "lasting condemnation of the North"
of which Booth wrote was turned on its head.

Booth immortalized himself by staging one of history's greatest dra-
mas. In the process, he accomplished what every actor aspires to do: he
made us all wonder where the play ended and reality began.

BOOTH'S DIARY

Ti Amo
April 13–14 Friday the Ides[1]

Until today nothing was ever *thought* of sacrificing to our country's wrongs. For six months we had worked to capture. But our cause being almost lost, something decisive & great must be done. But its failure was owing to others, who did not strike for their country with a heart. I struck boldly and not as the papers say. I walked with a firm step through a thousand of his friends, was stopped, but pushed on. A Col. was at his side. I shouted Sic semper *before* I fired. In jumping broke my leg. I passed all his pickets, rode sixty miles that night, with the bone of my leg tearing the flesh at every jump. I can never repent it, though we hated to kill; Our country owed all her troubles to him, and God simply made me the instrument of his punishment. The country is not what it *was*. This forced union is not what *I* have loved. I care not what becomes of me. I have no desire to out-live my country. This night (before the deed), I wrote a long article and left it for one of the Editors of the National Inteligencer, in which I fully set forth our reasons for our proceedings. He or the Govmt[2]

[*The text stops abruptly here, followed by a crudely drawn calendar in Booth's own hand. The dates begin at April 17 and continue through June 18, with April 17–25 crossed off. The entry for April 20 is marked "on Poto[mac]," the 21st says "swamp," and the 22nd is again marked "Poto." The diary text resumes after several blank pages.*]

After being hunted like a dog through swamps, woods, and last night being chased by gun boats till I was forced to return wet cold and starving, with every man's hand against me, I am here in despair.[3] And why; For doing what Brutus was honored for, what made Tell a Hero. And yet I for striking down a greater tyrant than they ever knew am looked upon as a common cutthroat. My action was purer than either of theirs. One hoped to be great himself. The other had not only his country's but his own wrongs to avenge. I hoped for no gain. I knew no private wrong. I struck for my country and that alone. A country groaned beneath this tyranny and prayed for this end. Yet now behold the cold hand they extend to me. God *cannot* pardon me if I have done wrong. Yet I cannot see any wrong except in serving a degenerate people. The little, the very little I left behind to clear my name, the Govmt will not allow to be printed. So ends all. For my country I have given up all that makes life sweet and Holy, brought misery upon my family, and am sure there is no pardon in the Heaven for me since man condemns me so. I have only *heard* of what has been done (except what I did myself) and it fills me with horror. God try and forgive me, and bless my mother. To night I will once more try the river with the intent to cross; though I have a greater desire and almost a mind to return to Washington and in a measure clear my name, which I feel I can do. I do not repent the blow I struck. I may before my God but not to man.

I think I have done well, though I am abandoned, with the curse of Cain upon me, when if the world knew my heart, *that one* blow would have made me great, though I did desire no greatness.

To night I try to escape these blood hounds once more. Who, who can read his fate God's will be done.

I have too great a soul to die like a criminal. O may he, may he spare me that and let me die bravely.

I bless the entire world. Have never hated or wronged anyone. This last was not a wrong, unless God deems it so. And its [*sic*] with him to damn or bless me. And for this brave boy with me who often prays (yes, before and since) with a true and sincere heart. Was it crime in him, if so, why can he pray the same I do not wish to shed a drop of blood, but "I must fight the course." 'Tis all that's left me.

[Original in the Lincoln Museum, Ford's Theatre]

NOTES

Some of the citations below may require explanation. The records of the conspiracy trial prosecutors have been published by the National Archives on sixteen reels of microfilm, and are designated Microcopy M-599 by some authors. Here I refer to them as the Lincoln Assassination Suspect File, or LAS, and cite documents from them in this form: LAS [*reel number: frame number*]. This will distinguish them from other National Archives microfilms, documents from which are cited in the following form: [*Microcopy publication number*], [*reel number: frame number*].

Much of the information in this book has been published in the Official Records of the Union and Confederate Armies or its companion series, the Official Records of the Union and Confederate Navies. These sources are cited as O.R. and N.O.R., respectively, in the following form: O.R. [*series number*], [*volume number*] (*part number*) [*page numbers*].

Bound textual records in the National Archives are cited in this form: RG [*record group number*] (*record group part number*) [*catalog entry number*], [*book or volume number*]: [*page number*]. Unbound textual records are cited in the same manner, but without the book or volume number.

Legal sources are cited in accordance with standard legal notation, which gives volume number first, then a standardized abbreviation for the source, followed by page number. For example, a statute that appears in volume 12 of the United States Statutes at Large, page 320, would be cited as "12 Stat. 320." Court cases are cited in this form: *Plaintiff* v. *Defendant*, [*volume, series title, page*]. Cases decided by the United States Supreme Court are cited by [*case name*], [*volume* U.S. *page*].

Chapter 1: "By God, then, is John Booth crazy?"

1. Eyewitness biographies are derived from obituaries and Civil War pension files. The former prisoners of war were Obadiah Downing and Edwin Cooke; Downing also took part in the Dahlgren Raid. At least 250 eyewitnesses were combat veterans.
2. Welford Dunaway Taylor, ed., *Our American Cousin: The Play That Changed History*

(Washington: Beacham Publishing, Inc., 1990), 14. The play débuted in October 1858 in New York, and it became a turning point in the careers of Laura Keene, Joseph Jefferson III, and E. A. Sothern. *Autobiography of Joseph Jefferson* (Cambridge, Mass.: The Belknap Press of Harvard University Press, 1964), 147. As the original Dundreary, E. A. Sothern ad-libbed a lisp and stutter-step. His improvisations, and a ridiculous wig, made the play a hit. It was thereafter known as a comedy. Taylor, *Our American Cousin*, 14. See also Rebecca Lea Ray, "Stage History of Tom Taylor's 'Our American Cousin' " (Ph.D. dissertation, New York University, 1985).

3. The playbills were already being printed when the Lincolns' notice arrived, so stage manager John B. Wright ran over to Polkinhorn's Printing Shop and had the printing stopped. A stanza from "Honor to Our Soldiers" was inserted into the copy block, and the rest of the bills included that revision. Thus, two separate playbills existed for the performance that night. "Music and Drama," *Boston Transcript*, June 15, 1898. Ford's Theatre may not have been full that night. Though the orchestra (ground level) section seems to have filled up at about curtain time, many people showed up late, but still managed to find good seats. Of more than 350 eyewitnesses I've tracked, not a single one claimed to have sat in the upper balcony, or family circle. The house had a capacity of just over 1,700, and if the two lower levels were full, the audience would have numbered about a thousand patrons.

4. A Park Service historian listed ten prior visits of Lincoln to Ford's Theatre, but two more were subsequently discovered. George J. Olszewski, *Restoration of Ford's Theatre* (Washington: Government Printing Office, 1963), 105; James P. Ferguson statement in the National Archives, in the Lincoln Assassination Suspects File, a part of Record Group 153, and reproduced on microfilm in Microcopy M-599, reel 7, beginning at frame 487. Ferguson gave detailed statements to various newspapers as well. See Washington *Evening Star*, April 17, 1865, 1; Generally, theaters of the day continued to keep the houselights raised during the performance, and late arrivals were common. The practice of dimming the lights to draw attention to the stage was an innovation of the 1890s, though it was not unknown in 1865.

5. The Grants had been renting a house at 309 Wood Street, Burlington, since September 1864, and their daughter Nellie attended school at St. Mary's Hall nearby. William E. Schermerhorn, *The History of Burlington* (Burlington, NJ: Enterprise Publishing Co., 1927), 136–37. Both the house and school are still standing. Taylor, *Our American Cousin*, 14; Much of my information on Henry and Clara came through the kindness of their granddaughter, the late Louise Randolph Hartley.

6. The account of Mrs. Lincoln comes from Helen Bratt DuBarry in a letter to her mother, dated April 16, 1865, in the Illinois State Historical Library; Isaac Jacquette in LAS 2:104.

7. James P. Ferguson statement in LAS 4:339, and in the *Evening Star*, April 17, 1865, 1.

8. Taylor, *Our American Cousin*, 82. "Sockdologizing" is one of those quaint Americanisms Taylor made up for the play. A "sockdologer" was a fish trap with two hooks that close upon each other by means of a spring. *Bartlett's Dictionary of American English*, 2nd ed. (1848), as cited in the *Oxford English Dictionary*, 2nd ed. (1989).

9. Hawk's April 16 letter to his father, William J. Hawke, was published in *The New York Times*, April 26, 1865, 2. The distance from the rail to the stage varies owing to the downward slant of the stage floor. Measurements taken from the April 17 photographs were used in the restoration of the theater in the 1960s. See Olszewski, *Restoration of Ford's Theatre*, 45.

10. H. Clay Ford statement in LAS 5:459; James L. Maddox in LAS 5:275.

11. Edwin Bates letter, April 15, 1865, to his father, Jacob Bates, of Derby, Vermont. Files of the National Park Service; Charles Addison Sanford letter to Edward Payson Goodrich, April 15, 1865, published in Bulletin 47 of the Clements Library, University of Michigan.

12. Joseph B. Stewart statement, sworn before Justice A. B. Olin, April 15, in LAS 4:58.

13. Isaac Grantham Jacquette statement, April 26, in LAS 2:103.

14. Ferguson, *Evening Star,* April 17, 1865; Ferguson in Maxwell Whiteman, *While Lincoln Lay Dying* (Philadelphia: The Union League of Philadelphia, 1968), 2.

15. John J. Toffey letter to his parents, dated April 17, 1865. I am indebted to William Toffey, a direct descendant of the lieutenant, and to Stephen J. Wright for putting me in touch with him.

16. E. D. Wray in LAS 3:1043; James P. Ferguson claimed the woman who said, "They've got him" was Laura Keene. Ferguson testimony in Ben: Perley Poore, *The Conspiracy Trial for the Assassination of the President* (Boston: J. E. Tilton and Company, 1865), 2:537. Hereinafter Poore.

17. Isaac Jacquette in LAS 2:103; Letter dated April 16, 1865, from Helen DuBarry to her mother, in the Illinois State Historical Library; Dr. Charles Leale reported hearing cries of "Shoot him!" and "Kill the murderer!" Report of Dr. Charles A. Leale dated July 21, 1867, for the Butler Committee in the House of Representatives, Benjamin Butler Papers, Manuscripts Division, Library of Congress.

18. James L. Maddox, April 28, in LAS 5:275; Pandemonium: Theodore S. McGowan statement, LAS 5:317; Helen DuBarry letter. Mayor Richard Wallach also tried to calm the crowd. See John E. Buckingham, *Reminiscences and Souvenirs of the Assassination of Abraham Lincoln* (Washington: Rufus H. Darby, 1894), 15. Joseph B. Stewart and others heard hoofbeats trailing off in the alley, toward F Street. A new streetcar line was under construction there, and Stewart later reported hearing the horse cross over the wooden planking that covered the construction area. Joseph B. Stewart in *The Trial of John H. Surratt in the Criminal Court for the District of Columbia* (Washington: Government Printing Office, 1867), 125 (hereinafter *Surratt Trial*).

19. Sarah Hamlin Batchelder letter dated April 15, in the Hannibal Hamlin Papers, Fogler Library, University of Maine at Orono, MSS40758.

20. John T. Bolton's recollections were not published until nearly fifty years after the fact, so take them for what they are worth. He appears to be the officer mentioned in several contemporary accounts. Norfolk (Virginia) *Ledger-Dispatch,* January 28, 1911. Hereinafter Bolton, *Ledger-Dispatch.* Thanks to James O. Hall.

21. Henry Rathbone statement dated April 17, LAS 5:83; Leale Report; An excellent composite of Leale's career and education is in John B. Mulliken, M.D., "Charles Augustus Leale: Lincoln's Young Physician," *Surgery* 71, no. 5 (May 1972): 760–70.

22. Blotter entries for April 14 in the records of the Washington Metropolitan Police. Record Group 351, entry 126, National Archives.

23. Richards would later (1878) claim to have been present in Ford's Theatre, but he asked questions that no eyewitness would have had to ask. Detective James A. McDevitt's later account recalled that Richards ordered him to send out a telegraphic message. *Washington Star,* April 14, 1894, and an undated clipping in the George Alfred Townsend Papers, Maryland State Archives, claimed that Richards "jumped for the telegraph" when James Ferguson brought him the news. However, the Metropolitan Police Force didn't have a telegraph system until after July 23, 1866, when Congress appropriated $15,000 to build one. 13 Stat. 206; Maddox in LAS 5:277. The Maddox and Ferguson 1865 accounts predate the others, and I tend to give them more credence.

24. Bolton, *Ledger-Dispatch;* Annie Wright in "President Lincoln: His Assassination Described by an Eyewitness," Dorchester (MA) *Beacon,* April 11, 1896. Clipping in the papers of John T. Ford, Maryland Historical Society; Original notes of Dr. Charles S. Taft, written immediately after the events, are in the Joseph Nathanson Lincolniana Collection at McLennan Library, McGill University, Montreal. Though several accounts by Dr. Taft exist, these notes have never been published in their entirety. The author discovered them there in 1996. Courtesy of Dr. Richard Virr.

25. Jesse Weik, *Century Magazine,* February 1913, 562.

26. In his contemporaneous notes, Taft said that he didn't know anyone had been wounded until he heard the calls for a surgeon; Daniel Beekman manuscript dated February 11, 1915, National Park Service files.

27. Leale Report. Dr. Taft was a half-brother of Julia Taft, governess to the Lincoln children; Bolton, *Ledger-Dispatch.*

28. Dr. King's parents were enthusiastic supporters of the Colonization Society, hence the name. King graduated from the University of Pennsylvania Medical School in 1865, but had an earlier medical degree from the National Medical College. He and Leale both had experience with battlefield casualties long before the assassination. Howard A. Kelly, *Dictionary of American Medical Biography* (Baltimore: n.p., 1928), 697. This source credits Dr. King with the discovery that mosquitoes transmit malaria. Judging from his notes, Dr. Taft seems to have taken little notice of Leale, and could not even remember his name, but he later praised Leale's work; J. Willard Brown, *The Signal Corps, U. S. A. in the War of the Rebellion* (Boston: U.S. Veteran Signal Corps Association, 1896), 665 (hereinafter Brown, *Signal Corps*); Letters to Edwin Bedee on this subject are in the James A. Hardie Papers, Manuscript Division, Library of Congress.

29. The motto of Virginia, adopted on July 5, 1776, was generally translated as "Thus Ever to Tyrants," and was subsequently placed on the commonwealth's seal and flag. "Report on the Great Seal of Virginia," House Document No. 7, Virginia House of Delegates, dated February 20, 1930, Virginia State Library, Richmond. DeForrest P. Ormes and Benjamin F. Gilbert, eyewitnesses to the shooting, were typical in that they did not understand what Booth said on the stage, but agreed he had spoken twice. Their undated joint statement is in LAS 3:832.

30. Ferguson spoke to a reporter for the Washington *Evening Star* (April 15) and gave three separate statements over the next few days, including one at the Petersen house (LAS 4:339); Details on his life are given in an 1876 interview published in the *Chillicothe Advertiser,* date unknown, a copy of which is in the papers of George Alfred Townsend at the Maryland State Archives.

31. James L. Maddox statement in LAS 5:342.

32. Maddox was described as a witness at police headquarters, though any statement he gave at that time seems to have been unrecorded. In this and other cases, I assume the witnesses gave essentially the same information that they provided soon afterward. The information used here came from Maddox's April 27 memorandum and his April 28 interrogation at the Old Capitol. LAS 5:346 and 5:275, respectively; Joseph Borrows statement in LAS 4:64. "Peanuts" has never been identified, and his family name is given as "Burroughs," "Bohrar," and "Burrus" in the records. Though I cannot prove it, I believe he may have been the son of Dr. Joseph Borrows III, a prominent physician who lived just around the corner from Ford's on E Street. Dr. Borrows's property abutted Baptist Alley, behind the theater. The only information given about the boy himself was that he lived with his father, whom police did not see the need to identify specifically; Ferguson in LAS 4:339 and 5:384.

33. Samuel J. Koontz and Captain Joseph Robinson Findley letters in the files of the National Park Service; Dr. George B. Todd letter dated April 15, copies of which were distributed. One is in the Henry Bass Collection at the University of Oklahoma, Norman; Letter by James A. Tanner to Hadley Walch, April 17, 1865, published in *American Historical Review* 29, no. 3 (April 1924): 514. Tad Lincoln's escort has often been identified as Alexander Williamson, but in an interview given two years before his death, Williamson said he was at home when he learned of the assassination. His son, William B. Williamson, was an eyewitness at Ford's. From an unidentified obituary dated June 8, 1903, in the papers of actor Owen Fawcett, University of Tennessee at Knoxville. I thank William B. Williamson's granddaughter, Grace Hand, for Williamson family information.

34. Sterling in Washington *Evening Star,* April 14, 1918 (4), 1.

35. Seaton Munroe, "Recollections of Lincoln's Assassination," *North American Review* 162 (March 1896): 425. A few eyewitnesses recalled that six soldiers carried the president, but only four of them have been identified. The other two had apparently served in different units, and were thus strangers to the other four. See "Shot That Killed Lincoln Still Rings in Memory of Soldier Who Saw Him Die," Washington *Daily News,* February 11, 1933.

36. Jacob Soles gave many interviews, in which he identified his companions in the procession. Personal information is from Jacob Soles's pension file and from the service records of those he identified. For information on the soldiers' artillery unit, see Frederick H. Dyer, *Compendium of the War of the Rebellion* (Des Moines, Iowa: Dyer Publishing Company, 1908).

37. Munroe, 425; Isaac Jacquette in LAS, 2:103; Bolton, *Ledger-Dispatch;* Some eyewitnesses disputed the story that Laura Keene ever got into the box. Clara Harris was quoted as saying, "Laura Keene did not enter the box from first to last. She might have been with the crowd who were trying to get in at the door, but only a very few were admitted and she was not among the number." Miss Keene's daughter responded in the December 29 (year unknown) issue of the Philadelphia *Weekly Times,* claiming she still has the blood-spattered dress. Clipping in the Laura Keene Papers, Manuscript Division, Library of Congress. A swatch from Miss Keene's bloody dress was once in the Colorado Historical Society, and a stained cuff from it is in the Smithsonian Institution. The staining is more extensive than one would expect if Lincoln's wound did not bleed profusely while he was in the box.

38. In later years, Taft even paid tribute to Leale, saying, "It was owing to Dr. Leale's quick judgment in instantly placing the almost moribund President in a recumbent position the moment he saw him in the box, that Mr. Lincoln did not expire in the theatre within ten minutes from the fatal syncope." *Century Magazine,* quoted in Brown, *Signal Corps,* 667; Taft notes.

39. John Devenay identified the hat. April [15], 1865, LAS 2:154. E. D. Wray, LAS 3:1043. Capt. John Rankin Gilliland, 51st Pennsylvania Infantry, found that spur, though several other spurs have surfaced over the years. Thanks to Gilliland's descendant Winifred S. Dynes. A drawing of the hat and spur appeared in *Frank Leslie's Illustrated Newspaper* on May 6, 1865. Detective Corps Blotter for April 14, 1865. The full list of names also included Andrew C. Manwaring, William Brown, C. W. Gilbert, and James B. Cutler—none of whom were called to testify in either trial.

40. Much of this was not put on paper until Maddox was interrogated on April 28 at the Carroll Annex. LAS 5:275. Baptist Alley got its name from the Tenth Street Baptist Church, which John T. Ford converted to a theater early in 1862. Sergeant Johnson re-

turned with a saddle cover, a halter, and three fishing lines that had belonged to Booth. The Metropolitan Police detective blotter entry for April 17 says that these items were collected on the morning of the fifteenth, but had not yet been claimed.

41. Henry S. Safford letter to Osborn H. Oldroyd, June 25, 1903, in the files of the National Park Service. The Petersen house address is now 516 Tenth Street. Another Petersen child, Louisa, was attending the Moravian Academy in Bethlehem, Pennsylvania, at the time; Bersch died in 1914, but his account appeared in the *Washington Star*, April 16, 1933 (6), 12. He later painted the scene in oils, and his painting shows an American flag carried on a pole near the president. Neither his nor any other contemporary account mentioned anything about the president's head being cradled in a flag. That story, just now gaining currency, seems to be a twentieth-century creation.

42. George A. Woodward, "The Night of Lincoln's Assassination," *United Service: A Monthly Review of Military and Naval Affairs* (May 1889): 472–73 (hereinafter Woodward, *United Service*).

43. Lawrence A. Gobright, *Recollections of Men and Things at Washington* (Philadelphia: Claxton, Remsen, & Haffelfinger, 1869), 348. The special was printed in papers throughout the country, including for example, *The Baltimore Sun*, April 15, 1865, 2.

44. Laird and Maynard in *The Washington Post*, April 11, 1915 (2), 5.

Chapter 2: "It all seems a dream—a wild dream"

1. The determination of the timing of the attack is based in part on the fact that Lafayette Park was to be locked just before the time of the attack, and William H. Bell had just heard the announcement. Washington *Evening Star*, April 15, 1865, 1. Testimony of William H. Bell, *Surratt Trial*, 247.

2. Details of the attack and the injuries are from a letter from Frances (Mrs. William) Seward to a Mr. Alward, dated May 11, 1865, as published in Frederick W. Seward, *Seward at Washington, as Senator and Secretary of State* (New York: Derby and Miller, 1891), 279–81. Most of the victims left good accounts of this incident. William and Frederick Seward gave their impressions to the London *Spectator*. This previously unnoticed interview was republished in the Cincinnati *Commercial*, December 8, 1865, 1. Fanny Seward made copious notes in the April 14 entry of her diary, and she wrote another account in addition to that. Seward Papers, University of Rochester, microfilm reel 198. George Robinson's earliest account was published in the Washington *Evening Star*, April 18, 1865, 1. Frederick Seward's detailed account was given in testimony at the 1867 trial of John Surratt. *Surratt Trial*, 249–51.

3. Washington *Evening Star*, April 14, 1918 (4), 1.

4. The brace, with nicks, is mentioned in the *New York Tribune*, April 17, 1865, 1. Frances Seward letter, May 11, 1865; Cincinnati *Commercial*, December 8, 1865, 1.

5. Theodore F. Bailey in the *Delaware* (Ohio) *Gazette*, undated clipping from the papers of Bailey's grandson, Theodore Selke, of Laurel, Maryland. I am grateful to Nancy Griffith for a copy of this article.

6. In *Reminiscences and Souvenirs of the Assassination of Abraham Lincoln* (Washington: Rufus H. Darby, 1894), 19–24, John E. Buckingham recounts Cartter's firsthand recollection, told many years later. In this account, Cartter and Surgeon General Barnes left Seward's together, and found Welles and Stanton already at Petersen's. My rendition is drawn from the diary of Gideon Welles, which was written just after the fact. I used Cartter's story of the frightened driver because it does not conflict with the Welles account. *Diary of Gideon Welles* (Boston: Houghton Mifflin & Co., 1911), 2:283–86.

7. April 5, 1865, letter of George Francis, a boarder at the Petersen house, to his niece,

Josephine. Chicago Historical Society. An interesting monograph on Clark was published in W. Emerson Reck, "The Riddle of William Clark," *Lincoln Herald* (Winter 1982): 218–221.

8. George A. Woodward and others remembered the bugle call of "Boots and Saddles," but that call was for ordinary occasions. "To horse" was the emergency call for mounted troops; "To arms" called infantry to battle. Philip St. George Cooke, *Cavalry Tactics* (Philadelphia: J. B. Lippincott & Co., 1862), 7; Woodward, *United Service,* 474. The order is in the National Archives, Record Group 393 (I), Entry 5375. Letters sent by the commanding general, XXII Army Corps, Department of Washington. Bound volume 22, 231. Orders to halt all persons also went out from General Henry W. Halleck to General Morris in Baltimore, O.R. I:46 (3), 776; another went to General Cadwallader in Philadelphia, *ibid,* 779.

9. Rumors were reported in nearly every contemporary source. The Grant story came from the letter of B. Eglin, in the Historical Society of Great Falls, Virginia. The Usher, Speed, and Stanton rumors were reported in a letter from Usher to his wife, dated April 16, in the Manuscripts Division, Library of Congress. Hubbell account is in Marc Newman, ed., *Potomac Diary: A Soldier's Account of the Capital in Crisis, 1864–65* (Charleston, SC: Arcadia Publishing, 2000), 90.

10. Maunsell B. Field, *Memories of Many Men and of Some Women* (New York: Harper & Brothers, 1874), 325; Henry Ulke, an artist who lived in the Petersen house, was under the impression the doctors wanted hot water to keep the president's legs from stiffening. Washington *Evening Star,* January 24, 1903 (4), 2.

11. Leale report; Dr. Charles S. Taft notebook; Virtually everything connected to the assassination is a matter of dispute. Doctors at the president's deathbed disagreed on which eye was swollen, as well as the ultimate location of the ball. See John K. Lattimer, M.D., and Angus Laidlaw, "Good Samaritan Surgeon Wrongly Accused of Contributing to President Lincoln's Death: An Experimental Study of the President's Fatal Wound." *Journal of the American College of Surgeons* 182 (May 1996): 440. Like Dr. Lattimer, I adopt the view of Dr. Barnes, who said that the bullet stopped above and slightly behind Lincoln's right eye.

12. Lyman Sprague's testimony in the Surratt trial gave the locations of the Johnson and Atzerodt rooms at the Kirkwood House. *Surratt Trial,* 324. Farwell's account has been told many times, including once at the conspiracy trial. Poore, 3:174–75; Washington *Daily National Intelligencer,* April 21, 1865, 2.

13. Testimony of John Lee in Poore, 1:62–63, and his reward claim in the National Archives, Microcopy M-619, reel 455, frame 874. This series of records is from Record Group 94, from the Adjutant General's Office (hereinafter M-619). Michael Henry memorandum to James R. O'Beirne, July 20, 1865, in the collection of Scott Balthaser, of Harrisburg, PA; my thanks to him for a copy. Henry found another suspicious character named William Graham, and reported his actions at the hotel on April 24. LAS 3:90. William R. Nevins also claimed to have helped point Atzerodt out to authorities. Poore, 2:277–81.

14. John Lee testimony in Poore, 1:64–65, and LAS 2:529. James O'Beirne's memorandum list of items found is in LAS 2:526. The name on one handkerchief, as Lee read it, was "Mary R. E. Booth," but that seems to be an error; the assassin's mother was Mary Ann Holmes Booth. The original handkerchief is now lost. The entire balance of $455 came from two deposits made the previous October. One was in the amount of $200 Canadian, and the rest was deposited by check.

15. Henry Atwater's recollections in *The Washington Post,* April 11, 1915 (2), 5.

16. Undated statement by Lyman H. Bunnell, LAS 3:665; W. S. Burch, inventor of a heating and air-conditioning system, was a wealthy man. Last Will and Testament dated March 1, 1869, Register of Wills, Washington, D.C.; John Pettit testimony in *Surratt Trial*, 127; Stebbins's report was recorded in LAS 6:264.

17. Richards telegram to "The chief of Police Baltimore" in Box 175, Benjamin Butler Papers, Manuscripts Division, Library of Congress. The same message went out to police chiefs in Philadelphia, New York, and Alexandria, Virginia.

18. Arthur F. Loux, "The Mystery of the Telegraphic Interruption," *Lincoln Herald* (1979). Mr. Loux based his article on interviews with Heiss's descendants and on newspaper articles about him. One descendant, Carrie Schaetzel, told substantially the same story to Philip Van Doren Stern in a letter dated March 8, 1939. Stern Papers, Manuscript Division, Library of Congress.

19. James R. Ford in *The Baltimore Sun*, April 15, 1897.

20. Leale report. To give some idea of the conspiracy paranoia that prevailed just then, a man who signed himself "Death to Traitors" wrote to Judge Advocate General Holt inquiring about the names of the doctors who preceded Dr. Stone in the treatment of the president. He and his friends assumed these surgeons were "Conspirators in disguise prepared for the express purpose that if Booth failed in completing his Hellish purpose or act, They under the guise of friendship or professional duties might accomplish what he in his haste failed to perform." That was a common rumor of the time. Joseph Holt Papers, Manuscript Division, Library of Congress, 47:6326; *The Washington Post*, April 11, 1915 (2), 5.

21. *New York Herald*, April 15, 1865, 1.

22. C. C. Bangs in *The Washington Post*, April 12, 1896, 20. Others claimed to have broken the news to Robert Lincoln as well—Thomas Pendel, for example, in *The Baltimore Sun*, October 30, 1901. I chose Bangs because contemporary sources corroborate the rest of his account, with minor discrepancies. Robert Todd Lincoln served on the staff of General Grant.

23. Spangler's own statement in Nettie Mudd, *The Life of Dr. Samuel A. Mudd* (New York: The Neale Publishing Co., 1906), 326 (hereinafter *Life of Mudd*); Hawk in Cincinnati *Enquirer*, April 16, 1881, 2. His friend was Charles DeCosta Brown, an embalmer who would help prepare Lincoln for burial. Keene in the Washington *Star*, February 7, 1937.

24. One of the Confederate prisoners, C. T. Allen, paid tribute to Congressman Smith with an article about this in his own newspaper, *The Princeton (Kentucky) Banner*, April 14, 1881. The manuscript, with additions, is in the Perkins Library, Duke University. One of the 12th V.R.C. soldiers, F. L. Hickok, gave his side of the story, including troop strength figures, to the *Allegan (Michigan) Press*, and it was subsequently printed in the *National Tribune*, May 6, 1909. My thanks to Katherine Dhalle for the *Tribune* article.

25. Woodward, *United Service*, 473–74; George A. Cassidy, of the 9th Veterans' Reserve Corps, commanded the men on Tenth Street. Johnstown, Pennsylvania, *Tribune*, December 6, 1922. Courtesy of Ken Beck, a Cassidy descendant. Nearly all books refer to the rainy or drizzly weather, but the Signal Corps, and sailors in the Potomac, kept meticulous records of the visibility and weather conditions in their logbooks, and these documents indicate that rain did not begin until well after midnight on April 15. At the last count, on March 1, 1865, the Department of Washington had 26,056 soldiers. O.R. III, 5:506. Reference to the 13th New York is in Augur's order to Maj. George Worcester, April 15, in National Archives, Record Group 393, Part 2, book 186. Notification to various other cities can be found in Microcopy M-473, Telegrams Sent by the

War Department, reels 88 and 89. The train order is now privately owned; it is quoted from *The Collector,* an auction catalog. Fire Brigade notification is mentioned in the testimony of William Dixon, *Surratt Trial,* 584.

26. Clara Harris letter of April 25, 1865, to "My dear Mary," in the New-York Historical Society.

27. Field, 322–23; *Chicago Tribune,* April 17, 1865, 1.

28. The term "navy revolver" goes back to 1851, when Colt began making a medium-caliber weapon with a naval battle scene engraved on the cylinder. This decoration gave the pistol its nickname, and soon after, other manufacturers issued revolvers of the same (.36) caliber. They came to be known generically as navy revolvers. Courtney B. Wilson, "Terms Army, Navy Refer to Caliber Not Revolver's Use," *Antique Week,* July 10, 1989, 9.

29. Description of the hat is in a report dated April 16 from Britten A. Hill to Secretary Stanton, in the Edwin Stanton Papers, Manuscript Division, Library of Congress, Microfilm reel 9. The condition of the revolver was described in detail by Frederick Seward in *The New York Times,* April 13, 1913.

30. For the letter of Dr. William A. Child to his wife, Carrie, dated April 14, 1865, I am indebted to the doctor's great-grandson, Everett Sawyer; Woodward, *United Service,* 476.

Chapter 3: "The President's case is hopeless"

1. *New York Herald,* April 17, 1865, 1.

2. Edwin M. Stanton annual report to Andrew Johnson, November 22, 1865. O.R. III, 5:494–535.

3. *The Baltimore Sun,* April 18, 1865, 1. The area was near the present Lincoln Square, though some sources place this incident a little north of there. From there, Tennessee and Maryland avenues both gave easy access to the Benning Bridge, which was the commonly used route to Baltimore.

4. According to Gideon Welles, General Montgomery Meigs and Major Thomas T. Eckert both warned Stanton not to visit the deathbed. Both times, he seemed to be mulling it over. Welles, *Diary,* 2:283–86.

5. Britten Armstrong Hill biography courtesy of Bellefontaine Cemetery, St. Louis, MO; Olin biography in *Biographical Directory of the American Congress* (Washington: Government Printing Office, 1961), 1405. This panel seems to have taken in witnesses passively, and without regard to the evidentiary value of their statements.

6. Tanner's original notes were published by Maxwell Whiteman, ed., *While Lincoln Lay Dying: A Facsimile Reproduction of the First Testimony Taken in Connection with the Assassination of Abraham Lincoln* (Philadelphia: Union League, 1968), 2.

7. Theodore Roscoe, in *The Web of Conspiracy* (Englewood Cliffs, NJ: Prentice-Hall, 1959), 180, refers to Stanton as a "generalissimo, Commander-in-Chief, National Dictator, Supreme Police Superintendent, High Judge, Captain, King, all in one. A one-man junta, in effect . . . ," and this reflects the typical exaggeration of Stanton's role in the crisis.

8. *New York Herald,* April 15, 1865, 1.

9. William H. Bennett statement to Justice Olin, April 15, LAS 4:122; Henry B. Phillips statement, LAS 7:490; "The Assassination of President Lincoln, 1865. James A. Tanner Letter to Hadley F. Walch." *American Historical Review,* 29. 3 (April 1924), 516.

10. Hawk in Whiteman, 1; Rathbone in *Surratt Trial,* 125. Walter Burton, a clerk at Booth's hotel, knew the actor well. Though he got a clear look at the man on the stage, Burton later said he did not recognize him at the time. Washington *Evening Star,* January 24,

1903 (4), 2; Others who said it wasn't Booth, LAS 2:466; Sarah Hamlin Batchelder letter, University of Maine (her emphasis).

11. Spangler and others confirmed that the shot came about fifteen minutes after Booth's arrival. LAS 6:201. I have assumed, here and elsewhere, that the information given to police by any given witness was substantially the same as that produced in the conspiracy trial, though it wasn't recorded on the earlier occasion. Rittersback's testimony is in Poore, 2:461.

12. Joseph Borrows memorandum, LAS 4:64; Joe Simms in LAS 6:166. H. B. Phillips said that Spangler had disappeared. He did not refer to Spangler by name, but he clearly meant Ned, who had just sold the buggy as a favor to Booth. LAS 7:490.

13. Ezra J. Warner, *Generals in Blue: Lives of the Union Commanders* (Baton Rouge, LA: Louisiana State University Press, 1964), 12.

14. Theodore McGowan in LAS 5:317.

15. Emerson in the Washington *Evening Star,* February 9, 1913. According to a story attributed to Emerson, Elnathan Meade found the "Reserved" sign. Emerson himself claimed to have found a bloodstained playbill in the box. *Evening Star,* July 31, 1934, B1. The sign is now owned by Dr. John K. Lattimer. Isaac Jacquette in LAS 2:103. Eventually, Jacquette did cut off a small end section of the bar, but Lafayette Baker recovered both pieces before the trial.

16. William T. Kent statement, LAS 5:129. Extra caps: *The Baltimore Sun,* April 17, 1865, 1. The manufacturer was Henry Deringer, but the name was often misspelled "Derringer" when applied generically to any small pistol.

17. John J. Toffey letter to his parents, dated April 17, in the possession of his great-grandson, William Toffey.

18. The opera glasses are now in the Forbes collection. Harold Holzer, "Remembering the Lincoln Assassination—120 Years Later," *The Antique Trader Weekly* (Dubuque, Iowa), April 17, 1985, 83.

19. Dr. May's presence at the deathbed is previously unknown, but Dr. Charles Taft's notebook lists him among those who were there.

20. Petersen's young daughters, Anna and Julia, were buried at Prospect Hill Cemetery in February 1863. A sermon delivered by Rev. Abram Dunn Gillette on April 23, 1865, mentioned the girls' deaths and the reverence with which the family treated that back room. A. D. Gillette, *God Seen Above All National Calamities: A Sermon on the Death of President Lincoln* (Washington: McGill & Witherow, 1865), 5. Gillette's source was the Petersens' minister, Rev. Samuel Finckel, of the German Lutheran Church, who was a personal friend. Souvenir hunters were mentioned in the *Evening Star,* April 17, 1865; Henry Ulke and Thomas Proctor, who boarded in the house, claimed to have helped the doctors. Ulke in the *Evening Star,* January 24, 1903 (4), 2. Petersen's political views might be inferred from the family tradition that John C. Breckinridge, the vice president who ran against Lincoln in 1860, once boarded in the Petersen house. This information was given to me by a Petersen descendant, but city directories do not confirm the story. William Petersen filed a claim for $550 to replace "sheets, pillow-cases and carpets" damaged on the night of the assassination. I found no record that he was paid. He charged tourists fifty cents admission to see the back bedroom. *Pacific Commercial Advertiser* (Honolulu), September 16, 1865, 3.

21. Dr. Abbott's notes appeared in *The New York Times,* April 15, 1865, 1.

22. Bangs, *The Washington Post,* April 12, 1896, 20. The same story is told from Mrs. Dixon's point of view in a May 1, 1865, letter to her sister Louisa, a copy of which was provided to me by the recipient's great-grandson, David C. Andrews, of Andes, New

York. Where discrepancies exist, I have preferred Mrs. Dixon's contemporary account to that of Bangs.

23. O.R. I:46 (3), 783. The original is in M-473, 88:996.

24. The observation about government boats is by D. C. Forney, "Thirty Years After," *Washington Evening Star,* June 27, 1891, 11. Notifications to General E. O. C. Ord, commanding the U.S. forces in Richmond, and others can be found in O.R. I:46 (3), 750 *et seq.*

25. See O.R. I:46 (3), 744–45. Samuel H. Beckwith, in the *Boston Post,* April 11, 1915 (2), 2, identifies the veteran as George W. Porter. One of Porter's co-workers at the American Telegraph Company also claimed to have delivered the message. See Charles Bolles, "General Grant and the News of Mr. Lincoln's Death," *Century Magazine* 18 (June 1890): 309. Dana's warning is in O.R. I:46 (3), 756. This story is pieced together from War Department telegrams from Microcopy M-473, 88:991 *et seq.,* and Horace Porter, *Campaigning with Grant* (New York: The Century Co., 1897), 499–500. General Porter was also present at the time, and his account is consistent with contemporary sources. Fifty years had passed before Beckwith wrote the account cited above, and his version was riddled with inaccuracies.

26. "A Silent Witness: President Lincoln's Cane?" by John H. Saylor. Scrapbook in the Military Order of the Loyal Legion of the United States (MOLLUS) Civil War Museum and Library, Philadelphia.

27. Cloughly's statement is in Whiteman, 1. The documents published in this book are in the Union League of Philadelphia, but another copy of the Cloughly statement can be found in the Chicago Historical Society. The officer of the company at the White House said that only a few men were still around that night.

28. Roger D. Hunt and Jack Brown, *Brevet Brigadier Generals in Blue* (Gaithersburg, MD: Olde Soldier Books, 1990), 308; Pension file for Timothy Ingraham, Jr., National Archives.

29. The incident occurred on June 4, 1864, when Tyrrell took custody of Lt. P. S. Early, of the 13th Pennsylvania Cavalry. In addition to that wound, Tyrrell had also been shot five times while serving as color sergeant of the 116th Pennsylvania Infantry in the battle of Fredericksburg. William H. Tyrrell pension file, National Archives.

30. The room description comes from the *Daily Constitutional Union,* April 15, 1865, 2, and *The Baltimore Sun,* April 18, 1865. The cartridges, coat, and handcuffs were never used as evidence in the conspiracy trial, so Tyrrell wrote to the War Department asking if he could keep the handcuffs as a memento. Permission was granted, and today they are displayed at the Grand Army of the Republic Museum in Philadelphia. See also the statement of Asahel Hitchcox, M-619, 455:807. None of the published accounts mentioned a gimlet, but George W. Bunker testified in the conspiracy trial that he had found such a tool in the trunk on the day after the assassination. Poore, 3:60. Another desk clerk, Charles Dawson, testified about the contents of the valise and trunk at the trial of John Surratt. *Surratt Trial,* 337–38.

31. Henry Atwater in *The Washington Post,* April 11, 1915 (2), 5.

32. James Tanner once indicated he had also recorded an interview with Laura Keene. If that is true, no transcript survives. He was the only person to mention Miss Keene in that connection. Whiteman, 5.

33. This telegram was marked "Rec'd 1.45 am" at the War Department, and "sent 2.15 am." The original is in the National Archives, reproduced in Microcopy M-473, 88:997–98. Published versions, such as those appearing in the newspapers and in the Official Records, were edited by telegraph operators and others. See O.R. I:46 (3), 780.

34. Johnson commented on his "arduous and embarrassing" duties in a June 18 letter to Rev. W. A. Buckingham, moderator of the National Council of Congregational Churches in Boston. His letter was published in the Washington *Daily National Intelligencer,* June 21, 1865, 1.

35. James A. McDevitt in the *Washington Star,* April 14, 1894; the liquor ban was posted in the Washington *Evening Star,* April 15, 1865.

36. Gobright, 349. *The Baltimore Sun,* April 18, 1865, 1; Detective blotter, entry for April 15.

37. William Withers sworn statement, n.d. [April 15] taken by Nehemiah Miller, LAS 6:468, National Archives; Letter of William E. Morgan to Edwin Stanton, dated April 22. LAS 2:68. The accusation was not specific, but over the years, Withers told of being seriously wounded by Booth's knife, and eventually he claimed to have received "a six-inch scar, which I carry to this day." But Withers received a pension as former leader of the 62nd Pennsylvania's Regimental Band, and in records of his physical exams, his doctors noted no scars on his body.

38. Fletcher gave several statements to the authorities, and he testified in the conspiracy trial. His most detailed account is the previously unknown claim he sent to Congress on May 17, 1866, for a portion of the reward money offered. This is in Record Group 233, House of Representatives, Thirty-ninth Congress, First Session, Committee of Claims file HR39A-H4.1. Some details here are taken from a memorandum in LAS 5:415 and from a letter to Edwin Stanton, sworn and dated September 23, 1865, in M-619, 456:297.

39. John C. Proctor, Sr., sworn affidavit dated May 13, 1865, in M-619, 456:579.

40. McDevitt in the Washington *Evening Star,* April 14, 1894. Richards in Louis J. Weichmann, *A True History of the Assassination of Abraham Lincoln* (New York: Alfred A. Knopf, 1975), 177. The Surratt boardinghouse was built by Jonathan T. Walker in 1843. Surratt acquired it on December 6, 1853, from Augustus A. Gibson. Washington, D.C., Recorder of Deeds record for Lot 20, Square 454, in Liber JAS 70, folio 251. It is now the Wok 'n' Roll Restaurant at 604 H Street.

41. Weichmann later recalled that he told Mrs. Surratt that detectives had come to search the place, and she said, "For God's sake! let them come in. I expected the house to be searched." *Surratt Trial,* 450.

42. Louis J. Weichmann mentioned Susan Mahoney's place in the household in *Surratt Trial,* 398. He described the layout of the house in *Surratt Trial,* 376. Mahoney's fiancé was not named, but Washington marriage records show that a black woman named "Susan Mahorney" married Samuel Jackson on April 27, 1865. The Holohan children were Charles and Mary.

43. Weichmann, 175–76, gives a slightly different version of this late-night raid, and I have taken most of the Mary Surratt quotes from this version. Otherwise, this account is from the testimony of John A. W. Clarvoe in *Surratt Trial,* 697–701, and from Weichmann's testimony in *Surratt Trial,* 394.

44. This is based on Fletcher's House claim, along with that of Charles Stowell, in the same file. Additional information comes from M-619, 456:303.

45. Unsigned order dated April 15, 1865, in National Archives, Record Group 393, Part 1, entry 6714, Letters Sent and Received by the 22nd Army Corps, Book 162, 224. One such order sent to Major George Worcester at Fort Baker was sent out at about midnight (*ibid.,* Book 186).

46. O.R. I:46 (3), 778. Fry's border guards were still on duty days after Booth's death. See National Archives, Record Group 110, Records of the Provost Marshal General, entry 79, letter from S. B. Hayman to Fry, April 29, 1865.

47. Arrest of the Booth look-alike was reported in the Washington *Evening Star,* April 17,

1865, 2; The Navy Department telegram: National Archives, RG 45, on Microcopy M-149, 80:333.

Chapter 4: *"Arrest every man, woman, or child attempting to pass"*

1. James R. O'Beirne claim, filed with the House Military Affairs Committee, January 12, 1866. House Committee of Claims, file HR39A-H4.1, in RG 233, National Archives.

2. The document was marked "Sent 3.20 a.m." M-473, 88:999. Published in O.R. I:46 (3), 780–81.

3. The Eastern Branch was a more common name for what is now called the Anacostia River. General DeRussy's order is in RG 393, Part I, entry 5459, box 413, page 93. It was sent out at 3:00 A.M. on April 15. John J. Toffey letter to Joseph Holt, dated December 5, 1865, in M-619, 456:422.

4. This account comes mostly from Fletcher's House claim. Some details are added from Fletcher's claim to the War Department, in M-619, 456:304.

5. References to the weather are taken from ship logs of the Potomac Flotilla in RG 45, National Archives, and from observations of the Signal Corps in Washington. Soldiers who communicated by flag were especially dependent on weather, and their logbooks made frequent references to visibility. For example, April 14–15 entries in RG 393, Part I, entry 5459, Messages Sent and Received by the Signal Corps, book 413:92; Leale report.

6. Stanton's placing of Grant in charge of security, in O.R. I:46 (3), 757; Grant telegram from Newark, dated April 15, in the National Archives, RG 393, Part I, entry 2343, Letters Received by the 8th Army Corps, box 8; Clearing the way at Havre de Grace was from 1st Lt. H. E. Hazen, *ibid.*; The picket system discussed in an April 15 letter to Gen. Lockwood by Assistant Adjutant General Samuel B. Lockwood, *ibid.*

7. Most of these items were deemed irrelevant to the investigation, and were set aside. They were microfilmed in LAS 2:290–378. Those set aside as important will be discussed below.

8. LAS 2:294. The address was 71 West 45th Street, New York. Its significance has not been determined.

9. The original is in LAS 15:343. When Arnold suggests Booth meet him "in Balto, at B——," he refers to Barnum's Hotel. The letter was dated on the twenty-seventh, but the envelope was not postmarked until the thirtieth.

10. Leale report; Taft notes. Leale's report, written two years after the fact, mentions nothing of Dr. Taft, and seems to run this sequence of events together. It is all given more explicitly in the Taft notes. Though even contemporary accounts disagreed on the path of the bullet, again I accept Dr. John K. Lattimer's conclusion that the ball rested above the right eye. Lattimer and Laidlaw, 440.

11. Letter of James A. Tanner to Hadley Walch, April 17, 1865. The bedside details are from Mrs. Dixon's letter to her sister, May 1, 1865.

12. O.R. I:46 (3), 775.

13. According to the (Washington) *Daily Constitutional Union* of April 15, "The Metropolitan Police saw two men riding rapidly towards the Anacostia bridge at 11 o'clock." This seems to have been forgotten, and no record of the sighting exists in official files. The exchange of horses was a favorite theory of some officials. It was reported in *The New York Times*, April 16, 1865, 1. Newspapers seemed to favor the theory that decoys had been sent out over the city. See *The Baltimore Sun*, April 18, 1865, 1.

14. Court-martial hearing of Lewis Chubb, 13th Michigan Light Artillery, case MM2513, RG 153, National Archives.

15. O.R. I:46 (3), 776. It should also be noted that standard times did not exist until 1873,

so local time varied from one city to another. General Henry H. Lockwood, in Baltimore, received several copies of the same order, and in exasperation, he sent back an itemized list of the places his men already patrolled. Lockwood's memo shows how thorough the army's efforts were. Letters Received by the Eighth Army Corps, RG 393, Part I, entry 2343, box 8. Sent 5:00 A.M. April 15.

16. Leale report; Taft notes.

17. Bushrod M. Reed in M-619, 456:565.

18. Accounts of Lincoln's instructions are in *Seward at Washington*, 274. Telegrams from Stanton, or at Stanton's direction, went out at 4:10 and 4:40 A.M. ordering the arrest of Thompson. M-473, 88:1001.

19. Original, marked "Sent 4.44 a.m.," is in M-473, 88:1000; O.R. I:46 (3), 781.

20. David T. Z. Mindich, "Building the Pyramid: A Cultural History of 'Objectivity' in American Journalism, 1832–1894," doctoral dissertation in the American Studies Program, New York University, 1996, 100–115. Mindich points out that journalists were not influenced by Stanton's use of the inverted pyramid, as they did not begin using it until many years later.

21. Statements of Herbert T. Staples, 3rd Massachusetts Heavy Artillery, in LAS 6:157, and of Charles Ramsell, LAS 6:116; Ramsell in *Surratt Trial*, 498.

22. The only known sample of this original reward poster is in the Columbia Historical Society, Washington, DC. The story of its creation was told secondhand by Hack's former colleagues at *The Washington Times* in that paper's edition of February 12, 1937, 8. I have corrected some details to conform to the contemporary record.

23. Stowell statement in M-619, 456:505.

24. R. Chandler, Assistant Adjutant General, to Maj. George Worcester, April 15, 1865. National Archives RG 393, Part 2, entry 6714, book 186. Dana arranged for a detail of ten more men to meet him later in the morning. Dana to Joseph Holt, October 3, 1865, in M-619, 458:467.

25. Woodward, *United Service*, 476.

26. Diary of Benjamin B. French, entry for April 15, 1865, 386–87, Manuscripts Division, Library of Congress. As this entry indicates, the Capitol was left open, even overnight. This was the standard practice with public buildings, including the White House.

27. Ferguson passed the story about Spangler on to police a few days later. LAS 5:385. Detective Sergeant Charles Skippon brought Spangler and Rittersback to the station house on E Street. The arrest and interrogation were described by Spangler himself while locked up in the Carroll Annex. John T. Ford Papers, MS 371, at the Maryland Historical Society. A brief reference to the interrogation appears in the police detective blotter, RG 351, Entry 126, in the National Archives.

28. Spangler to Justice Olin, April 15, LAS 6:201; Spangler memo in Ford Papers; William P. Wood memorandum on Rittersback, LAS 6:48

29. Dr. Abbott's detailed accounting of the president's vital signs is in *The New York Times*, April 15, 1865, 1; Brooke Stabler in LAS 6:122; the note itself is in LAS 15:306. It has always been misquoted, even in verbatim trial transcripts, as "Atzerodt" rather than "Azworth," but the latter is the only name Stabler ever heard applied to the suspect.

30. Dr. Taft said that he stood with his hand over the president's heart, closely observing the time on the surgeon general's watch. Breathing stopped at 7:21:55, and the heartbeat stopped fifteen seconds later. Taft notes, McGill University.

Chapter 5: "A singular combination of gravity and joy"

1. San Francisco *Daily Dramatic Chronicle,* April 17, 1865, 2; *The Chicago Tribune* was typical in laying blame at the door of its competitors. On April 29, 1865, the *Tribune's* editor called the Chicago *Times* a "vile manufacturer of Booths," and said that the *Times's* editors were just as responsible for the killing as Booth.

2. Mrs. Elijah Rogers, a longtime neighbor of the Booths, responded to a series of inquiries about the family by Dr. William Stump Forwood, of the Harford County Historical Society, in 1886–87. Mrs. Rogers told of the beech spring and the log house in her letter of August 16, 1886. Almost all information about Junius and Mary Ann's first home in Harford County can be traced to Mrs. Rogers's letters. Manuscripts Division, Library of Congress, cataloged as the Junius Brutus Booth Family Papers.

3. Junius Jr. was born in Charleston, SC, before his parents ever came to Maryland. Rosalie was born on the Hall farm before her family purchased the adjoining land. Joseph was born in a house on High Street, Baltimore. New York *Sun,* June 9, 1893, 7. According to Asia Booth Clarke, the household included her aunt, Jane Booth Mitchell, and her aunt's ten children. By 1850, they had moved to Baltimore, where the census showed only five children: George, twenty-five; Robert, nineteen; Maria, fifteen; Charlotte, thirteen; and Richard, eleven.

   Richard Booth eventually moved out to live with the Woolsey family nearby. He died alone on December 29, 1839. In her privately printed book, *Personal Recollections of the Elder Booth* (London, n.d.), 19–21, Asia Booth Clarke discussed her eccentric uncle, Jimmy Mitchell, who lived with the family for a time. "His children married and died around him; on the latter occasions he never failed to publish the honor of his ancestry . . . and boasted a title in his own family." I am indebted to Stephen M. Archer for telling me about this little-known source. Research by Mary Beth Jameson shows that Mitchell's father was Sir Robert Mitchell, a fellow of the Royal Antiquarian Society. *The Baltimore Sun,* April 4, 1855, 2.

4. Following is the order of their birth: Junius Jr., born December 22, 1821; Rosalie Ann, born July 5, 1823; Henry Byron, born 1825, died December 28, 1836; Mary Ann, born 1827, died 1833; Frederick, born 1829, died 1833; Elizabeth, born 1831, died 1833; Edwin, born November 13, 1833; Asia, born November 19, 1835; John Wilkes, born May 10, 1838; Joseph Adrian, born February 8, 1840.

5. Dr. William Stump Forwood, unpublished manuscript on the Booth family, in the Manuscripts Division, Library of Congress, 146.

6. In *Personal Recollections,* 34, Asia Booth Clarke discusses her family's dealings with slavery. In a letter to William Winter dated July 17, 1886, Edwin Booth reminisced about the servants in the family. He quoted his sister Rosalie as saying that their father had bought a young woman "because he could not hire an obedient one, but as she threatened to beat Mother's brains out with a fence-rail, he gave her free papers three days after purchase & sent her away." Quoted by Daniel J. Watermeier, ed., in *Between Actor and Critic: Selected Letters of Edwin Booth and William Winter* (Princeton, NJ: Princeton University Press, 1971), 274–75. Annie Hall, who died in July 1904, told stories of the Booths that were incorporated into a book written by Ella V. Mahoney, who lived in Tudor Hall for seventy years. Ella V. Mahoney, *Sketches of Tudor Hall and the Booth Family* (Bel Air, MD: Tudor Hall, 1925).

7. Asia Booth Clarke, *The Unlocked Book: A Memoir of John Wilkes Booth by His Sister Asia Booth Clarke,* edited by Eleanor Farjeon (New York: G. P. Putnam's Sons, 1938), 41–43.

8. Archer, 238; Asia Booth Clarke, *The Elder and the Younger Booth* (Boston and New York: Houghton Mifflin and Co., 1881), 98.

9. *Spirit of the Times,* April 5, 1851, quoted in Archer, 324, n.47; Walt Whitman letter to Edwin Booth, August 21, 1884, published in Edward Haviland Miller, ed., *Walt Whitman: The Correspondence* (New York: New York University Press, 1961), vol. 3, 88. The listing of books is from Clarke, *Personal Recollections,* 37–38.

10. The notion of cigar-induced insanity is in *The Philadelphia Inquirer,* April 26, 1865, 1.

11. *The Baltimore Sun,* May 3, 1838, 2. I can find no record of an explanation offered for Booth's absence, but note that this occurred a week before the birth of John Wilkes Booth. Perhaps Mary Ann's health became a pressing concern to the expectant father.

12. *Charleston Courier,* March 12, 1838; The *Baltimore Transcript,* quoted in the *Georgetown Metropolitan,* April 11, 1836. Transcript in the Stanley Kimmel Collection, Merle Kelce Library, University of Tampa; "Stories About Booth," *The Philadelphia Inquirer,* April 21, 1865, 1. Stephen M. Archer has suggested that pain resulting from an infection may have exacerbated the problem. Archer, 239.

13. For advice about flies: Clarke, *Personal Recollections,* 25; Diary of Dr. James Rush, entry for September 28, 1835, Pennsylvania Historical Society, Philadelphia.

14. Clarke, *Personal Recollections,* 28–29.

15. William Purdie Treloar, *Wilkes and the City* (London: John Murray, 1917), 14. Treloar gives an excellent overview of Wilkes's career. Despite the heroic efforts of genealogists, no direct connection has been confirmed between Richard's mother, Elizabeth Wilkes, and "the agitator." However, letters to John Wilkes from both Richard Booth and his father, John, mention a family connection. Perception may be more important here than fact. I am indebted to Nancy Williams and Carita Curtis for their information on the family of John Wilkes, from whom they are descended.

16. The letter to Jones, dated November 5, 1832, is in The Players, New York; The friendship with Jackson is mentioned in Asia Booth Clarke, *Booth Memorials: Passages, Incidents, and Anecdotes in the Life of Junius Brutus Booth (the Elder)* (New York: Carleton, 1866), 91, 110. Actor Charles Pope later described the odd sight of Junius Booth and Sam Houston as they strolled around Washington together. See "The Eccentric Booths," *New York Sun,* March 28, 1897, clipping in the Harvard Theatre Collection. Booth gave Andrew Jackson a pair of Egyptian mummies, though as historian John C. Brennan once told me, the gift was puzzling in light of General Jackson's fondness for "shooting people and producing his own cadavers." They were subsequently given to the Smithsonian Institution, though no record of the donation can be found there. Edwin's description of his father is in Watermeier, 274. The threatening letter is in the Andrew Jackson Papers, Manuscripts Division, Library of Congress, microfilm reel 46.

17. My friend Stephen M. Archer believes the "Brutus" came from another pseudonym used occasionally by one of the men suspected of being the author of the "Junius" letters. I believe Richard named his son for Lucius Junius Brutus, who expelled the Tarquins from Rome, and Marcus Junius Brutus, whose assassination of Caesar was supposed to restore the Republic. Algernon Sydney Booth died at the age of five, and daughter Jane later became Mrs. James Mitchell. Another John Wilkes Booth lived in London in the 1790s, and he appears to have been a nephew of Richard Booth.

18. Gary Lawson Browne, *Baltimore in the Nation, 1789–1861* (Chapel Hill: University of North Carolina Press, 1980), 161–65. "Family flour" was made from a new strain of wheat that kept better in hotter climates.

19. Names of boys on Exeter Street are given in "The Civil War Note-book of Washington Hands," unpublished manuscript, Maryland Historical Society. Testimony of Philip H.

Maulsby tells of the connection between Booth and the O'Laughlens through a school run by a Mr. Smith. Maulsby had many relatives in Bel Air, and was married to a sister of the O'Laughlen boys. Poore, 2:226.

20. Walter Edgar McCann, "The Booth Family in Maryland," *Our Newsman*, n.d., 410, copy provided by Stephen M. Archer; *The (New York) Weekly Press*, June 7, 1893, 2; *Boston Transcript*, July 7, 1923; George L. Stout's Recollections, Baltimore *American*, July 27, 1902. Stuart Robson in "May's Dramatic Encyclopedia," unpublished manuscript by Alonzo May, in the Maryland Historical Society, Jacket 16, 28.

21. June had attended St. Mary's School, run by the Sulpician Order, in Baltimore. Stanley Kimmel and others have said that Clementina was eleven years older than Junius, but death records in St. Louis show that when she died on March 25, 1874, she was sixty-six years old.

22. Stanley Kimmel and others have said that the headmaster of the Bel Air Academy was Edwin Arnold, but Arnold was elsewhere throughout this period. The old academy still stands, at 24 Pennsylvania Avenue in Bel Air; School life was described in *Circular of the Milton Boarding School* (Baltimore: James Lucas & Son, 1859), Maryland Historical Society. I have assumed that the offers made in 1850–51 were nearly identical to those published in this pamphlet. The old Milton School building still stands, and is currently a restaurant called the Milton Inn, at 14833 York Road in Sparks, Maryland.

23. John Milton, "The Tenure of Kings and Magistrates," as quoted in *Areopagitica and Other Political Writings of John Milton* (Indianapolis: Liberty Fund, 1999), 83; "A Defence of the People of England," as quoted in *Areopagitica*, 123.

24. "Giaour" is an Arabic word meaning "infidel," or non-Moslem. Though the original version of the poem, published in 1813, had fewer than seven hundred lines, Byron's final version was nearly twice as long. Frank D. McConnell, ed., *Byron's Poems* (New York: Norton Critical Editions, 1978), 94.

25. For a discussion of the Seward speech in historical context, see Michael F. Holt, *The Rise and Fall of the American Whig Party* (New York: Oxford University Press, 1999), 489–91. The controversial law is in 9 Stat. 462.

26. For political consequences, see W. U. Hensel, *The Christiana Riot and the Treason Trials of 1851* (Lancaster, PA: The New Era Printing Co, 1911), 51. Castner Hanway was the only person tried for treason, and after the judge instructed the jury that the crime did not rise to the level of treason, they returned a quick verdict of not guilty. Hensel, 98–99. *Circular of the Milton Boarding School* lists four Gorsuch boys as alumni, including Thomas Gorsuch. It also listed Joshua Gorsuch, who was present at the Christiana incident, and Jacob Pearce, whose father had been there. The 1850 census, taken June 24, caught "J. M. Booth" at the Milton School, but none of the Gorsuch boys was listed with him there; as they lived so close by, they probably did not board at the school.

27. Frank A. Burr, "Booth's Wife Adelaide," New York *Press*, 1891.

28. The tale came from the March 14 journal entry of James Winston, of the Covent Garden Theatre. It was a good story, but Robert Holmes actually died on December 23, 1823. According to Stephen M. Archer in *Junius Brutus Booth: Theatrical Prometheus* (Carbondale, IL: Southern Illinois University Press, 1992), 296, n. 32, Winston's notes in the Harvard Theatre Collection are inaccurate.

29. Stanley Kimmel erroneously thought that Junius had somehow kept the families a secret from each other for more than twenty-five years. But as Stephen M. Archer has shown, the Maryland family's 1827 visit to London sparked a moral exposé in the London *Sunday Monitor*, and Mary Ann and Adelaide must have been aware of those articles. The Stanley Kimmel Collection includes neighborhood recollections of these

tantrums at Bel Air, and at the Bel Air Market in Baltimore. The marriage certificate indicates that a wedding took place at the home of "the Hon. Mrs. [Jane] Chambers." The document is owned by a descendant of Edwin Booth.

30. The divorce became final on April 18, 1851. A copy of the decree is in the Maryland Historical Society, Manuscripts Division.

31. Clarke, *Unlocked Book,* 59.

32. The book was *The Architect* by William H. Ranlett (New York: Dewitt and Davenport, 1849). See James T. Wollon, Jr., "Harford County Architectural Notes: Tudor Hall, Fountain Green: Home of the Booth Family," *Harford Historical Bulletin* 3 (Spring 1973): 11. The author is indebted to Mr. Wollon, whose great-grandmother occupied Tudor Hall for seventy years. Gifford, the architect, gained an eccentric reputation when, after returning from college in Europe, he placed nude statues in his yard at Spring and Fayette streets. The Baltimore city government threatened to arrest him for public obscenity, and Gifford forestalled the problem by erecting a wall around the property. Perhaps his spunk is what attracted Booth's notice. The present author recalls many pleasant afternoons in the company of Gifford's grandson, Hugh Robert Gifford, who supplied this information.

33. Junius Jr. did not believe that little Blanche was his biological daughter, and he divorced her mother, Clementina DeBar, eventually marrying Harriet Mace. The St. Timothy's quotes are from *Rules and Regulations for the Government of the Students at St. Timothy's Hall* (Baltimore: Joseph Robinson, 1852), supplied by Percy E. Martin.

34. St. Timothy's Hall produced three Civil War generals: Fitzhugh Lee and Steven Elliott for the Confederacy, and Charles Phelps for the Union. Erick F. Davis, "Saint Timothy's Hall," *History Trails* [Baltimore County Historical Society newsletter] 11, no. 3 (Spring 1977): 14.

35. *Rules and Regulations;* Asia Booth Clarke and others have said that the students were artillery cadets, but as Erick F. Davis has shown, the school's three artillery companies were organized beginning in 1856. *St. Timothy's Hall,* 13.

36. Clarke, *Unlocked Book,* 75–76.

37. "A Marylander," December 3, 1878, quoted in Clarke, *Unlocked Book,* 152–53. This article has glaring inaccuracies, probably attributable to the passage of twenty-five years, but the author knew a great deal about life at St. Timothy's Hall. He erroneously remembered that Senator Thomas Bayard attended the school; it was actually Thomas Baynard, of Savannah, Georgia. A third student included in this memoir was William Morris Orem, of Baltimore.

38. E. Anthony Rotundo, *American Manhood: Transformations in Masculinity from the Revolution to the Modern Era* (New York: Basic Books, 1993), 35.

39. An eyewitness account of Junius's death was published in *The New York Times,* August 1, 1856.

40. The destruction of Tudor Hall's roof chilled relations between Booth and Gifford, who witnessed the assassination in Ford's Theatre. See John T. Ford in LAS 5:441; William P. Wood memo in LAS 6:447.

41. Clarke, *Unlocked Book,* 67, 72–73, 99–191; Cola di Rienzi entry in *The Catholic Encyclopedia,* vol. 13 (New York: Robert Appleton Co., 1912). Most likely, Booth was familiar with the novel *Rienzi* by Edward Bulwer-Lytton (1835), and perhaps with the Wagner opera of the same name (1842). Both were sympathetic to the memory of Rienzi. The historical figure, however, was not so laudable. He became intoxicated with power, and was ultimately killed by the public he started out to serve.

42. John Wilkes Booth letters to S[amuel]. William O'Laughlen, April 30, 1854, and Au-

gust 8, 1854, both in the collection of Dr. John K. Lattimer. This last incident may be the same one Asia described, involving a sharecropper. Booth's eight surviving letters to O'Laughlen are published in John Rhodehamel and Louise Taper, eds., *"Right or Wrong, God Judge Me": The Writings of John Wilkes Booth* (Urbana and Chicago: University of Illinois Press, 1997), 36–44.

43. *Ibid.*, 72, 76. The present author owns dozens of books that came down through the families of Junius Jr. and Joseph Booth. Many were owned by John Wilkes, and are inscribed in his own hand.

44. *Ibid.*, 63–65.

45. The process of realignment is best described by Michael F. Holt in *The Political Crisis of the 1850s* (New York: John Wiley & Sons, 1978). For an excellent study of the American Party, see Jean H. Baker, *Ambivalent Americans: The Know-Nothing Party in Maryland* (Baltimore: Johns Hopkins University Press, 1977). Officially, the Know-Nothings called themselves the American Party.

46. The Kerney incident became a highlight of his brief political career; William G. Brownlow, as cited in Joel H. Silbey, *The Transformation of American Politics* (Englewood Cliffs, NJ: Prentice-Hall, 1967), 53; Thomas R. Whitney, *A Defence of the American Policy*, as quoted in Michael F. Holt, "The Antimasonic and Know-Nothing Parties," *History of United States Political Parties*, Arthur M. Schlesinger, Jr., ed. (New York: Chelsea House and R. W. Bowker, 1973), 1:681–82; Horace Greeley said this in a letter to Schuyler Colfax, August 24, 1854, as quoted in Holt, *Political Crisis*, 167.

47. Clarke, *Unlocked Book*, 105.

Chapter 6: "He wanted to be loved of the Southern people"

1. Clarke, *Unlocked Book*, 106–7; *The Baltimore Sun*, August 14, 1855, 3.

2. Family and friends called Edwin "Ned" until 1864, when his partner, William Stuart, reshaped his image and insisted he drop the nickname. New York *Press*, May 20, 1893, 25. Asia Booth letter to Jean Sherwood, August 1, 1855, Peale Museum. According to Asia, Ned claimed to have made a fortune, but expected to lose it before returning home.

3. *The Baltimore Sun*, August 14, 1855, 3. John Ford Sollers, "The Theatrical Career of John T. Ford," Ph.D. dissertation, Stanford University, 1962, 57–59. The Baltimore Museum was established in the days when theater was not yet socially acceptable. Patrons could go to the first-floor museum, then slip quietly upstairs for a "moral lecture." Baltimore, New York, and Boston still had such establishments.

4. As the evening's proceeds went to Clarke, it appears his recommendation of Booth was not without self-interest.

5. See Ben Graf Henneke, *Laura Keene: Actress, Innovator, and Impresario* (Tulsa, OK: Council Oak Books, 1990), 34. Eventually, insiders also learned that Miss Keene's "nieces," Emma and Clara, were actually her daughters. Another Keene biographer sees the Keene-Booth animosity as a clash of personalities, explaining that Laura Keene had contrived the whole Australia tour as a search for her husband, from whom she sought a divorce. See Vernanne Bryan, *Laura Keene, a British Actress on the American Stage* (Jefferson, NC: McFarland, 1993), 43–45.

6. The Bel Air *Southern Aegis*, July 18, 1857, 14. The ad also ran in the July 25, August 1, August 8, and August 15 editions. Nobody took Booth up on the offer, and Tudor Hall remained vacant for several more years. Thanks to Dinah Faber for supplying the dates of the ad.

7. Bruce Erwin Woodruff, "Genial John McCullough: Actor and Manager" (Ph.D. dissertation, University of Nebraska, 1984), 1; Coincidentally, Philadelphia's Central High

School had three students who would enter the assassination story later: writer George Alfred Townsend, court reporter Edward V. Murphy, and witness Louis J. Weichmann. All, coincidentally, took "phonography," or shorthand, courses at the school, but they were unknown to one another.

8. Letter from William F. Johnson (McCullough's intimate friend) to William Winter, November 8, 1885, in McCullough Papers, Folger Shakespeare Library. A fuller discussion is in Woodruff, 11–13; White's teachings were based on the technique of Thomas Sheridan, a son of playwright Richard Brinsley Sheridan (*The School for Scandal*). Much would be made of Booth's lack of formal voice training, but in fact he may well have received the standard lessons. There seems to be no contemporary record one way or the other, because this did not become an issue until well into the twentieth century, after all of Booth's contemporaries had died. See Stanley Kimmel, *The Mad Booths of Maryland* (Indianapolis: Bobbs-Merrill, 1940), 179, 180–81.

9. A playbill in the Crawford Theatre Collection at Yale University shows "Mrs. Wilks," "Mast. Wilks," and "Mast. J. Wilks," all in the cast of *Masks and Faces; or, Before & Behind the Curtain* at the Arch Street Theatre, November 23, 1855; George Alfred Townsend, *The Life, Crime, and Capture of John Wilkes Booth* (New York: Dick and Fitzgerald, 1865), 21–22 (hereinafter Townsend).

10. Townsend, 21–22.

11. To be fair, it was Townsend alone who painted a bleak picture of Booth's apprenticeship. Others simply copied Townsend's story. Thanks to Arthur F. Loux and Stephen M. Archer for character searches. Dr. Archer also supplied a copy of Harold S. Sharp and Marjorie Z. Sharpe's *Index to Characters in the Performing Arts* (New York: The Scarecrow Press, 1966).

12. Baltimore land records show that in the second half of October 1860 (immediately after the elections in Maryland), Richard Junius Booth sold all of his property, evidently with the intent of leaving the country. His properties were at the southeast corner of French Lane and South Charles Street; two lots on the north side of Preston Street; a lot on the west side of Amity, north of Fayette; and a corner house at German and Green streets. These 1860 sales are recorded in Liber GES 199 folio 39; Liber GES 199 folio 393; Liber GES 199 folio 445; and Liber GES 217 folio 235. Richard and his wife, Sarah, moved to London. According to William Winter, Edwin Booth befriended his half-brother there. *Life and Art of Edwin Booth* (New York: Macmillan and Co., 1894), 396. (Earlier editions do not mention this.) As Stephen M. Archer discovered, Sarah Booth died in London on November 18, 1868, and Richard followed a month later, on December 16. Both are buried in Highgate Cemetery, Grave 16340, Square 111. Edwin later became the target of an extortion attempt relating to the release of the Adelaide story.

13. The play tally comes from my own database, taken from a full run of Arch Street Theatre playbills in the Roland Reed Collection, Howard University. For an additional discussion of the Arch at this time, see William D. Coder, "A History of the Philadelphia Theatre, 1856 to 1878," (unpublished doctoral dissertation in English literature, University of Pennsylvania, 1936). An excellent look at the changing image of one tyrannicide can be found in Max Radin, *Marcus Brutus* (New York and London: Oxford University Press, 1939).

14. Townsend's comments about Booth are in *Townsend*, 22. Star system and management of the Marshall Theatre: Charles F. Fuller, "Kunkel and Company at the Marshall Theatre, Richmond, Virginia 1856–1861" (master's thesis, Ohio University, 1968), 106. Information on specific Booth performances is published in Arthur F. Loux, *John*

Wilkes Booth: Day By Day (n.p., privately printed, 1990). This listing is the most complete and reliable available, but only twelve copies were printed.

15. Biographical information on John T. Ford and his associates (including Marshall company actors) can be found in *Sollers,* 79. Dr. Sollers was Ford's grandson, and I am indebted to him and his wife, Grace, for their friendship, generosity, and support.

16. John M. Barron, "With John Wilkes Booth in His Days As an Actor." *The Baltimore Sun,* March 17, 1907.

17. Edward M. Alfriend in *The (Washington) Sunday Globe,* February 9, 1902, clipping in the papers of David Rankin Barbee, Lauinger Library, Georgetown University.

18. Alfriend, *Sunday Globe.* In a private letter to Jean Sherwood, Asia Booth Clarke described the Booth eyes as "black and brilliant, the white ball is bluish from the excessive darkness of the pupil." Letter of June 19, 1859, Peale Museum.

19. Townsend, "Philistine's Diary"; Ralph Brooks, M.D., "Insane or Ill?" *Surratt Courier* 22 (August 1997): 9. According to Margery Boorde, R.N., tertiary syphilis patients are unable to form coherent sentences, and are clearly dysfunctional.

20. Clara Morris, *Life on the Stage: My Personal Experiences and Recollections* (New York: McClure, Phillips & Co., 1901), 100.

21. Mary Devlin letter to Edwin Booth, August 24, 1859, in the New York Public Library, Theatre Collection; Edwin Booth letters to Junius Booth, October 31 and December 12, 1858, supplied by Franklyn Lenthall.

22. Richmond *Dispatch,* October 15, 1858, 2.

23. Frederick Bancroft, *William H. Seward* (New York: Harper and Brothers, 1900), 1:458, 461. Emphasis added.

24. *New York Herald,* October 28, 1858, 2; *The New York Times,* October 28, 1858, 2.

25. Richmond newspapers for February 28 through March 12, 1859, show *Our American Cousin* playing every night but March 11. What part John Wilkes Booth played is not known. Laura Keene sued Clarke again, and the litigation only intensified in 1865, after *Our American Cousin* found a place in history. See *Keene* v. *Clarke,* 28 N.Y. Super. Ct. 38, *Keene* v. *Wheatley et al.,* 14 F. Cas. 180 (no. 7644), and *Keene* v. *Kimball,* 82 Mass. 545. Clarke's defense was that he had bought an independent copy of the script from the widow of Joshua Silsbee, a co-author of the play. Depositions taken in London showed that Taylor was the sole author, and Silsbee was not authorized to have a copy of the script. Keene was an alien herself at the time, and was not naturalized until October 5, 1859.

26. Clarke, *Unlocked Book,* 110–11; Asia Booth Clarke letter to Jean Anderson, May 17, 1859, in Peale Museum, Baltimore. Asia sometimes signed her letters "Asia Booth Sleeper" at this time. Eventually she would express her regret at ignoring her brother's advice about Clarke. However, private letters show that the marriage was very happy for a few years. "The square" is now Logan Circle.

27. *Richmond Whig,* October 18, 1859, 3.

28. *Ibid.,* 2; Israel Green, "The Capture of John Brown," *North American Review* 141 (December 1885): 564–69.

29. *New York Herald,* as quoted in John P. Hale's response, published in *The New York Times,* November 2, 1859, 1; *Richmond Whig,* December 3, 1859, 2. On this same page, the *Whig* editor suggested the formation of a Southern confederacy.

30. *The New York Times,* October 24, 1859, 1; Letcher's message to the Virginia legislature, January 7, 1860, as quoted by Allan Nevins in *The Emergence of Lincoln* (New York: Scribner's, 1950), 2:176; Richmond *Dispatch,* December 3, 1859, 1.

31. Even though Brown had attacked a federal installation, there were no laws making his

act specifically a federal crime; thus he was tried in a state court. "Monomania" is discussed by Isaac Ray in *Treatise on the Medical Jurisprudence of Insanity* (Boston: Little, Brown, 1853), 170–71; The political angles are examined by Robert E. McGlone, "John Brown, Henry Wise, and the Politics of Insanity," in Paul Finkleman, ed., *His Soul Goes Marching On: Responses to John Brown and the Harpers Ferry Raid* (Charlottesville: University Press of Virginia, 1996), 216. The spelling of "Charlestown" was subsequently changed to "Charles Town."

32. Libby is familiar to Richmonders as the name of the warehouse at Twentieth and Dock streets. In 1861, it was leased by Luther Libby, ship chandler and father of the man who lent Booth his trousers in November 1859. Their building became Libby Prison during the war. See George W. Libby letter to John H. Ingraham, August 15, 1913, in Mss6:1L6144:1, manuscript collections of the Virginia Historical Society; Lt. Louis J. Bossieux was a manufacturer of "double refined steam candies"; Richmond *Dispatch*, October 18, 1859, 2; George Crutchfield letter to Edward Valentine, July 5, 1900, in the Valentine Museum, Richmond; George W. Libby, "John Brown and John Wilkes Booth," *Confederate Veteran* 37 (April 1930): 138; Richmond *Dispatch*, October 17, 1859, 2. In 1865, Edwin Adams said that Booth had forced himself into the Grays and was made an assistant commissary or quartermaster. This makes perfect sense, as no military unit wants to bring along "dead weight," and Booth had no rifle. Adams, a leading man at the Marshall, did not say how he learned this. LAS 2:60. For information on the Grays, I am indebted to Howard E. Bartholf and Al Bossieux.

33. *Richmond Daily Whig*, November 28, 1859, 2; Washington *Evening Star*, November 25, 1859, 2; Washington *Evening Star*, November 28, 1859, 2.

34. Unpublished recollections of Philip Whitlock, Mss5:1W5905:1, manuscript collections of the Virginia Historical Society, 87; Clarke, *Unlocked Book*, 113, 124.

35. The "Secret Six" who financed him were Samuel Gridley Howe, Thomas Wentworth Higginson, Franklin B. Sanborn, George Luther Stearns, Gerrit Smith, and Theodore Parker. See Edward J. Renehan, Jr., *The Secret Six: How a Circle of Northern Aristocrats Helped Light the Fuse of the Civil War* (New York: Crown, 1995). The notion that conspirators kept the masses ignorant of their intentions had become a staple of conspiracy literature as early as 1747, when anti-Masonic tracts began to assert that secret authorities were manipulating their subordinates and exploiting their naïveté. Fear of secret societies would bloom again during the Civil War, unhampered by the need or expectation of factual proof. See Daniel Pipes, *Conspiracy: How the Paranoid Style Flourishes and Where It Comes From* (New York: Free Press, 1997), 61–62.

36. Edward M. Alfriend, an actor and member of the Grays, recalled the theater confrontation in *The (Washington) Sunday Globe*, February 9, 1902. Asia Booth Clarke, undated letter [ca. December 1860] to Jean Anderson, in the Peale Museum, Baltimore. In a letter dated November 28, 1859, Mary Devlin tells Edwin, "I told you I thought he would seize the opportunity," and predicts the hard life of a soldier would dissuade him from further service. (She apparently did not know about St. Timothy's Hall.) New York Public Library at Lincoln Center, Theatre Collection.

37. Roy P. Basler, ed., *The Collected Works of Abraham Lincoln* (New Brunswick, NJ: Rutgers University Press, 1953), 3:541.

Chapter 7: "The *man of genius in the Booth family*"

1. Columbus *Daily Sun*, October 3, 1860, 3; Morris, *Life on the Stage*, 99.

2. Columbus *Daily Times*, October 5, 1860, 3.

3. The wound was described in different sources as both serious and minor and as being "in the thigh," in the "fleshy part of the leg," "in the side," and "in the rear." The standard account comes from the Columbus *Daily Sun,* October 13, 1860, 2, but this comes from Canning's interview with George Alfred Townsend, published in the Cincinnati *Enquirer,* January 19, 1886, 1. Though it was recorded long after the fact, it is by far the most detailed, and does not conflict with earlier versions of the story. Later, Canning's wife said that according to her husband, the scar left by the bullet was "not to be mistaken once described."

4. Montgomery *Daily Mail,* October 30, 1860, 3.

5. Montgomery *Advertiser,* November 7, 1860; Baltimore *Daily Republican,* November 8, 1860; *New York Herald,* November 8, 1860, 1; and *New Bern (NC) Progress,* as quoted in Robert S. Harper, *Lincoln and the Press* (New York: McGraw-Hill, 1951), 67.

6. *The New York Times,* December 14, 1860, 1.

7. Buchanan's message was published in *The Philadelphia Inquirer,* December 5, 1860, 1.

8. *Ibid.*

9. Edwin discovered the speech years later in his own house, which is now The Players in New York. The speech is in the Hampden-Booth Theatre Library there. The full text appears in John Rhodehamel and Louise Taper, eds., *"Right or Wrong, God Judge Me": The Writings of John Wilkes Booth* (Urbana and Chicago: University of Illinois Press, 1997), 55–64.

10. *Ibid.,* 55.

11. Albany *Argus,* February 18, 1861; New York *Clipper,* February 23, 1861; Albany *Journal,* February 24, 1861; Albany *Express,* March 5, 1861.

12. Norma B. Cuthbert, *Lincoln and the Baltimore Plot, 1861* (San Marino, CA: Henry E. Huntington Library, 1949).

13. 12 Stat. 1258.

14. *The Baltimore Sun,* February 27, 1861; The James Buchanan incident brought suggestions that an alternate railway should be built to avoid Baltimore. *New York Tribune,* March 11, 1857, 5. A congressional committee looked into the so-called Baltimore plot and various other threats against Lincoln, focusing on Cipriano Ferrandini, a barber at Barnum's Hotel. No criminal charges were ever brought in the case. See House Report No. 79, Thirty-sixth Congress, Second Session, 2:3–19, 125, 132–38, 166–78; and Richard G. Reese, "Lincoln and the Baltimore Barber," *The Baltimore Sun,* February 26, 1961.

15. *The New York Times,* December 14, 1860, 1. The circumstances surrounding Baltimore in April 1861 are covered in O.R. I:2: 580 *et seq.*

16. Assault on Baltimore, O.R. I:2, 607, 608; *ibid.,* 601–2; *The Baltimore Sun,* May 14, 1861, 1. Publicly, the administration denied having ordered Butler to occupy the city, but the following day, Lincoln promoted him to major general. *Ex parte Merryman* 17 Fed. Cas. 144, no. 9,487. Taney thought that only Congress could suspend the writ.

17. Incremental moves: *The Baltimore Sun,* April 29, 1861, 4; Basler 4:346–47. O.R. I: 2, 601–2. Subsequent proclamations extended the suspension throughout the United States. Basler, 5:436–37 and 6:451–52. Lincoln said, "In my opinion I broke no law." Basler, 4:430; His response to the House is in Executive Document no. 16, Thirty-seventh Congress, First Session; Arrest of mayor George W. Brown, O.R. II: 1, 587 and 619–21, and of police marshal George P. Kane, *The Baltimore Sun,* June 28, 1861, 1, and O.R. II: 1, 620, 623, and Kane's own report, *ibid.,* 628–30; orders for arrests of legislators: O.R. II: 1, 589, 678. Generals Nathaniel Banks and John A. Dix complained about their orders, but complied nevertheless, *ibid.,* 586, 589.

18. The order prohibiting legal counsel is in O.R. II:1, 613–14. Seward's statement to Lord Lyons was quoted by John A. Marshall in *American Bastille* (Philadelphia: Thomas W. Hartley & Co., 1881), xiii, which ran an engraving of "Seward's little bell" as its frontispiece.

19. Of all states, Maryland had the lowest rate of response to draft calls, providing only 46,638 of the 70,965 men requested. O.R. III:4, 72.

20. Actor William A. Howell claimed to have roomed with Booth on High Street in 1861, but his account is confused, and undoubtedly refers to a later period. Undated clipping from *The Baltimore Sun* in the Stanley Kimmel collection, University of Tampa; In *Fraser's Magazine,* June 1865, 791–806, an anonymous source claimed that Booth was caught tearing up rails and was released by the president's own order. A Boston paper quoted Baltimore attorney W. G. Snethen as saying that Booth helped burn the bridges. *The Commonwealth,* April 22, 1865, 2. Booth allegedly told William H. Garrett that he had been present at the Pratt Street Riot. "Wilkes Booth" in the Philadelphia *Press,* December 17, 1881; An unidentified clipping dated October 4, 1861, lists "John Wilkes" as one of ten men released from jail on taking an oath of allegiance, but Booth had been long gone by that time. LAS 3:123; See also Albany *Argus,* April 22, 1861.

21. "The Civil War Note-book of Washington Hands," MS 2468, on microfilm at the Maryland Historical Society. Hands did not mention the Booths, except to say that Charles Claiborne was living in their Exeter Street house.

22. In a letter to Nahum Capen dated July 28, 1881, Edwin Booth said, "I asked [John Wilkes] once why he did not join the Confederate army; to which he replied, 'I promised mother I would keep out of the quarrel, if possible, and I am sorry that I said so.'" Published in Clarke, *Unlocked Book,* 202–4. Edwin and Joseph both moved to England, and Edwin returned after a year abroad. Joseph, however, continued on to Australia, and for a while even his family was unable to locate him. With Edwin and Joe out of the country, John Wilkes was providing his mother's principal support. His residence officially changed to New York City when Mary Ann moved there, and all subsequent legal instruments (including estate papers) were filed accordingly; Though Lincoln had been conscripting soldiers since July 1862, the draft was not actually authorized under the law until Congress passed the Enrollment Act on March 3, 1863. 12 Stat. 731. About half of all eligible Northern men avoided service, and more than 2.25 million men on enrollment lists had not yet been called by the war's end. James W. Geary, *We Need Men: The Union Draft in the Civil War* (DeKalb, IL: Northern Illinois University Press, 1991), 82.

23. Henrietta survived, married actor Edward Eddy, and lived until November 1905.

24. Edwin's comment was in an 1858 letter to his brother Junius in the collection of Francis Wilson, quoted in Wilson's book *John Wilkes Booth: Fact and Fiction of Lincoln's Assassination* (New York: Houghton Mifflin, 1929), 17. Buffalo *Morning Express,* October 31, 1861; Leavenworth, Kansas, *Conservative,* December 27, 1863; Washington *Daily National Intelligencer,* April 30, 1863; New Orleans *Times,* March 18, 1864.

25. Boston *Daily Advertiser,* May 19, 1862; *Cincinnati Enquirer,* January 19, 1886, 1; John T. Ford in *The Washington Star,* December 7, 1881.

26. Chicago *Times,* June 3, 1863; Mary Devlin Booth to Edwin Booth, February 12, 1863, in the New York Public Library, Theatre Collection; *Spirit of the Times,* April 5, 1862; Chicago *Times,* December 3, 1862; Philadelphia *Press,* March 9, 1863; *Daily National Intelligencer,* May 2, 1863. My own unpublished survey of more than eight hundred reviews shows that all but a handful were positive.

27. *New York Tribune,* March 25, 1862; Cleveland *Plain Dealer,* November 30, 1863; When Booth fell on the stage at the Holliday Street Theatre, notices in the *Spirit of the Times* (March 8, 1862, 13) said he had broken his nose. Though he finished the play with blood "streaming from his nose," he was right back on the stage the following night, and nothing further was said about it. The New York *Clipper* called it a sword fight incident. Edwin had been injured several times on stage; see, for example, Asia Booth Clarke letter to Jean Anderson dated March 3, 1861, Peale Museum.

28. Brooklyn, New York, *Standard,* October 31, 1863, as quoted in Loux, 359; Louisville *Journal,* January 20, 1864; New York *Clipper,* January 25, 1862. The supposed best sword fight involved Booth and Thomas L. Conner.

29. Sollers, 113–14; original playbill in the John T. Ford collection, Manuscripts Division, Library of Congress. The entire passage, from act I, scene 1 of the Cibber version, was:

> *I have no brother, I am like no brother*
> *And this word Love, which gray beards call divine,*
> *Be resident in men like one another*
> *And not in me—I am,—myself, alone*

Booth's innovations are marked in one of his own prompt books for *Richard III,* now in the Harry Ransom Humanities Research Center, University of Texas at Austin. An unidentified clipping in the Harvard Theatre Collection gives H. A. Weaver's detailed description of the sword fight. Examples of the critical praise: *St. Louis Democrat,* December 23, 1862; *Spirit of the Times,* March 22, 1862; Louisville *Journal,* June 30, 1862.

30. No accurate accounting of Booth's travels is possible, but mileages noted here are based on modern roads, and calculated with the help of MapQuest.com. Booth traveled on railroads and steamboats much of the time, which adds to the total given. Brooklyn Academy of Music: Brooklyn, New York, *Standard,* October 31, 1863.

31. Canning in *The Cincinnati Enquirer,* January 19, 1886, 1; Adam Badeau, *The Vagabond* (New York: Rudd & Carleton, 1859), 329. "Furore" playbill for May 19, 1862, in the Princeton University Library Theatre Collection; The Boston *Advertiser,* February 1, 1863, quoting the New York *Programme.* Boston was the home of choice for most of the Booths. Edwin and Mary lived in Dorchester, and Mary died there in 1863. Junius settled just north of the city, and ultimately died in Manchester. Richard and Kellie Gutman, "Boston: A Home for John Wilkes Booth?" *Surratt Society News* 10, no. 9 (September 1985): 1, 6–8. The lot purchase was completed in October 1864, and the title was put in Mary Ann's name. The lot remained undeveloped for as long as the Booths owned it.

32. The reasoning behind the Supreme Court law was to allow for one new justice to cover the geographically remote western states (California and Oregon) in their circuit riding capacities. Stephen J. Field was appointed to fill that opening. 12 Stat. 794. Before this, Attorney General Edward Bates advised the secretary of war to keep the habeas corpus issue away from the Supreme Court, as the administration would probably be defeated. Letter to Stanton, dated January 31, 1863, in Stanton Papers, document 52223. Lincoln escaped revocation of his other war powers by a single vote, when the "Prize Cases" gave him a 5–4 victory in 1862. 67 U.S. 635. When the unpopular Andrew Johnson became president, Congress let the number of justices drop to seven.

33. For a fuller discussion of the war's effect on state governments, see David E. Long, *The Jewel of Liberty* (Harrisburg, PA: Stackpole Books, 1994).

34. Saulsbury in *Congressional Globe*, Thirty-seventh Congress, Third Session, 230.

35. Louisville *Journal*, June 20, 1862, 2. The Richmond editorial was actually directed at John C. Frémont, for his actions in Missouri.

36. Indianapolis *Daily Sentinel*, November 29, 1862, 2.

37. The state of morals in the District of Columbia was covered in Lafayette C. Baker, *The Secret Service in the Late War* (Philadelphia: John E. Potter, 1874), 217, 222; Matthew Canning quoted by George Alfred Townsend, the Cincinnati *Enquirer*, January 19, 1886, 1. May gave his own accounts of this in several places. Here, I've used his testimony from *Surratt Trial*, 270. May could have been known to Booth previously, as his brother Henry was a former member of Congress from Baltimore and was among those arrested with state legislators in 1861.

38. John F. May manuscript, "The Mark of the Scalpel," in the Manuscripts Division, Library of Congress, 4. An edited version was published in *Records of the Columbia Historical Society* 13 (1910): 53–87. Booth letter to Simonds, April 19, 1863, in the André de Coppet Collection, Princeton University Library; Canning to Townsend in the Cincinnati *Enquirer*, January 19, 1886.

39. Herold's own statement mentioned the bullet operation, and dates this initial meeting on the night that Booth played in *The Marble Heart*, which would be April 13, 1863. LAS 4:442. He did not say how he got backstage, but he traveled with friends in the Marine Band, who would have been able to give him such access. Musicians moonlighted because their salaries, which were set at only $22 per month, forced them to seek additional income. 13 Stat. 144. Nearly every member of the Ford's Theatre orchestra was also a member of the Marine Band, and I assume this was true of other playhouses in Washington; When Adam George Herold died in October 1864, he left a will that specified "under no circumstances should the duty of settling my estate devolve upon my son, David." For more on Herold see Michael W. Kauffman, "David Edgar Herold, the Forgotten Conspirator," *Surratt Society News* 6 (November 1981): 4–5.

40. Historians have speculated that Booth's "failure" as a manager was due to Union reverses in the war, and this, they said, was a factor in his growing despondency. But before he began the Washington venture, Booth wrote to Joe Simonds, "I am idle this week but stay here in hopes to open the other theater next Monday for a week or two before going to Chicago." Booth letter to Joseph Simonds, April 19, 1863. André de Coppet Collection, Princeton University Library.

41. Maj. Henry L. McConnell claimed that he had arrested Booth in St. Louis but released him on his taking the oath. McConnell's account is not very specific, but it must have happened between December 22, 1862, and January 3, 1863, when both were in St. Louis. LAS 4:75. Ed Curtis, who was present at the New Orleans incident, published an account in an unnamed newspaper. It was subsequently quoted by John S. Kendall in *The Golden Age of the New Orleans Theater* (New York: Greenwood Press, 1968), 498; The New York incident is recounted in Jennings, *Theatrical and Circus Life*, 489–90. For details of Kane's arrest, see *The Baltimore Sun*, June 28, 1861, and O. R. II:1, 620–30. This is another example of Booth's tendency to exaggerate. He did not really know Kane, though the marshal's joint ownership of the Howard Athenaeum, in which the elder Booth had played, probably brought him in contact with Booth's father. Adam Badeau, "Dramatic Reminiscences," St. Paul and Minneapolis *Pioneer Press*, February 20, 1887; Clarke, *Unlocked Book*, 118.

42. Tyler Dennett, ed., *Lincoln and the Civil War in the Diaries and Letters of John Hay* (New

York: Dodd, Mead & Co., 1939). Fanciful accounts were written long after the assassination, but without benefit of contemporary evidence. See, for example, Stanley Kimmel, "Lincoln Had Deep Appreciation of Acting of John Wilkes Booth," Washington *Sunday Star,* April 15, 1941.

43. *True Delta,* March 19, 1864, 1; "Booth's Appearance in Washington, November 1863," *Lincoln Lore* 1301 (March 15, 1954).

44. "John Wilkes Booth," Boston *Advertiser,* May 19, 1862, clipping in the Harvard Theatre Collection.

45. Boston *Courier,* May 13, 1862; The 1864 New Orleans engagement was tainted with hoarseness, but as one paper said, the weather had been severe the whole time Booth was in town. New Orleans *Times Picayune,* March 24, 1864. He had traveled almost nine hundred miles to get there from his previous engagement in Cincinnati; what followed was another long run in Boston, more than fifteen hundred miles away, and that was also plagued by violent rainstorms and cool weather. Historians have never considered these factors in assessing Booth's health, but the Boston *Transcript* did. On May 16, the paper's critic said that Booth was "over-taxing his physical power" by pushing himself too hard. In *The Albion,* March 22, 1862, 139, "Mercutio" (William Winter) characterized Booth's voice as a "severe case of larynx," implying it was a deliberate effect. The Boston-to-Chicago trip was mentioned in a June 10, 1862, letter from Mary Ann Booth, at The Players. June's vocal lapse was recorded in his own diary for 1864. This remarkable document, discovered by the author, was tipped into an 1864 *Frank Leslie's Lady's Almanac,* and gives a wealth of detail about the Booth family. It is in the Folger Shakespeare Library, Washington.

46. Morris, *Life on the Stage,* 103.

47. *Ibid.,* 104; Alfriend, "Assassin Booth," Washington *Sunday Globe,* February 9, 1902; Edwin Booth to Richard H. Stoddard, January [22,] 1863, quoted in Otis Skinner, *The Last Tragedian: Booth Tells His Own Story* (New York: Dodd, Mead and Co., 1939), 71.

48. Raymond in "Raymond's Recollections," *The Washington Star,* April 7, 1883; Wyndham in the *New York Herald,* June 27, 1909; Kate Reignolds Winslow, *Yesterdays with Actors* (Boston: Cupples and Co., 1887), 140.

49. Earl Schenck Miers, *Lincoln Day by Day* (Washington: Lincoln Sesquicentennial Commission, 1960), *passim.* The plays Lincoln saw were *Richard III, Julius Caesar, The Merchant of Venice / Don Cesar de Bazan, Hamlet, Richelieu, The Fool's Revenge,* and *Richard III* again. Fanny Seward wrote a detailed account of the March 11 meeting, and it has been preserved with her diary. Anna told Fanny that she always felt predestined to marry Edwin Booth, but married Frederick Seward instead. Seward Papers, University of Rochester Library.

50. Booth letter to "Dear John," dated June 17, 1864. Illinois State Historical Library, John Wilkes Booth collection, SC 157.

51. Bradley Tyler Johnson, "My Ride Around Baltimore in 1864," *Journal of the United States Cavalry Association* 2:6 (September 1889): 250, 253–55.

52. *Ibid.,* 256–57.

53. A copy of the letter is in the Abraham Lincoln papers in the Library of Congress, and was published in Basler, *Collected Works,* 7:451; Confederates denied initiating the episode. See Clement C. Clay's report to Judah P. Benjamin, O.R. IV:3, 584–87.

Chapter 8: "My profession, my name, is my passport"

1. Johnson, "My Ride Around Baltimore in 1864," 257.

2. Booth traveled while still recovering from erysipelas that summer. His August 22 letter

to "Dearest" [Isabel Sumner], evidently written in New York, says, "My arm is a little better," and other sources show him in Philadelphia and Baltimore with the same condition. Virginia Historical Society, MSS1 D9345a 29; Clarke, *Unlocked Book*, 119, 115–16. A letter was sent to the Confederate War Department by "Dr. J. W. Booth," but only an index entry was found, and not the letter itself. House Report 104, Thirty-ninth Congress, First Session (1866), 13.

3. All mileages given here are a bare minimum, based on modern road travel. Steamship and rail travel would have added to the distances, but we do not always know what form of transportation Booth used. His travel sequence is taken from Loux, *John Wilkes Booth: Day by Day*.

4. For draft numbers, see McPherson, *Political History*. The Kilpatrick-Dahlgren raid, which was broken up on March 2, has been covered extensively in several books, among them Virgil Carrington Jones, *Eight Hours Before Richmond* (New York: Henry Holt and Co., 1957). For a good discussion of the hard war policy, see Mark Grimsley, *The Hard Hand of War: Union Military Policy Toward Southern Civilians, 1861–1865* (Cambridge: Cambridge University Press, 1995).

5. For more on prisoner exchanges, see O.R. II:3, 222–24, and II:4, 174, 266–68. The cartel was formalized in General Orders 142, Adjutant General's Office, on September 25, 1862. The issue of exchanges was also complicated by the administration's wish to avoid any formal recognition of the Confederacy. When the general exchange was halted in 1863, commanders were given "field discretion" to issue paroles and thus avoid the responsibility of caring for their captives. See House of Representatives, Executive Document no. 124, Thirty-seventh Congress, Second Session. Grant's quote is from a letter to Gen. Ben Butler, August 18, 1864, in O.R. II:7, 607. He expressed a similar view the following day in a letter to Seward. O.R. II:7, 614–15. The contents of Lincoln's pockets are in the Library of Congress, and include several newspaper clippings.

6. Stanton to the Joint Committee on the Conduct of the War, May 4, 1864. O.R. II: 7, 110.

7. O.R. II:7, 111. Prisoners on both sides suffered from diseases such as typhoid fever, and not only from starvation, as charged. O.R. III: 5, 523. Stanton recommended "precisely the same rations and treatment" for rebel officers. O.R. II: 7, 113. In ordering retaliation, Stanton was supported by a list of senior officers who endorsed the cut in rations. O.R. II: 7, 150–51, and O.R. II:7, 183. Stanton's own figures showed that 26,436 Confederates died, out of 220,000 held in captivity, while 22,576 of 126,940 Union prisoners died in the South. House Report no. 152, Thirty-ninth Congress, First Session, July 28, 1866.

8. The circumstances leading up to Booth's reunion with Arnold are unknown, but inferred by Ford's knowledge of Billy Arnold as a "bad boy" who got drunk around the theater, and by Booth's known habit of dropping by the same theater when in town. John T. Ford in LAS 5:441.

9. Statement of Samuel B. Arnold, sworn on December 3, 1867, Benjamin F. Butler Papers, Manuscripts Division, Library of Congress (hereinafter Arnold-Butler). Arnold attended St. Mary's Seminary, St. Timothy's Hall, and Georgetown College. Though some of these were Catholic schools, Arnold was a Methodist. His January 1864 request for a pass to return to Baltimore noted that Arnold and his brother Charles had done honorable service and were "still ardently devoted to the cause." RG 109, Confederate Records, M-437, file 23A 1864, National Archives. My thanks to Michael Musick. Switching sides, as Arnold tried to do, was not uncommon; in 1865 alone, 1,955 captured Confederate soldiers were released upon joining their former enemies. O.R. III: 5, 531–32.

10. Samuel B. Arnold, *Memoirs of a Lincoln Conspirator* (Bowie, MD: Heritage Books, 1996), edited by Michael W. Kauffman, 42–43.

11. Arnold, *Memoirs,* 43. Both sides took hostages during the war, the legality of which was recognized in sections 54 and 55 of General Orders No. 100, the army's guide to the laws of war.

12. *New York Herald,* June 20, 1867; Thomas Nelson Conrad, *A Confederate Spy* (New York: J. S. Ogilvie, 1892), 69. Conrad believed there was a Mosby plan, but the story he cited appears to have come from a dubious source. According to John B. Jones of the Confederate War Department, proposals to assassinate Lincoln were never answered. Jones mentioned an 1863 letter from Henry Clay Durham, whom he called "a mad private, and Northern man." Davis sent his letter to the War Department without comment. *A Rebel War Clerk's Diary* (Philadelphia: J. B. Lippincott & Co., 1866), 2:24.

13. Conrad, *Confederate Spy,* 69–75. Conrad attributed the sudden vigilance to a security leak by drunken soldiers involved in the Mosby plot. He got this story from William H. Crook, an unreliable source who called himself a friend and bodyguard to the president.

14. Seward's letter quoted in John Bigelow, *Retrospections of an Active Life* (New York: Baker & Taylor Co., 1909), 2:547–48.

15. In September 1862, Companies D and K of the 150th Pennsylvania were assigned to the Soldiers' Home as well as the White House. Thomas Chamberlin, *History of the One Hundred and Fiftieth Regiment Pennsylvania Volunteers* (Philadelphia: F. McManus, Jr. & Co., 1905), 38–41. My thanks to Michael Cavanaugh. The Union Light Guard of Ohio did not actively guard the president until the fall of 1864, though some of its members recalled doing so much earlier. See George Ashmun, "Recollections of a Peculiar Service," *Magazine of History* 3 (April 1906). Depredations on the White House were reported regularly. On December 24, 1864, for example, the *Evening Star* said that gilded tiebacks, cords, and tassels from the curtains had all been carried away by tourists. For the Cabinet meeting incident, see Gideon Welles, *Diary,* February 19, 1864.

16. Washington Hands listed Harry Inloes Jackson, Charles Clark, Charles Claiborne, and John Rooney as members of the Baltimore Light Artillery, and as residents of Booth's block on Exeter Street. "Civil War Note-book of Washington Hands," Manuscripts Department, Maryland Historical Society.

17. Gen. Lew Wallace, in Baltimore, had issued General Orders No. 30 in April 1864, stepping up confiscation in Maryland. The War Department's policy was spelled out in General Orders No. 257, O.R. III:4, 721. Joseph H. Simonds, LAS 2:739; Booth's quitclaim deed giving the shares to Junius was executed on October 21, 1864. It is in the Pearce Collection at Navarro College, Corsicana, Texas. Richard and Kellie Gutman, "Boston: A Home for John Wilkes Booth?" *Surratt Society News* 10 (September 1985): 6–7.

18. Joseph H. Simonds letter to Capt. David V. Derickson, April 25, 1865, in LAS 2:738. Simonds said that the property given to June and Rosalie had since become "moderately valuable."

19. L.P.D. Newman in LAS 2:574 and LAS 2:928.

20. The slaves in question ranged in age from four to forty-five. *The Baltimore Sun,* March 10, 1864.

21. Election results were 29,536 to 27,541 against the constitution, exclusive of absentee votes, and the final count was 30,174 to 29,699 in favor. Reverdy Johnson, *Opinion of the Honorable Reverdy Johnson* (Baltimore: n.p., 1864); Lew Wallace, *Lew Wallace: An Autobiography* (New York: Harper and Brothers, 1906), 674, and Henry Bascom Smith, *Be-*

tween the Lines (New York: Booz Brothers, 1911), 80. Smith points out that Wallace was the only commanding general in Baltimore who was never sued for false arrest. New York *World,* October 20, 1864; New York *Daily News,* October 10, 1864.

22. The estimate of Confederate strength in Canada probably included escaped prisoners. H. Rossman, "To whom it may concern," dated September 29, 1864, in Joseph Holt Papers, 45:5925, Manuscripts Division, Library of Congress; Regarding the Kane plan, Lee wrote to Jefferson Davis on June 26, 1864, urging caution. Clifford Dowdey and Louis H. Manarin, eds., *The Wartime Papers of Robert E. Lee* (New York: Bramhall House, 1961), 808. On October 25, 1864, Lee wrote to Davis swearing off on a project of Reverend Stewart's. "I have not a high opinion of Mr. Stewarts Discretion, & could not advise any one to join him in his enterprize." Douglas Southall Freeman and Grady McWhiney, eds., *Lee's Dispatches: Unpublished Letters of General Robert E. Lee, CSA, to Jefferson Davis* (New York: Putnam, 1957), 302–4.

23. Jacob Thompson report to Judah P. Benjamin, December 3, 1864, in O.R. I:43 (1), 930–36. This document summarizes all of Thompson's activities in Canada during 1864.

24. St. Lawrence Hall Arrival Book, Ms. Group 28, Public Archives, Ottawa.

25. Poore, 2:268–74; It has been asserted that Martin wrote a letter of introduction to Dr. Samuel Mudd as well. However, the evidence for this consists of a secondhand account of what Arnold said at the time of his capture. But his remarks were transcribed and signed at the time, and they said nothing of the kind. When asked years later, Arnold said he didn't remember whether the letter had been written to Dr. Mudd or Dr. Queen. Testimony said it was Dr. Queen. See Steers, *Blood on the Moon,* 73; Testimony of Eaton G. Horner in Poore, 1:430, and Arnold-Butler. In the *New York Daily Graphic,* March 22, 1876, and the Cincinnati *Enquirer,* April 18, 1892, George Alfred Townsend mentions an interview with Kane, who said he destroyed his letter. It will be remembered that Booth once said he was a friend of Kane's, but this letter would have shown that claim to be false. Kane never divulged its contents.

26. Cincinnati *Enquirer,* April 18, 1892; Robert Anson Campbell in Poore, 2:87–88, and *Surratt Trial,* 1:193. Booth's application for the bill of exchange is in LAS 3:139. A Mr. Davis was also with Booth at the bank; he was never identified. Booth covered his Montreal trip with a false story about having an engagement at the Theatre Royal. See Thomas B. Florence in the New York *Sun,* April 19, 1865, 1.

27. *The New York Times,* May 28, 1864, 2. Many examples came to the public's attention only after the assassination. The Syracuse parade mottoes were copied from the Syracuse *Courier* into the Detroit *Advertiser and Tribune,* May 25, 1865.

28. In the popular vote, Lincoln received 2,330,552 votes to McClellan's 1,835,985. The electoral vote was 212 to 21, and the soldier vote was 116,887 to 33,748, which reversed the outcomes in New York and Connecticut. Lincoln also took Maryland with 40,171 votes to his opponent's 32,739. The soldier vote there was 2,799 to 321 in favor of the president.

29. This was reported to the War Department only after the assassination. Most of the *Enquirer* article was directed at Seward. LAS 4:186.

30. Clarke, *Unlocked Book,* 124.

31. Occupation forces in Maryland were usually commanded by prewar Democrats: Ben Butler, George Cadwallader, Nathaniel Banks, John A. Dix, Robert Schenck, and Lew Wallace. Banks, who arrested the state legislators in 1861, had been a Know-Nothing before becoming a Republican. Forney, Philadelphia *Press,* July 30, 1862; Hunter, August 31, 1863, letter to Stanton, O.R. III:2, 740. Stanton did not reply. Booth evidently

believed that Seward was still in charge. In one of his political tantrums, he told Asia, "Other brains rule the country." Clarke, *Unlocked Book,* 124.

32. Sylvanus Cadwallader, *Three Years with Grant* (New York: Alfred A. Knopf, 1955), 231–32.

33. In Charles County, Nathan Burnham's presence was deemed "intolerable" in a public resolution, while the other five Lincoln supporters were conditionally forgiven "as an earnest expression of our moderation." *Port Tobacco Times,* December 27, 1860, 2. Burnham later joined the 196th Pennsylvania Infantry. Gen. John A. Dix to S. P. Chase, O.R. I:51 (1), 442, and T. B. Robey to the State Department, O.R. II:2, 864–68; Report of E. J. Allen [Allen Pinkerton] to Andrew Porter, October 26, 1861, in O.R. II:2, 866.

34. Information on smuggling was supplied by Rev. Lemuel Wilmer and others in letters to the War Department. O.R. II:2, 863, 864. The author has rowed these waters, and was surprised to learn how easily one loses sight of a boat on the river. See *The Washington Post,* April 18, 1999, F5. Plugs in the boats were mentioned in Smith, *Between the Lines,* 67–68; Quote from General Robert Schenck in Wallace, *Autobiography,* 675; For a good account of a "commercial" smuggling trip, see Philip Whitlock's notebook, Virginia Historical Society, 111–20. The river was blockaded by executive proclamation; 12 Stat. 1262, August 16, 1861. Acts of July 13, 1861, May 27, 1862, and March 12, 1863, could also be invoked in the Maryland smuggling cases. The confiscation law was disseminated to troops in General Orders No. 257, O.R. III:6, 722. William P. Wood, the keeper of the Old Capitol Prison, claimed to have put a stop to Baker's depredations, thus earning the gratitude of local citizens. Washington *Sunday Gazette,* November 4, 1883, 1. According to Jeremiah T. Mudd, few citizens were much inclined to talk about the war in the last two years. Poore, 2:265.

35. Thompson in Poore, 2:270. A recent account of this visit claims that Booth had arranged to meet Dr. Queen, because the doctor's son came up to get him in Bryantown. However, eighteen to twenty-four hours passed between Booth's arrival at the tavern and Joseph Queen's arrival to pick him up. That was more than enough time to notify the doctor that he had a visitor in town, and far too much time to keep someone waiting intentionally. If the Queens had prior knowledge of Booth's intentions and whereabouts, they would have hustled him out of town as quickly as possible. See Steers, *Blood on the Moon,* 74; J. Dominick Burch was the son of Henry Burch, the tavern's owner. He was about the same age as Booth, and the two apparently got on well during the latter's visit. The friend who lived on Fayette Street has never been identified, and there are many possibilities. Special Collections, Georgetown University Library; This scenario leaves out the visit to Dr. Mudd, which has traditionally been seen as a part of the November visit. I no longer believe Booth met Mudd on this occasion. See chapter 9, note 9, below.

36. Booth's Jay Cooke & Company bankbook, Chicago Historical Society, entry for November 16. For the conspiracy assumptions, see Steers, *Blood on the Moon,* 73. An alternate explanation was given by Sam Arnold, who said that Booth told him the money he got there was borrowed.

37. The original four officers were Sgt. John R. Cronin, and Privates Alphonso T. Donn, Thomas F. Pendel, and Alexander C. Smith. Later, William H. Crook and John F. Parker replaced Pendel and Cronin. The character of these men is drawn from their police service files in Record Group 351, National Archives. Examples of vandalism were given in the Washington *Evening Star,* December 24, 1864, 1. White House watchmen were subsequently paid directly by the commissioner of public buildings. 1866 appropriations, 13 Stat. 206.

Chapter 9: "I have a greater speculation . . . they won't laugh at"

1. Owen Fawcett Scrapbook, Kefauver Library, University of Tennessee; Clarke, *Unlocked Book,* 126–27.

2. Junius Booth, Jr., in LAS 4:118; Edwin Booth to Nahum Capen, July 28, 1881, quoted in Edwina Booth Grossman, *Edwin Booth: Recollections by His Daughter* (New York: The Century Co., 1894), 227; Clarke, *Unlocked Book,* 118. The feelings remained for many months, as John Wilkes referred to them in a letter to June, dated January 17, 1865, in the Seymour Collection, Princeton University. The question of Booth family loyalties was deliberately clouded after the assassination. John Wilkes and Joseph were unambiguously pro-Southern, and it might be argued that Mary Ann, Junius, and Asia showed some Democratic leanings.

3. The Winter Garden is described in Joseph Jefferson, *Autobiography,* 158; Both quotes: *Julius Caesar,* III.i.

4. Edwin Booth served on the fund committee with William Wheatley and Leonard Grover. His correspondence mentions several attempts to book John Wilkes in the summer of 1864, but scheduling problems kept him from committing to a date. June's diary entry for November 26 said the *Julius Caesar* performance had raised $3,500, while the New York *World,* on November 28, put the figure at "almost $4,000." Other benefits held at the same time raised a total of $22,000. Anthony Deering, "L. Grover Busy at 94," undated clipping in the Aloysius Mudd Theatre Collection, Historical Society of Washington, D.C. John Wilkes Booth was never tied to the hotel-burning incident.

5. New York *Press,* May 7, 1893, 25. Adding to his success was his ownership of the Winter Garden, which Edwin and Clarke bought in August. They already owned the Walnut Street Theatre in Philadelphia, and were negotiating to buy the Boston Theatre. Together, they were the probably the wealthiest men in the theater business. For a full discussion of the Booth-Clarke dealings, see Donald E. LaCasse, Jr., "Edwin Booth: Theatre Manager" (Ph.D. dissertation, Michigan State University, 1979).

6. Chester in LAS 4:144–47.

7. There has been some dispute over the date of Mudd's introduction to Booth. John C. Thompson testified that it occurred "by chance" in November, but he did not say how he fixed the date in his mind. Two sisters of Dr. Mudd's confirmed the November date, but both got it from reading the testimony, not from personal knowledge. The church meeting, house visit, horse purchase, and return to Bryantown clearly describe a sequence of related events. But Booth did not own that horse until December, and that is when he bought a saddle and bridle for it in Bryantown. If the introduction took place in November, then we have no idea what he did in the second half of that meeting, or in the first half of a second one. It is easier to assume that Thompson was mistaken, and that the introduction to Mudd took place in December. All witnesses agreed there was only one meeting in Bryantown between the two men. See Thompson in Poore, 2:271.

8. Much was made at the trial, and again in recent years, of the fact that Dr. Mudd did not hold legal title to his farm, but Mudd's brother Henry testified that he could get a deed to the property at any time. Dr. Mudd had in fact sold a portion of this same tract to John F. Hardy some years before, and he kept the proceeds for himself. Poore, 2:434. See Charles County land records, Liber JHC-1, folio 62 (December 29, 1858).

9. The evidence of Booth's December visit has been interpreted in vastly different ways. Given the backgrounds of the people in Charles County, and of Booth himself, I find that Dr. Mudd's own account, written on August 28, 1865, makes the most sense. It was

published by Mudd's daughter Nettie in *The Life of Dr. Samuel A. Mudd* (New York: Neale Publishing, 1906), 42–48 (hereinafter *Life of Mudd*). A couple of sources describe the one-eyed horse as a dark bay, but others refer to it as brown. I use the latter word to avoid confusion with the bay horses Booth and Surratt later rode. Brooke Stabler described the horse as a good pacer. LAS 6:131; Mudd's own initial statement gave the price. LAS 2:1025; George Alfred Townsend gave the only known account of Booth's introduction to Harbin. He said, "[Harbin] told me that Dr. Mudd introduced him to Booth, and said that Mr. Booth wanted some private conversation with Mr. Harbin. They took a room on the second floor. . . ." Whether Mudd went along to the upstairs room is a pivotal point in the case against him. It sounds as if he did not, but as Townsend did not make it any more explicit, we are left to split hairs over a second-hand account written twenty-eight years after the fact. Their relationship was one of mutual distrust, and I seriously doubt that Mudd would have divulged such damaging secrets. Cincinnati *Enquirer,* April 18, 1892; For the case of Jones, see Thomas A. Jones, *J. Wilkes Booth: An Account of His Sojourn in Southern Maryland* (Chicago: Laird and Lee, 1893), 13, and O.R. II:2, 861.

10. Statement of Edman Spangler in the papers of Benjamin F. Butler, Manuscripts Division, Library of Congress (hereinafter Spangler-Butler); James L. Maddox in LAS 5:250 and 5:276.

11. Jeremiah T. Mudd in Poore, 2:259–60. Weichmann in Poore, 1:70 and 1:135. John Surratt, Jr., was appointed postmaster on September 10, 1862. He applied for work in the Paymaster General's Department in October 1863, and was dismissed as postmaster the following month. *Surratt Courier* 25 (August 2000): 3, and Postmaster Appointments, Microcopy M-601, National Archives. See also Maj. W. B. Lane to General James B. Fry, April 23, 1865, in the records of the Provost Marshal General, Record Group 110, entry 38, National Archives.

12. *Life of Mudd,* 42–43. At first, Weichmann insisted that this meeting took place on January 15. Circumstances proved him wrong, and when questioned by a congressional investigator on May 25, 1866, he corrected himself as to the date. Butler Papers, Box 175, Library of Congress; Apparently, Surratt encouraged Weichmann to seek a government position. Augustus Howell, the spy, said that Weichmann took the job "with the express understanding . . . that he . . . was to furnish Surratt with all information that came under his notice. . . ." John T. Ford Papers, MS 371, Maryland Historical Society. Hoffman's office was at 1925 F Street and Weichmann had been working at St. Matthew's Institute, only a block away. *Surratt Trial,* 369 and 403. Issues touching on Weichmann's college career are in the Sepulcian Archives in Baltimore. For more, see Louis J. Weichmann, *A True History of the Assassination of Abraham Lincoln* (New York: Alfred A. Knopf, 1975), *passim* (hereinafter Weichmann, *A True History*).

13. *Life of Mudd,* 43–44; Poore, 1:94, 96–97, 104. The lines in Booth's drawing were wavy, and resembled streams more than roads, with indistinct squares placed alongside two of them. Though very familiar with Southern Maryland, I cannot make out what locality it was supposed to represent. The envelope had been addressed in Booth's hand, to "Jas. V. Barnes, care of T. Zizinia, Box 1344, N. Y." and "T. Zizinia, 15 South William Street." It had never been used, and was evidently outdated; Zizinia had moved to 68 Beaver Street by then. Little is known of Thomas Zizinia, but his address was just around the corner from a brokerage used as a cover for Eddy Martin. The government had no files on any subversive by that name. LAS 2:292.

14. *Life of Mudd,* 45. Weichmann denied giving out government secrets from his office. Regulations for the office were established by General Orders No. 190, issued May 3,

1864, and they show how important the office was to the flow of information on prisoners. O.R. II:7, 106–8. Weichmann was specifically charged with keeping accounts of the money found on the prisoners at the time of their capture. Weichmann, *A True History*, 376–77. Jeremiah T. Mudd in Poore, 2:262. Francis Lucas, who was to have taken the stove to Bryantown, had no room on his wagon. Poore, 2:267.

15. Chester in LAS 4:147–50; A list of broken engagements, found in Booth's trunk, included a week in Cleveland, five in St. Louis, two in Chicago, and two in Cincinnati. LAS 2:296; John H. Jack in LAS 5:49, 55. Canning to George Alfred Townsend in the Philadelphia *Evening News*, January 8, 1886; Clarke, *Unlocked Book*, 127; Though this conversation is described as taking place in Washington, that may have been a mistake by the officer who reported it. Canning and Booth were both in Philadelphia just after the Chester discussion.

16. Simonds to Booth, December 31, 1864, in LAS 2:314; Information about Adams Express is from Dan Loughran testimony, *Surratt Trial*, 206, Henry McDonough testimony, *Surratt Trial*, 356, and Weichmann, *A True History*, 31. Surratt's quitclaim deed is in Prince George's County Land Records, Liber FS2, folio 368–70, Maryland State Archives. Booth had divested himself in a similar way, yet the practice did not seem to be common among Confederate agents.

17. Herold appreciated the trust Booth put in him. His own father, who died in October, refused to let him have anything to do with the management of his estate. Will of Adam George Herold in Register of Wills, District of Columbia; Arnold statement of April 17, 1865, from M-619, 458:309, with additional details from Arnold's December 3, 1867, statement in the Butler Papers, Library of Congress; Chester in LAS 4:148–50.

18. Charles C. Dunn in *Surratt Trial*, 437. Two years later, a hotel clerk went through Booth's trunk and found a note that said, "I tried to secure leave but failed. J. Harrison Surratt." *Ibid.*, 337. Richard M. Smoot in the *Fort Smith (Arkansas) Times*, May 9, 1906, 4; Register of births and baptisms of the Lutheran Church of Dorna, now in the state of Langensalza, Germany, show that Atzerodt was born at 5:30 A.M. on June 12, 1835. Transcriptions were provided by Hans Falckner, of Thuringen, Germany. The *Port Tobacco Times*, March 12, 1857, recorded the arrival of George and John in the village; The *National Intelligencer*, July 9, 1865, gives additional details of the business. The partnership was dissolved February 4, 1861. LAS 7:510. Henry Atzerodt served in the Maryland Line, and was captured near Petersburg on April 3, 1865. LAS 7:006.

19. Observations of John C. Atzerodt in LAS 3:558, 566; Memoranda of Nicholas B. Crangle, Henry Bailey, and Edwin Middleton are in the Records of the Provost Marshal General, RG 110, Entry 38, National Archives. Atzerodt's own account of Surratt's recruiting pitch is in LAS 3:597. Details on Eddy Martin are from his own account in LAS 5:330 and *Surratt Trial*, 214, as well as Smith, *Between the Lines*, 259–70.

20. *Daily National Intelligencer*, January 22, 1865, 2. Recall that others have claimed Booth gave up acting because he had lost his voice through abuse. This review said, "To be sure he suffered from huskiness of voice—but then, what perfect acting! . . . His elocution was faultless. . . . His readings were perfect. On no occasion was he tempted to mistake the passion of his hero, and to launch forth into mere elocution, that he might display a quality so inferior to the *genius of acting*, and for which the role of Romeo offers so many alluring opportunities."

21. Washington *Evening Star*, February 10, 1864, 2; Starvation of troops was discussed at length in the February 1865 report of Gen. Lucius B. Northrup, Commissary General of Subsistence, as published in the *Southern Historical Society Papers* 2.1 (July 1871): 85. Details of Eddy Martin's dealings are in Smith, *Between the Lines*, 269. A more thor-

ough discussion of the cotton trade can be found in William C. Harris, *Lincoln's Last Months* (Cambridge, MA: The Belknap Press of Harvard University Press, 2004), 175–88.

22. Weichmann in *Surratt Trial,* 373; Parr in LAS 5:519, 528, and 6:20; Smith, *Between the Lines,* 258; Maggie Branson in LAS 3:189; Mary Branson in LAS 3:197. In September 1863, Maggie Branson allegedly brought Powell a federal uniform when he was in the hospital. He put it on and simply walked out of the place. After the assassination, Samuel S. Bond claimed that Maggie Branson was widely suspected of helping prisoners escape from the hospital in Gettysburg as well. LAS 3:274–75; Mary Branson in LAS 3:198 mentions the blue uniform Powell wore on his first visit to the house after his escape. The "skedaddle" was explained by John H. Alexander in *Mosby's Men* (New York: Neale Publishing Company, 1907), 20. Gen. William H. Payne letter to Bradley T. Johnson, September 6, 1894, typescript in the Virginia Historical Society; See Betty J. Ownsbey, *Alias Paine: Lewis Thornton Powell, the Mystery Man of the Lincoln Conspiracy* (Jefferson, NC: McFarland & Company, 1993). Ms. Ownsbey speculates (p. 30) that the man Powell saw in Richmond was Joseph Branson, Mary's father. She and others have wondered if Powell was brooding over an important "secret service" assignment, but to me, the mood suggests a romantic despondency. Mary Branson conceded her intimacy with Powell in LAS 3:199; Lewis Edmonds Payne, son of Powell's host, Dr. Albin S. Payne, gave a detailed account of this period in "Lewis Powell's Exploits: Reminiscences of the Remarkable Youth Who Stabbed Secretary Seward," Philadelphia *Weekly Times,* June 3, 1882.

23. The sale of his horse was mentioned in the Alexandria, Virginia, *Gazette,* June 23, 1865; Smith, *Between the Lines,* 258; Though she did not identify the Greenback raid by name, Mary did recall something about a raid in which newspapers were captured. In fact, newspapers were taken in large quantity during the Greenback raid, and were spread over the floor of the railroad car as part of a threat to burn the car. If Powell had been involved, he would have received a large sum of money for his participation (estimates vary; in *Mosby's Men,* p. 113, John H. Alexander claimed that each got $2,200). Powell's brothers, George and Oliver, were not actually killed in the war, as he had thought. According to the family Bible, George Powell lived until June 8, 1923, and Oliver died April 25, 1928. Courtesy of George's descendant Jewell Powell Fillmon.

24. General Robert Schenck advised General Lew Wallace to watch out for the women in Baltimore; they were "cunning beyond belief," and did most of the espionage work. Wallace, *Autobiography,* 675. Maggie and Mary Branson both admitted to sending provisions to Confederate prisoners—Maggie in LAS 3:192, Mary in LAS 3:202; Though many of Mrs. Egerton's letters were found in the Branson house, no one by that name was listed among the residents at the time of the assassination. She was in touch with Major Allen G. Brady, a Connecticut officer whom she (and possibly Maggie Branson) had attended in the hospital at Gettysburg. Brady had been wounded in the shoulder, and was assigned to the same hospital as Powell. As an officer in the V.R.C., he was appointed provost marshal of the Point Lookout Prison, and Mrs. Egerton was in close communication with him throughout the following year. LAS 2:672–75. A. G. Brady pension file, National Archives.

Mrs. Parr's relief efforts were mentioned in her husband's obituary, *The Baltimore Sun,* November 15, 1900, 7. Powell's initial contact with Parr might have come about in another way: a daughter of Dr. Alban S. Payne, in whose house Powell had lived, was a sister-in-law of Nannie (Ann Corbin Lomax) Green, an intimate friend of Annie Parr. Thus, a family visit in Fauquier County could have led to a series of recommendations. Gen. William H. Payne letter, Virginia Historical Society, and Preston Parr in LAS 5:528.

25. Preston Parr tried to downplay his connection to Surratt after the assassination, describing him as "a troublesome visitor" who annoyed him by using the china shop as a rendezvous point for lewd women and others whom Parr did not know. Parr in LAS 6:26, 5:518–23, and 5:533.

26. Every known letter of Mary Surratt's deals with the education of her children and with the drunkenness of her husband. As she wrote to Father Joseph M. Finotti, she felt her husband would kill her if she did not become what he wished. Undated letter, New-York Historical Society; The Surratt house was generally thought to have been intended as a tavern from the beginning, but a letter from Father Leonard Nota to Father Bernardin Wiget dated January 3, 1855, explained that the family's circumstances derived from severe losses, which obliged Mrs. Surratt "to keep a public house, where the public stage stops but occasionally." Maryland Province Archives of the Jesuit Order, Georgetown University Library.

27. The boardinghouse had six large bedrooms and two small ones. Washington *Evening Star,* November 11, 1864, 3. Similar ads were placed on November 30, December 8, and December 27. A consolidated report of the Signal Corps, C.S.A., for the quarter ending March 31, 1864, described the recommended stops for mail runners going by way of Mathias Point: "Allen's Fresh, Newport, Bryantown, Surratt's Tavern, to Washington." Captured Confederate records, Record Group 109, National Archives. Thanks to Erick Davis.

28. For more on Mrs. Slater, see James O. Hall, "The Saga of Sarah Slater," *Surratt Society News* 7, no. 1 (January 1982): 3-6 and 7, no. 2 (February 1982): 3-6; also Alexandra Lee Levin, *This Awful Drama: General Edwin Gray Lee, C.S.A., and His Family* (New York: Vantage Press, 1987), 145–47; Her fluency in French would have enabled Mrs. Slater to claim Canadian citizenship, had she been caught. The description came from Atzerodt, and was published in the Baltimore *American,* January 19, 1869.

29. Just before this, Surratt had brought Atzerodt from Port Tobacco and put him up at the Pennsylvania House for a night. In the conspiracy trial, Weichmann testified that Atzerodt came to Surratt's alone, and Surratt showed up later. Poore, 1:72. Atzerodt, however, said that Surratt brought him there, and Weichmann later said the same. LAS 3:597, Weichmann, *A True History,* 75. I suspect Atzerodt went to the door, while Surratt delayed his entrance. For Howell's presence, see Poore, 1:88, and for Mrs. Slater's visit, see Weichmann in LAS 6:506 and 6:473. Howell and Slater crossed the Potomac on that trip, and Atzerodt rowed them across. See James Fowle's statement, papers of Benjamin F. Butler, Box 175, Manuscripts Division, Library of Congress.

30. Poore, 1:89, 1:73, 1:106; Mary Surratt in LAS 6:170, Anna Surratt in LAS 6:212, and George Atzerodt in LAS 3:596.

31. Arnold, *Memoirs,* 24.

32. Arnold-Butler; Junius Booth diary, entry for February 7, 1865, Mugar Library, Boston University; Washington *Evening Star,* February 11, 1865, 2. As John Sleeper Clarke was the star of the play, it is entirely possible that Junius knew the Lincolns were planning to attend. He made up the premonition story because he suspected his brother would do something that night.

33. Clarke, *Unlocked Book,* 120, 121; Alfred Smith in LAS 2:12; McCullough told George Alfred Townsend that he and Booth kept their trysts secret by using the code names "Jack" and "Bob" for the ladies. San Francisco *Chronicle,* July 30, 1882; John and Letitia

McCullough had been married since April 8, 1849, and their two sons were fifteen and five years old in 1865. Woodruff, 15, 17.

34. Simonds to Booth, February 21, 1865, in LAS 2:318–19; Chester in LAS 4:161.

35. McVicker to Booth in LAS 2:349.

36. The Maryland trips were mentioned in Henry Merrick's memorandum, based on entries in the National Hotel register. Poore, 1:48; For Chester's specific role, see LAS 5:496; Booth had evidently done his research, and he knew that Forrest insisted on keeping the back door to Ford's locked for fear that he might catch a chill. Borrows in LAS 4:70; Chester's figure of $4,000 for horses is in LAS 4:154.

37. *Surratt Trial*, 375; Martin in *Surratt Trial*, 217; Smoot in *Ft. Smith Times*, May 9, 1906, 4.

38. Weichmann in Poore, 1:75–76, 1:88, 1:109.

39. McCullough related the incidents to Townsend a few years after the assassination. San Francisco *Chronicle*, July 30, 1882, 1. John Surratt also made a point of telling Lou Weichmann that Booth was out riding with McCullough. Weichmann in LAS 6:499.

40. Louis Weichmann letter to Thomas Donaldson dated April 20, 1886, in the collection of Monsignor Robert L. Keesler. In his memoirs, written much later, Weichmann changes the place of their meeting, and says they were sitting in the Surratt parlor when *he* suggested they go to the Capitol. Weichmann, *A True History*, 88. This version is based on the one he gave in *Surratt Trial*, 379.

41. Booth told David Herold that Miss Hale had obtained a pass for him. John A. Bingham in the *Chicago Tribune*, November 23, 1873, 9. Some writers believe the story of John W. Westfall, an officer of the Capitol Police, who later claimed to have held Booth back as he lunged for the president. Benjamin B. French recorded his recollection of the incident just after the assassination. According to French, a man lunged at the president, and he (French) ordered Westfall to grab him. The man insisted he had a right to be there, and thinking he might be a new member of Congress, French told the policeman to let him go. Benjamin French to Francis O. French, April 24, 1865, French Papers, Manuscript Division, Library of Congress. See also Weichmann, *A True History*, 90–93. A photograph of the event purporting to show Booth and his conspirators standing close to the president may have been misinterpreted. The man standing near Lincoln may or may not be Booth; in some photographs of the scene, he does not look much like him. However, Powell was in Baltimore at the time, and Herold may have been laid up with a sprained ankle in Piscataway, Maryland. Atzerodt had spent the previous night rowing across the Potomac. Though he spoke freely about the activities of his fellow conspirators, Atzerodt never mentioned their presence at the Capitol that day. See Dorothy Meserve Kunhardt and Philip B. Kunhardt, Jr., *Twenty Days* (New York: Harper and Row, 1965), 34–35.

Chapter 10: "You can be the leader . . . but not my executioner"

1. On the envelope, franked for California senator John Conness, was an "endorsement" by John Parker Hale Wentworth, a cousin of Lucy Hale and occasional roommate of Booth's. Wentworth, a newspaper publisher, had received a political appointment from Lincoln, and was in town for the inauguration. *Daily Alta California*, January 7, 1891. The document was part of the Oliver Barrett Collection, and a photograph of it was published in the Parke-Bernet auction catalog of February 20, 1952.

2. Shuffling horses: Spangler-Butler, Stabler in LAS 6:142A, James Pumphrey in LAS 6:5, William Cleaver in *Surratt Trial*, 206, John Fletcher in LAS 5:416, Arnold, *Mem-*

oirs, 24–25, John A. Foster in LAS 5:348; Mary Van Tyne referred to meeting places in LAS 6:437, as did Stabler in LAS 6:130. Surratt's bay horse is mentioned by Mary Surratt in LAS 6:253.

3. Chester in LAS 4:161; LAS 4:403, 434, 512; LAS 6:271; Arnold, *Memoirs,* 46; The O'Laughlen debt is mentioned in LAS 4:197.

4. D. C. Forney says in the Washington *Evening Star,* June 27, 1891, 11, that Booth occasionally stayed at the Herndon House, and though it rests on his word, this does account for those periods when Booth was known to be in Washington, but not at the National.

5. Surratt's appearance was commented upon in the Washington *Evening Star,* August 29, 1865; Stabler in LAS 6:125, Grillet in LAS 3:502 and LAS 3:507, and John C. Atzerodt in LAS 3:565 all remarked on the clothing of the conspirators; Stabler in LAS 6:127 and John A. Foster in LAS 3:538 noted how Atzerodt did not fit in.

6. Stabler in LAS 6:127-128, 139; Weichmann in LAS 6:505, *Surratt Trial,* 406, and LAS 6:501.

7. St. Lawrence Hall register, Ms. Group 28, vol. 10, National Archives of Canada; Weichmann in LAS 6:499; diary of Brig. Gen. Edwin Gray Lee, C.S.A., microfilm in the papers of the Southern Historical Society, University of North Carolina; Stabler in LAS 6:127; Weichmann in *Surratt Trial,* 381, 789; Martha Murray in the Joseph Holt Papers, 93:7009, Library of Congress. Mrs. Murray recalled Powell using the alias of "Kinsler," but printed versions of her account gave it as "Kincheloe." Since the previous November, former slaves had come under military protection in Baltimore, so the beating incident was investigated by Col. John Woolley. Wallace, *Autobiography,* 692; Smith, *Between the Lines,* 255–56; James L. Stevens in LAS 3:184; Powell's oath certificate is in LAS 4:397.

8. Surratt-Parr telegrams in LAS 3:1046 and 1048; The urgency of this exchange can be inferred from the use of real names, which were required for a quick home delivery. Weichmann in Poore, 1:90, 96, *Surratt Trial,* 428, and Poore, 1:109; then again in Poore, 1:77, and *Surratt Trial,* 399; Booth telegram in LAS 15:352.

9. Nora Fitzpatrick in *Surratt Trial,* 234, and Weichmann in *Surratt Trial,* 411; William P. Wood in LAS 5:413; Weichmann in LAS 6:499 and *A True History,* 98–99; Miles in LAS 5:292; Arnold, *Memoirs,* 25.

10. John Howard in LAS 6:429. Herold and Booth had friends who worked there, which may account for the staff's allowing them to have the place to themselves. Waiter Michael Hayden had known Booth. *National Tribune,* January 11, 1917; Thomas Manning, the night watchman, lived in Herold's neighborhood, and sometimes took drinks with him. LAS 4:474; Arnold, *Memoirs,* 25.

11. Arnold, *Memoirs,* 25–26; *Evening Star,* March 15, 1865, 2. The exchange went back into effect on January 18, and was to take place at the rate of three thousand per week. General Grant later testified to a congressional committee that it had gone into full swing within a month. In fact, Grant's February visit to Ford's Theatre was made on the occasion of this Capitol Hill appearance. *The New York Times,* February 12, 1865, 1; Rep. Com. No. 119, Thirty-eighth Congress, Second Session; Whether Arnold was aware of the Grover's Theatre visit depends on how closely he and the others were trailing the president. It was reported in the following day's *Evening Star,* March 16, 1865. Clara Harris was their guest, and she was escorted by Gen. James G. Wilson.

12. Arnold's original account of this is in Record Group 94, Records of the Advocate General's Office, on Microcopy M-619, 458:305–12; additional details are in Arnold, *Memoirs,* 26–27; Thomas Manning in LAS 5:286.

13. Weichmann in Poore, 1:90, 106, 108, 110, *Surratt Trial,* 399, and LAS 6:499.

14. Mathews in Philadelphia *Press,* December 4, 1881; Washington *Daily National Intelligencer,* March 18, 1865. Mathews was not in the cast of *Still Waters Run Deep.* The same cast performed this play the following night in the city. Original playbill for March 18 is in the Crawford Theatre Collection, Box 28, Yale University Library. Harry Clay Ford later recounted a political discussion with Booth in the same bedroom (LAS 5:456). Mathews may have been misquoted in this article. He begins his interview by saying that he and Booth had grown up together in Baltimore, but he actually met Booth for the first time on January 1, 1865, and spoke to him only a few times (LAS 5:304). He testified in 1867 that he grew up in Cumberland, Maryland. *Surratt Trial,* 824.

15. Arnold, *Memoirs,* 26; Arnold-Butler; The Surratt Tavern involvement is in LAS 2:200; The boardinghouse rendezvous is in Poore, 1:370.

16. Atzerodt gave some details of the escape route, saying Booth wanted to avoid toll roads and vigilant toll takers (LAS 3:596); T.B. is just north of the intersection of Maryland Routes 5 and 301 in southern Prince George's County. It got its name from Thomas Brooke, a colonial landowner, who marked his boundaries with stones bearing his initials. Richard M. Smoot identified Joseph Eli Huntt as the man with the fresh horses. Huntt's house still stands at T.B., and is occupied by his granddaughter. *Ft. Smith (Arkansas) Times,* May 9, 1906, 4; Details of the so-called kidnap attempt are given in Arnold-Butler, and in John Surratt's Rockville lecture. Surratt later claimed to have intercepted a carriage with Chief Justice Salmon P. Chase inside. Chase, however, was probably in Baltimore that day. An unidentified newspaper article recounted a brief conversation at the hospital between Booth and Davenport, in which the latter told Booth the president was not there. See Margaret Leech, *Reveille in Washington* (New York: Harper and Brothers, 1941), 375. The Surratt house rendezvous was mentioned by Weichmann in Poore, 1:370.

17. The ceremony was a planned event, undoubtedly known to at least some of the National's residents in advance. The flag in question had been captured by the 140th Indiana at Fort Anderson, North Carolina. *Evening Star,* March 18, 1865, 1. Long before the details of a kidnap attempt were known, Thomas E. Richardson, editor of the *Constitutional Union,* said that he was with Booth on that occasion. *New York Herald,* June 18, 1878, clipping in the papers of John T. Ford, Maryland Historical Society.

18. Weichmann in Poore, 1:370–72, 374, LAS 6:502, and *Surratt Trial,* 399. Maybe that's when Booth told Surratt that he was a good actor. Weichmann was not sharing a room at this time, and I can imagine no reason why anyone would need to go into *his* room, instead of a private one.

19. Lloyd in LAS 5:157–62 and LAS 165–66; Norton in LAS 6:309–10. Norton gave the date as April 1, but that was inconsistent with other evidence.

20. John Lloyd in LAS 5:167; John Atzerodt in LAS 3:558–62. This coincidence was brought to light by computer analysis of the records. Lloyd in LAS 5:167–68.

21. Mrs. Van Tyne in Poore, 1:142; Herold's clerkship has been given in several conflicting versions, but this is the earliest one. Herold in LAS 4:442; Atzerodt in LAS 3:598; George Bateman had known of the boat's purpose all along, but now he and Charles Yates were expected to keep an eye on it for Booth. Smoot, *Ft. Smith Times,* May 9, 1906, 4.

22. Woodruff, 9; Richard Lalor Shiel, *The Apostate* (New York: French's Standard Drama, 1846), 16–17; Weichmann in Poore, 1:73 and 1:102–3.

23. W. B. Lyndall to Mary A. Lyndall, November 14, 1866, in the Lyndall Papers, Duke

University; J. J. Reford to Booth, February 20, 1865, in LAS 2:354; Weichmann in *Surratt Trial*, 380; R. D. Watson to Surratt in LAS 3:114; *New York Tribune*, May 17, 1865; Edwin Booth told Henry Magonigle that he had not planned to make it a long run, but William Stuart kept pushing him. Booth letter dated November 14, 1874, Folger Shakespeare Library, Washington.

24. A report on Atzerodt by John A. Foster, published in the *Daily National Intelligencer*, July 9, 1865, mentions New York only once, despite the many references by Atzerodt in his "confessions." Actor Charles Pope claimed that in February, Booth hinted at some enterprise he wanted Pope to join. New York *Sun*, March 28, 1897. Actor John M. Barron told nearly the same story in *The Baltimore Sun*, March 17, 1907. Chester in LAS 4:145; Junius in LAS 2:263; Arnold, *Memoirs*, 46; Atzerodt in the Baltimore *American*, January 18, 1869; Lone Star is mentioned in *Surratt Trial*, 241; prostitutes are in LAS 3:693; Lux in LAS 2:157; James Gordon, of Mississippi, later claimed to have been involved in the capture plan, though his account is vague and unverified. See *Goodspeed's Biographical and Historical Memoirs of Mississippi* (Chicago: Goodspeed Publishing Company, 1891), 1:805–7.

25. Telegram is in LAS 15:331; Weichmann in LAS 6:499; In 1867, Weichmann said the post office visit happened on about the twentieth. *Surratt Trial*, 380, 381; Poore, 1:78 and 3:221.

26. Weichmann in LAS 6:501; D.H.L. Gleason, "Conspiracy Against Lincoln," *Magazine of History* 13, no. 2 (February 1911): 59–65; In his published account, Gleason mistakenly gave the date as February, evidently thinking it had to have been before the inauguration. Gleason in LAS 4:373; Gilbert J. Raynor in LAS 6:101; In LAS 6:463–64, Col. John A. Foster said that Weichmann suggested he might join the blockade-running scheme "for the fun of the thing," but that his fellow clerks told him to stay away from it. Weichmann later said he was just "blowing," and all of his remarks were made "in a spirit of fun." His figure of $30,000 apparently came from Atzerodt, who expected to make that amount from his participation in the plot. Weichmann may have recanted because he came to feel he had become an "insider."

27. J. B. Menu in LAS 2:381; Menu's letter was grouped with others found in Booth's trunk after the assassination, while Lou Weichmann's papers were grouped elsewhere. Had Weichmann known it existed, he certainly would have used it to bolster his claim that he had tried to report the plot.

28. Weichmann in LAS 6:457, 499, 503; The blank on the note comes from Weichmann's account, which never identified the person who was supposed to have the money. Smoot, *Ft. Smith Times*, May 9, 1906, 4. Surratt took up the habit of avoiding Smoot by pretending he had gone to New York.

29. Atzerodt in LAS 3:596; John H. McOmber, clerk of Barnum's Hotel, certified that on March 25, Booth arrived in Baltimore on the 3:30 A.M. train from Philadelphia and left on the 7:00 A.M. train to Washington. His eight o'clock arrival in the capital coincided with Mrs. Slater's appearance at Surratt's. M-619, 458:333; Edwin G. Lee Diary, March 22 entry; Weichmann in Poore, 1:80; Stabler in LAS 6:121 and 142, Weichmann in LAS 6:472; George Atzerodt was quoted as saying that "Major Barron, formerly of the rebel army" was on this trip, but Atzerodt got the story secondhand, and evidently misunderstood the name; it was Barry, not Barron.

30. Weichmann in LAS 6:472; Augustus Howell statement, John T. Ford Papers, Maryland Historical Society; Barry in *Surratt Trial*, 751–52, 754. Barry wanted to meet Charles Cawood, a signal service officer, at Port Tobacco.

31. Atzerodt in LAS 3:596; Surratt's original note is in LAS 6:145; Stabler in *Surratt Trial,* 217.

Chapter 11: "There is going to be some splendid acting tonight"

1. Ford in LAS 5:485.

2. Notice in the *Evening Star,* March 27, 1865, 2 (emphasis added). Mrs. Lincoln had invited Senator Charles Sumner to be their guest in "a large private box" for the opera. Justin G. Turner and Linda Levitt Turner, *Mary Todd Lincoln: Her Life and Letters* (New York: Alfred A. Knopf, 1972), 209; Booth telegram to O'Laughlen in LAS 15:356; In *Surratt Trial,* 401, this telegram was erroneously reported as having been sent from New York. Williams in Poore, 1:145–46, LAS 3:611, and LAS 6:497. The Fayette Street address was the bakery owned by Arnold's father.

3. Thomas Wallace statement in the Joseph Holt Papers, 93:7014, Library of Congress.

4. Crangle in LAS 4:109, John Atzerodt in LAS 3:561, Nicholas B. Crangle statement in Record Group 110, Entry 38, National Archives; John Atzerodt in LAS 3:563, Bailey in LAS 4:53. Bailey told authorities that he quit his job merely to "take a little turnaround." Henry M. Bailey statement in Record Group 110, Entry 38, National Archives.

5. Martha Murray first recalled the name as "Kensler," but all subsequent transcripts of her testimony gave it as "Kincheloe." A detective clipped the signature from the hotel register, and it has not been seen since. Martha Murray in *Surratt Trial,* 247, and Joseph Holt Papers, 93:7009. Arnold letter in LAS 15:343, reproduced here in full in chapter 4, pages 65–66.

6. Greenawalt in LAS 2:1052 and LAS 3:633; Bailey in LAS 4:53; Walter M. Barnes in LAS 4:98; William P. Wood in LAS 6:460; John Atzerodt in LAS 3:557; Charles Bostwick in M-619, 456:532. Edwin Middleton also visited them.

7. John Atzerodt in LAS 3:565. Years later, Atzerodt's brother-in-law, John L. Smith, claimed to have reported those remarks to Seward, but no action was taken. Baltimore *American,* December 12, 1903; Stabler in LAS 6:130; Greenawalt in LAS 2:1052. In another version, Greenawalt said that Atzerodt only claimed his friends could get him out of financial trouble. *Surratt Trial,* 273; Stabler in LAS 6:130 and 6:127–28.

8. Herold in LAS 4:442; Greenawalt in LAS 2:1055, Mary Van Tyne in LAS 6:442, Herold in LAS 4:451; George W. Baird, who once attended school with Herold, remembered him as a chubby boy who joked his way out of trouble. November 29, 1921, letter published in Burke McCarthy, *The Suppressed Truth About the Assassination of Abraham Lincoln* (Washington: privately printed, 1922), 110.

9. Fitzpatrick in LAS 5:404, 410.

10. Weichmann in Poore, 1:76. Lloyd said he had seen John Surratt at the tavern about fifteen or twenty times in the early months of 1865. LAS 5:162; Stabler in LAS 6:127, and Greenawalt in LAS 2:1054, Stabler in LAS 6:127, Arnold, *Memoirs,* 34, LAS 6:439, John R. Gile in Poore, 3:215; Weichmann in LAS 6:422. Rullman's had recently been acquired by Henry Lichau, whose Lichau House was around the block on Louisiana Avenue. The conspirators were in the habit of calling both places by the name "Lichau's"; I have made them consistent here. Arnold and O'Laughlen moved out of Rullman's just after they inadvertently encountered Surratt in Booth's hotel room. Mary Surratt in LAS 6:236 and LAS 6:172. The thirty-five-day cycle in Surratt's route was estimated by Col. John A. Foster, who questioned Preston Parr about it (LAS 5:534).

11. Arnold-Butler, and Arnold, *Memoirs,* 36, 28–29.

12. City Point is at the confluence of the Appomattox and James rivers. It is now the town of Hopewell, Virginia. Mary Ann's letter is in LAS 2:352.

13. *New York Herald,* May 19, 1863; comments by Sen. Lazarus Powell (KY) in the *Congressional Globe,* Thirty-seventh Congress, Third Session, 1061.

14. Col. John A. Foster in LAS 5:348; John Fletcher said that Booth came in with Atzerodt and said that he was leaving town, but consented to the sale of his horses. Record Group 233, House of Representatives, Committee of Claims, Thirty-ninth Congress, First Session, HR39A–H4.1, National Archives; Stabler in LAS 6:121, 130–31; Greenawalt in LAS 6:633 and *Surratt Trial,* 273.

15. Weichmann in *Surratt Trial,* 387, 453. Surratt and Weichmann belonged to a draft club that charged $50 for each call. They pooled the money, and used it to buy exemptions for any members who had been called up. Mary Surratt in LAS 6:238–39; Nora Fitzpatrick in LAS 5:400; Weichmann in LAS 6:170, 174, 237, 454, and 501, and again in *Surratt Trial,* 388.

16. Report of Gen. Lucius B. Northrop, February 1865, in *Southern Historical Society Papers* 2, no. 1 (July 1871): 85; Financial incentives are contained in the Records of the Richmond, Fredericksburg, and Potomac Railroad, Virginia Historical Society. It should be pointed out that bounties were high, in part, because they were offered in Confederate scrip, which was nearly worthless by that time. Civilian poaching from the "government farm" was mentioned in a clipping in the Lincoln Obsequies Scrapbook, Library of Congress. The authors of *Come Retribution* believed these measures were taken to prepare for Lincoln's abduction, not to provide food to Confederate troops.

17. Greenawalt in LAS 6:633 and *Surratt Trial,* 273; Atzerodt told John Fletcher he had sold the horse to John F. Thompson, driver of the Port Tobacco stage line. But the line was based in the Pennsylvania House, and perhaps it fell under Greenawalt's control. LAS 5:415; Stabler in LAS 6:142A.

18. Alfred Smith to Edwin Stanton, April 16, 1865, in LAS 2:11; Providence *Press,* April 18, 1865, 2. Thanks to James O. Hall. The original signature clipped from the register is now in the collection of Dr. John K. Lattimer.

19. *The Rail Splitter* 8, no. 1 (Summer/Fall 2002): 4. O'Beirne wrote back for confirmation. Some conspiracy buffs have taken Mrs. Lincoln's note as an appointment of Parker to the "bodyguard" detail. See Otto Eisenschiml, *Why Was Lincoln Murdered?* (Boston: Little, Brown, 1937), 11–21.

20. Nelson D. Lankford, *Richmond Burning* (New York: Viking, 2002), 161–67.

21. *Evening Star,* April 6, 1865, 2; Frances Seward letter to her sister, as quoted in Frederick Seward, *Seward at Washington* (New York: Derby and Miller, 1891), 271. Stanton asked the president to return to Washington, but Lincoln thought better of it. Details of the accident are in M-473, 88:801, telegrams sent by the secretary of war.

22. Surratt was listed in Rooms thirteen and fifty; St. Lawrence Hall register, National Archives of Canada; Diary of Edwin Gray Lee, Barney Devlin in LAS 2:124; James Sangster in *Surratt Trial,* 166. As a courier, Surratt had the option of declining all espionage work. See Confederate Signal Service quarterly report, Record Group 107, National Archives. See also John Surratt's lecture in Rockville, Maryland, in 1870 (hereinafter Surratt Lecture). Washington *Evening Star,* December 7, 1870.

23. "Some Newly Collected Facts About John Wilkes Booth," typescript by Quincy Kilby, in William Seymour Collection, Princeton University; Chester in LAS 4:160. Though Lucy Hale left Newport with Booth, she disappeared from the story when he got to Boston. I have assumed she stayed with friends there while Booth conducted his busi-

ness and went on his way. However, she might have continued on to her family's home in Concord, New Hampshire.

24. Chester in Poore, 1:48–51, and LAS 4:155–64; Booth spent much of the afternoon with other friends: David Harkins, late of the Virginia cavalry, Thomas Johnson of the Winter Garden, and actor Harry Pierson were with him and Chester by the time they reached the saloon. Owen Fawcett, C. W. Taylor, and John E. Owens drank with him as well. The latter encounter was mentioned in the April 7 entry of Owen Fawcett's Diary, Kefauver Library, University of Tennessee.

25. Chester in LAS 4:164; William E. Sinn, "A Theatrical Manager's Reminiscences," in *Abraham Lincoln: Tributes from His Associates* (New York: Thomas Y. Crowell & Company, 1895), 170.

26. Bunker in Poore, 1:32, and LAS 15:261; *Evening Star*, April 10, 1865, 1, and April 11, 1865, 2.

27. N.O.R. I:5, 550; O.R. III:5, 508.

28. Lincoln's speech in the *Evening Star*, April 10, 1865, 2; Weichmann in LAS 6:499.

29. Pierson in LAS 3:168; Weichmann, *A True History*, 131; Thomas Otway, *Venice Preserved; or, A Plot Discovered* (Lincoln: University of Nebraska Press, 1969,) edited by Malcolm Kelsall. The hero is politically ambiguous, and the play is not strictly a celebration of tyrannicide.

30. Henry B. Phillips in LAS 7:491; Tracy in LAS 4:437. The other men were H. R. Tracy, of the Attorney General's office, and B. F. Pleasants, of the Treasury Department.

31. Foster in LAS 4:8; Spangler-Butler; Mathews in LAS 5:310.

32. The sale of 287 acres was recorded in Equity Case 623, Prince George's County, and Administration Docket 593, Maryland State Archives, Annapolis. Weichmann in *Surratt Trial*, 389; Calvert's letter is in LAS 15:418; The amount of the debt is in *Surratt Trial*, 390; Acreage is given in Poore, 2:250. Zadock Jenkins testified about the two judgments in *Surratt Trial*, 759, and said (p. 758) that Nothey lived three or four miles from Surrattsville, in the direction of Piscataway (toward the west). Trip to Surrattsville: Weichmann in LAS 6:454 and Poore, 1:74; Lloyd in LAS 2:199, LAS 5:148, 157, 169–70; Weichmann in Poore, 1:136–37, Emma Offutt in Poore, 1:305–6; Lloyd in *Surratt Trial*, 295. Riding with Lloyd were his sister-in-law, Emma Offutt, her little son, and Dave Herold's friend Walter Griffin. The child was not identified, but he may have been her four-year-old son James, who died on April 27.

33. Nothey in LAS 4:411; Gwynn in LAS 4:420; Lloyd in LAS 5:157, and 162; Weichmann in LAS 6:456.

34. Spangler-Butler.

35. *Evening Star*, April 12, 1865, 1; Frederick Stone supposedly told George Alfred Townsend that his client, Herold, was with Booth that night at the White House. Townsend published it in his novel *Katy of Catoctin* (Cambridge, Maryland: Tidewater Publishers, 1959), 490. Another source puts Powell, not Herold, at the scene, but the author of that version (John Clampitt) was even farther removed from the event than Stone was. Powell was said to be paranoid about going out in daylight, and if that was true, he would not have gone to this very public event.

36. Sale of carriage: Spangler-Butler; Ford in LAS 5:456, 459, 484.

37. Smoot, *Ft. Smith Times*, May 9, 1906, 4. Smoot said that Mrs. Surratt showed him a letter from her son that mentioned his return on Friday. The letter was addressed to "Miss Mitchell," who was not further identified. Perhaps this was actually Anna Ward, who had recently received a letter from John Surratt, and who brought it to the Surratt

house on the evening of April 10. Weichmann saw that letter, but took no notice that it mentioned Friday night. Weichmann, *A True History,* 131.

38. O.R. III:5, 509–10; Mary Todd Lincoln's invitation to Grant, dated April 13, 1865, was published in *The Papers of Ulysses S. Grant,* 14:483. The original is in the Berkshire Museum, Pittsfield, Massachusetts.

39. Like Shakespeare, Booth probably got his information on Brutus from Plutarch's *Lives.* It remains available in many editions, including one rereleased in two volumes, entitled *Fall of the Roman Republic* and another as *Makers of Rome.* Both have been published in softcover editions by Penguin Classics.

40. Booth did not target Seward for strictly legal reasons; the secretary of state was not in line to succeed the president, except in the absence of the vice president, president pro tempore of the Senate, and speaker of the House. Had Lincoln and Johnson both been killed, their successor would have been Senator Lafayette S. Foster, of Connecticut. The "meddlesome" quote is from Welles, *Diary,* 2:76. Early in the war, it was commonly believed that Seward would actually run the government. Lincoln proved to be his own man, but because he and his secretary of state agreed on so many issues, the notion of Seward's dominance persisted throughout the war. Asia Booth Clarke quoted her brother as saying, "Other brains rule the country," and he undoubtedly had William Seward in mind. Clarke, *Unlocked Book,* 124.

41. Powell at Seward house: *Evening Star,* April 18, 1865, 1; Robinson in LAS 6:96; Someone calling himself "Justice" reported seeing Booth talking to O'Laughlen in Baltimore, and said that O'Laughlen was supposed to accompany Booth to Washington that day. The story has the ring of truth, and makes O'Laughlen's trip to Washington appear less coincidental. It also shows how Booth tried to keep his summons off the written record, in deference to their friendship. The letter, dated May 6, 1865, is in Record Group 393, Part 1, entry 2347, Letters received by the Secret Service of the 8th Army Corps, Old Book 19, p. 224, National Archives.

42. George Wren in LAS 6:495; Dwight Hess in LAS 4:381 and Poore, 2:539.

43. Anonymous report in LAS 3:611 and Murphy in LAS 5:242; Early in LAS 4:318, Henderson in LAS 4:420. Henderson's uniform was mentioned by George R. Grillet in LAS 3:505.

44. Atzerodt in LAS 3:535 and 596; Hess in LAS 4:385. Long before the thirteenth, D. A. Strong overheard people talking about the theater exits (LAS 6:261). Hess told George Alfred Townsend that Booth explored the exits and alleys around his theater. San Francisco *Chronicle,* July 30, 1882, 1.

45. *Evening Star,* April 14, 1865, 1; Murphy in LAS 5:244; Early in LAS 4:318, Henderson in LAS 4:420.

46. Atzerodt in LAS 3:535; Atzerodt's "confession" in the Baltimore *American,* January 18, 1869. All accounts of this meeting came from Atzerodt, and he changed the details with every retelling. He had been staying at the Pennsylvania House since March 18. Greenawalt in LAS 2:1052.

47. Mary Todd Lincoln's note to General Grant was published in Turner and Turner, *Mary Todd Lincoln: Her Life and Letters,* 219; Hatter in Poore, 1:246; Knox in Poore, 1:242, 244–45.

48. *New York Tribune,* May 1, 1865, 4. The original has apparently been lost.

49. Huntt visit: Smoot, *Ft. Smith Times,* May 9, 1906; Laurie Verge, "That Trifling Boy," *Surratt Courier* 27, no. 1 (January 2002): 4. Herold had left behind a nightshirt that had the name of John Surratt sewn into its neckband. The shirt, still owned by Huntt's de-

scendants, is on display at the Surratt House museum. Atzerodt: James Kipp in LAS 2:658; Lyman Sprague in *Surratt Trial,* 324; Powell: Robinson in LAS 6:96.

50. Thomas H. Carmichael in LAS 4:197. Nobody explained why O'Laughlen should collect a debt for his brother Billy, who lived and worked in Washington. Sam Arnold said that Mike himself had lent Booth the money. Murphy in LAS 5:240; Early in LAS 4:317.

51. Booth had breakfast with Carrie Bean. *Daily National Intelligencer,* April 29, 1865, 2; Murphy in LAS 5:240; Early in LAS 4:317; Harry Ford in LAS 5:467; John T. Ford manuscript in MS 371, Maryland Historical Society. James Maddox referred to the White House messenger as a "detective," and he probably inferred that from seeing the same man outside the president's box that night. He was Charles Forbes. Maddox in Poore, 2:110.

52. Fletcher in LAS 5:418, 420, *Surratt Trial,* 227, and M-619, 456:299.

53. Welles, *Diary,* 281–83.

54. Smoot in *Ft. Smith Times,* May 9, 1906, 4; Weichmann in *Surratt Trial,* 443, 445, and LAS 6:454.

55. John Miles in LAS 5:211; Frederick Seward overheard Lincoln ask the general as he was leaving the Cabinet meeting. *Seward at Washington,* 276; *Evening Star,* April 14, 1865, 1.

56. Murray in *Surratt Trial,* 249; Margaret Rozier in LAS 3:659; William P. Wood in LAS 6:47; Pumphrey in LAS 6:01–4; Foster in LAS 5:348; Pumphrey in Poore, 1:175.

57. Mary Lincoln to Francis B. Carpenter, as quoted in Turner, *Mary Todd Lincoln,* 218; William Wallace Lincoln (b. 1850) had died in the White House on February 20, 1862, of bilious fever. *Evening Star,* March 19, 1865, 2; April 15, 1865, letter by Dr. George B. Todd, surgeon of the *Montauk.* Copies in the Chicago Historical Society and the University of Oklahoma Library. Knife incident: Grillo in *Surratt Trial,* 176–77.

58. *Evening Star,* April 15, 1865, 3; April 13 memo from William F. Potter to Thomas Ingraham, Record Group 393, Part I, entry 5444, National Archives; *National Intelligencer,* July 18, 1867. Mrs. Grant noticed a dark-haired man "with a wild look" peering into the carriage at her. She told her husband he was the same man who had followed her into the Willard's Hotel dining room earlier and stared at her there. Horace Porter, *Campaigning with Grant* (New York: The Century Co., 1897), 498–99.

59. Fletcher in *Surratt Trial,* 227; Robert R. Jones in LAS 2:655; The card is at LAS 15:312. Nevins in LAS 3:48; Lyman Sprague in *Surratt Trial,* 324; Johnson was in Room 68, at the top of the stairs by the desk. Contrary to rumors, it was nowhere near Atzerodt's room.

60. Harry Ford in LAS 5:456. Dick Ford came back from the Treasury Department with one flag, and a man from the department brought the other one over later.

61. Weichmann in LAS 3:1154 and Poore, 1:75; Lloyd in LAS 5:151, 170–73, LAS 14:162, LAS 14:141, and *Surratt Trial,* 298. The defendant at Upper Marlboro was Edward L. Perrie, who had stabbed Lloyd on or before February 17. Office Dockets, Case 85, April Term 1865 of the Circuit Court. Maryland State Archives. Emma Offutt, who was at the tavern when Mrs. Surratt arrived, said that Lloyd was more drunk than she had ever seen him before. LAS 14:145.

62. Lloyd in LAS 5:151; Gwynn in LAS 4:420 and *Surratt Trial,* 755. The note is in LAS 15:414 and was mistakenly dated 1864 in *Surratt Trial,* 402; Mary Surratt in LAS 6:178; Weichmann in LAS 6:454 and *Surratt Trial,* 392; Lloyd in LAS 14:140; Mary Surratt in LAS 6:182; Gwynn in *Surratt Trial,* 756; Lloyd in *Surratt Trial,* 288. The field glass was distinctive in that it had adjustable settings for field, marine, and theater use.

63. Ferguson in LAS 7:489. In a more publicized version, he quotes Booth as saying, "See what a nice little horse I have?" LAS 5:384; Merrick story in *The Baltimore Sun*, April 18, 1865, 1; Atzerodt: John A. Foster in LAS 3:535, 5:348.

64. The Ashmun note was first quoted in *The Philadelphia Inquirer*, April 15, 1865, 1; John T. Ford had arranged for a police officer to stand duty there regardless of Mr. Lincoln's presence, and this had been his practice for many years. Gifford in *Surratt Trial*, 559; LAS 4:83.

65. Weichmann did not see Booth in the parlor, but said he heard a man's footsteps, and inferred it had been Booth from a remark made by Anna Surratt the following morning. LAS 3:1155–56. He later refuted Holohan's testimony that this was just a friend of the family, who was never identified. Weichmann in Holt Papers, 92:444, December 18, 1883. Mary Jane Anderson in LAS 3:488; Spangler in LAS 4:64 and Spangler-Butler; Frederick Seward, *Seward at Washington*, 276. The doctor was Basil Norris; John E. Buckingham in LAS 4:50, 51; Peter Taltavull in LAS 6:368; John Miles in LAS 5:210.

66. William H. Bell in LAS 4:78; Fletcher in LAS 3:1154; Weichmann's quote of Mrs. Surratt in LAS 5:417 and *Surratt Trial*, 451; Theodore McGowan, who sat a few feet away from the entrance to the president's box, said that Booth had shown a card or an envelope, he wasn't sure which. I assume that McGowan had seen Simon P. Hanscom enter the box, and since he paid little attention at the time, he wasn't sure which man showed an envelope and which showed a card. We know that Hanscom brought the president an envelope.

Chapter 12: "Sic semper tyrannis!"

1. This version of the shooting differs from Harry Hawk's, but is more in line with the typical eyewitness account. James P. Ferguson also heard Booth say, "I have done it" as he passed beneath him. See LAS 4:340.

2. Cobb's account is from LAS 4:173, with minor details from his trial testimony in Poore, 1:251–55. The assassination occurred at 10:20 P.M., and Cobb thought that Booth reached the bridge about twenty minutes later. According to the U.S. Naval Observatory, Astronomical Applications Department, the moon rose at 10:10 in Washington that night, four days past the full moon. Thirty-one years later, an imaginative witness recalled that it looked slightly reddish, and Lincoln biographer Carl Sandburg exaggerated this in naming his account of the assassination "Blood on the Moon." Philadelphia *Press*, April 12, 1896, 29–30. Farm wagons were allowed into the city at any time, even after the assassination. For these and all orders pertaining to the bridge guards, see Record Group 393, Part 1, National Archives.

3. Samuel Smith in Poore, 2:510; James Walker in Poore, 1:391; Washington Briscoe in Poore, 1:403.

4. John Lloyd in LAS 5:152, LAS 5:173–75, and *Surratt Trial*, 296.

5. Henderson in LAS 4:418. John Mathews kept quiet about Booth's letter, and never referred to it in questioning. But Booth himself mentioned the letter in the course of his escape. In 1867, the editor of the *National Intelligencer*, to whom it was addressed, was accused of suppressing the letter, and Mathews came to the man's defense. He was called to testify about it at John Surratt's trial, but he could not produce the original document, and his mental reconstruction of it was not deemed competent evidence. *National Intelligencer*, July 18, 1867. By April 14, Mathews no longer lived in the Petersen house.

6. A statement written by Col. Henry H. Wells is in LAS 5:226. Mudd refused to sign the Wells statement (hereinafter Mudd-Wells), and wrote his own, which is in LAS

2:1025. Edward Steers has confused Wells's work with Mudd's, and claimed that both were in Mudd's own handwriting, though clearly they were not. He and others have held Mudd accountable for differences between them. See Steers, *His Name Is Still Mudd,* 106, 111. Frank Washington (farmhand) in LAS 6:485, 489; Thomas Davis fed the horses, but did not see the visitors at all. Davis in LAS 4:255–56. Mudd claimed that Booth kept his face to the wall, and if so, Booth would have been able to see out the front window—the one with a view of the road leading up to the house; Mudd told Colonel Wells that Herold had given Booth's name as "Tyson or Tyser," and that he called himself "Henson." Herold himself stated that Booth had gone to a doctor by himself, and had told the doctor his name was Tyson. Later in the same statement, Herold claimed that, according to Booth, there was a man in the plot named Henson or Hanson. No such person existed, and both "Tyson" and "Henson" were products of Herold's imagination. LAS 4:458, 463; Mrs. Mudd's statement, sworn on July 6, 1865, was never admitted into any public record, as the testimony of a spouse was inadmissible. It is in the Ewing Family Papers, Manuscripts Division, Library of Congress. All information from Mrs. Mudd comes from this document and another, written on June 16, also in the Ewing Family Papers.

7. *National Intelligencer,* April 15, 1865, 2; *New York Herald,* April 15, 1865, 1; Clarence Seward's death reported in Record Group 393, Part 1, entry 5459, 413:96. The same source reported "Booth captured this a.m. ten miles this side of Baltimore." James A. Hardie's message is in M-473, telegrams sent by the War Department, 88:1015, National Archives.

8. Trains stopped: *The Baltimore Sun,* April 15 and 16, 1865, 2, and O.R. I:46 (3) 778; *ibid.,* 776 and Weichmann in Poore, 1:377. Baltimore police notified: *The Baltimore Sun,* April 16, 1865, 1, and O.R. I:46 (3) 777. The original Richards telegram is in the Butler Papers, Library of Congress. McPhail in M-619, 456:319. McPhail to Charles A. Dana, M-619, 458:280.

9. Stanton's warning to Sherman, M-473, 88:1017, and Halleck's details. O.R. I:47 (3) 221. Their information came from a secret agent referred to as "B" stationed in Paris. On March 17, F. H. Morse, at the U.S. consulate in London, informed Seward of the impending attack. Morse considered the whole story improbable, since the Confederates had other agents who were closer to the general's location. LAS 7:315–26.

10. O.R. I:46 (3) 767; M-619, 458:466; RG 393, Part 2, entry 6714, book 186. Thomas H. Watkins was murdered on March 25 by John H. Boyle, who was captured on April 15 in Frederick, Maryland. See James O. Hall, "The Guerrilla Boyle," *Surratt Society News* 10 (April 1985): 1, 5–6. Dana in M-619, 458:467. The identification of Mr. Anderson came from George Cottingham in his affidavit for the Committee of Claims, RG 233. Regarding Lloyd's denials, see A.C. Richards to Henry L. Burnett, May 9, 1865, in LAS 2:940; Clarvoe in LAS 2:199; Lloyd in LAS 5:148 and LAS 5:180.

11. O.R. I:46 (3) 783; Dana quote in M-473, 88:1029; McPhail in M-619, 458:338; The *Harriet DeFord* was hijacked at Fair Haven on April 5 and burned shortly thereafter. It is possible that Booth had sent the men to keep an eye on O'Laughlen, who had just left the plot. The O'Laughlen house was a few doors away from the home of Mrs. Henry, where they stayed. Barnes's explanation—that he had gone to pick up liquor for his business—did not explain why he was there for two weeks (LAS 6:461).

12. Greenawalt in LAS 2:1056 and Poore, 1:342–46; James Walker in Poore, 1:392; William Clendenin in Poore, 1:395–96; Dana in M-473, 88:1029 and O.R. I:46 (3) 783.

13. Weichmann had met John Holohan on the street, and they agreed to tell authorities about Atzerodt. See Weichmann in *Surratt Trial,* 442, 453, and *A True History,* 122.

14. Tiffany's story in the Utica *Saturday Globe,* clipping in an unidentified scrapbook, courtesy of Mark S. Zaid; Ellen Starr suicide in *The Baltimore Sun,* April 17, 1865, 2, and LAS 6:259; W. B. Lyndall to Mary A. Lyndall, November 11, 1866, in Lyndall Papers, Perkins Library, Duke University; St. John was sentenced to six months at hard labor. His case was discussed in House Report 559, Fiftieth Congress, First Session; Husband in the *Cleveland Leader,* April 17, 1865, 4; Springfield case: Utica *Daily Observer,* May 4, 1865, 2; The Hilton Head shooting was mentioned by Pvt. William L. Mead, 127th New York Volunteers, in a letter to "Dear Friend Louise," April 19, 1865, Cornwell-Mead Letters, Maryland Historical Society; The hanging in Iowa: Eugene Marshall letter to his sister, Mrs. F. L. Trow, dated April 23, 1865, in Eugene Marshall Papers, Perkins Library, Duke University; The Fort Jefferson incident: Henry B. Whitney Diary, April 22 entry, Perkins Library, Duke University; A survey of twenty-five newspapers found reports of eighty mob incidents relating to the assassination. Charles J. Stewart, "A Rhetorical Study of the Reaction of the Protestant Pulpit in the North to Lincoln's Assassination" (Ph.D. dissertation, University of Illinois, 1963), 11.

15. John J. Toffey was assigned to guard prisoners at Lincoln Hospital. Letter of April 17, courtesy of William Toffey; O.R. I:46 (3) 778; The announcement was given in General Orders No. 66, Adjutant General's Office, O.R. I:46 (3) 788, issued April 16.

16. Dispatch 194, John F. Potter to Seward, April 24, 1865, in RG 59, microcopy T-222, reel 6, National Archives; *The Examiner* was quoted in *Forney's Progress,* November 22, 1879, 22. Reactions in Richmond are described in a letter from Charlie Morrell to his brother Isaac, dated April 17, 1865, courtesy of the recipient's granddaughter, Gertrude Beidler. Ewell's reaction is in the *New York Herald,* April 17, 1865, 1, and his note to Grant is in O.R. I:46 (3) 787; Special Order 56, issued on April 17 by Sherman's adjutant, L. M. Dayton, on the general's orders. O.R. I:47 (3) 239.

17. Greeley incident is from Edward Everett Hale, ed., *James Russell Lowell and His Friends,* as quoted by the Frederick, Maryland, *Citizen,* clipping provided by Mark S. Zaid; *The Baltimore Sun,* April 19, 1865, 2; Shaw's killing has always been presented as a case of political retaliation, but Jesse Glass, who has studied the case, believes it was the result of a personal feud. *The Baltimore Sun,* September 13, 1992, and personal correspondence with the author; William T. Clark to his sister Ida, April 19, 1865, in the files of the National Park Service.

18. Telegrams relating to Keene and Harry Hawk: Butler papers, Library of Congress; Thomas Quinn, of Baltimore, quoted by William F. Morgan in a letter to the War Department, LAS 2:70; Richards to Ingraham, April 15, in RG 393 (1) entry 5454; "Dixie" punishment is given in RG 393 (1), entry 2347, old book 17, p. 302. Ford defended his staff by explaining that Mr. Lincoln himself had called it a "captured tune" the night before they played it. *The Baltimore Sun,* April 19, 1865, 1.

19. Junius Booth Diary, Mugar Memorial Library, Boston University; LAS 4:117; Washington *Daily Constitutional Union,* April 21, 1865, 1; Quincy Kilby typescript, Princeton University Library. Kilby was an intimate friend of the Tompkins family. Edwin's letter to Asia is quoted in Clarke, *Unlocked Book,* 130; Winter, *Life and Art of Edwin Booth,* 400–1; Mary Ann's reaction is reported by Mrs. Thomas Bailey Aldrich, *Crowding Memories* (Boston: Houghton Mifflin Co., 1920), 70–73.

20. Clarke, *Unlocked Book,* 127.

21. Elizabeth Dixon letter; *National Intelligencer,* April 17, 1865, 2.

22. Reminiscences of Robert Brewster Stanton, Manuscripts Department, New York Public Library; unidentified clipping in the Columbia Historical Society. The six men were John C. Weaver, William Reith, Eli Morey, David Frantz, John Richardson, and

Antonio Bregazzi. Mose Sandford, a Quartermaster Department worker, wrote to a friend on April 17 describing the clothes left in the coffin. Sandford enclosed a swatch from the bloody shirt. Files of the National Park Service, Ford's Theatre.

23. John P. Usher letter, April 16, in the Manuscripts Division, Library of Congress; William T. Clark letter, April 19, National Park Service files, Ford's Theatre; *Whig Press* (Middletown, New York), April 20, 1865, 2, in LAS 7:623; Richardson, *Messages and Papers of the Presidents*, 6:305; Welles, *Diary*, 252.

24. Cabinet meeting is mentioned by Edwin Stanton in M-473, 88:1020; Notes of Dr. Charles S. Taft, at McGill University, identifies those present as Dr. Joseph K. Barnes, Dr. Charles H. Crane, Dr. Robert King Stone, Dr. Joseph J. Woodward, Dr. Edward Curtis, Dr. William Notson, and himself. Autopsy report of Dr. Woodward is in Record Group 94, TR11 Special File 14, D776, in the Treasure Room of the National Archives; Dr. Robert King Stone testimony in Poore, 1:250; The ball was often described as .41 caliber, and Dr. Barnes said that it was made of Britannia metal, an alloy of tin, antimony, copper, and lead. However, it was actually made of plain lead. It is now too corroded for an accurate measurement, but a recent examination by the FBI laboratory showed it to be consistent with a .41-caliber ball typically used in the .44-caliber weapon. The ball is now on display in the Armed Forces Institute of Pathology at Walter Reed Army Medical Center, along with the skull fragments and probe. NPS File for catalog number 3224, Accession 190. For a modern study of Lincoln's wound, see John K. Lattimer and Angus Laidlaw, "Good Samaritan Surgeon Wrongly Accused of Contributing to President Lincoln's Death: An Experimental Study of the President's Fatal Wound," *Journal of the American College of Surgeons* 182 (May 1996): 431–48; Helen R. Purtle, "Lincoln Memorabilia in the Medical Museum of the Armed Forces Institute of Pathology," *Bulletin of the History of Medicine* 32 (January 1958): 73–74; Original memorandum on the bullet is in LAS 7:666.

25. *The Baltimore Sun*, April 18, 1865, and Turner, *Mary Todd Lincoln*, 224; On Sunday, Stanton ordered the 22nd U.S. Colored Troops up from Petersburg to participate in the funeral. O.R. I:46 (3) 816, and James Otis Moore, letter of April 23, in Perkins Library, Duke University.

Chapter 13: "I believe he would have murdered us, every one"

1. Various rumors circulated in Bryantown. Daniel Monroe heard that the assassin was Edwin Booth (Poore, 3:491); John H. Ward said that foreign-born soldiers with Dana could not pronounce Booth's name, and called him "Boose" (Poore, 2:64); Eleanor Bloyce heard the news, but did not hear any name given for the assassin (Poore, 2:48); Leonard S. Roby said that the soldiers he spoke with did not know who the assassin was (Poore, 3:207). For Boyle's reputation, see E.D.R. Bean in Poore, 3:211; Leisurely ride: see George Booz [Booth] in Poore, 3:336–37. See also testimony of John F. Hardy in Poore, 3:432, and Francis Farrell in Poore, 3:419.

2. Sarah Frances Mudd affidavit dated July 6, 1865, in the Ewing Family Papers. A copy is in the records of the Pardon Attorney, RG 204, file B596, National Archives; Captain R. Chandler, acting on Dana's information, ordered the arrest of "Boyd or Boyce" and John Surratt, the two supposed assassins. RG 393 (2), entry 6714; book 186, Mudd in LAS 2:1029; Samuel Cox, Jr., wrote about the contraband mail in the margins of his own copy of the Thomas A. Jones book, now in the Maryland Historical Society. I have used Cox's account of Booth's departure rather than Mudd's original version. Though Cox got the information from Mudd secondhand, it seems more candid and perfectly logical, given the doctor's predicament. For Mrs. Mudd's plea to delay re-

porting, see the affidavits of Sarah Frances Mudd, Elizabeth A. Dyer, and Sylvester Mudd, all dated June 16, 1865, in the records of the Pardon Attorney, RG 204, file B596, National Archives.

3. Jim Ferguson and Mary Ellen Cecil were not married until 1867. Unidentified 1876 clipping in the George Alfred Townsend Papers, Maryland State Archives, and District of Columbia marriage records; The "Ephesian dome" was the temple of Diana (or Artemis) at Ephesus, which was allegedly burned by Herostratus in 356 B.C. For Booth's quote, see New York *World,* April 25, 1865, 1. An unidentified schoolmate from St. Timothy's later gave the same story. See Clarke, *Unlocked Book,* 155–57; The mainstream view of Booth's motives remains that expressed by Stanley Kimmel in *The Mad Booths of Maryland, passim.*

4. The description of Prince George's County was dated four years after the assassination, but little had changed there (and nothing for the better) in the postwar years. Unidentified clipping in the Lincoln Obsequies Scrapbook, Rare Book Room, Library of Congress; Regarding Herold's photograph, see Van Benthuysen and James A. McDevitt in M-619, 456:567 and 456:574, and an April 22 letter from Brevet Brigadier General Charles H. Crane, of the Surgeon General's office, which mentioned the photo lab's work. Robert E. Batchelder Autographs catalog number 63 (1987). The photos were printed by a lab in the Surgeon General's office.

5. An interview with the Sewards was reported in the *Cincinnati Commercial,* December 8, 1865, 4; Dr. Verdi gave his prognosis in the *Western Homeopathic Observer* 2 (May 15, 1865), for a copy of which I thank Dr. Blaine V. Houmes; Thomas B. Gunning, "Treatment of Fracture of Lower Jaw by Interdental Splints," *New York Medical Journal* 4 (1867): 23–29; For an excellent overview of Secretary Seward's treatment, see John K. Lattimer, M.D., "The Stabbing of Lincoln's Secretary of State on the Night the President Was Shot," *Journal of the American Medical Association* 192 (April 12, 1965): 99–106; Frederick Seward in *Surratt Trial,* 252; A previously unused source on the Sewards' progress were the morning and evening reports of the Surgeon General. For some reason, General Barnes telegraphed these reports to Stanton, whose office was in plain sight of his own. On April 20, Stanton began forwarding them to General Dix for dissemination to the press. They appear in M-473, reels 88 and 89. Frederick Seward returned to work in October.

6. Samuel Beckwith in *The Washington Post,* April 1, 1915, 2:5. Though Grant ordered the arrest of John T. Ford, most of his attention was directed at demobilizing the army and advising General Sherman on terms of surrender for Johnston, Mosby, and others still under arms. B. A. Hill's investigation was reported to Stanton on April 16, Stanton Papers, reel 9, Library of Congress; Resumption of the rail service in Stanton to Morris, April 15, in M-473, 88:1022; Edward Murphy in LAS 5:241–47; John Caldwell lent Atzerodt the money (Poore, 2:148). Lucinda Metts lived at 182 West Street (now 3213 P Street). Atzerodt's connection to Mrs. Metts has not been determined, but Montgomery County marriage records connect several people of her family (with its variant spelling "Metz"; here I use her own spelling) with the Richters. Atzerodt's aunt was married to Frederick Richter. High Street is now Wisconsin Avenue, and the Cunningham Tavern still stands at Wisconsin and O streets. Details on the events at Tennallytown (now Tenleytown) are in the court-martial records of Lewis F. Chubb in RG 153, case file MM2513, National Archives.

7. Philadelphia *Evening Bulletin,* November 1, 1911. My thanks to Steven J. Wright.

8. Thomas in LAS 6:377; It is often suggested that Booth and Herold avoided going through Bryantown because Dr. Mudd had warned them of the military presence

there. In fact, we have no reason to suppose they ever intended to go through a populated area in the first place. Herold said that he had relatives at Patuxent City, and he
might have gone there in search of a carriage. It is not far from Hughesville. Herold in
LAS 4:451, 460.

9. For Major Waite's report on the "skirmish," see O.R. I:46 (3) 870; Dr. Richard Neale
and two other men were committed to the Old Capitol, charged with attempting to
assassinate Union soldiers. I found no record that they were prosecuted. Commitments
to the Old Capitol, RG III. Swan in LAS 6:227; Charles County land records give the
name as Oswell Swann, but I take the spelling from the family, and from Swan's death
certificate. For family information, I am indebted to Swan's grandnephew, Ricky
Robinson.

10. For the story of Jack Scroggins's death, see Donald Yacovone, ed., *A Voice of Thunder:
The Civil War Letters of George E. Stephens* (Urbana and Chicago: University of Illinois
Press, 1997), 163–64, 190–91; a refutation appeared in the *New York Tribune*, March 4,
1862; One variant gave the slave's name as Jackson Smook, and another named Thomas
Jones as the killer. For variants on the story, see Cora Frear Hawkins memorandum,
February 4, 1953, in the Stern Papers, Library of Congress, and George Alfred
Townsend, "How Wilkes Booth Crossed the Potomac," *Century Magazine*, April 1884.
Mrs. Hawkins took notes from her many conversations with Bettie Johnson, a former
servant of the Coxes.

11. The house still stands, but has been altered since Cox's time. It originally had wings on
either side of the main structure, but the left wing was destroyed before the Civil War,
and the right was torn down in 1975. Rich Hill was deeded to Samuel Cox (1819–80) in
1849, including 845½ acres. A letter from Rudolph Carrico to J. Matthews Neale dated
July 24, 1959, gave a full title abstract. It is in the papers of Philip Van Doren Stern,
Manuscripts Division, Library of Congress; Samuel Cox interrogation report by
Colonel Olcott, in Holt Papers, vol. 92, document 6769; Swan in LAS 6:227. According to Lafayette Baker, Mary Swann (no relation to Oswald Swan) saw Booth holding
his hand up to the lantern, showing Cox the tattooed initials on the back of his hand.
The story is suspect, however, because it originated with Baker, and because Mary always claimed to have protected her master. In a statement to Colonel Wells, Mary said
that she saw the fugitives, but they did not come into the house. See Cora Frear
Hawkins memorandum; Swann to Baker in LAS 6:162 and Swann to Wells, LAS
6:160.

12. Cold front: RG 393, Part 1, entry 5459, 413:102. Samuel Cox, Jr., letter to Mrs. Bradley
T. Johnson, July 20, 1891, in Virginia Historical Society; Jones, *J. Wilkes Booth*, 73–74.

13. *The Nation's Sacrifice: Abraham Lincoln. A Sermon Preached at the Church of the Redeemer,
Cincinnati* (Cincinnati: Robert Clarke & Co., 1865), 7–8, 13, 14; *Cleveland Leader*, April 17,
1865, 4. Reverend Thome preached at the Detroit Street Congregational Church.

14. Edwin Booth to Adam Badeau, April 16, copy in the Sterling Library, Yale University;
Edwin returned to New York that day with Orlando Tompkins and Henry Jarrett, according to the diary of William Warren, in the Roland Reed Collection, Howard University; Asia did not explicitly state that she looked through the papers beforehand, but
she implied it by saying, "I opened the packet alone, and destroyed an envelope. . . ."
Clarke, *Unlocked Book*, 127; Sleeper Clarke in LAS 7:410; Both letters are in the Treasure Room of the National Archives.

15. Cottingham in M-619, 458:391 and claim report, RG 233, file HR39A-H4.1; Jones's
smuggling case was laid out in O.R. II:2, 861, and his plea to Seward is on p. 860. His
release was delayed by a letter from Frederick Seward dated December 20, 1861, advis-

ing that he be transferred to Fort Lafayette in New York Harbor. O.R. II:2, 874. I assume this was urged by Seward's father, who had received Jones's pleas for mercy, as well as Allen Pinkerton, who considered Jones a dangerous character.

16. Some of those summoned: William P. Wood in Washington *Sunday Gazette,* February 22, 1885, 1; Lafayette Baker and New York Police, O.R. I:46 (3) 783; Stanton to Baker in M-473, 88:1018; George H. Sharpe, O.R. I:46 (3) 851–53; Robert Murray, M-619, 456:358; John Young, O.R. I:46 (3) 783; Stanton relieved James O'Beirne of his regular duties on Sunday. M-619, 458:106 and O'Beirne in claim file, RG 233.

17. Roger D. Hunt and Jack R. Brown, *Brevet Brigadier Generals in Blue* (Gaithersburg, MD: Olde Soldier Books, 1990), 212, 658; Howard Murphet, *Hammer on the Mountain: The Life of Henry Steel Olcott* (Wheaton, IL: The Theosophical Society, 1972), 7–8, 15–21; Welles, *Diary,* 265. Welles also said that Olcott probably acted with good intentions.

18. Cottingham in M-619, 458:391–92; Joshua Lloyd in M-619, 456:492.

19. Voltaire Randall and Eaton Horner in claim file, RG 233; M-619, 458:291.

20. John H. Jack's report on Canning is in LAS 5:50–57. Jack's youngest child, incidentally, was a two-year-old boy named Edwin Booth Jack.

21. Harry Langdon in the Baltimore *American,* March 17, 1907; comment in *The Philadelphia Inquirer,* April 28, 1865; Rogers's arrest was mentioned in *The Baltimore Sun,* April 24, 1865; Washington *Evening Star,* April 21–24, 1865. Some of the best sources on the "Pennsylvania Booth" are in a collection of newspaper clippings at Lincoln Memorial University, Harrogate, Tennessee. *National Intelligencer,* April 18, 1865, 1. A few sources identify the man as Capt. Jacob Haas, but Haas was arrested in western Pennsylvania, not in the northeastern part of the state.

22. During the day, McPhail went with Horner to arrest Mike O'Laughlen, but found that he had not yet returned from Washington. *Memorial,* in the Voltaire Randall claim file, RG 233; Van Tyne in Poore, 1:140; Brooke Stabler in LAS 6:136; Cobb in LAS 4:174, and Loughran in LAS 5:135.

23. The amount on Baker's handbill included the $20,000 offered by the Common Council of Washington, so the large "$30,000" heading was misleading. M-619, 455:732; Allen and Kirby in M-619, 455:599. When Baker suspected that Kirby had been holding out on him, he had both men arrested. Aquilla Allen and William Washington Kirby in M-619, 455:601 and 455:620; RG 393 (1), entry 5459, book 413, p. 96.

24. Thomas Price in LAS 6:32–35 and Poore, 2:23–24; Clara Harris in the Washington *Evening Star,* April 17, 1865; The knife belonged to Harry Ford, who inadvertently left it behind after inspecting the box on Friday afternoon (Ford in Poore, 2:550–51). The items found in Lincoln's pockets are now in the Rare Book Room, Library of Congress. For the disappearance of the flags, see Michael W. Kauffman, "The Revenge of Old Glory: History vs. Myth in the Lincoln Assassination," *Lincoln Herald* 104, no. 4 (Winter 2002): 143. Olin in Poore, 1:409–11, and *Surratt Trial,* 786; *Evening Star,* April 17, 1865, 1. James J. Gifford went into the box with Secretary Stanton on Monday, and observed that the hole in the door was hurriedly made with a left-handed augur bit. Gifford in *Surratt Trial,* 327.

25. They may have gotten their instructions from Jones, or from Stoughton W. Dent. Just after putting Jones in touch with the fugitives, Sammy Cox informed Dr. Dent of what was going on. Cox letter to Mrs. Bradley T. Johnson, July 20, 1891; Jones, *J. Wilkes Booth,* 80; Margaret Powers letter to Stanley Kimmel, 1940, in Kimmel Papers, University of Tampa (Mrs. Powers had been a neighbor of Franklin Robey, and heard the details directly from him).

26. James Leamon in Poore, 2:505.

27. Junius Booth to Edwin, April 17, 1865, in the Hampden-Booth Library, The Players.

28. H. W. Bellows letter to Police Superintendent John A. Kennedy, April 17, 1865, original in the Massachusetts Historical Society; Clarke, *Unlocked Book,* 131–33.

29. Randall and Horner in claim file, RG 233; M-619, 458:322 and M-619, 458:291; Randall's telegram is in M-345, reel 30; As Percy E. Martin discovered, Benedict Arnold had his name legally changed by the Maryland courts in 1840.

30. Cottingham claim file, RG 233; Lovett in M-619, 456:488; Joshua Lloyd in M-619, 456:493.

31. Mississippi River warning is in M-473, 88:1052; Chesapeake sighting was reported in the *Intelligencer,* April 16, 1865, 1; Adams to William H. Seward, dispatch number 969, published in *Diplomatic Correspondence* (Washington: Government Printing Office, 1866), 386.

32. Lue Porterfield in *Century Magazine,* February 1913, 562; LAS 3:873; Gifford in *Surratt Trial,* 327; William H. DeMotte lent them one flag, and the National Democratic Association provided another. The photographer's assistant did not return either flag, and in a few days DeMotte wrote to the War Department asking for the return of his own. He said it could be identified by a triangular rent in the blue field. LAS 2:127. A receipt for the second flag was signed by Mr. John Miller on April 28. LAS 4:1238. Neither Harry Ford nor Gifford commented on the accuracy of Brady's re-creation, as far as I can tell.

33. LAS 4:197 and M-619, 458:247; There is no official statement attributed to O'Laughlen, but these few scraps were published in the *New York Herald,* April 19, 1865, 1; M-473, 88:1039 and O.R. I:46 (3) 821.

34. Chicago clue in LAS 2:17; Booth taunts: LAS 3:590, LAS 2:433; George Surratt in LAS 3:111; Mercy Abbott in LAS 7:202–4; Mrs. Van de Water in LAS 7:357; Young in LAS 2:35; Addison F. Brown in Ft. Delaware, RG 110, entry 38; "Loyalty" in the Joseph Holt Papers, vol. 92 (he was identified later as T. A. Marshall); Quinn, quoted by William E. Morgan in LAS 2:71.

35. Henry Clay Young letter to Stanton, April 20, 1865, in LAS 2:34; Sewer report: Gen. James A. Hardie to Col. Timothy Ingraham, RG 393 (1), entry 5444; Search Delaware City ships: M-473, 89:37; Search 9:30 train from Baltimore to Philadelphia: M-473, 88:1109; Search all trains there for three days: M-473, 88:1111; Mance raid: M-473, 88:1066; Most people believe the Canada trip was ordered by Police Superintendent A. C. Richards, but it was actually ordered by Baker.

36. Clark's report: John A. Kimball affidavit for the Committee of Claims, House of Representatives, Thirty-ninth Congress, First Session, HR39A–H4.1, Record Group 233, National Archives (Kimball overheard Clark's story, and escorted him to Augur's office); Smith in M-619, 455:919–20.

37. Spangler in LAS 2:903 and Spangler's own account in the John T. Ford papers, MS 371, Maryland Historical Society.

38. Henry W. Smith in M-619, 455:919–25; Wermerskirch in *Surratt Trial,* 486–87; No writer has questioned Powell's appearance in a coat, even though his bloody overcoat had already been found in the woods. The explanation may lie in the observation of Private Price, who had recently noticed a few overcoats lying on the ground, evidently discarded by careless workers. See LAS 6:33; For the contents of Powell's pockets, see LAS 5:542.

39. Olivia Jenkins in *Surratt Trial,* 748; Mary Surratt interrogation in LAS 6:235–36, 239–50.

40. Bell described his identification of Powell in Poore, 1:477–78. The photo found at Surratt's is in LAS 15:370; Wermerskirch in *Surratt Trial,* 487.

Chapter 14: "Let the stain of innocent blood be removed from the land"

1. Two different sources suggest that Powell intended to head northeast. Richard M. Smoot said that conspirators in Southern Maryland were expecting three horsemen—Booth, Herold, and Atzerodt—to go through T.B. And Mary Surratt's attorney, John Clampitt, quoted Powell as saying he intended to escape to Baltimore. Smoot in *Ft. Smith Times,* May 9, 1904, 6; Clampitt, "The Trial of Mrs. Surratt," *North American Review* (September 1880): 223–40.

2. Louis J. Weichmann suggested that Powell had been hiding in Congressional Cemetery, but the coat was found miles from there. Powell was wearing a "drab coat" when captured, and I assume it was one of the coats Thomas Price saw abandoned along the road. Price in LAS 6:33, Charles H. Rosch in LAS 6:92; log of the U.S.S. *Saugus;* J. B. Montgomery to Gideon Welles, April 18, 1865, in the Missouri Historical Society.

3. The government farm incident was investigated and found to be a "humbug." See Waite, LAS 3:881; Dr. Richard Neale, sixty-four, was arrested as a suspect in what turned out to be an ambush, not a skirmish. He was released on May 14. LAS 2:192; RG 110, commitment book of the Old Capitol Prison, 153, 165; M-473, 88:1086–87; Andrew Von Robey had succeeded John Surratt, Jr., as postmaster, and moved the post office to a new location west of the tavern. The three cavalrymen were Peter McNaughton, James A. Rankin, and George B. Seymour. M-619, 456:398–402; In an October 1865 letter to Joseph Holt, Dana seemed preoccupied with that raid on the government farm, and continued to believe the incident involved Booth, even long after the facts proved otherwise. It appears he pursued the matter vigorously, while ignoring Mudd's report. Dana to Holt, in M-619, 458:467 and RG 110, commitment book of the Old Capitol, 153; and RG 393 (2), 20:22. George Dyer Mudd, who reported to Dana, was a second cousin of Samuel Alexander Mudd.

4. *Ibid.;* Dr. George D. Mudd in Poore, 2:392–93. Darkness fell, and they never made it to Wilmer's house that day. Joshua Lloyd in M-619, 456:494.

5. Daniel S. Camenga to Kate Camenga, April 30, 1865, in Kate Camenga Papers, Perkins Library, Duke University.

6. Washington *Evening Star,* April 15, 1865, 2; and quoting the *Whig,* April 18, 1865, 4.

7. *National Intelligencer,* April 16, 1865, 1; There are many conflicting ideas about what "the Ides" actually means, but in ancient Rome it referred to the day of reckoning—the date on which the taxes came due. Here Booth writes as if the assassination of Lincoln has just occurred, but in reality his first passages were written several days later. The original Booth diary is on display in the Lincoln Museum at Ford's Theatre.

8. John Mathews testified about the letter at the Judiciary Committee hearings on President Johnson's impeachment. See James O. Hall, "That Letter to the *National Intelligencer,*" *Surratt Courier* 18 (November 1993): 4–8. A skeptical view of Mathews's testimony appears in Thomas G. Shaffer, "The Gospel According to John Matthews," *Surratt Courier* 18 (October 1993): 3–9.

9. Booth landed on the stage on his right foot, not his left. On April 15, John Devenay said that Booth "fell with his face towards me" (LAS 2:154). Charles Hamlin said the same thing. *The New York Times,* July 9, 1883, 1 (citing the *Cincinnati Enquirer*). Frederick Sawyer noted Booth's quickness in a private letter, quoted in *Civil War History* 22 (March 1976): 64. The lieutenant was John J. Toffey, and his letter was dated April 17.

Courtesy of William Toffey. The "real theatrical manner" was the phrase used by Sarah Hamlin in an April 15 letter (University of Maine at Orono). Twenty years later, General Roeliff Brinkerhoff still remembered the "swift stage walk" that Booth had evidently studied for effect. Brinkerhoff also recalled, "It is said his leg was broken by the fall, but I saw no evidence of it in his gait." *The Mansfield (Ohio) Herald,* April 16, 1885.

10. Borrows in LAS 4:67 and Poore, 1:225; Stewart in LAS 4:58 and Poore, 1:70; Cobb noted no distress in Booth, and said that he "seemed to be very gentlemanly in his address and style." LAS 4:171; Lloyd in LAS 5:148, and Poore, 1:115, 137. He also told the story to John A. Foster, who reported it in LAS 4:8.

11. Because of his gentle gait, Charley, the roan horse, was normally reserved for ladies. Thomas Davis, who worked at the Mudd farm, described the horse's injuries (LAS 4:247). Aquilla R. Allen and William Washington Kirby believed they had discovered the switch, based on the word of Gabriel Thompson, a black man who saw the fugitives just before they reached Surrattsville (M-619, 455:608). Allison Nailor, son of Thompson Nailor, explained the horse switch in the Washington *Evening Star* on January 10, 1885; 2; This type of leg fracture is commonly seen in horseback riders, and generally occurs when the horse rolls quickly, giving the rider no time to remove his feet from the stirrups. The girth of the horse exerts a sideways pressure on the lower leg, snapping the smaller (outside) bone straight across. This accords perfectly with the injury Booth suffered. See the autopsy report by Surgeon General Barnes in Record Group 94, entry 623, file B, in the Treasure Room of the National Archives.

12. Herold in LAS 4:463, 483–84, 479.

13. Distribution of troops, O.R. I:46 (3) 870; Sleep rotation: R. Chandler to Maj. G. Worcester, April 16, in RG 393 (2), book 186, entry 6714; Extra rations: Capt. Musser, of Hardin's Division, *ibid.;* James Otis Moore (22nd USCT) to his wife, Lizzie, April 23, 1865, in Moore Papers, Perkins Library, Duke University; Wood in M-619, 455:574. Aquilla R. Allen, who was working for Wood on the pursuit, had worked for many slave owners as the most celebrated "slave catcher" before emancipation.

14. Adeline (Mrs. Austin L.) Adams in LAS 2:908, RG 393 (2), entry 6709, and Old Capitol commitment book, 139; Conrad arrest in *ibid.;* Celestino's arrest was witnessed by Weichmann, who mentioned it in *Surratt Trial,* 397. The captain was not prosecuted, but he was deported. Case of Benjamin Ficklin: LAS 7:414, LAS 7:405, and RG 110, entry 38; Bedee arrest order: M-473, 88:1057, and Stanton's apology: M-473, 89:284.

15. The mobbed prisoners were identified in the press as Judson Jarboe, Grafton Suit, and William Berry. *The Baltimore Sun,* April 18, 1865, 2; Old Capitol commitment book, 139, identifies them as Jarboe, Berry, and George A. Baden; Powell's being stolen as a child: unidentified clipping in the Lincoln Obsequies Scrapbook, Rare Book Room, Library of Congress; A. B. Newcombe was assigned to track down the Kentucky rumor, and he even brought the wife of George B. Payne down to identify the prisoner. Newcombe to Burnett in LAS 2:731; M-619, 456:355.

16. Seward in Poore, 2:9; Wells in Poore, 2:45.

17. Grant's presence when the news came: Randall and Horner claim file, RG 233; Stanton to Wallace in M-473, 88:1058; Stanton to McPhail (through Wallace) M-473, 88:1061; McPhail's prohibition on reporting leads was issued through his brother and assistant, William McPhail. M-619, 458:254; Augur's order: J. H. Taylor, April 18, 1865, in Letters Received by the Provost Marshal, District of Columbia, RG 393 (1), entry 5444; McPhail's defense in M-619, 458:247–52; Fulton's letter in M-619, 458:256.

18. Surratt escape in Weichmann, *A True History,* 335; The description of Atzerodt was

vague; James O'Beirne was told only that he was "of medium height, black hair . . . looks like a German, a smiling man." O'Beirne's diary, formerly in the papers of Otto Eisenschiml, now owned by Donald P. Dow; Francis Curran in LAS 3:518.

19. Sunrise salute: RG 393 (1), entry 5459, 413:109; Mrs. Lincoln's preference for Illinois was not announced until eleven P.M. on the nineteenth, and she finally chose Oak Ridge Cemetery, Springfield, on the night of the twenty-eighth. The remains had been in Cleveland most of that day. Stanton to Dix, M-473, 88:1090 and Stanton to John L. Stuart, April 28, 1865, in M-473, 89:190; Description of the scene: Washington *Evening Star*, April 19, 1865, 1; The Guard of Honor consisted of one captain, three lieutenants, and twenty-five first sergeants. Upholsterer John Alexander: *Evening Star*, April 20, 1865, 2; Honor Guard appointments in O.R. I:46 (3) 845; More escorts were to be added by state officials. Gen. John A. Dix was ordered to supplement the guard as he saw fit while the remains were in the state of New York. Stanton to Dix, M-473, 88:1113; Description of the corpse by George Alfred Townsend in San Francisco *Chronicle*, n.d. [1882?], clipping in Box 100, George Alfred Townsend Papers, Maryland State Archives; Brown and Alexander assigned the embalming to Henry Pratt Cattell, who used a method developed by Professor Suquet in Paris. Cattell quoted in Allen E. Roberts, *House Undivided: The Story of Freemasonry and the Civil War* (New York: Macoy Publishing, 1961), 76–77. Gurley's eulogy was published in John Gilmary Shea, ed., *The Lincoln Memorial* (New York: Bunce and Huntington, 1865), 120, 122.

20. The hearse was built by George R. Hall, and the thousand-dollar coffin was made by R. F. Harvey and G. W. Harvey. *Evening Star*, April 17, 1865, 3; The costs of the funeral was borne by the government, and a treasury warrant was issued in the amount of $30,000 to the Interior Department on April 11, 1866, to cover the costs. See Treasury Department, Comptroller records, warrant 4976, National Archives. (My thanks to Markus Ring.) Transfer of the 22nd U.S. Colored Troops: O.R. I:46 (3) 816. Order of march in Washington was set in O.R. I:46 (3) 807–8, and more specifics were published in Shea, *Lincoln Memorial*, 129–34. Arrangements in Baltimore alone were staggering. See RG 393 (1), entry 2343, box 8. Marshal scandal: *Chicago Tribune*, May 4, 1865; Last-minute adjustment: Signal Corps records in RG 393 (1), entry 5459, 413:109.

21. John Walter Lee to his father, April 19, 1865, in Iowa State Historical Society; Troop estimates varied, but Edwin Stanton's report to the president in November 1865 gave the following figures for Confederate troops in the field as of April 10: Richard Taylor, 42,293; Edmund Kirby Smith, 17,686; Joe Shelby, 200; and Joseph E. Johnston, 31,243. That meant that 91,222 men were still fighting for the South after Lee surrendered his 27,805 men. O.R. III:5, 532. Johnston began negotiations with Sherman on April 14, but Confederates remained on the run throughout the period of the talks. It should be noted that Mosby's Rangers had not yet surrendered, but had been observing a truce during negotiations. Washington *Daily Constitutional Union*, April 26, 1865, 1. By executive proclamation, President Johnson declared the war over in every state except Texas on April 2, 1866, and on August 20, 1866, in that state as well. The U.S. Supreme Court deferred to those proclamations. See *The Protector*, 79 U.S. 700.

22. Sherman's telegram in O.R. I:47 (3) 287; John C. Breckinridge to Davis, April 19, 1865, in LAS 15:451; This version of Davis's reaction is drawn from William C. Davis, *An Honorable Defeat: The Last Days of the Confederate Government* (New York: Harcourt, 2001), 173–75. Davis made an exhaustive survey of the firsthand accounts, and concluded that the best-known version of Davis's response—that of Lewis Bates—was a fabrication.

23. The five were Edward McHenry, Michael O'Callaghan, Henry T. Bevans, Lorenzo

DeAngelis, and Charles Bostwick. DeAngelis in M-619, 456:523; McHenry in M-619, 456:516–17; O'Callaghan in M-619, 456:513; Bevans in M-619, 456:526; In RG 45, order of Assistant Secretary of the Navy Gustavus V. Fox to Commodore J. B. Montgomery, for the use of a ship for Capt. Samuel Beckwith and six men to go to Chapel Point. (Beckwith brought the detectives and a telegraph repairman along.) The constable in question may have been John W. Wise. A fragment of a letter from him to "Dear Friend Surratt" was found during the investigation. LAS 7:688.

24. Smith in the Baltimore *American,* December 21, 1903; Two examples will illustrate the difference between Southern Maryland and Montgomery County. When William Harvin, a sawmill worker near T.B., guided some cavalry to Dr. Mudd's house, he was threatened for cooperating with the Yankees (LAS 5:201). By contrast, Sgt. George Lindsley wrote to James Purdom on April 19, acknowledging his report of Atzerodt. He closed his letter, "Give my love [to] all the family And believe me Your friend. . . ." (LAS 2:233–34); Purdom's source was a neighbor, Nathan Page (LAS 2:227–28); *Delaware State Journal,* April 28, 1865, 3; The original conversation at Metz's was reported by James Leamon in Poore, 2:505. His brother, Somerset Leamon, gave a slight variation in Poore, 2:503. O'Daniel in M-619, 455:835; Purdom in M-619, 455:893; Gemmill in LAS 2:1014; The soldiers on the detachment were Privates David H. Barker, Albert Bendler, James Longacre, Christopher Ross, Samuel J. Williams, and George W. Young. More details on the Atzerodt pursuit, as well as their pass from General Tyler, are in Committee of Claims files, HR39A–H4.1, Record Group 233, National Archives.

25. Purdom in LAS 2:228; Gemmill in LAS 2:1015; John L. Smith said that Gemmill was suspicious because a cousin snickered when Atzerodt gave a false name. That may be true, but contemporary sources did not mention it. Gemmill in LAS 2:1017–18; Smith in Baltimore *American,* December 21, 1903.

26. Col. Timothy Ingraham issued Special Order No. 68, which sent detective James A. McDevitt to New York with Weichmann and Holohan, but Lafayette Baker was actually behind the order and the subsequent trip into Canada. Detectives Clarvoe and Bigley were with them there. Order in LAS 7:597; Weichmann in *Surratt Trial,* 443; Weichmann, *A True History,* 398.

27. *The Philadelphia Inquirer,* April 19; Clarke, *Unlocked Book,* 127–28; John Sleeper Clarke in LAS 7:410; Correspondence of the Attorney General, RG 60, National Archives; Washington *Evening Star* editorial, April 20, 1865.

28. Remains in the Rotunda: anonymous letter, Huntington Library, San Marino, California, HM 19954.

29. Lovett in claim file, RG 233; O.R. I:46 (3) 847; Original draft, in Stanton's hand, is in M-473, 88:1092; This account of Lloyd's interrogation is spliced together from testimony, letters, and memoranda submitted in support of reward claims. The original sources are contradictory, and cannot be reconciled completely with one another. Cottingham in M-619, 458:362–366; M-619, 458:391–395; and Poore, 2:192–93. My emphasis is in Cottingham quote; Lovett in M-619, 456:488; Joshua Lloyd in M-619, 456:492–93; Williams in M-619, 456:501; and John M. Lloyd in LAS 2:199; Hidden guns were discussed in Cottingham's claim file, RG 233.

30. Thomas Jones later claimed to have told Henry Woodland to return his boat to Dent's Meadow every evening, but Woodland's 1865 account indicates the boat was kept at Allen's Fresh until Wednesday night. Jones, *J. Wilkes Booth,* 85; Woodland in LAS 6:451; William Tidwell used tide and weather data to determine the forces Jones might have taken into account as he planned Booth's departure. However, as local watermen

pointed out to me, the currents here are complex, and as Jones would have known, eddy currents can flow south along some parts of the crossing, then north on others, regardless of the tide. See William Tidwell, James O. Hall, and David Winfred Gaddy, *Come Retribution* (Oxford, MS: University of Mississippi Press, 1988), 456 (hereinafter *Come Retribution*).

31. The St. Mary's sighting may have been related to the arrest at Great Mills of a man dressed in women's clothing. Gen. James Barnes to Stanton, April 23, 1865, in M-109, naval historical files, 44:1133. Weather information comes from the logs of ships in the Potomac Flotilla. Jones, *J. Wilkes Booth*, 98–110. The Huckleberry farm is now privately owned and operated as the Loyola Retreat. David Herold recalled having only one paddle and one oar (LAS 4:464).

32. Murray in LAS 5:263; William H. Runkle, a newspaper editor working as a clerk to General Tyler, transcribed the conversations. M-619, 455:854; Stanton's telegram to Tyler: M-473, 88:1106; Atzerodt and Richter on the *Montauk:* ship's log; Atzerodt was moved on the twenty-third to the *Saugus* and placed in the windlass room. RG 45 and M-149, 80:385.

33. Log of the U.S.S. *Juniper,* National Archives. Though many authors have accepted Jones's recollection that Booth crossed on the twenty-first, contemporary evidence suggests otherwise. The calendar in Booth's diary is marked "On Poto[mac]" for April 20. Henry Woodland said that Jones was gone from noon on April 20 to dawn on the twenty-first (LAS 6:451); William R. Wilmer, of Port Tobacco, reported that two men, one answering the description of Booth, had been seen in Nanjemoy on the twenty-first. For the other side, see William Tidwell, "Booth Crosses the Potomac: An Exercise in Historical Research," *Civil War History* 36 (April 1990): 325–33.

Chapter 15: "I must fight the course"

1. The funeral train has been the subject of several books, the latest and perhaps most comprehensive being *The Lincoln Funeral Train* by Scott D. Trostel (Fletcher, Ohio: Cam-Tech Publishing, 2002).

2. This entry appears to have been written at the Indiantown farm, near Nanjemoy, on April 23. Original is in the Lincoln Museum, Ford's Theatre.

3. Townsend, *Life, Crime and Capture,* 55. Lafayette C. Baker repeated this passage verbatim, and without attribution, in *The History of the United States Secret Service,* 492.

4. Dr. Samuel Mudd in LAS 2:1028; Sarah F. Mudd in a sworn affidavit, July 6, 1865, in Ewing Family Papers, Manuscripts Division, Library of Congress; John F. Hardy in Poore, 2:435–36. Hardy was with Mudd at the time. He counted twenty-eight horses outside.

5. Stanton's declaration was published in *The Baltimore Sun,* April 24, 1865, 1; Allen and Kirby in M-619, 455:609.

6. RG 393, Part 1, entry 2778, Letters sent regarding Secret Service, Department of Missouri, 559:203; The St. Louis order is in M-473, 89:42; RG 393, Part 1, entry 2778, 559:207–9.

7. Spangler statement in the John T. Ford Papers, Maryland Historical Society, MS 371; similar content is in another statement, published in the Harrisburg *Daily Telegraph,* June 24, 1869.

8. Log of the *Ella* for April 23 showed her passing the *Casko,* the *Jacob Bell,* the *Resolute,* and the *Juniper* in this vicinity. Commander Foxhall Parker to Gideon Welles, O.R. I:5, 559; Lt. Cdr. E. Hooker to Parker, *ibid.;* loophole: O.R. I:46 (3) 818. Lincoln's original blockade had been lifted, but was effectively reinstated after the assassination.

9. Quesenberry in LAS 5:557–59; *New York Herald,* May 4, 1865. I am deeply indebted to several of Mrs. Quesenberry's descendants, particularly Nicholas Payne and Betty Houghton, for genealogical information and photographs. Alice Yturbide regained custody of her son, and kept him at Rosedale, the house in which she and her sister Elizabeth had been born. During a more recent international custody dispute, seven-year-old Elian Gonzalez stayed in the same house. Louise Mann Kenney, *Rosedale* (Washington, D.C. Youth for Understanding, 1989), 51; Just before the assassination, Gen. Lew Wallace went to Texas on Lincoln's behalf to study the Mexican situation. Wallace and others were determined to start a war with Mexico, having annexation in mind. Herold in LAS 4:462, and John M. Garrett in M-619, 457:506; Wallace, *Autobiography,* 812–46; Andrew F. Rolle, *The Lost Cause: The Confederate Exodus to Mexico* (Norman: University of Oklahoma Press, 1965), 9. Most of the ten thousand Confederate exiles who went south ended up in Mexico. Maximilian was defeated and put to death in 1867. Juaristas slaughtered many of those Confederate mercenaries.

10. William Bryant in LAS 4:95–97.

11. *The Philadelphia Inquirer,* April 23–25, 1865; Details about the second funeral-related death were not given in the papers. Phillips Brooks House Association, *Columbia Encyclopedia;* A. V. Allen, ed., *Life and Letters of Phillips Brooks* (Boston: n.p., 1900).

12. Burnett's letter books appear in LAS reel 1.

13. Bryant in LAS 4:95–97; Stuart family information comes primarily from the doctor's papers in the Alderman Library, University of Virginia, and from the kind help of descendants, especially Courtney McKeldin, Eugenia Thirkield, Julia Lindsay, and Rosemarie (Mrs. Richard Stuart) Hunter; Mosby's men were dispersed over a wide area, and they tended to surrender piecemeal, as word of their commander's wishes reached them. The colonel himself was holding out for guidance from federal authorities. See Ulysses S. Grant to Stanton, April 17, 1865, in O.R. I:46 (3) 817–18; Hunter's comments in Grinnan Family Papers, Mss1 G8855a 179–86, Virginia Historical Society; Dr. Stuart did not identify all his visitors by name, but they were probably S. T. Stuart, Major Hunter, and the doctor's daughters Ada (widow of Lt. Col. William Randolph), Rosalie (Mrs. S. Turbeville Stuart), and Margaret (fiancée of Major Hunter). It is possible that his daughter Julia Jones and son Richard Henry Jr. were also present. In a letter to *Century Magazine* in 1895, someone signing himself "E.G.D.G." claimed to have been present, and says that Dr. Stuart was away at the time of Booth's visit. Elise Skinner, who identified herself as a Stuart cousin, also claimed to have been present. T. C. DeLeon, *Belles, Beaux and Brains of the Sixties* (New York: G. W. Dillingham Company, 1907), 251.

14. Stuart in LAS 6:206–10. The doctor did not say who asked him about his neighbors, but I assume Herold did the talking. Lucas in LAS 5:145–47.

15. *The Baltimore Sun,* April 27, 1865, 1.

16. William Lucas in LAS 5:145–47.

17. The officers' car, which followed the *United States* in line, was also ferried across by boat. Information on Peter Relyea comes from family clippings, copies of which are in the Surratt House library, and from clippings in the Abraham Lincoln Scrapbook, Manuscripts Division, Library of Congress. The photograph issue was not finally decided until May 1, when Stanton ordered Dix to comply with the original order. M-473, 89:145–46, 177, 220; *The New York Times,* April 25, 1865.

18. O'Callaghan in M-619, 456:514; DeAngelis in M-619, 456:523; O'Beirne and Beckwith affidavits, in RG 233, claims file HR39A–H4.1; M-619, 458:449.

19. Wood in LAS 7:368; Hall in LAS 4:139–40. Years later, a story was told that when the

cavalry searched Tudor Hall, a daughter of William Heuisler's, who had been renting the place from the Booths, defiantly told them that John Wilkes would have been welcomed there. However, Thomas Hall described the search as fruitless, and he said that Heuisler "nearly came to blows" with Booth over politics. See Ella V. Mahoney, *Sketches of Tudor Hall and the Booth Family* (Bel Air, MD: Franklin Printing Co., 1925), 50.

20. Rollins in M-619, 457:552–54, and in LAS 6:79–80; Jett in LAS 5:88–92; This was the first time the fugitives mentioned Orange Court House. This town was about sixty miles away, and just beyond it was Gordonsville, an important railroad hub still in Confederate hands. Evidently, Harbin recommended that Booth find his way there; Though Jett said Booth had used the alias "James William Boyd," most of the earliest sources claim he was calling himself "John William Boyd." People often use their correct first name in order to avoid slipping up, and in different places along the escape, Booth and Herold were doing exactly that. Jett in Poore, 1:311. Jett did not serve with Mosby, as often claimed. His story is given in G. W. Beale, *A Lieutenant of Cavalry in Lee's Army* (Boston: The Gorham Press, 1908), 230. Beale knew Jett well; For information on the Gouldman family, I am indebted to my good friend Harold M. Gouldman, Jr., whose grandfather shared a room with Jett on April 25; At the end of the war, former Confederates were examined to determine which form of amnesty, if any, would apply in their cases. Each was required to obtain a certificate from the examining officers.

21. Doherty entry in the *Army List, 1815–1900*, 285. *The Annual Report of the Adjutant General* gives April 22 as the date of his promotion, retroactive to April 3; Doherty in M-619, 456:274 and 456:284; Schneider in M-619, 456:286. The order for men was copied into M-619, 456:273. The detachment consisted of two sergeants, seven corporals, and seventeen privates.

22. Herold said that as soon as he identified himself to Jett, "he gave me a book and asked my signature." I have assumed Jett would have wanted Booth's as well. In the *New York Herald*, May 4, 1865, William N. Walton said that Herold copied something on a paper he took from Booth. Walton had just come from retracing the escape with members of the 16th New York. They had been ordered to collect evidence, and this poem seems to fit that description, though it was never marked or identified. It was discovered by the present writer, and is published here for the first time. LAS 7:661; The handwriting is Booth's, and the second part is consistent with Herold's, though the only known example of his writing is a signature in LAS 4:433; Herold statement in LAS 4:467; Rollins in LAS 6:80–81. Incidentally, the lines "I could not love thee, dear, so much / Loved I not Honor more" were taken from "To Lucasta, Going to the Wars," by Richard Lovelace (1618–57).

23. Jett in LAS 5:94–98.

24. Richards told this to Colonel Olcott, who recounted it in a memo to Colonel Burnett on April 25. LAS 2:129; Kelly and Clarvoe were already gone: LAS 3:323.

25. Jett in LAS 5:94–98; Herold in LAS 4:467; A deed dated September 17, 1846, described a 517-acre tract that included "Locust Hill." Caroline County land records, Liber 45, folio 293. Cecilia Fleetwood Garrett was living with an uncle in Lexington, Missouri; Mary Elizabeth Garrett was teaching school in South Carolina; and Julia Garrett died in infancy. John Muscoe "Jack" Garrett served in the Fredericksburg Artillery, and was traded to the Caroline Artillery on April 15, 1864, in exchange for a wounded soldier. William Henry Garrett served in the latter unit. The Gouldman-Jett conversation was recounted by Henry C. Bell in a letter to Finis L. Bates, December 20, 1914, in E. H.

Swaim Papers, Georgetown University. Bell interviewed George Jesse Gouldman and his mother several times, and his own recollection was certified by a son of Jesse's.

26. Records of Massachusetts General Hospital, 1857; RG 94, Entry 112, Order Book of the 16th New York Cavalry, Special Order 32, January 31, 1865, announced the promotion of Corbett, retroactive to March 1, 1864; Frederick H. Dyer, *Compendium of the War of the Rebellion*, 1380; I am indebted to Steven G. Miller for sharing his unsurpassed knowledge of the regiment's history.

27. According to Lucinda Holloway, "Mr. Boyd" offered an opinion that the killer had only wanted notoriety. However, her account was not written until many years later. L.K.B. Holloway, "An Eyewitness Account of the Death of John Wilkes Booth," manuscript in the Confederate Museum, Richmond. See also Jack Garrett in M-619, 457:502.

28. Luther Byron Baker in M-619, 455:669–70. Baker said that other people in King George County had already pointed them in the direction of Port Conway. However, nobody else on the expedition recalled meeting such people. William McQuade in M-619, 456:237; David Baker in M-619, 456:245; Abram Snay in M-619, 456:219; Charles Zimmer in M-619, 456:234; The split tactic is mentioned by Doherty in M-619, 456:276; Capt. Wilson's orders: Baker in M-619, 455:669. Baker claimed that an old man said Booth and Herold had crossed the previous day. Doherty said it was a black man, and Rollins mentioned the presence only of Dick Wilson, who was an African American. Doherty in M-619, 456:276; Sources also disagreed on who mentioned Jett's courtship of Izora Gouldman. Baker claimed they heard it from some ladies at a "house of entertainment" ten miles down the road, while Doherty attributed it to Mrs. Rollins. The latter makes more sense, as they were hell-bent for Bowling Green long before they saw the ladies mentioned by Baker. Doherty, *ibid.*, frame 277; Baker and Conger in M-619, 455:676.

29. Jack Garrett in M-619, 457:507–9; Herold in LAS 4:467–69; At the suggestion of Mrs. Rollins, the cavalry pretended to have William Rollins under arrest. Rollins in M-619, 457:559 and Baker in M-619, 455:674; Details of the Star Hotel encounter are given by Conger in Poore, 1:313, and M-619, 455:726, and by Baker in M-619, 455:677.

30. Richard H. Garrett claim in Committee of Claims, RG 233; Jack Garrett in M-619, 457:514–17; Herman Newgarten in M-619, 456:227; Conger in Poore, 1:314.

31. Jack Garrett in M-619, 457:515; L. B. Baker, 680; Conger in Poore, 1:314; Lewis Savage in M-619, 456:224; Oliver Lonkey in M-619, 456:222; John Winter in M-619, 456:229; Godfrey Hoyt in M-619, 456:236.

32. Herold in LAS 4:470; Jack Garrett in M-619, 457:519–20. This whole sequence is compressed in Garrett's account. He remembered being in the barn for just a brief word with Booth, while Baker and Conger recalled ordering the fugitives several times to give themselves up to Garrett.

33. Will Garrett in M-619, 457:530–31; Conger in Poore, 1:315; Herold in LAS 4:470–71; Baker in M-619, 455:680; John Winter in M-619, 456:231.

34. Herold in LAS 4:470–71; Baker in M-619, 455:681; Boston Corbett in M-619, 456:256. In nearly all of the soldiers' accounts, the fire starts only seconds before Booth was shot. However, Conger himself stated, "At 1:30 A.M. we set fire to the barn, and Booth was shot at fifteen minutes past three A.M." It is hard to square this with Conger's assertion, on the very next page, that he set the fire after Herold surrendered. Adding to the mystery is an experiment I once undertook to resolve this issue. In September 1996, I enlisted the help of cavalry reenactors and burned down a genuine Civil War–era tobacco

barn. We duplicated the Garrett farm conditions as best we could, starting at 1:30 A.M. on a relatively still night. Though we eventually resorted to using gasoline, our barn took about twenty minutes to get a noticeable flame going; Everton Conger in M-619, 455:726; Boston Corbett, M-619, 456:257.

35. Young Lillian Garrett remembered Herold being taken out, and she thought it looked painful, being tied with his back to a tree. Philadelphia *Press*, December 4, 1881; Conger in M-619, 455:728; Corbett in M-619, 456:258; Conger in M-619, 455:729.

36. Conger in Poore, 1:317–18; Baker in M-619, 455:684–86.

Chapter 16: *"These people around here contradict each other so much"*

1. Clarke, *Unlocked Book*, 130–31; *New York Tribune*, April 28, 1865, 1. L. B. Baker thought Booth kept the shavings to start a fire. *Surratt Trial*, 320; The *Tribune*'s favored treatment might have had something to do with its Washington bureau chief, Aaron H. Byington, who was a particular favorite of Stanton's. The actresses pictured were Fanny Brown, Alice Gray, Helen Western, and Effie Germon. For many years, authorities left the name of Miss Hale unspoken; It was Dan Bryant who commissioned his musical director, Dan Emmett, to come up with a new "walk-around" for the end of his show. Emmett's "Dixie" became an instant success. *Richmond Dispatch*, March 19, 1893; Effie Germon also earned a footnote in history. She spent much of the spring of 1865 posing for her brother-in-law, Constantine Brumidi, as he painted the interior of the Capitol dome. Her face can be seen on the allegorical figure at the right hand of George Washington. My thanks to the woman (raised in the Germon family) who first tipped me off to the story; my apologies for misplacing her name. Beckwith in M-619, 458:449; Wells to Augur, April 26, 1865, in M-619, 458:424.

2. Corbett turned down as much as $100 for the pistol, saying it didn't belong to him. *The Baltimore Sun*, April 28, 1865, 2. It was stolen from him within days, and has never been seen since. Corbett, quoted in *The Lincoln Log*, December 1975.

3. Log of the U.S.S. *Montauk* in RG 24, National Archives. Burial suggestions: A. S. Lathrop to Stanton, April 27, 1865, in Stanton Papers, reel 9. The photographs were used to make woodcut drawings for the illustrated newspapers, and they have since disappeared. Baker's statement is in M-619, 455:666, and Conger's is in M-619, 455:725. The medical specimens are still on display at the Armed Forces Institute of Pathology at Walter Reed Army Medical Center. A small piece of thoracic tissue is in the Mutter Museum in Dr. Woodward's hometown of Philadelphia. The excision of chest and neck samples caused a lot of comment, and Marine Private Henry Landes, standing nearby, wrote in his diary that the head and heart had been cut out. My thanks to his great-grandson, Joseph Landes, for a copy. The *Boston Advertiser* reported the same thing on May 3, and this became a general understanding for years.

   A report on Booth's neck wound is in the *Catalogue of the Surgical Section of the United States Army Medical Museum*, specimens 4086 (third, fourth, and fifth vertebrae) and 4087 (spinal cord section). The accession cards refer to the *carbine* wound, but the official descriptions given in the *Medical and Surgical History of the War* (Washington: Government Printing Office, 1866), first surgical volume, p. 452, refer to a *pistol* ball. Dr. Barnes gave an imprecise report, saying only that "a gun shot wound" was found in the neck. Barnes to Stanton, April 27, 1865, in Record Group 94, entry 623, file D, Treasure Room of the National Archives.

4. Freckling was described by May in LAS 4:360 and in his personal recollections of the autopsy, now in the Manuscripts Division, Library of Congress. A Washington reporter described the blood settling "in the lower part of the face and neck." *Evening*

Star, April 27, 1865, 2; Initials on the hand: Charles Dawson in LAS 4:353; Jett in LAS 5:92; Richard Baynham Garrett to Gen. A. R. Taylor, 1907, published in "An Interesting Letter About the Death of John Wilkes Booth" (Peoria, Illinois: Oakwood Lincoln Club, 1934), 10, courtesy of William Hallam Webber; Emory Parady, of the 16th New York Cavalry, mentioned them in a letter to his parents, April 28, 1865, courtesy of Steven G. Miller; Sgt. Joseph Hartley, of the marine guards, also remembered the initials. His letter on that subject is in the Marine Corps Historical Center Library, Washington Navy Yard. My thanks to the sergeant's great-grandson, John Hartley, for this information.

5. Seaton Munroe in *The North American Review* 162 (March 1896): 431. See also LAS 4:356. Gideon Welles asked Commodore Montgomery for a report on who had been allowed to view the body, and whether hair was taken. M-149, 80:442–43; Stone's reply said that no orders had been issued with regard to the corpse, and that the hair was cut by an assistant to the surgeon general. Commodore Montgomery confirmed that his orders referred only to the prisoners, not the corpse. RG 45, Washington Navy Yard papers, Commandant's Letters to the Secretary of the Navy, documents 194, 195. Pvt. Marcus Conant, of the 3rd Massachusetts Heavy Artillery, took a portion of the splint from Booth's leg, and it is now in the collection of Dr. John K. Lattimer. A lock of hair was clipped by Marine Sgt. John M. Peddicord, whose grandson kindly showed it to the author in 1995. See Roanoke, Virginia, *Evening News,* June 6, 1903, 3.

6. Creation of Judge Advocate General position: 12 Stat. 598; records summary for Record Group 153, p. 327, National Archives; Herold in LAS 4:442. Contrary to recent statements, Herold never denied that the man killed in the Garrett barn was Booth. He mentioned him by name ten times in the verbatim transcript of this interview. *Evening Star,* April 27, 1865, and January 5, 1907; The penitentiary had been shut down in 1862, and its prisoners sent to New York. The old building was then absorbed into the arsenal for storage purposes. Stebbins originally ordered Sgt. Joseph Campbell to bury Booth under the stone floor of a prison cell. Hours later, Campbell reported that the ground was too hard there, so the major found a more practical site in a storage room. Suzanne Deitrich, a great-granddaughter of Major Stebbins's, provided these details. Besides Sergeant Campbell, only one other member of the burial detail has been identified: Corporal Florin Harbach. Coincidentally, a great-great-grandson of Harbach's commanded the same military installation (now Fort Lesley J. McNair) in the 1990s. My thanks to Vincent H. Harbach.

7. Charles Merrill made eight or ten trips over Atzerodt's escape route. Merrill to Joseph Holt, September 4, 1865, in M-619, 458:508; A public meeting in Bryantown resolved to cooperate with Wells. *National Intelligencer,* April 27, 1865, 2. Wells to Joseph H. Taylor, April 28, 1865, in M-619, 458:418; The officers who went with Baker were Capt. Francis M. Baker (no relation to the detectives) and Lt. Peter McNaughton. William N. Walton, of the *New York Herald,* went along to the Garrett farm, and reported the trip in the May 4 edition. Lieutenant Dana was sent by Burnett. RG 393 (2), entry 6709, p. 29, National Archives.

8. Washington *Evening Star,* July 7, 1865. Ford's fire: Nashville *Colored Tennessean,* May 6, 1865, 3. Ford eventually got $100,000 for the theater, which opened as a three-story office building late in 1865. Someone proposed to make Ford's Theatre a public lecture hall. *National Intelligencer,* June 27, 1865, 2. It would be hurriedly converted, and its myriad uses included space for the Army Medical Museum, which housed specimens from both Lincoln and Booth.

9. Virginia Lomax, *The Old Capitol and Its Inmates,* 67. Mrs. Lomax was there at this

time. Ford's two unpublished memoranda are in the John T. Ford Papers, MS 371, Maryland Historical Society. For the record, he and others noted the kindness of Superintendent William P. Wood, who allowed most prisoners to upgrade their furniture and food beyond what he could supply. As a friend of Mary Surratt's family, Wood was ordered to keep some distance from his most notorious female prisoner. William P. Wood to Mrs. Franklin Rives, March 8, 1899, in Blair Rives Collection, Manuscript Division, Library of Congress. My thanks to Gayle Harris for spotting this.

10. McPhail in LAS 2:962. Smoot later said that they were indeed in on the plot, and that Bateman destroyed Booth's boat on hearing of the assassination. Smoot in *Ft. Smith Times,* May 6, 1904; Parr in LAS 5:530. In an 1898 newspaper interview, Surratt said that he met Booth through a letter of introduction written by a friend. He did not identify the friend. *The Washington Post,* April 3, 1898.

11. Young: LAS 1:105; Burnett's KGC theory: LAS 7:211. The Frankfurt consul, William W. Murphy, sent back a copy of the *Gothaisches Tageblatt* of May 9, which notified the citizens of Thuringen that one of their own was a strong suspect in the Lincoln conspiracy. Baron von Berlepsch remembered Frederick's nephew, Ernest Hartmann Richter, as "a very ill-principled scoundrel and a notorious thief," but this was actually a cousin of the man in custody. Consular dispatches no. 470, dated May 17, and no. 474, dated May 31, in Record Group 59, microcopy M-161, National Archives.

12. Junius Booth and Sleeper Clarke arrests: M-598, reel 110, records of the Old Capitol Prison; Joseph Booth in M-345, reel 30. Joe Booth was questioned and released, per Stanton's orders. M-473, 89:369. When a business partner inquired into Clarke's case on May 19, Holt endorsed the letter: "I have no knowledge of any testimony implicating John S. Clarke." He was released. T. J. Campbell to J. B. Fry, RG 110, entry 38, National Archives; RG 393 (4), entry 2139, book 1; Saulsbury case: Thomas M. Wenie to J. R. Kenly, in LAS 2:220, and to James A. Hardie, RG 393 (1), entry 2347, old book 17:236. For more on Blackburn, see Nancy Disher Baird, *Luke Pryor Blackburn, Physician, Governor, Reformer* (Lexington, KY: The University Press of Kentucky, 1979).

13. The Booth note quotes a passage from *Macbeth* III.iv in which Lady Macbeth says that giving food does not constitute good hospitality in itself. The note, now lost, was produced and read by Thomas T. Eckert at the impeachment hearings. *Impeachment of the President* (Washington: Government Printing Office, 1867), 677.

14. Forty marines were assigned to guard duty, with two placed over each prisoner at a time. They served under Capt. Frank Munroe, brother of Seaton Munroe, and Sergeants Joseph Hartley and John Peddicord; The order from Gustavus V. Fox to Montgomery is in a bound volume of telegrams published in M-149, reel 80, page 385. A subsequent telegram orders a ball and chain for Powell. Hoods are described in a National Park Service Textile Laboratory memorandum, May 29, 1990. The originals are in the collection of the Smithsonian Institution. Spangler and Arnold had the same experience with the hoods. See Spangler's unpublished manuscript in the John T. Ford Papers, MS 371, Maryland Historical Society, and the Philadelphia *Evening Telegraph,* June 24, 1869; Also Arnold, *Memoirs,* 56–57; Eisenschiml, 176; Yossi Silverman, handcuff expert and collector, provided the Dr. Lilly story in e-mail correspondence with the author, January 2003.

15. Weichmann anecdote is from James R. Ford, "Recollections of Carroll Prison," unpublished manuscript in the John T. Ford Papers, MS 371, Maryland Historical Society. James J. Gifford also heard a guard threaten Weichmann. *Surratt Trial,* 820.

16. The prisoners were kept in the cell block built for women inmates. Michael W. Kauff-

man, "Fort Lesley J. McNair and the Lincoln Conspirators," *Lincoln Herald* 80 (Winter 1978): 176; Stanton's orders, as well as the list of prisoners transferred, are in Stanton Papers, vol. 43, 101–2; The *Keyport* was identified in the log of the *Saugus*, RG 24. Hancock was also ordered to take charge of Mary Surratt at this time, but she was not transferred over from the Old Capitol until the following day. Dr. George Loring Porter, "How Booth's Body Was Hidden," *Columbian Magazine* (April 1911): 65. My thanks to Dr. Porter's great-great-granddaughter, Marcia Maloney.

17. Eighty defendants: *Chicago Tribune*, May 4, 1865; The law admitting non-white testimony was passed on July 2, 1864; 13 Stat. 351; Only Maine allowed a defendant to testify in his own behalf, and they passed the law on March 25, 1864; 1864 Maine Acts. 214, Chapter 280. A similar federal statute was passed in 1878 (20 Stat. 30). A brief history of this rule is given in *DeLuna* v. *U.S.* 308 F2d. 140, 150–51, and 324 F2d. 375. For the history of plea bargaining, see Albert W. Alschuler, "Plea Bargaining and Its History," in *Crime and Justice in America* (Westport: Meckler, 1978), 2:3–45 and Mark H. Haller, "Plea Bargaining: The Nineteenth Century," *ibid.*, 188–94.

18. Atzerodt lied: Robert Murray in LAS 5:263. An item in the Baltimore *American*, January 19, 1869, is termed a "confession," but it is only a memorandum in the style and manner of those written by Foster. Atzerodt's proffer is now in the collection of Floyd E. Risvold; Wells's promise was mentioned in the *Evening Star*, July 7, 1865, 2; The New York conspirators planned to gain access to the White House, then blow it up during an "entertainment" they had staged for the president. In *Come Retribution*, this is transformed into a Confederate plot whose chief operative, Thomas Harney, was captured en route to Washington. It is worth noting that the War Department did nothing to prosecute Harney, who was still in custody, or Thomas Green, whose house was supposed to have been used in this scheme. They almost certainly looked into Atzerodt's story; Powell checked out: Martha Murray in Poore, 1:470; The statements attributed to Atzerodt are in LAS 3:597, and 3:536 (Foster's report); *National Intelligencer*, July 9, 1865 (Wood's report); Baltimore *American*, January 19, 1869; and *Surratt Courier* (October 1980). The original statement, taken by William M. Runkel, has never surfaced. See M-619, 455:854.

19. Olcott on Chester: LAS 5:492; The Weichmann interrogation was described by the witness himself in *A True History*, 224, and *Surratt Trial*, 398. Mudd was actually taken to the penitentiary on May 4, and not immediately after this interview, as Weichmann claimed. See Hartranft log, 9; Capt. M. A. Clancy, of Ingraham's staff, recommended no action against Mudd. Both draft indictments omitted Mudd's name. The first omitted John Surratt and included João Celestino. The revised draft reversed that. Joseph Holt Papers, 93:7023, 7028. Mary Surratt in LAS 6:170–200; Olcott's report in LAS 5:495; Fitzpatrick in LAS 5:403, 410.

20. For examples of case summaries, see Foster's report in LAS 4:08 and Olcott's in LAS 5:492; Stanton to Edward Carrington in M-473, 89:389. Stanton in M-473, 89:284–85; Hardie's apology is in the Hardie Papers, Library of Congress.

21. Johnson's proclamation is in 13 Stat. 756; Clippings of the Montreal newspapers are in the Hagley Museum and Library, Wilmington, Delaware; Thompson in the *New York Tribune*, May 22, 1865, 5

22. Collier's name is on the original order, in Stanton's hand, but never appeared in print. Stanton Papers, reel 9, Library of Congress. "In Memoriam: Frederick Hill Collier," MOLLUS pamphlet. My thanks to Roger D. Hunt. Comstock believed the accused should be tried in civilian court, and General Kautz was upset that the assignment in

Washington would further delay his wedding in Ohio. General Porter kept his reasons to himself. Cyrus Ballou Comstock diary, May 9 entry, Library of Congress; August V. Kautz Papers, Library of Congress; Special Orders No. 216, copied into O.R. II:8, 696.

23. Benn Pitman described the recording process in a letter to Holt, November 22, 1873, in Holt Papers, 67:259. They actually used Benn Pitman's American variant of his brother's system. Charges in Poore, 1:14–19. The names of Harper and Young were supplied by a witness who later proved to be a fraud. These men may not have existed. General Hartranft read the charges to each prisoner just before the commission met (Hartranft log, 16). Holt's recommendation was recalled by Spangler in the Philadelphia *Evening Telegraph,* June 24, 1869; The published rules said nothing about secrecy, but limited attendance to those with passes, and specified that testimony could be published only at the discretion of the Judge Advocate General. Benn Pitman, *The Assassination of President Lincoln and the Trial of the Conspirators* (Cincinnati: Moore, Wilstach, and Baldwin, 1865), 21.

24. William E. Doster, *Lincoln and Episodes of the Civil War* (New York: G. P. Putnam's Sons, 1915), 257 (hereinafter Doster).

Chapter 17: "Nothing short of a miracle can save their lives"

1. Alfred C. Gibson recollections, from the Civil War Library and Museum, Philadelphia. Thanks to Steven J. Wright. Clement Clay Papers in the Perkins Library, Duke University; O.R. I:49 (2) 733.

2. Von Steinacker in Poore, 1:20–25; Montgomery in Poore, 3:84; Merritt in *ibid.,* 98–100, 103. Recall that John Yates Beall was hanged in February 1865, for piracy on Lake Erie. His mythical connection to Booth was probably asserted first at this time, and it survived for many years. In reality, Booth was not related to Beall and had not attended the University of Virginia with him as some people claimed. Though the two might have crossed paths in Beall's hometown of Charlestown, it is unlikely they ever knew each other at all.

3. Godfrey J. Hyams claimed to have been involved in the yellow fever plot. Poore, 2:409; A newspaper ad from the Selma, Alabama, *Dispatch* was traced to George W. Gayle, a former federal prosecutor, who told investigators he was only joking. Gayle was brought first to Washington, then to Hilton Head, South Carolina, as a prisoner. He was supposed to stand trial at Fort Pulaski, near Savannah, but was released without trial a year later. Stanton Papers, Reel 9, 43:140, O.R. I:49 (2) 922; *The New York Times,* April 10, 1875. The ad itself is in LAS 15:557; Grant and Comstock's visit to Johnson is in the Comstock Diary, May 12 entry.

4. Department of Washington forces were said to be 26,056 men at the most recent count. O.R. II:5, 506; April 13 orders: O.R. III:5, 509; Stop asking for passes: RG 393 (1), entry 5375, 22:228; Lincoln's note in Basler, *Complete Works,* 8:410; Stanton's report: O.R. III:5, 532; The assassination law was passed in August 1965: U.S. Code, Title 18, Chapter 84, Section 1751, 79 Stat. 580, plus later amendments.

5. Johnson in Poore, 1:54; Johnson's apologists insist he was there only to plead to the jurisdiction, but in the passage quoted above he said he was there to do everything that the evidence would justify. Pitman to Holt, in Holt Papers, 93:7036, Library of Congress; Cazauran had a long-standing feud with the Booths, and had recently caused trouble for Blanche DeBar and others. See the Brooklyn *Eagle,* April 23, 1913.

6. Defendant descriptions are from clippings in the Lincoln Obsequies Scrapbook, Library of Congress; Courtroom crowding: Benjamin B. French Diary, June 18 entry, Library of Congress; Some writers have claimed that the defendants were not allowed

to speak privately with their attorneys, but this was not so. General Hartranft was ordered to be present during these meetings, but not within hearing distance. Hartranft suggested they have attorney conferences in the courtroom instead of the cells. Hartranft log, 28.

7. Harris case: RG 153, Records of the Judge Advocate General, case MM1957. He was charged with a violation of the 56th article of war, not "the laws of war." Frederick Stone was one of Harris's attorneys, and his appearance for Mudd and Herold was delayed until the end of the first trial.

8. Conover in Poore, 3:116–17, 120–21, 141.

9. Kennedy's guess: LAS 3:843; Ethan Allen Hitchcock to Elizabeth Peabody, June 11 and June 29, 1865, in the Massachusetts Historical Society; General Hitchcock believed that Powell was Dan Murray Lee, a son of Admiral Smith Lee. He took a personal interest in the issue, and eventually tracked down the Powell family near Live Oak, Florida, to confirm the story that came out. See Ethan Allen Hitchcock Papers, Library of Congress. Windson in LAS 3:104; The War Department spelled his name "Payne" because they believed he was one of the Kentucky Paynes. RG 110, entry 38; Doster, 264–65; Powell's two brothers had not actually been killed, but he believed they had (see chapter 9, note 23). Entries from the family Bible in the possession of Jewell Powell Fillmon.

10. Prisoner descriptions are from clippings in the Lincoln Obsequies Scrapbook, Library of Congress; Constipation and pulse: Dr. James C. Hall in Poore, 3:544; Weeping was noted by Rev. A. D. Gillette, clipping in the Lincoln Obsequies Scrapbook; Junius Booth letter to Edwin, dated October 20, 1862, at The Players; Joe Booth interrogation by General Dix, May 12, 1865, in M-345, reel 30, National Archives; Allen D. Spiegel and Merrill S. Spiegel, "William H. Seward and the Insanity Plea in 1846," *American Journal of Forensic Psychiatry* 19 (1998): 5–26; Dr. Isaac Ray, *A Treatise on the Medical Jurisprudence of Insanity* (Boston: Little, Brown and Company, 1853). My thanks to Dr. Allen D. Spiegel for information and guidance on Civil War–era insanity cases; Doster on insanity: Poore, 3:76–77.

11. Barnes in LAS 14:222–23.

12. Motive for attacking Seward: Poore, 1:15; Frederick Hatch, "The Seward Problem," *Journal of the Lincoln Assassination* 16 (August 2002): 25; Succession law: 1 Stat. 240, most of which was repealed in 2 Stat. 295 (March 25, 1804); Under laws existing in 1865, the office of president would have fallen to the president pro tempore of the Senate, Lafayette S. Foster, of Connecticut.

13. Benn Pitman, "Some Facts of the Assassination Trial," unpublished manuscript in the Jerome B. Howard Shorthand Collection, New York Public Library; "Special treatment" pertained to Dr. Mudd being allowed to sit outside the prisoners' dock, which Hartranft explained by saying the dock was already full by the time Mudd was brought into the room (Hartranft log, 62, 20–21); Powell was caught playing with the iron ball, and Hartranft had it removed. *Ibid.,* 49. Spangler in *New York Tribune,* quoted in an unidentified clipping; Stanton to Hancock, June 19, 1865, in Stanton Papers, reel 10, Library of Congress; Doster, 276; transfer of Mrs. Surratt: Hartranft log, 9, 70–71; Mrs. Surratt's condition was "diagnosed" recently by Dr. William Coyle, a longtime member of the Surratt Society. Spangler in Philadelphia *Evening Telegraph,* June 24, 1869; Adjournment in LAS 14:294; Dr. George Loring Porter examined the prisoners twice every day, and his recommendations for lighter treatment were always granted. See Porter, report of June 20, 1865, in Stanton Papers, reel 10, Library of Congress, and Mary Walker Porter, *The Surgeon in Charge* (Concord, NH: Rumford Press, 1949).

14. Request for witnesses: Poore, 3:517; Holt had often discharged prisoners for such "fatal defects" as a failure to swear in a commission member in the presence of the accused. See Gayla M. Koerting, "The Trial of Henry Wirz and Nineteenth Century Military Law" (Ph.D. dissertation, Kent State University, 1995), 41. This work is full of useful insights on Holt and his operation of the Bureau of Military Justice. Attorneys allowed: 1 Stat. 118. Prosecutors working both sides: 6th Article of War, in 2 Stat. 360; Benet, 245–51; DeHart, 308–14; Coppee, 20–21, 56–59. All three prosecutors held military rank: Holt was a brigadier general, Bingham a major, and Burnett a brevet lieutenant colonel. When the U.S. Supreme Court finally held that the right to counsel in a capital case was also binding on state courts, they based their decision on the Fourteenth Amendment, which was written, ironically, by John A. Bingham. *Powell* v. *Arizona*, 287 U.S. 45. Bingham's authorship of the due process clause is examined in Bernice R. Hasin, "John A. Bingham and Due Process" (master's thesis, California State University, Long Beach, 1976).

15. DeHart 288–89, 364–65; Benet 353–54; Cox in LAS 14:675, 708; Ewing in LAS 14:235–36. Holt's response in LAS 14:242–43; Habeas Corpus Act of 1863, section 2 in 12 Stat. 755. The convoluted wording allows for argument about the meaning, but Congress certainly intended to force the secretary of state, or the secretary of war, to turn over non-political prisoners to the courts. Failure to do so could result in the secretary's imprisonment.

16. Holt in Poore, 2:542; Cox in Poore, 3:347; Ewing quoted in Poore, 3:342; Bingham in Poore, 3:345; Cox quoted in Poore, 3:346–47; Bingham response in Poore, 3:352; A transcript of the letter appears in Poore, 3:271.

17. Jenkins in Poore, 3:387; Holohan in Poore, 3:369; Howell in Poore, 2:342, 347; Cipher machine: Dana in Poore, 2:56; Burnett quoted in Poore, 3:373; Wallace-Aiken exchange in Poore, 2:177.

18. Cox quoted in LAS 14:708–9; William Winship, ed., *Digest of Opinions of the Judge Advocate General* (Washington: Government Printing Office, 1865). Secretary of Defense Donald H. Rumsfeld published a more detailed and explicit set of rules for military commission trials in his "Military Commission Order No. 1" dated March 21, 2002, and "Military Commission Order No. 2" dated April 30, 2003. If followed to the letter, these orders would give defense attorneys a reference that lawyers did not have in 1865. Though no detainees have been brought to trial as of this writing (2004), military authorities insist that such trials be held in secret. My thanks to Professor Ruth Wedgewood for copies of the above orders.

19. Herold was allowed to remain in the courtroom after hours to write out a confession. It was never made public, and has not been found. Atzerodt's confession was allowed as part of his lawyer's closing summation. Hartranft log, 32, 33; Also comments in Poore, 2:514; Booth's diary might have been admitted for other purposes, but not to prove the truth of anything he wrote in it. Bingham quoted in Poore, 2:183; An exception is found in the case of treason, for which a court might hear a defendant's confession in court. Francis Wharton, *Wharton's American Criminal Law* (Philadelphia: Kay and Brother, 1853), 1:358.

20. Ewing-Holt argument in Poore, 2:396; Afterward, John Bingham reverted to the charge that Mudd's extended concealment was part of the crime. Wells in Poore, 1:282–93; Wells's own statement on behalf of Mudd is in LAS 5:226.

21. Poore, 3:446; Rule on character evidence: Benét, 287; Grover's Theatre: Poore, 2:541. Ewing brought this up again in his summation. LAS 14:602–3; By statute, they were

required only to provide a copy of the charges and a transcript of the previous day's testimony. Cottingham in Poore, 2:216.

22. Changed story: compare Mary Van Tyne in LAS 6:438 and Poore, 1:139–43; Misquotes: see Wells's report on Greenawalt compared to Greenawalt's sworn testimony, LAS 3:635 and Poore, 1:347. Alexander Lovett said on the stand that Booth left the Mudd farm on foot, yet no one said any such thing before the trial. Lovett, Gavacan, Joshua Lloyd, William Williams, and A. R. Allen contradicted one another. See Poore, 1:260, and M-619, 455:598 and 456:488, 492, 497, 501; The envelope, with the name of Thomas Zizinia, was apparently found in Booth's trunk. The lines on it do appear to represent roads, but the locality has not been identified. See LAS 2:292; Alexander Lovett and George Cottingham reward claims in RG 233; Lovett said that Lloyd had confessed to being an accessory (LAS 5:193).

23. Suspicions: Joseph N. Clarke in LAS 2:922; Sympathizer: Gilbert J. Raynor in LAS 6:102–6; Howell statement in the John T. Ford Papers, MS 371, Maryland Historical Society; Foster in LAS 6:463; Weichmann to Burnett in Poore, 1:377; LAS 6:500; Sworn testimony later established that officers had threatened Weichmann directly. See Gifford in *Surratt Trial*, 820; *Tribune* article mentioned in Poore, 1:385; See Joseph George, Jr., "Nature's First Law: Louis J. Weichmann and Mrs. Surratt," *Civil War History* 28 (February 1982): 101–27.

24. Clara in LAS 3:135–37. I would guess that Sarah Slater wrote the letter.

25. Joseph George, Jr., "Subornation of Perjury at the Lincoln Conspiracy Trial? Joseph Holt, Robert Purdy, and the Lon Letter," *Civil War History* 38 (1992): 230–41; Norton in Poore, 3:195, 439; Evans in Poore, 3:236–61; Ewing, 17.

26. Prince George's County Circuit Court, *Accounts* vs. *the Estate of J. H. Surratt,* vol. WAJ, No. 1:277, Maryland State Archives. An entry for November 9, 1865, shows "One open a/c in favor of Jno H. Nothey" for $30.00.

27. The government's embargo on the "suppressed testimony" was about to be lifted when Mrs. Pitman handed a transcript to the *Commercial*. Benn Pitman explained the mixup in an unpublished memorandum, now in the New York Public Library. Montreal *Evening Telegraph,* June 10, 1865; Gen. John A. Dix to Stanton, June 24, 1865, in Stanton Papers, reel 10; Levi C. Turner's report on the Conover perjury is in O.R. II:8, 855–61, and Holt's reply follows in *ibid.*, 962.

28. Hall in Poore, 3:542–43; In all, four doctors examined Powell: Basil Norris, James C. Hall, Joseph K. Barnes, and the prison doctor, George Loring Porter. See LAS 14:216–29. Dr. Nichols testified earlier in order to establish the validity of the defense. Some of his testimony supported the notion of Powell's insanity, and some detracted from it. He had not examined the prisoner. Nichols in Poore, 3:143–53; The law did not then provide for an examination of the accused. See Poore, 3:498; Powell probably did not realize that his mother's relatives were also Powells; hence the apparent ignorance. See Hall testimony in Poore, 3:545.

29. *Wharton's American Criminal Law,* 618, and 1 *Bingham on Criminal Law,* section 265, both cited by Cox in LAS 14:691–92; The rule today, generally, is that conspiracy is a felony, and regardless of intention, a death that results will invoke the "felony murder rule," by which all are guilty of "felony murder." In 1865, conspiracy was only a misdemeanor, and in any event, the aim of this plot was to take a hostage, which was recognized as a legal act of war. See General Orders No. 100, Articles 54 and 55; O.R. II:5, 674.

30. Herold argument: Stone in LAS 14:808, 815, 818–19, 823; Spangler argument: Ewing in

LAS 14:550, 558–59, 603; Cox in LAS 14:674–75, 680–89, 711, 732–33, 777; Atzerodt argument: Doster in Pitman, 300–7; Powell argument: Doster in LAS 14:629–30.

31. For more on Hunter, see Edward A. Miller, Jr., *Lincoln's Abolitionist General: The Biography of David Hunter* (Columbia, SC: University of South Carolina Press, 1997).

32. Lew Wallace to Susan Wallace, n.d. [June 26, 1865], in Indiana Historical Society; Powell's defense in LAS 14:611, 613, 635–38, 645; John A. Bingham, *Argument of John A. Bingham, Special Judge Advocate* (Washington: Government Printing Office, 1865), 35–36.

33. Bingham, 94–95, quote on horses: *ibid.,* 113.

34. Burden of proof: *ibid.,* 82 (emphasis added); Johnson's other clients included Robert E. Lee; Quote on liberty: *ibid.,* 60; Bingham's attack on defense counsel: *ibid.,* 11–13; In August 1863, Ewing issued General Order No. 11, which nearly depopulated four Missouri counties by ordering all rebel sympathizers not living in designated cities to leave. He also ordered a subordinate officer to make sure that certain rebels "are not to be captured under any circumstances, but to be killed when found." O.R. I:22 (2) 473 and O.R. I:34 (4) 260.

35. R[ichard]. A. Watts, "The Trial and Execution of the Lincoln Conspirators," *Michigan History Magazine* 6 (1922): 99; Prosecutors in deliberations: Benét, 95–96; DeHart, 94; Findings are published in General Court-Martial Orders No. 356. O.R. II:8, 698.

36. Statistics: clipping in the August V. Kautz Scrapbook, Library of Congress; Meal figure is from the Hartranft log, 80; Henry Kyd Douglas, *I Rode with Stonewall* (Chapel Hill: University of North Carolina Press, 1940), 342; Bingham in LAS 14:167.

37. Payment of a per diem was normal for witnesses, but Conover, Purdy, and others were given money from the secret service fund as well. A three-dollar per diem was authorized by statute. See 1 Stat. 216; Conover's payment: Book W, Index to Secret Service Payments by disbursing clerk, Turner-Baker Papers, RG 94, National Archives; The Lew Wallace Library in Crawfordville, Indiana, has many of the general's courtroom drawings. Another, discovered by the present writer, is in the Howard Shorthand Collection at the New York Public Library. Lobbying for war with Mexico was consistent with the views of both the Lincoln and Johnson administrations, and had the full support of Stanton, who considered it was way to "intensify national feeling . . . thousands, once misled [by secession] would rejoice to atone their error by rallying to the national flag." Stanton to Andrew Johnson, in O.R. II:5, 511. The sapphire ring was mentioned in a letter to Susan Wallace from "Zayde," dated October 29, 1865. At that time, her husband was president of the commission trying Henry Wirz, commandant of Andersonville prison.

38. Benn Pitman letter to Joseph Holt, November 22, 1873, in Holt Papers, 67:9259; Browning and Thomas Ewing, Sr., helped in the drafting of the writ; Ewing Family Papers, Library of Congress.

39. *Evening Star,* July 7, 1865, 2; Gillette's account is in an unidentified clipping in the Lincoln Obsequies Scrapbook, Library of Congress.

40. *Evening Star,* July 7, 1865, 2; Unidentified clipping in the George Alfred Townsend Papers, Manuscripts Division, Library of Congress. Townsend got the Mussey quote from Johnson himself. Herold's mother "had tried in vain to teach him better counsels, and now he must take the results of his wicked conduct without expecting sympathy from her." Unidentified clipping in the Lincoln Obsequies Scrapbook, Library of Congress. The notes written by Herold's sisters were not delivered because Mrs. Johnson and her daughter were ill. *Evening Star,* July 7, 1865, 2; The rule on executions was changed by both statute and court decisions. On March 3, 1869, the U.S. Congress

passed a law requiring lower courts to suspend executions until they received a mandate from the U.S. Supreme Court (15 Stat. 338). Not until 1883 would the courts confirm that a "supersedeas" would prohibit enactment of the lower court's decree. *Hovey* v. *McDonald,* 109 U.S. 150. The 1863 law creating the Supreme Court of the District of Columbia (formerly the U.S. District Court of the District of Columbia) gave one of its four justices the power to act as a federal judge in matters such as this. Wylie was evidently the designated judge. 12 Stat. 763.

41. Suspension of writ: *Evening Star,* July 8, 1865, 3: Original order is in the Treasure Room, National Archives.

42. Arnold, *Memoirs,* 61; *Evening Star,* July 7, 1865; 16th New York orders are in RG 393 (1), entry 5375, 23:51; Lt. D. F. Landon, letter dated July 11, 1865, transcript in the David Rankin Barbee Papers, Georgetown University; Relay: Hartranft log, 85.

43. *New York Tribune,* July 8, 1865, 1; John L. Smith's duties were to deliver the death warrants to General Hancock, then to remain on "death watch" until the sentences were carried out. He had once been ordered to arrest his own wife and take her to the prison as a witness, but she was excused for illness. Smith in the Baltimore *American,* December 21, 1903; Father Walter was from St. Patrick's church, and Father Wiget was from Gonzaga College. Rev. Mark Olds, of Christ Church, and Reverend Vaux, chaplain, U.S. Army, stood with Herold.

44. Gillette's story is in Amy Gillette Bassett, *Red Cross Reveries* (Harrisburg, PA: Stackpole Co., 1961), 91. Mrs. Bassett was the minister's granddaughter, and used his journals in the preparation of her account. *New York Tribune,* July 8, 1865, 1; The four soldiers were William Coxshall, David F. Shoup, George F. Taylor, and Frank B. Haslett. They were identified by Coxshall in the Milwaukee *Free Press,* January 31, 1914.

Coda

1. No other federal execution: see *Surratt Courier* 22 (May 1998): 6–7. The petition was signed by Hunter, Kautz, Foster, Ekin, and Tompkins. The original is in LAS 14:526. According to Holt, General Ekin copied it into his own hand, after John A. Bingham and Supreme Court Justice David Davis wrote it. Cincinnati *Enquirer,* December 15, 1883, 1; A Brophy affidavit is in the Butler Papers, Library of Congress, and his charges are in LAS 7:399–401; Weichmann response: *The Philadelphia Inquirer,* July 29, 1865, 1; Hartranft was rather emphatic that Powell "states that she had no knowledge whatever of the abduction plot, that no hint was ever said to her about it. . . ." *New York Herald,* July 12, 1865, 5; Brophy's explanation of the Hartranft statement is in a letter to James Croggon of the *Evening Star,* July 10, 1865, in Crosby N. Boyd Papers, Library of Congress. The general's own explanation is in Hartranft Papers, Gettysburg College. Less publicized was the remark of David Herold, who had said, "That old lady is as deep in as any of us" (Doster, 277); Gen. James A. Hardie and Father Jacob A. Walter both explained the execution flap in letters (dated July 22) to Archbishop M. J. Spalding. The archbishop ordered Walter to refrain from talking publicly on the subject. Both letters are in the archives of the Baltimore Archdiocese, and additional material is in the James A. Hardie Papers, Library of Congress.

2. Arnold, *Memoirs,* 62; The prisoners had originally been sentenced to the Albany Penitentiary, but that was changed to Fort Jefferson, a military installation, at which they could not be reached by civilian courts. Stanton Papers, 10:55523, Library of Congress; Holt's *Digest of Opinions,* 93, says that if the offense is punishable by the laws of the state wherein committed, a civilian penitentiary is recommended over a military one. But the offenses in this case were not specified in any civilian statute.

3. Semmes was a prisoner of the Navy Department. RG 393 (4), entry 2139; Richard Garrett sought restitution for damages to his barn, but Congress rejected his claim. Richard H. Garrett in *The Fredericksburg Herald*, April 27, 1868, and his claim, dated April 10, 1872, in RG 233. The official response is in House Report No. 743, Forty-third Congress, First Session. Jett and Rollins were also rumored to have taken blood money. When Rollins died in 1901, he left several large plantations, which he had bought, according to family tradition, in postwar tax sales. Rollins's will, filed in King George Court House; My thanks to William Rollins's great-grandson Garland Clarke. For information on A. R. Bainbridge, I thank Robert Cabot Bainbridge IV.

4. *The Unlocked Book* appeared in 1938, and a later edition, edited by Terry Alford, was published under the title *John Wilkes Booth: A Sister's Memoir* (University Press of Mississippi, 1996); Theater receipts: New York *Clipper*, February 3, 1866; Assassination attempt: See "May's Dramatic Encyclopedia" (manuscript), Jacket 16, p. 28, in the Maryland Historical Society. Comment on Edwin's fame: Eleanor Ruggles, *Prince of Players* (New York: Norton, 1955), 206; Edwin did not burn his brother's costumes, as is so often stated. The true story is given in many accounts, among them a clipping from the Boston *Sunday Herald*, November 14, 1891, clipping in the Harvard Theatre Collection, and the *Boston Herald*, August 7, 1927, clipping in Record Group 107, War Department Administration Files, National Archives. Government correspondence on Booth's trunks is in RG 59, and published in Microcopy T-482, reel 2. An inventory of the items was sent to Stanton by Consul General John F. Potter (LAS 7:229).

5. Ford's Theatre disaster: *Washington Star*, June 10, 1893, and New York *Press*, June 10, 1893; files on the disaster are kept by the Architect of the Capitol.

6. *Ex Parte Milligan*, 71 U.S. 2.

7. Dunham pardon file in RG 204, Records of the Pardon Attorney, file B-576, National Archives. Holt endorsed Albert G. Riddle's recommendation for parole, based on Dunham's secret contribution to the prosecution of John Surratt. For the case against Dunham, see House Report 104, Thirty-ninth Congress, First Session, 33–41. Because the conviction was for House testimony, Holt and Dunham always maintained that it had no bearing on other cases. William H. Gleason, of the Freedman's Bureau, visited the Dry Tortugas at the behest of Butler. Each prisoner gave a statement on his own terms. Butler Papers, Library of Congress; The diary was often mentioned in newspaper reports right after Booth's death. *The New York Times*, April 28, for example. According to Gideon Welles, the president and Stanton were "violently opposed" to its publication. Welles, *Diary*, 2:95; Butler in the *Congressional Globe*, Fortieth Congress, First Session, 363. The FBI laboratory examined the diary in 1977 and concluded that forty-three sheets (eighty-six pages) were missing. FBI report D-770615073, dated October 3, 1977. The Secret Service performed an indentation analysis in 1998. Secret Service Report 175-865-34837, dated June 30, 1998.

8. Lafayette C. Baker, *History of the United States Secret Service* (Philadelphia: King and Baird, 1867). Baker in House Report No. 7, Fortieth Congress, First Session, 32–33; Remarks on honesty: *ibid.*, 111. Thomas Eckert and Everton Conger both insisted the diary was just the same in 1867 as when it was taken from Booth. Eckert in *Surratt Trial*, 828–34, Conger in *ibid.*, 308–9, and House Report No. 7, 324–25. Byron Baker also held the diary for "about a minute." *Surratt Trial*, 320. Stanton's own memoranda on the diary are in the Stanton Papers, 11:56773 and 11:56424. They were published in the *Daily Morning Chronicle*, May 22, 1867, 1. At the impeachment hearings, Stanton denied that Booth's burial was secretive, and Thomas Eckert revealed the exact whereabouts of the grave. Review in the *Brooklyn Eagle*, May 21, 1867, 2.

9. Rejected claims are listed in M-619, 457:32–164; Runkel in *ibid.*, 455:854; West Virginia Cavalry: *ibid.*, 455:559; Rollins statement in LAS 6:76; Doherty claim in M-619, 456:216, and complaint, *ibid.*, 455:769. Adolph Singer's claim quoted Doherty as saying, "Go up as quick as possible for the rest of the men and Conger. I am on Booth's track." *Ibid.*, 456:252; Byron Baker repeated his own version in *Surratt Trial*, 316; The fight continued into the courts, where the last of the lawsuits was dismissed in October 1878. See Supreme Court for the District of Columbia, Equity case no. 790, National Archives. Thanks to Paul Kallina, via Steve Miller.

10. War Department recommendations: House Exec. Doc. No. 90, Thirty-ninth Congress, First Session; Committee amendments: House Report No. 99, Thirty-ninth Congress, First Session; Final awards, 14 Stat. 341; Navy guidelines were set by law on June 30, 1864. 13 Stat. 309; Checks were issued on Treasury warrant No. 156952, dated August 4, 1866, in RG 217, Miscellaneous Treasury Accounts, National Archives. Baker in *Surratt Trial*, 319; Conger statement of April 27, M-619, 455:728, 729.

11. Holt's remarks: Cincinnati *Enquirer*, December 15, 1883, 1; Denials in *New York Tribune*, September 11, 1873; Holt's *Vindication* (Washington: privately printed, 1873), and a letter from Holt to Secretary of War William Belknap, August 1873, in Holt Papers, Box 9, Huntington Library, San Marino, California; Reuben D. Mussey wrote a twenty-seven-page account of the clemency petition, Holt Papers, 67:9165, Library of Congress. Father Walter's comment is in a July 22 letter to Archbishop Spalding, cited above; The "nest" comment was made by President Johnson to a group of ministers on the night of July 7, and recorded in a letter by Rev. John G. Butler of the Lutheran Church; Dr. William P. Tonry, a government chemist, was fired on June 19, 1869, two days after his wedding. Special Orders No. 149, HQ of the Army, June 21, 1869, paragraph 3.

12. Robinson's medal: 16 Stat. 704; The Secret Service Division of the Treasury Department began under executive authority in 1865, and was given statutory recognition in 1882. It was not actually a permanent organization until Public Law 82-79 was passed on July 16, 1951. Correspondence of H. Terrence Samway, U.S. Secret Service, with the author. For Olcott's life, see Howard Murphet, *Hammer on the Mountain: The Life of Henry Steele Olcott* (Wheaton, IL: Theosophical Publishing House, 1972); For Wallace's life see *Lew Wallace: An Autobiography* (New York: Harper & Brothers, 1906). The general died while writing his memoirs, and his wife completed the second volume. The trial account is thus hers, and not his; On Harris, see H. E. Matheny, *Major General Thomas Maley Harris* (Parsons, WV: McClain Printing Co., 1963). Asia Booth Clarke seemed to believe her brother had converted to Catholicism, but the evidence is not convincing. Booth and Herold were Episcopalians, Atzerodt was a Lutheran, Arnold and O'Laughlen were Methodists, and Powell was a Baptist. Spangler was German Reformed, but converted to Catholicism on his deathbed.

13. On the life of Mrs. Lincoln, see Jean H. Baker, *Mary Todd Lincoln: A Biography* (New York: Norton, 1989); Grave-robbing plot: Bonnie Stahlman Speer, *The Great Abraham Lincoln Hijack* (Norman, OK: Reliance Press, 1990).

14. Lincoln and Booth: Chicago *Daily Inter-Ocean*, June 18–21, 1878; On Lucy Hale, see Richard Morcom, "They All Loved Lucy," *American Heritage* 21 (October 1970): 12–15.

15. For Blackburn, see Nancy Disher Baird, *Luke Pryor Blackburn: Physician, Governor, Reformer* (Lexington, KY: University Press of Kentucky, 1979). For Tumblety, see J. H. Baker to Charles A. Dana, May 11, 1865, in RG 393 (1), entry 2778, book 559:226.; Francis Tumblety, *Kidnaping of Francis Tumblety. By Order of the Secretary of War of the U.S.* (Cincinnati: n.p., 1866), and Stewart Evans and Paul Gainey, *Jack the Ripper: America's*

First Serial Killer (New York: Kodansha International, 1995). Dunham in the New York *World*, December 2, 1888. Tumblety was never charged in the London murders. He died in 1903 at Rochester, New York.

16. Corbett's paranoid behavior got him court-martialed in 1865. Case OO1128, in RG 153, National Archives. His pension file includes criminal case documents on the impostor, John Corbit; The Rathbone story was given to me by Henry and Clara's granddaughter, Louise Randolph Hartley, and it is much like the version that appeared in German papers at the time. The *Hannoverscher Courier*, December 24 and 25, 1883, and the *Hannoversche Allgemeine Zeitung*, November 29, 1979, were provided (with translations) by Ulrike K. Baumann, a Hildesheim native. My thanks to Mrs. Baumann.

17. For prison conditions, see Arnold, *Memoirs, passim*. O'Laughlen's remains were later transferred to Green Mount Cemetery in Baltimore. *Ex parte Mudd*, 17 F. Cas. 954 (S. D. Fla., 1868, No. 9,899); Boynton said there was enough of an argument in the petition itself to assure him that the defendant would not make a valid argument in court. Holt in Poore, 2:140; Pardons are in the State Department pardon files, vol. 9, National Archives, and on Microcopy T-967, reel 4: Mudd on 395–401, Arnold on 469–74, Spangler on 474–77. A petition with 35 signatures was sent to Washington on Mudd's behalf. It was not acknowledged, and in October 1867 another one, bearing the signatures of 258 enlisted men, was forwarded for action. See Mudd's pardon file in the records of the Pardon Attorney, RG 204, file B-596, National Archives.

18. Correspondence between Holt and Ste. Marie is in RG 59, Microcopy T-222, reel 6, National Archives; Congressional documents are published in *The Pursuit and Arrest of John H. Surratt* (Media, PA: Proofmark Publishing, 2000); Additional details, drawn from Papal Zouave records, are in Alfred Isacsson, *The Travels, Arrest, and Trial of John H. Surratt* (Middletown, NY: Vestigium Press, 2003). The extradition of Surratt may have been a show of gratitude by Pius IX, who was then losing a civil war and had been offered asylum in the United States. See Leo F. Stock, ed., *United States Ministers to the Papal States: Instructions and Despatches, 1848–1868* (Washington: n.p., 1933), xxxii. The details of Surratt's escape and capture were investigated by George H. Sharpe, whose report was printed as House Executive Document 68, Fortieth Congress, Second Session. Seward's own report was published as House Report 33, Thirty-ninth Congress, Second Session. The $25,000 reward offer for Surratt had been rescinded before his capture, so Congress appropriated a special award of $10,000 for Ste. Marie (15 Stat. 234). He sued for the $15,000 difference, but died in 1874, leaving his interest in the suit to William Shuey, who took the case to the Supreme Court and lost. *Henry B. Ste. Marie* v. *U.S.* in C. of C. Dec. T., 1873, 415; *Shuey, Executor* v. *United States*, 92 U.S. 73; Ste. Marie's will, dated July 26, 1874, Philadelphia Register of Wills.

19. Trial papers are in Record Group 21, criminal case no. 4371, National Archives. Judge Holt was interviewing witnesses behind the scenes. His role was exposed in the testimony of Edward L. Smoot, *Surratt Trial*, 191, and Bradley's protest in *ibid.*, 219. William H. Seward procured the services of Albert G. Riddle as one of the prosecutors, after failing to get John A. Bingham for the job. RG 60, Papers of the Attorney General's Office, National Archives; Surratt's letter to his cousin, Bell Seaman, was dated April 10, but was mailed on the twelfth. It is in LAS 3:759–60. Additional letters from Surratt to Bell were evidently taken away (or perhaps fabricated) by Lafayette C. Baker, who quoted them in his *History*, 388–91; Acrimony: Fisher in *Surratt Trial*, 469; Weichmann's accusers were Lewis Carland, John T. Ford, James J. Gifford, and James Maddox; Dye charges: *Surratt Trial*, 1180; Cleaver testimony: *Surratt Trial*, 206; Ashley's jailhouse promise: House Report No. 7, Fortieth Congress, First Session, 1203–4.

Cleaver charges: District of Columbia Criminal Court, case no. 5481, in RG 21, National Archives.

20. Merrick comments: *Surratt Trial*, 838; Fisher in *ibid.*, 839–40; The story of coached witnesses was explained more fully after a participant, Benjamin Spandauer, died in prison. *The Baltimore Sun*, August 10, 1889, 4; The Fisher-Bradley controversy escalated into a lawsuit for lost income. The U.S. Supreme Court decided in the judge's favor. *Bradley v. Fisher*, 80 U.S. 335 and *Ex Parte Bradley*, 74 U.S. 364. Joseph Bradley was readmitted to the bar in 1874. See *Washington Star*, September 28, 1874; Lobbying: undated letter from A. G. Riddle to William Seward, in RG 60, Records of the Attorney General's Office, National Archives; Dr. Lewis McMillan testified that Surratt admitted getting a summons from Booth on April 6. *Surratt Trial*, 208; The second indictment papers, including arguments, can be found in RG 21 under case no. 5920. The appeal decision is in 6 D.C. 306; The third indictment was labeled case no. 6594.

21. The present writer located Spangler's grave site in 1986, and it has since been marked by the Surratt and Dr. Mudd Societies. Spangler statement: Mudd, *Life of Mudd*, 322–26. Hawk in *Boston Herald*, April 11, 1897, 27. Rittersback spoke about claiming a reward, but none had been offered for Spangler. Arnold's articles were published as a limited edition book in 1943, and more recently as *Memoirs of a Lincoln Conspirator* (Bowie, MD: Heritage Books, 1995). Thanks to Dennis Doyle, great-grandnephew of Arnold, for additional details.

22. Atzerodt's burial, under the name of Gottlieb Taubert, was discovered by Percy E. Martin in 1979. The Smithsonian received Powell's skull in 1896 from the Army Medical Museum, but there was no record of what happened to the rest of the bones. Anthropologist Stuart Speaker made the discovery. He had once worked at Ford's Theatre, and knew the significance of the find. The author notified Powell's relatives, and they in turn asked him to participate in the burial.

23. Vacation: John H. Surratt letter to William Norris, dated June 24, 1869, in the William Norris Scrapbook, collection 2562, Alderman Library, University of Virginia; Rockville lecture, *Washington Star*, December 8, 1870; Surratt's dramatic escape from the Zouaves has been described in heroic terms, but Henry Lipmon, one of his guards, later admitted that he and the others had let Surratt use the privy, and he merely slid through the sewer to freedom. *New York Tribune*, February 21, 1881, 3; Surratt's arrest: *Richmond Daily Enquirer*, January 3, 1871, courtesy of Betty Ownsbey; Surratt's wife, Mary Victorine Hunter, came from a Rockville family that later included F. Scott Fitzgerald.

24. Charles A. Leale, "Address Delivered Before the Military Order of the Loyal Legion of the United States," February 1909, 5–6; Beckwith in the *Boston Post*, April 11, 1915, 2:2; Whitman actually toured the country with his first-person account, though he was in Brooklyn on the night of April 14. See *New-York Daily Tribune*, April 15, 1879.

25. Matilda Todd on WOR Radio, New York, February 12, 1928; transcript in the E. H. Swaim Papers at Georgetown University; Guard budget: 13 Stat. 206; No attendants at Ford's: Harry Ford in LAS 5:483; See John F. Parker's record in the office of the D.C. Corporation Counsel, Washington. William H. Crook and Thomas Pendel criticized Parker, but neither is a reliable source. Francis Burke, the president's coachman, said that he went next door to have a drink with the "special police officer," but that referred to a uniformed officer who was assigned to the front of the building, whether Lincoln was there or not. See Forbes, LAS 4:84, and Gifford in *Surratt Trial*, 559. The debunking process is tedious, and would make up an entire volume. Since anyone would have allowed Booth into the box, the issue strikes me as moot.

26. The original suit was filed by researchers Nathaniel Orlowek and Arthur Ben Chitty,

joined by a first cousin (twice removed) of John Wilkes Booth and a great-great-granddaughter of Edwin. The researchers were stricken in the first round of motions. *Virginia Humbrecht Kline and Lois Rathbun* v. *Green Mount Cemetery*, case no. 94297044/CE187741; Michael Kauffman testimony, May 19 and May 25, 1995.; The appeal to the Maryland Court of Special Appeals was rejected; see case 1531, 110 Md. App. 383 (1996).; See also Francis J. Gorman, "The Petition to Exhume John Wilkes Booth: A View from the Inside," *University of Baltimore Law Review* 27 (2): 47–57.

27. Decoration Day: editorials in the Baltimore *American*, June 9–10, 1870; Autograph prices: "Lincoln note sells for $21,850; Assassin's note sells for $31,050," Associated Press report, May 10, 2001.

28. Surratt in *The Washington Post*, April 3, 1898. Citing many errors of fact, some people have suggested that this interview may have been fraudulent. After being repeatedly misquoted myself in newspapers, I am inclined to consider it genuine. Surratt himself did not issue a disclaimer. Menu letter in LAS 2:379; Clara letter: LAS 3:135; For Weichmann's story, see Joseph George, Jr., "The Days Are Yet Dark: L. J. Weichmann's Life After the Lincoln Conspiracy Trial," *Records of the Catholic Historical Society of Philadelphia* (December 1984): 67–81. I am indebted to Dr. George for many insights on Weichmann and the trials; Dutton statement: Pitman, 421. William F. Keeler, the ship's paymaster, claimed to have heard something similar. His motives may be inferred from the fact that he appended a copy of his report to his pension application. Hunter's remarks were sworn by James L. Henry, a friend of Hunter's and a fellow West Pointer, on August 19, 1865, and published in *The New York Times*, April 15, 1867, 4.

29. Mudd pardon in the State Department pardon files, on Microcopy T-967, 4:395–401; Army board: Docket no. AC91-05511, January 22, 1992; Civil action: United States District Court for the District of Columbia, case no. 97-2946; Final disposition: *USA Today*, March 7, 2003, 3A; Stone in the *New York Tribune*, June 17, 1883, 4; Richard M. Smoot in *Ft. Smith Times*, May 9, 1906. Smoot soon put his account into a small book. My thanks to Barbara F. Plate, a Smoot descendant, for a copy of the book.

Appendix: Booth's Diary

1. There are many conflicting ideas about what the phrase "the Ides" actually means, but in ancient Rome it referred to the day of reckoning—the date on which the taxes came due. Here Booth writes as if the assassination of Lincoln has just occurred, but in reality his first passages were written as he hid in a pine thicket several days after the shooting.

2. Actor John Mathews later admitted Booth had given him a letter to the *Intelligencer*, but he destroyed it. He testified to this at the Judiciary Committee hearings on President Johnson's impeachment, and at the trial of John H. Surratt.

3. This entry appears to have been written at the Indiantown farm, near Nanjemoy, Maryland, on April 23. Booth had been unable to cross into Virginia, and here he attributes his failure to the active pursuit of federal gunboats. The actual date of this attempt is in dispute. The diary says he first tried to cross on April 20, but the traditional accounts (based on the writings of Thomas A. Jones) put the first attempt one day later. See William A. Tidwell, "Booth Crosses the Potomac: An Exercise in Historical Research," *Civil War History* 36.4 (1990): 325–33, and Jones, *J. Wilkes Booth*, 98.

BIBLIOGRAPHY

Much of this book is based on the Lincoln Assassination Suspects (LAS) File, which is published in Microcopy M-599 in the National Archives. This publication consists of sixteen reels of microfilmed documents gathered by Lt. Col. Henry L. Burnett for use in the conspiracy trial.

The second most useful group of records is M-619, letters received by the Adjutant General. For a year after the assassination, much of this material pertained to claims for the reward money offered in connection with the Lincoln conspiracy. In most cases, the claimant was asked to provide an account of services rendered, and these recollections (often written within hours after the fact) are often detailed and very informative. They appear on reels 455–58 of the series.

After the reward money had been distributed, many of the unsuccessful claimants petitioned Congress for a second chance at having their services recognized. These claims were batted around for a time, eventually finding their way to the Committee of Claims, where they were all tabled. All were filed with the records of the Thirty-ninth Congress, First Session, file HR39A–H4.1. They were discovered by the present writer, and are used here for the first time.

The military response to Lincoln's assassination, and the efforts made through army personnel, are contained in the records of the army's continental commands, Record Group 393. These papers (typically bound volumes) are among the most valuable sources of information, yet they are also used here for the first time. The pages are divided into four parts, then subdivided into the National Archives' catalog entries.

Edwin Stanton's most important telegrams were collected and bound, then copied into Microcopy M-473. The papers shown here are original drafts of the secretary's messages, and are arranged chronologically, with the assassination-related material beginning near the end of reel 88 and continuing through reel 89. They have not heretofore been used effectively, in part because writers have tended to rely on the published versions, which appeared in the Official Records in edited form.

NATIONAL ARCHIVES AND RECORDS SERVICE

Textual records

Record Group (RG) 21 Records of the District Courts of the United States

RG 24 Records of the Bureau of Naval Personnel

RG 28 Records of the Post Office Department

RG 29 Census Records

RG 42 Records of the Public Buildings and Public Parks of the National Capital

RG 45 Naval Records Collection of the Office of Naval Records and Library

RG 56 Records of the Department of the Treasury

RG 59 Records of the Department of State

RG 60 Records of the Department of Justice

RG 94 Records of the Adjutant General's Office

RG 107 Records of the Office of the Secretary of War

RG 109 War Department Collection of Confederate Records

RG 110 Records of the Provost Marshal General's Bureau

RG 111 Records of the Chief Signal Officer

RG 127 Records of the Marine Corps

RG 153 Records of the Office of the Judge Advocate General

RG 233 Records of the U.S. House of Representatives

RG 351 Records of the Government of the District of Columbia
      Records pertaining to Washington Metropolitan Police start at Entry 116.

RG 393 Records of the U.S. Army Continental Commands

Microfilm publications

M-30 Despatches from U.S. Ministers to Great Britain

M-44 Despatches from U.S. Ministers to Germany

M-90 Despatches from U.S. Ministers to the Italian States

M-149 Letters Sent by the Secretary of the Navy to Officers

M-161 Despatches from U.S. Consuls in Frankfort on the Main, Germany

M-345 Union Provost Marshal's file of papers relating to individual civilians

M-416 Union Provost Marshal's file of papers relating to two or more civilians

M-432 1850 Census

M-473 Telegrams Collected by the Office of the Secretary of War (bound)
      Stanton's correspondence is grouped in several ways, but nearly all the relevant
      material is filed here or in the Stanton Papers.

M-599 Investigation and Trial Papers relating to suspects in the Lincoln assassination
      (LAS file)

M-619 Letters Received by the Office of the Adjutant General
      Reward claims for the capture of the conspirators are on reels 455–98.

M-653 1860 Census

M-797 Case Files of Investigations by Levi C. Turner and Lafayette C. Baker (Turner-
      Baker Papers). Not all Turner-Baker papers were microfilmed.

M-1274 Disapproved pension applications

M-1279 Approved pension applications

M-1546 Petitions submitted to the Senate requesting restoration of rights for former
      Confederate officers

T-45 Despatches from U.S. Consuls in Alexandria, Egypt

T-222 Despatches from U.S. Consuls in Montreal, Canada

T-224 Despatches from U.S. Consuls in Naples, Italy
T-252 Mathew Brady Collection of Civil War Photographs

COURT AND COMMISSION RECORDS

The *Our American Cousin* lawsuits:
  Keene v. *Clarke*, 28 N.Y. Super. Ct. 38
  Keene v. *Wheatley et al.*, 14 F. Cas. 180 (No. 7,644)
  Keene v. *Kimball*, 82 Mass. 545
Public laws and executive proclamations are recorded in *The Public Statutes at Large of the United States of America* (Boston: Little, Brown & Co.). Civil War legislation is contained in volumes 12 and 13, cited as [*volume* Stat. *page*].
Commission records are in Record Group 153
Benjamin Gwynn Harris trial, case MM1957
Lewis F. Chubb court-martial, case MM2513
Boston Corbett court-martial, case OO1128
Conspiracy trial, case MM2251
John Surratt's first indictment, DC Criminal Court, case no. 4371
          second indictment, case no. 5920
          third indictment, case no. 6594
Henry B. Ste. Marie v. *U.S.*, C. of C. Dec. T., 1873, 415
Ste. Marie's appeal:
  Shuey, executor, v. *U.S.,* 92 U.S. 73
Joseph H. Bradley lawsuits
  Ex Parte Bradley, 74 U.S. 364
  Bradley v. *Fisher,* 80 U.S. 335
Reward money suit:
  Baker v. *Doherty,* D.C. Equity 790
Dr. Mudd case:
  Ex Parte Mudd, 17 F. Cas. 954 (S. D. Fla., 1868, no. 9,899)
Dr. Mudd appeal:
  Army Board for the Correction of Military Records, docket no. AC91-05511
Mudd family lawsuit:
  Richard D. Mudd v. *Togo West,* U.S. District Court for the District of Columbia, case 97-2946
Petition to exhume the remains in Green Mount Cemetery:
  Virginia Eleanor Humbrecht Kline and Lois Rathbun v. *Green Mount Cemetery,* Circuit Court of Baltimore City, 94297044/CE187741
Exhumation appeal:
  Maryland Court of Special Appeals, no. 1531, 110 Md. App. 383 (1996)

CONGRESSIONAL REPORTS

Thirty-ninth Congress, First Session
House Executive Document No. 63. *Message from the President of the United States. Distribution of Rewards for Arrest of Assassins of President Lincoln.*
House Executive Document No. 86. *Awards for the Capture of Booth and Others. Letter from the Secretary of War, in Answer to a Resolution of the House of the 10th Instant,*

Calling for the Findings of the Commission for the Capture of John Wilkes Booth and David E. Herold, April 19, 1866.

House Executive Document No. 90. *Awards for the Capture of Booth and Others. Letter from the Secretary of War, in Answer to a Resolution of the House of the 10th Instant, Calling for the Findings of the Commission for the Capture of John Wilkes Booth and David E. Herold, April 19, 1866.*

House Report No. 99. *Report Relating to Rewards for the Capture of Booth* [Issued by Rep. Giles Hotchkiss, July 24, 1866, to accompany H.R. 801.]

House Report No. 104. *Report Relating to the Assassination of President Lincoln* [George S. Boutwell's report on the possible complicity of Jefferson Davis and Andrew Johnson. The minority report of Andrew J. Rogers is included.]

Thirty-ninth Congress, Second Session

House Executive Document No. 9. *Message from the President of the United States, Transmitting a Report of the Secretary of State Relating to the Discovery and Arrest of John H. Surratt*

House Executive Document No. 25. *John H. Surratt. Message from the President of the United States, Transmitting Further Copies of Papers in Answer to the Resolution of the House of 3d ultimo, Relative to the Arrest of John H. Surratt*

House Report No. 33. *John H. Surratt* [Report on the discovery and arrest of Surratt.]

Fortieth Congress, First Session

House Report No. 7. *Impeachment Investigation: Testimony Taken Before the Judiciary Committee of the House of Representatives in the Investigation of the Charges Against Andrew Johnson*

House Executive Document No. 36. *H. B. Sainte-Marie; Letter from the Secretary of War* ad interim, *Relative to a Claim of Sainte-Marie for Compensation for Information Furnished in the Surratt Case*

Fortieth Congress, Second Session

House Executive Document No. 68. *Assassination of President Lincoln. Message from the President of the United States, Transmitting a Report of George H. Sharpe Relative to the Assassination of President Lincoln*

House Executive Document No. 150. *Trial of John H. Surratt. Message from the President of the United States, in Answer to a Resolution of the House of 27th January, Relative to the Trial of John H. Surratt*

MANUSCRIPT COLLECTIONS

Library of Congress
 Ray Stannard Baker Papers
 Amy Gillette Bassett Papers
 Junius Brutus Booth Family Papers
 Crosby Noyes Boyd Papers
 Benjamin F. Butler Papers
 Cyrus Ballou Comstock Papers
 Ewing Family Papers
 George P. Fisher Papers
 John T. Ford Collection

    William Stump Forwood Papers
    Benjamin B. French Papers
    James A. Hardie Papers
    Herndon-Weik Papers
    Ethan Allen Hitchcock Papers
    Joseph Holt Papers
    Andrew Johnson Papers
    August V. Kautz Papers
    Laura Keene Papers
    Robert Todd Lincoln Papers
    Lincoln Obsequies Scrapbook
    Letitia B. Martin Scrapbook
    Phillip Phillips Papers
    Edwin Stanton Papers
    Alfred Whital Stern Collection
    Philip Van Doren Stern Papers
    Gideon Welles Papers
Historical Society of Washington, DC
    Aloysius Mudd Theater Collection
Folger Shakespeare Library, Washington, DC
    Booth Family Scrapbook
    Junius Booth, Jr., 1864 Diary
    Owen Fawcett Scrapbook
    John McCullough Papers
National Park Service, Ford's Theatre, Washington, DC
    J. B. Wright Scrapbook
Office of the Architect of the Capitol, Washington, DC
    Ford's Theatre Disaster Files
Office of the Historian of the U.S. Senate
Lauinger Library, Georgetown University, Washington, DC
    David Rankin Barbee Collection
    Margaret K. Bearden Collection
    Aaron H. Byington Papers
    E. H. Swaim Collection
    Maryland Province Archives, Jesuit Order
Martin Luther King Public Library, Washington, DC
    Washingtoniana Collection, Lincoln Scrapbooks
    Washington Star Collection
Marine Corps Historical Center, Navy Yard, Washington, DC
Naval Historical Center, Navy Yard, Washington, DC
Auburn University, Auburn, AL
    Thomas T. Eckert Diary
Henry E. Huntington Library, San Marino, CA
    Joseph Holt Papers
    Gideon Welles Collection
Hagley Museum and Library, Wilmington, DE
Merl Kelce Library, University of Tampa, Tampa, FL
    Stanley Kimmel Papers
Chicago Historical Society, Chicago, IL
    William E. Barton Papers
    Charles Gunther Collection

Chicago Public Library, Chicago, IL
    Otto Eisenschiml Papers
Illinois State Historical Library, Springfield, IL
    John Wilkes Booth Collection
    Henry Horner Collection
    Robert Todd Lincoln Collection
Indiana Historical Society, Indianapolis, IN
    A. G. Porter Papers
    Lew Wallace Papers
Lilly Library, Indiana University, Bloomington, IN
    Osborn H. Oldroyd Papers
Notre Dame University, South Bend, IN
    O. H. Bronson Collection
University of Iowa, Iowa City, IA
    Judge James Wills Bollinger Collection
    Otto Eisenschiml Papers
Fogler Library, University of Maine, Orono, ME
    Hannibal Hamlin Papers
Maryland State Archives, Annapolis, MD
    George Alfred Townsend Papers
Maryland Historical Society, Baltimore, MD
    John T. Ford Papers
    The Civil War Note-book of Washington Hands
    William H. Marine Scrapbook
    Alonzo J. May Papers
Peale Museum, Baltimore, MD
    Asia Booth Clarke Letters
Surratt House Museum and Library, Clinton, MD
Harvard Theatre Collection, Harvard University, Cambridge, MA
Mugar Memorial Library, Boston University, Boston, MA
    Junius Booth, Jr., 1865 Diary
Massachusetts Historical Society, Boston, MA
    H. W. Bellows Letters
Smith College, Northampton, MA
    Sophia Smith Collection / Clara Morris Papers
Oakland University Library, Rochester, MI
    Frederick L. Black Papers
Missouri Historical Society, St. Louis, MO
    William K. Bixby Collection
Long Branch Historical Society, Long Branch, NJ
Princeton University Library, Princeton, NJ
    André de Coppet Collection
    William Seymour Collection
Butler Library, Columbia University, New York, NY
    Edwin Booth Scrapbook
    Thomas Ewing, Jr., Papers
    Theodore Roscoe Papers
New-York Historical Society, New York, NY
    Clara Harris Letters

New York Public Library, New York, NY
    George S. Bryan Papers
    Jerome B. Howard Shorthand Collection
    Edwina Booth Grossman Collection, Lincoln Center
Hampden-Booth Theater Library, The Players, New York, NY
    Edwin Booth Papers
Rochester University, Rochester, NY
    William H. Seward Papers
Perkins Library, Duke University, Durham, NC
    Kate Camenga Papers
    Clement C. Clay Papers
    Lyndall Collection
    Eugene Marshall Papers
    James Otis Moore Papers
    Green Clay Smith Papers
    Henry B. Whitney Diary
University of North Carolina, Chapel Hill, NC
    Southern Historical Society Papers
    Edwin Gray Lee Papers
    Weedon-Whitehurst Papers
Ohio Historical Society, Columbus, OH
    John A. Bingham Papers
Civil War Library and Museum, Philadelphia, PA
    MOLLUS Scrapbooks
Grand Army of the Republic Museum, Philadelphia, PA
U.S. Army Military History Institute, Carlisle Barracks, PA
    August V. Kautz Papers
    Julian E. Raymond Collection
Drake Well Museum, Titusville, PA
Musselman Library, Gettysburg College, Gettysburg, PA
    John F. Hartranft Papers
Lincoln Memorial University, Harrogate, TN
    Theodore Roscoe Papers
Kefauver Library, University of Tennessee, Knoxville, TN
    Owen Fawcett Papers
Harry A. Ransom Humanities Research Center, University of Texas, Austin, TX
    John Wilkes Booth Script for *Richard III*
Alderman Library, University of Virginia, Charlottesville, VA
    William Norris Papers
    Richard H. Stuart Papers
University of Richmond, Richmond, VA
    Southern Baptist Historical Collection
Virginia Historical Society, Richmond, VA
    Grinnan Family Papers
    Philip Whitlock Reminiscences
McLennan Library, McGill University, Montreal
    Joseph Nathanson Collection
Public Archives of Canada, Ottawa
    St. Lawrence Hall Register

REFERENCE BOOKS

Benét, Stephen Vincent. *A Treatise on Military Law and the Practice of Courts-Martial.* New York: D. Van Nostrand, 1864.

Biographical Directory of the American Congress. Washington: Government Printing Office, 1961.

Coppee, Henry. *Field Manual of Courts-Martial.* Philadelphia: J. B. Lippincott, 1863.

DeHart, William C. *Observations on Military Law and the Constitution and Practice of Courts-Martial.* New York: D. Appleton, 1863.

Dyer, Frederick H. *Compendium of the War of the Rebellion.* Des Moines, Iowa: Dyer Publishing Company, 1908.

Hunt, Roger D., and Jack Brown. *Brevet Brigadier Generals in Blue.* Gaithersburg, MD: Olde Soldier Books, 1990.

Loux, Arthur F. *John Wilkes Booth: Day by Day.* Limited edition. N. p.: privately printed, 1990.

Official Records of the Union and Confederate Armies in the War of the Rebellion. 128 vols. Washington: Government Printing Office. The entire series is available in an excellent CD-ROM version by the Guild Press of Indiana.

Pitman, Benn. *Assassination of Abraham Lincoln and Trial of the Conspirators.* Cincinnati: Moore, Wilstach and Baldwin, 1865. Pitman himself called this "a great heap of rubbish," and since it is paraphrased and heavily edited, this trial transcript is nearly worthless. However, it does contain portions of the transcript not available in the Poore version. The attorneys' arguments are presented verbatim.

Poore, Ben: Perley. *Conspiracy Trial for the Murder of the President and the Attempt to Overthrow the Government by the Assassination of Its Principal Officers.* Boston: J. E. Tilton, 1865.

Pursuit and Arrest of John H. Surratt. Media, PA: Proofmark Publishing, 2000.

Ray, Isaac. *A Treatise on the Medical Jurisprudence of Insanity.* Boston: Little, Brown and Co., 1853.

Rhodehamel, John, and Louise Taper, eds. *"Right or Wrong, God Judge Me": The Writings of John Wilkes Booth.* Urbana and Chicago: University of Illinois Press, 1997.

Stock, Leo F., ed. *U.S. Ministers to the Papal States: Instructions and Despatches, 1848–1868.* Washington: 1930.

Taylor, Wellford Dunaway, ed. *Our American Cousin: The Play That Changed History.* Washington: Beacham Publishing Company, 1990.

Trial of John H. Surratt in the Criminal Court for the District of Columbia. Washington: Government Printing Office, 1867.

Warner, Ezra J. *Generals in Blue: Lives of the Union Commanders.* Baton Rouge, LA: Louisiana State University Press, 1964.

Wearmouth, Roberta J. *Abstracts from the* Port Tobacco Times *and* Charles County Advertiser. 4 vols. Bowie, MD: Heritage Books, 1990–1996.

Wharton, Francis. *Wharton's American Criminal Law.* Philadelphia: Kay & Brother, 1853.

Winthrop, William W., ed. *Digest of Opinions of the Judge Advocate General of the United States Army.* Washington: Government Printing Office, 1865.

THESES AND DISSERTATIONS

Bogorad, Alan B. "A Rhetorical Analysis of the Speaking of John A. Bingham with Emphasis on His Role in the Trial of the Lincoln Conspirators." Ph.D. dissertation, Ohio State University, 1963.

Busch, Walter E. "General, You Have Made the Mistake of Your Life." Master's thesis, California State University at Dominguez Hills, 2001.

Coder, William D. "A History of the Philadelphia Theatre, 1856 to 1878." Ph.D. dissertation, University of Pennsylvania, 1936.

Fuller, Charles Franklin, Jr. "Kunkel and Company at the Marshall Theatre, Richmond, Virginia, 1856–1861." Master's thesis, Ohio University, 1968.

Hasin, Bernice R. "John A. Bingham and Due Process." Master's thesis, California State University at Long Beach, 1976.

Koerting, Gayla M. "The Trial of Henry Wirz and Nineteenth Century Military Law." Ph.D. dissertation, Kent State University, 1995.

LaCasse, Donald E., Jr. "Edwin Booth: Theatre Manager." Ph.D. dissertation, Michigan State University, 1979.

Mauldin, Michael L. "Edwin Booth and the Theatre of Redemption: An Exploration of the Effects of John Wilkes Booth's Assassination of Abraham Lincoln on Edwin Booth's Acting Style." Ph.D. dissertation, Ohio State University, 2000.

Mindich, David T. Z. "Building the Pyramid: A Cultural History of 'Objectivity' in American Journalism, 1832–1894." Ph.D. dissertation, New York University, 1996.

Ray, Rebecca Lea. "Stage History of Tom Taylor's 'Our American Cousin.'" Ph.D. dissertation, New York University, 1985.

Sollers, John Ford. "The Theatrical Career of John T. Ford." Ph.D. dissertation, Stanford University, 1962.

Steward, Charles J. "A Rhetorical Study of the Reaction of the Protestant Pulpit in the North to Lincoln's Assassination." Ph.D. dissertation, University of Illinois, 1963.

Woodruff, Bruce Erwin. "Genial John McCullough: Actor and Manager." Ph.D. dissertation, University of Nebraska, 1984.

BOOKS AND PAMPHLETS

Aldrich, Mrs. Thomas Bailey. *Crowding Memories*. Boston: Houghton Mifflin Co., 1920.

Amator Justitiae [John P. Brophy]. *Trial of Mrs. Surratt; or, Contrasts of the Past and Present*. Washington: n.p., 1865.

Arnold, Samuel B. *Memoirs of a Lincoln Conspirator*. Edited by Michael W. Kauffman. Bowie, MD: Heritage Books, 1996.

Baird, Nancy Disher. *Luke Pryor Blackburn: Physician, Governor, Reformer*. Lexington, KY: University Press of Kentucky, 1979.

Baker, Jean H. *Ambivalent Americans: The Know-Nothing Party in Maryland*. Baltimore: Johns Hopkins University Press, 1977.

———. *The Politics of Continuity*. Baltimore: Johns Hopkins University Press, 1974.

Baker, Lafayette C. *History of the United States Secret Service*. Philadelphia: King and Baird, 1867.

Balsiger, David, and Charles E. Sellier, Jr. *The Lincoln Conspiracy*. Los Angeles: Schick-Sunn Classics Books, 1977.

Basler, Roy P., ed. *The Complete Works of Abraham Lincoln*. 8 vols. New Brunswick, NJ: Rutgers University Press, 1953.

Bates, David Homer. *Lincoln in the Telegraph Office*. New York: D. Appleton–Century, 1907.

Bates, Finis L. *Escape and Suicide of John Wilkes Booth*. Memphis: Pilcher Printing Co., 1907.

Bingham, John A. *Argument of John A. Bingham, Special Judge Advocate, in Reply to the Arguments of the Several Counsel*. Washington: Government Printing Office, 1865.

Brown, J. Willard. *The Signal Corps, U.S.A., in the War of the Rebellion*. Boston: U.S. Veteran Signal Corps Association, 1896.

Browning, Orville Hickman. *Diary of Orville Hickman Browning*. 2 vols. Edited by Theodore Calvin Pease and James G. Randall. Springfield: Illinois State Historical Society, 1925 and 1933.

Bryan, Vernanne. *Laura Keene: A British Actress on the American Stage*. Jefferson, NC: McFarland, 1993.

Buckingham, J. E. *Reminiscences and Souvenirs of the Assassination of Abraham Lincoln*. Washington: Press of Rufus H. Darby, 1894.

Clarke, Asia Booth. *Booth Memorials: Passages, Incidents, and Anecdotes in the Life of Junius Brutus Booth (the Elder)*. New York: Carleton, 1866.

———. *The Elder and the Younger Booth*. Boston and New York: Houghton Mifflin and Co., 1881.

———. *Junius Brutus Booth*. New York: Carleton & Co., 1865.

———. *The Unlocked Book: A Memoir of John Wilkes Booth by His Sister Asia Booth Clarke*. Edited by Eleanor Farjeon. New York: G. P. Putnam's Sons, 1938. A recent edition, edited by Terry L. Alford, is entitled *John Wilkes Booth: A Sister's Memoir* (Jackson, MS: University Press of Mississippi, 1996).

Conrad, Thomas Nelson. *A Confederate Spy*. New York: J. S. Ogilvie, 1892.

———. *The Rebel Scout*. Washington: National Publications, 1904.

Crook, William H. *Through Five Administrations*. Edited by Margarita Spalding Gerry. New York: Harper, 1905.

Davis, William C. *An Honorable Defeat: The Last Days of the Confederate Government*. New York: Harcourt, 2001.

Dennett, Tyler, ed. *Lincoln and the Civil War in the Diaries and Letters of John Hay*. New York: Dodd, Mead and Co., 1939.

Doster, William E. *Lincoln and Episodes of the Civil War*. New York: G. P. Putnam's Sons, 1911.

Douglas, Henry Kyd. *I Rode with Stonewall*. Chapel Hill, NC: University of North Carolina Press, 1940.

Eisenschiml, Otto. *Why Was Lincoln Murdered?* Boston: Little, Brown, 1937.

Evans, Stewart, and Paul Gainey. *Jack the Ripper: America's First Serial Killer*. New York: Kodansha International, 1995.

Ewing, Thomas, Jr. *Argument of Thomas Ewing, Jr., on the Jurisdiction and on the Law and Evidence in the Case of Dr. Samuel A. Mudd*. Washington: H. Polkinhorn & Son, 1865.

Field, Maunsell B. *Memories of Many Men and of Some Women*. New York: Harper & Bros., 1874.

Finkleman, Paul, ed. *His Soul Goes Marching On: Responses to John Brown and the Harpers Ferry Raid*. Charlottesville, VA: University Press of Virginia, 1995.

Fishel, Edwin C. *The Secret War for the Union*. Boston: Houghton Mifflin, 1996.

Gambone, A. M. *Major-General John F. Hartranft: Citizen Soldier and Pennsylvania Statesman*. Baltimore: Butternut and Blue, 1995.

Geary, James W. *We Need Men: The Union Draft in the Civil War.* DeKalb, IL: Northern Illinois University Press, 1991.

Gobright, Lawrence A. *Recollections of Men and Things at Washington During Half a Century.* Philadelphia: n.p., 1869.

Grant, U. S. *Personal Memoirs of U. S. Grant.* New York: Charles L. Webster, 1885.

Grossman, Edwina Booth. *Edwin Booth: Recollections by His Daughter and Letters to Her and His Friends.* New York: Century, 1894.

Gutman, Richard J. S., and Kellie O. Gutman. *John Wilkes Booth Himself.* Dover, MA: Hired Hand Press, 1979.

Hanchett, William. *The Lincoln Murder Conspiracies.* Urbana: University of Illinois Press, 1983.

Harris, Thomas M. *Assassination of Lincoln: A History of the Great Conspiracy and Trial of the Conspirators.* Boston: American Citizen, 1892.

————. *Rome's Responsibility for the Assassination of Abraham Lincoln.* Pittsburgh: Williams, 1897.

Henneke, Ben Graf. *Laura Keene: Actress, Innovator, Impresario.* Tulsa, OK: Council Oak Books, 1990.

Holt, Joseph. *Vindication of Judge Advocate General Holt, from the Foul Slanders of Traitors, Confessed Perjurers and Suborners, Acting in the Interest of Jefferson Davis.* Washington: Chronicle Printing, 1866.

————. *Vindication of Hon. Joseph Holt, Judge Advocate General of the United States Army.* Washington: Chronicle Publishing, 1873.

Hyman, Harold M. *Era of the Oath: Northern Loyalty Tests During the Civil War and Reconstruction.* Philadelphia: University of Pennsylvania Press, 1954.

Isacsson, Alfred. *The Travels, Arrest, and Trial of John H. Surratt.* Middletown, NY: Vestigium Press, 2003.

Jones, Thomas A. *John Wilkes Booth: An Account of His Sojourn Through Southern Maryland.* Chicago: Laird and Lee, 1893, and various reprints.

Kimmel, Stanley. *The Mad Booths of Maryland.* Indianapolis: Bobbs-Merrill, 1940.

Lattimer, John K. *Kennedy and Lincoln: Medical and Ballistic Comparisons of Their Assassinations.* New York: Harcourt Brace Jovanovich, 1980.

Levin, Alexandra Lee. *This Awful Drama: General Edwin Gray Lee, C.S.A.* New York: Vantage Press, 1987.

Lomax, Virginia. *The Old Capitol and Its Inmates.* New York: E. J. Hale, 1867.

Long, David E. *The Jewel of Liberty.* Harrisburg, PA: Stackpole Books, 1994.

Mahoney, Ella V. *Sketches of Tudor Hall and the Booth Family.* Bel Air, MD: Tudor Hall, 1925.

Marshall, John A. *American Bastille.* Philadelphia: James W. Hartley & Co., 1881.

Metheny, H. E. *Major General Thomas Maley Harris.* Parsons, WV: McClain Printing, 1963.

Miller, Edward A., Jr. *Lincoln's Abolitionist General: The Biography of David Hunter.* Columbia, SC: University of South Carolina Press, 1997.

Morris, Clara. *Life on the Stage: My Personal Experiences and Recollections.* New York: McClure, Phillips & Co., 1901.

Mudd, Nettie, ed. *The Life of Dr. Samuel A. Mudd.* New York: Neale Publishing, 1906.

Murphet, Howard. *Hammer on the Mountain: The Life of Henry Steel Olcott.* Wheaton, IL: Theosophical Publishing Co., 1972.

Oldroyd, Osborn H. *The Assassination of Abraham Lincoln.* Washington: n.p., 1901.

Olszewski, George J. *Restoration of Ford's Theatre.* Washington: Government Printing Office, 1963.

Ownsbey, Betty J. *Alias Paine: Lewis Thornton Powell, the Mystery Man of the Lincoln Conspiracy.* Jefferson, NC: McFarland & Co., 1993.

Porter, Horace. *Campaigning with Grant.* New York: The Century Company, 1897.

Porter, Mary Abbie Walker. *The Surgeon in Charge.* Concord, NH: Rumford Press, 1949.

Rolle, Andrew F. *The Lost Cause: The Confederate Exodus to Mexico.* Norman, OK: University of Oklahoma Press, 1965.

Roscoe, Theodore. *The Web of Conspiracy.* Englewood Cliffs, NJ: Prentice-Hall, 1959.

Ruggles, Eleanor. *Prince of Players.* New York: Norton, 1955.

Seward, Frederick W. *Seward at Washington: A Memoir of His Life with Selections from His Letters.* 3 vols. New York: Derby & Miller, 1891.

Skinner, Otis. *The Last Tragedian: Booth Tells His Own Story.* New York: Dodd, Mead and Co., 1939.

Smith, H[enry] B[ascom]. *Between the Lines: Secret Service Stories Told Fifty Years Afterwards.* New York: Booz Brothers, 1911.

Smoot, R[ichard] M[itchell]. *The Unwritten History of the Assassination of Abraham Lincoln.* Baltimore: John Murphy, 1904.

Speed, James. *Opinion on the Constitutional Power of the Military to Try and Execute the Assassins of the President.* Washington: Government Printing Office, 1865.

Speer, Bonnie Stahlman. *The Great Abraham Lincoln Hijack.* Norman, OK: Reliance Press, 1990.

Steers, Edward, Jr. *His Name Is Still Mudd.* Gettysburg, PA: Thomas Publications, 1992.

———. *Blood on the Moon.* Lexington, KY: University of Kentucky Press, 2001.

Tidwell, William A. *April '65: Confederate Covert Action in the American Civil War.* Kent, OH: Kent State University Press, 1995.

Tidwell, William A., James O. Hall and David Winfred Gaddy. *Come Retribution: The Confederate Secret Service and the Assassination of Abraham Lincoln.* Jackson, MS: University Press of Mississippi, 1988.

Townsend, George Alfred. *The Life, Crime, and Capture of John Wilkes Booth.* New York: Dick & Fitzgerald, 1865.

Trostle, Scott. *The Lincoln Funeral Train.* Fletcher, OH: Cam-Tech Publishing, 2002.

Turner, Justin G., and Linda Levitt Turner. *Mary Todd Lincoln: Her Life and Letters.* New York: Alfred A. Knopf, 1972.

Wallace, Lew. *Lew Wallace: An Autobiography.* New York: Harper and Brothers, 1906.

Watermeier, Daniel J., ed. *Between Actor and Critic: Selected Letters of Edwin Booth and William Winter.* Princeton, NJ: Princeton University Press, 1971.

Weichmann, Louis J. *A True History of the Assassination of Abraham Lincoln, and of the Conspiracy of 1865.* Edited by Floyd E. Risvold. New York: Alfred A. Knopf, 1975.

Welles, Gideon. *Diary of Gideon Welles.* 3 vols. Edited by John T. Morse, Jr. Boston: Houghton Mifflin, 1911.

Whiteman, Maxwell, ed. *While Lincoln Lay Dying.* Philadelphia: Union League of Philadelphia, 1968.

Wilson, Francis. *John Wilkes Booth: Fact and Fiction of Lincoln's Assassination.* Boston: Houghton Mifflin, 1929.

Winslow, Kate Reignolds. *Yesterdays with Actors.* Boston: Cupples & Co., 1887.

ACKNOWLEDGMENTS

This book was shaped by years of interaction with friends and researchers from across the country. The first among these was John C. Brennan, who never liked to be called a "researcher," but who tirelessly gathered and disseminated information on this case for more than thirty years. John had an infectious passion for the subject, and anyone who knew him would agree that his daily bulletins were more informative, helpful, and entertaining than any book could ever be.

I am fortunate to have many friends who freely contributed research and ideas as well. Stephen M. Archer, Katherine Dhalle, Joseph George, Nancy Griffith, Richard and Kellie Gutman, James O. Hall, Dr. Blaine V. Houmes, Monsignor Robert L. Keesler, Dr. John K. Lattimer, Franklyn Lenthall, Arthur F. Loux, Stephen G. Miller, Dr. Richard D. Mudd, Michael Musick, Betty J. Ownsbey, Richard E. Sloan, and Laurie Verge have always kept me in mind when something new and interesting came to their attention.

I cannot possibly name all who have helped in this effort, but others who come immediately to mind are Helen Alderman, Terry L. Alford, Louise Mudd Arehart, Robert Cabot Bainbridge IV, Deirdre Barber, James L. Barbour, Sally Barley, Bill Barnett, Edmond Bastek, Ulrike K. Baumann, Margaret K. Bearden, Stephen W. Benjamin, Margery Boorde, Garth Bowling, Sharon Brahmstadt, Samuel Carter III, Michael Cavanaugh, Joan L. Chaconas, Frederick Chesson, Arthur Ben Chitty, Kenneth Clark, Michael Coccia, Peggy Colony, Robert W. Cook, Kathryn Coombs, Carita Curtis, Margaret Wilson Dean, Suzanne Dietrich, Garland W. Clarke, Everton E. Conger, Jeannine Clarke-Dodels, Bob Dodson, Carol Garrett Donohue, Donald P. Dow, Robert Eager, Vivian Edelen, Mary S. Elbert, Clark Evans, Dinah Faber, Rev. Ralph E. Fall, Jewell Powell Fillmon, Mrs. Edwin C. Fishel, Danny Fluhart, Howard and Dorothy Fox, Nancy Galbreath, Al Gambone, Carleton H. Garrett, Christopher Garrett, John A. Garrett, Hugh R. Gifford, Sherrie Gilbert, Leslie Goodier, Frank Gorman, Harold M. Gouldman, William Hanchett, John and Valerie Handy, Michael Harman, Gayle T. Harris, Louise Randolph Hartley, Frederick

Hatch, Frank Hebblethwaite, Ann Hoover Holcombe, Michael F. Holt, Betty Houghton, Jeff and Joan Huffman, Erin Hulme, Roger D. Hunt, Rosemarie Hunter, George L. Kackley, Paul Kallina, Suzanne Kelley, Dorothy E. Kelly, Arthur Kincaid, Virginia Kline, Elizabeth Nuckols Lee, Judy Lewis, Rebecca Livingston, Walton Mahon, Michael Maione, Marcia Maloney, Jonathan Mann, Percy E. Martin, Charlotte Gurley Mattern, Elysabeth Huntt Mays, Jerry McCoy, John and Mary McHale, Courtney McKeldin, Ernest C. Miller, Ronald Moffat, Guy W. Moore, Annette Morriss, Tony O'Connor, Louise Oertley, Nicholas Payne, Angus Phillips, Barbara F. Plate, Pat Purcell, Carolyn Quadarella, John Quinnette, Emerson Reck, Markus Ring, Emily Mudd Rogerson, David E. Roth, Nicholas B. Scheetz, Lew Schmidt, Bert Sheldon, Ron and Helen Shireman, Gene Smith, Mike Snyder, John Ford Sollers, Dr. Allen G. Spiegel, John F. Stanton, Candida Ewing Steel, David M. Sullivan, Warren Taltavull, Bill Taylor, William Toffey, Lois Rathbun Trebisacci, Bob Wadsworth, John and Roberta Wearmouth, William Hallam Webber, Betsy Webster, Penny Weiner, David Whellams, Nancy Williams, Chris L. Witherspoon, James T. Wollon, Jr., Marie Worster, Steven J. Wright, and Mark S. Zaid. These people have all been a tremendous help to me, even though many would not agree with my approach to the case, or with my conclusions.

My thanks to the professional and accommodating staffs at the National Archives; Library of Congress; Folger Shakespeare Library; Historical Society of Washington, D.C.; Martin Luther King Memorial Library, Washington; Lauinger Memorial Library, Georgetown University; Enoch Pratt Free Public Library, Baltimore; Maryland Historical Society; Johns Hopkins University Library, Baltimore; Maryland State Archives, Annapolis; Maryland Court of Special Appeals Library, Annapolis; Surratt Society, Clinton, Maryland; Philadelphia Free Public Library; Civil War Library and Museum, Philadelphia; Pennsylvania Historical Society; U.S. Army Military History Library, Carlisle Barracks, Pennsylvania; Princeton University Library; Delaware Historical Society; New Castle Historical Society; New York Public Library; New-York Historical Society; Houghton Library, Harvard University; Massachusetts Historical Society; Mugar Memorial Library, Boston University; Sterling Library, Yale University; Connecticut Historical Society, Hartford; John Hay Library, Brown University; Pike County Historical Society, Milford, Pennsylvania; University of Pennsylvania Library; Swarthmore College Library; Alderman Library, University of Virginia; Virginia State Library; Lewis Egerton Smoot Library at King George, Virginia; King George Historical Society; Rappahannock Library, Fredericksburg; Southern Maryland Room, College of Southern Maryland; Williamsburg Foundation Library, Williamsburg, Virginia; Perkins Library, Duke University; Library of the University of North Carolina at Chapel Hill; DuPont Library, University of the South, Sewanee, Tennessee; Lincoln Memorial University, Harrogate, Tennessee; Chicago Historical Society; Illinois State Historical Library, Springfield; Lincoln National Life Foundation, Ft. Wayne, Indiana; Indiana Historical Society; Missouri Historical Society; Arkansas State Archives, Little Rock; University of Iowa Library, Iowa City; University of Oklahoma Library, Norman; Enid Public Library, Enid, Oklahoma; Granbury Public Library, Granbury, Texas; Harry A. Ransom Humanities Research Center, Library of the University of Texas at Austin; Huntington Library, San Marino, California; San Francisco Public Library; and all the county clerks, cemetery superintendents, and librarians who had to chase me away at closing time.

My thanks to all the many people who took the opportunity, while on my Booth Escape Route tours, to offer new leads and insights. Thanks to our drivers, especially Darwin Engle and Carol Brown.

I am especially indebted to Jim Donovan, who brought me into the world of publishing, and to Robert Loomis at Random House for his patience, faith, and expert guidance.

Finally, I thank my wife, Mary, and our children, Emily and Brian; my parents, Russell and JoAnn Kauffman; and my in-laws, Frank and Margery Patten. I am grateful for their support and understanding through some very challenging times.

INDEX

PHOTO: GAMMON PHOTOGRAPHY

MICHAEL W. KAUFFMAN has had a particular interest in Lincoln's assassination for three decades. He has published numerous articles on the subject, and for nearly twenty years he has guided bus tours of Booth's escape route. His research has unearthed a wealth of new material on the assassination, and his computer analysis of the government's case files has brought to light many facts previously unnoticed in the literature. He has appeared on A&E, C-SPAN, the Discovery Channel, and the History Channel, and testified as an expert witness in the 1995 Booth exhumation hearings in Baltimore. He lives in Southern Maryland.

ABOUT THE TYPE

This book was set in Caslon, a typeface first designed in 1722 by William Caslon. Its widespread use by most English printers in the early eighteenth century soon supplanted the Dutch typefaces that had formerly prevailed. The roman is considered a "workhorse" typeface due to its pleasant, open appearance, while the italic is exceedingly decorative.

HUNTED

Also by
MEAGAN SPOONER:

Sherwood

MEAGAN SPOONER

HUNTED

An Imprint of HarperCollinsPublishers

HarperTeen is an imprint of HarperCollins Publishers.

Hunted

Copyright © 2017 by Meagan Spooner

All rights reserved. Printed in the United States of America.

No part of this book may be used or reproduced in any manner
whatsoever without written permission except in the case of
brief quotations embodied in critical articles and reviews. For
information address HarperCollins Children's Books, a division of
HarperCollins Publishers, 195 Broadway, New York, NY 10007.

www.epicreads.com

ISBN 978-0-06-242229-3

Typography by Sarah Creech and Erin Schell

18 19 20 21 22   PC/LSCH   10 9 8 7 6 5 4 3 2 1

First paperback edition, 2019

To the girl
who reads by flashlight
who sees dragons in the clouds
who feels most alive in worlds that never were
who knows magic is real
who dreams

This is for you.

BEAST

We always know before the change comes. When a storm approaches, we feel it in the thickness of the air, the tension in the earth awaiting the blanket of snow. We feel the moment the wind changes direction. We sense a shift of power when it is coming.

Tonight there is hunger in the air. The forest waits for something. We pace, our steps stirring the early snows. Our frustration vents in growls and grunts. Each of us could read the change to come, neither hindered by the other. We could track it, or we could run with it. But we are trapped, and we can do neither.

We always know before the change comes—but we never know what the change will bring.

ONE

YEVA WATCHED THE SKY over the far-off forest, listening to the baronessa with one ear. The air was heavy and unfamiliar. *A storm?* she wondered, inhaling the strangeness. In the distance the treetops swayed as if in a gust of wind, but the rest of the forest was still.

She leaned forward, abandoning the sewing on her lap so she could nudge the glass-paned window open a fraction. The air outside was frigid, especially for Yeva in her finely embroidered dress, but she didn't mind—the glass distorted the distant woods, and she'd rather see clearly than be warm. *How large must a creature be to cause movement like that?* Larger than anything an arrow could bring down, unless the shot was beyond lucky. Here on the edge of the wood, there shouldn't be anything larger than a bear skulking beneath the canopy. Her father used to tell stories of larger, stranger things that hid in the heart of the wood, but she'd outgrown stories long ago. If only that sign of movement would come again, perhaps she'd be able to—

"Yeva, darling!" The baronessa's voice cut in, the world snapping back to the present. "You'll get your death in that draft. Close the window before we all catch a cough."

Yeva reached for the latch to pull it closed, trying to look less rattled than she felt. "Sorry, my lady. I thought I saw bad weather approaching."

"Not another storm," moaned the baronessa, clutching her fur wrap more closely about her shoulders. "It's too early for such snow, I don't know what we'll do this winter."

"Do you really think a storm is coming?" asked Galina, one of the baronessa's other ladies.

With her attention mostly on the far-off forest, Yeva noticed with a start that Galina had been speaking to her. "The air smells of it," Yeva replied, eyes shifting from Galina's face to the baronessa's.

Galina turned to whisper to the lady next to her, forgetting herself. The baronessa scarcely noticed, though, too busy wringing her hands. "Oh, what shall we do?" she murmured, not bothering to look outside herself, but staring around at the faces of her ladies.

Yeva glanced back at the window. There was still no sign of bad weather on the horizon, but uneasiness lingered at the back of her mind. The parlor had erupted into whispers, and with creeping dread Yeva realized that she could be here all night.

"My lady," she said, adopting for once the gentle voice she was meant to be cultivating, "perhaps the other ladies and I should retire, if we are to get home to our families before the storm arrives." A number of heads lifted among the circle of women.

"And leave me alone?" cried the baronessa as though Yeva had proposed taking her out into the storm and blindfolding her.

The baronessa was fairer skinned than most, claiming some

Varangian blood in her ancestry. Other nobles would have hidden those roots, but she owned them with pride, attributing some romantic hot-bloodedness to them. Combined with her plump face and bow-shaped mouth, it gave her a youthful appearance, childlike and sweet. For all her silliness, Yeva could not help but feel a twinge of pity for the woman. She wasn't that much older than Yeva herself, not even twenty yet, with her husband more than three times her age. The company of the wealthy ladies in the town was all she had in the dark months of the year.

Yeva smiled at her, for once not having to search for the expression. "The baron will be home soon, and of course Machna and Lada will be here." The two sisters were guests of the baron's household, visiting from the city.

The baronessa chewed at her lip, casting a glance for the first time at the tiny window. Yeva had secured the spot by being the most junior of the women in the baronessa's circle, and thus taking the coldest seat—but she preferred it to any other, with its view of the forest beyond the edge of the baron's property. Yeva felt impatience strum at her insides. She hated the indecisiveness of people in town, how they waited to make decisions, took weeks or months or years to settle, until the decisions were made for them by inaction.

"Oh, very well," the baronessa said finally, waving her hand in a sad, dismissive gesture. "If the snow has not marooned us all by morning, will you ladies return tomorrow afternoon? If it snows my husband will not be hunting, but he will be so cross that I would rather have company when facing him."

Yeva felt a sluggish stirring of dislike in her stomach. Only a nobleman, whose idea of hunting involved sitting high on a spotlessly decorated stallion while half-starved hounds did all the work, would be turned away by snow. *The snow is a canvas,* her father would say, *upon which the beast paints his past, his home, his intentions, his future. Learn to see the picture and you will know him as you know yourself.*

"Of course we will come back tomorrow," Galina replied, saving Yeva from having to formulate an answer. "Thank you, my lady."

The girls all stood, tucking their sewing away, preparing to leave until the next afternoon. Yeva hurried to follow suit, shoving her embroidery into its basket. She'd learned in her first few days that the baronessa often snared the last of the girls to leave, drawing them into conversations that could last for hours. It wasn't so much that Yeva disliked speaking with the baronessa, but rather that she'd prefer to reach home by nightfall.

And before the storm, if one was coming.

They left the baronessa mournfully describing her husband's hunting exploits to the hapless sisters from the city, and rushed to bundle up in their winter gear.

"Thank you," whispered Galina as she caught up to Yeva, jogging her elbow a little and casting her a smile.

Yeva shook her head, the corners of her mouth twitching. "I was only thinking of our safety, traveling in the weather."

One of the baronessa's ladies, overhearing Yeva, laughed. "We knew exactly what you were thinking of, Yeva. What time is Solmir meeting you?"

Yeva's smile vanished. "Solmir?" she echoed.

"Don't think we haven't seen how much attention he pays you at the baronessa's dinners." The lady raised an eyebrow. She was one of the older members of the baronessa's inner circle, soon to be engaged to a man in the baron's hunting party. "Don't give me that look. That is the point of this all, no? For us to see, and be seen."

Yeva looked over at Galina, who was watching quietly as she laced the ties on her cloak. Finding no answer there, Yeva could only shrug in response.

Galina fell into step beside Yeva, and they walked in silence through the high doors of the house and onto the street. Galina was the second-newest addition to the baronessa's collection, and somewhat more understanding of Yeva's peculiarities. She had never once blanched at the accidental mention of weaponry.

"Was it true?" Yeva broke the quiet as they passed the church.

"Was what true?" Galina looked up, brown eyes blank.

"What they said about Solmir." Yeva glanced behind them, checking that no one was near enough to hear. She felt her cheeks warming despite the cold. "About his attention to me."

Galina smiled. The expression was always sudden and unexpected on her small, solemn face. She was a relatively plain girl, but her smile was beautiful. "Yeva, you silly thing. You can't say you haven't noticed. They tease you only because they feel certain there is an understanding between you."

Yeva stopped short, abruptly enough that slush sprayed up onto the hem of her skirts. "An understanding?" She had tied her cloak too tightly—her breathing felt labored, uncertain.

"I am sorry to be the one to tell you," said Galina, dimming her smile with clear effort. Her expression was still brimming with amusement. "See you tomorrow," she added, before turning at the corner to make her way toward her own father's house, in the opposite direction. Yeva stood stirring the slush with the toe of her boot.

Solmir? He was nothing, barely more than a name in her mind. No, that was unfair; he was more than that. One of the baron's hunting party, he was without land or title, but his family was wealthy nonetheless. His father had been a respected cooper and manager of the baron's wine cellar until his death, at which point Solmir had become the baron's ward. Rumor had it that the baron, childless after two previous marriages, might confer his lands and titles to Solmir if the new baronessa failed to produce him an heir.

Yeva tried to picture Solmir in her mind, conjuring up hazy memories of dinners past. They'd always been a trial for her. The afternoons with the baronessa were one thing; they kept Yeva—for the most part—from longing for the forest trails. The dinners, however, were another. She'd always counted the moments until she could be back home again with her father, feeling like one of those ragged birds at the market beating halfheartedly against their wicker cages. The only image of Solmir her memory provided was of friendly hazel eyes and a soft voice that made her cheeks flush all the more. She recalled him broaching the strangest subjects, though she preferred his bizarre company to the dull conversation of the other gentlemen.

How long had the other ladies been talking about them, with Yeva completely unaware?

She tried to ignore how warm she was under her furs. It was not quite cold enough for full winter gear but she wore it anyway—a blizzard could rise swiftly and without warning, even this early in the winter. Sweat started to form between her shoulder blades and trickle down her spine; she set off down the road toward her father's house.

They lived toward the edge of town not because Yeva's father couldn't afford to live at its center, but because he, like Yeva, felt more comfortable with a house that bordered on nature. He'd given up life as a hunter to marry Yeva's mother, using his wealth to start a career as a merchant, but he couldn't wholly give up the need for the woods and the snow and the wild tang of the beasts.

Yeva felt a tension draining that she hadn't realized she was carrying. She liked the baronessa, and she appreciated having been taken into her circle, but some part of her still longed for the freedom she'd had even a year ago. Her father used to take her with him, training her, teaching her what he knew of hunting. It was all in fun, because what harm was there in teaching these things to a child? Echoes from a past life; things his own father taught him. Sharing them was the only way of keeping them real. Being a merchant held no passion for him, but it was safe, and it had made his wife happy until she died when the girls were young. It was only recently that her father had noticed Yeva's age, and thought that she ought to be a lady now, and no longer his wild little Beauty.

It was time to join her older sisters in society—such as it was.

The houses became smaller and more spread out as she trudged along, the laneways connecting them covered with snow once more instead of the slush churned up by many feet and carriage wheels. Yeva could see her father's house on the ridge and hurried her steps.

The sky was growing darker, though the hour was too early for the sun to set. The clouds were thickening. Perhaps there would be a storm after all. Yeva felt no shame at the fiction— there *had* been something in the air—but she would feel better able to face the baronessa tomorrow if some kind of weather came in the night.

The hill was steep enough to make Yeva's breath puff white in the cold air, and she sputtered an oath. Such terrible shape for a hunter to be in. She used to be able to run for hours, uphill or down, blood coursing through her and urging her onward. But then, she was not a hunter anymore. The roundness of face and limb she saw in the washbasin each morning, the sleek deep red of her hair, the full lips, the lazy gaze—every day she was more a lady. Every day less herself.

Yeva hurried through the door, trying to still her panting breath so no one would see her winded. One of the servants met her at the door, his lanky arms outstretched to receive her furs.

"Thank you, Albe," she told him with a smile that made him blush and duck his head. Albe had been with them since he was a boy, but lately he'd been inching around Yeva and her sisters as if they were made of glass.

All the merchants' daughters were spoken of as beauties. Yeva would have preferred to be admired for her skill, but she'd suffered the great misfortune of having been born a girl. And so no one would ever know. When she was younger, she used to dream of a husband who would love her all the more if she could hunt with him, side by side. But age, and time spent with the baronessa, had worn away that imagined future.

She could remain unmarried, but to do so would make her a financial burden to her father. To marry would be to leave the wood forever, surrendering what little freedom she still had.

But Solmir is a hunter, whispered a sinuous thought. *And a good one. If anyone were to admire your skill in the forest, it would be him. . . .*

"Your sisters are in the kitchen, mistress," said Albe, head still bowed. Yeva could see a flush on the back of his neck and the tips of his ears.

"Thank you," she repeated, and left the poor boy to recover.

As she headed down the hall, a thumping, clattering, wild noise exploded from the back corner of the house. Laughing, Yeva crouched down so that when a pair of dogs came barreling around the edge of the hall, they hit her square. Less painful than letting them catch an arm or a leg. Doe-Eyes whined eagerly, burying her face in the fold of Yeva's hip, while Pelei sniffed her all over, circling and circling and snuffling his aggravation at her collection of the day's scents.

Pelei was the scent hound, thick and shaggy and red-brown, named for the clay he so resembled. Doe-Eyes was the runner, slimmer and lighter built, less armored against the biting cold in winter. They were her father's hunting dogs, but any time the subject arose, he delighted in moaning about how his youngest daughter had stolen them from him, how they betrayed him every day they ran to her. But he loved to see them love her, and always spoke with a twinkle in his eye.

Yeva ordered the dogs back to their corner of the house, sending them reluctantly away, and went to the kitchen. She found Asenka and Lena kneading bread together, moving as one, each leaning down into the stroke as the other folded. They were closer in age to each other than Asenka was to Yeva, and so alike as to be nearly twins. Asenka's hair was two shades darker than Lena's chestnut brown, and her cheeks fuller and pinker, but from a distance the two were indistinguishable.

"Yeva," said Asenka warmly, looking up but not halting at her work. "You're home early."

"The ladies thought there might be a storm coming," Yeva replied, "and the baronessa dismissed us early."

"The ladies?" echoed Asenka, a smile lurking behind her black eyes.

Yeva grinned and lifted one shoulder delicately. "My seat is closest to the window—why shouldn't I notice incoming weather first?" She reached for the laces on her dress and tugged them loose, drawing in a long breath. Her blood was still pumping from her uphill walk.

"Oh, Yeva." Lena's voice was heavy with weary scolding.

"What are you doing? Father will be home soon—what if he should see you?"

"Father has seen me head to toe in men's clothing," Yeva reminded her, "and half covered in boar's blood. I don't think he will die from the scandal."

"But you were a child then," said Lena delicately. "Now you are grown. And anyway, what if Albe were to come in?"

"Then he shall probably explode on the spot."

Asenka let out a strangled laugh before turning her head aside to hide her mouth against her shoulder. Lena glared at her, the expression quickly dissipating in favor of a rueful smile. "Service to the baronessa was supposed to tame you, Beauty, not teach you new ways to torment us all."

Yeva smiled, turning away before Lena noticed her mistake. Yeva had been Beauty all through her childhood. Her father had named her on the day she was born after the old goddess of beauty, as he'd named her sisters after light and grace. Every few years, the holy men from the west came through to perform weddings and naming ceremonies, and the townsfolk would hide their heathen accoutrements, as the priests called them, and hang up their crosses.

The merchant's youngest daughter was renamed Yeva, after the temptress in the garden. She would have preferred Beauty, for at least there is beauty in all things, not only temptation, but Yeva she was to be. Her mother enforced the name as strictly as a warden minding his charges, but she died when Yeva was only five years old, so there was no one after that to insist her father use her proper name.

She had always been Beauty when they hunted together, always Beauty when he tucked her in at night. He called her Yeva now, because she was to be a fine lady someday, and her proper name was the one society knew. And yet there was always a half second's pause before he said that name, a tiny catch in his voice that was all that remained of who she'd been before.

Though the servants were responsible for preparing dinner, Yeva and her sisters often helped. The three spent their days apart—Yeva with the baronessa, Asenka at the leech's shop tending the sick, and Lena managing the household and spending time with her fiancé, Radak, whenever he was in town. He was a merchant like their father, and was both very much interested in merging empires and very much in love with Lena.

The evening was their time to be together, in the brief hour before their father returned, and they had little taste for sewing and gossiping as ladies were meant to do. Preparation of fresh bread to accompany the meal was tradition.

Yeva busied herself fetching herbs down from the racks, crumbling them between her fingers and breathing in the scent. Seasoning had been her job when she was too little to knead the bread, and so it remained even now she was old enough. Asenka shaped the dough, and Yeva rolled it in the crumbled herbs until there was a light crust coating the loaf. Then Lena wrapped it all in a cloth and tucked it close to the hearth to rise. She pulled out the risen loaf prepared the night before and slid it carefully into the oven, then she and Asenka washed their hands in the basin, pulling their aprons off, chattering.

Yeva drifted into the next room, preferring to leave the aroma of herbs on her skin. She took up her spot on the floor by her father's chair, crossing her arms on the footstool and resting her chin on her hands. The smell of herbs mingled with the smell of the bread as it warmed in the oven, and she closed her eyes. At some point her sisters joined her, still chatting and laughing. Lena helped Asenka into her chair before taking her own. It wasn't until a name caught Yeva's attention that she opened her eyes and lifted her head.

"Do you think there's any truth to it?" Asenka's voice was low, with the strange wobble in it that showed she was thinking intensely about whatever she was saying.

"It's everywhere. I can't see that there wouldn't be at least a grain of truth in the telling, if everyone is telling it. Yeva, have you heard anything at the baronessa's?"

Yeva swallowed. She'd heard the name, but not the context. "About what? I had my eyes closed."

They were used to her tuning out their chatter—Yeva was the quiet sister. Lena leaned forward, her face shining with interest. "There is a rumor that Solmir is going to speak for one of Tvertko's daughters." Her eyes sparkled as she spoke their father's name.

Yeva's heart seized. But before she could answer, Lena turned back to gaze at Asenka, whose own face carried a delicate pink flush. "Oh, it must be true. You've admired him for years, Ashka. And if he asks—why, then we can be married together! Think of it, a double wedding in the spring when the snows melt."

Asenka bowed her head, covering her face with her hands. "Stop that!" she protested. "My face will fall apart from the smiling. It's a rumor, nothing more. Leave it be, will you?"

Yeva kept silent, her stomach roiling. She prayed they wouldn't ask her again what she knew, for she couldn't lie to them. But how could she tell them that it was the youngest sister, not the eldest, who had caught Solmir's eye? How could Asenka bear to see her sisters spoken for, when no one had cast an eye in her direction?

Asenka always sat so that her twisted foot would be covered by the hem of her skirts, but Yeva found her eyes going there anyway. Her sister walked with difficulty and great pain, but managed everything else with such ease that most people tended to forget the malady she was born with. At the leech's office she was admired for her compassion, and for the long hours she spent limping along the beds, fetching down tinctures and salves without a word of complaint.

Yeva's fists clenched around handfuls of her skirt, fury replacing the uneasy roiling in her stomach. Why should it always be *beauty*? Why could her sister not be sought after for her kindness, her empathy, her strength? Why could she not be loved for that, instead of passed over because of one misfortune of birth that supposedly marred her?

Anger prompted her to rise, mouth opening to burst out with the truth, the injustice of it. Her sisters looked up at her, mouths forming identical Os of surprise. But before she could speak, the sound of the door opening in the hall interrupted her.

"Father's home!" cried Lena. "Yeva, how do you always know?" She helped Asenka to her feet, and the two sisters made their way to the hall. Someone outside the family might speak of the cruelty of naming a baby with a twisted foot after grace. But in everything but her step, Asenka was the most graceful girl Yeva had ever seen. Gentle of smile, long-fingered, slender and lovely. Her voice was always soft, her laugh never too loud in a quiet room. Even as she leaned on Lena, the way she walked was careful and smooth with deliberation.

Yeva stood clenching her jaw, tongue pressed against her teeth to still it. Let them believe she had leaped to her feet to greet their father. How could she break Asenka's heart with the truth?

"I was thinking of spending next summer in the city," her father was saying as he mopped up the last of the gravy on his plate with some of the fresh bread.

Yeva lifted her head, torn from the thoughts swirling around Solmir and Asenka. Her father had taken Yeva and her sisters with him to the city on business once years ago, and while they had lit up at the flood of new sights and experiences, Yeva had found it overwhelming. The streets stank and every face was strange, and she could not follow any paths or trails through the churned-up streets or across the uneven cobbles. She had spent every moment clinging to her father's hand.

Now, his glance passed between his older daughters before coming to rest on his youngest. "I have some business with the cartographers there, and it'll take some time to get my affairs settled. So I'll be required to take a house in the area for a few months. It'll be quiet there all by myself, so I was thinking of bringing you three to live with me."

The older girls exploded with glee, chattering and laughing, celebrating their good fortune. While none of the sisters was solely fixated upon fashions and society and standing the way the baronessa was, the prospect of being surrounded by so much of it for three months of the summer was a delight.

Yeva alone was quiet, watching her father. She knew how much it cost him to move away from the wilderness; it cost her the same. But she knew why her father wanted to go. None of the men here had spoken for Asenka. Perhaps somewhere new, her loveliness would catch a man's eye the way it hadn't here. Her father raised eyebrows peppered with gray, watching Yeva in return. She took a deep breath and summoned a smile. He nodded and leaned back in his chair.

"Of course," he said, speaking now primarily to his older girls, "you'll be required to bring along any husbands or fiancés you may have acquired in the meantime." This pronouncement brought on further shouting and laughing, and even Yeva's smile grew less stiff in the face of her sisters' glee.

"Pechta!" called her father, summoning the cook into the doorway. "I believe the girls would like some sweets to celebrate." The cook bobbed a curtsy and vanished back into the kitchen.

The dogs had crept in during the merriment, as if hoping they wouldn't be noticed. Lena, as lady of the household, objected to them in the rooms where people ate and slept, but for right now even she could not be distracted. Pelei stood watch beside her father's chair, and Doe-Eyes slunk over to Yeva, nose nudging up under her elbow and into her lap. Doe-Eyes had been purchased during that trip to the city all those years ago. Yeva sat stroking her absently, watching her sisters' excitement.

Outside, the wind had picked up, beginning to beat against the sturdy frame of the house. The servants had shuttered the windows already to prepare for the storm, but Yeva felt a flicker of the uneasiness she'd experienced at the baronessa's, a restlessness she could not name.

Suddenly, over the howl of the rising storm, a heavy pounding against the front door broke through the sounds of chatter and laughter. The sisters exchanged glances as their father leaned to the side to look around the edge of his chair toward the hall.

"Is it Radak?" wondered Asenka, glancing at her younger sister. It was unlike Lena's fiancé to come calling without first having made an appointment with their father.

"He is away on business. Maybe it's Solmir," whispered Lena before dissolving into quiet laughter again at the blush that crept over Asenka's face.

Yeva volunteered no guesses. She could hear the howling of the wind, and could imagine no one who would venture out in such weather except due to some terrible emergency.

The pounding came again, this time so urgently that the

smiles faded from the older girls' faces. Albe had finally arrived at the door and was nearly thrown back as he opened it by the force of the wind on the other side. Yeva couldn't recognize the man who stumbled through it, covered head to toe in winter gear. Only the tip of his nose was visible over his muffler, red and shiny from cold. He pawed at his face to free his mouth, gasping their father's name.

"Tvertko," he said, choking in the sudden heat of the house as Albe struggled to close the door again, "I need to see Tvertko. Where is he, I must see him immediately."

Albe gaped at him, stammering his usual greeting. The man glanced past him to see Yeva's father in his chair and shoved his way into the room.

"Tvertko," he said, throwing himself forward. "It's gone. It's all gone."

Her father's face became very still, brows lowered. "What's gone, Pietr? Speak clearly, man."

"All of it," the man moaned again, dropping to his knees. He was exhausted, that much was clear. And he was not a local, or Yeva would have recognized him the moment he pulled the muffler from his face. And yet, her father knew him. One of his contacts in the city, perhaps?

Her father was silent, watching the man gasping for breath and dripping melted snow onto Lena's immaculate floorboards. Then he lifted his head, addressing his daughters. "Girls, please go upstairs. Take the dogs. And please tell Pechta to boil some tea."

"But Father—" Yeva began, startled. He had never excluded them from his business discussions before.

"Go, Yeva." His voice was no louder than it had been, but so firm that it brooked no opposition.

Her sisters were on their feet, Lena clinging to Asenka as much as the other way around. Yeva leaned down to lay a hand on each of the dogs, murmuring to them to go upstairs. Sensing her urgency, they obeyed, slinking up the stairs with their tails low. As Lena guided Asenka to the first step, Yeva ducked into the kitchen.

She found all four of the servants there, wide-eyed and midgossip. Albe was still in disarray from having opened the door to the storm, his hair standing up roughly in every direction.

"Tea," said Yeva. "For my father and his guest." She was not usually so abrupt, but something cold had seized her belly and she couldn't find it in her to soften the order. Pechta merely nodded, forgetting to curtsy, and hurried to the fireplace and the kettle.

Yeva took the long way back around to the stairs, passing through the hallway instead of the living room where her father still sat, listening to his visitor. Halfway up she paused; some acoustical anomaly in the building of the house conspired to throw their voices so clearly she could hear what they were saying.

". . . and every man of them dead," the visitor was saying, his voice rough with exhaustion. "Barbarian swords in their guts, heads piled in the wagons and burned. All the goods stolen or destroyed."

"No one was left alive?" Her father's voice was full of quiet grief. Yeva could imagine his head bowed, eyes closed as he listened. "Not even the boys?"

"No one," repeated the visitor. "Are you hearing me, Tvertko? It's all gone. You're ruined."

Ruined. Yeva's ears rang with the word in the ensuing silence.

"Yeva!" a voice hissed. Yeva blinked, finding her eyes watering in the stillness, and looked up. Lena was at the top of the stairs, beckoning to her. "Come."

Yeva joined her sisters, not wishing to hear any more than she already had. They all piled into Asenka's bed, the three of them and the dogs too, and for once Lena didn't push them away. Doe-Eyes lay with her head trembling in Yeva's lap, keeping as still as possible in the hope that no one would notice her and make her leave. Pelei kept licking and licking at the hem of Yeva's skirt, scenting the nervousness in the air and trying to make sense of it.

They waited, none of them talking, although Asenka moved now and then to shift her weight and ease her twisted foot. It wasn't until they heard the front door open again, a brief gust of air howling through the house and tossing their hair back, that Yeva lifted her head. The door slammed again, leaving them in utter silence.

Lena spoke first. "Should we——?"

Yeva drew in a breath, trying to still the shaking in her legs as she slipped out from underneath Doe-Eyes's head. "I'll go." Both of her sisters relaxed a fraction—they had been waiting for her to offer. She was their father's favorite, though it was no source of angst or friction among them. It was part of her family duty to be her father's daughter.

She told the dogs to stay, although Doe-Eyes scrambled off the bed and followed her as far as the doorway of the room. Bare feet tingling against the chill of the floorboards, Yeva made her way back down the stairs.

She found her father still sitting in his chair, though he was leaning forward, feet braced against the ground. He looked somehow smaller, elbows propped on his knees, forehead resting on his balled fists. The firelight granted false color to what she could see of his pale face, the lines etched there throwing ghastly shadows. Yeva had never realized that her father's face was wrinkled.

Yeva swallowed and crept forward. Her father gave no sign that he was aware of her presence, but when she reached out and touched his shoulder with the tips of her fingers, he didn't jump or cry out.

He merely sighed, the breath leaving his body in a low groan. "Oh, Beauty," he said, without lifting his head. He raised one of his hands to grasp at hers, fingers wrapping around her hand with the strength of a drowning man. Saying nothing else, he only sat there clasping her hand against his shoulder, head pressed against his fist.

"Oh, Beauty."

BEAST

We are uncertain how many years it has been, or how many centuries. To half of us the passage of time is tiny and measured, and with no measuring devices it is impossible to track. To the other it is infinite, immeasurable, a stream in which all things drown in the end. We are at odds because of this and so many things, and when the sun fades and the dark returns we mark it only as a change in the light.

The storm that comes tonight is not the change we felt coming. But in the howl of the night wind and the blinding violet of the snow, there is nothing else to be sensed. And so we retreat, to pace inside our den, to remember sleep, to wait for another change in the light.

TWO

YEVA'S FATHER ASKED FOR the night to think of a plan, so Yeva did not share with her sisters what she had overheard, nor participate in their whispered speculation after they had blown out the candle in the room they shared. She lay awake after her sisters had drifted off to sleep, watching the ceiling and listening to the wind beyond the window.

At dawn she rose sandy-eyed and stiff and crept down to the kitchen, carrying her shoes so as not to wake her sisters. The kitchen was cold and empty—Pechta had declined to make an appearance yet, unsurprising after the previous evening's excitement. Yeva stirred the fire back up, checked on the bread rising in its nook in the hearth, and put the kettle on over the flames. Then she slipped her icy feet into her shoes, shivering and standing with her back to the kitchen fire.

After a time the household drifted to life again, the servants waking and accepting mugs of tea, her sisters joining them once the sunlight reached the edge of the window. The wind had tossed around the snow but the storm had not brought much more of it, leaving the world newly coated in a thin layer of white, with dark patches of frozen slush all up and down the sides of the buildings and the windowpanes. The ice shattered the light as it entered the house, sending it in knives and sunbursts across the rugs and floorboards.

No one spoke of the previous night, neither the sisters nor the servants. And yet there was an air of uneasy expectance, as if everyone were waiting, but too fearful to ask what they were waiting for.

Eventually Yeva's father appeared in the entryway to the kitchen. His eyes were red-rimmed and tired, his face drooping and mouth tight. He looked as if he'd gotten no more sleep than Yeva had.

"Girls," he said, the sharp-cut sunlight outlining his form in the doorway. "Staff. Would you all please come join me in the parlor?"

Yeva poured a mug of tea, then followed the rest of the assemblage out into the living room. Her father had relit the fire there, but only moments before. The room was still freezing, and she pressed the mug of tea into her father's hand before huddling close to her sisters by the fireplace.

He stood next to his chair and gazed at the floor near Yeva's feet for a time. He lifted his head. "A month ago," he began, "I sent out a caravan headed for Constantinople. If the venture were successful, it would mean a new trade route, which would bring you girls—and the town, and all the surrounding cities—countless luxuries. And perhaps the return of the priests and of books, education, maps, life from beyond our borders. The Mongols prevent us from making outside contacts, but I thought—" He shook his head, as if at the folly of such a dream.

"It was a foolish risk. A gamble I should not have taken."

Yeva wanted to look at her sisters to see if they had figured it out yet, if they were beginning to understand the meaning of the visitor in the night. But she could not take her eyes off her father's weary face.

"Our entire fortune was tied up in the caravan, along with investments from merchants and noblemen, vouchsafed by me. It is all gone."

The breath went out of the room. Yeva felt Lena go stiff, and from across the room she heard one of the maidservants stifle a gasp.

"I have thought all night on what to do, and spent some time adding up what I owe to the investors. Our only option is to sell the house and most of our possessions. For you, the staff, I will find positions with the neighboring households. You will all have outstanding references. I still own my hunting cabin in the north wood. The girls and I will move there, and I will take up hunting again, and attempt to earn enough to pay back our debts."

Silence followed this announcement, as though everyone in the room were waiting for him to continue. He stepped to the side and sank down into his chair, doubled over with his elbows resting on his knees, mug dangling between them from his fingertips.

Pechta began to wail, turning to one of the maidservants and burying her face in her shoulder. It seemed this was the cue for the entire household to break down—the two maidservants started to sob, as Albe stood gawking in shocked silence and Yeva's sisters put their arms around each other. Yeva stood alone, watching her father. Amid the chaos, he lifted his head to meet her eye.

Yeva had always longed for nothing more than to live at her father's hunting cabin, where she had spent so many happy days with him as a child on their expeditions. This—this meant she was free of trips to see the baronessa, free of figuring out how to deal with Solmir, how to tell her sisters where his interest truly lay. But at what cost? Would Radak still want to wed Lena if she had no wealth and connections to offer? And the hunting cabin was leagues from the nearest town. There were no eligible young men in the wilderness to speak for her and her sister, only the trees and the wind and the beasts.

She had seen the spirit die in her father's eyes. He sat doubled over, looking up at her like a man of eighty. How long could he continue to hunt? He had not had to provide for himself, much less a family, solely by hunting in nearly twenty years.

A chunk of ice detached itself from the roof and slid off, scraping loudly across the sniffles and sobs punctuating the quiet. Winter was coming fast.

Yeva's sisters watched their possessions and their futures being auctioned off to the highest bidders with no tears and with no outward signs of sorrow. Though in private Lena's face was often drawn with worry—for her fiancé, Radak, was away on business and would not hear of what had befallen them until after they had gone—to the outside world, she and Asenka were as sunny as ever. They cheerfully explained to prospective buyers why this mirror was their favorite, that dress the most stylish, this mother-of-pearl box the most beautiful. If Yeva had inherited her father's skill at hunting, they had inherited his ability to negotiate a deal. They earned more from their possessions than their father had calculated, but it still was not near enough to pay back the investors he owed.

In his youth, Yeva's father had been widely considered the best hunter in the land. Though there were many hunters who took advantage of the rich wilderness in the black wood, he was the only one who ventured into its heart. Yeva's father had told her stories when she was little of the things he claimed to have seen: the life-sucking *kudlak*, the great bears to the north who could change their fur to match the ice, the *stuhac*, who would steal the ligaments from a man's legs to make bindings for his own feet in the snow. Soaring above them all was the story of the Firebird—Yeva's favorite for as long as she could remember. Despite the darkness and danger of the black wood, the Firebird at its heart was a burning beacon. No hunter could catch it— the only one who had ever come close was nothing more than a legend of a hundred years or more. And he had only caught a single feather from its tail.

Yeva used to dream of being the one to catch the Firebird— she dreamed of it long after she stopped believing in the other tales her father spun for her. But even without the kudlak, without the monsters of the fairy tales she loved as a child, the depths of the wood were dangerous, far more deadly than the more commonly hunted perimeters of the wilderness.

Her father had once fearlessly ventured into the deepest reaches of the wood, but how could he return to such a life now? He had given up the danger of the hunt for love of Yeva's mother, who could not bear to see him disappear into the black wood day after day.

And what of his heart? He'd huddled in front of the fire that night like a broken man. He was proud, as proud of his mercantile empire as he'd been of his hunting abilities as a younger man. He could not hope to earn enough simply from pelts and meat of deer and rabbit; he would have to venture deep to bring back the heads and skins of trophy game. How could he hope to be so bold and so strong now, with this humiliation and ruin weighing on him like twenty extra years?

So Yeva's sisters tried to earn as much as they could from their treasures, parting with them readily. Yeva lacked their skill with people and was more than happy to leave the sale of her own possessions to them. She kept aside only a few of her plainest dresses to bring with her to the cabin.

There was talk of selling the dogs as well, for they were purebred and Yeva's father could still hunt without them. Yeva's heart nearly broke at the idea, but she recalled her sisters cheerfully handing over their cherished books and trinkets, and she agreed to meet a man who had asked about purchasing them. Pelei was cautiously interested in the prospective buyer, sniffing at his hand with great determination, but Doe-Eyes— the gentlest dog Yeva had ever encountered—flung her ears right back and growled when he approached, the fur standing up along her back in a ridge.

Yeva's father had shrugged after the buyer had left, and said only, "I suppose we will have to build them a kennel to sleep in at the cabin."

With the dogs safe, Yeva turned her mind to packing the family's few remaining belongings. At her father's instruction she had placed three of their four servants with new families—only Albe remained. He came to them one morning and dropped to the floor, knees striking wood with a loud thud.

"Please let me come, master, mistresses," he begged, taking hold of Tvertko's hand. "You know I'm no good, I'll only be thrown out of another house. I break things and I forget. But for you I'll be better. I can do a bit of cooking and cleaning and whatever you need, I'll make it worth keeping me, I will."

"But we can't pay you," Yeva said gently, as her father patted Albe's hand and tried to get him to stand back up.

"Don't care, miss," he protested. "Where else would I go? Been here since me mother died, been with you since I was seven. Where else would I go?"

From then on Albe oversaw the packing, and would relieve Yeva of anything she tried to carry out to the wagon. He generally made a nuisance of himself, always underfoot and performing his tasks with such enthusiasm that he nearly knocked the sisters over. But his antics caused them to smile more often than shout at him, and so when the family finally departed the house, their spirits were not quite as low as they might have been otherwise.

With the men walking and the dogs trotting alongside, and the wagon pulled by the plow horse they'd borrowed from a neighbor in exchange for a rug, they set off on the road north.

It was a three-day journey from their house in town to their father's hunting cabin. They stayed in inns along the way, an expense Yeva protested each night. But her father refused to allow his girls to spend the night in a barn, or worse, wrapped in their cloaks on the ground beside the road—they had not sunk that low, he said, in a too-calm voice that Yeva knew better than to question. On the third day the weather took a turn for the worse, the skies lowering and gathering gray until the air turned white with snow in the late afternoon.

As the day faded toward twilight Doe-Eyes began to stumble, her long legs shaking in the snow. Yeva hopped down in order to help lift the dog up into the back of the wagon, and joined her there. Doe-Eyes was built for speed, bred in a land far to the west, with a slim body and shorter fur; a summer dog, not bred for the winter hardships she'd face at the edge of the black wood.

Yeva rubbed and rubbed at the dog's body and legs until the

tremble left them. Doe-Eyes licked her wrist and curled herself into a nest Yeva made of her remaining few dresses. They'd be covered in hair and smell like dog, but what did Yeva care? Out here there would be no baronessa to notice. Yeva left the dog slumbering in her nest and rejoined her sisters atop the broad wagon.

Beside her she felt Lena tremble, and she glanced aside. Her sister's face was turned resolutely out toward the passing trees, but Yeva saw her hands, folded so tightly in her lap that the knuckles shone white. They had sent word of their misfortunes to Lena's fiancé, but they'd had no time to wait for a reply, especially since there was no guarantee the message would even find him. Radak would mostly likely return from his business trip to find Lena gone, and all reason for marrying her too. There was no good now to be had from an alliance with the family—to marry one of them would be to marry their debts, which could well cripple a young entrepreneur.

Yeva folded her hands over her sister's. They were nearly as cold as hers were, but they relaxed under her touch and after a time, both Yeva's hands and Lena's warmed to the company.

The weather worsened as they turned from the high road onto a smaller path into the woods, and they had to break their own trail through the snow, for no one had come this way since the storm had begun. Albe called out, suggesting they turn back and make for the inn several leagues behind. Yeva's father said something in reply that she could not hear, but Albe quieted, tugging his coat more closely about his shoulders. She jumped down from the wagon, landing calf-deep in snow, and shouted over the wind, "Take my seat awhile, Albe."

He protested, face flushing beet red, but she shook her head. "Please—I'd like to speak to my father in private."

Reluctantly Albe let her give him a leg up onto the wagon as it groaned along through the snow. Yeva stepped over to her father and linked her arm through his, for warmth as much as companionship.

"That was kindly done," he said, patting her hand.

"Right now, Albe is our only friend in the world."

Her father's hand stilled against hers, head bowing against the biting cold. For a time there was only the jingle of the horse's harness and the groaning of the wagon, the dull thud of hoof on snow, the occasional distant thump as a branch gave way and dropped its heavy burden to the forest floor.

"I was a fool." Her father's voice was a whisper, but the quiet of the snow did little to hide it. "Such a fool."

Yeva had never had to comfort her father before. Her heart squeezed with the kind of fear she never felt outside of nightmares, the kind of fear that made her blood pound. "It isn't your fault," she said finally, searching for any words that might ease the tension in the arm linked through hers.

Her father exhaled a grunt of a laugh, the mist of it hanging in front of his lips like a ghost. "We had enough. More than enough. That caravan—I was a fool to put everything we had into such a fragile venture. But I wanted more for you, for my girls—I wanted—"

His voice cracked, and with it Yeva's heart. For decades their town, along with a vast stretch of the country, had been cut off from other parts of the world by marauders who intercepted travelers and convoys alike. The books her father owned all came from a time before the Mongols; the priests who had blessed Yeva at her naming ceremony were some of the last to make it through on their pilgrimages.

"You wanted the world for us," Yeva whispered, hugging

her father's arm close against her body. "There's no shame in that." Still, her heart stirred uneasily. Had she not been berating herself the same way for wanting more than the life a husband like Solmir could offer her?

"I had the world," her father replied, his pace faltering for a few steps until Yeva stopped too. Her father's red-rimmed eyes met hers, the snow melting on his cheeks and trickling into his beard. "I was just too blind to see it."

Yeva swallowed hard. "You have us," she said softly. "We have you. That's all we need. Come, Father—you'll get stiff if you stop moving."

As they continued, Yeva found movement warmed her, and that walking was much more preferable to riding on the wagon— but she had not been walking for three days through ankle-deep snow. After just half an hour she found that little-used muscles had begun to ache and protest the exercise.

As dusk fell the cabin came into view, the same white and black with snow and wood as the forest. The huddled occupants on the wagon leaped down, Albe unhitching the horse as soon as the wagon pulled into the lee of the house. Exhaustion made them all slow and stupid, even those who had ridden on the wagon, for the cold and the swaying, jouncing movement were nearly as wearying as walking. Asenka could barely move, her bad leg was so stiff, and Lena helped her through the snow with some difficulty. Yeva collected Doe-Eyes from her sleepy warm nest and whistled for Pelei, who had roamed too far, dancing around the trees, sniffing and shivering with excitement at their new surroundings. Albe put the horse in a dilapidated shed to be tended later, and everyone made their way to the house. It had lain unoccupied for the better part of a decade, and with a long breath their father shoved the door open for the first time since

Yeva had been a child.

It was covered in dust and dirt, half the window shutters broken, drifts of fallen leaves and snow filling the corners. Something rustled in the back, its nest disturbed by the human arrivals. The only light came from behind the broken shutters and from a hole in the roof, plugged mostly with snow, allowing only for the cold blue glow of twilight through the ice. Flakes drifted down from the hole, glinting in the shaft of light.

This was not the cozy home Yeva had remembered from her childhood. She found herself wishing her father had listened to Albe back on the road—if he had, they would be warm and fed in an inn by now. But then, her father's too-thin purse would be several coins leaner.

They all stood inside the doorway, dripping snow and ice onto the floor, surveying the dank interior of the cabin in silence. Asenka spoke first, taking a limping step forward. "Albe," she said softly, "if you will be so good as to use the shovel there at the hearth and remove the snow from inside, I will lay a fire."

Lena, as if shaking herself from a dream, stumbled forward to take her older sister's arm and help her to the hearth. The two set to clearing leaves from the fireplace as Albe took the ash shovel and began hauling the snow out the windows. Yeva knelt and whispered to Pelei, one hand on his quivering shoulder, "Go on, I know you smell them. Remind them that this is our house." When she straightened and pulled her hand away, Pelei was off to the far corner of the cabin like a bolt from a crossbow, sending frantic rustles throughout the leaves there as the house's previous occupants fled before him. Yeva located the broad, sturdy table amid the debris and, with Albe's assistance, set it on its legs and then smoothed her hands over its top to wipe off the worst of the dust.

Yeva's father remained in the doorway, unmoving, watching his family get to work. When Yeva turned toward him he inhaled sharply through his nose, passing his hand over his face. "My girls," he said hoarsely, pressing his lips together. After a silence he shook himself and cocked his head toward Yeva with a smile. "I will go excavate the tea." And he left to begin bringing things in from the wagon.

Over the next few days the cabin slowly became habitable. Albe was put to work felling a few nearby trees and hewing rough timber to repair the worst holes and shore up the loft space to make it safe. There was one bedroom at the back of the house and two pallets in the loft. Tvertko and Albe took the beds in the loft, for Asenka could not manage the ladder—she and Lena took the bed at the back of the house, the one that had been their father's when he still used this as a hunting cabin.

Yeva herself made a pallet by the hearth. In the evenings it was warm from the day's fire, and as night grew thicker, the dogs curled up on either side, and she was as cozy as any in the house. Her father protested the arrangement, and her sisters too, but when Lena offered to take it in turns with her sleeping on the floor, Yeva turned her down.

"They are my dogs," she pointed out with a smile, "and you'll only complain in the mornings of their smell." Yeva was usually the first in the family to wake anyway, and so it became her habit to stir the fire at dawn so that the water was just beginning to boil for tea when Albe came down the ladder rubbing his eyes.

Yeva's father began making forays into the surrounding forest, learning the woods again. He'd taught Yeva that the key to being a good hunter was not to track a creature through the forest but to know the forest so well it was like tracking your prey through your own home. He rarely came back with much those early days, but he made imminent plans for trips deeper into the woods.

Yeva begged him to let her come along.

"You're not a child anymore," said her father with a sigh. "When I've paid my debts we'll move back to town. By that time, I fear, you'll have gone so wild that the confines of civilization will break your heart."

"Please," was all Yeva could think of to say. She had no argument against it—even years after the last time they had been hunting together, she still longed for the dark, cold cathedral of the wood.

He shook his head. "I won't be persuaded on this, Yeva." She still flinched to hear the use of her proper name from her father. "Besides, if you come with me, Doe-Eyes will try to follow, and you know she can't weather this cold."

And so he left her behind, traveling deeper and deeper into the forest each time with Pelei at his side. Sometimes he was gone two or three days, leaving Yeva and her sisters, and Albe, alone in the house. Yeva kept to her bed by the fireplace. Doe-Eyes would have whined and cried all night, unable to climb the ladder to the loft, had Yeva taken over her father's room in his absence.

It was during one of her father's excursions that they received their first visitor to the cabin, on an afternoon full of pale, cold sunlight. Yeva and Lena were blocking up the gaps in the timbers of the floor and the walls with clay, while Asenka sat by the hearth, mending one of their father's shirts. Doe-Eyes was executing a circuit around the house, as she did every hour or so, alert for Pelei's return. But instead of the perk of her ears and frantic lash of her tail that heralded his arrival, she went rigid, nose pointed toward the door and tail unmoving.

Yeva paused, her eyes on the dog. "Albe, is someone outside?"

The servant's head peeked out from the edge of the loft, where he was tidying. "I don't hear anyone, miss."

Yeva put a hand on Doe-Eyes's shoulder and found the muscles there solid as rock. "Could you please check?"

Albe slid down the ladder to land with a solid thunk on the floor. He opened the door a crack, peering out across the gleaming snow. "There is someone coming, miss," he said, surprised.

Lena dropped her bowl of mud, sloshing some of it on the floor. "Radak," she whispered, glancing first at Yeva and then over at Asenka, who had stopped mending and was staring back at her sister. "It has to be. Oh, what if he's come to break our engagement?"

"He hasn't," said Yeva firmly. "He wouldn't. And if that was his intention, he would hardly travel three days for it, he would just never come at all."

"It isn't your young man, miss," said Albe. Yeva regretted having spoken—now each day that Radak didn't come, Lena would be more convinced he never would.

Albe stepped into the gap of the door, straightening his shoulders. "Welcome, sir. May I help you?" He spoke to someone Yeva couldn't see, his form silhouetted by the blinding light off the snow behind him.

"Is this Tvertko's new house?" asked the visitor. "I've come to see him—and his daughter."

Albe stepped back, allowing the man inside. As soon as the door closed behind him and shut out the daylight, his features became clear. It was a young man, perhaps five or six years Yeva's senior, with dark hair and an easy smile. He had friendly hazel eyes that cast over the room, going first to Asenka at the fireplace and then to Lena by the wall, and then to Yeva. And there his eyes stayed. There was a gasp from the hearth, and Yeva turned to see that Asenka had gone white, staring at the man in the doorway.

It was Solmir.

BEAST

Something comes.

A man and a beast, moving slowly, scanning the ground. We watch from only a few feet away—we know how to disguise our scent from the canine. The man is surefooted and strong, if old for his kind, and we watch with interest. Something about him is familiar; we have encountered him before.

Yes, we know him. He would not have been the first hunter we turned to our purposes but he was the most promising. We were so certain he would be our salvation, until one day he vanished and never returned to the wood. It was years ago—or weeks? Perhaps generations. His hair has changed and his face has grown lines, but he walks with the same knowledge of the lifeblood of the wood.

We growl, the sound blending with the wind and the groaning of the trees under their weight of snow. We are patient. We still remember our plan.

As the man makes his way through the forest, the dog blowing steam at his side, we move on silent paws to follow.

THREE

YEVA STOOD ROOTED TO the spot, staring at Asenka as she stared at Solmir. Yeva was closest to the door, and knew she ought to greet him properly, but she felt that if she looked at him everything would unravel.

Finally Lena stepped forward, smoothing down her skirts as if they were made from fine silk, and not mud-spattered wool. "Welcome, sir!" she said, brushing past Yeva and holding her arms out for Solmir's heavy cloak. "Please forgive us, you're the first visitor we've had since we moved."

Solmir let her remove his cloak with a murmur of thanks, glancing at her briefly before shifting his gaze back to Yeva. "I apologize for not sending word, but by the time a messenger arrived and returned, it would be a week gone at least. I have a room at the inn some leagues back—I can return another time if I'm inconveniencing you."

"Of course not," said Lena. "You must be cold. Please, sit

here by the fire." She pulled one of the chairs from the table over to the hearth, placing it nearer to Asenka's than was necessary. Asenka, whose white face had gone red as she twisted her hands together in her lap, flashed Yeva a look of alarm.

Solmir shifted his weight from one foot to the other. "Actually, I don't have much time. Your father is not at home?"

Lena shook her head. "He is hunting," she explained, one hand still on the back of the chair, as if hoping to usher him there by willpower alone.

His face fell a little. "Well, I will have to come back another time to speak with him—but that wasn't my sole purpose." Solmir had dropped his gaze to the floor, as if he might find his next words written there.

"Yes?" said Lena expectantly, the hand on the back of the chair creeping over to rest on Asenka's shoulder.

"I—had hoped to be able to speak with Yeva." His eyes flicked up, meeting Yeva's before she looked away, startled. "Alone."

Heart straining against her rib cage, Yeva could not help but look at her sisters. Lena's face was blank, confused . . . but Asenka understood. Her lips parted, but no sound emerged; the flush of nervous excitement warming her face fled; her hands went still in her lap. She caught Yeva's eye, and after a long, heavy second, the corners of her mouth turned up in a smile.

Unable to stand it any longer, Yeva darted forward, fumbling for the latch of the door. "As you can see," she said harshly, "we have only the one room aside from the bedrooms. I will speak with you outside, if you please."

She stumbled out into the snow without waiting to see if Solmir would follow. *Why*, she thought furiously, *could it not have been Radak?* In her haste she'd left her cloak behind. For now, hot humiliation and distress coursed through her, immunizing her against the cold.

Solmir's horse stood obediently by the snow-covered trail, snorting steam into the air. Well trained, that it required no hobbling or tying. A voice cut through her thoughts. "Yeva?" Solmir was closing the door behind him, having grabbed his cloak back from the hook on which Lena had placed it.

"What are you doing here?" Yeva turned abruptly enough to send up a spray of snow.

Solmir's mouth opened in surprise, his brows furrowed. "I— why are you so angry?"

Yeva had not known her emotions were so obvious. She closed her eyes, sucking in a frigid breath of air that burned the insides of her nose. "I am sorry, you came at an awkward time. Please, sir—why have you come?"

"Solmir," he corrected her. "I hate it when people call me *sir*. I came—" He paused, brows lowering further as he peered at her in the winter sunlight. "You really don't know?"

The fury ebbed, leaving her with only confusion and dread creeping through her as quickly and surely as the cold. "No." She shivered.

"Here." Solmir stepped forward and draped his cloak over her shoulders before she could protest. Taking a step back, restoring a respectful distance between them, he leveled his scrutiny at her again. His eyes were friendly, warm—it was unsurprising that they were what Yeva remembered most about him from the dinners they spent together.

"I apologize. I thought you had understood." Though he spoke softly, he spoke with confidence. "I know we haven't spent much time together but of everyone at those dinners, you were the only one I wished to speak to. The other ladies spoke of weather and fashion, and of the baronessa's silver. You explained the proper way to skin a leopard so as not to mar its fur."

Yeva felt the bottom falling out of her stomach. "I—never—"

"Not to me," he said, with a smile. "To one of the huntsmen in the baron's service. I overheard you. I tried in vain to talk about hunting with you but I think the baronessa had you too well trained. Never before have I so envied a mere huntsman."

Now that he spoke, Yeva remembered more clearly the evenings they had both attended dinner. He had always sat at her elbow, always spoke of the huntsmen and asked if she knew any of them. She had thought he was engaging in some form of gossip, and had deflected the questions as best she could. Yeva closed her eyes again. How had she been so blind?

"Please," said Solmir. Yeva heard a soft footfall, knew he had taken a step toward her. "When I got the news of your father's caravan, your family was already gone and I had missed my chance. And now I've come all this way, instead. I will have to come back and speak with your father but everyone knows how he loves you. If you want something, he won't refuse you. Please, Yeva. Consider my offer. I would like to take you back with me—as my wife." He had run out of breath, forced to gulp down another before his last words.

Yeva felt as though the weight of his cloak on her shoulders might drive her to her knees. She forced herself to meet his eyes and immediately wished she hadn't. He was too earnest, gazing at her with such feeling. How had she never noticed?

"I can't marry you," she mumbled, shivering again despite the warmth of his cloak. "I'm sorry."

"Why not?" He looked merely puzzled, not comprehending what she was saying.

"I can't marry anyone." As the words came out, Yeva realized how much truth they held. Of all the men in the world who might ask for her hand, she could not hope to find someone more suited for her than this one—and yet the thought of marriage made her want to startle like a wood thrush and fly away into the forest. "I'm not—I'm not a wife. You should marry my sister, Asenka, she's kind and good and—"

Solmir shook his head, moving forward and reaching for her hands. Yeva, too dumbfounded to protest, stared as he enclosed them in his. "It's not your sister I want, Yeva."

She looked up, caught by the longing in his voice. The depth of it left her speechless.

He met her eyes and the corners of his mouth drew up in the tiniest of smiles. "Yeva," he repeated softly.

"I can't." She pulled away, dragging the cloak from her shoulders and presenting it to him at arm's length. "I'd offer you refreshment but we've only just moved and we aren't ready to receive company. Please, go." If she weren't so thrown, she'd be shocked at her own behavior. She was being unforgivably rude.

But Solmir only gathered up his cloak, hugging it to his chest. He kept hold of her outstretched arm with one hand, his fingers encircling her wrist. He was watching her as though wishing it was she, and not the cloak, pressed against him, but he made no attempt to draw her nearer. "I must come back to speak with your father. A fortnight, perhaps. That will give him time to return. Please, only think about it until I come again. We can hunt together, travel together, until the baron names me his heir. Then you will be my baronessa, and no one will dare tell us what we should do."

Yeva could say nothing, breath stuck in her throat, heart thrashing against her rib cage.

Solmir bowed over her captive arm, and Yeva expected him to kiss her hand the way a gentleman would kiss a lady's. But then fingers as dexterous as a weaver's turned her wrist over, and he bent her hand back gently so that her fingers opened like a flower. Then he placed a kiss in her palm. Yeva shivered again—and this time not from the cold.

"Please give my regards to your sisters," he said, releasing her hand. "And tell them I'm sorry I can't stay longer to speak with them." Then, pulling his cloak over his shoulders, he made his way back to his horse and mounted with practiced ease. He sat like someone born to the saddle, which was plain and unadorned—worn with use and care. Solmir saw her looking and smiled.

Yeva dropped her gaze to the snow, but felt his eyes on her for long moments before he turned his horse and disappeared back into the forest.

She longed to remain where she was, neither returning to the house nor going after Solmir, but cold inevitably drove her indoors. She opened the door as quietly as she could, slipping inside, but stealth was useless. They were all waiting for her.

Her eyes went immediately to the figure standing in the house's center, one hand steadying herself on the table. Asenka smiled, and Yeva could see no hint of anything but pleasure in her sister's face.

"I'm so happy for you, Beauty," said Asenka, raising her arms. Yeva went to her, ducking her head against her shoulder, and felt her sister's arms wrap tightly around her. "He's a good man."

Late that night, as Doe-Eyes dreamed of fat rabbits and twitched at her side, Yeva heard a sound from the back bedroom. Whispers, barely audible over the wind and leaves—and then a sob, low and quickly muffled. Just once, a single cry in the quiet.

Yeva spent the rest of the night awake, arms wrapped around Doe-Eyes, the palm of her hand burning in the darkness.

Yeva rose before dawn, dressing in the dark and wrapping herself up well against the chill. She took a slice of day-old bread and slipped it into her pocket, then made for the door. Doe-Eyes scrambled up from her nest by the fire and trotted after her, toenails clicking on the wood, but Yeva held out a hand and the dog dropped to her haunches. "Mind the house, Doe-Eyes," she whispered. Doe-Eyes cocked her head, trembling with the desire to accompany her mistress, but when Yeva slipped out, the dog remained obediently still.

The sky was beginning to lighten in the east as she crossed the snow-covered yard toward the run-down shed that butted up against the edge of the property. Albe had taken the borrowed horse back to town, but the wagon was theirs, and some of what they had brought had yet to be unpacked. Yeva hoisted herself up into the back of the wagon and threw aside the heavy canvas that covered its contents, tossing up wayward snow as she did so.

There—a long wooden chest, one of the few things of value that her father had not parted with. It was carven with intricate depictions of ash and oak, rowan and hickory. Amid the tangle of leaves and branches there were eyes peeking out, a flash of a tail there, a glimpse of a paw. Yeva ran a hand along the box and then opened it.

Her father had taken his heavy bow with him and his ax, but the lighter bow was there, unstrung, and a quiver of fine goose-feathered arrows. These were hers, had been since she was young. Her father's bow had always been much too heavy for Yeva to draw, and anyway, she'd never needed the power the strong bow offered. He was a large-game hunter, while Yeva was quick and resourceful, with good aim and well-hidden traps.

Yeva pulled out the bow, testing the wood with her thumb. She had neglected it these past years. When was the last time she had oiled the wood? And yet it was smooth to the touch, and when she bent it across her shin it curved gracefully. Someone had been caring for the bow. And who other than her father would know what it needed?

She strung the bow with some difficulty, bracing the wood against her leg and discovering that the muscles she'd had when she was twelve had atrophied over the years. Her arms shook as she slipped the string into its groove at the bow's tip. After retrieving her knife and her spool of wire from the bottom of the chest and tucking them into the band of her skirt, she hopped down from the wagon. She slung the bow and the quiver of arrows over her shoulder and slipped back out of the shed, shutting the door behind her.

Yeva glanced to the east, where the rosy violet sky over the trees had grown several shades lighter. Albe would be rising soon, and he would find the hearth cold and the kettle empty. But if Albe woke to find her there, she would be drawn into the daily life of the cabin, and she could not bear to face her sisters, not yet.

And her father had not forbidden her to hunt—only to accompany him.

She set off through the silent, snowy forest, blood coursing past her ears. Though she'd slept little, energy flowed through her and drove her onward. She stopped now and then to set a wire snare in the snow. Her fingers fumbled with the task at first, but they soon remembered the trick of it, growing more sure as she went. Her skirt hampered her more than she'd expected; she would have to make herself a pair of trousers out of one of her dresses, if she was to do this regularly. And now that she'd tasted again the fresh air, felt the snow-covered world enclose her, smelled the crisp brightness of the ice underlain with spicy fir, she knew she would do it every day she could.

She saw little sign of anything nearby in the forest, coming across only old tracks: deer and fox, and occasionally the strange hopping troughs in the snow that told of rabbits. The day passed quickly, the morning turning to noon almost without her noticing. Just after noon she stopped to rest, wishing she'd been thinking clearly enough to bring food for lunch.

She would have to turn back soon, retracing her route to see if any of her snares had borne fruit. And at the end of her trail: the house, with Albe and Lena—and Asenka.

Yeva breathed deep, despite the way the cold air stung her nose and lungs. She thought of Asenka, the tiny sting of a smile on her face when Yeva had reentered the cabin after Solmir left. Her voice, without recrimination, as she congratulated her little sister on a match well made. That same voice, lost in a single sob in the darkness.

Yeva would have to turn back—but not yet. She stalked off, deeper into the forest, heels kicking up snow as she moved. This was not a hunter's gait, but she was too angry, too unsettled, to care.

How could Solmir have come, with no warning and no announcement, to ask Yeva such a thing? And when she had scarcely ever spoken three words together to him. And yet, he'd been watching her. Listening to her chat so easily with the lowly huntsmen. *Envying* them—because they were the ones to whom she chose to speak.

And wasn't Yeva always criticizing the townsfolk for their skittish indecisiveness? Hadn't she wished for them to be more certain about their decisions, to act quickly and with strength and confidence?

She stopped, placing a hand against the tree trunk at her side. *Speaking of wishes,* whispered her thoughts, *who wished for a man who would love her for her skill?*

Marriage. To Solmir.

It would mean that she, her father, her sisters—all would be taken care of, no matter what might come. She would be baronessa, and her family secure on the baron's estates. They would be safe. Happy. Solmir would take her hunting, would love her for her abilities. It was what she wanted. More than anything she'd dared to hope for.

So why did it feel as though a hollowness was crouched inside her? Why did she feel as though the bindings of a cage were closing in around her?

She tore the bow from her shoulder, nocking an arrow to its string with ease. She'd had no opportunity to test the bow that morning, but found that her body still remembered the motion. Her shoulders would ache later, but she could still draw it. She sighted along the arrow's shaft, wrist straight and strong, elbow level.

A cascade of sound exploded from the right, and she nearly sent the arrow whistling off into the forest in shock. She managed to lower the bow instead, instinct preventing her from loosing an arrow she could not afford to lose. She whirled to face the sound, only to see something burst out of the brush toward her.

"Doe-Eyes!" exclaimed Yeva, knees weakening. The dog collided with her leg and ricocheted off, shaking snow from her short fur and beaming at her with a wide, gap-jawed smile, tongue lolling out to one side.

Adrenaline drenched Yeva's thoughts, narrowing them into

one furious torrent. It could have been a boar, a wolf, a bear; she had been paying so little attention. "Go home!" she ordered the dog, her voice cracking.

Doe-Eyes stared at her, tongue going still. She cocked her head in confusion.

"Bad dog!" Yeva shouted, waving the arrow at the creature. "Go back home, *now!*"

The dog backed up a step and then lay down tentatively in the snow, dropping first her front paws and chin and then her hindquarters. Eyes rolled upward, she gazed desperately at Yeva, tail thumping once in pathetic appeal.

Yeva passed a hand over her face, the rush of fear fading and with it, her anger. She dropped to her knees; recognizing forgiveness, Doe-Eyes leaped up to throw herself at her mistress. Yeva ran a hand down the dog's spine as a cold nose thrust itself against her neck.

"You shouldn't be out here," Yeva whispered, pressing her hand flat against the dog's body. Doe-Eyes was trembling, but whether from cold or from eagerness and delight, Yeva could not tell. "What possessed you to burst out of the wood like that?"

As if the dog could understand her, Doe-Eyes wriggled from her grasp and went dashing back into the bushes. Yeva could hear her thrashing, and was about to step closer when something small and brown came shooting out of the undergrowth, cutting back across the path Yeva had trampled.

Before she had time to think about it, Yeva had an arrow nocked to her bow and drawn back. When Doe-Eyes flushed out a second rabbit, she let the arrow fly.

The rabbit's scream sent a thrill of satisfaction down Yeva's spine. Elation coursed through her as she lowered the bow and slung it over her shoulder. The thrill faded as she approached and saw that the rabbit was still thrashing—not a clean kill. Her aim was not what it used to be, and she'd drawn a sharp, piercing arrow—a deer-hunting arrow. She'd have to relearn her own fletching codes to tell by feel which were the blunter-tipped arrows for small game.

She quickly reached out and wrung the creature's neck, putting an end to its suffering, then lifted her head. No sign of Doe-Eyes, although she could hear a faint rustle in the distance.

Retrieving her arrow, she wiped it off, staining the snow bright crimson in the dappled afternoon sunlight. She ran a loop of her wire around the rabbit's hind legs and hung it from her belt. *Stew*, she thought happily, *or roasted on potato mash.* It would be the first fresh meat they'd had since moving to the cabin. She began to retrace her trail, humming a marching song her father had given her to sing while she ran to keep time with his steps.

Doe-Eyes caught up to her a few moments later, shivering her delight and licking her chops. The first rabbit had clearly fared no better than its fellow, and Yeva would not have to feed Doe-Eyes scraps of bread and dried meat tonight.

She made her way back home, all thoughts of Solmir banished the second her arrow found its mark.

"Beauty, you didn't." Lena held the skinned, cleaned rabbit at arm's length, although there was an undeniable eagerness in her voice at the prospect of fresh meat. "Father said you were not to go hunting."

Yeva had stowed her bow once more in her father's chest outside, and removed any trace of the day's work. Her snares had turned up empty, but she would check them again at first light tomorrow. "I laid a few traps," she said. It was not a lie—the traps were laid, after all.

Lena sighed. "And the checking of the traps is what kept you out most of the day?"

Asenka had not risen from her chair by the fire, but had smiled at Yeva when she came. It was like nothing had changed between them, despite the chasm Yeva felt stretched there. She saw that Asenka no longer sat with her skirt covering her feet, but had her twisted leg stretched out to the warmth of the fire.

No need any longer to hide her flaws.

Yeva closed her eyes. "I will go check my snares again," she blurted, turning to make for the door.

"Yeva," said Asenka. Her voice was soft, but it was enough to stop Yeva dead in her tracks. "Will you wind my wool for me?"

Yeva wanted nothing less. Except, perhaps, to upset her sister. So she went, sinking down onto the floor at Asenka's side as Lena began to dismember the rabbit for stew. She picked up the loose skein of wool from the basket at Asenka's feet and wound loops of the yarn around her hands, holding it so that it would feed easily as Asenka knit.

Asenka began to hum a tune their mother had favored. Yeva remembered it more from her sister, for she had been too young when their mother died for clear memories of her to take root. Yeva sighed and turned her head to the side, laying it against her sister's knee. She felt the slight movements of Asenka's body as she wound the wool around a needle, dipped it through the fabric, wound again.

After a time, under the sounds of Lena cooking dinner, Asenka whispered, "If you are happy, Beauty, then so am I." She bent and pressed her lips to the crown of Yeva's head.

Yeva said nothing, eyes burning and blurring as she stared resolutely at the uneven floor. If only she were as selfless.

Yeva took to spending her days in the forest, under the tall straight pines in the snow and the silence. Her skill at the bow returned quickly, muscles remembering what the rest of her did not. Her fitness was slower to return, forcing her to stop for rest far more often than she would have liked. She came to know the forest again, finding it as familiar and as comfortable as an old friend.

Doe-Eyes accompanied her on days when the sun was high, the temperatures otherwise too harsh for her slight build. Though Asenka promised to lavish her with affection on the days Yeva left her behind, the sight of the dog with her head slung low, haunting the doorway, often made Yeva relent at the last minute and allow the dog to come. She was grateful for the company, and for Doe-Eyes's ability to flush prey out of brush and thicket that Yeva might never have discovered on her own.

She never came back to the house empty-handed, and often with more than they needed for the day's meal. Albe constructed a rudimentary smokehouse by the shed, and they began to supplement their stores of food rather than deplete them. The prey Yeva took was too small and unremarkable for saleable pelts, but she cleaned and scraped each hide anyway in the evenings, to save for their own uses in the burgeoning winter. They could not afford to waste anything.

She made a point of rising early enough to avoid her sisters, but once she woke to find Asenka kneeling at her side, stirring the fire. Yeva started to rise, but her sister set the poker down and laid a hand on her arm.

"Yeva," she whispered, her eyes anxious. "Stay. You don't need to go out every day. We have food. Stay with us today."

Yeva's eyes blurred, and she blinked hard. "I can't," she whispered back.

Asenka's hand shifted to touch Yeva's cheek, then brushed some of her sleep-tangled hair out of her eyes. "What is it you're looking for out there?"

Yeva blinked again, about to reply that she wasn't looking for anything, just game for their survival—but her throat closed. How was it her sisters knew her so well, better even than she knew herself? She drew a shaking breath. "I don't know," she breathed. "Something more."

After a week had passed, their father returned. He arrived in the evening, knocking his feet against the doorframe to dislodge the snow on his boots, a thick, wild growth of stubble half masking his face. Pelei came barreling in so that he and Doe-Eyes could turn circles around each other, sniffing and sniffing and remembering.

Yeva's father threw himself into his chair by the fire while Lena made tea. "It knows I'm here," he said, stabbing a finger at the arm of the chair. "It is driving the other animals from me. Tracking me. I've seen not even a single rabbit all week."

Yeva exchanged glances with her sisters. Not one of them mentioned the gradually increasing store of dried meats in their larder. Yeva took her father's chilly hand in hers, as much to keep him from harming himself in his frustration as to comfort him. "Perhaps you are still learning the forest again," she said carefully, "and that's why you haven't come across any game."

"No," grunted her father, sinking back into his chair and watching the fire, pulling his hand free of Yeva's in order to rub at his bristly face. "No. There is something out there. Something cunning."

"Father, surely there can't be—"

"I have seen it before."

Yeva glanced up to find Asenka watching them, her expression bathed in concern. Yeva tried again to touch her father's hand, but he would not be calmed.

"What did you see before?" she asked softly.

But her father only shook his head, and shook his head again.

Eventually Albe and her sisters ambled off to bed and it was only Yeva and her father by the fire. And after a time, because she was tired from her day's hunt, Yeva too drifted off to sleep. She had no memory of her father leaving the chair for his own bed.

He could not be convinced to stay, planning to depart again with Pelei at his side when the morning dawned clear and cold. He took food from the stores, not noticing that they had grown since he was last home. The single-mindedness with which he planned his return to the forest chilled Yeva. Always, he had confided in her. She had seen hints of this passion in him when she was very young, when he would tell her stories of the things he had seen in the heart of the wood. Things he'd hunted— things he'd killed. Things that had escaped.

The creatures he used to tell her about—the monsters and the wonders hidden deep within the forest, where the other hunters refused to go—they were stories. Fantasies invented to teach children good manners, to fascinate them on cold winter days when they could not play outside. Her father had always spoken of them as if they were real, but that was to delight Yeva, to let her believe, when she was still too small to know better. The way he was acting now, muttering about the thing tracking him, pacing as he recounted the old stories to himself, still acting as though they were true—it no longer delighted her. She was frightened.

"Father!" she shouted finally, on the morning of his planned departure. "Father, you must stay. Something is wrong. Please—let Lena make you some tea."

"I don't need tea," he said, strapping his crossbow to his back and stamping his feet into his boots. He rubbed at his arm, which had been stiff and sore all morning.

"Then bring me with you," she said, moving forward to take his hand. "If there is some creature out there with intelligence then two sets of eyes, two minds, will be better than you alone."

"Too dangerous," Tvertko grunted, jerking his hand away.

"You don't know that," she argued.

He stopped, looking up from his pack to meet her gaze, though he seemed to be staring through her at a distant memory. "It is a Beast," he said. "A monster unlike anything in any story. It was there twenty years ago. When your mother asked me to give up hunting, it was the one thing I had not, could not catch. And it is there still. When I kill it, its head will bring such a price that we will be able to return home."

Yeva heard one of her sisters, she could not tell which, stifle a gasp behind her. There was madness in her father's face, and Yeva fought for control of her voice. "Let us just live here," she begged. "Leave the Beast to the forest. We will hunt for food and sell pelts when the snow leaves in spring, and we will be happy. This is a fine home." She wanted to tell him of Solmir's offer, but the words stuck in her throat.

Her father only shook his head and moved to leave, calling Pelei to his side.

Yeva darted around him, putting her body between him and the door. "Daddy," she whispered. "Please."

"Step aside," he ordered, the harshness of his face nothing like the smiling one she knew best. Pelei's tail was tucked firmly between his legs, his head low as he watched.

"No."

Her father barely gave her time to react, brushing her aside with an easy sweep of his arm. His physical strength had more than returned—but the wildness of his gaze frightened Yeva far more than the effortless way he knocked her to the ground. Pelei tried to lick her face, but her father gave a piercing whistle and the dog dragged himself away, slinking with his belly low to the ground in unhappiness.

Lena rushed forward to help her up, but by the time Yeva struggled to her feet again, their father was gone.

BEAST

We should not have let him see us.

He is mad with memory now, crashing through the forest loudly enough to frighten away the slowest and most dim-witted of creatures. He leans on his dog, who nudges him upright in the snow when he stumbles. We watch from some distance behind him as he forces his way through the forest. There is no beast in him left, no predator—there is only man. A madman.

He is useless now. When he was young he saw us and lived to dream about us. He could see the edges of the other world, the one that binds us. But now age has turned him, and we cannot use him for our purpose. We want to howl our rage and frustration, want to tear him limb from limb for making us hope, even the tiniest flicker, after all these long years. We want to destroy every part of him.

We follow him on silent paws.

FOUR

A COLD DREAD SETTLED in Yeva's belly after her father left. Her sisters looked to her when it came to their father, for she knew him better than anyone. Yeva could not afford to let them see how frightened she was, or else they too would live with the same heavy tension at every moment, the feeling of the ax overhead, of waiting for it to fall. And so when she was at home, she smiled and asked her sisters about the inconsequential events of the day, and saved her fears and worry for the hunt.

Yeva saw his face as she moved through the forest, the distant gaze that had looked right past her, the negligent sweep of his arm as he shoved her from the doorway. She feared for whether he would come home—and she feared for what he might be when he did.

Despite her dread, the hours she spent in the wood were like light in the darkness. There was no Asenka, with her broken heart, no Lena to scold Yeva about muddying the floors. The weight of pretending all was well, that everything was normal and as it should be—it fell away. She knew she should be with her sisters, should be grateful they were all well and together and safe. Running to the quiet of the forest was selfish. But that shard of guilt, that tiny flicker of shame, fell silent when she stepped outside each sharp-frosted morning.

She felt herself growing stronger each day, moving more quickly, more quietly. Her breath no longer puffed loudly in the air when she paused, and the soles of her feet no longer ached when she returned home in the evenings. Albe and her sisters ate rabbit, fox, brush-hen, and deer. They cured the hides, and Asenka put her skill with the needle, learned from the leech, to work on leather instead of wounded flesh. She fashioned Yeva trousers, and the freedom they offered made her faster still.

Yeva was forced to leave Doe-Eyes at home more and more often as winter took hold of the forest. She kept her own trails clear, walking them each day there was new snow to tamp them down, but elsewhere in the forest the snow deepened. If the slim dog, bred for far warmer climates, tried to wade shoulder-high all day long, she'd risk frostbite or worse.

Yeva was striding down one of her trails one afternoon on her way back to the cabin, a trio of rabbits hanging from her belt, when the hairs on the back of her neck lifted in warning. She kept moving, but her senses went on alert, one hand shifting toward her bow. Her father's words came back to her as if he were standing at her elbow.

There is something out there, he'd said. *Something cunning.*

Then, the words had sounded like madness. But here, in the silence of the forest, with her instincts speaking far more loudly than her good sense, his warnings were fresh in her mind. Here it seemed possible that every tale he'd told her as a child could be true.

Yeva disguised her movements by striding faster, letting the bow slip down off her shoulder and swatting at it as though it inconvenienced her. She always carried an arrow free of the quiver, in order to shoot quickly should a rabbit dart in front of her. Now, her fingers wrapped around it.

Behind her and to her right came a dull thud as a clump of snow slid from a pine bough. The image flashed in her mind of a shadow behind the tree she'd just passed, its thick branches weighted heavy with snow. Four steps behind her, maybe five.

Her right hand tightened around the bow's grip as she stepped over the snow-covered shape of a branch along her path. Two steps farther, and the branch cracked behind her.

She whirled, nocking the arrow and drawing it back in one movement, sighting down it at the figure in front of her before she registered what it was.

"Yeva!" it cried, throwing itself backward onto the ground.

Yeva was following it down with the point of her arrow by the time the voice registered. "Solmir!" Her hands tried to let go of bow and arrow both, in surprise and relief. She managed to throw the bow aside instead, sending the arrow to thump harmlessly into the ground.

"What are you doing?" she cried, heaving a breath into lungs that were fighting to work properly.

"Looking for you," gasped Solmir, still sprawled on his back in the snow, staring up at her. "What are *you* doing?" Wild-eyed, hair in disarray from his tumble, he looked more like a boy of twelve than a man of twenty-five.

Yeva lifted her hand to brush it, shaking, across her forehead. "I thought you were—something else."

He picked himself off the ground, brushing the snow from his cloak. "Something else? What, a bear tiptoes over your path to catch up with you?"

She shook her head, adrenaline leaving her angry, but not without relief. "Why are you here?"

Solmir's expression was blank for a few long seconds. "It has been a fortnight," he said. "I came as I promised. Your sisters said you were out gathering barks and winter herbs for remedies. The trails are not hard to follow." His eye fell on her bow, chin lifting to point at the rabbits dangling from her belt. "I see your medicine chest will be full indeed."

Yeva fought against the flush rising to her cheeks. "Why did you sneak up on me?"

"I had thought to surprise you," Solmir said. "Foolish. Don't worry, I don't intend to try it again. At least not unless I am certain you are unarmed."

She began to bristle, but he held up his hands, palms outward. A gesture of peace. "Please, I didn't come to argue. I know that Yeva comes armed. I would not have her any other way."

Have her. The blush won, and Yeva cast her glance away to focus on the snow trampled by his body when he fell. "My father is out again. You have missed him by more than a week."

"I know, your sisters told me." Solmir paused, the hesitation betraying that he was choosing his words carefully. "Did you speak to him? About what I asked two weeks ago?"

"It—did not come up." Yeva could not quite bring herself to look at him.

"Oh. I see." The silence stretched between them, only the distant sound of snow falling from another branch to lessen it.

"He was only here for a short time," Yeva burst out, the silence drawing the words before she could stop them. "I am sorry. It wasn't because—because I intended to refuse."

"But you do intend to refuse?"

Yeva lifted her eyes at the catch in his voice to find him looking at her, gaze full of that same mute appeal it had held when he first made his offer. "I know I should not." Her voice was a whisper.

Perhaps Solmir saw something in her face to give him hope, for he strode forward to bridge the gap between them. "I am not asking you to love me," he said, his voice ringing in the quiet winter air. "Only that you let me love you. As I do."

Yeva wished she could remove her cloak—the cloying warmth of it stifled her thoughts. "You don't even *know* me," she protested.

"I know enough," said Solmir. "You and I are the same."

"That is not reason for marriage!"

"It *is*!" he countered.

"I am not gentle and wifely, I am coarse and—and impossible! *This* is impossible."

"But you will *learn* those things, Yeva! There is time for you to learn gentleness after we've had our adventures, after I become baron. When there are children you will—"

"Children!" she exclaimed. Suddenly the forest seemed to close in around her like the woven bonds of a cage.

"Yes! Children. You act as though I'm trying to hold you captive. If you would only cool your temper and listen to me, I am trying to offer you a life beyond *this*!"

"I don't *want* a life beyond this!" She paused, breath steaming on the frigid air as she panted. Even as she spoke them, she knew the words were not entirely true. There was a yearning in her, something that had lodged deep in her heart since the first time her father had told her of the wonders that lived in the forest's heart. But what she wanted, Solmir could not offer. She drew another breath, slower this time. "I'm not what you want."

"I'm not trying to fight you," he said quietly, breath misting in the air between them. "You must know how hard it will be to survive this winter here. I would wait, and bide my time, and let you come around, but neither of us has that time. Every week that passes could bring a storm that makes travel impossible. If someone in your family should become unwell, what would you do?"

Suddenly it was not Solmir's face that Yeva saw, but the wild, unnatural focus of her father's stare before he left, determined to catch the thing that he imagined was tracking him. Yeva closed her eyes. Her heart fluttered against her rib cage like a bird trying to beat its way free.

"Please," said Solmir. "Let me help your family. Let me help you."

Yeva remained silent for some time before opening her eyes. Solmir's face was inches from hers. Only her breath steamed the air, as he held his and waited.

"I cannot accept your offer," she began in a whisper. His face went wooden, and she hurried to continue. "Not without making clear my situation. My family's situation."

"There's nothing that would change my mind." His voice was tense with cautious anticipation.

"M-my father is unwell." Her voice broke, to her horror. Yeva found her throat closing, the anxiety that had hunted her the past week bubbling up without warning. She had discussed it with no one, not even her sisters, but now the need to speak overtook her. "I fear—I fear he is going mad."

Solmir stepped forward, his hands going to her shoulders. He gently pulled her close. "Then we will find him help. Together."

Yeva wanted to pull away, but the fear lodged inside her since her father shoved her down fought its way out. And Solmir was warm, and as his hand pressed at the small of her back, pulling her closer still, she found that part of her didn't mind his touch at all. She knew she could not reasonably spend her life wandering these forest trails in search of something she could not even name—not when Solmir's proposal offered answers to every misfortune her family had suffered.

"Then I accept," she whispered, mumbling the words into the leather of his tunic.

His arms tightened, robbing her of breath, and then released her again. "Come. Let us get your barks and herbs into the stewpot, and tell your sisters the happy news."

Solmir visited almost daily after that, joining Yeva at her tasks. She stuck to her snares in his company, bringing her bow along only for defense. Her daylong hunting expeditions turned into pleasant strolls, Solmir at her side, discussing horses, and hunting, and how to skin leopards. Though she longed for the solitude to which she'd grown accustomed, she found herself growing fond of Solmir nonetheless, with his boyish enthusiasm for all things hunting. At first Yeva feared he might take advantage of the quiet, empty forest to embrace her again, but he remained a respectful distance from her, only offering her his hand now and then to help her over a log or across a frozen stream.

The relief that he was willing to help her father was dampened, however, by the uneasiness still haunting her. She could not quite place it—true, she did not love Solmir, but that was hardly reason not to marry him. She was fond of him, and growing fonder every day. The life he'd spoken of was a far better and richer one than Yeva ever could have hoped for, and yet there was a shadow over her heart, a tight emptiness she could feel every time she took a deep breath. She told herself it was fear for her father. She told herself it would pass once her father returned. She told herself she would be happy, then.

Solmir left in the afternoons to return to the inn where he was staying, giving Yeva a few precious hours before dusk in which to do some real work, checking her traps a final time and using her bow on any stragglers heading back to their dens for the night. She was not as productive as she had been before he began accompanying her, but she still brought home enough food for her sisters and Albe.

The days stretched on into weeks, and there was still no sign of Yeva's father. She watched for marks of him in the forest, but the trail of his passage from the house had long since been erased by snowfall, and she could not tell in which direction he had traveled.

Her dread grew. It woke her at night with a pounding heart, distracted her during the day when she ought to be listening to Solmir. Her sisters said nothing, and she offered nothing in return, but the tense silences in the evenings were eloquent nonetheless. She felt stretched as taut as the wires of one of her snares, waiting for the tiniest shift to send her springing into action.

So when a commotion outside interrupted the quiet just before dawn, Yeva was up off her pallet by the fire and halfway to the door before Doe-Eyes had even lifted her head.

Yeva threw open the door, but before she could scan the area for signs of her father, a shape launched at her out of the inky blackness. Behind her Doe-Eyes yelped recognition. Someone lit a lamp, and as its illumination fell upon the doorway, Yeva recognized what had thrown itself at her.

"Pelei," she whispered, dropping to her knees and not

bothering to reprimand the dog when he began mopping her face with his tongue. She was too busy staring through the night beyond him, searching for her father's form, waiting for him to emerge out of the darkness.

The dog was whining insistently, shoving his nose against Yeva's neck and sniffing anxiously. Yeva dropped her eyes. "Where's Father?" she whispered, her heart constricting. The dog began to wriggle away but she gripped his front legs, holding him still. "Pelei? Where's Father?"

She could say nothing else, repeating the words over and over until she felt hands at her shoulders drawing her back. "Yeva! He cannot answer, Father isn't here!" It was Lena, her voice choked with fear.

"No!" Yeva tore her arm from Lena's grip. "Pelei, why did you leave him? Father!" she called, into the night, knowing at any moment she would hear his voice call back to her.

"He's not here," whispered Lena. "Yeva—he's not here."

Yeva turned to see a trio of pale faces in the lamplight, all staring at her. "He has to be," she whispered back. "Pelei would not have left him. Pelei *never* would have left him. Something has happened."

She rose to her feet and began to dress in silence, not even bothering to warn Albe—he whirled around, turning his back as she traded her night shift for her trousers. Lena tied the dogs by the bedroom as Asenka tried to speak to Yeva, her voice shaking.

"What are you doing?"

"Go back to sleep," Yeva said calmly. She was putting things into a leather bag Asenka had made from rabbit skins. A water flask, flint and tinder, dried meat and some tubers wrapped in an extra cloak. Lengths of wire, goose feathers, a pot of glue for arrow fletching in the field. Needle and thread. Bandages.

Medicines for pain, bleeding, frostbite, broken bones, every eventuality she could think of.

"Yeva, you don't know where he is."

"I will find him."

"It's dark—please, calm down—wait until morning."

"No time. His trail may be lost by then."

Asenka grasped at Yeva's arm with uncharacteristic strength. "Yeva, *stop*. We need you here. You can't go tearing off into the woods. I am as worried about Father as you are, but *we* need you too."

Yeva hesitated, arm flexing under Asenka's grip. Her sister was right—if something had happened to their father, then she was the only one who could ensure her family would not starve this winter.

But if something had happened to their father . . . Yeva's heart shriveled, and her instincts took over. She shook her sister's hand off, then closed up the satchel and swung it onto her back. "You have enough food for several weeks. I'll be back before then, I promise."

"Yev—"

"*I promise.*"

She took one last look at the house: Lena with her arms around the dogs, holding them back; Asenka, white-faced and leaning against their father's chair by the cold hearth; Albe in the corner, hands clenched together and hair sticking straight up. All of them still, round-eyed and frightened as they watched her.

A sharpness stung her heart in the brief, heavy silence while she stood in the doorway. She could not leave them—and yet she had to find her father. If he was alive she would bring him home. Solmir would help her find a doctor for him, and together they would take him away from the wood that had driven him mad.

And she and her family would have peace. *If* he was alive . . .

If he was not—then she would find him anyway. She stepped out into the predawn gloom and let the door close on the lamplight behind her.

Pelei's tracks through the snow were obvious despite the darkness. The dog had been moving quickly, bounding across deep snow and leaving a trough created by his body. Yeva followed the trail, grateful for the dog's large size, and that he had forged such a path for her. She fell into the rhythm of her stride, mind reverberating with each step and each breath that steamed away behind her.

Keep moving. Keep running.

The sun rose behind a heavy curtain of clouds, leaving the forest in a false twilight that threatened to play tricks on her eyes. She kept her head down and kept moving, ignoring the burning in her legs that began just after noon. If her father was injured or trapped somewhere, she would not have much time to find him. This cold could kill someone within hours if they were not properly prepared—and even her father, master of these woods, could falter.

Pelei's tracks grew fainter as the day wore on, hidden under a light dusting of snow that had begun to fall. By the time twilight crept in again she was forced to stop and make camp, as much to rest her burning legs as to wait for daylight to show her the way onward. She slept little, fear shrieking at her to keep moving despite logic telling her she must rest. She passed the time mending holes in her cloak with the needle she'd brought with her.

As soon as the sky lightened, she packed up the camp and doused the fire. She sucked on some of the dried meat until she was able to chew it as she moved out. She had not gotten more than ten steps, however, when a voice cried her name. She stopped, the sound ringing in ears that had grown used to hearing only the quiet evenness of her own breath.

She stopped long enough to let Solmir catch up with her, his breath coming in great ragged gasps. "Wait," he panted. "Wait. Wait."

"I can't," she said tightly. She could not afford to dwell on her fear, or else she felt she might be paralyzed by it. "He could be hurt."

"I've been following you all night," he gasped, hands on his knees as he struggled for breath. "Please. Your sisters explained. Let me help."

"How?" Yeva shook her head. "I'll move more quickly on my own."

"Two sets of eyes," he managed, lungs still heaving.

Yeva felt the hairs on the back of her neck prickle. Had she not used the same justification to try and convince her father to let her come with him? She closed her eyes. "I am sorry, Solmir," she said quietly. "I have to go on alone. I can run farther than you—you're in no shape to continue on. And I must."

He coughed breathlessly, but could manage no more words, merely lifting his gaze enough to watch her with silent appeal.

Yeva's lungs constricted and she clenched her hands into fists, trying to fight the urge to give in. "If you would help me," she murmured, "then—would you look after my sisters while I'm gone?"

"But—"

"Please," she said simply. "Please, Solmir."

"But what about Albe?"

Yeva's lips twitched—the first hint of a smile she'd felt since Pelei had returned. "Yes," she agreed. "You will need to look after Albe too."

"That's not what I meant." He was regaining his breath somewhat, but his face still burned with the flush of exertion, and his voice was still ragged.

"I know. But he is more brother than servant, and he doesn't know these woods. He can't provide for them. You can." She stepped forward to clasp his hands in hers. She had never voluntarily reached out for him before, and he seemed almost as surprised by the gesture as she was herself. "This is what I'm asking you to do."

Solmir was silent for a time, breathing hard through his nose. "When you return—"

Yeva nodded. "When I return I will marry you. And we will see my father settled, and go out hunting as often as you like, and sit at the baron's table together. But for now I have to find my father. And I need your help—at home."

Solmir freed one hand from Yeva's grasp and lifted it to take hold of her chin in his fingers. He leaned forward and brushed his lips against hers, the briefest of touches before he pulled away again. "For luck."

She knew she ought to feel changed by his kiss, that her lips ought to tingle or her heart swell—but her lips felt only numb with cold, and her heart pounded only with urgency and exertion.

Yeva let go of him and staggered back so she could retrieve her pack and her bow. "Thank you," she whispered, and then turned and stumbled off again.

She put as much distance as she could between her and Solmir, praying he didn't change his mind. If he kept his word—and she had no reason to think he wouldn't—then it would buy her some time. If she could not return in the next few days, then at least her sisters would be taken care of, and Solmir would not come blundering after her through the woods.

She had no time to think of Solmir. She knew, now, what she was searching for in these woods.

By the end of the day her vision was blurring with exhaustion. She knew she needed sleep, but after so long moving she found it hard for her limbs to settle. She put her head down on her pack, wrapping herself in the extra cloak by her meager fire. Her tired eyes sought patterns in the flames, saw wings of fire stretching skyward, and she fell asleep hearing her father's voice telling her stories of the Firebird deep in the heart of the wood.

In her dreams a serpent glided toward her, red-gold eyes capturing and holding her as if she were a rabbit facing its death. Unable to run or cry out, she could only watch as it slithered across her chest. Its skin was ice cold and smooth as it reached her face, sliding over her lips and cheeks like a frigid kiss. It hissed as its head brushed her ear, jerking her out of her daze.

She sat bolt upright, gasping for air and clawing at her face, trying to throw the serpent away only to find her fingers closing around half-melted snow. The fire was nearly dead, its last embers hissing desperately under the onslaught of a new storm. Yeva blinked and looked up to find heavy snowfall drowning the camp, covering the whole lower half of her body.

"No," she gasped, numb lips struggling to form the word. "No, no—Pelei—"

She scrabbled under the snow for her bow and her pack, then stumbled over onto her hands and knees. Dawn was breaking, pale light cast diffusely across the wood. Pelei's trail was only visible as a faint series of hollows in the snow, almost indistinguishable from other features, obscured by the new snow—and filling fast.

Yeva scrambled to her feet and bolted down the trail, still shaking off the remnants of her nightmare, mind barely functioning. But Pelei's trail was nearly gone, and without it she would only be one person in a vast, uncharted wood, with no way of ever finding her father. She could not afford to waste half a second collecting herself.

The snow fell more and more thickly, the wind picking up to toss it against her face and blind her at every turn. Pelei's trail had also become more twisted, reflecting some confusion in the dog's original path. Twice she had to stop and go back, retracing her steps to the point where she had mistaken a dip in the terrain for the trail.

She lost all track of time in the storm, the clouds and the falling snow too heavy for her to see any sign of the sun. The trees were growing together more thickly here, allowing little of the snow through. It meant there was less snow to cover Pelei's trail, but that there had also been less snow to preserve it in the first place.

Eventually she stumbled over a hidden log, falling hard onto her stomach. Her breath stopped, leaving her groaning and trying to force her lungs to suck in new air. She rolled onto her back and lay there until she could fill her lungs normally, head spinning. She sat up, casting about for Pelei's trail—and could see nothing. There was only the uneven expanse of snow in every direction, and her own scattered trail leading back the way she'd come.

Yeva dragged herself to her feet, shivering now that she'd stopped moving and the perspiration from exertion settled on her skin. Though the denseness of the trees prevented the snow from being too blindingly thick, she could no longer see any distinct path to follow. She stood there, eyes straining through the gloom, heart pounding and breath steaming the air.

As she turned in a slow circle, something stung at the insides of her nose, distinct from the icy burn of falling snow. Tracking by scent was usually impossible in such cold—everything was wiped clean by the frozen air. But Yeva could smell a faint, metallic tang that made the hairs rise on her arms.

Blood.

BEAST

Blood everywhere. It burns us, horrifies us, sets us ablaze. We hunger. We roar. We want to revel in it, and we want to run. We pace across the blood-soaked snow, our heart thrumming in our ears.

But something comes. We pull back and hide our scent, waiting. Another hunter—so like the first, but younger, smaller. We slink closer through the thick trees to look.

It is female. We stop abruptly, sniffing again. Her scent is unmistakable. A mate? No. She is young and he was old.

Offspring.

Perhaps our plan is not lost. We watch her from our hidden place, breathing her smell and listening to the silence of her steps. She moves like an animal in a woman's body.

She moves like beauty.

FIVE

YEVA DROPPED INTO A hunter's stance. Where there was blood there would be scavengers—and wolves fed as a pack. And while wolves would ordinarily flee a human's presence, if they felt their kill was being threatened, they might try to defend it. With her every sense tuned, she crept forward, feet feeling for any hollows or obstacles that might trip her up.

Whatever had been killed here was much larger than a rabbit or a fox. Blood splashed the area, painting the trees and the snow red in the half-light. The falling snow had covered large portions of it—she estimated that the blood had been spilled only hours before.

Had her father been here? Had he encountered the Beast of his stories, and killed it? Yeva dropped to one knee to touch a finger to the ground. The blood was frozen. Perhaps it had been longer than she'd guessed. A shadowy irregularity caught her eye a few steps away, and she reached down and cleared the snow from the object.

It was her father's ax.

Yeva stared at the weapon, her mind refusing to process what it was seeing. A sense of wrongness built up in her gut. Why would he have abandoned it? Its handle was specially-carved, shiny-smooth from use, and fitted to his hand. Had he dropped it after killing the Beast?

And then Yeva saw what the sense of wrongness was trying to tell her.

The blade of the ax was clean, unbloodied. It had not shed the blood staining the ground.

Some distance beyond, a familiar shape dragged her forward—she uncovered his bow, then a few feet farther she found his pack, the leather torn and the contents strewn about beneath the snow.

With shaking hands she knelt over the next snow-covered hump, brushing the snow aside. She glimpsed something like raw meat, the white of bone glinting in the dim light.

A moan tore itself from her throat as she hurled herself away from the thing, which was too small to be a whole body. She fell onto her hands and knees, gasping for breath, staring blindly at the red snow before her eyes. There was only the rushing in her ears and the agony in her chest as her lungs fought for air.

She realized she was clutching his bow, its string pressed against her cheek, its long curves digging into her chest. Her numb arms refused to let it go. Her body shook, nausea clawing its way up from her belly.

A smell made its way into her awareness and her mind seized on it, grasping for anything with which to distract itself. This scent wasn't blood, but something wilder, richer. Musky, but not unpleasant. Yeva opened her eyes, staring through the gloom of the forest. Her blood surged through her, a wild flood of fury.

The bow was still in her hand. She gripped it hard enough for her knuckles to shine white as bone.

All at once an immense shadow moved, and Yeva was stunned into momentary inaction. She had been searching for a creature the size of a wolf, but it was as though an entire section of the forest had suddenly thrown itself backward through the clearing.

Without further pause she swung her father's bow around and drew it in one smooth movement. The arrow flew straight and true. There was a bone-shaking roar of fury and pain that threw her to the ground with its intensity, and then the shadowy giant bounded off through the wood.

She lay there stunned, brain trying to understand what it had seen. No natural animal could have made that sound or loomed so huge. It wasn't until the smell of her father's blood reminded her of where she was that she shook her head to clear it.

Yeva strapped her father's ax to her back, then lurched to her feet and took off after the Beast. She left her own bow behind, gripping her father's bow white knuckled, no space left for rational thought. There was only the hunt, the need to kill, to spray the creature's blood across the snow. The blizzard had stopped, and the sun was setting behind its concealing layer of clouds. The forest grew darker by the second, but she didn't care. The Beast who had slain her father was here. And she was going to destroy it.

Just there—a spatter of fresh blood some distance from where she stood. Too fresh to have belonged to her father. Droplets led from the spot, and a trough in the snow told of something large moving away.

She broke into a long, smooth run, her eyes on the ground, intent on the trail. Even if the tracks of its great body dragging through the snow weren't a clear path, she would have been able to track its scent. Its blood was a black, wild tang of metal in the back of her throat. Were it a smaller creature she would've guessed it to be an arterial hit, but she had seen the size of the Beast as it loomed up, before she pulled the trigger. For an animal so huge, the quantities of blood spattering the ground would not be fatal. If she was lucky, she'd punctured a lung, and the Beast would be slowly suffocating. If she could track it far enough, she'd be able to kill it.

Her father had taught her this stride, steady and low to the ground, covering distances smoothly and quickly and quietly. She raced along behind the Beast. The smell of it grew stronger with each step as she closed the gap between them.

All was silent save for the occasional dull thud of snow sliding from the pine boughs. With the storm now passed, the forest was still and dry and aching with the weight of winter. There were no other animals, only the Beast and, closing on its heels, its hunter.

The dusk leached the color from the world, and the spots of blood on the snow were a rich gray. Not long now.

Up ahead she heard a sound. Something coughed. Wet, labored breathing rippled through the air. Yeva's pulse beat fiercely in her temples. Her father's bow held at the ready in her right hand, she reached up with her left to finger the handle of her father's ax. The weight of it was a comfort.

A clearing opened up ahead of her. The gloom of the forest lightened to a treacherous twilight, revealing the massive shadow slumped in its center. The rise and fall of it was uneven. It heaved labored, rattling breaths that caught and gasped on the exhale. Great clouds of condensation rose, catching the mix of moonrise and sunset.

She crept forward, searching under the snow with the tip

of her boot until she found a stick. She stepped on it smartly, sending a sharp crack into the air, no quieter for its muffling white blanket.

The lump of shadow twitched, its breath wheezing. It extended a forepaw and tried to rise, only to collapse to the snow again, where it lay still but for its heaving breath and quivering fur.

Yeva could wait for it to die, for the air and the blood to run out. But she could not bear to wait, and that was too gentle a death—a gradual slowing of the body that ended in sleep. That death was too kind for this monster. The lust was rising in her, the wild hiss of revenge bubbling up to replace the hunter's cold reason.

She wanted to feel the crunch of its skull through the handle of the ax, see its life spill onto the snow in a steaming torrent. She wanted to see the face of the Beast that killed her father in the moment it understood it had lost. She wanted to watch it die.

Slinging her father's bow over her shoulder, she reached up to free her ax from its strap, gaze intent, every step pillow-soft in the powder. As she drew nearer she saw that it was not a monstrous bear, as she had thought, but something different and strange. She decided she would sever its spinal cord and take its head, which had the delicate elegance of a wolf's with the bone-crushing jaw muscles of a wolverine's. This trophy she would not sell. This one was hers.

She shifted her grip on her ax, careful to stay back out of range of its claws, which now dug into the snow, grasping for salvation.

Closer still, and she could see its eyes in the gloom. It rolled them at her, baleful, pleading, animal. The bloodlust swelled.

How had her father ever given up this life? In her mind's

eye a tapestry unfurled, the life she could have led as her father's daughter, side by side with him. If only he had brought her on his final hunt. If only he had then not found this Beast on his own. If only.

The Beast growled and the tapestry vanished like the ghost of its breath in the air. The growl turned to a whine, and she guessed her earlier shot had indeed punctured its lung. It tried once more to rise, but buckled again with a thump, its fur dusted white with snow. Its eyes rolled shut, mouth hanging open as it gasped and bled.

She was close enough now that the force of its breath stirred the fur lining her hood. The air smelled of blood and damp, and wild musk. She inhaled, nostrils flaring.

"For you, Daddy," she whispered, lifting her ax.

Her only warning was the glitter of its eyes as they opened. Too late she saw that the Beast's hind legs were crouched beneath its bulk, muscles tense and ready. Too late she saw the corpses of several rabbits, decapitated and cooling in the fresh blood that led her to the clearing. Too late she realized how close to the Beast she was standing.

The Beast lunged at her, knocking her ax aside with a blow that numbed her from the shoulder down, arm falling uselessly to her side. The sound of its roar was the sound of the forest, the vibrations shaking snow from every branch and flinging it to the ground in a perverse echo of the winter storm that had brought it. The impact of the Beast's body hitting hers sent her head snapping forward out of its concealing hood, as it lifted her from her feet.

Her last thought, strangely rational as their bodies sailed through the air, was: *This is no Beast, to lay such a trap for me. This is a hunter.*

And then its body crushed hers into the ground and it was to the dull snap of her bones breaking that she lost consciousness.

Yeva woke in utter darkness. The air was heavy with the sense of earth pressing in on her. She blinked several times, convincing herself that her eyes were working—there was no difference between having them open or closed.

She was lying on her back, spread-eagled on stone. Staving off the panic that she'd gone blind, she attempted to sit up. Shooting pain pierced through her right side, causing her to gasp aloud. She tried to clap her hands to the spot, but only her right arm moved. The left twitched with the clanking sound of metal, a frigid cuff cutting into her wrist.

Yeva slowly took inventory of the rest of her body. With careful fingertips she found not one but three ribs that made her eyes water when touched. She could move her legs, bend her spine—with great pain in her side—and her neck. Her head ached, and when she moved it she felt an agonizing tender spot at its back. Whoever had put her here had dropped her without care. She must have hit her head on the stone floor. She could smell blood in the air, and wondered if it was hers.

I am chained underground with broken ribs and no light, she told herself, closing her eyes and letting the fear wash through her. Her father had always told her that no matter the predicament, a hunter should never lie to himself. Only by understanding the problem can one see past it. Her father—Yeva clamped her lips together, eyes prickling behind closed lids. She could not afford to think of him now.

The last thing she remembered was the roar of triumph before the Beast had flung itself at her. She swallowed, neck prickling. *It should have torn out my throat.* By comparison, captivity and broken ribs seemed trivial.

Had someone saved her before the Beast could finish killing her? But why save her only to chain her in a cave?

Before she could think of an explanation there came a grating rasp of metal and stone. She inhaled sharply, feeling the stab of the breath in her broken ribs, and lifted her head but could see nothing in that direction. Something clattered to the floor and then scraped across it, as if it was being shoved toward her. Yeva strained and blinked in the blackness. Before her eyes could discern anything except the faint outline of a rectangle, the grating shriek of hinges came again, followed by the sound of something slamming closed.

Forcing herself to take shallow breaths, Yeva tried to calm herself. Not a cave, then, if there was a door—although the sensation of being underground remained. She tried to think if she had seen a figure in the doorway, but the darkness had been too complete.

She tried to sit up again, gritting her teeth against the pain, and managed to lift herself up on an elbow. Reaching out with one leg, she hooked her heel over the edge of the object that had been placed in her cell, and dragged it toward her. She was barefoot—someone had removed her boots. And her cloak and pack too, she realized.

And her weapons.

She got the object close enough to reach it with her fingertips, and then drew it the rest of the way to her. It was a tray, she discovered, exploring its contents with her fingers in the dark. She recognized the texture of dried meat, as well as uncooked tubers and a skin of water. They were from her own supplies.

There were also two strips of something rough and semistiff under her fingers. She picked one up, holding it to her nose and then brushing it with her lips, which were far more sensitive to touch than her fingers. Tree bark.

Her heart surged with confusion as she touched the strip to her tongue. Willow bark. For pain. She broke a bit off with her teeth and chewed, the bitterness so strong she had to fight the urge to spit it out again immediately. *Chew, don't swallow.* She sucked at the bark, head aching with the foul taste of it—but the pain began to ease, both in her head and her side. She spat out the pulpy mass and reached for the water skin to wash away the taste.

Why would someone lock her here and then bring her food and medicine for pain? She ate the rations, some part of her mind asserting itself and reminding her that if she hoped to escape, she'd need her strength. With difficulty she followed the manacle chaining her left hand back to the wall and tried to prop herself up against it—but the pain in her ribs was still too great, despite the dulling effects of the willow bark.

The food and the medication had arrived only seconds after she'd awakened. Could someone have heard her gasp?

"Hello?" she called to the darkness, her voice rasping like the scrape of a knife cleaning leather. The sound of it was small, dull and without echo. The room she was in couldn't be large. She swallowed and tried again, her voice a little stronger. "Hello? Thank you to whoever gave me the bark."

Perhaps it was a servant of whoever held her, feeling sorry for her. "Please, I need light. I'm injured, but I can't tell how badly without being able to see."

There was no answer. She let her head fall back against the wall to which she was chained. The blackness spun around her, though she could not tell if it was from fear or pain or an overdose of the willow bark. She closed her eyes, and fell into a doze.

Her sleep was fitful at best, haunted by monstrous images

and flashes of light. She dreamed she was blind, able only to see red streaks as though trying to see behind closed eyelids.

The streaks became a pair of eyes, the serpent's eyes from her dream in the forest, but also the Beast's—they stalked her and she found she was paralyzed as well as blind. The Beast moved closer, and when she tried to scream her voice had fled, and she jerked upright and felt the sting of fangs in her lungs and cried out, eyes flying open.

Yeva stared, gasping, at the ceiling as the dream fell away. Her side ached where her sudden movement had jarred her injured ribs. She blinked at the gray stone ceiling for long moments before her mind caught up with her.

The gray stone ceiling? She could *see*.

She rolled over onto her side with difficulty, her chain scraping the stone below her. A few feet away, sitting on the floor by the door, was a tiny oil lamp.

Someone had brought her light.

Yeva reached out and dragged the light closer, unable to take her eyes from it despite the way they burned and watered after so long in darkness. "Thank you," she whispered to her invisible ally. "Thank you."

She eased herself down again onto her back, unlacing her tunic so that she could raise her undershirt. Angry red and blue bruises spread across her side, tinged with the yellow of a stormy sky. She explored their edges with her fingertips and shuddered against a stab of pain. Broken, as she had feared. She slowly eased her shirt back into place and looked around.

The light allowed her to see that her cell was roughly square in shape, a bit longer than she was tall. There were no windows, only a solid timber door bound with iron and a thick lock. In the corner adjacent to the one where she was chained was a wooden hatch, no more than half a foot square. Though she could smell nothing, Yeva assumed she was meant to relieve herself there. The room was otherwise empty but for Yeva, her light, and the tray of uneaten, raw tubers.

She considered trying to roast the tubers over the oil lamp, but after a few halfhearted attempts decided that the flame was not hot enough. Whoever had left her food had merely taken the supplies from her pack and deposited them on the tray, with no thought for whether they were actually edible uncooked.

The lamp gave off a tiny amount of heat, and so she drew it in close to her body, trying to ignore the monstrous shadows she cast on the four walls of her tiny cell. The shadows reminded her far too much of the creature in the clearing before it had struck.

Yeva took in a deep breath, stirring the air enough to make the flame flicker across the walls. "I know you can hear me," she said, voice sounding much more certain than she felt. "I don't know who you are, or why you're helping me. But I need medicines from the pack I brought with me. The willow bark was good but it is not enough."

She waited, but there was only silence.

Yeva glanced her fingers over her ribs again, wincing at the pain but unable to leave it alone. "I need the salve from the small red pot. It will help me heal. Please." She strained to listen, ears ringing with the quiet. There came a light scrape as of fabric or leather on stone, so faint she would have dismissed the sound, if it hadn't been followed by a voice.

"You will have to put out your light."

The voice was a rumbling bass, heavy and musical and rich. Yeva shivered in spite of herself—if anything she had expected a meek, gentle voice. Someone sympathetic enough to help but too weak to actually set her free. Everything about this voice spoke of strength, and very little of compassion.

"But it is the only light I have," she replied, her free hand moving instinctively to the lamp. "I have no way of lighting it again."

"I will leave you flint and tinder," said the voice. The swish of leather or skin or cloth on stone came again, as though someone was shifting, unseen in the small cell. "But you must put it out."

"Why?"

"No questions."

Yeva shivered. The thought of being left alone in the dark again was enough to make her eyes sting, but she had no reason to distrust her benefactor. He would not leave her a light only to take it from her again.

"Very well," she whispered, and turned the wick down, the light shrinking and quivering. Yeva almost didn't see it go out, afterimages dancing before her eyes and blinding her.

The door squealed open, the noise of rusty hinges shredding the quiet. Yeva clapped a hand over her ears, grimacing. Then came that tiny sound, a footfall. The person, whoever it was, was wearing the softest of shoes. Or else they were barefoot, like she was.

"Are you a captive too?" she asked the darkness.

The voice didn't answer right away. There came a quiet clatter as something was placed down on the tray of food. "Yes," said the voice then, the word emerging like a sigh.

"And yet you are free to move around and see other prisoners?"

"I said *no questions.*"

There was a growl to the voice, a hint of anger that made Yeva want to scramble backward. She held her ground, calling on hours spent waiting outside rabbit dens to aid her in keeping still. "Thank you for helping me," she said softly. She could not afford to alienate the one person who could give her aid.

"I wish you to get well." Though the words were kind, the voice was not.

Yeva swallowed. "These roots. They must be cooked before I can eat them."

"I care not," said the voice. The door slammed shut with a screech of angry hinges, leaving her, once again, in silence.

Yeva's breath left her in a gasp, her heart pounding. She crawled toward the tray, ignoring the pain in her side, and retrieved the salve. Then she felt around the tray's surface until her fingers found what they were looking for: a pair of flints and a braided strip of wool for tinder. Yeva tightened her hand around them, not caring how the stones dug into her palm. At least she would not be left in the dark.

BEAST

We had no intention of hurting the female, but the bodies of humans are fragile. Even broken, she will serve. We will keep her alive until a hunter comes to retrieve her, and then we will take him to serve our purpose.

We stand often outside her door, listening to her breathe and learning the scent of her. This way if she tries to run we will be able to hunt her down. The light in the room is no more than a sliver along the bottom of the door. Very rarely it flickers as she passes between it and the door, a shadow of movement.

"Thank you," she whispers when we leave her things.

We do not understand this gratitude—we

are her captor. We will be her death. We are
beast and she is as fragile as the other one
was. We should show her our face and let her
scream until she breaks. They will come for her
whether she has her mind or not.

We do not do this. We ask her to put out
the light when we open the door so she will
not see our face.

Why?

SIX

HER RIBS HEALED SLOWLY, in large part due to her inability to sit still. Yeva tested the confines of her cell, able to reach the hatch in the corner only by stretching as far as the chain would let her go. She could barely touch the edge of the door, fingertips grazing the iron bindings. When her meals arrived she never heard the sound of a lock turning. The chain kept her here—the door itself was unlocked. Which explained how it was that her ally could come and go.

Yeva asked questions of the darkness, hoping for the voice's return. Though its tone had offered nothing of kindness or sympathy, the invisible ally had brought food, medicine, light. It didn't speak again, but now and then Yeva's requests were granted. She was given bandages for her wrist, which had gone raw and bloody within its manacle. The fuel in her lamp was replaced. The hinges on the door were oiled and no longer shrieked. And after one particularly cold and fitful stretch of sleep, she woke to find that a blanket had been deposited at her side.

But the voice never spoke.

She understood that if she wished her requests to be granted, she had to turn out her light and wait. The darkness then was so heavy, so stifling, she'd speak to fill the empty blackness.

Yeva had always preferred silence to the chatter of others, daydreaming of the forest quiet while the baronessa's ladies laughed and gossiped. Her thoughts came to life in the stillness of the wood, nurtured by the air and the scent and the vividness of it. But as the days crept by in her cell, she discovered that she had never known silence—not true silence. In the forest the air was alive with smells of wood and wet, the sounds of her steps echoing in the vastness. Always there was the possibility of movement and life, a rabbit flashing out of a burrow or the briefest glimpse of a fox's tail as it disappeared from sight.

The silence of her cell was small and stagnant. Heavy air pressed in on all sides, and any sounds she made were swallowed up by the weight of the earth overhead. She longed to hear the sound of a human voice, even if it was her own.

She took to speaking of anything and everything that came to mind, to fill the hungry silence. She described her featureless cell: the way the gray stone fitted together so seamlessly she could not see the mortar, the aching chill of the rock beneath her, the musical clatter of the tray, the frigid brush of her fingertips against the iron bindings on the door. She spoke of her lamp, gazing at its flame for hours, breathing in the faint burning scent and making it flicker with the breath of her words.

She imagined that the owner of that deep, rumbling voice was listening to her, and that when she spoke she was in some small way offering an exchange. His help, for her words.

When she ran out of things to describe she spoke instead of her family. Though she could not bring herself to remember her father, she talked about her sisters. She described Asenka's twisted foot and explained how five minutes with her smile and her laugh made anyone forget her disability. She recalled Lena's silly moodiness with a smile, though there was no one to see it. She even spoke of Albe and his clumsiness, and how his desire to please more than made up for his bumbling attempts to help.

"I left them," she confessed to the shadows. "They begged me to stay, and I promised I'd return. I *promised*." Her eyes burned. If only she had listened. She had not been able to help their father, and now . . . now it seemed likely she would never see any of them again. *What is it you're looking for out there?* Asenka had asked her. Yeva's throat closed.

Not this.

When she could no longer talk about her family without crying, her mind wandered to the stories her father used to tell her of the creatures that lived in the heart of the black wood. At first the stories were disjointed. It had been so long since she'd heard them, and the silence edging in on her was a distraction. Her cell was always cold, and the chill had weakened her, a gradual decay of strength that she had no way of preventing.

She told of the poor working boy who made the princess laugh and stole her heart, and of the girl who was polite enough to Father Winter to be rewarded with a chest of treasures. She told of Vasilisa the Beautiful, and how in one tale she bested her wicked stepsisters with Baba Yaga's magic light; and in another, how she fooled a king who wanted to marry her into believing she was a boy by riding and hunting better than any man.

It was one of her favorite stories. Her voice had a tendency to go hoarse after she'd been speaking into the darkness for more than a few hours. She was half whispering by the time she neared the end of this last story, with her lamp turned low to conserve the oil. She sat leaning against the wall, eyes closed.

"And so finally the king commanded that the 'young man' take a bath with him," she whispered. "But Vasilisa—" Her voice caught in her throat and turned into a cough, and she reached for the water skin to soothe it.

From the corridor beyond the door came a sound that she'd come to recognize: that lightest of scrapes signifying the step of bare feet or soft leather. Yeva froze, listening over the sound of her pounding heart. The invisible ally was outside.

The silence stretched until, so quietly Yeva felt it in the stones more than heard it, the voice said, "Go on."

A smile tugged at the corners of Yeva's mouth. She swallowed a mouthful of water and then whispered, "But Vasilisa was too quick for him. She changed and bathed and left before the king had finished taking off all his finery. She left a note for him, saying that for all his wealth and power he was not as quick or as smart as she, for she was not Vasili but Vasilisa, and he'd been fooled by a girl."

Again there was silence, and then a melancholy sigh from beyond the door.

Yeva swallowed, crawling forward until she was as close to the door as her chain would allow. "Will you not help me escape?" she pleaded, voice cracking again into a whisper. "I don't even know where I am, or who has captured me, or for what purpose."

She heard him shifting his weight on the other side of the door. "I cannot."

"Why risk helping me then?"

Silence. Then: "Why has no one come for you?"

"For me?"

"To rescue you. A brother or a mate. There is a trail to find you if they look."

Yeva swallowed. "I don't think they know I'm caught. They believe I'm looking for my father." Her throat tightened at the mention of him.

"That is not how it should be." The hint of a growl was back in his voice, the sound of barely controlled anger. "Someone should have come."

Yeva stretched her hand toward the door, her fingertips touching the iron. "No one will come for me. You are all I have. Please, help me?"

There was no answer but the sound of footsteps fading down the corridor again.

The next time Yeva woke from her troubled dreams, she found by her head a plate full of tubers, roasted in their skins with oil and salt. They were still hot, steaming gently in the lantern light.

Her lungs and throat worsened over the next few days until speaking prompted a rattling cough that forced her to brace herself against the stone wall. The unrelenting chill of her cell had settled into her bones, and not even the blanket was enough to shield her from it. Her ally provided her with more of the willow bark from her supplies, but before long the store of medicine gave out, and no more bark turned up on her tray.

She knew she was showing signs of fever, but there was little she could do. She stopped telling stories, for they required more energy than she had, and she could not speak without coughing. Her head throbbed when she put it down to sleep, and ached when she sat up again.

"I am sick," she whispered, stubbornly sticking to her father's advice to be honest with herself about her predicament. It had been several days since she'd heard from the voice, and only the fact that food still appeared in her cell told her he was even there anymore. She strained to hear the sound of his footsteps in the corridor beyond, but heard only silence punctuated by the throbbing of her head.

She sipped at the water skin until the rawness of her throat triggered more coughing, and then put her head down. The lamp burned at her eyes even closed, so she put out the light, bathing her eyelids in blessed darkness. Yeva rolled onto her back, lungs rattling with the effort of breathing.

"Can you walk?"

She had not heard the door open. Since her ally had oiled the hinges the door was quieter, but not silent; it was the labored sound of her own breathing that had masked it. Her eyes flew open, struggling to peer through the gloom. She could see nothing in the complete blackness, but she could sense him there nonetheless, no more than a few feet away.

"I think so," she whispered.

Something soft fell against her ribs where she lay. "Put this on." The voice held no emotion, though it was far from flat—full of richness and depth. There was no disobeying it.

Yeva sat up with difficulty, reaching for the object to discover that it was a strip of cloth, finer than any she'd felt in months. Silk, folded many times over. Her fingers closed around it.

"Over your eyes," the voice clarified, impatience emerging in the barest hint of a snarl.

She hurried to comply, fingers shaking. Was he going to take her out of the cell? Was the blindfold so that she could not see him, and implicate him later if she were to be caught again?

The manacle around her wrist clanked open, and for the first time in weeks Yeva was able to press her naked arm against her body without the chafe of iron. She felt like collapsing with relief. But the voice commanded her to rise, and she did so by holding on to the wall and standing on quavering legs. How had she lost so much strength so quickly? And after she'd fought so hard to win it back again. Behind the blindfold she shut her eyes more tightly.

"Follow me," ordered the voice, before the sound of his footsteps whispered against the stone.

"Wait." Yeva turned her head this way and that in the doubled darkness of cell and blindfold. "How can I follow if I cannot see?"

"Can you not track by sound and smell?" There was a brief silence, and then his footsteps again. "Put your hand against my shoulder and I will lead you."

Yeva stretched out a trembling hand until her fingertips found fur. What she wouldn't give for her rich fur cloak, now gracing the shoulders of an opportunistic buyer's wife. She dug her cold fingers deep into her invisible ally's coat and moved away from the wall.

He led her out of the cell and turned left, down what Yeva guessed was a corridor. They turned again, and again, until she lost all sense of direction. She tried to count their steps, but her head spun from fever and cold, and she gave up tracking their route.

From fever and cold—and from the scent. She smelled something musky and wild, something familiar that she could not place. *His fur coat*, she thought, but as soon as she thought it she knew it was not true. This was no dead pelt. *Perhaps my captor owns dogs.* But that could not explain it either, for Yeva knew the smell of dogs well enough to know this was not the same. The hairs rose along her arms, and she was grateful for the solid warmth under her hand, the slow movement of his body beneath his coat.

Her escort came to a halt, forcing her to stop as well. There came a faint whoosh of air, as of a door sliding open, and then a wall of heat struck her. She gasped, lifting her hand from the coat and reaching without thinking for her blindfold.

"Don't." It was more growl than word, spoken so close to her ear that the force of his breath stirred her hair.

Her hand froze, and she fought the burning need to flee blindly back down the corridor. *He is my ally,* she reminded herself, face turning to the unseen heat. *He is my ally. He is not to be feared.*

"Come."

She found his shoulder again, and he led her forward into the room she could not see. Behind her the door slid closed again with a scrape and a click. The cold stone under her bare feet gave way to lush carpet, sending a wave of unexpected pleasure through her. How long since she'd felt such riches? Not for the first time, she wondered where she could possibly be.

Her ally led her forward and then bade her sit. Yeva relinquished her hold on his shoulder with reluctance. The fur had been warm and soft, and she'd found herself enjoying the feel of another person under her hand. She felt around with her feet and discovered a pile of cushions, and sank down onto them. To her left was the crackle and hiss of a fire, heat hammering at her skin.

"You may stay in this room as long as is necessary for you to recover your health," said the voice. Yeva's heart surged. "On one condition."

"What condition?"

"That you never remove the blindfold for any reason. If you do, you will die. Do you understand?"

Yeva swallowed. She would rather die warm and comfortable than cold and ill. But better not to die at all. "Yes. I will not remove it. You have my word."

* * *

"Tell me about your father."

Yeva paused midmeal, swallowing her mouthful of roasted pheasant. "My father," she echoed.

"You speak of your sisters, your servant, your mother. But never your father. Do you hate him so much?"

She blinked behind her blindfold, trying to read the hazy shapes beyond it. Some light made it through the silk, but she could not track anything unless it stood between her and the light. "No. I loved him."

"Then, do you not speak of him because he is dead?"

Yeva's throat closed again, despite having recovered over the past three days from the chill from the cell. Her cough remained, but mostly when she slept. Now, her throat constricted with grief instead.

"How do you know he's dead?" she whispered.

"You said you loved him." The voice emphasized the word *loved*, the past tense sounding final and heavy.

Yeva fell silent, listening to the fire, meal forgotten. Her ally had managed to source more food for her since her reprieve from the cell, the richest of game cooked to perfection. Perhaps he, too, was a hunter. Perhaps he'd understand.

"Before my father met my mother he was the greatest hunter in all of Rus. Maybe the world. He stopped to please her, for it was dangerous work, but in his heart he loved the forest. He was the only one who could venture into its heart, hunt the wildest and strangest of creatures who lived there."

"You have only mentioned sisters. Had he no sons?"

Yeva shook her head. "Only my sisters and me, the youngest." She hesitated. But what did it matter what her ally thought of her? He would not risk the anger of her captor to help her and then turn away because of scandal. She took a slow breath. "When I was young he treated me as he would a son, teaching me what he knew. I hunted at his side. I was happiest there."

"He trained you to hunt? Hunt as he did? With the same skills?" For the first time something colored the heavy voice—surprise, perhaps. Or dismay. Yeva found it difficult to read the emotion.

She lifted her chin. "You disapprove," she commented. "Because I'm a girl?"

"No." The voice paused. "Females are often the best hunters. They must provide for the young and survive when the males are too busy posturing to do so. But this is not the way with humans."

"Humans?" Yeva's thoughts ground to a halt. How could he speak as if he weren't one?

Another pause. "I apologize. I spend all my time here in the forest, and find myself more at home here among the beasts than among men. By now I am more beast than man myself."

This time Yeva had no difficulty reading the emotion there. Bitterness, thick and black and bringing the color to her cheeks. "I don't think that's true," she found herself saying.

"No?"

"No," she replied firmly. "You've helped me when you didn't have to. When whoever put me in that cell could return and punish you for letting me leave."

The air stirred, and Yeva saw a shadow move beyond the blindfold. The shape was huge—her ally must have been closer than she had thought.

"You know nothing," snarled the voice. His steps moving away were heavy on the carpet. The door opened and closed, and Yeva was left in silence again.

BEAST

We pace, more at home right now in our den of earth and cold than within four walls of stone and fire. Over our head the earth trembles with our steps, showering our fur with dirt.

He trained her to hunt as he did. She has his skills. We have been waiting for someone with the skills to rescue her, the skills to serve us, when she has been within our grasp all along. And we nearly let her rot to death in the cell.

Our breath comes in short, angry growls. We must show her what we are, force her to do our will now. We must not waste any more time. And yet . . .

And yet she tells us stories. And it has been

so long since we have heard a voice that was not screaming.

She put her hand on us and did not pull away.

She told us we were not a beast.

We growl, coming to a halt. Even our den smells of her now, and part of us thrills to it, sensing prey. Our mouth fills with saliva and we flee to the world above, to find something on which to feed.

We are always the beast.

SEVEN

"AND SO TO REWARD him for his love and faithfulness, the ghost gave Ivan the chestnut horse. With it he was able to leap higher than any other rider in the kingdom and win the heart of the princess. She knew him by his kiss."

The crackle of the fire at her back was the only applause Yeva received for finishing the tale, but she had grown accustomed to silences from her ally—her friend, as she was coming to think of him. She still had not dared ask his name, for it was clear he wished to remain anonymous. She had long since grown well again, but neither of them had suggested a return to her cell, and so she spent her days by the hearth, relishing its warmth.

The presence at her side shifted, shadows moving across her blindfold. Again she caught the faint tang of wildness, making her heart constrict. She missed the forest, for all she could not complain about her treatment here.

"This Ivan," rumbled the voice, its heavy bass tone weighted still more by deliberate thoughtfulness. "You have mentioned him several times."

To pass the time, she had asked for, and been granted, her arrow-making supplies. The small knife for trimming the wood and feathers was not enough for her to fight her way free, even if she wished to harm her friend. She'd learned to work by touch and feel, and just now she was fitting the fletching at the arrow's end. "He is the hero in many stories," she replied, running the edge of her finger along a strip of fletching, judging its straightness. "Sometimes it is Vasilisa who is the heroine."

"Vasilisa the Beautiful," echoed her friend, the uplift of his voice turning it to a question.

"Yes."

"What is your name?"

The question came suddenly, and Yeva's fingers froze at their work, feathers falling to her lap. "Beauty." Perhaps it was the task she was performing. The word came without thinking. Her father's name for her.

"Beauty?"

"No—no. My name is Yeva. The other is only a nickname. Yeva is my given name."

The voice was silent for a while, and then moved again. This time Yeva felt the brush of fur at her arm and shivered. Why did he continue to wear his coat despite the roaring blaze behind them?

"I shall call you Beauty," he said finally.

Yeva opened her mouth to protest, sure that the sound of her other name would stab deeply into the still-raw wound of her father's death. But in her friend's warm voice it merely felt true, and right, and she exhaled without speaking instead. "What is yours?" she whispered.

"I do not remember."

Yeva longed to pull her blindfold away, read the expression on his face. "How can you not remember your own name?"

"I said I have been here, alone, for many years. When you do not use a thing it withers and becomes dust."

"What does your master call you? The one who captured me?"

Silence.

Yeva swallowed. "I must call you something," she protested gently. "Shall I call you Ivan then?"

His exhale was almost a growl, although the sound no longer frightened Yeva—the thrill had changed from fear to something else entirely. "I am not a hero."

The heat of the fire rose to Yeva's face. She could feel it radiating against her blindfold at the curve of her cheeks. Forcing her voice to remain even, she said softly, "You are to me."

The presence at her side moved abruptly, the sound of footsteps leading away. Yeva clenched her jaw, arrow lying half made in her lap. But just as his footsteps would have reached the door they stopped and came close again, bringing with him that spicy wildness on the warm air.

"Tell me more of this Ivan."

Yeva fought to keep the relief from her tone. "He's in many of the old stories. He's often the youngest of several brothers— and often foolish. But he usually has a kind heart. The most famous story of Ivan is probably the tale of him, the Firebird, and the gray wolf."

The pacing stopped, air going still. Yeva suddenly felt tension snap into place in the room, the hairs on her arms standing up in response. She could not even hear her friend breathe. "Shall I tell that one?" she whispered.

"Yes."

Yeva closed her eyes behind her blindfold as her ally sat down again, fur coat brushing her arm. She began as her father had often started the story, and found she remembered it as clearly as if she'd read it yesterday.

There was once a king who had the most magnificent garden in the world. At the center of the garden was an enchanted tree that bore golden apples. But every time an apple would ripen, the Firebird would come in the night and steal it away.

Furious, the king called his two older sons and told them that whoever caught the Firebird would gain half of his kingdom and become his heir. His youngest son, Ivan, begged to help, but the king saw him as weak and foolish while his brothers were strong, and he refused. So the older brothers set out to catch the bird, and drank and caroused all night in celebration of their impending rewards. But they passed out in the early hours of the morning and when they woke, the apples were gone again.

So the king allowed Ivan to try. True, Ivan was not as strong as his brothers, but he was clever and resourceful. He stayed awake all night and did not touch a drop of wine, and so when the Firebird came he was ready. The bird was quicker than he, however, and so Ivan was only able to catch a single feather from the bird's tail.

The king sent his sons out into the world to catch the Firebird, and again Ivan had to beg to go. When his father finally relented, Ivan set out alone and came to a crossroads with a sign. Whoever took one path would learn hunger and cold, whoever took the second would survive but his horse would die, and whoever took the third would die, but his horse would live. Ivan chose the second path, and soon a huge gray wolf came out of the forest and ate his horse, forcing Ivan to walk. But Ivan was determined, and walked until he fell over with exhaustion.

The wolf took pity on him and offered to carry him on his back, and together they found the kingdom where the Firebird lived in a golden cage.

The wolf warned him not to take the cage, but Ivan was greedy and took both, setting off alarm bells throughout the castle. The ruler of that kingdom caught Ivan and, after hearing his story, said that he could have the Firebird if he would bring him the horse with the golden mane.

And so the gray wolf carried him farther still until they came to the next kingdom, where the horse with the golden mane lived, wearing a beautiful golden bridle. Again the wolf warned him to take the horse without the golden bridle, but Ivan did not listen, and again he was captured. This ruler listened to his story and said that he would let Ivan have the horse if he would agree to capture Yelena the Beautiful, a princess in yet another kingdom, and bring her back to him.

And so the gray wolf brought him to the next kingdom, and warned him not to fall in love with Yelena when he carried her off. Again Ivan did not listen, and when they returned to the second kingdom, Ivan begged the wolf to help him. The wolf agreed to take the form of Yelena to be given to the king, and so Ivan took the horse and kept the woman he loved. The wolf escaped the king and accompanied Ivan, Yelena, and the horse back to the first kingdom, where Ivan again persuaded the wolf to change shapes. Ivan pulled the same trick exchanging the wolf in the horse's form for the Firebird, and again the wolf escaped and met up with him later.

And so Ivan returned to his kingdom with Yelena, the horse, and the Firebird. He and the wolf parted ways, but when he lay down to sleep, his brothers found him. They had been confounded by the very first crossroads and so had done nothing. Jealous of their youngest brother's success, they killed Ivan in his sleep and cut his body into pieces. They agreed that one would marry Yelena, and the other would exchange the Firebird for half their father's kingdom.

But again the wolf felt sorry for Ivan, and so with the help of the water of life, he restored Ivan's body. Ivan awoke in time to ride once more on the wolf's back to stop the wedding and regain his share of the *kingdom, while the wolf ate his treacherous brothers whole.*

After the last words of the story, Yeva fingered the newly shaven shaft of the half-made arrow, listening for signs of life from her companion. He was even quieter than usual; Yeva thought he must be able to hear her heart pounding.

"So it is a happy ending for Ivan?"

Yeva nodded. "He kept the horse and Yelena and the Firebird, and inherited his father's kingdom as well."

"Why did you not tell me this story in the beginning?"

Yeva's fingers closed around the arrow shaft. "It is the most popular, but it's one of my least favorites," she admitted. "It doesn't end right."

"Why?"

She hesitated, trying to think of a way to explain. "Fairy tales are about lessons. Those who are virtuous and true are rewarded, while those who are wicked and greedy are punished. Ivan is said to be clever and resourceful but in this story he seems only greedy and careless. The wolf warns him over and over and Ivan never listens. And yet, Ivan never gets punished. The wolf helps him every time, and neither he nor the wolf have to pay for what they've done. In the end Ivan gets everything he wants and lives happily ever after."

Silence from her companion, though Yeva could hear the soft, rich sound of his breathing not far from her elbow. "You may call me Ivan," he said finally, surprising her.

"Because of that story?"

"Because your Ivan is not a hero."

Yeva turned toward the sound of the voice, arrow craft forgotten. She reached out toward where she guessed his hand or arm might be, fingers closing around fur.

"What are you doing?" The fur pulled away from her abruptly.

Her heart pounded against her barely healed ribs. "I was going to take your hand."

"No." The snarl had returned, but it no longer made her want to scramble back in fear.

"I would never betray you. I want only to see your face."

"You promised," came the voice, low and dangerous. "You gave me your word."

Yeva reached up for the blindfold anyway, only to have her arm knocked back so forcefully that it tingled, numb at her side. "I don't care," she said. "I've come to care for you, Ivan, or whoever you may be. I want to see your face."

She reached up again and this time something huge flung itself at her, knocking her back onto the ground. Her head struck hard enough to stun her, despite the carpet to cushion it. The knotted silk gave way under the blow.

"*You gave your word,*" snarled the voice, his breath hot against her cheek. His weight, fur coat warmed by the fire, pinned her underneath him.

Her heart pounded with fear and longing both, knowing that Ivan's face was only a hand's breadth from hers. Yeva turned her head, the knot loosening yet more—and the silk slipped down from her eyes.

Inches from her face was a nightmarish visage, snarling fangs and red-gold eyes. She screamed, every muscle going rigid as she tried to struggle free, but claws dug into her skin on all sides, giving her no room to move. She stretched out with one arm anyway, ignoring the tearing pain of it, fingers brushing the hilt of her fletching knife.

"*YOU GAVE US YOUR WORD.*" The voice was almost unrecognizable, the roar tangible against her face as the teeth flashed in the firelight. The claws tightened, piercing her skin all over and causing her to cry out in pain and terror.

Yeva's hand closed around the knife, and with a scream she brought her arm up in an arc, sinking the knife to its hilt in the Beast's shoulder. Its roar of rage and pain overtook hers, and she let her arm fall again as the room spun into blackness.

Yeva woke once more in darkness, body cold and stiff. She dragged herself to her knees, her aching body prompting recognition—she was back in the cell. Her fingers found multiple puncture marks across her shoulders and chest and legs. The blindfold was gone, but she was in darkness again. She explored the confines of the cell by feel and found nothing, no manacle and chain, no blanket, and no tray—and no lamp. This time, the door was locked.

No fire, no blanket, no lamp; she had little heat to conserve, but little was better than none. She sank onto the floor and drew her knees up to her body, ignoring the way the movement sent aches screaming down her limbs. She dropped her head, clenching her teeth together.

I am locked in a cell, she said to herself, mind stuttering and unfocused as she tried to follow her father's advice, *with no food and no light and no hope of escape. And the one friend I had is the monster that killed my father.*

Her eyes burned, but when she lifted her head they were dry. Carefully she stretched out her legs one at a time, biting her lips when the movements tugged at sore muscles and punctured skin alike. Then her arms, then her back, then her neck. She had no weapons and no plan but she was quick, and maybe—just maybe—if the Beast thought she was wounded it would give her a chance to run.

She was doing her best to clean the dried blood from her skin when the door swung open, a huge blackness filling the space.

She had never seen the massive shadow before, but then, she had not been looking for it. She had been looking for a shape the size of a man.

"Get up," said the Beast.

Every muscle was rigid. The voice was still the one she knew, the musical bass with hints of wildness. But she recognized its ferocity now—and the voice no longer warmed her. Her bones were like ice.

"No."

"Get up or we kill you now."

Yeva clenched her jaw so tightly it ached. She dragged herself to her feet, playing up the soreness of her muscles and acting more stiffly than she felt.

"Come." The shadow threw the blindfold at her and then moved from the doorway.

Now was her chance. Its back was turned, and she could try to run. Yeva glanced at the lighter area of shadow that told of the empty corridor. *I am the captive of the monster who killed my father,* she thought with sudden crystal clarity.

She hadn't left her sisters behind for nothing. She hadn't tracked her father and discovered him dead, only to die herself the captive of a Beast.

She knew now why she was here. She would see the monster dead.

Yeva fell into step behind it, following it by smell and sound down the corridor. From the sound of its steps it was limping. Her knife had wounded it. She felt a surge of satisfaction so strong her ears rang with the triumph.

"Where are you taking me?" she whispered, lifting the blindfold into place and securing it behind her head.

Into the quiet came its despicable voice once more. "Training."

BEAST

We were wrong. There is no animal in her. The way she speaks to us now, so full of fury, is more human than anything we have experienced in many long years. Animals don't hate. That is the rightful domain of humanity.

It is better this way, that she see us for what we are. We are pleased. She is strong still, despite her illness, and skilled. She will do what we require of her, and it will be done. We will be free.

There is no more subterfuge, no more pretending at humanity. We do not have to provide her assistance or hide in the shadows.

We do not have to listen to her voice or her stories, we do not have to suffer her giving us a name as though we are a man. We do not have to feign feeling.

It is better this way. She has seen us and that, too, is freedom. It will go quickly now. We know this.

It is better.
It is better.
It is better.

EIGHT

YEVA FOLLOWED THE BEAST as it led her through a maze of corridors. She stumbled more than once, but the Beast did not offer its shoulder to guide her, and she did not ask. She thought there was a slight upward slant to their path, but she could not be sure until cold, clear light burst upon her, bright enough to see even through the blindfold.

The sensation of the heavy underground fell away, the air coming alive again with movement, smells, and distant sounds of life. The sun, pale and cold in the winter sky, was tangible on her skin.

For the briefest of moments Yeva forgot her fury, stumbling along through the snow and breathing the sharp freshness of the air as someone who'd been suffocating to death. But her relief faded with each step, as she struggled blindly in shin-deep snow. She focused on each breath, the stabbing of air in her lungs, trying to memorize how far they were going, what turns they made.

"Remove your blindfold."

Yeva halted, reality slamming back into her and jarring loose her half-formed mental image of where they were. She forced her hands to steady as they pulled the blindfold from her eyes. She stood, blinking, half blinded. The sky was overcast but the snow was brilliant enough that she could barely see.

At her feet she made out a familiar shape. Her father's bow, and next to it her quiver.

"That is your target." The Beast sat on its haunches like a huge wolf some distance from her, its immense body in no way diminished now that it was outside instead of in the confines of the corridors. Its thick, shaggy tail wrapped neatly around its body like a cat's.

"You will shoot the target, and if you succeed we will try at a farther distance."

Yeva reached down for the bow, not bothering to shift her gaze from the creature long enough to see what target it was indicating. She ought to have felt relief and triumph that it had provided her with a weapon—but she felt only ice. She fitted the grip to her palm, and though she turned her eyes toward the target, she saw nothing but a red mist descend over her vision.

"Shoot when you are ready."

Yeva drew in a deep breath as she nocked an arrow, mind calculating the arc between the target she was meant to hit and the Beast to the side. Not far. She blinked the haze from her eyes, the bloodlust rising in anticipation. Releasing the breath she was holding, she drew and twisted to the side to aim at the Beast, then released the arrow in one smooth motion.

The Beast barely moved. It lifted one paw and flicked the arrow aside in midair, where it buried itself in a tree.

Yeva stood staring and panting, the hands holding the bow

suddenly nerveless. It was impossible. Nothing could move that fast, animal or man. The Beast stared back at her, the red-gold of its eyes unperturbed.

"Again," it said, with no sign of the fury it had displayed when she'd pulled the blindfold away by the hearth.

For all its power, the bow would not help her. She let her arms fall and dropped the weapon into the snow at her feet.

"No."

The tip of the Beast's tail flicked. Irritation. "You will try it again, or die."

"Kill me, then." Yeva knew she ought to be afraid, but there was only room inside her for anger.

With careful deliberation the Beast rose to its feet, the size of it once again robbing Yeva of breath. It came toward her, each paw landing so softly that it made no sound in the snow. Yeva stood her ground, even when the Beast halted only inches from her face.

"You will do it again," it said in its low, dangerous growl, "or we will kill your family."

Yeva froze.

The Beast sat back down, the musky-sweet smell of its fur nearly overpowering in the frigid cold. "Ah," it said, bitter satisfaction coloring its otherwise emotionless voice. "Yes. You will do as we order from now on, or we will kill them all."

She had told him about each of them, about Lena's scolding and Asenka's twisted foot, Albe's clumsiness and well-intentioned gestures. She had described the trees around the cabin, how it nestled at the fork of a stream that ran to either side of it. She had *described the house*.

"Pick up the weapon." The Beast's eyes bored into hers.

Yeva's began to water from strain and cold, burning in the

freezing air. She stooped, not taking her gaze off the monster as she retrieved the bow. She pulled another arrow from the quiver at her feet, fingers closing around its shaft like she was clinging to her last hope of survival in a howling blizzard.

The Beast rose and turned its back, moving toward where it had been sitting when she removed her blindfold. Yeva lifted her arm to stab the arrow down into its spine.

"If you try to kill us again," said the Beast without turning around, "make certain you succeed."

Yeva froze again, her arm suddenly heavy as lead.

"For if you try and fail, your sisters will pay the price. You we will keep alive long enough to watch."

"Again."

The Beast's voice had become so familiar that Yeva's ears almost didn't register it. She felt it like a vibration deep in her chest, a stirring of the fury still surging through her veins. He brought her outside day after day to shoot at the same target, an old, gnarled tree with a blackened spot of rot the size of her fist. First he made her shoot at thirty paces, then forty, fifty. Her accuracy with her father's stiffer bow was not what it had been with her own, but she'd abandoned her lighter bow when she took up her father's weapons to pursue the Beast that killed him. As her strength improved, though, so did her aim with the old, heavy bow. Each day she was made to practice, and each night she was returned to the frigid, dark cell to eat cold rations and sleep. At first she stayed wakeful and restless, pacing, thoughts thrashing against the confines of this prison, seeking a way out—but as the days passed she could not help but fall into exhausted, dreamless sleep.

Instead of loosing the arrow she'd drawn in numb response

to the command, she lowered her bow and closed her eyes.

"I said *again*." The Beast's voice rose, and though there was no anger in it, Yeva could sense the quickening, the intensity of it. "Your aim today is worse."

"I cannot," Yeva said, dropping both bow and arrow into the well-trodden slurry of ice and snow at her feet. "My shoulders ache—I've had no rest, no time for my muscles to repair themselves."

The Beast—sitting, as it always did, just far enough away that she could not lunge for it—rose up from its haunches and narrowed its red-gold eyes. "The need for rest is a human weakness."

"And I'm human," Yeva snapped, exhaustion robbing her of good sense. For the moment, she couldn't bring herself to care if she angered her captor. For the moment, she forgot about the cabin nestled at the fork of the river, her sisters and her friend, her dogs, the lives she had to protect. For this moment she could only think of the bone-deep ache in her body and the certainty that she could not aim even one more arrow.

"An illusion," the Beast snarled. "You only imagine you need rest."

"Is it an illusion that my arrows cannot strike their target today?" Yeva braced her feet against the ground, determined not to give in to their desire to buckle beneath her and send her sprawling in the slush. "Is it imagination that yesterday I missed the tree entirely and lost one of my arrows?"

The Beast was silent, continuing only to stare at Yeva with that unnerving, unblinking animal gaze. She stood her ground, willing herself not to shiver. Days, maybe weeks, had passed and she still could not reconcile the animal eyes with the fact that its fanged mouth formed speech, that its lips could purse and flatten and curl around words like a man's.

Yeva drew her cloak around herself, stepping back from the bow. "You tell me I am training, but you do not tell me what I'm meant to be training for."

"Because you do not need to know yet."

Yeva clenched her jaw. "You insist I shoot at a dead tree, but unless it is some archery competition in some distant kingdom, this training is worthless. No target stands there, waiting to be shot at again and again."

The Beast didn't answer immediately, and if it were a man, Yeva would think him hesitant. But it only looked at her. Unblinking. Unmoved. Then, ponderously, it replied, "We have need of a hunter."

Yeva's skin prickled, and she suppressed the surge of anticipation threatening to show itself in her features. It was the first hint of an answer she'd ever received from the creature. "Why?"

"There is a certain quarry we require captured." The Beast's bass rumble of a voice was as unruffled as ever.

Yeva scanned the Beast's face for some time before realizing she was searching for some hint of its thoughts in its expression— some *human* hint. But this was no human. She swallowed hard on the white-hot anger that had sustained her since she learned the identity of her captor. "Capture your quarry yourself. You lay traps as efficiently as any hunter."

"We cannot." The Beast's face rippled for the space of a heartbeat. In the lupine features, the glint of teeth, the red-gold eyes—for the tiniest instant, Yeva recognized it. Frustration. Anger.

Helplessness.

"Why not?" Yeva whispered.

"Because we—" The Beast's words halted as suddenly as if its lungs had no air. Its brows drew in, brows Yeva hadn't noticed before. It shook its head, the movement traveling down the creature's body like a shiver until it hunkered low, belly nearly resting in the snow.

Perhaps, if she had not spent so much time in the cell telling stories, bringing to the surface the tales she'd heard as a child, or if she had not spent these last weeks the captive of a creature that could only exist in such tales, Yeva would not have had the thought that came next: *He cannot tell me, for he is under a spell.*

In every fairy tale there were rules. Even the monsters could not break them.

And where, except in fairy tales, did there exist talking beasts?

BEAST

We thought hatred would make it easier. That if she continued to believe we were her father's death, her fear and her fury would free us from our human side. We thought she would become no more than a tool, a weapon to be wielded, an arrow to be loosed from a bow.

We thought . . .

We thought too much.

Because while hatred is a fire only man feels, he does not hate the beast that comes in the night. Mankind fears it, fights it, drives it off, but he does not hate it. No one hates the bear, the wolf. They don't hate the wind or the snow. They don't hate death.

They hate each other.

NINE

YEVA HUDDLED IN THE corner of her cell, cloak drawn tightly about her as she sank into a half doze. The cold seeped from the stones into her body like poison, making her curl more against herself, despite the protests of her muscles. The strain of drawing her father's heavy bow day after day was tearing at the joints in her shoulders, ripping at a knot of tension between her shoulder blades that re-formed tighter and tighter each night she spent in the cold.

She knew she ought to stand, ought to pace the room and stretch and remain as limber as she could. And at first, she had done so each night. But she couldn't bring herself to move anymore. Perhaps if she tore a muscle so she could not draw the bow at all, the Beast would let her rest.

Her mind, as it often did during these dark, silent hours, tried to turn toward thoughts of her family. Of her sisters, and how they would worry; of Solmir, and how long he would continue to care for them; of how long it would take them all to believe she was dead. But she could not afford to think of them, for she could not imagine her home without her father there too, and remembering him was a stab of pain as real as her broken ribs, her aching muscles. She refused to think of them, of any of them. There would be time for grief later, once she had killed the Beast.

A sound beyond the door of her cell brought her sharply back to the present. It was nothing more than the barest whisper, but it was a sound she knew well, from days, weeks, maybe months ago. A sound that meant it was time to resume the story she'd been telling to her invisible ally, waiting in silence just beyond the door.

Her invisible ally. Yeva could have laughed at her blindness. Ally? He was always her captor.

Yeva shivered so violently a sound escaped her lips, a tiny moan snatched up by the hungry stones of the empty room.

"You said you required rest." The Beast's voice was quieter, and for a moment there were two faces in Yeva's mind: the one she'd imagined belonging to her friend, and the one she had seen snarling and roaring in front of her eyes when her blindfold fell away.

She didn't answer.

The Beast's footfalls came again, the soft scrape of his footpads against the stone. He was pacing in front of her door. "You require rest, and we require—" The pacing halted for a heartbeat, then resumed. "*I* require . . . I require talk."

It was the first time since she'd learned what he was that he hadn't referred to himself as "we." Yeva had always imagined there must be others in this place, servants or perhaps other creatures out of the old stories. Someone had cooked the potatoes she'd eaten. Someone had opened her pack and sorted through the medicine bundle, prepared trays for her, lit an oil lamp. The Beast could not have done it, not with the great velvety paws now pacing back and forth before the door.

But the two faces flashed again before Yeva's eyes, and suddenly she wasn't so sure. She swallowed, her throat dry. "Talk?"

"Yes."

Yeva's head spun, and she slipped one hand free of her cloak to press her cold fingertips to her temple. "You want me to *talk* to you? In exchange for rest?"

The footfalls ceased, and silence spread through the stones like the cold. Then the Beast's ferocity returned in the form of the reverberating growl that made some primitive part of Yeva's mind recoil and send urgent commands through her body to flee, hide, defend herself.

"Never mind," he snarled.

And the footsteps retreated, back into the silence and the dark, and Yeva was left alone.

"You may begin."

They were the same words the Beast used every day to signal that Yeva could remove her blindfold for the day's target practice. He always led her to the same spot, far enough from the building that held her cell that she could not see it, could see nothing but trees.

But when she pulled the silk down around her neck this time, it was different. The old, gnarled tree she'd used as a target was nowhere in sight, and the forest around her was new. She hadn't noticed how familiar the other clearing had become. She could see her tracks leading off through the snow, and the Beast's beside hers, the snow indistinct around his paw prints where his fur and his tail had swept it aside.

Her bow and quiver were at her feet as usual, but there was

no clear target. She hesitated, turning toward the Beast, who sat watching her as he always did. "I don't understand," she said slowly.

"You were correct." Only the tip of the Beast's tail moved, flicking side to side where it curled around his haunches. "Real prey does not stand still, waiting to be shot. Today you will hunt."

A spark jumped in Yeva's heart. She stooped to retrieve her father's bow from the snow without taking her eyes from the Beast. "What am I hunting?"

"Whatever you wish."

Yeva's fingers curled around the bow grip, feeling where the carving was suited to larger hands, hands that would never draw it again. "And what's to stop me from running?"

"I will be watching you."

Yeva straightened, feeling a frown crease her forehead. "You'll drive away the game," she protested. "They'll smell you, hear you. They'll know there's a predator after them."

The Beast's tail stirred again, the only outward sign of any impatience. "They will not know I am there."

"It happened when my father was hunting," Yeva argued, hand tightening still more around the bow. The fingers of her drawing hand itched to reach for an arrow—the instinct could not be reasoned with, or convinced of the futility of trying to fire upon the creature.

"No." The Beast's reply was curt, the red-gold eyes the only color besides his fur in the snow-covered wood. But as he stared back at her, he seemed to soften, something about the pupils changing, the roundness of the eyes elongating into features more like a man's. He blinked, then dropped his gaze from hers. "He drove the game away himself."

Yeva opened her mouth to protest, but a flash of memory prevented her from speaking. She saw her father bursting into the house after weeks in the forest, shedding snow as he stomped here and there, wild-eyed and impatient. The same madness that had him shoving her to the ground could have swallowed his skill and stealth as well.

Then a thought stirred, falling into place. "You were watching him," she whispered. "In the wood, before he died."

"Yes."

"You have need of a hunter."

"Yes."

A surge of anger so hot she could not swallow it down flooded Yeva's mouth with the bitter taste of metal, and her hand shook where it gripped her father's bow. "He was the best hunter in this country, perhaps in any country. You were following him, you could see his skill—why kill him? Why tear him to pieces and leave him for scavengers to pick over?"

The Beast's head snapped back up, eyes fixing on Yeva as they narrowed. He didn't answer, but instead went still. Even his flicking tail stopped moving, leaving him so statue-frozen that the snowflakes caught in his fur, quivering with each beat of his heart.

"Why?" gasped Yeva, her voice cracking, passion making her vision blur and body shake. "Answer me!"

The Beast abruptly rose from his haunches and stalked a few paces, tail sweeping long troughs in the snow behind him. By the time he turned, Yeva felt she must have imagined that she'd seen something other than his bestial nature—his wolflike head hung low, gap-jawed, as a predator might scent prey on the wind. "Why we do anything is no concern of yours," the Beast snarled, the words distorted as though speaking around his fangs had suddenly become difficult. "You may begin."

Time seemed to slow, as if caught by the roar of Yeva's blood rushing past her ears, held back by the tension singing through every muscle. Her body stirred before her thoughts did, as if the hand reaching for an arrow from the quiver were giving the commands, and not her heart. She'd fitted the arrow to the string and stepped back on her left foot and drawn the bow before the impulse traveled deep enough to reach her thoughts, and by that time all she could think was *I will kill him, kill him, kill him.*

And by the time she turned toward the Beast, he was gone.

Yeva stood panting, bow still drawn, shoulders shaking with effort and breath steaming the air. The spot where he'd been was trampled, its outer edge more distinct with paw prints, the center only flattened snow and mud. There were no tracks leading away. And as she stood there, even his smell, that strange, ferocious musk, faded into the frost until all that was left was the sting of winter in Yeva's nose while she struggled to catch her breath.

She lowered the bow slowly, the tip of the arrow inscribing an arc through the snow as she moved. *If you try to kill us again,* the Beast had told her, *make certain you succeed.* He'd vanished before she could make that attempt and test the threat behind those words.

Woodenly, jerkily, Yeva slung the bow over her shoulder and slipped the arrow back into the quiver, gathering herself to move. She didn't know whether the Beast's disappearance was magic or skill, whether he could will himself invisible or if he was simply so in tune with the forest that he could use it to mask even his scent. It didn't matter. Either way his ability was greater than hers, and she had no choice but to do as he'd ordered.

So she would hunt.

Yeva looked up at the sky, what she could see of it through the spindly black arms of the trees. The sun's position was concealed by a thick gray blanket of clouds, but she thought one spot of the sky seemed brighter than the rest. She'd been unconscious when the Beast brought her to the cell, and she'd been blindfolded each time she was led away, so she could not know where in the forest she was. But her father's hunting cabin was north through the wood from the town where they'd once lived, and Yeva knew the Beast's lair had to be farther into the dark heart of the forest than the cabin. So she chose the direction she thought might be south—and struck out.

Despite the weeks of captivity, she fell into her old habits like she'd fall into a comfortable bed—the long-legged strides that ate up the ground without overtaxing her, the tuning of her ears to register each new sound and file it away as part of the background canvas. Compared to the silence of her cell the forest was alive with color and sound—the shading of the snow beneath an old gnarled tree, ranging from palest ice blue to deeper lilac, told of a hollow there, and a burrow beneath. The stirring out of the corner of her eye of a branch, far above her, betrayed the path of a squirrel leaping treetop to treetop. The harsh cry of a distant jay warned his fellows of an intruder, and told Yeva to move more carefully, more quietly.

And all around, crossing this way and that like trails on a map of the invisible roads of the forest, were animal tracks. Some were fresh, like the long hopping troughs left by rabbits, or the delicate holes of dainty-pawed foxes trotting circles around their territories. Others were older, half filled with snow blown across them, more difficult to read.

Yeva's nose caught a faint, quick breath of a musky scent and her heart jumped, thoughts immediately conjuring an image of the Beast—but this scent was different, duller and more familiar. A few moments of searching uncovered a tree with long rents in its bark and tufts of brown-black fur caught in the splinters. Somewhere nearby a bear was hibernating with her young. Yeva could read that signpost as clearly as if it were spelled out with letters, and she gave the area a wide berth.

Time passed, impossible to track without a clear view of the sun—an hour, maybe two, and the back of Yeva's mind began to prickle, summoning thoughts that more and more she couldn't ignore. *Where is the Beast? It's been hours since I saw or smelled even a hint of him.*

And then, *Perhaps I can run. . . .*

He'd promised that he could disguise his presence from the animals whose senses were so much sharper than Yeva's, and it was true that the only creatures startled from burrow and den were driven out by Yeva's steps, not some unseen predator's. But did that mean he was telling the truth? Or did it mean that he was no longer following her?

There is something out there, her father had whispered, as he stared mad-eyed and wild at the fire in the hearth. *Something cunning. Tracking me.*

Yeva, alone in the forest, shivered because she knew she wasn't alone.

Despite the hairs lifting on the back of her neck, her heart seemed to lift too, surrounded by the world she knew, the world she loved. Though she was still a captive, for these few hours she was free, and freer than she'd ever been on her hunting forays from her father's cabin. Something about this world, the Beast's valley, made her life at home seem like a far-distant memory. Her steps came easier, and the ache in her ribs seemed to ease as she breathed the fresh winter air. The tiniest tendril of a feeling flickered in her heart, licking out like flames to warm her freezing toes and aching fingers. She felt . . . at *home.*

She came across the fresh tracks of a solitary deer almost by accident, her thoughts preoccupied. She had rarely hunted deer on her own before—her bow was not heavy enough to consistently puncture a deer's thicker hide. But her father's bow was. She pointed her boots in the direction of the deer's tracks and set off.

Without knowing when the last snow had fallen, or whether there had been recent wind to disturb the top layer of snowfall, it was impossible to know how long ago the deer had passed this way. It could have been an hour, or days. But she had no other choice than to follow where the tracks led, and hope it would bring her some success. By whatever measure the Beast was using.

She'd been following the trail for an hour or two when a sound, distinct from the background tapestry of noises she'd cataloged, interrupted her. She paused midstep, one hand reaching for the bow over her shoulder, and listened.

Something was coming toward her, and coming fast. Too large for fox or rabbit, but too small for bear or boar. The cracking, crashing noise of underbrush told of a creature with great, leaping strides, and as the seconds stretched, she heard labored breath coming in great renting gasps.

A wolf?

Yeva grabbed for the bow, pulling it off her shoulder and nocking an arrow to the string in a second. She braced herself, facing the sound of the oncoming animal, eyes searching the frozen wood.

There. A torrent of motion, a furrow of flying snow and twigs. She caught a brief flash of fur amid the underbrush, not the shaggy gray she'd expected, but a pale gold. A wheezy yelp split the air, and Yeva froze, confusion washing through where certainty and had been moments before. *That's no wolf, that's . . .*

The creature burst out of the bushes and flung itself at Yeva, knocking her backward into the snow. All was fur and yelps and whines and a tongue bathing her face, and freezing-cold paw pads stabbing at her gut, her thighs, a tail beating at her knees, her face, as the creature turned and turned and barked and panted hot breath on her skin.

"Doe-Eyes!" Yeva cried, her voice tearing, grief and love and relief and fear tangling in her throat. How long must her dog have been searching for her? And in the kind of snow and cold she was not bred to withstand. "Oh, Doe-Eyes—you bad dog, you wonderful, terrible thing—"

Then Doe-Eyes stomped on her chest in her enthusiasm to get as close to her mistress as possible, and Yeva's ribs, still only partially healed, seared white-hot. Yeva let out a shriek of pain before she could stop herself.

And then the Beast was there.

He came from nowhere, snarling rage and fury, fangs bared and fur bristling with readiness. He leaped toward Yeva, turning her yelp of pain to a scream of genuine terror, and she pulled herself in tightly to shield herself from the blow she knew was coming—

And then she opened her eyes to find the Beast standing over her, growling and shaking himself, staring down Doe-Eyes, who was now only a pace or two from her, all four legs planted in the snow, her own teeth bared.

She felt the Beast gathering himself to attack, felt it like she could feel her own intentions, and she threw herself forward, grabbing for his shoulder, too suddenly fearful to realize it was the first time she'd touched him since the blindfold fell away and she saw who—what—he was. Too fearful to process what she'd seen—that he was protecting her.

"No!" she cried, and felt his muscles bunch and halt under her hand. "No! She's my friend—don't—"

The Beast paused, the lupine head turning so he could fix his eyes on Yeva once more. The pupils, dilated with the rush of the hunt, suddenly contracted in the snowy glare as the fight left his gaze.

"I—" he said, and then Doe-Eyes leaped.

She was a fraction of his size, and built for speed, not for fight—her long slender limbs let her vault as high as his shoulder, her teeth sinking into the flesh there and gripping. Her eyes were frantic, wild, full of fury toward the Beast she thought was attacking her mistress.

The Beast gave a little roar, no more than a sluggish ripple of annoyance, and gave his great body a shake that dislodged the dog and sent her flying. Yeva's heart shriveled, then snapped as Doe-Eyes collided with a tree and dropped into a heap in the snow, unmoving.

BEAST

I moved without thought.

Instinct. Animal. Nothing more. The actions of a predator defending its kill, its territory, its property.

And yet we did not decide to act, I did. Alone. I heard her voice, her stories, her softness as she spoke of her family, and her iron as she spoke of me—I heard her scream, and I moved without thought.

We need her skills. That is all. Only she can free us from this torment, and that is what we were protecting. Our freedom. Our lives. Our hope.

And yet . . .

TEN

"NO!" YEVA SCRAMBLED FROM beneath the Beast,
who was still standing over her. Ignoring him, she lurched to her
feet and sprinted to the spot where Doe-Eyes had fallen.

Her dog lifted her head, and Yeva gasped for a breath as her
heart started once more. Doe-Eyes whined at her, tail thumping
once in pathetic appeal. She tried to stand, fumbling in the snow
and yelping in pain.

"No—stay." Yeva pressed her hand against the dog's head,
firm and warm. "Lie down, don't move." That she was hurt
somewhere was obvious, but Yeva could not see where. If she was
bleeding, it was internal.

She felt the Beast move up behind her, but could not find any
spare feeling for him—her attention was on Doe-Eyes.

The Beast rumbled once, an echo of the growling roar he
gave when he reappeared. "She will die," he said, voice as still and
calm and emotionless as it ever had been.

Yeva whirled, the movement kicking up snow. "No! She will *not.*"

The Beast dropped onto his haunches, staring at her with those disconcerting eyes, wrapping his tail around himself and tilting his head like a great cat, unconcerned. "Why should it matter?"

"Because I love her," Yeva snapped back. "She's mine. She came here searching for me. She's my responsibility. Do you not understand loyalty? Love? Do you have no concept of anything other than the hunt?"

The Beast did not answer, continuing to stare, continuing to sit, continuing to exist in that hateful way, as though everything Yeva said was of no consequence. As though everything she thought or felt or did was a minor irritation to him, an annoyance to be borne and dismissed.

Yeva spat a wordless cry at him and turned back to Doe-Eyes, reaching out to run a light hand down her dog's body, watching her and trying to see if any spot caused her pain.

The Beast's voice came again after a moment. "Her leg is broken."

Yeva glanced over her shoulder. "How can you know that?"

The Beast blinked. "How can you not?"

Yeva ran her hand down first one foreleg, then the other— then jumped as Doe-Eyes yelped, her tongue lolling out immediately after, as if apologizing for having felt the pain at Yeva's touch. "That's the only injury?" she asked, eyes still on her dog.

"Yes," said the Beast.

"You said she would die," Yeva protested, stroking her dog's head, doing her best to keep her still.

"She will. In this cold, unable to walk or feed herself, she will die of starvation or exposure. It is . . . it is merciful to end her suffering." The Beast paused, his gaze troubled again, that same look as before, like a man would furrow his brow. "I will do it if you wish."

Yeva's hands trembled, and she kept one on Doe-Eyes as she stared at the Beast. One part of her longed to scream at him for his callous dismissal of life, to rail against the cold heartlessness of his offer to kill her beloved Doe-Eyes, her only friend in this bleak wood. But there was another part of her, the same corner of her heart that could read the scratches in a tree and tell the difference between the rustle of a rabbit and that of a squirrel. And that part of her heart ached with sudden understanding.

In the wild, in *this* wild, it would be merciful to kill a wounded animal. And more merciful still not to make her be the one to deliver the killing blow to her own companion.

But what could a Beast know of mercy?

Yeva drew in a shaking breath. "How far are we from—from your home? I will carry her."

The Beast paused, either calculating the distance or hesitating to share the information, Yeva did not know. "You cannot carry her if you are blindfolded."

"No," agreed Yeva, gazing back at him.

The Beast's tail twitched, darting one way, then the other. "It is not far," he said finally. "Follow me."

Doe-Eyes was not a small dog, and though the weeks of drawing her father's bow had strengthened her shoulders, Yeva still staggered under her dog's weight after the first hour. The Beast did not offer any help, and Yeva did not expect him to—if she ever drew too near him, Doe-Eyes would stiffen in her arms, legs flailing about as her instincts told her to get her feet on the ground in order to defend herself and her mistress.

After casting a few glances her way, the Beast stalked on ahead of them, as if he were frustrated by Yeva's slow pace. But as he moved, his bulk trampled the snow ahead of Yeva's steps, making her journey considerably easier. Though he clearly had some way of traveling through the forest without leaving a sign, now he walked like any common beast, forging a path ahead.

Now and then Yeva set Doe-Eyes down in order to rest her back, and the dog would hobble a short distance on three legs. Though Yeva knew she must be in considerable pain, Doe-Eyes kept gazing up at her with that gap-jawed smile of hers, tongue lolling out, eyes seeking assurance.

The Beast led them up a long slope, a slope Yeva did not remember descending while blindfolded. She assumed he must have led her away by some other route, and was now taking a more direct path. Up ahead the trees thinned, telling Yeva that they were approaching a ridgeline overlooking one of the many valleys in the forest. She set Doe-Eyes down again in anticipation of pausing at the top of the ridge, and was unable to prevent the groan that escaped her lips. The bones in her spine popped in protest as she straightened, and she pressed her hands into the small of her back to stretch the muscles.

When she opened her eyes again the Beast had stopped. He was watching her. That unblinking stare was still unnerving, but the rush of terror that ran through Yeva every time the massive creature looked her way had dwindled to a trickle. He was still frightening, alien, unpredictable—but she found she could return his stare now without shivering.

As if sensing her thoughts, the Beast broke his eyes away first and looked toward the thinning trees. "My home is in the . . . valley," he said haltingly, as though he had to pause to remember the right words. "You will not ask me questions."

Yeva knit her brows and took a step toward the ridge. "What do you mean? Why would I—"

"Did I not just tell you there were to be no questions?" The Beast's voice quickened with irritation.

"You did. But I didn't agree to your terms."

The Beast drew himself up on his haunches. "There is no negotiation. I gave you an order."

"How nice for you." Yeva clicked her tongue at Doe-Eyes, who was sniffing furiously at a patch of yellow snow left by a passing fox. The dog left the spot reluctantly, falling into hobbling step beside her mistress as Yeva set off for the ridge.

She felt the Beast's consternation, heard it in the wordless rumble of protest as she passed him. She regretted moving ahead instantly—it had been some time since she'd had to break her own trail through the snow, and she'd grown used to the trampled path left in the Beast's wake. But she wouldn't let the creature see her struggle. She fought her way through the snow, keeping her eyes down.

It wasn't until a flicker of light caught her eye that she looked up and found a valley opening below her. The overcast sky was clearing in spots, letting trickles of sunlight out to wash the vista ahead. A river ran through the valley, only a narrow ribbon of treeless white expanse in the frozen winter. The trees thinned off to one side of the valley, suggesting a meadow or marsh beneath its blanket of snow, and on the far side stood a ridge of small mountains, barely high enough for their peaks to clear the tree line and stand stark white in the patches of sun.

But none of this was what held Yeva's gaze. Because in the

bottom of the valley, straddling the river nestled in the foothills, was a castle.

Yeva stood stunned, dimly aware of Doe-Eyes leaning against her legs. The castle sat dark and gray, as much a part of the landscape as the trees or the distant mountains. Its peaked roofs were coated with snow, and from this distance it hardly seemed real—like a picture of a castle that, as soon as Yeva moved, would betray itself as fake.

The Beast waded past her, his great body low to the ground and churning up the snow like a plow in the fields. He did not pause to admire the sight, or to take in Yeva's shock, but rather began making his way down into the valley. Yeva stood until Doe-Eyes gave the tiniest of whines, and jerked her out of her confusion. She swallowed hard, stooped to pick up the dog, and moved to follow the Beast.

BEAST

We will not break the terms of our sentence. We cannot explain, or we risk remaining trapped together for the rest of eternity. But the girl's face, when we turn to look at her, carries a thousand questions, and she is clever. We must tread with care.

Do you not understand loyalty, she asked us, or love?

We wanted to answer: no. They are human concerns, and we have not been human for centuries. We are, we have always been, beast.

But the question hangs on the air like the smell of a coming storm, and we fear the change the storm brings.

ELEVEN

AS THEY NEARED THE castle, Yeva saw that it was in terrible disrepair. Crumbling stone, cracked by centuries of freezing and thawing, was covered in frozen lichen, and many of the great carved gargoyles lining the eaves were broken or missing altogether. The windows were dark and cold, and many of them shattered, leaving only carved stone frames around the blackness beyond.

The palace looked like it had been abandoned for centuries.

Most of the building lay on the other side of the river, with a gatehouse on the near side, connected to the rest by a bridge. Though Yeva hesitated at the idea of crossing such an ancient, crumbling structure, the Beast continued on ahead without pausing.

If it can hold his weight, Yeva thought dubiously, *it must be able to hold mine.* But then, the Beast seemed able to make himself as light as air when he chose, to leave no prints in the snow and make no sound as he moved.

Yeva walked very, very carefully.

On the other side of the bridge, a section of the palisade lining the walk had crumbled away, and Yeva saw a well-trodden path leading down toward the river. Churned mud and snow led to a hole in the rock foundation supporting the castle, some dank hollow or cave. A home befitting a Beast. Yeva half expected the Beast to turn and lead her down the slope, but instead he set his shoulder to one of the great doors at the far end of the courtyard and shoved until the rotting wood groaned open wide enough for them to slip through.

The only light inside came from a row of grime-coated windows high above, centuries of cobwebs and dust turning the pale winter sunlight the color of dusk. The Beast kept moving without pause, able to see in the dark with those animal eyes, but Yeva stumbled when her feet encountered a broken stone in the floor. She gasped and nearly dropped Doe-Eyes, who yelped as Yeva's grip shifted and she jostled the injured leg.

Yeva heard the Beast stop, no more than a change in the way the air moved. She couldn't see him, only a shift in the shadows ahead. "Wait here," he said, and before Yeva could answer, he was gone.

Yeva dropped to her knees on the cold stone floor, uncertain what the Beast meant her to wait for, but grateful for the rest. Doe-Eyes settled beside her and laid her head in her lap, and though it was too dark, Yeva saw in her mind the look the dog was giving her: eyes rolled up, seeking Yeva's face, tail thumping in the dust. She stroked Doe-Eyes's ears, and stared up toward the thin gray light trickling down from the windows high above.

The castle was not large—or rather, it was far larger than any building Yeva had ever seen, including the baron's estate, but it was far smaller than the castles Yeva had seen depicted in paintings and tapestries. The castles of old stories were vast and sprawling, with fantastical turrets and buttresses that stretched toward the sky. This one was more compact, lacking the ornamentation and fancy of the ones in pictures. *This was the sort of castle that could have been defended in a siege,* she thought.

The Beast was gone so long that Yeva considered lying down right there on the stones to sleep. But just as she started to lean over, the shadows ahead of her moved abruptly. A flame sprang to life—a lantern, unshielded. Yeva could not quite see how the Beast managed it without fingers, and yet there he stood, sitting on his haunches, the lantern hanging from one massive paw.

"Here," he said, blank-faced.

Yeva pulled herself up, getting to her feet with some difficulty, as her abused muscles had stiffened. She reached out for the lantern, willing her arm to steady despite its desire to tremble, so close to the Beast's claws.

The Beast turned again without speaking, and led Yeva across what must have once been a grand foyer. The lantern only cast enough light for Yeva to see the floor beneath her feet and the barest hint of the room around her, but she spied a great stone staircase off to the right, so wide she could have lain down across each step many times over. She got the impression of vast tapestries against the wall, and she veered off in that direction a little, keeping one eye on the Beast as she lifted the lantern higher.

She saw only faded cloth and dust, too old and too dirty to reveal any images underneath, and a twinge of disappointment took the place of her curiosity.

"This way," said the Beast, voice quickening in that way it did when he was annoyed.

Yeva saw that he was standing before a smaller door that

stood ajar, opening onto a narrow staircase leading down. Yeva knew what lay in the dark under-places of castles. She drew back, and Doe-Eyes, hobbling at her side, dropped to her haunches.

The Beast halted when she did, and Yeva saw the gleam of his eyes catching the lamplight.

"Don't make me go back to that cell," Yeva blurted, before she had even fully resolved to speak. "You bring me out, you make me hunt for you, but you keep me locked away where I cannot see the sky, cannot tell what weather has come and gone in the night—how can I know how old a set of tracks is if I don't know when the last snow fell, or whether the wind has been strong enough to stir snow from the tree branches? How can I learn the forest well enough to track its creatures if I never know where I am, or where I'm going?"

The words came out in a rush, her voice rising with the strength of her plea. She could not live out the rest of this existence, however long it took before the Beast was done with her, in a locked room of stone.

"I'll die in there—the part of me that hunts will die, anyway—and I'll be useless to you. And Doe-Eyes—she wasn't built for cold. Her leg will ache in there, with no warmth, and she'll never heal properly if I can't see her to treat her and make her well. I—"

"The dungeons," said the Beast calmly, interrupting her, "are through the door on the other side of the hall."

The rest of Yeva's breath fell out in a stuttering gasp, punctuated by the wavering light of the lamp dangling from her hand.

"My home," the Beast went on, "when I choose to live there, is down here."

Yeva swallowed. *Here*, where the Beast had been leading her.

She shifted her weight, her tired muscles trembling and making the flame dance and shiver. "All right, then."

The narrow stairway curled around and around, and as they descended farther into the depths beneath the castle, the air grew colder and heavier. Yeva began to shiver in earnest— not from exhaustion or fear, but from a cold more penetrating than the bitter wind outside. This cold crept in from everywhere, chilling all of her, even her bones, despite her cloak and thick wool undergarments. Doe-Eyes managed the stairs with great difficulty, but it was too narrow for Yeva to carry her, and even if she could, she needed her hands to keep from slipping. The steps were worn low in their centers, bowing inward by centuries of feet carving smooth hollows in the stone that threatened to send Yeva's boots sliding.

The staircase ended in a narrow hallway with doors on either side. Yeva guessed that this area must have once housed the castle's servants, and she wondered again how the Beast came to live here; whether the castle was in ruins when he found it, or whether—and this made her shiver all the more—he was the reason the castle had been abandoned.

The Beast halted in front of a door a few down from the staircase, and lifted one paw for the latch. Yeva raised the lantern, determined this time to see the trick of it, how he mastered human tasks with nothing but his claws—but despite the light on him and the door latch, her eyes couldn't quite grasp what they were seeing. Her gaze kept trying to slide from what was happening. However he managed it, he opened the latch as easily as she would have done, and pushed the door open.

Beyond, the room was dim and cold. But as Yeva stepped forward, her boots hit carpet. She paused. Below her feet was a lush red rug, and as she looked around, she realized it was the room the Beast had brought her to when she was ill. It was furnished with dilapidated, mismatched furniture, obviously from various rooms of the castle. Some of it seemed in better care, if faded, while other items, like a crooked, battered table that stood on three legs and a stack of moldering books in place of its fourth leg, wouldn't have been fit for a hovel. The floor was covered by overlapping rugs of clashing colors. Along one wall was a fireplace, and though it held only ashes and blackened charcoal, next to its hearth was a stack of feathers and hafts—Yeva's arrow-making supplies. And there, some distance from them, was her fletching knife. Its blade was stained rusty brown, and with a jolt, Yeva remembered stabbing it down into the Beast's shoulder as he railed at her for removing her blindfold.

You gave us your word, he'd roared. At the time, she'd been too terrified to think. But now, as the Beast stood aside while she explored the room, she wondered at the depth of his fury. He scarcely seemed to notice her stabbing him, but the betrayal, the breaking of her word, sent him into such a fury that the memory of it made Yeva's body grow colder still.

Yeva halted in the center of the room, trying not to think of the faded blue divan a few paces away, and how easy and lovely it'd be to drop onto its moldering cushions and close her eyes. But the Beast was still there, and as exhausted as she was, that primitive part of her brain would never be able to dismiss the presence of a predator in the room with her.

"You may remain here," the Beast said coolly, "as long as you give your word that you will not try to escape, and that you will not try again to kill us. Remember that we know where your family lives, that we have watched them, that we could kill them at any time."

Yeva swallowed hard, this time forcing her hand to still.

"I give you my word," she said slowly, "that I will not run away."

"You lied to us once," the Beast said softly.

"Perhaps I regret doing so." Yeva's own voice quieted. For it was true. Maybe, if she had not let curiosity get the better of her, she would never have learned the identity of her captor, and she could have gone on in ignorance, telling stories to her friend by the fire.

The Beast was silent for a long time, so long that Yeva's eyes began to play tricks on her. His form melted back into the shadows cast by the lantern, and she began to wonder if he was even still there. When he spoke again, she nearly jumped.

"You promised not to run," he murmured. "You did not promise not to try to kill me."

"No," Yeva agreed. "I didn't."

The Beast stood in silence again for a few seconds. Then came the oddest, most unexpected of sounds—a bass rumble, a quick burst of rich velvet, lacking the somber chill his voice usually carried.

He was *laughing*.

Before Yeva could react, the Beast was gone.

BEAST

She believes she can kill us. She wants to avenge her father's death, letting hatred and fury fuel her. Her word not to run comes easily because she has no desire to flee—not until we are dead.

She has a fire to her that we have not seen, have not felt, in a long time. That the fire wants to consume us makes no difference— that passion will make her stronger, faster. More useful to us. That is all that matters. Fire cannot hurt us.

And yet, when we light her a lantern, there is a moment as we watch the wick flare in the darkness—a moment in which I want to touch the flame.

Just to see if I can still be burned.

TWELVE

YEVA DID WHAT SHE could for Doe-Eyes. After lighting a fire in the cold hearth from the flame of the oil lamp, she broke an arrow haft in two for splints, which she bound to the broken leg with strips torn from her tunic. If she'd had the medicines she'd brought with her, she could use the cypress salve she'd applied on her own ribs, but she had no way of summoning the Beast to return. Nor did she feel like pressing her luck with him further.

As Doe-Eyes heaved a noisy sigh and rolled onto her back, all four paws in the air and belly exposed to the fire, Yeva leaned against the edge of the divan and closed her eyes.

That laugh.

Beasts did not laugh. True, Doe-Eyes smiled at her—but it was not a smile the way most humans would recognize it. Yeva knew she was seeing happiness when her dog's mouth fell open and the tongue lolled out, and it translated into a smile in her mind because she knew Doe-Eyes, knew each twitch of her tail or flick of her ears, and what they meant. But the laugh from the

Beast required no translation, no learned interpretation of his body language.

The laugh was *human.*

It was one thing to wish to hunt down and destroy the animal that killed her father. It was entirely another to think that what had killed him was, in some small way, human. It made his death something else.

It made his death murder.

A rabid animal, a man-eater, deserves nothing more than a swift death to spare anyone else the fate her father had suffered. But a murderer?

That deserved a kind of vengeance that turned Yeva's heart to ice.

Behind her closed eyes, images played like light through colored glass. Fragmented, flashing so quickly from one to the other that her thoughts became as scattered as the light itself. The Beast's snarling maw, inches from her. The calm with which he spoke of her family's torture and death if she betrayed him. The anguish in his eyes when the blindfold fell away and she saw his face. The swath of trampled snow carving a path for her to carry her wounded dog with greater ease.

At some point the still images became moving scenes of things remembered and things imagined, and soon the scenes became dreams, and Yeva slept.

Yeva was awakened the next morning by Doe-Eyes's urgent whining and a cold nose digging into the crook of her elbow. Though she could not tell in the windowless room whether it was morning, she felt like she'd been asleep for days. But as she rubbed at her eyes, she saw that her bow was missing, and her quiver of arrows. He'd taken her weapons. Even the fletching knife that had lain on the floor ever since she'd stabbed him was gone, leaving only a spatter of old blood where it had been.

Doe-Eyes whined again and Yeva slipped off the divan and into a crouch, assuming she'd see her favoring the injured leg. Instead Doe-Eyes gave an awkward, urgent sideways hobble, which, after a moment of confusion, Yeva recognized with a burst of clarity.

"You'll have to hold on," Yeva told the dog, thinking with dread of the long flight of stairs required to reach the outdoors. "And promise not to wet my tunic if I carry you, because I only have the one."

The Beast had not forbidden her to leave the room, only to flee the castle entirely, but her hand trembled anyway as she reached for the latch. It gave under her touch, and the door swung outward. Doe-Eyes hobbled past her, galloping in a stiff-legged, slipping way up the staircase ahead of Yeva. At least she would not have to try to carry her and the lantern.

Yeva felt as wobbly as her dog as she followed in Doe-Eyes's wake. She found that the staircase was not as long as she'd remembered from the day before, that exhaustion had stretched the distance out in her memory. Doe-Eyes remembered the way, and as soon as Yeva opened the door at the top of the staircase, Doe-Eyes scrambled forth, making for the massive front doors.

They still stood open, and a faint spray of snow blown in by the wind glistened in the sunlight cast upon the floor. She had not noticed yesterday that the floor was a polished marble, smooth except for the places where the stone had cracked after centuries of the castle settling and shifting. Doe-Eyes bolted toward the sunlight, and Yeva trailed after her.

The clouds had cleared in the night, and the glare of the sun on the snow was so blinding Yeva had to stand just inside the doors, holding her arm across her eyes to shade them and squint to track her dog's progress. Doe-Eyes went only a few paces down the outer wall of the castle before dropping into a crouch to relieve herself.

Yeva turned her face toward the brilliant morning. The sun was only a few handspans above the far mountains, but it was still bright enough reflected on the snow to make her eyes water and nose itch with the urge to sneeze. She wiped at her eyes and scanned the valley, tracking the river from where it passed under the bridge before her, on toward where it vanished in the trees to the west.

There was no sign of the Beast. No new tracks led from the door except those Doe-Eyes had just made, and though it was difficult to tell new tracks from old, Yeva didn't think any of the churned frozen slush leading down to the cave was fresh. So where had the Beast spent the night?

Somewhere in the castle, Yeva knew, she'd find whatever she needed to survive. Kitchens, latrines, perhaps even some room not too badly decayed for her to sleep in. The Beast might prefer to live deep underground, but Yeva could not bear the thought of spending one more night with the weight of all that stone over her head. And if nothing else, it would be impractical to bring Doe-Eyes up and down those stairs every time she needed to go out.

Yeva decided to explore. A part of her shrank from the idea, uncertain what horrors she might uncover in a castle prowled by a cursed Beast. But the rest of her thrilled to the thought, curiosity settling in and overwhelming her fear.

Because there was another reason to search the corners of this crumbling, ancient castle. Somewhere, somehow, she would find the key to destroying this Beast. He was too fast and too strong for axes or bows, but she would find a way. She *would* discover the secret to killing him.

Now that her urgency had eased, Doe-Eyes was moving much more stiffly on her wounded leg. But Yeva could not order the dog to stay put. Whenever she tried, Doe-Eyes would drop down onto her haunches, tail wagging furiously—and then, as soon as Yeva turned her back to leave the great foyer, she'd hear Doe-Eyes's toenails click-clicking against the marble and then feel her hot breath on the backs of her calves.

"Fine," Yeva told her finally, in fond exasperation. "You can come along. But don't complain to me when your leg hurts tonight."

Doe-Eyes only grinned at her, hobbling along, lolling tongue jouncing with every step. In truth, Yeva was glad for the company.

She kept her explorations to the ground floor for Doe-Eyes's sake. She found room after room of faded tapestries and grand marble floors. One room held piles of rusted, ancient armor scattered at regular intervals—a display room, a decorative armory. Another room held a dining table so long Yeva could not have thrown a butter dish from one end to the other. Some of the chairs were missing—others were broken into pieces, or rent apart, their cushions spilling stuffing like entrails onto the floor.

She came to another hall, lined on one side with what had once been a series of stained-glass windows, most of which were smashed now. Snow had blown in through the empty stone frames, lying in wispy drifts in front of each window. Yeva crossed over toward one that still had some pieces of the original glass clinging to its edges. She reached up to trace her fingers over the vivid gold tips of a bird's wing. There'd been no illustrations in her father's book of tales, but Yeva had always imagined the Firebird this way: wings outstretched, golden, shining even in the palest winter light. She felt a sudden pang of loss for the images the windows had once held.

Her boots squeaked against the blown snow as she turned, but the sound made her pause. True, her steps had crunched against the snow, but not on the broken glass that should have been scattered everywhere if centuries of storms had blown the windows in. Yeva crept to the edge and gripped the window frame as she leaned out, peering down below. There was only the empty expanse of a snow-covered courtyard. But she knew that somewhere beneath the drifts of white would be the remains of these windows. Because someone had broken them from the inside.

Yeva left the snowy hall and moved on. She found the latrines, and the kitchen, covered in cobwebs, each pot and dish dull with dust and age. She found no bedrooms, for they must have been on the second or third floor, but she did stumble across enough sitting rooms with moldering divans and sofas that she could certainly make a bed for herself if she could stand the smell of mildew and age. Given a choice between the cleaner divan in the Beast's room underground and a pallet on the floor of a sitting room within reach of the outdoors, she'd choose the latter without hesitating.

Her stomach was growling unhappily, but Yeva had seen no sign yet of the Beast, or of food he'd left for her. She'd given her word not to run away, but did that include leaving the castle to find something to eat? He'd confiscated her bow and she had no wire for snares, but even in winter she might be able to find edible roots if she searched. Though roots would do little to satisfy her hunger.

If only she had some way of finding the Beast and asking for her bow.

As if the thought had summoned him, a roar echoed through the halls, vibrating through the soles of Yeva's boots. Her heart jumped into a flurry, and Doe-Eyes pressed in sideways against her leg, ears flung back flat against her skull. Yeva pushed the instinctual flash of fear down.

He needs me, she reminded herself. *He won't hurt me.*

And yet he'd killed her father.

The sound came again, and this time Yeva thought she heard words in it. *"Girl!"* the Beast was roaring. "Where are you? Come."

Irritation rose up, warming her where fear had frozen her feet to the ground. "Who does he think I am?" she asked Doe-Eyes. "Some quivering servant? To be summoned whenever he wishes?"

Doe-Eyes didn't answer.

"Girl!" the roar came again. "COME."

Yeva's hands balled into fists, and she took off back the way she'd come. From the many-faceted echo of the Beast's roar, she guessed he was in the grand foyer. She burst into the hall, Doe-Eyes skittering along beside her, and drew in a breath to shout back at the monster as soon as she saw his great bulk silhouetted by the pale light coming from the open door.

But the Beast was laden with something, leaning backward and dragging a large burden in his teeth. He stepped sideways, ears flicking straight up as he heard her footsteps, and halfway turned. The thing he was dragging was a deer, glassy-eyed as its head lolled toward Yeva. The Beast stopped, his great red-gold eyes rolling toward Yeva, his teeth clamped around the base of the young buck's neck. He opened his mouth to drop his burden, working his jaw for a moment as if relaxing the muscles there.

"I have brought you food." The Beast staggered a step to the side, then dropped onto his haunches, jaw still hanging slightly open as he tried to conceal his quicker breathing.

Yeva was struck so suddenly and so vividly by a memory that her own mouth fell open. He looked so very much like Pelei, her other dog, whenever he brought home a dead squirrel or rabbit he'd caught—where Doe-Eyes was tidy, Pelei would bring the mangled carcasses straight into the house, deposit them on Lena's clean rug, and then stand there amid the blood and the fur, panting and grinning proudly as if to say, *Aren't I a good dog?*

The Beast was still watching her, clearly waiting for some response. When Yeva didn't say anything, his face darkened, the brows lowering and his jaw closing. "Well?" he demanded.

Yeva's breath caught up with her and she frowned. "Well, what? Do you expect thanks? You've made me your prisoner. I'm not going to thank you for feeding me."

"Eat or don't," growled the Beast. "I care not."

Yeva took a deep breath. There was no question: no animal could be this temperamental, this . . . childish. There was *without a doubt* an element of humanity, however deeply buried, within this Beast. "You care because you have gone to all this trouble to catch and train me, for whatever purpose you won't explain."

The Beast just snarled at her, and turned to stalk away, toward the opposite side of the castle from the one she'd explored.

"Beast!" Yeva called. "Wait!" And when the Beast paused, she did as well, gathering her thoughts. "Do you know how to dress a carcass, or only how to devour it?"

"I am not your servant," the Beast replied, glaring at her over his shoulder.

"No," Yeva agreed. "But I have no knife, nothing with which to carve meat from these bones. I cannot simply rip off chunks with my teeth as you would do."

The Beast was frowning still, but his aggravation turned to

consternation. "If I give you a knife, you will try to kill me."

Yeva's stomach growled again, and she could not help but roll her eyes. Just now, killing the Beast was not foremost in her mind. "I won't try to kill you when I'm hungry."

The Beast stared at her. She stared back at him. Doe-Eyes looked between them, still ill at ease in the Beast's presence and pressing close to her mistress. In the end, the Beast grumbled low in his throat and led Yeva outside, lugging the deer with him, dropping it in the snow some distance from the door. He vanished and then reappeared some time later with her pack, in which Yeva found everything she'd brought with her. Though the food stores were nearly gone now, and the willow bark too, the other medicines were there, and her wire for snares, and the fletching knife as well.

Dressing squirrel and rabbit was one thing—butchering the carcass of a deer was another. It was always her father who'd done this work when she was a child, and by the time she had its innards in a pile beside the carcass, she found she wasn't hungry anymore after all. Her bloody hands shook, and she wiped at her brow with her sleeve to buy time. She would not show weakness in front of the Beast, who stood some distance apart, watching her carve up his offering.

Doe-Eyes, who'd been snatching up various organs and then hobbling away to gulp them down with one wary eye on the Beast, finished eating the deer's liver and skipped back to press against Yeva. She paused before reaching to scratch at the dog's ears, her eyes on her blood-coated hands.

The Beast gave a low rumble. "You are inefficient."

"Yes, with you staring at me," Yeva mumbled back, too worn out and drained by the task to worry about angering him.

"Return indoors," the Beast ordered.

"I need to finish—"

"Return!" the Beast's voice rose, and he drew himself up taller, looming so that Doe-Eyes wheezed an inaudible whine against Yeva's arm.

Yeva fought the instinct to flee. "I have to eat!"

The Beast drew one deep breath, then two, and Yeva realized she had too. *Patience,* she thought. *That's what I'm reaching for with each breath—could he be doing the same?*

Finally, the Beast dropped his head. "I will finish your task," he said slowly. "That is what I meant."

"Then say that. Don't command me as if I were your property."

The Beast growled low and dangerous. "You *are* mine."

"You may have me captive," Yeva said. "You may control when I can leave and what I eat and how long I'm allowed to live. But you don't own me." She paused, then added with irritation, "And don't call me *girl*, like I have no name."

The Beast's tail flicked aside, twitching with anger. "You call me *Beast*."

"That is what you are. Have you given me reason to call you anything else?"

The Beast hesitated, scowling across the blood-soaked snow at her. "I will call you Beauty then," he said. "For that is what you are."

Yeva remembered her stories, and her decision to call her invisible friend Ivan, and her thoughts could not reconcile that name with the monstrous visage a few paces away. Her father's nickname for her sounded strange from this creature, this thing that had murdered him. And yet she could imagine him calling her nothing else. From someone else it would be flattery, but there was no falsehood in the Beast's face. Yeva wouldn't have been surprised if he were incapable of lying, if his animal nature kept him to the truth at all times.

The compliment caught her so off guard that her response came before she could stop it. "Thank you," she mumbled, dropping the knife to wipe the blood from her hands against the snow.

BEAST

She calls you Beast, for that is what you are.
  And Beauty.
  The surprise is not the compliment, not the
truth, that she is beautiful. The surprise is
not that we wish to help her. The surprise is
not even the electric warmth that rises at the
sound of her voice, even when she is shouting.
  The surprise is how much I long to hear
her call me, just once more, Ivan.

THIRTEEN

FROM THEN ON THE Beast brought her meat that had been dressed and carved. She didn't know how he managed such delicate work with only claws and teeth, because he never let her watch. Sometimes she killed the game herself, as he continued to take her into the wood to practice her skills. Other times, when her game was scarce, he'd go out on his own. He never failed to bring something home.

She cleared a space of dust and cobwebs in the vast kitchen, and cleaned out one of the four hearths so she could use the roasting spit. A few of the pots and pans she scrubbed clean, and a few plates and bowls as well. One of the sitting rooms she took as her own, and the Beast did not object when she began to sleep there instead of in his lair below. She imagined she was carving off a piece of the lifeless castle itself for her own use—or else bringing that tiny piece to life again. All around her was the dead, decaying carcass of whatever court had once existed here, and she was only living in a tiny corner of its shell.

With Yeva's cypress salve, Doe-Eyes's leg began to heal as the days stretched into weeks. She still hobbled, due to the splints keeping her leg straight, but she could move much faster, and no longer favored it the way she had been. Yeva could bring her along when the Beast took her hunting, and though Doe-Eyes was still too slow to catch anything herself, she delighted in galloping after the little scurrying things in the brush that caught her sight, and she slept much more soundly for the exercise. She bore up far better against the cold than Yeva would have thought, although that might have had as much to do with the dog's loyalty as her hardiness.

Yeva tracked the days with a bit of charcoal on the wall. Though she could not know how long she'd been down in the cell, she estimated it had been at least a month. Which meant that by now, her sisters must think she'd met the same fate as their father. And Solmir must believe the same. How long would his word last? She knew him to be a good man, but if he came to understand that Yeva would never return to marry him and repay him for taking care of her family, how long would he continue to do so? Her sisters had never learned to hunt as she had, and Albe certainly knew nothing about it. How would any of them survive without her?

She remembered her sister's words to her as she prepared to rush into the wood in search of their father, the words she'd ignored without a second thought. *We need you here.* And she'd abandoned them anyway.

No. *No.* She would not think of them. Not until it was done, and their father's death was avenged. She couldn't afford to. She forced her heart to harden, pushed her sisters from her mind.

It was two weeks after she'd moved into the castle above when the Beast came as usual to fetch her for the day's work. This time, however, he stopped at the far edge of the bridge and sat down, fixing his eyes on Yeva.

She fingered the bow over her shoulder and eyed him back, uncertain at this change in their routine. "What is it, Beast?"

"Your skill at hunting in your wood is sufficient," the Beast announced. "Now you will begin hunting in mine."

Yeva's brow furrowed. "Yours? I don't understand."

The Beast hesitated, his gaze sliding toward the forest beyond the overgrown road leading to the castle. "It is difficult to explain without——" He stopped short, as if someone had stolen his breath.

Yeva's pulse quickened, curiosity tingling its way up her spine. "Without violating the terms of the spell?"

The Beast's jaw fell open, and if it weren't for the number of sharp, menacing teeth his mouth held, Yeva might have laughed at the shock written across his animal features. He went absolutely still, even the tip of his tail that was usually so expressive. For an instant he was so like one of the crumbling gargoyles on the battlements of the castle that Yeva thought maybe just speaking of his secrets had turned him to stone.

But then he heaved a breath and dropped lower to the snow, crouching like a wounded animal, forelegs bent and breath stirring the top flakes with each puff. "You are clever," he mumbled.

"I know stories," Yeva corrected. "The bespelled can never speak of what afflicts them—that is always part of the curse."

The Beast's eyes flicked up. "You believe I am cursed?"

It was Yeva's turn to hesitate. Her mind still could not decide whether he was a man who had murdered her father or a beast who'd given in to animal instinct and torn him to pieces. And it still couldn't decide which would be worse. Either way he would have to answer for what he'd done.

"I know you aren't natural," she said finally. "And you can clearly hunt far better than any human hunter could, so your need for me must mean you have a task you cannot complete on your own."

The Beast said nothing, didn't confirm her guesses. But neither did he deny them.

"And this existence is clearly . . ." Yeva paused, swallowing. "It's clearly miserable."

The Beast stayed silent.

"So, yes." Yeva took a deep breath. "Yes, I believe you are cursed."

Still the Beast gave no reply, which gave Yeva time to study his face. Though he'd dropped his eyes again, there was something about his features that caught her attention. He seemed different today, and not only because he'd changed their routine by halting at the end of the bridge. His muzzle seemed somehow less elongated, his eyes less bestial, his mouth more expressive and less fanged. The longer she stared at him the more it seemed, in the sun-dazzled glare, that he was somehow also a man kneeling in the snow. She blinked, and blinked again, and could not dismiss the image.

"Enough," the Beast said abruptly, giving himself a shake that seemed to cause that humanity to fall away like shed fur. "It is enough for you to know that there is another world inside these woods, one you have not been trained to see. It is in this world that you will find your eventual quarry, so it is this world with which you must become familiar."

"Another *world*?" Yeva glanced out toward the wood as the Beast had done.

"The easiest way to explain is . . . think of your stories." The

Beast's face was turned aside, revealing only a sliver of his profile. "The stories you told of Ivan. That is the world you must learn to see."

Yeva found herself clutching at the grip of her bow, not in fear but in a sudden thrill of excitement. Her father had mentioned seeing flashes of things that could not exist—he'd told her of spirits and demons and creatures that had no names. But all children were told such stories, and all children grew out of them. She had never imagined the things her father told her might be reality.

"So what am I hunting today?" Yeva asked, a million imagined images flashing before her eyes. She thought of the glass wing tips still clinging to the window frame in the long, shattered hallway.

The Beast's lips pulled back, and Yeva could not decide whether it was a smile or a snarl. "Today," he said, "you will be hunting me."

Yeva felt like throwing her bow down in frustration. After three days of hunting the Beast, she could find no trace of him until he appeared close to sundown to bring her back to the castle. She knew now that it had to be magic, and her thoughts screamed at the unfairness of it. After all, she was human. Only a girl with a bow and a pair of strong arms and eyes. And none of those things could help her when tracking a magical creature through a forest that, for her, held only squirrels and deer and jays.

She'd been so sure this was a step toward achieving what she needed to do, that learning to track the Beast would be part of learning how to kill him. But that seemed farther away than ever, now that she knew how truly impossible it was to get the advantage on him.

The Beast was as frustrated as she was. She could read it in the gathering tension in his voice each day when he ended the hunt by revealing himself to her. So when, on the fourth day, he appeared early—no more than an hour or two after midday—Yeva's heart flickered with a beat of panic. Was she to be punished?

But the Beast merely sat there, appearing from behind a tree as she walked. He stared at her, contemplatively, and for once, Yeva refused to let the stare unsettle her. Instead she stared back, fingering the fletching on the arrow she kept nocked to her bow.

"Come," the Beast said finally.

"Come where?" Yeva asked warily.

"Here, to me."

Yeva didn't move, only gripped the bow more tightly and eyed the Beast sidelong, swallowing down fear.

The Beast's brows lifted. "I will not harm you."

"Your word?" Yeva asked.

"My word."

Yeva's hands shook as she returned the arrow to her quiver, and she stepped closer to the Beast. She stopped when she was near enough to feel the heat of his fur in the cold, near enough to smell that wild smell and see the flecks of red that gave his gold eyes their hue.

The Beast inclined his head, a melding of nod and bow that left Yeva more confused than before—a courtly gesture, so familiar from her time among the baronessa's retinue, but so alien from this creature. "Turn around."

Yeva did as he asked, though every nerve in her body told her not to turn her back on him, told her that she was mad to let such a predator so near.

She heard the Beast move closer behind her, and a warm paw

came to rest in the center of her back. She suppressed the urge to shiver, certain at any moment she'd feel his claws. Instead she heard his voice.

"Close your eyes and listen." His voice was very quiet, and despite the vast open wood all around, his words felt intimate, private. Yeva thought that even if someone were standing a few paces away, they wouldn't hear him. It was as though he was speaking directly into her ears. "Tell me what you hear."

"I hear you," Yeva replied. When that got no response, she took a long, slow breath and let her attention move outward. It was difficult to listen with the reminder of the Beast right behind her, but as the sounds of the forest settled into the quiet she almost forgot about his touch.

"I hear jays," she whispered. "Calling to one another. There is a wind some ways to the east, making the trees sigh against each other, but it's not coming our way. Snow sliding from a branch."

"Is that all?"

Yeva, eyes closed, felt her brows knit. "What else am I supposed to hear?"

"Listen."

Yeva listened. She listened until her ears started to ring in the quiet. She was about to speak, and drew breath to tell him she heard nothing, when something made her stop. The skin at the back of her neck prickled, and not from the Beast's presence. She felt her head turn, making the prickling stronger. "I hear . . ." Her thoughts emptied as she tried to name the sensation. Something was pulling at her, drawing her attention northwest, and it *was* a sound. Except it wasn't a sound, at the same time. "I hear . . . music."

The Beast's breath caught, then started again. "Music?" he

repeated, sounding surprised.

"I can't describe . . ." Yeva's ears strained. It wasn't music, not really. But her mind could not interpret it any other way, this feeling, this sweeping, rhythmic pulse that kept drawing her attention off through the woods. "It calls to me the way music does."

"Music," the Beast echoed again, his voice low and musing, almost wondrous. "That is not what I hear."

"What do you hear?"

"That is not important. For now, just concentrate on the sound."

Yeva wanted to know the answer to her question, but she wanted to listen to the music more. Though the sensation was new and alien, it also felt strangely familiar. *I've heard this sound before,* she realized, her entire body tingling. She'd caught glimpses of it, like a distant haunting refrain, in her deepest moments of silence in the wood. When the long days stretched timelessly on, and her mind emptied of thoughts until there was only her footsteps in the snow, only the feel of the bow in her hand, the bite of cold on her cheeks. When everything else faded away, this sound was what was left.

What is it you're looking for out there? Asenka had asked her.

"I hear it," she whispered, mesmerized.

"Hold the sound in your mind," the Beast murmured in her ear. "Imagine that it is not only a sound, but that it is a vision as well. Imagine that you will be able to see it when you open your eyes."

She instantly saw colors playing against the backs of her eyelids, pulsing in time with the not-quite-music. Blue and white and green streaks of light shot across her vision. She did not dare breathe to speak, but nodded instead, slowly, as though moving too quickly would jar the vision free.

"Now," the Beast whispered. "Open your eyes."

Yeva did as she was told. All around were the trees, and the snow, and the underbrush, and the light in her mind's eye was transposed against the scene. There was a focal point, a spot from which the light seemed to emanate, and Yeva stared at it. Suddenly a woman stood there, leaning against one of the trees. Her hair was long and raven black, and she was naked, as though the cold meant nothing to her. Yeva felt her face warming, suddenly all too aware of the rough wool on her own skin, and of the Beast's presence behind her. The woman was beyond beautiful, and she stood running her long fingers through her hair like a maiden waiting for a lover. Then she paused, and turned her head. She looked straight at Yeva, and when their eyes met Yeva felt something inside her shatter.

She cried out and stepped back, falling against the warm bulk of the Beast. She fumbled with the bow at her shoulder, trying to grab for an arrow but getting only handfuls of the Beast's fur. She gasped for breath, fear coursing through her veins, and looked back at the woman—and she was gone. There was only a pair of startled thrush that burst from the underbrush, crying and fluttering off into the distant wood.

Yeva stood, heart pounding. All at once she noticed how much she was leaning against the Beast, and that all her fear was for the strange woman in the wood, and that rather than terrifying, the Beast's warm presence behind her was reassuring.

She had forgotten for an instant that the Beast was her enemy, that she existed now only to kill him. It had been only a few heartbeats, her thoughts flooded with the music of this strange other world, but she'd *forgotten*. Her stomach lurched, sickened, and she stumbled away from him.

When she turned, he was calm, watching her as though nothing strange had happened.

"What was that?" Yeva fumbled with her quiver strap to adjust it, disentangling her cloak from about her, trying to compose herself.

"Her name is Lamya," the Beast said. "She and her sisters live in the next valley but they travel often, and Lamya prefers lying by the side of my river to shed her skins in the sun."

"Shed her . . ." Yeva blinked, trying to understand. "Shed her *skins*?"

"She is a dragon." The Beast's brow furrowed. "Have you not seen a serpent's shed skin before, in the wood?"

"But . . . but she was a woman, not a serpent at all."

"She is that too."

Yeva stared into the trees, trying to summon back that burst of color and music. She thought she heard a distant, rhythmic pulse, like the leathery flapping of great wings, but then it seemed nothing more than a far-off gust of wind. Yeva's head spun. "Beast, what . . . what is this?"

The Beast sank down on his haunches. "This is my world."

"The . . . the thing you need me for," Yeva said. "You want me to hunt a creature from this world, your world."

The Beast nodded.

"Lamya?"

"No, not Lamya."

"But you won't tell me what it is?"

"I cannot."

Yeva let her breath out in a rush. "How can I hunt a thing if I don't know what it is?"

The Beast was silent. Yeva had come to know him well enough to see from the set of his face that he was troubled. "I . . .

I do not know," he said finally. "But if you can see Lamya, then you will be able to see her, too."

Her.

Yeva filed the tidbit away, tying it down in among the other scraps she'd collected. For now they were shreds of next to nothing, but perhaps, if she gathered enough of them, she'd be able to stitch them together into a tapestry with answers. For now, she would wait and listen for that far-off music. For maybe, somewhere in its rhythmic pulse, in the way it seeped into the empty spaces of her heart like warm honey into dry bread . . . maybe in that music she'd find the way to kill the Beast.

"Beast," she said, making her voice steady, letting it warm.

"Yes?"

"You said that you didn't hear music." Yeva watched his face. "What do you hear?"

"For me," the Beast replied, "it is like a heartbeat."

Yeva fought a smile pulling at the corners of her mouth. "The heartbeat of the forest."

The Beast gave himself a little shake, then tilted his head eastward. "That is enough for today. We will return now."

As he turned to pass her, the Beast moved on top of the snow, his paws not even stirring the loose snow dusting the icy crust. Yeva's boots crunched through, but he moved like wind, like spirit. He was showing her how he could travel through the forest without leaving a trace, and Yeva watched each step as if hypnotized.

"It is the same sound I heard," the Beast said as he passed her, "when I first saw you."

BEAST

We remember a time of such clarity. We were Beast, we ran with wolves and hunted prey, we lived on the wind and breathed the forest. We wanted nothing but to be, to run, to endure. Want didn't exist.

And we remember another time, too, a time of longing and desire, where we existed as nothing but want . . . always the next unattainable thing. There was no joy in what we had, only in what might come.

And now these two selves, these two minds cursed to exist as one, every day grow more at odds. We return to our den to pace and end up railing against the darkness and the dirt—we lie before the fire in our room and itch at the confines of stone and mortar.

Only she frees both of us. She moves like beauty, she whispers to us of wind and forest—and she tells us stories, such stories that we wake in the night, dreaming dreams of a life long past. She reminds us of what we used to be.

She whispers to us of what we could be.

FOURTEEN

YEVA AND THE BEAST fell into a pattern as the weeks began to stretch. Though she still could not track him through the forest, even as she developed an ear for magic, she discovered other wonders living in the Beast's valley. Trees that had faces, voices, peeping at her one instant and gone the next. Lights dancing in the distance, riding the storm winds, laughter calling her to join them. A fox that stopped and smiled at her. Birds that flocked together this way and that on the wind, painting shapes in the sky over the meadow: a face, a cresting wave, a herd of running deer.

She asked the Beast about them all. Sometimes he had names for them, and sometimes he did not. Sometimes, very, very rarely, she'd tell him of a creature even he had never seen. Yeva thought, privately, that those moments seemed to delight him. She asked him each time, at each new wonder, whether that was what she was meant to hunt. Each time he said no.

It was nearly two months after moving into the castle, by her charcoal tally on the kitchen wall, that she woke to find the Beast crouched in the corner of her room.

At first she didn't see him, and rose half sleeping from her nest of blankets to add a few logs to the fire so the room would heat while she woke the rest of the way. Doe-Eyes never bothered to wake when she did, grumbling happily from her part of the pallet until the fire drew her out to bask in its heat. Yeva wrapped herself back up in her blankets and jiggled her knees up and down to bring the blood back to her toes, and waited for warmth.

The shadows in the far corner moved, and Yeva let out a shriek before she could stop herself. She'd seen dark, frightening things in the musical wood, and her dreams had been more troubled since she'd begun to see this other world. She reached for the fire poker before she could think.

The Beast stepped forward into the light and blinked his round eyes at her. "We did not mean to frighten you."

Yeva gulped back her panic, her pounding heart starting to calm as she saw it was only the Beast and not some monster from her dreams.

It was only *the Beast? When did that happen?*

"You can't come in here like that, while I'm asleep," she gasped, lingering fears prompting irritation to sharpen her voice.

The Beast's brows lowered. "Why not?"

"It's not polite," Yeva retorted, then took a breath as the ridiculousness of that sank in. What were manners to a Beast?

But as she struggled for a reason he would understand, the Beast merely tilted his head a fraction to the side. "Very well. Do you wish us to leave?"

Yeva's voice sputtered to a halt. *Yes,* she thought. *Or else let me kill you and end all of this.* But aloud, she said only, "What do you want?"

"Polite," the Beast echoed, murmuring the word as if to himself. But there was a wicked gleam in his eyes that made Yeva stop short, a realization snapping into her mind like a spark from chafing wool.

He was *teasing* her.

"It is time for training."

Yeva's head ached. She was weary, but more than that, she was frustrated. The more she understood of this world the Beast had shown her, the more she saw how little hope she had of avenging her father unless she could discover a weakness, some secret that would give her the upper hand.

But it was clear she would not find the Beast's weakness by ordinary means, and she could not afford to keep growing complacent, to let the days slip by unmarked. She would track these creatures in the wood, the ones she'd learned to see with the Beast's help. One of them had to know something, anything, that would help her kill the Beast. And she'd hunt down every last one of them if it came to that.

Quickly, she rose to her feet and crossed the room to splash frigid water from the basin onto her face. "Beast," she said, earning herself a faint grunt in response. "I want to go into the forest on my own today."

The Beast's brows lifted, but he said nothing, clearly waiting for an explanation.

"I need to be able to navigate this world of yours alone, without your guidance." Yeva could see the Beast shift his weight from one side to the other, see him start to reply. "And," she added quickly, "whatever quarry I'm meant to find, we haven't found it yet. Perhaps it won't reveal itself to you. But maybe it will to me if I'm alone."

That brought the Beast up short, and he gazed at her with

those steady eyes, tail swinging side to side like a slow, gentle pendulum. He stared at her so long that Yeva's own eyes began to water with the effort of not looking away. When he spoke, his voice was low and careful. "I still have your word that you will not attempt escape?"

Yeva swallowed at that reminder, bitterness on her tongue. "You still have my word. Since you will kill my family if I do."

Silence again, broken by the hiss and intermittent pops of the fire in the hearth. "Yes," he said finally.

Yeva hesitated. "Yes, you will kill my family if I escape? Or yes, I may go alone?"

"Both." The Beast's brows lowered. "I accept your word. If you were given to lying, you would have promised not to kill me at the start. Since you did not, I believe you when you say you will not flee."

His voice was so low, so bitter, so full of loathing, that Yeva almost took a step back. The fire no longer seemed to hold any warmth for her, and she shivered. "You killed my father," she whispered. "I can never let his death go unanswered."

The Beast's eyes were flat and dull. "And that is why you stay. Not because of threats or fear. Because you believe one day we will drop our guard, and you can avenge him."

Yeva's jaw clenched. She had little hope of convincing him otherwise, not when he saw through her so easily. So let them be enemies. She'd find a way to destroy him regardless. "Yes."

The Beast's tail stilled. The flat eyes softened, his face suddenly so human that Yeva *knew* he had changed, that it was no trick of the light or her own eyes. He seemed torn between two warring natures, and whichever ruled him at any given time, that aspect took over.

Just now, his face, his expression, was so full of anguish that

Yeva's fury vanished and her heart ached so much that she bit her lip.

"We did kill him," the Beast said after an eternity, and his face closed over again as he looked away toward the door. When he looked back, he was the Beast once more. "And maybe one day we *will* drop our guard. Then you will get what you most desire."

He turned and was gone.

Yeva fought the instinct to wipe the frigid wash water from her face. She wanted to hold in the chill, wanted to remind herself she could not, *would not* be comfortable here. She was a prisoner in this decaying castle, tied to the thing that had destroyed the person she loved most in all this existence.

But something, an ache that Yeva would not name, stirred deep in her heart. With those words the Beast had renewed her dedication to vengeance, shored up her determination to remain here. Even if he said she could go free tomorrow, she would stay, and wait, and find a way. . . .

With those words he had ensured she would not try to leave him. It was a human thing to tell a person what they want to hear. A human thing to manipulate and hide the truth to serve one's own ends. A human thing to lie.

And in the moment he admitted to killing her father, he had seemed so very human.

Though the sky was clear and sunny, the air was bitingly cold, and Yeva set a brisk pace to keep her blood pumping. Doe-Eyes trotted at her heels, her leg so improved she could accompany Yeva all day if necessary. Her father's bow at hand, her pack filled with her own gear, Yeva felt more at home, more truly free, than she could remember ever feeling. Even without the Beast's threats against her family, she would return to his castle

by choice. Vengeance, not fear, would bring her back. And if all
went well, she would return armed with knowledge of the Beast's
weaknesses.

She could hear the music always now, a constant thread that
lingered in the very back of her mind, unless she summoned it
to her attention. It was not unlike the way she'd always heard
the forest before, its tiny noises and breezes weaving together
automatically to paint a picture beyond what she could see. It
unnerved her, how easily the music became a part of that picture.

She shoved those thoughts aside and concentrated, turning
her head this way and that to locate the different threads of
magic, like scent trails. She twisted toward the nearest, giving
Doe-Eyes a sharp whistle to stay close, and set out.

Yeva had learned from her excursions with the Beast that the
creatures in this wood were rarely evil—and neither were they
good. They simply *were*, the way animals were. Spirits that led
travelers astray could also help them find the road again. Birds
that warned of dangers ahead could also cry out and betray a
person's presence to waiting beasts.

This was a world governed by balance. Evil deeds begot
evil consequences. Blessings used for ill purposes could quickly
become curses. Though Yeva would tread carefully, and knew
any information she sought would require some kind of payment,
she felt certain that even in this realm she could only be rewarded
for seeking to destroy the Beast.

She was several hours out from the castle, over the ridge and
into the valley beyond it, when a movement caught her eye and
made her stop. She put a hand on Doe-Eyes's head, signaling
silently for her to be still.

Just ahead, mostly hidden by the trees, was a face. An old man
was watching her, as still as the snowy world around him. His

skin was lined and grooved like bark, his hair long and tinged green like moss, his eyes the pale blue of an icy pool. She had never seen him before.

She took a breath and moved forward a step, but the instant her weight shifted the face vanished behind the tree again.

"Wait!" she called, breaking into a run, eyes scanning for a shape darting through the woods. But when she reached the tree behind which the man had been standing, she found a fox there, sitting calmly in the snow and gazing up at her.

Yeva, breathless, stared at it, and it stared back. At her side, Doe-Eyes sniffed interestedly—but didn't go stiff as she would have done had an ordinary fox appeared in their path.

"Well?" said the fox.

Yeva yelped, and couldn't help but take a step back, half lifting her bow. She caught her breath, noticing the fox had the same pale-blue eyes the man had had. She swallowed. "What are you?"

"I am Borovoi."

Yeva shifted her grip on her bow, forcing herself to relax lest the fox—or old man, or whatever he was—sense her nervousness. "Is that your name, or what you are?"

The fox's head tipped to the side. "I am Borovoi. What a waste of a question. You only have one more."

Yeva's mouth opened to protest, but she stopped herself before she could speak. In her father's tales, the number three was always important. Three sons, three wishes . . . this world was ruled by the laws of those stories. She took a deep breath, choosing her words carefully, and asked, "Can you show me how to destroy the Beast?"

The fox paused for a long moment. Then his lips drew back into a wide, toothy grin, and he whirled with a flash of his red tail and darted off into the forest. Yeva broke into a run without thinking, shoving her bow onto her shoulder and sprinting as fast as she could. She could see no tracks, but the fox was always just ahead of her, visible as a flash of red fur against the white canvas of snow. She ran until she stumbled into a dense thicket, which tangled about her legs; her momentum tried to keep her moving and she went crashing down into the dry, leafless branches.

Gasping, she crawled forward, detangling herself as best she could, ignoring the scratches on her face and the branches snagging her hair. When she finally stumbled free, she found herself in a snowy clearing—and the fox, Borovoi, was nowhere to be seen.

Yeva stood panting, trying to catch her breath as Doe-Eyes came wriggling through the thicket after her. Tongue lolling, gap-jawed, Doe-Eyes gazed up at her mistress as though to say, *What fun! Again!* Still winded, Yeva dropped into a weary crouch. She rubbed at Doe-Eyes's ears as she scanned the clearing.

There had to be a clue here, some importance to this section of the wilderness. Though tricksters were everywhere in fairy tales, they rarely lied—any misfortunes were always the fault of the hero or heroine, misunderstanding what was really being said. So Yeva doubted she would find some weapon buried beneath the snow that could kill the Beast, but she knew some piece of the answer must lie here.

She set off across the clearing, steps cautious, eyes scanning. It wasn't until she was nearly halfway across that she noticed a flat expanse that was lower than the rest, and mostly clear of snow.

When she drew closer she found that it was a pool, a woodland spring that had frozen over in the cold. Yeva strode halfway around it, peering at the ice, which showed little but black water beneath it. Ordering Doe-Eyes to stay put, Yeva gingerly stretched a foot out to test the ice's surface. It gave only the tiniest groan in response as she shifted more of her weight onto that foot.

She was about to take another step when a flash of gold beneath the ice made her stop short. Heart pounding, she stared into the black depths, hoping for another glimpse. It came again, a sweep of fire gold, and then abruptly it was there.

The Firebird.

Yeva gasped and threw herself down onto her knees to stare beneath the ice. The Firebird was trapped there, its golden wings outstretched, beating futilely against the ice's surface. With a cry, Yeva drew her fletching knife from her boot and chipped at the ice—she forgot about Borovoi, forgot about her reason for coming to the wood alone, forgot even the Beast himself. She could see only the Firebird, hear only its muffled cries, each one a stab at her heart.

All her life she'd longed for the tiniest glimpse of this creature. She would not let it drown—she would free it, take it for her own, feel the heat of its fiery wings on her face. She stabbed down at the ice again and again, feeling it shudder beneath her. Each groan of the ice made her work harder, faster. Doe-Eyes's frantic barking at the pool's edge faded to a distant buzzing in her ears. All she heard, all she was, was the Firebird's song.

The ice gave a mighty crack, and a spray of water flecked Yeva's face. She moved so she could drive down at the hole with her boot, putting every ounce of strength she had behind it— and then the entire sheet gave way with a roar.

Yeva was in the water before she knew what was happening, air driven from her lungs and rushing back in a huge gasp before her head went under. For a long instant she felt nothing—no cold, no wet, no fear at the sudden darkness—only the need for the Firebird, the longing to touch it even once, even if it flew away and she never saw it again.

Something wrapped around her from behind and she turned, joy flooding her heart as she expected to see the Firebird at last, whole and in front of her, not obscured and blurred by the ice. Instead, a rotting face loomed out of the blackness at her, bony arms pulling her close. It had once been a woman, her long hair still clinging to what remained of her scalp, and the flesh of her cheeks had sunken and rotted so that Yeva could see her teeth in profile as the thing leaned forward to whisper in her ear.

"Stay with me," the dead woman sighed, holding on to Yeva with unnatural strength. They were sinking, down into darkness, far deeper than a meadow pool should be. The thing's hair curled around Yeva, wrapping around her neck, slithering along her skin beneath her clothes.

Yeva tried to scream, but all that came was a torrent of bubbles. The spell broken, her longing for the Firebird gone, Yeva's body struggled for survival. Her lungs were burning even before she'd wasted air trying to scream, and she struggled to pull one of her arms free from the thing's grip. When she'd hit the cold water her muscles had seized, and in her hand was still the knife she'd been using to chip at the ice. Yeva's mind felt slow and sluggish, and every second they sank deeper made it harder to think.

She lifted her head and saw the distant glimmer of the pale winter sun, and with a wrenching effort that drove another flood of bubbles from her lungs, she tore her arm free of the dead thing's grasp. She stabbed the knife down as hard as she could, driving it into the thing's shoulder until it grated against bone. It howled, a cry as much of grief and despair as of pain, but its grip only tightened. Yeva stabbed again, her vision growing blurry, and again, and again—finally the knife crunched through the thing's skull, and abruptly its arms fell away. Yeva tried to swim upward, her own body barely responding to her mind's commands. When she looked down, all she saw was a ghostly pale form sinking slowly, quietly, into the black depths.

She clawed her way up, the glimmer of light above her seeming farther with every stroke—but eventually her arms remembered how to swim, and just as her lungs readied to breathe water if she could not find air, she broke the surface with a gurgling cry.

The pool itself was small, and though the ice was too thin for her to climb on top of it, she could make her way to shore, the ice shattering around her. She fell into the snow, dizzy and shivering, sobbing for air. The roaring in her ears began to fade, replaced by Doe-Eyes's frenzied barking; Yeva opened ice-crusted eyelashes to find her dog dancing above and around her, nudging her from all sides. She couldn't even feel it when Doe-Eyes began licking the water from her hands.

All she wanted was to lie there in the snow and breathe and stare at the sky, which was turning gray with clouds. Some distant part of her mind knew, though, that this was wrong. She must move, or die from the cold. With a moan, she rolled over onto her side and drew her knees in close to her body, then slipped her pack from her shoulders. Most of her supplies were wet, including her tinder for starting a fire, but she had no firewood or kindling anyway, and that wasn't what she was after. She kept her sleeping-roll blanket at the bottom of the pack, and the pack's leather and the layers of supplies had protected it somewhat. It was damp, but far drier than anything else.

She peeled off the sopping outer layers of her clothes, moving as quickly as her numb, shaking fingers would allow.

Her shivering began to slow, but rather than making movement easier, it seemed harder and harder to move. She knew that was bad—that all of this was bad—that she would die of exposure. She wondered what would happen to her family, whether the Beast would kill them for her failure, or if they'd simply go on living in that cabin forever. She imagined Lena learning to hunt, then found herself laughing at the thought of her prim sister trying squeamishly to retrieve an arrow from a deer.

It was a sharp bark from Doe-Eyes in her ear that brought her back to herself, wrenching her thoughts from home with an effort. A surge of fear that she was losing her ability to think got her the rest of the way out of her cloak and clothes until she was only in her wool undershift—that she kept on, for even wet the wool would help her somewhat. Then she tried to call Doe-Eyes, her voice cracking and whispery thin. The dog tucked her body in close and Yeva wrapped herself around her, and the blanket around them both, and tried to think.

Her tinder was soaked but if she could make it to the forest perhaps the thicket she'd fallen into on her way to the clearing would have wood dry enough to ignite from sparks. If she could get her hands working she could shave curls from it with her knife. If she had a lantern she could warm some water to drink . . . she ought to ask her invisible friend to bring her one, to unlock her manacle, to let her out of the chilly cell and into the room with the blue divan, and the hearth. She curled more tightly around the warm body alongside hers and mumbled, "Asenka, your toes are so cold. . . ."

Doe-Eyes's barking roused her and she groaned, "Hush, it isn't dawn yet!" But there was light against her eyelids, and a shadow moving across them. She tried to open her eyes but her lids wouldn't listen; she tried to lift a hand to pry them open but couldn't tell if her arm was moving. "Where's my arm—I need that to shoot. . . ."

"Hush," said a voice in her ear, tense and deep. Not her father's voice. But familiar somehow. Warm like velvet. "I will carry you on my back. But you must hold on or you will fall off."

"I'm not a child," Yeva protested. The voice ignored her, and she expected to feel a pair of arms lifting her. Instead something clamped onto her shoulder, a firm pressure, and dragged her back and halfway up onto a soft slope.

"Climb," the voice ordered.

Yeva grabbed automatically, fingers closing around handfuls of fur. Her muscles seemed weak for some reason as she dragged herself upward, a task that should've been easy. The soft thing beneath her moved, staggering to the side and half knocking her upward. Then it rose, making her stomach lurch.

"Hold on." This time the voice came from beneath her, rumbling against her chest and cheek like a house cat's purr, or the stirring of distant thunder. The thing began to move, slowly at first, then faster and faster until Yeva pressed her face in against the spicy fur so the wind would not sting her cheeks.

As Yeva's consciousness slipped away, she heard the voice again, murmuring, *Hold on.*

BEAST

We are not afraid. We are never afraid. It has been centuries since we knew fear, even longer since there was any being, beast or man, strong enough to harm us.

And yet our heart pounds like thunder in our ears, echoing like a voice shouting at us to run harder, move faster. Our paws feel clumsy, and half the time we sink into snow that we long ago learned to cross without leaving a trace. Though we always know exactly how far we are from the castle it feels twice, three times as far as it ought to be.

The body against our back is cold. She is no longer moving. Only that she has not fallen, that her hands still grip our fur, tells us that she is still alive.

Hold on, Beauty.

Hold on.

FIFTEEN

YEVA WOKE BECAUSE HER skin was on fire. Her voice was cracked and she found she could barely move, and that when she did, it made her body burn all the more.

"Go slowly," said a low voice. She knew that voice. The Beast.

She opened her eyes to find him crouched several paces from her, his eyes narrowed onto her face. The tip of his tail twitched as she met his gaze, then twitched back as though he wished to hide that tiny hint of reaction.

Yeva was lying on the floor before the hearth in her room, on top of several layers of blankets, the uppermost of which was of soft fleece—and yet it scratched against her skin like burlap. Some detail prickled at her mind sluggishly, and it wasn't until she looked away from the Beast that she realized what it was.

She was naked.

Yeva gave a low, horrified cry and snatched up the blankets to gather them around her body. Her fingers felt clumsy and swollen, but she forced them to grip the blankets.

The Beast's eyes narrowed all the more, lips curling back. Yeva could not tell if he was snarling or smiling. "You are improved," he said.

"Did you *undress me?*" Yeva demanded, starting to shiver—the fire in the hearth had been warming her far more than the blankets around her were doing now.

"If I had not you would likely have died." The Beast's tail lashed once. "Would you have preferred death over preservation of your modesty?"

Fragments of memory were coming back now: the shocking cold of the icy water; the flood of terror when she turned to find not the Firebird, but a haunted wraith before her eyes; the smell of the Beast's fur as he carried her on his back. She gulped for air, remembering the burning in her lungs as she began to drown. Doe-Eyes was at her side, and crept in close—Yeva opened the blanket enough for the dog to crawl in alongside her, giving off heat like a furnace.

When Yeva didn't answer, the Beast gave a low growl and sat up, leaning back on his haunches so that he once more loomed over Yeva, prone on the floor. "What should it matter? I am a beast no different from the hound at your side."

Yeva clenched her jaw a moment, gathering Doe-Eyes in against her body and then glaring up at the Beast. "We both know that's not true," she snapped.

The Beast's hair lifted along the ridge of his spine, a crest of irritation Yeva had come to recognize as plainly as the furrow in a man's brow or the thinning of his lips. He turned toward the door.

"Wait." Yeva's breath caught as the Beast halted. She knew she ought to thank him for saving her, but the words stuck in her throat. To thank her father's murderer? Her captor? He had only saved her because of his need for a hunter, and yet she'd felt the urgency in the Beast's gait as he ran, the raggedness of his breath as he pushed himself harder, faster, to get her back into the shelter of the castle.

Thank you.

But when Yeva opened her mouth again, she said only, "What was it? The thing in that pool?"

The Beast turned back, eyeing her before settling onto his haunches again. "The pool belongs to one of the Rusalka, a girl killed long ago by a lover or a father or brother. She appears to men as their heart's desire to lure them to their deaths."

Not just men, Yeva thought bitterly. "And what of Borovoi?"

"Borovoi?" The Beast's brows lifted in that expression so like surprise that it almost made Yeva forget about the teeth, the eyes like a wolf's, the ears that pricked toward her when she spoke. "You met him? He rarely shows himself."

"He brought me to the Rusalka's pool."

"Borovoi is one of the leshy, the forest spirits. He grants answers, though the answers he gives often lead travelers astray. What did you ask?"

Yeva's lips pressed together. She'd asked him how to destroy the Beast, but if she was to have any hope of lulling the Beast into lowering his guard, she certainly could not tell him that. "I . . . I cannot remember."

The Beast was silent for a time, long enough that Yeva wondered if he might know she was holding back the truth. But then he bowed his head and took a step backward. "I will let you recover. You will not have to train tomorrow."

Yeva, still shivering despite Doe-Eyes's trembling warmth, watched as the Beast padded softly toward the door, tail sweeping gently behind him. She'd asked the leshy how to destroy the

Beast, and it had brought her to a place that, had it not been for the Beast, would have been her death. She knew that the Beast needed her skills as a hunter, that he hoped she'd play some part in unlocking his curse. But her death would hardly destroy him, only delay his freedom until he found some other hunter to use.

The Beast paused in the doorway for a few seconds before glancing back over his shoulder. "What did you see?" he asked quietly. "In the Rusalka's pool. What was your heart's desire?"

Yeva's pulse sounded quick and loud in her ears. She could still see the Firebird there, its great gold wings sweeping against the ice, calling to her. "I—I saw my family." The lie came so haltingly she felt sure the Beast would see it.

But he only inclined his head once, eyes dropping to the floor before he vanished, leaving her alone.

Yeva crept closer to the hearth, making sure the Beast was gone before opening the blankets to let the fire warm her. She shouldn't have had to lie. She should have seen her family, or Solmir, or her father alive again. She should have seen home, her old life, the comfort of a world without monsters and curses and Beasts. But instead, she'd seen the one thing that most symbolized the world she'd dreamed of as a child.

Instead, she'd seen magic.

As if the Beast could somehow control the weather, no sooner had Yeva recovered enough to venture outside again than the dead of winter hit like an iron fist, and it was no longer safe for Yeva to brave the woods. Blizzards howled through the castle, forcing her to shut up the doors and huddle with Doe-Eyes close to the fire. She half expected to find the Beast waiting behind her, as he did in the wood when she hunted, but he never came. She did return once from the kitchen to discover that layers of tapestry had been fixed over the high window frames, which had been letting in the cold. She could not think how the Beast could have reached them, and for an instant the image of him trying to climb a ladder with four paws and a tail made her want to laugh. But her room was much warmer, and she'd fall asleep on the rugs before the fire gazing up at the high tapestries and imagining what stories lay hidden beneath the centuries of fading and dust.

She saw very little of him during those dark weeks. For a time, the only sign he was even there was the occasional refreshed store of game in the larder. Every now and then she'd catch a flash of red-gold eyes vanishing into the shadows as she explored the castle, or a glimpse of a tail disappearing around the corner, but he never stayed or sought her out.

Doe-Eyes was her constant companion, following her everywhere. Even if the dog was dead asleep, rolled over on her back in front of the fire, if Yeva rose so much as to visit the latrines, Doe-Eyes would wake, scramble to her feet, and trot along at Yeva's side. Her leg had healed almost as good as new, only a slight limp left behind when Yeva failed to keep the fire burning hot enough and the cold crept in. Yeva was glad Doe-Eyes had found her so miraculously in the wood that day, saving her from the ache of loneliness.

And yet, despite her dog's warm body leaning against her as she slept, something twinged deep in her psyche, a discontent that Yeva could not—or would not—name. She'd watch the windows as she wandered the empty castle, the landscape sometimes obscured by storms, sometimes a white, crystalline stillness. Once she saw the silhouette of a distant bird of prey circling the wood—then saw it turn, and the flash of a long, forked tail made her breath catch. *She is a dragon*, the Beast had told her after her brief encounter with Lamya in the wood. Now, as

Yeva blinked, and the silhouette stooped into a dive after some prey unseen behind the next ridgeline, she could not be sure of what she'd seen. Cooped up indoors, surrounded by snow and emptiness, her eyes could easily play tricks on her.

I miss the outdoors, she told herself, turning her back on the window. *I miss hunting. I miss my family.*

Only occasionally, when she let herself dwell too long on the feeling of being unsettled, incomplete, did she remind herself, *He killed my father. He is a murderer. He is a Beast.*

I do not *miss his company.*

The castle itself was enough of a mystery to keep Yeva's mind occupied during the long, dark weeks of winter as she waited for her chance to roam outside again. With Doe-Eyes at her side, she took to exploring by lantern light the endless corridors and rooms. Some, especially on the top floor, were in such disrepair that the roof had caved in. In those places all was snow and rubble and it was impossible to tell what the room had once been used for. Others were almost entirely intact, and but for the centuries of dust and cobwebs, could have been abandoned only yesterday.

From the look of the pristine, freshly fallen snow outside the castle doors each morning, she could tell the Beast was not spending his nights in the lair beneath the castle. Yeva supposed he could be concealing his tracks, but he'd never done so before on his way to the cave, so she couldn't think why he would now. She assumed he must be living in the castle, but the room down the long spiral stair where she'd convalesced and told her stories was empty, and the hearth cold.

She told herself she was searching for his new lair so she'd be able to keep an eye on him, monitor him, perhaps even catch him unawares while he was asleep. But as she turned each corner, stepped through each doorway, it was curiosity that drove her. And while it was a softer, gentler flame than fury, it burned far more slowly and never guttered out.

Yeva knew that the Beast was cursed in some way, and that the answer to his curse involved capturing or killing some creature that lived in the magic world of the wood. Though she imagined that he'd once been human, sometimes her certainty faltered. The ferocity in his gaze when he'd drag home the day's dinner, the alien stare of his eyes as he surveyed the wilds, the moments of utter abandon when he ran through the trees.

Perhaps instead he'd once been an animal, cursed now with human traits. Either state must be a torment. For an animal to be haunted by human conscience, human guilt, human loneliness and fear and desire, would be maddening. And for a man to have his humanity stripped away by the endless onslaught of animal instincts and predatory impulses would be heartbreaking.

The mystery of the castle *was* the mystery of the Beast, and she roamed for days on end with Doe-Eyes's toenails clicking on the cracked marble at their feet.

Though it was nowhere near as large as the castles depicted in illuminated stories and fantastical tapestries, Yeva kept discovering new rooms that she had somehow missed in her previous wanderings.

She found the remains of an old workroom, full of spools of faded thread and a loom and spinning wheel draped in cobwebs. A single gray thread still ran from the rim of the wheel through the spindle, but when Yeva reached out to run her finger along it, it crumbled into dust at her touch.

She found a vast suite of rooms clearly meant for the master and mistress of the castle, with a bed so large she could have lain down crosswise upon it and not reached the edges even if she stretched her fingertips over her head. The bathing chambers held a tub sunk into the marble floor and a chute in which to dump coals to keep the water warm for hours on end. Yeva had never had such luxury—even at the height of her father's wealth, she and her sisters would draw straws as to who would get the tub first, and get the hot, fresh water all to herself. Yeva almost never drew the longest straw, and often shivered her way through her bath. Without servants to draw water, it would take her hours, if not days, to bring enough water to fill this tub—but the thought of it made Yeva smile. She'd been bathing with cloth and buckets of water, and the idea of submerging in warmth, of being entirely, utterly, totally clean . . . she sighed and moved on.

It was on her third or fourth survey of the castle that she stumbled across the library.

She stopped dead and lifted her lantern high to illuminate every shadowy corner. Yeva and her sisters all knew how to read, and though Asenka was certainly the most learned of the three sisters, Yeva had always loved to be read to. Most of her father's books were scholarly texts, but one of them held some of the old stories he'd told her when she was a child, and though she could read the words herself, there was a magic to having them spoken aloud to her, so she could close her eyes and simply listen, and weave images in her mind as the stories unfurled.

Her father had owned over a dozen books, the most of anyone in the town including the baron himself. And as Yeva scanned the walls, each one lined with shelves and each one full of leather-bound books, at least a hundred books, more than she knew existed in one place, she felt her heart might simply burst.

The room itself was dank and cold. It was an interior room with no outside windows, but leaks in the ceiling had allowed moisture to drip onto the floor, and Yeva's nose filled with the smell of rot and mildew. But even that couldn't dim the flare of excitement as she hurried across the room to set the lantern down on one of the end tables in order to reach out and pull one of the books from the shelf.

Its spine crumbled at her touch, and she lifted the cover gingerly. It broke apart in her hands, and the page beneath was so stained with rot that she could not make out any of the text. She set it aside and reached for another, and another—but each one had been so tainted with age and damp as to be unreadable. Yeva was so unprepared for the swell of anguish at the thought of the knowledge lost in this room that she sat down hard on the floor, gasping for air. Doe-Eyes pressed in against her—though she didn't know why, she knew her mistress was upset, and gave her ear a tentative lick.

"You are unhappy." The somber voice came from behind her, but Yeva had grown so accustomed to the Beast's abrupt appearances that she felt only a flicker of surprise.

She turned to see him filling the doorway, a large shadow with gleaming eyes. She wiped at her face and cleared her throat. "I'd hoped to be able to read these," she said quietly. "I used to love hearing my father—" Her voice stuck, and as she gazed back at the Beast, a dull flicker of that angry despair rose up. She'd never hear her father read to her again.

The Beast let the silence stretch, the only sound the gentle scrape of his paw on the stone as he shifted his weight from one foot to the other. "Come," he said, and without waiting for her to answer, turned and vanished from the doorway.

Yeva considered ignoring the order out of spite, but she'd begun to sense differences in the Beast's voice. Sometimes his orders were heavy and sharp and designed to make her feel small and helpless. But at other times, like this one, there was a plea evident in the tone, and though he never said "please" or "will you" or "might I suggest," there was nonetheless room in his voice for her to refuse.

So she rose to her feet, one hand on Doe-Eyes's back to steady herself, and followed the Beast out into the corridor.

He led her clear to the other side of the castle, walking in silence. Yeva's lantern didn't cast its light far enough to illuminate his path, but the darkness didn't seem to bother him. He never put a foot wrong or hesitated or clipped a wall.

He padded into the master suite of chambers, which had no other exit as far as Yeva was aware. But instead of coming to a halt, he crossed toward one of the tapestries. An instant before he reached for it, Yeva saw that it was brighter and cleaner than the others, having collected less dust—and when the Beast lifted it aside, she realized why. It concealed a thick ironbound door that swung soundlessly inward at the Beast's paw.

The secret door led to another stair, and as Yeva transposed her mental image of the castle as seen from the ridge above the valley onto the corridors she'd begun to learn, she thought they must be ascending into one of the thick round turrets. The Beast climbed the stair ahead of her, always just vanishing around the curve of the wall as she glimpsed him, but she saw enough to discover that he was climbing the staircase on two legs, not four, and her heart began to slam against her rib cage. Though the joints of his legs were all wrong, and his tail still swept after him, and his fur still caught the lantern light, to see him walking like a man caused all her questions to surge up again until she almost forgot the lost library below.

The stair led to another door, and this time the Beast stopped. He dropped back down onto all fours as Yeva approached, and he paused. His eyes flicked back over his shoulder at her, and she saw indecision written there, recognized his hesitation as clearly as she would've on one of her sister's faces. Then he gave himself a shake and reached out with one paw toward the latch.

She'd never quite seen how he managed many of the things he did—though it'd become quite obvious that no one else lived in the castle and that the Beast must have cooked her food while she was in the cell, lit her lanterns, locked and unlocked her chains. No beast with only paws and teeth could do such things, and Yeva had to admit the role that magic played in every aspect of the Beast's existence. Perhaps he merely did it with a wave of his paw, the same way he simply walked on top of the snow as if it were solid ground, or turned his own scent off like a tap to hide himself from nature.

But this time, as she watched, he *changed*. His paw seemed to shimmer before her eyes, rippling like hot air escaping a door into a frosty morning. Her eyes ached with the need to look away, but she forced herself to watch, ordering herself not to miss it this time. The furry toes lengthened, the claws shortening, the whole wrist joint shifting up. It was not a hand, nor a paw, but something in between. And it held a key.

He unlocked the door deftly, and the key vanished somewhere about his person. By the time he put his hand back down it was a paw again, and he glanced back at her as if nothing strange had taken place. "Come," he said again, more gently this time.

She followed him into the room.

The room was round and held four windows, shuttered tightly against the winter outside. The ceiling above was peaked, supported by wooden crossbeams that had been repaired and replaced over the years, each one stained a slightly different shade by time. Like the one below the castle, this room was obviously lived in. Unlike that one, however, the furnishings here were not cobbled together from whatever bits and pieces were least destroyed throughout the castle's many rooms—here they were of a kind. A low daybed divan stretched along one wall below a shuttered window, bordered on each side by matching end tables. Odds and ends scattered their surfaces: a rabbit's skull hung with beads and feathers; a tiny box inlaid with mother-of-pearl; a small stone figurine of a knight such as a child might play with, worn shiny with use. Rugs of thick blue shag covered the floor, and the hearth at the far side of the room glowed with fresh coals.

The Beast turned to a wardrobe that stood near the divan, and sank bank on his haunches so he could reach with both paws to open the wardrobe doors. The air shimmered again, but this time it was easier to watch as he shifted enough to grasp at the door handles. She expected to see what one normally finds inside a wardrobe: cloaks, dresses, shoes, hatboxes—or else, she supposed, tunics and leggings, if the masculine decor spoke to the room's original occupant.

Instead the wardrobe was full of books.

Unlike those in the library below, the leather of these spines was bright with color, showing the original dyes, and their titles were stamped deep. Though the gold and silver leaf was worn from some of them, others she could read. Still others were written in languages she had never seen before.

She felt her breath leave her, and before she knew what she was doing, she came up beside the Beast so she could lift the lantern higher and scan the collection. There were maybe thirty or forty of them—nothing to how many were in the ruined library—but these had been cared for, protected and preserved against the years. And though they showed wear, cracked spines and corners rubbed such that the dye had faded, it was the kind of wear from use, the wear her own family's books had shown before they sold them. These books were read, many times. These books were loved.

The Beast shifted at her side, his fur brushing her arm and making her shiver. He was warm, warmer even than the coals in the hearth.

Yeva's mind spun. The spines that she could read bore the names of old knights' tales, the cataloging of magical creatures, adventures in distant lands she'd never heard of. No dry scholar's texts—all stories.

"You . . ." Yeva was so taken by surprise that she found it difficult to speak. "You—you saved these?"

The Beast's eyes slid from the contents of the wardrobe to Yeva's face, then back again. "Someone else used to live here," he said finally. "It was he who rescued these from the damp."

Yeva tore her eyes from the books so she could study the Beast's profile. When she looked again at the room she saw details she hadn't noticed before. The shag carpet lying before the fire was worn more than the others, flattened and thickened with fine pale-gray hairs, the same color as those coating the Beast's underbelly. The inside of the door was grooved with scratches, such as might be left by someone with claws before he remembered how to use a latch.

"You live here," she whispered, turning in a slow circle as her gaze flew about the round tower room. "This is where you stay when you don't stay in the cave."

The Beast's eyes fell to the floor. "Yes."

"But . . . why show me this now? These books, the trinkets . . . they're yours. Why keep it from me before?"

The Beast didn't answer. She could not see his eyes, for his head was dropped down and gaze fixed to the floor. The Beast remained silent for a time, and if it weren't for the way his chest rose and fell with increasing speed, Yeva would think he was ignoring her. But his emotions were rising, his breathing quickening, and she waited.

"You would not have cared," he burst out in a snarl. "We have no desire to change your opinion of us. You are our weapon. Nothing more. That you stay because you are waiting for the chance to kill us only serves our ends, to keep you here for our task."

Once, Yeva would have shrunk from his temper. Once, that snarl would have made her tremble. Now she just stared at him, a thousand questions spinning in her mind. Though her lips kept trying to shape the questions into words, there were too many for her to sort through, and she could only stand there, mouth opening and closing.

The Beast looked up finally to see her dumbfounded expression, and the too-human eyes faltered for an instant, brows lifting from fury into pain. Then he turned on his heels and stalked toward the door.

"Beast!" Yeva tore her feet from the ground and ran to throw herself between him and the door. "Wait."

The Beast paused, head dropping low, so low his muzzle nearly brushed the carpet. Yeva knew the body language from years of caring for Doe-Eyes and Pelei—shame. He regretted his outburst.

"Thank you . . . for showing me this," Yeva said.

The Beast's head swung round until he could fix those staring eyes on her, and this time they were round with surprise. Yeva had never thanked him for anything before, not since learning the truth of what he was. "You—" His voice deepened. "You may come here to read whenever you wish. I will leave the door unlocked."

Yeva's heart pounded as the Beast made his departure, his paw pads whispering against the stone as he went. She was wrong— she *had* thanked him once before, when he'd brought her a deer and called her Beauty.

She'd meant it then.

She meant it now, too. And that, more than the Beast's temper, more than the snarl of his fangs and the snap of his jaws, made her shiver. The reason he'd never shown her this room before was because he had no reason to do so. She was his captive, kept for his purpose. And he'd revealed this room now, this part of himself, simply because she had been sad . . . because he'd seen, in the way she looked at the ruined library, how much a room like this would mean to her.

Her vision blurred and she swiped angrily at her eyes. She ought to throw every one of these cared-for books into the fire. She ought to smash every keepsake and memento in this room. She ought to want to hurt the Beast in any way she could.

She crouched on the floor, burying her face in her arms. She couldn't stay here any longer. Each answer she found led her further from destroying this creature, this murderer, this thing that had killed her father. *He* was the reason she'd never hear her father read to her again. *He* was the reason her sisters must believe she was dead. *He* was the reason for everything. She could not let a place like this change any of that.

Doe-Eyes nuzzled at her elbow until she lifted her head, stroking absently behind her dog's ears. Her eyes fell upon the hearth, on the rug before it and its coating of fine hairs from the Beast's coat. She gazed at it for a long time, enough time for her thoughts to still and her pulse to quiet. The pieces were slow to connect, and she felt them sliding into place with something almost like dread.

For in showing her this room, the Beast had given her exactly what she'd been trying to find all these long months.

She'd known from the lack of tracks outside that he was not spending his nights in the dark den below the foundation. But she knew now where he slept in the castle, where he was at his most vulnerable.

She wasn't fast enough or skilled enough to kill him, not when he was awake and watching her, alert to her every movement. But if he were asleep . . .

Yeva forced herself to remember that moment in the forest all those weeks and months ago when she'd found her father's body. She forced herself to remember the surge of nausea when she realized that the Beast had killed him, that the blood spattered around that clearing was her father's. She made her mind flood with images of blood, and revenge, and hatred. She'd never hear her father read to her again, and the Beast had reminded her of it. Perhaps he felt guilty, and that was what prompted these little kindnesses, and there was a part of Yeva that needled her to think of using them against him—but she was stronger than the Beast, and she was harder, and she could outlast his guilt without caving to her own sympathy for his plight. She let the needles stab at her, again and again, until she felt numbed to their sting.

Because now she had the means to make everything right. She'd be able to go home, to her sisters and to Albe and to Solmir, though she could not think of them, not yet, not until it was done. It would not be tonight, nor tomorrow, but soon.

Soon she'd be able to kill the Beast.

BEAST

We see the way she looks at us. We are not blind.

She hates. When she forgets herself the hate retreats, like the river's waters in summer, but the damp sandy scars that stretch through the valley tell of the groundwater still there, still carving its course through the forest. And her hatred is still there, and its scars mark her face every time she sees us.

She must not know the truth. All we need is for her to stay, and complete her task, and if the thirst for revenge is what will keep her at our side, well, then we've thirsted enough to know she will stay until time robs her of youth and leaves her bent and trembling.

I wish just once she would look at me without hate.

But wishing is for men. Wanting is what brought us here. Desire and greed are human traits.

We are the Beast.

And yet . . . I wish.

SIXTEEN

WHEN THE STORMS RETREATED, the Beast began to take Yeva hunting again. Yeva had expected the weather to shift, for by her makeshift calendar she'd spent many months here, and spring ought to have begun creeping delicately in at the edges of the forest. But the valley remained blanketed with snow, a new dusting falling every few days to erase their tracks and give them a fresh canvas from which to work.

Yeva began to use that glimpse of magic the Beast had shown her, and slowly she became better at it. Soon she could track the Beast for leagues before she lost his trail, and the thrill of hunting prey that could outwit her, outsmart her, quickened her steps and sharpened the air in her lungs. She slept more soundly and deeply than she had in weeks cooped up in the castle.

Sometimes the Beast would spring from nowhere, shortly after she lost his trail, and demonstrate that he'd been two paces behind her for the last half hour, and Yeva would let herself laugh. The sound seemed to hearten the Beast, and Yeva felt his body language shifting, his manner warming. Spring had not come to the wood, but it was coming to the Beast's heart. And at the same time, she hardened her own.

It was no different from tracking him through the wood. Day by day she grew better, faster, more sensitive to the hints of magic that would alert her to his presence. And day by day, inch by grueling inch, he let down his guard.

One night Yeva returned to the castle after giving up on the Beast's trail to find that he had beaten her back, and had moved a number of pieces of furniture from the underground room into the one she'd chosen for herself. The blue velvet divan was there, and the table, and a big flat cushion stuffed with wheat husks and hay had appeared before the hearth. It was onto this cushion that Doe-Eyes sprang immediately and rolled around until she could stretch all four snow-covered paws out toward the fire, which crackled merrily.

Yeva stood in the doorway, fingering the tip of her bow, which she had not yet unstrung. She stared, feeling vague and uneasy, heart rebelling at how swiftly she felt at home here. This was not, could never be, home.

"Is there anything else you wish for?" The Beast spoke from a few paces behind her.

Yeva swallowed. "It's wonderful."

The Beast hovered just beyond the doorway. His gaze was on her hands, which still gripped her father's bow.

She took a deep breath and then slipped her leg between bow and string so she could bend it across her thigh and unstring it, there while the Beast watched. She set it in its corner and turned her back. She had to stop to remember how, and then, with effort, turned to smile at the Beast. "Thank you."

The Beast's ears flicked, flattened, then shot up again, which spoke to Yeva of surprise, then pleasure. He shuffled back a step, and before her eyes, he shimmered. It was the same eye-straining blur that occurred when he needed dexterity for locks or latches, but this time it was all of him, and for a moment he seemed like something else, some*one* else. Yeva heard a swell of music, like that she heard in the wood—only this was a song all his own, a thread she could separate and listen to and know.

Then the Beast shook himself and the mirage fell away like a shower of stray hairs. He took another step back.

"Good night, Beauty," he said, and quickly hurried into the shadowy corridor.

Yeva waited, controlling her breathing with an effort. She knew the Beast would hear the sound of her quickening breath if she let him.

"Sleep well," she whispered—then sat down to wait.

"Stay," Yeva whispered to Doe-Eyes, catching and holding the dog's gaze. She didn't like asserting her dominance, for it made Doe-Eyes unhappy and uncertain, but Yeva couldn't risk the dog coming after her anyway and alerting the Beast. Still, the fleet hound rose up, head cocked uncertainly, as Yeva moved toward the door. "Mind the house," Yeva said automatically, the command that had for years stood for two things: that Doe-Eyes must stay, and, most importantly, that Yeva would return.

Doe-Eyes sat back down and then, with reluctance, dropped her head onto her paws.

Yeva slipped into the corridor, knife resting comfortably in her palm. It was the blade the Beast had given her for butchering and carving, and if it was not quite as sharp as her fletching knife, it was much larger, and she'd grown familiar with it over the months. She let it hang from her hand beneath her cloak, easy to hide should the Beast be awake and spot her.

He could be watching her even now, from the shadows—but Yeva did not think so. She felt certain if he were near, she'd hear that thread of magic, that song that was all his own. If he were watching her, she'd hear the way that song quickened when he saw her, quickened to match the rate of her own heartbeat. And though her heart was racing now, she could not hear the Beast's song.

As she reached the hidden spiral stair leading to the turret, her heart pounded even harder. She wished she could control it as she could her breath, but she settled for controlling her speed, and moved quickly up the stairs and through the door. She slipped to the right and pressed her body against the side of the wardrobe. The room was lit dimly by the remains of a fire, and she saw the bulk of the Beast on the daybed along the wall. The steady rise and fall of his outline told Yeva that he slept.

Or pretends to sleep.

She'd thought of bringing her bow, so she then wouldn't have to risk crossing the room and getting close to the Beast. But even if her arrows could penetrate his hide, her best shot would be to perforate a lung, and it would take him far, far too long to suffocate to death. Enough time, certainly, to kill Yeva for what she'd done. Further, Yeva didn't know the extent of his magic, and whether he'd be able to heal such a wound. Her attack would have to be decisive, and brutal in order to be final.

If she could kill him from here, though, she would not have to see his face. And he would never see hers. Never know who had struck the killing blow. Never know it was his Beauty that had ended him.

She forced herself to shed those thoughts. She would have to be close to him when she struck. Her best chance was to cut his throat. He would kill her instinctively unless she penetrated deeply enough to nick his spinal column and deaden his movements. But even a Beast would bleed to death in seconds if she could open his jugular. Too quick for any magic he might summon.

She crept closer, watching for the slightest change in the rise and fall of his body. She breathed silently, forbade herself from taking any deeper breaths, forbade herself from swallowing her nervousness, for the tiniest sound could wake him. Something tickled at the back of her mind that the scene wasn't right, something about the proportions of the room that made her feel as though she were in a dream and watching the world distort. She felt too large, and the room too large as well. . . .

She realized what it was: the Beast was smaller.

And then he rolled over, and she saw why.

His form was human.

Not entirely human—it was as if the aspect of the wolf was laid overtop him like a costume. And like a costume, it didn't seem real. The ears and the teeth and the claws were but shadows. Yeva froze, staring down at his face with the knife clenched in her hand.

She'd long known that the Beast had two natures, and that they fought within him. She'd seen him use his hands, seen him shift a little when she treated him with kindness, saw the humanity in his eyes when he was at his softest.

He seemed to shift without thinking, without comment, and Yeva had wondered if it were possible he wasn't aware of it, or if his outward appearance shifted as involuntarily as the beating of his own heart. The knife felt like lead in her hand.

Do it, said the vengeful voice in her heart. *Before he catches your scent and wakes. Now! He is your father's murderer no matter what face he wears.*

Yeva lifted the knife.

The Beast's lips parted, his eyelids flickering. "Yeva," he mumbled. "Beauty."

She froze. He was dreaming about her. She swallowed before she could stop herself, body flooding with every ounce of uncertainty she'd been pushing into the dark, unseen corners of her mind where she wouldn't have to face it.

She swallowed, and the Beast heard it, and his eyes opened.

They met hers, still clouded with dreams, hazel-gold reflecting the firelight and holding no other hint of red. "Beauty," he said again, more distinctly, and his mouth was human, and Yeva could not move. His mouth. She couldn't look away.

The Beast's face cleared of sleep, and he blinked, and then he saw the knife. For an instant his eyes snapped back to Yeva's, shock and confusion and hurt mixing together, and in that moment he *was* human, and Yeva saw it, that only his human aspect could register and respond to this kind of betrayal.

She knew in another heartbeat he'd be the Beast again. And because she knew she'd die when he was, and because the animal instinct deep in her heart knew what to do, she struck.

The knife stabbed deep into his throat, and hit bone, and Yeva gasped aloud as she jerked the knife sideways, trying to slice. It wasn't quite sharp enough and it met with resistance, all the tissues and tendons in his neck fighting her. His gasp turned to a gurgle and to a whimper. And then the knife was out, and there was blood everywhere, blood on the rug and blood spattering the wardrobe. Blood spattered the pages of a book that had been left open by his bedside, as though he'd been reading just before he slept. Blood hissed and spat in the coals. Blood mixed with the tears Yeva suddenly found coursing down her cheeks and dripped, watery red and thin, onto her tunic.

The Beast moaned again, and he was once more every inch the wolf, except that Yeva thought she heard a word in the horrible hissing gurgle: "Beauty." Was it her name? Or was her heart searching for the word, somehow wanting to find it in that sighing death rattle?

A final breath. And then he was still.

Yeva dropped the knife, discovering that part of the moan echoing through the tower had been her own, and her voice petered out into a thin, reedy cry until she gulped for air. She staggered back and fell, landing on the plush carpet. The room spun as she lifted her hand to her face, and she inspected herself, because she could not be sure the Beast hadn't struck her before he died.

But she was whole.

She gasped again, the sound emerging hesitantly, like her body needed to confirm the Beast was really dead and she was really alive, despite the evidence before her eyes. Yeva could not look at the body and so stared at the bloodstained book until its image was burned into her eyes. She waited for a sense of victory. Triumph. Elation. Anything.

But she felt . . . nothing.

No, that was wrong. As the room quieted and her heart settled and her mind slowly, slowly began to uncurl itself and reinhabit her body, she *did* feel something. Hear something. Very faint, but growing with every breath.

Music. The song of magic.

The Beast opened his eyes.

Yeva cried out and scrambled backward until she hit the wall. The knife was out of reach, but she could not even think of it now. The Beast had been dead, she was sure of it, yet now she was staring at this impossible thing as it happened in front of her.

The Beast's gaping throat knit itself together neatly, as though she was watching a seam ripping in reverse. His lungs filled in one great, wet, rattling breath, and he coughed more blood onto the rug, and then he breathed again, and this time coughed pink foam, and then he lifted his head and, reeling as from a great blow, rolled onto the floor and onto his feet.

He gave a muted roar, sounding almost more inconvenienced and befuddled than furious, and stumbled forward a step. Then his head, still moving haltingly as the bones and tendons in his neck repaired themselves, swung over until his eyes found Yeva.

She could not even brace herself. She'd known he was magic, but this was sorcery beyond anything she could have imagined. This was nothing she could fight. She'd never felt so utterly helpless. The Beast would leap upon her soon and end it, and her terror was so real and so complete that she found herself praying that he would, and now, so that she would not have to feel this all-consuming fear an instant longer.

"Do not be afraid," he whispered, then fell over, sideways, and slumped to the floor.

Yeva sat gasping, staring at the Beast. She did not imagine him speaking to her instead of simply tearing her apart, and she certainly had not expected his words to be . . . *kind.*

She found her shoulder blades peeling from the wall. Her body seemed to move on its own, crawling on all fours closer to the Beast.

He groaned, and lifted his head. His mouth was half open, panting like an animal who's been too long in the sun and must cool itself—but these gasps were for breath, and Yeva knew there was still blood in his lungs, and that he'd fallen over from lack of air. "Do you think . . . ," he said haltingly, stopping to pant, "I had not tried . . . to end my life . . . already?"

Yeva could not speak, only stare at him numbly.

"I suppose . . . ," he wheezed, "it never occurred . . . to you." He let his great head drop onto his paws, exhaustion closing his eyes.

"What?" Yeva managed to whisper.

"That I am a prisoner too. And have been far longer than you."

Yeva was suddenly, keenly, brutally aware of her body; of the muscles strained and screaming; of the pounding in her own head from too much air, hyperventilated; of the way blood stuck her fingers together, the way it had somehow gotten inside the leg of her trousers, and was sticking the back of her knee to itself when she crawled. Her eyes burned, and she didn't know whether they held tears, or if some of the Beast's blood had gotten into them.

The Beast drew several long breaths, and each one slid a little bit more smoothly into his chest than the one before. "For a time—I do not know how much time—I tried everything I could think of. I threw myself from my tower. I opened my veins. I walked out into the cold and lay down in the snow and waited for the winter to take me, but it never did. I stopped eating, starved for months and waited to sleep and sleep and never stir again, but I woke every morning the same, emptiness within me. I begged Lamya, and the others, to kill me. But they also failed."

He stopped for another breath before opening his eyes to look at Yeva, a great sadness in them that cut through her shock, finally, and left her on the verge of weeping. "If I thought you would have succeeded I would have let you kill me that day in the forest, when you found your father, and followed me into my trap."

"Why?" Yeva trembled, her voice as raspy as if it had been her throat slashed. "Why forbid me to try to kill you, why threaten my family . . ." She swallowed. "Why lie?"

"Because we know wanting. We know desire. We know need."

"Need . . ."

"You needed to believe you had a purpose. You needed to believe that you could kill me. You needed . . . hope." The Beast watched her, the great sad eyes empty of all that rage, all that bestial ferocity that she'd seen that first day in the wood. "Now you understand that there is none."

They stared at each other across the bloodied rugs, the spattered pages of the book, the glinting, sticky knife. The coals in the hearth glowed steadily, and outside the winter wind sang through the mouths of the gargoyles and blew snow against the castle stones, and somewhere down below Doe-Eyes waited, ears pricked and eyes closed, for the sound of Yeva's footsteps returning.

"Tell me," the Beast said softly. "If you had known, from the start, that I could not be killed, that you would never have your vengeance . . . would you have stayed?"

Yeva didn't answer. She could not answer. Her heart had emptied. Her desire for revenge had nowhere to go. Without it, what did she have? What was she? What had she become?

But the Beast's words had stung her, touching a buried current she'd been ignoring for days. For weeks. Ever since he'd brought her a deer and, over its carcass, had called her *Beauty*.

"Beast," she whispered, numb. "Did you kill my father?"

His eyes flickered, the ghost of something passing before them so that for a moment he wasn't looking at her anymore, but at some memory, some thought she could not see. He didn't answer, but rose unsteadily to his feet. Before she knew what she was doing, Yeva stood as well and crossed to his side.

The Beast froze. His gaze dropped from Yeva's face to where

her hand had come to press against his chest to keep him from leaving.

She swallowed, abruptly aware of how infrequently she touched him, and forced herself to fight the instinct to withdraw. He moved as if to brush past her, but Yeva didn't take her hand from his chest, and dug her fingers into the soft fur.

"Let me go," the Beast said quietly. Then, so soft she almost missed it: "Please."

"He was already dead, wasn't he?" Yeva said. "When I came upon him in that clearing. You were coming to find him, to track the hunter you needed for your task, and you came upon his body moments before I did. The scavengers had gotten to him. He was already dead, wasn't he?"

The Beast shifted, the muscles stirring beneath her hand, reminding her that if the Beast truly wished to leave, he could brush her aside with an easy swat of his paw.

He did not answer. There was no need.

"Why take me?" Yeva asked.

The Beast's eyes closed, as if it might be easier to speak without Yeva's face before them. "Because I thought hunters like your father would come after you if you disappeared. I thought I could take one of them for my task. I knew I had to find someone else, someone younger, but still possessing his skill. I did not know then that you . . ."

The Beast's breath hitched. Yeva could feel it under her hand, and the beat of his pulse, so very like the music she heard in the wood. For the first time she understood how the Beast could hear it as a heartbeat.

"I did not know," he began again, "that you were the one I'd been searching for."

Before she could respond he slipped past her. Yeva could hear his steps for once, halting as he continued to recover from the mortal wound she'd given him, fading down the long curved stair of the tower. She thought they sounded like the rhythm of two feet rather than the gallop of four.

Nothing in her body was working, not her lungs nor her legs, and Yeva dropped to the floor with a feeling like knives in her chest. She began to sob so violently her body felt as if it might shatter. The fury that had sustained her, the burning need for revenge that had kept her alive in the cell, that had driven her in the wood to hone her archery and her tracking—what did she have now? Her fire had gone, and she felt its loss as keenly as if she were mourning a death.

And she was. When her father's death had been a murder, when he'd died because a savage Beast had ripped out his throat, she didn't have to grieve. She could find his killer and destroy him, stand over him, watch him die. She could have shaken the very earth with her vengeance and filled the gaping hole in her heart with blood.

She could have killed death itself.

But all that was gone now. Instead her father had died an old man's death, from a weakened heart and an unsound mind. He'd died cold and alone in a wood that he no longer knew. And there was no one who could pay for it, no one whose blood could dilute Yeva's grief.

She lay there on the floor, weeping into the blood-soaked rug, surrounded by the books her father would never read to her, the castle he would never see, the approaching spring that, for him, would never come. And as if by the same magic that had transformed the Beast, she became nothing more than a little girl who'd lost her father.

BEAST

The sound of her weeping follows us to the farthest reaches of the castle, even into our den below, back, back into the earth and the deep. We curse our animal's hearing and we curse our man's knowledge of what grief is and we curse the unfamiliar ache of regret that creeps ever deeper, ever deeper.

We curse everything, for we are cursed, and we have no arms to shelter her and no lips to press to her hair and above all no words to tell her that we know loss and we know pain and if they were monsters we could fight we would have slain them in her name long ago like the heroes of old.

But we are not a hero. We are cursed.

SEVENTEEN

EVENTUALLY YEVA'S WEEPING SLOWED, for though the lancing pain in her heart remained, her eyes could produce no more tears. She could not bring herself to stand, feeling as weak as if she'd been in bed for weeks—instead she crawled to the divan and slumped into its velvet cushions.

She slept.

Later she woke to a tiny sound, no louder than a whisper, but a sound she knew so well. A single footstep, the slip of paw pads against stone. The Beast was on the other side of the door. She waited, but he did not speak, and did not enter. After a time, she heard his footsteps retreating again, and she rose shakily to her feet. When she opened the door, she found food and a water skin and, wrapped in a roll of faded linen, her arrow-making supplies—and Doe-Eyes, having grown anxious waiting for her below, hoping to be allowed inside.

And then she found she could still weep, for the Beast who knew she did not want company and gave her that solitude, for

the Beast who could not know how badly she *wanted* him to speak
with her, about anything other than her father, and nothing but
her father. She wept because she did not know what she wanted,
and because she wanted everything, and because her father was
dead.

She could not eat, so in time she slept again. This time hunger
woke her, and Doe-Eyes's nosing at her elbow. Yeva stumbled
toward the bowl of stew the Beast had left for her. It was cold
now when she uncovered it, but she ate it anyway, ate until she
forced herself to stop so she could offer the rest of it to Doe-
Eyes, who sat at her feet trying not to stare longingly at the food
in Yeva's hands.

Yeva sank back down onto the divan to the sounds of Doe-
Eyes noisily cleaning out the rest of the bowl. Her eyes fell once
more upon that book, the one the Beast had been reading where
he slept, the one whose pages were stained with his blood. Her
mind felt numb with the truth.

The Beast had not killed her father.

She had no more reason to stay, for each time the Beast had
repeated his threat to punish her family if she escaped, she had
believed it less and less. Now, as she thought of the pain in his
eyes as he finally told her the truth, she knew he would not harm
them, as surely as she knew the rhythm of her own heartbeat.
She could leave. She could walk now out the door and down the
bridge and out of the valley and never look back. She could go
home.

As if the thought of them had summoned their spirits, Yeva
felt the absence of her family so keenly, so abruptly, that she
bent over at the waist and rested her head on her balled fists. She
wanted Asenka, and her warm smile, and the feel of the wool
between Yeva's fingers as Asenka knit. She wanted Lena's energy

and spirit, and even her scolding, and could not help but imagine what she would say of Yeva's appearance if she could see her now, bloodstained and thin. She wanted Albe's fumbling attempts at kindness, his endearing grin, his devotion to the family that had raised him from childhood. She even wanted Solmir—the simplicity of him, how easy it would be to go with him back to the town to be his wife and ride horses through the trees and have servants to draw her baths, and books, and her sisters, and her dogs, and a life without magic and mysteries, and in that instant she knew she *could* do it. She could live that life. And just now she wanted it more than anything else.

She left the high tower room. She descended the twisting spiral turret, and walked through the master bedroom suite and into the long corridor, and down the next staircase and into the foyer and down the wide marble steps onto the wide marble floor. She pushed against the broad doors until they opened enough to send her stumbling and gasping and blinking into the harsh glare of the sun and the snow. She went sliding and stumbling down the snow-covered slope until she stood at the mouth of the Beast's cave, breathing hard, breath steaming the air, and sun-dazzled eyes conjuring wraiths out of the gloom to swim and twist beyond the edges of her vision.

"Beauty." The voice came from the depths of the cave, low and soft, velvet bass that echoed in the same place deep within her that heard the music of the magic wood.

"Beast," she answered, still breathing hard. "I must go."

Silence. She could not see him, only darkness, but she knew he could see her silhouette against the daylight at the mouth of the cave. Then, softly, his voice came again. "I know."

Yeva's heart shrank. It would have been easier if he'd roared at her, if he'd knocked her to the ground, locked her up, given her reason to hate him again. It would have been easier if he'd been the Beast. She swallowed. "My family. They're all alone. I have to go to them."

"You do not have to explain."

But I want to. Yeva stood, hands twisting in the fabric of her cloak, listening to Doe-Eyes pace around behind her, uncomfortable so close to the Beast's den.

Some part of the shadows moved, and she saw his eyes, gleaming briefly with reflected sunlight—then he moved again and the glimpse was gone. "Will you give your word to return someday?" the Beast said, so softly Yeva could not be certain she hadn't imagined it.

Yeva's mouth opened, but all she could think of was the echo of the conversation they'd had long ago, when they first stood face-to-face. "I will give you my word I won't try to kill you again."

"You did not promise to come back," the Beast said, and his voice was a lament, so shattered that Yeva almost began to weep again.

"No," she whispered instead. "I didn't."

She closed her eyes and listened with her soul, and from deep within the hollow of the cave she heard the Beast's song, the pulse of magic he'd taught her to hear. It was low and sweet, heavy with pain and age and the blurring of time. It held hints of things long forgotten, of stories and words and dreams and, most of all, desires.

The song *wanted*. It wanted in the way Yeva had always wanted, wanted not so much a thing as *everything*, something beyond naming, something *more than*, different, deeper. It was the want that kept her from saying yes to Solmir, though he offered her everything she could have named aloud; it was the want that brought her to the woods each day, the want that filled her dreams of some other life, something beyond what others desired; it was the want that screamed to the sky that she'd give everything, all of herself and all she'd ever be, to live one moment of that other life, the one she could not explain, not even to herself.

She closed her eyes and listened to the Beast's heart.

And before she could begin to weep again, she turned and she ran.

BEAST

Beauty. We feel her running, the spark of her life in our senses speeding southward, but growing no less dim for distance. We feel her like a star in the thick darkness of our valley, but she draws near its edge.

We thought we would have more time.

We should not have let her go.

We had to let her go.

Beauty. Beauty.

Hunter, hunted. We no longer know which she is, which we want her to be, which we need her to be. We know only that we need her. We must bring her back.

You must bring her back. You desire her. You want her.

Yes. But she is Beauty. She will be free. I wish her to be free.

The spark of her teeters on the edge of our senses, the edge of the valley, and then twinkles out. In every direction there is only the long, dark cold of winter.

Beauty.

Beauty.

Beauty.

EIGHTEEN

FOR A LONG TIME Yeva was only aware of the pounding of her feet and the soles of her boots and the crunch of the snow, and the icy air cutting deep into her lungs with every breath, and Doe-Eyes's joyful panting as the dog ran at her side. If she had not been training with the Beast almost every day she would not have been able to breathe the frigid air so easily, but she'd hardened her lungs against the cold and she ran like a deer, like a wolf, like Beauty.

Eventually the ache in her thighs and the tightening of her lungs slowed her, until she walked, numb, her muscles crackling with energy and pinging like red-hot metal cooling slowly after being pulled from the blacksmith's forge. Then, abruptly, she stopped.

She was sweating. The sun was warm on the top of her head, through the dappled leaves—*leaves?*—and she was no longer wading through snow.

There *was* no snow. Anywhere.

There were leaves on the trees.

It was spring.

No—she blinked, then blinked again, then stared upward, uncomprehending. The leaves overhead were golden and red, and fire orange, and her feet crunched as she walked, but not from snow. The toes of her boots disturbed piles of fallen leaves, and through the long arcs of the trees she saw a shimmer of gold here and a flash of red there as individual leaves tumbled and fell here and there in the still, autumn air.

Autumn.

Yeva's heart shrank.

She realized that time, like so many things in the Beast's valley, did not work there as it did in the outside world. But what she didn't know, what she could have no way of knowing, was how much time had passed. Had she missed only one summer? Or had a thousand years slipped away, so that her sisters' children, and their children's children, had all long since crumbled to dust?

Doe-Eyes, heedless of the strangeness of winter becoming autumn on the other side of the mountains, was leaping from leaf pile to leaf pile, sinking up to her shoulders and then bounding free, tongue flying from her gap-jawed grin.

But none of that could lift Yeva's heart, which felt small and tight and cold in her chest.

It took her days to find a familiar landmark, and it was no more than the proximity of a rabbit's den to a particular evergreen that triggered her memory. She'd seen that burrow before, many months—or perhaps many centuries—ago. She knew the forest in the Beast's valley now better than she'd ever known the one surrounding her father's cabin, but as she stood, turning slowly in a circle, she felt her instincts click a sense of her surroundings into place.

Home is that way.

Another two days, and she and Doe-Eyes found the stream that ran to a fork around the clearing. And as the sun set, they emerged into the clearing and saw the cabin.

It was empty.

Yeva's breath caught and for a while she merely stood there, blank, her thoughts coming in strange fragments. She was too tired to put them together with sense. But as Doe-Eyes began to sniff around the cabin, then sniff more urgently, then paw at the door with enthusiasm, a few things began to settle.

The clearing was still clear, and bigger than it had been, with only a few leaf-covered lumps to tell of the trees that had been hewn down for firewood. The wagon was gone, and as Yeva opened the door, she saw that much of the furniture was as well. And the floor, but for a few cobwebs in the corners, was tidy and clear.

The cabin might be empty, but it was emptied recently. Yeva strode back out into the clearing, scanning the ground for any sign of the wagon, or of horse tracks. But while the tidiness meant that the cabin had not lain abandoned for more than a few months, it would have taken only a few weeks, or even days if there was rain, for all trace of her family's path to vanish.

Yeva spent that night in the cabin, shivering in front of a small fire not because the air was cold, but because her heart was, and she could not warm it up. She resolved to return to the town, and ask if anyone there had heard from Tvertko's daughters, or knew in what direction they'd traveled, or of anything that had become of them.

For all she knew she *had* been gone centuries, and it was some other family, some other wagon, some other life that had moved away from this cabin and given her hope.

Hope, the Beast had said.

Yeva clenched her jaw and refused to think of him, and of the great sadness in his eyes, and of the way he'd simply let her go, because he had nothing else with which to hold her.

But while she could control her thoughts to some degree, she could not control her dreams once she fell asleep, and while her guard was down every thought was of the Beast, and her ears rang with the song of magic, and the beat of wings, and she woke sandy-eyed and weary at dawn.

She stopped at the first farmstead she reached and traded a brace of rabbits for some brown bread and apples and a mug of cider, and though the farmer's wife stared at her and surreptitiously made a sign to ward off evil, Yeva asked them nonetheless what year it was, and found that only one year had passed since her father's ruin, and that she hadn't spent a century in the Beast's company.

She moved on, and paid for a night in an inn with a handful of quail's eggs and an archery lesson for the innkeeper's son, and was so thrown by the feel of sheets and linens against her skin that she ended up sleeping on the rug before the fire with Doe-Eyes.

She reached the outskirts of town on a gray afternoon, fits of rain bursting from the sodden clouds to wet Yeva's hair and weight her cloak. She was aching to find someone who might know of where her family went, or what had befallen them, but after the farmer's wife's reaction, she did not want to start rumors of a crazy madwoman associated with them—for on the chance that her family was alive and well, she wanted them to stay that way.

It wasn't until she spotted a familiar face that she darted out from the alley into the street. "Galina!" Yeva exclaimed, shocked by her old friend's face. She looked so young, her skin so light and clean, not a hair out of place. Even the line of mud edging her skirt from the street was orderly, and civilized—everything Yeva had lost over the past year.

Galina jumped, startled, and then stumbled backward upon seeing Yeva. Yeva knew she must look alarming: muddy, scratched, weatherworn, and wet. Her arms and legs were lean with muscle now, and her hair was coarse with its own oils and dust from leaves and wind. Her clothes were still the bloodstained ones she'd worn when she'd tried to slay the Beast, and though the stains were old and brown, they were not hard to identify. The dog at her side was as wet and muddy as she was, and stiff with the tension she was picking up from her mistress.

"I—I carry no money," Galina said, fear written clearly across her face. "Please, I am with child—for his sake, don't . . ."

Yeva blinked and lifted a hand, freezing when the movement seemed to frighten Galina more. "Galina—" She stopped, registering the utter blankness with which her old friend regarded her. She didn't recognize Yeva at all. She swallowed. "You're married?"

Galina nodded, wide-eyed, arms hugging herself. "This past spring. Who—"

"I mean you no harm," Yeva said. She wondered who Galina had married, tried to think if she'd ever mentioned a passing fancy. With a pang, Yeva realized she knew very little about her friend, and almost nothing about the secret desires of her heart. She'd always been so eager to get away from the baronessa's entourage that she'd never truly gotten to know Galina. She tried to stifle the sting of regret and softened her voice. "I only want information."

Galina's fear had subsided only enough for her to breathe. "How do you know my name?"

"I . . . I asked someone." Yeva thought quickly. "You look about the age of the people I seek, and I thought you might have heard of them. Do you remember the merchant Tvertko, who lived here until last fall?"

"Of course," Galina said, the fear ebbing and leaving room for sympathy. "But I am sorry to tell you that he is dead."

Yeva's heart flinched. "I know. I wanted to ask if you knew where his daughters went. After the cabin. They went to the cabin, Tvertko's hunting cabin, and then . . . ?"

Galina's brow furrowed as she inspected Yeva, this dirty, bloody, wild thing that had stepped from the shadows and onto the bustling street, and who was attracting stares and oaths from passersby. "Two of his daughters live here, in town. They live in Tvertko's old house, up on the rise." Galina swallowed, face flickering with an old, remembered pain. "The other, his youngest—she is dead, too."

Yeva stared, too numb and dumbfounded to answer or to conceal how much Galina's words had affected her. So her sisters believed her dead. Not surprising, given Yeva's disappearance in the middle of winter with no sign of her for nearly a year. But to learn that they were alive and well, and living in their old house again, was beyond what Yeva could have hoped for them. She felt her eyes filling, a little of that tight, cold, hard thing in her chest easing.

When she saw the tears, Galina leaned forward, her breath catching. "Why do you ask me these questions? Who . . ." She trailed off, her brow still furrowed. A spark, the tiniest flicker, of recognition ignited behind her blank gaze.

"Thank you," Yeva mumbled, and hurried away with Doe-

Eyes at her heels before Galina could have a chance to see through the months of wilderness and cold stone floors to find the girl beneath. She didn't know why she ran—except that it would be hard enough to face her sisters, who believed her dead and had been mourning for her and her father both all these long months, and she did not want to run through it first with Galina.

Walking up the rise to their old house left Yeva with the most curious quiver in her heart, a mix of fear and anticipation that made her hands jittery. She wanted to reach for her bow— her hands kept twitching with the desire to pull her weapon off her shoulder—but there was no enemy to fight other than her own nervousness. Doe-Eyes seemed to remember the way, her steps growing lighter with excitement.

Yeva halted several paces from the door, her eyes sweeping the house as Doe-Eyes investigated the shrubbery lining the path. Her father's home looked exactly as it had a year ago, spent peonies littering the ground cover by the kitchen door, vines climbing up the trellis by her old bedroom window. Instead of reaching for the door knocker she stepped off the path and peeked in a window. There was the furniture they'd brought from the cabin, though some of it had been replaced with newer, nicer pieces. She saw someone move from one room to the next—a servant, she thought, but could not tell who. She circled the house, peeking through window after window until, without warning, her sisters were there.

They were in the kitchen, and they were baking bread. Lena was humming—though Yeva could not hear it through the warped and rippled window glass, she could see from the rhythmic tilt of her head to and fro that she was hearing music as she worked. Asenka was with her, her shoulder brushing Lena's from time to time as they worked. She had flour in her hair.

Lena reached for the mix of herbs to roll the dough in and Yeva's eyes swam with unexpected tears. Crusting the loaf with herbs had been Yeva's job since childhood, and to see her role in the family so neatly eliminated—she fought for breath and dashed her arm across her eyes, her cloak so heavily weighted with rain that she nearly sank to her knees.

They'd had no choice but to try to carry on. They believed she was dead. Yeva knew this. But here they were, happy and settled in the house they loved, clearly the recipients of some immensely good fortune. Perhaps Yeva should not walk back into their lives—perhaps it would be better if they simply went on as they were.

She stood, indecisive, the image of her sisters side by side rippling with tears and distorted glass.

Then a voice behind her demanded harshly, "Don't move." It was a man's voice, and Yeva froze. She was still so unused to hearing any voice but the Beast's that she felt a thrill of fear. "What are you doing there?"

"I'm sorry." She lifted her hands to show they were empty of weapons. Doe-Eyes was still on the other side of the house, sniffing at the trees and plantings. "I . . . I know this house and I was only trying to—I mean them no harm," she said, lamely repeating what she'd told Galina.

"A woman?" The man sounded surprised as he identified her gender from her voice. "Turn around."

Yeva swallowed and obeyed—and then stared. It was Solmir.

His hard gaze didn't flinch, and he eyed her suspiciously. "If you'll pardon me for saying so, madam, you don't look like someone acquainted with the ladies of this house."

Yeva's tongue wouldn't work. When she'd found that a year had passed while she was with the Beast, she'd assumed Solmir had long gone. He'd agreed to look after her family in exchange for her hand in marriage when she returned, and Yeva had taken it as certain that when she was given up for dead, Solmir would have politely and quietly withdrawn to search elsewhere for a wife.

But here he stood, a year later, clad in fine leathers outside Tvertko's home, protecting the sisters from the mud-soaked madwoman staring at them through the window.

When Yeva didn't speak, Solmir took a step toward her, then stopped. The tension left his body, arms falling to hang limp at his side. His brows lifted and his eyes grew round, and an expression strangely suspended between horror and hope touched his features. "I don't believe it," he whispered, face draining of color.

Unlike Galina, Solmir had seen through the dirt and the blood and the leanness of limb and face. He knew her at a glance, even as she was.

"Hello, Solmir," Yeva said weakly.

BEAST

Despair. Despair. Cannot. Must go. Cliff. Water. Bleeding. Ending.

The animal does not understand, cannot understand the need to end our existence but I am here now, I control us. I have let it take me for so many years, so very many long years, but she has brought me back.

And I cannot descend again into that madness, the in-betweenness of animal and man, the combination of which leaves us less than the sum of us, less than who and what we once were. I cannot lose myself to instinct now I remember . . . now I remember . . .

End, our heart cries. Stop. Empty. Please.

Let us die human. Let us die remembering Beauty.

NINETEEN

SOLMIR DIDN'T MOVE, RECOGNITION petrifying him to the spot. He stared at Yeva as though she were the Firebird itself, myth turned real, magic become mundane and standing in someone's front garden. When it became clear he would not speak again, Yeva tried to clear her throat, and the sound interrupted whatever spell held Solmir and made him gulp for air.

"I'm alive," Yeva said, aware that this was a rather silly thing to say given that she was standing there before him.

But it seemed to hearten Solmir, who took a step forward, and then another, and another until he could reach out. His hand seemed uncertain where to rest, though, and after hovering by her shoulder, by her cheek, tracing the outside edge of a muddy lock of hair, it fell to his side again. "Yeva," he breathed finally. And there, at the edges of his eyes, Yeva saw something unexpected: sorrow. "I don't . . . I thought . . ."

Surely she must be imagining the sadness there—it was his confusion trying to steer him one way or the other. Yeva took the first of what she felt would be many long, steadying breaths. "I will tell you what's happened, and where I've been," she said. "And I will want to hear what has happened to you. But—but I would like to see my sisters first. And I'd like to tell you all at once."

She didn't think she could tell the story twice.

Solmir started, and the way he shoved his hand through his hair in sudden chagrin was abruptly so familiar to Yeva, and so completely human, that she felt a smile tug insistently at her cheeks. "Of course," he said, backing toward the door, as if loath to turn away from Yeva for fear she might vanish again. His face was so changed, so marked by emotions that Yeva could not interpret them all. Joy, disbelief, confusion, relief . . . and again, that conflicted flash of torment she could not place.

He groped for the latch and then disappeared, bursting through the house and leaving Yeva to trail after him, feeling strangely like a visitor in her own home, like she ought to wait by the door to be shown into the parlor. As if on cue a servant appeared, someone who had not worked for them before and who Yeva didn't recognize.

"May I take your cl . . . ," the maid began, then trailed off as she saw Yeva's warlike appearance. "Your cloak?" She paused, then hazarded, "Miss?"

Yeva gulped and reached for the clasp at her throat instinctively before thinking to point out that she was as muddy and wet beneath the cloak as on top of it, and it would do little good. But the maid was already gingerly taking the dingy thing into her arms, and rather than hanging it with the much cleaner—and more expensive—garments on the pegs by the door, she vanished into the next room.

She heard Asenka's voice firing off questions, growing nearer. "What are you saying? *She* who? Solmir, I don't understand. . . ."

Yeva turned to see Lena standing in the doorway to the front room, white-faced and frozen, and Asenka following, leaning on Solmir's arm to steady herself. Before Yeva could speak Lena screamed and fell back, half collapsing against the doorframe so that Solmir had to drop Asenka's arm or let Lena go crashing to the floor.

Asenka's eyes met Yeva's and clung there, round and dark, and, after a few long seconds, filling with tears. "I knew it," she whispered, so that Yeva could barely hear her over the sounds of Solmir attempting to revive Lena, who was still half senseless at the sight of her dead sister. "I knew you were alive." Asenka limped forward.

Yeva found she could not speak, could not even move, and it wasn't until she felt Asenka's arms go around her that she broke into a storm of weeping. Lena recovered herself and staggered toward them and threw her arms around them both, but her knees were still buckling, and after a moment of unsteadiness all three sisters sank into a heap on the floor, sobbing and hugging one another and all getting so muddy from Yeva's clothing that it was no longer easy to tell who was who.

By the time they made it to the sitting room before the fire, the rest of the household had heard the commotion, and word had spread that Tvertko's youngest daughter had returned from the dead. A few of the servants Yeva knew, for they'd been employed by their father and had returned. The cook screeched when she saw Yeva and then, just as loudly, announced she'd have the kettle on for tea. Others were new, and more confused about what was happening, for all they knew was that both the merchant and his youngest daughter had perished during the winter they'd spent at his hunting cabin.

Albe had stayed, too, but he was so bashful of Yeva—or

perhaps fearful of her, she could not tell which—that he hovered in the hall, peeking around the open doorframe at her whenever she spoke, and vanishing again whenever she looked his way.

Slowly, very slowly, with pauses for more tears and for explanations, Yeva learned what had befallen her family after she disappeared.

Solmir had faithfully continued to help feed and protect Albe and the sisters, monitoring the perimeter around the house for any sign of Yeva's return. After a little more than a week Radak, Lena's fiancé before their father's financial ruin, had appeared at the cabin, wild-eyed and demanding to see Lena. So flustered and distressed was he that he kept repeating his demand even after Lena stood in front of him repeating, "I am Lena! I am she! Radak, what is it?"

He had heard of her father's plight while traveling back from a business venture and had left his wagons and hired the fastest horse he could find, and arrived at the house in town to find another family living there, with no clue of Tvertko's whereabouts, nor his daughters'. Eventually he'd found a hunter who'd worked with the merchant long ago who knew the approximate location of the cabin, and from there he'd found Solmir's tracks, which led him to the door.

When Lena's voice brought him out of his cold and exhaustion, he dropped to his knees and asked her to marry him again, there in the open doorway of the cabin, soaked to the knee with melting snow and face chapped raw by wind and travel, and she had cried, and kissed him, and said yes. Radak, in possession of a fine new fortune as a result of his venture, had bought Tvertko's house back. They were wed immediately, so that he could bring her and her sister both to live with them—but they were unwilling to leave the cabin yet, hoping that Yeva and their father might return.

Yeva could not tell them about finding their father's body, her voice refusing to form the words—but when Lena's drawn face lifted and she whispered, "Father?" they could all see Yeva's answer in her eyes as they fell, in her hands as they twisted together, in the set of her lips as she turned her face away.

It was from that vantage point that she saw Solmir's hand twitch, a gesture she recognized as the urge to help, to touch, to comfort. And when she looked up, his eyes weren't on her, and her grief—they were on Asenka, who sat still as silent tears dripped from her chin and onto her folded hands.

Yeva was so caught by this that she was almost distracted from the reversal of her family's fortunes—but then Radak appeared in the doorway, having been fetched by one of the servants to come home and see Lena's long-lost sister.

"By God," he exclaimed in the doorway. He was a tall, thin man with terrible hay fever and a perpetually reddened nose that got chapped and flaky from the constant rubbing of his handkerchief. But he'd always been very kind, and after the story she'd heard of his devotion to her sister and to her family, Yeva thought that his face was perhaps one of the most handsome she'd ever seen. He joined them by the fire and kissed her cheek and then took Lena into his arms, wrapping them around her from behind, and it was only then that Yeva noticed with a jolt the curve of her sister's stomach.

She gasped wordlessly, and Lena, seeing Yeva's eyes go to her belly, grinned. "I did always like things to be prompt," Lena said, making Radak laugh softly in her ear. "The baby's no exception. He should be along in another four months."

Yeva gaped. She was still getting used to being a sister again, and now she would have to learn to be an aunt. "I've missed so much," she said, passing a hand over her eyes.

"Where *were* you?" Solmir burst out. He'd been quiet through most of the story, contributing only to dismiss the sisters' descriptions of his devotion to them during Yeva's absence with shakes of his head and flicks of his hand. He wouldn't look at Yeva directly, not if she was looking at him—he'd drop his eyes like a guilty man, as though his care and protection of her sisters was an act he ought to be ashamed of.

Yeva was slow to answer, at first because she was distracted by Solmir, and then because she could not think how to start. Each minute that she spent in her house, with her sisters, surrounded by the trappings of home, of wealth and security and all that had been stripped from her over the last year, made her life in the Beast's valley seem more and more distant.

Like it was no more than a fairy story, to be read in an old leather-bound book, from the safety and comfort of a warm bed.

Yeva accepted a cup of tea from the cook and blew on its steaming surface to buy herself time to order her thoughts. She took a sip to wet her throat, and began. "Do you remember the Beast Father spoke of, before he vanished?"

As the afternoon passed into evening and evening into night, Solmir left to return to the baron's household, where he was staying. As an eligible bachelor, it was hardly proper for him to stay too late in a household with two unmarried girls. The baron had been ailing from a chill caught over the last winter, and as his heir apparent, Solmir was a great comfort to him.

The servants brought dinner, and then tea, and then sweet-meats, and then cordial and brandy, all the while lingering a little too long in the sitting room as Yeva told her story. She imagined them gathering in the kitchen, each contributing what they'd overheard as they tried to patch together, thread by thread, the tapestry of Yeva's time with the Beast.

"I heard he was no Beast at all, but a man under a curse . . . ," one would say, while another would interrupt, "But I heard her say he had fangs and claws, and a roar so loud it shook the very earth beneath her feet."

At first her sisters, and Radak and Solmir as well, interrupted her with questions. But after Solmir was forced to depart, the questions grew fewer and fewer, and her sisters and her brother-in-law fell quiet, listening to the story. After its end they sat together there in front of the fire, digesting what Yeva had told them, and watching her with an even deeper, more profound disbelief and awe than when they'd first seen her, risen from the grave.

When it had been some hours since the last servant had appeared to eavesdrop, Yeva cleared her raw throat and stood in order to put another log on the fire, which was burning low in its grate. Radak had fallen asleep on the love seat beside his wife, head thrown back, breathing audibly through his mouth in deference to his hay fever. Lena threw him a fond look from where she sat curled in the now-limp circle of his arm, and nudged him gently until he settled to the side and his snoring ceased.

"He works too hard," she murmured into the quiet, the first anyone had spoken in some time.

Yeva sank down onto the rug before the fire, turning so that the coals warmed her back, and hugged her knees to her chest. "I knew he loved you for more than Father's wealth."

Lena's smile widened, and she sneaked another glance at the man sleeping next to her. "I had hoped. But that time was so awful, so full of unhappiness, it seemed all our luck had fled and everything that could go sour would."

"Our father died," Asenka said softly. "And with him, our little sister."

Yeva had always been closer to Asenka than Lena, in spirit as well as age. And it had always been Asenka to whom Yeva had confessed her heart. From the time Yeva could talk, Asenka had always been the one to listen to her when her little soul could no longer bear the weight of everything she wanted, the adventure and magic and the wide, wide wood, and all the things she could not name, that no one else seemed to understand.

Yeva's eyes stung, but she'd shed so many tears that day that none fell now, the well inside her dry. "If I could have sent word I was alive, I would have. I didn't think I would ever see any of you again."

"We waited as long as we could," Lena said, smile fading now. "But after summer ended, we knew we could not spend another winter in the cabin, not when Radak had this place for us again. And not with your new nephew on the way."

Yeva knew Lena was hoping for a boy, but she could hear a sound beneath everything else, a tiny, pulsing rhythm like the one she'd heard in the Beast's valley, and when she closed her eyes her sister's afterimage seemed to glow against her eyelids. And in that glow Yeva could see that the child would be a girl, though she could not have explained how she saw it. It was magic, and it frightened Yeva that she could see it even here, in town, as removed from the Beast's valley as it was from the far eastern sea.

Yeva watched her sister, and her unborn niece, and said nothing.

The quiet broke as Radak's breath caught and he harrumphed in his sleep, half waking. Lena took his hand and kissed his cheek and sent him off to bed and he went, only after she promised she would come soon.

"Yeva, this story . . ." Lena shook her head, her brows drawn in. "If it were anyone but you I would call her a liar."

"It's the truth," Yeva said. And yet there were pieces of the story she hadn't told them, fragments she kept to herself without knowing why: the way the Beast's voice changed when he said *I* instead of *we*; the way he smelled of spice and wind, except when snowmelt dampened his fur, when he smelled a little like a wet dog; how familiar the soft whisper of his paws on the stone floors had become; his eyes, as they met hers, right before she cut his throat.

She told herself it was because they would not believe those details, but in her heart she knew that wasn't the reason. Though she could not put the real reason into words.

"I believe you." Asenka slid from her chair onto the rug next to Yeva with a sigh, and stretched her feet out toward the fire. "But it will take some time before any of us understand."

"I know." Yeva's lips twitched. "I don't even understand yet. I just know that seeing you, and knowing you're here and safe . . . when I saw the empty cabin I feared something terrible had befallen you."

Lena had been avoiding Yeva's eyes—watching her, but looking away whenever her youngest sister glanced up. She finally let her breath out in a rush and bent over, face in her hands. "Oh, Yeva. I'm so sorry." She burst into tears.

Alarmed, Yeva glanced at Asenka, but she wouldn't meet her eyes either. "It's all right," Yeva said, sliding forward on the rug toward the love seat until she could take Lena's hands. "I'm fine. None of this was your fault."

Lena lifted her head, eyes brimming and face starting to redden and swell. "No, no—Yeva, I w-wanted to leave the cabin when spring came. I believed you were dead and I wanted to come home, and I was the one who told Solmir to stop. . . ." Her voice petered out, and she shook her head, unable to continue.

"You were the one who told him to stop looking for me," Yeva finished for her, gently.

Lena glanced at Asenka, then nodded.

"You did right." Yeva squeezed her hands. "You couldn't know I was alive."

"Asenka did!" Lena blurted through her tears. "She begged us to stay through the summer. She refused to believe you had died."

Yeva squeezed Lena's hands again and looked across the rug to Asenka, whose eyes were on the fire. Yeva bent her head and kissed her sister's hands. "None of that matters," she said firmly. "I don't think anyone can find the Beast's valley unless he wants them to—Solmir would not have found me if he had searched for a thousand years. Lena, you did the right thing. I'm so happy to find you all here."

Lena mumbled something and wrapped her arms around Yeva's neck, and they stayed that way for a time until Yeva told her to go join her husband, and sleep. She did so reluctantly, pausing on the third step to look back toward the fire, and the sister she'd thought she'd lost, before vanishing upstairs.

Yeva crawled back over by the hearth until she was near enough to Asenka to curl up as she used to do when she was a child, head in her older sister's lap, fingers grasping at her skirts as though they were a comforting blanket. Asenka bent her head and kissed Yeva's temple, and Yeva felt a tremble in her lips. She felt the patter of a tear hitting her cheek, and then another, but before she could look up, Asenka's hand began to stroke the dirty, muddy hair back from Yeva's face, and Yeva did not want to move for fear she would stop.

She fell asleep like that, and her last thought was of waiting to feel the next tear fall from Asenka's face to hers.

BEAST

I cannot continue.

*The wolf is too strong. With her I could . . .
I was . . . but the animal within is angry and
his anger makes him strong. He wants us to
hunt, and feed, and run through the wood.
He wants us to exist as instinct and whim,
quick and brutal as winter. My thoughts
drive his mind as mad as his instinct poisons
mine. But I remember what I was, and it
makes me weak. My despair is mine alone,
and I am so tired.*

*Can't keep . . . no point. Curl up. Let
him. I'll fade.*

Disappear.

TWENTY

YEVA ASSUMED SHE'D FEEL the itch to hunt, after it had become such a habit. That the town would seem crowded and dirty and loud, that the house would feel small after having lived in a castle. Instead it surprised her how easy it was to come back from the dead.

News spread through the town like the howling winter wind, so quickly that Yeva did not have to tell her story to anyone, because they already knew. Most of them had heard it entirely wrong, for the stranger the story, the more elaborate it became in the retelling—but she felt no urge to correct them.

And while her body was used to far more exercise than she could get strolling around town, it soon understood it was not being called upon to prowl through snow-covered forests or sprint after wild beasts, and settled.

She was not invited to rejoin the baronessa's circle of ladies, no doubt because no one quite knew what to make of her, whether she had spent the winter with an unmarried man under a curse or if she'd spent it in the bed of a wicked monster. Though neither was true, Yeva was hardly surprised that such doubts would prevent her from reentering high society. And since the baronessa's solarium was the one aspect of her life at home that she hadn't missed at all, that suited her perfectly.

After all, it didn't matter if the townsfolk were unsure about Yeva's honor, or whether her fantastical tale was the truth. She wasn't anticipating marriage proposals from any of them.

And then there was Solmir.

He visited daily, and though Yeva felt as fond of him as she'd been before her father's death, she also couldn't deny there was an odd gulf between them now. They'd grown close during their afternoon walks through the forest, checking Yeva's traps and talking about hunting, but he seemed stiffer around her, uncertain of himself. At first she thought it might be her new reputation making him ill at ease, and after a week she finally found the courage to ask him about it.

"Will you not tell me what's the matter?" Yeva burst out, after they'd sat in utter silence together under the peony tree, wrapped up against the autumn chill and watching the fire-gold leaves fall all around them.

Solmir started, looking for an instant like he'd forgotten Yeva was there at all. "What—what's the matter?"

"You're unhappy," Yeva said softly, and though it was the first time she'd used that word even to herself, she knew from the look on Solmir's face that she was right.

"No," he said swiftly. "I'm glad you're home."

"I know. But you can be happy about a thing and sad about it at the same time. Feeling one thing in your heart doesn't stop you from feeling another." Yeva pulled her cloak more tightly around herself. If her time in the Beast's castle had taught her nothing else, it was that anything—be it Beast or her own heart—could have more than one nature.

"I'm not unhappy that you're safe," Solmir said, so firmly he almost snapped the words. "Yeva, please. I'm only tired, and the baron is ailing, and I worry about him."

Yeva swallowed. "I know he once planned on naming you his heir. And I know the rumors that have been circulating about me. For you to be tied to such a woman would surely hurt your chances of—"

"Enough of that!" Solmir scowled at her, the first flicker of real, bright emotion beyond that distant melancholy she'd seen. "If you think I give a damn—sorry—about the silly rumors people whisper in the streets, you must not think very highly of me."

Yeva couldn't help but smile, for he was his old self again just then. But then her smile faded and she sighed. "I *do* think highly of you," she said softly. "I want you to be happy. Which is why—all I mean to say is that I don't intend to hold you to a promise you made a year ago. You believed I was dead. For all I know, you've begun courting someone else, some other girl in the baronessa's court."

Solmir's scowl smoothed, his face going blank. "You don't want to marry me anymore?"

Yeva's breath stuck in her throat, and as she saw hurt flickering behind that expressionless mask and her heart responded with a painful flutter, she realized she *did* love him. She loved him like she loved her sisters, like she loved Albe. She loved his heart, and his kindness, and the devotion he'd shown her family even after they all believed her dead. She didn't love him as a wife loved a husband, but she knew she could learn to do so, that she could be happy with him. If it would make him happy.

"You saved my family," Yeva said. "You helped my sisters

through the winter even after you thought I was dead and would never fulfill my end of the promise." Greatly daring, she reached out and took his hand. "I'll do anything you ask of me."

Solmir stared at her, his boyish face suddenly haggard. Weakly, his fingers squeezed hers back.

Yeva smiled. "Including releasing you from our engagement if that is what you want. You have your own reputation to think of, and I know that."

Solmir was silent, watching her. Beyond him and around him the peony leaves fell, drifting to and fro like feathers on the wind. *Yes*, Yeva thought. *I could love him.*

But though she struggled not to, she found herself listening with all her might for the tiniest glimmer of a song in him, of the magic the Beast had taught her to hear. All she heard was the sighing rustle of a breeze through the branches, and the crunch of leaves as Doe-Eyes and Pelei frolicked in the back garden, and the distant ring of the blacksmith's hammer in town, echoing back through the buildings.

And then Solmir's voice, saying, "I want nothing more than to continue keeping your family safe, as I promised." He squeezed her hand again, and this time there was strength to his grasp, and his smile was warm. "You are one of the most remarkable women I've ever known, Yeva, and it would be a fool who would let you go." He lifted her hand, and Yeva's heart flickered, and she waited for him to turn her palm over and kiss the inside of her wrist as he'd done that day in the forest. But he just brushed his lips against her knuckles, and then helped her to her feet and led her back inside.

Yeva dreamed that night of the peony tree. She was kissing Solmir beneath its branches, and its leaves fell around them like a rain of fire. His arms were around her and his palms pressed warm against her back, and all through her body ran a burning torrent she felt might consume her at any moment.

Solmir ducked his head to kiss her throat, then behind her ear, breathing in the scent of her hair and pulling her closer against him. Her head tipped back and she opened her eyes, and gasped.

The leaves falling all around them were not leaves after all, but feathers, feathers of red-gold fire. Yeva knew that if one of them touched her it would be too much, that just that tiny spark of heat would be enough to push her over the edge into the fire and she would burn. Her mind filled with the song she'd been searching for, and she felt magic in his pulse, and in the rhythm of his breath, and in her skin everywhere he touched her.

Then Solmir lifted his head and she saw his eyes, and they were gold, gold like the Firebird, gold like the feathers swirling around them in a blizzard of fire. His face wasn't Solmir's after all, but one she'd seen only once, and only by the faint light of a dying fire. But his eyes . . . those eyes were as familiar to her as her own heartbeat.

"Beauty," he whispered, tracing his fingertips along the contours of her face.

She woke gasping as if from a nightmare, but her body felt flushed and feverish and the pounding of her heart was not telling her to flee. Her thoughts flooded with regret, and for an instant she wished more than anything that she could return to that dream, for never in her life had she felt so awake.

Abruptly she realized three things: that she was sweating, that the window had blown open in the night, and that she was shivering. The heat and longing of the dream vanished and she groaned, sliding out of her bed and hurrying to the window. She was about to pull it closed when she heard something that made her stop.

It was still well before dawn, and the town was silent. She ought to hear only the noises of the night and the wind, but as she strained, she caught the faintest sound that made the fire of that dream sweep over her again.

She thought she heard distant music.

song

fire

beauty....

TWENTY-ONE

GALINA HAD COME TO visit Yeva a few days after word had spread through the town that Tvertko's youngest daughter had returned. She'd figured out the identity of the strange, wild-looking woman who'd accosted her in the street, and came full of apology and embarrassment that she hadn't recognized Yeva at once. But after a few visits, Yeva had managed to convince her that the lack of recognition was hardly Galina's fault. And since Galina was one of the few women around Yeva's age who didn't avoid her and her reputation like the plague, Yeva was glad for her company.

Aside from her sisters, who were all too eager to pretend nothing had changed, and Solmir, who responded to any mention of Yeva's absence with visible distress, Galina was the only other person who didn't turn every conversation into a stream of questions about the Beast. She'd talk about her new husband, a tailor on Market Street who had shyly designed a beautiful gown for her to wear at one of the baronessa's parties. She'd talk about how exhausting and frustrating her pregnancy was, as she was currently suffering through an endless run of mornings where she could not eat a bite without throwing it back up again. She'd talk about the current fashions, and the other ladies, and who was leaving for the city and who was moving into the vacant house on the eastern edge of town, and whether there would be an early frost to damage the harvests.

Perhaps it was *because* she didn't ask about the Beast that Yeva wound up speaking of him herself.

They were strolling through the marketplace, where the vendors were pressing their wares on passersby with renewed vigor, determined to sell as much of their stock as possible before winter shut the marketplace down for the year. Galina found that walking eased her nausea, and Yeva was all too glad to stretch legs that had been accustomed to long days of running through the woods.

"Yeva, is something the matter?" Galina's voice was soft, a change from the laughter with which she'd been talking about her husband's latest experiments with brocade.

Yeva lifted her gaze from the ground, where she'd been separating and categorizing the layers upon layers of footprints in the dried-mud street. "What? No, I'm merely feeling quiet today." But when she saw Galina's face, gentle and concerned and entirely without artifice or anything hidden, she sighed. "I've been dreaming about him."

"Solmir?" Galina asked, eyebrows lifting.

Yeva shook her head. "The Beast."

Galina was quiet, stride not even pausing. Yeva waited for the standard reassurances—*oh, the nightmares will fade, you've been through such a trial, give it time and you will learn you've nothing to fear anymore*—but Galina just asked, "What kind of dreams?"

Yeva felt her face warming despite the chill in the air and kept her eyes down. "They aren't bad dreams. In fact, I . . . I like them. They're nice dreams. They make me . . ." She stopped before she could finish the sentence, unwilling to utter the words she was about to say.

They make me miss him.

Galina nodded toward the square up ahead, and claiming weariness, suggested they sit on the rough-hewn fountain over the well. It wasn't the most private of places, but just now nobody was fetching water, and the blur of activity about the town offered its own cloak of anonymity.

Yeva sat, feeling the cold stone seeping through her layers of skirts. She'd been thinking of the Beast's valley more and more as winter approached, and though there'd been no frost yet, she wasn't sure if she'd be able to see the town blanketed in snow without longing for the forest and its music.

Galina let her breath out in a rush as she sat, and watched people moving to and fro for a time before she spoke. "I have a cousin in Kiev," she said finally, "who got married very young, because she wasn't wealthy enough for a large dowry and her parents didn't know if she'd ever get another offer like the one she'd received."

Yeva wondered if Galina had forgotten about her dreams, and nodded.

"Her husband wasn't a good man. He hit her when she didn't do everything exactly to his liking—if the bread was burned, or if the house wasn't spotless, or if he thought she'd looked too long at another man. He always hit her where it wouldn't show, until one day he lost his temper and blackened her eye and her brother recognized what was happening. But when he prepared to deal with the husband, to bring the matter to the magistrate and get the marriage annulled, my cousin begged him not to. She defended her husband and said he only had a terrible temper, that he was so loving and so apologetic afterward, and that no other man could possibly make her feel so special, so loved. She said that without her he'd be lost, and that he needed her."

Yeva listened in silence, her own thoughts troubled. She'd known other women who'd formed attachments to men who were cruel to them, though she'd never known any in such dire situations. She'd always thought them foolish, weak, lacking in the self-assurance to know they were better than the men whose backhanded compliments made them flush so. But perhaps they were simply in love. Perhaps their hearts had betrayed them, and not their courage.

Galina leaned back. "I tell you this because I wonder . . . I wonder if something like that has happened to you."

Yeva bit back a quick reply, forcing herself to absorb the story, and closed her eyes. "He never hurt me. Well, he did once, but to be fair, I had shot him with an arrow and was about to kill him with an ax."

Galina's expression flickered, but she managed not to blanch too visibly. "Maybe not, but you were his prisoner. That's a different kind of hurt, but hurt nonetheless."

"And I wanted to kill him," Yeva said, "when I was his prisoner. It was my whole reason for existing, surviving. I didn't fall in love with him because he hurt me—the idea is absurd."

Galina's eyebrows shot up. "In *love* with him? Heavens, Yeva, that's not what I meant at all. Who could even imagine such a thing?"

Yeva's face burned hot. "I thought—I mean, you were talking about your cousin—"

Galina shook her head quickly. "Good lord, no." Now she

was watching Yeva closely, voice dropping despite the noise of the bustling streets. "You care about him."

Yeva blinked hard, the words ringing in her ears, words she'd never dared say even to herself, even in the deepest, quietest parts of the night when she woke sweating and longing. "I—I feel for him," she whispered. Her eyes burned at the admission, and she looked up, barely able to meet Galina's eyes. "What does that make me?"

Though she tried to hide it, Galina's expression held the tiniest glimmer of horror, and it made Yeva shrink. But Galina drew a breath and when she let it out, her reply came in a sigh: "Human."

Yeva balled up her fists and ground them against her eyes, punishing them for their betrayal, making sure there'd be no more tears. "I hated him. I hated him more than anything, like I've never hated before. I didn't know I could hate until I hated the Beast."

"So what changed?"

Yeva had to pause to breathe until her voice steadied. "I found out he was a prisoner too," she whispered. "And that he was as lonely as I had been."

"Lonely?" Galina echoed. "But Yeva, he was the reason you were lonely, cooped up all alone in that old castle—"

"No," Yeva interrupted. "I was lonely before. I was lonely in the cabin, with my sisters. I was lonely here, with the baronessa."

Galina bit her lip, eyes dropping. Too late, Yeva realized she was saying that even her friendship with Galina in the past had left her lonely, but it was the truth, and she couldn't take it back.

"I was always lonely, and I never knew it until I met the Beast. The real Beast, the one beneath the fangs and the claws and the rage. The one who reads, who listens to fairy stories, who comes alive in the forest, who hears music. . . ."

"Music?" Galina frowned.

Yeva started. "No, I just meant—I don't know what I meant."

"But Yeva . . . he held you prisoner. He threatened your family."

"I know." Yeva's eyes crept up toward the hill, and though she couldn't see her father's house from here, she could imagine it just on the other side of the ridge. "And I took advantage of his trust and tried to kill him. We have both hurt each other."

"What makes you think he wouldn't have kept trying to hurt you if you hadn't escaped?"

"Because I didn't escape," Yeva replied simply. "He let me go."

Galina's face was troubled. "Give it time," she suggested softly. "You have your sisters, and me, and you have Solmir. Think of Solmir—you won't be lonely here, Yeva. You're surrounded by people who love you."

Yeva knew she was right. She thought of Solmir, and of his warm eyes, and of the tremendous kindnesses he'd shown her family. She tried to ignore the bite in the air as she and Galina stood and began the walk back to her home. It smelled like snow.

Asenka still spent most of her days at the leech's shop, helping to nurse the sick. The leech himself was good enough at treating illnesses, but he was an arrogant, officious man with no patience or interest in people—his passion lay in disease itself, in making endless lists of symptoms and treatments and linking them together. So it was Asenka, and her smiles and her unflinching sympathy in the face of horrific injury or disease, to whom many of the townsfolk quietly attributed their recoveries whenever they fell ill.

Yeva came now and then to share the noonday meal with her. Though Asenka was given lunch by the leech, it was more often than not cold meat on cold bread, so when Yeva brought hot stew from home, the change was more than welcome. Asenka's little corner of the upstairs loft in the shop was quiet, and unless the leech had patients so ill as to need full-time care, the beds in the loft were empty. It was a respite from the bustle of town, and even from their own home, which was full of servants, and Radak and Lena. Yeva had come to understand why Asenka enjoyed her time here so.

Sometimes they talked about the Beast. Sometimes they talked about Lena, and how increasingly irritable she was becoming due to the baby growing in her womb. Occasionally they spoke of their father, but most often they simply ate together quietly, enjoying the rare, precious company of silence shared.

It was the latter Yeva was hoping for when she decided to wrap up a tureen of dumplings in mutton broth and cabbage and walk down to the leech's shop. Lena was overseeing the redecoration of their sewing room as it was being converted into a nursery, and Yeva felt she might shout at her if she were asked one more time to choose between two nearly identical tapestries to cover the walls.

But as she climbed the stairs to the leech's upstairs, she heard voices.

"I asked you to go." Though Asenka's voice was quiet, the pain in it carried easily down the stairs and made Yeva stop short.

"I don't believe you mean it." It was Solmir. Yeva stifled her breath of surprise with her hand, and though her conscience told her she ought to creep away again, she couldn't help but stay to listen. Solmir sounded every bit as sad and hurt as he'd seemed lately, and she'd do anything to discover the cause.

"You can't keep coming here," Asenka said, voice rising. "It's improper. Someone will see you, and talk, and our family's had more than its fair share of rumor and gossip lately."

"What do I care?" Solmir burst out, with that same passion Yeva had come to find endearing.

"It's not you!" Asenka cried, making Yeva teeter on the stairs in surprise. She couldn't remember the last time Asenka had raised her voice to anyone. "*I* care, Solmir. Lena and Radak care. Yeva cares."

Solmir let out a frustrated, wordless sound, and Yeva heard his boots clomping first one way, then the other. "Asenka," he said, more quietly now. "Asenka, please. We must tell her the truth. If we don't, you'll be miserable, I'll be miserable—no one will be happy if we go through with this."

"Yeva will be," Asenka whispered.

"Asenka—"

"Go."

"No, I won't—"

"I said *go*." Asenka's voice held such steel as Yeva never knew she possessed, and Yeva ended up gawking at the empty landing ahead of her. It wasn't until she heard Solmir's slow, leaden footsteps heading for the stairs that she started and hurried away as quietly as she could.

That night Yeva waited until the household grew silent, and all the servants had retired and Radak and Lena were asleep. She crept out of bed, shivering as she pulled on a pair of woolen stockings, and then took up the quilt on her bed to wrap around her shoulders before slipping into the hall. She padded down to Asenka's room, where the door was open a crack as it always had been when Yeva was a child, and crept inside.

When she was young Yeva would crawl into Asenka's bed to tell her about her dreams of fairy-tale monsters and wicked spells, as thrilled and excited as she was frightened. Tonight her heart quickened as it used to, and for a moment she thought her throat wouldn't work until her whisper burst out: "Asenka?"

Her sister mumbled unintelligibly, then sat up. "Yeva, what is it?"

"Can I come in?"

"Always." Asenka slid sideways to make room for Yeva on the bed.

Yeva darted over and under the covers, warmed by Asenka's body heat. She turned on her side and wrapped her arms around her sister, pressing her forehead against her shoulder. "I need advice," Yeva said.

"About what?" Asenka tilted her head to the side until her temple rested against Yeva's hair.

"Solmir."

Asenka's body stiffened—so close, it was impossible for her to hide it from Yeva, and she knew it. "Please," she said eventually, sounding tired. "I can't."

Yeva's arms tightened, and she reminded herself that she needed to know what was happening, even if asking made her sister unhappy. "Something is wrong. I want him to be happy, but he's not, and he won't tell me why."

"Why would you think I could answer, when you can't?" Asenka's words were careful. She was never able to lie well, and certainly not to her own family.

"Because," Yeva said. "Because I think you're still in love with him."

Asenka's breath tangled in her throat, audible with Yeva so close to her. For the first time Yeva could remember, her sister pulled away from her and sat up, retreating to the corner of the bed and drawing up her knees. "Yeva," she gasped, anger tinting her voice. "He's your fiancé. I would never—it was a girlish whim, a childish fancy I set aside long ago."

Yeva's heart ached, because she could see the lie even in the dark, shining from Asenka's eyes more brightly than the moonlight from the window. "Asenka—has he fallen in love with you, too?"

Asenka's eyes flashed. "Of course not," she spluttered. "He loves you, he's marrying you. He wants to spend the rest of his life with you, he always has, since he met you."

"Even when he thought I was dead?" Yeva asked gently.

"It doesn't matter!" Asenka's voice was suddenly fierce. "I never believed you were gone. I knew you were alive. I knew you would come back, and I knew he must be here, waiting for you, when you did."

"Oh, Asenka." Yeva reached out, groping until she found her sister's hand. "If you love him, and he loves you, you must accept that. I won't be the one who comes between you."

"No," Asenka snapped, her voice as steely as when she'd sent Solmir from the leech's shop. "He was meant for you."

"I don't want him." Yeva spoke as gently as she could. "Oh, I care for him—I care for him very much. I can never repay all that he did for us. But Asenka, I've realized . . . he wasn't doing all of it for me. He was doing it for you."

Asenka had begun to cry, and was shaking her head again and again. "No," she said, voice thick. "Yeva, you are my sister. I love you. I love you more than anything. You and Lena are the most important things in all the world." She finally squeezed Yeva's hand back, swallowing audibly. "I would give up a thousand Solmirs for you."

Yeva crawled forward and slid her arms around Asenka's waist. "I know. But I'm not in love with him. Not the way you are. Asenka, I want you to be with him. I want it for you both."

Asenka's tears overflowed and she gave a wordless sob. A memory hit Yeva, the force of it robbing her of breath: a single sob, lost in the darkness in the back of the hunting cabin, the night Solmir had come to propose to Yeva and Asenka had seen where his heart lay. Yeva pulled her sister close, and they sat that way, rocking together, bound and twisted up in the bedclothes and murmuring to each other.

Finally Asenka's tears slowed, and she lifted her head. Yeva brushed her hair from her eyes and touched the tears from her cheeks, just as Asenka used to do for her when Yeva would come crying to her for comfort.

"But you must marry Solmir," Asenka whispered, her eyes intent.

"Why?" Yeva shook her head, unable to think why her sister was so insistent.

"Because if he doesn't hold you here, you will go back." Asenka reached up to lay her hand against Yeva's cheek. "Back to the Beast."

Yeva's heart twitched and leaped, and she caught her breath. "What? Don't—don't be absurd. Why would I go back?"

But as they sat there together, and Yeva held Asenka until she drifted off to sleep, her sister's words echoed in her mind over and over, until they settled into place, like a missing piece that filled the exact shape of the hollow in her heart she'd been trying to ignore.

Back to the Beast.

BEAST

We run. We hunt. We feed.
*   We are of the forest and of magic, and we*
have always been. We glory in the kill.
*   We are the Beast,*
*   and we will always be.*

TWENTY-TWO

THAT NIGHT YEVA'S VISION of the Beast was a nightmare. She dreamed she was the deer, and that the Beast was stalking her through the wood. She could not see or hear or smell him, but some deep-rooted instinct knew he was there. She knew she was prey.

But when she woke gasping, it was not the thought of being caught and consumed that echoed in her fear-muddled mind. All she could see were the Beast's eyes, red and fixated on her, full of bloodlust and nothing more. They held no humanity, no sense—not even the careful cunning of a predator. The eyes were simply mad, like those of a rabid animal. They were not the eyes of the creature, man or Beast, she'd come to know in the castle.

She rose before any of the servants and stoked the fires in the sitting room and the kitchen, and put a kettle of water on to boil for tea. The tasks reminded her of her life in the hunting cabin with her family, and she felt a twinge of loss as she stood warming her fingers and toes before the flames. She knew her sisters would remember those few months as a time of terrible hardship and fear, but Yeva couldn't help but see them as the start of a journey that would change her forever.

For she *was* changed. Yeva knew that to live here, among her family and the townsfolk and the bricks and mortar and steel and bustle, would require diligence and focus. She could not think of the forest, of Lamya and the music and the things she'd seen deep in the castle valley, of the thrill of that other world. She would not remember how alive she'd been when she was the animal, focused on nothing but the hunt.

Because Asenka was right. Without Solmir, without the knowledge that she must keep her promise, that she must make him happy to repay him for all he'd done, that she must make herself happy and pretend that this life still held a place shaped for her to slip into . . . without all that, what her heart most wanted was to return. Her nightmare needled her, a gnawing worry for the Beast himself. Though it was only a dream, she could not shake the fear that there was some truth in it—that without her, the Beast's humanity was slipping away.

She could not banish the thought that the Beast needed her.

By the time the rest of the household had woken, Yeva had packed a few meager possessions into a bag. Her father's bow, which had been unstrung since the day she'd returned, stood next to it, string dangling from one notched end as if in invitation. She'd brought her fletching knife, some day-old bread and apples and dried meat, flint and tinder, a new cloak to replace the torn and muddy one Lena had insisted on burning. She brought only what she thought she'd need on the journey back to the Beast's castle.

Except for one thing, which served no practical purpose: she'd brought a book, one of the few volumes her sisters had managed to track down and buy back from the townsfolk who'd purchased Tvertko's possessions before the family departed a year ago. It was the book of fairy tales that her father had read to her when she was very small, so small that it was his voice telling her stories that colored her very earliest memory. She remembered perching on the sill of her bedroom window with the pane opened a crack so she could let the winter in, and she remembered letting it sting her nose and wash over her until she was shivering and blue.

"Ah, my little Beauty!" her father had cried when he lowered the book and saw her. "You'll be frozen to the core! Come away. What are you doing?"

"I'm listening for the Firebird," little Beauty had replied, voice shaking with cold. "Can't you hear it, Daddy?"

Her father set the book aside and strode to the window beside her. He wrapped her up in his warm arms, but rather than close the window and bring her back to bed, he stood listening too. And after a moment, she felt his whiskers scrape at her cheek as he nodded. "Aye," he said gravely. "I hear it."

"How sad it sounds," little Beauty said.

"Why is it sad?" her father asked.

"Because it is lonely."

Her father stayed quiet for a while, then sighed. "Perhaps we will give it some company. When spring comes, how would you like to come with me to my cabin? I used to live there, before I met your mother and we were given you girls. It lies deep in the forest, and I can teach you all about the things that dwell there."

"Does the Firebird live there?" Beauty had asked, brimming with sudden excitement.

"The Firebird, aye, and many other wonders. Would you like that, my little Beauty?"

Beauty had squealed and turned from the window and thrown her arms around her father's neck, making him laugh and fall back as though she'd been a wild beast whose weight had driven him to the floor. She was five years old.

Now, Yeva shivered despite the fire surging back to life before her. *How sad it sounds,* she thought, remembering the Beast's low, somber voice. *How lonely.*

Pelei, while overjoyed to see Yeva again, had nonetheless developed a quick and surprising preference for Radak. Lena said it was because of everyone, Radak had been the least generous with his affections for the dog, which seemed to make Pelei work all the harder to win him over. Though Radak protested he cared nothing for the creature, Lena privately confessed that most nights it was Radak who covertly invited the big shaggy scent hound up on their bed, to fold himself up in the hollow behind Radak's knees.

Doe-Eyes, however, still rarely left Yeva's side. It was Doe-Eyes who woke with her when Yeva bolted upright out of her dreams, and it was Doe-Eyes who padded downstairs with her when she woke early or wandered the back garden aimlessly.

And it was Doe-Eyes who lay across the front door now, trying to look easy and relaxed, but watching Yeva's every movement with an intensity that betrayed her. Even as servants stirred and began the morning's tasks, Doe-Eyes didn't move. Yeva wondered how she could possibly know this morning was different from any others, how she could possibly read Yeva's heart, but her time with the Beast had taught her how a creature could shout its intentions to the sky without ever making a sound. She knew Doe-Eyes could see Yeva meant to leave.

"If you wish to come," Yeva whispered, crouching down by Doe-Eyes and laying her cheek against the top of the dog's warm head, "then I will be glad for the company. But here you'll be warm and fed, and there I can't guarantee what we'll find. He might be—we might be on our own."

Doe-Eyes heaved a great sigh, blowing hot, wet air across Yeva's neck, and didn't shift from her spot guarding Yeva's belongings by the door.

"What are you doing up?" Lena stood at the bottom of the staircase, rubbing at her eyes. She was wearing a dressing gown over her nightclothes, and her hair was flattened on one side from her pillow.

Yeva searched for the words to tell her sister that she was leaving, that she was afraid for the Beast, but could find none. But after a few breaths Lena's sleepy eyes widened, traveling from Yeva, to Doe-Eyes skittering urgently from side to side, to the pack at Yeva's feet.

The sleep left Lena's face and she stumbled down the last few steps toward her sister. "Yeva! Where are you going?"

Yeva shook her head mutely, and gathered the cloak in her arms more tightly against her chest.

"No." Horror colored Lena's voice. "No, you *can't*. He's a monster."

Yeva closed her eyes. "I know," she murmured. When she opened her eyes again Asenka had emerged, drawn by the sharpness of Lena's tone, and stood on the stairs watching them. "He is a monster. But I believe he's a monster because of something that was done to him. I believe I can save him."

"You don't owe him anything!" Lena cried. "He's done nothing but hurt you!"

Yeva shook her head. "He let me go. And if I return to him now, we'll be on equal terms. I won't be hunting him, and he won't be hunting me."

"Why would you *want* to go back?"

"I . . . I can't explain it." Yeva sighed. "But . . . the Beast is not the monster. The monster is what he's become. He took me because he thought I could free him, and I mean to find out why."

"You mustn't." Lena, stubborn as always, stalked across the floor and snatched up Yeva's pack, as if she might prevent her sister from leaving if she could take away her supplies. "This makes no sense."

"Yes, it does." Asenka's voice came quietly from where she'd sunk down to sit on one of the steps leading to the upstairs. Her eyes never left Yeva's. "She's going to rescue him."

Lena stared from Asenka to Yeva, spluttering. "R-rescue? Yeva! You're no knight from an old story, and he's certainly no maiden in distress."

"No," agreed Yeva, fighting back the irrational urge to smile. "But I mean to try, nevertheless."

Lena's expression clouded. "You left us once before," she said intently, well aware that she was resorting to unfair tactics. "If it weren't for Radak and Solmir . . ."

Her sister's words cut. She had abandoned them in pursuit of revenge. But it was different this time. "But you have them now, for always," Yeva said gently. Her eyes flicked toward Asenka, whose face flushed, guilt and longing mingling in her features. "Solmir was never for me, Lena."

Lena, too, glanced over her shoulder at Asenka. Yeva knew from the look on Lena's face that she'd been right to release her fiancé from his promise.

Lena drew a shaky breath. "At least stay one more night," she begged. "One more dinner, one more evening before the fire. Please?"

Yeva hesitated, but even Asenka's expression was pleading, and her resolve crumbled. "One more night," she agreed, then turned for the door.

"Wait! Where are you going?"

"I must speak to Solmir." Yeva didn't have to look at Asenka to know what she'd find on her sister's face. "I promise, I'll come back. Here," she added, when Lena didn't look convinced. "Take Father's bow. I wouldn't leave it behind."

Lena took the long, curved staff of the unstrung bow in hands that were unused to holding weapons of any kind, and cast Yeva an uncertain look. "One more night," she repeated.

"I promise."

The baron's manor house stood on a rise on the other end of town, and Yeva took the long path that circumnavigated the busier streets. Though she often preferred to avoid the crowds who still looked at her like she was half spirit, half saint, today she simply wanted the time to gather her thoughts.

The Beast had been waiting hundreds, if not thousands, of years to break his curse. One more day would not be the end of him. And yet Yeva's heart felt tight and uncomfortable, and her feet itched for the soft give of the forest's carpet of leaf mold instead of the hard-packed mud of the town streets.

The gates of the baron's estate stood open, as they almost always did, and Yeva was not stopped until she reached the manor itself. The doorman showed her inside; Solmir must have given the staff instructions in advance. She was brought to a sitting room hung with tapestries—one of the baron's rooms, and not one she frequented as part of the baronessa's retinue—and left to wait.

She couldn't help but compare this room to those of the castle in the valley. Though this room had no hint of mildew or age, nothing worn or cracked or shabby, there was an obvious grandeur that Yeva found off-putting. The pieces in the room had been selected to show off the baron's wealth, and whoever had done the selecting lacked the taste of the castle's decorator, whoever he'd been, all those centuries ago.

She was inspecting the books displayed prominently on one of the shelves when Solmir appeared in the doorway. Last year, whenever he arrived to accompany Yeva on her walks through the forest, he'd appear disheveled and out of breath, eagerness flushing his face and quickening his steps. Now, she couldn't help but notice his face was grave, his steps unhurried.

He inclined his torso a few degrees when Yeva turned. "Good morning," he greeted her, crossing the room to take her hand and lead her to one of the couches.

She thanked him and sat, then abruptly found that everything she'd planned to say on her walk here had vanished from her memory. She stared at Solmir dumbly.

He stood by the fire, leaning one elbow on the mantel and looking exactly like a painting, a single frame from a story of lost love and tragedy. When Yeva didn't speak, his brows knit, concern coloring that grave face. "Yeva? Are you all right?" His eyes widened. "Is it your family? Is something wrong?"

"No," Yeva was quick to reassure him, finding her tongue again. "No, everything's fine." She hesitated, then glanced around the expansive room. "I've never been in this part of the manor," she said finally, "only in the baronessa's wing and the grand hall. It's . . . big."

At that, Solmir grinned, some of his stiffness relaxing. "Coming from you, I'm pretty sure that's not a compliment."

Yeva's smile came out in response, and she chuckled. "You know me too well."

"Well, you are to be my wife," Solmir replied, the grin softening and easing away. "I should know you well."

Yeva's throat tightened. "That's what I came to talk to you about."

"The baron's told me in confidence that I will be his heir." Solmir said it without much surprise, or pleasure, and Yeva could see the grief there. The baron was dying, and Solmir truly did care for him—far more than for the riches he would inherit. "He wants me to marry before he announces it publicly. He feels the people will be most comfortable if the new baron is taking steps to produce an heir, so that this period of uncertainty won't repeat itself."

Though the words were mercenary, even callous, Solmir's hollow voice said everything Yeva needed to know in order to be finally, utterly certain that she was right.

"Solmir," she blurted, "I know you're in love with Asenka."

Solmir's face froze, then drained of color as his lips thinned. "I'm not—that isn't what—I won't sit here and . . ."

Yeva wouldn't look away, though he squirmed under her gaze like a schoolboy being taken to task for misbehavior. "Solmir, I'm glad. I'm *glad*, you understand? I want you to marry her."

Solmir's face tightened further, and his voice was strained. "Yeva, I made a promise to you."

"And I to you." Yeva got to her feet and crossed to the mantel. "But why hold to a promise that benefits no one?"

Solmir's expression flickered, the boyishness peeking through his newfound gravity, before he shook his head and looked down. "It doesn't matter."

Yeva felt a flicker of annoyance. Asenka and Solmir were both so determined to be miserable—she shouldn't have to fight this hard to make them see she wanted no part of standing between them. "If it doesn't matter to you, then it certainly matters to me. I have no interest in being married to a man who's in love with my sister."

"I love you," Solmir said fiercely, as if he could make it so by saying the words with enough force behind them.

Yeva took his hand. "And I love you." She leaned forward, rising on her toes enough to press her lips to his cheek. "And want nothing more than to call you brother."

Solmir's face crumpled, and he pulled back, striding from the fireplace and shoving both hands into his hair. "It doesn't matter," he repeated. "It doesn't matter, because she won't have me."

Yeva stopped short. "What?"

"I asked her." Solmir turned, and Yeva could see guilt in every line of his face. "I asked her to marry me, months ago, when we believed—" His voice caught.

"When you believed I was dead," Yeva whispered.

Solmir nodded wordlessly.

"And she refused?"

Solmir cleared his throat, then cleared it again when the words still wouldn't come. "She told me she wouldn't marry me because she knew you were alive, and that you'd come back to us, and she wouldn't betray you."

Yeva's eyes closed, heart swelling. She didn't know whether she wanted to throw her arms around her sister or pinch her for being so stubborn. "You must ask her again."

Solmir glanced at Yeva, face agonized, so moved by feeling that Yeva almost felt music in it. "I couldn't bear to hear her refuse me a second time."

"Solmir," Yeva said gently. "Ask her again."

❊ ❊ ❊

That night Lena threw an elaborate dinner, conspiring with the cook to create a feast far beyond anything they'd eaten before, even at the height of their father's wealth. Though she said it was to celebrate Asenka's engagement to Solmir, Yeva suspected it was in no small part an attempt to keep her there. She'd promised Lena she would only stay this last night, but it was obvious they would be having the exact same argument all over again in the morning.

As it turned out, Lena was not the one she'd have to fight. Asenka and Solmir barely seemed to notice the rest of the family, or indeed the food. Solmir stared at her so dreamily that at one point he put his elbow into his bowl, and only noticed when soup soaked through his coat and burned his skin. And Asenka sat still as a statue, barely eating, flushing beet red each time she glanced up to meet his dreamy stare.

It was at the end of the meal, when Yeva was offering the last of her stew to Doe-Eyes under the table, that Asenka finally drew a breath and broke away from Solmir's gaze. "We're to be married in a week," she said, interrupting a conversation about the spring planting to come after winter's end.

Yeva started. She couldn't think when they'd had time to decide upon the date, but there they were, Solmir nodding eagerly and Asenka beaming down the length of the table at her.

"The baron wants a swift marriage," Asenka went on hurriedly, "so he can announce Solmir as his heir. Otherwise we wouldn't be so hasty."

"There's no need to explain," said Yeva, feeling a warmth inside her that hadn't come from the stew.

"We all know why you're pushing for a swift wedding," Radak added, laughing and earning an elbow in the ribs from his wife.

Asenka ignored this, her gaze on her little sister. "You must stay," she blurted, her normally soft voice peaking with urgency. "I know you planned to stay only one more night, but—Yeva, you have to be at my wedding."

Yeva glanced from Asenka to Lena, whose wedding she had missed, and her heart ached. That itch in her feet, the hollow in her soul that called for the forest and the valley and the Beast's song swelled. The animal ferocity of the Beast in her nightmare tugged at her heart. Autumn would soon become winter, and once winter came, it'd be too perilous a journey to attempt in the bitter cold and the waist-deep snow. But, gazing at her sisters, surrounded by her new brothers and the warmth of her old home and the dog at her feet, she found that the music seemed more distant than ever, more like a dream than a memory, and she found herself nodding.

"Of course," she whispered, and Asenka's eyes filled. "Of course I'll stay."

BEAST

He is gone forever now.
I am the WOLF.

TWENTY-THREE

THOUGH BOTH ASENKA AND her betrothed would
have been most pleased with a small ceremony, Solmir's new
status as the baron's heir required a certain degree of festival
when it came to his wedding. Yeva found herself so occupied
with preparations that she had little time to think of the Beast,
nor his valley and how she could break his curse. There were
holly branches to weave into garlands, dishes to arrange for the
feast, gowns to fit, dignitaries to greet.

Yeva continued to dream, but each day kept her so busy that
the nightmares seemed to vanish like morning mist in the sun.
She still had time; the days were long, and though they grew
gradually shorter, they hadn't yet seen the first frost to herald
the start of winter. And after her sister was married, she was so
exhausted from all the preparations that she convinced herself
that she needed rest before she set out. Her sisters said nothing,
though she knew it was on Lena's mind, for her father's bow
had vanished from its corner, no doubt hidden away to avoid

reminding Yeva of what she'd intended to do.

Asenka moved into Solmir's quarters at the baron's manor, and one week to the very hour after their wedding, the baron died. His funeral was a grand, solemn event, for he'd been a good landowner, and his people had prospered under his guidance. The last of the autumn leaves fell in a sorrowful shower of red and gold as Solmir spoke to the gathering across his predecessor's coffin. The shower of color reminded Yeva of . . . something. Something she couldn't quite pin down in her mind.

Though the baron's young widow made motions to move out of the wing of the manor that had been her home, Asenka wouldn't hear of it. She insisted that the former baronessa stay, and that as the new baronessa, she only needed a few small rooms for herself. Yeva came daily to visit her sister, and found the baron's widow often at Asenka's side, the two of them becoming fast friends. It was after such a visit that Asenka confessed to Yeva that she'd underestimated the baronessa, judging her from Yeva's descriptions of lavish parties and court gossip, and that the baronessa had done much of the governing while her husband had been ill. She was proving to be a valuable advisor for Solmir, who was considering throwing tradition to the winds and adding her in an official capacity to his council.

Asenka and Solmir set aside a suite of rooms for Yeva, asking her to come live with them, for Asenka had little interest in hunting and Solmir remembered his walks with Yeva as fondly as she did. Now the looming prospect of their marriage was gone, Yeva found her friendship with Solmir to be one of the closest she'd ever known.

Lena insisted that Yeva stay with them, in her old room, and Lena even stopped scolding Yeva for allowing the dogs up onto her bed. She said nothing when the laundrywomen complained of the difficulties of getting dog hair out of the linens.

Radak, surprising Yeva by showing her he knew her at least as well as her sisters did, quietly offered to purchase Yeva her own little cottage by the northern edge of town. It would ordinarily be an act of social suicide for a young, unmarried woman to live alone in her own home, but Yeva was such an odd figure in the town as a result of her time with the Beast that it wouldn't cause too many ripples.

She'd so longed to come home, but now that she was here, and with a flood of different homes to choose among, Yeva could not banish the twinge of discontent inside her. She no longer dreamed of the Beast, having managed to train herself to wake at the start of the nightmares when they came. But the town had no song, not like the forest or the Beast or his castle. And she was restless.

Lena's belly grew rounder each week, and Asenka's happiness was so infectious that Yeva couldn't bear the thought of leaving them. *A few more weeks,* she told herself, stubbornly watching the weather and telling herself winter was still far away. She had plenty of time to make it back to the Beast's valley before the snows came and made travel impossible.

And so Yeva, choosing to remain in her old room in Radak and Lena's house, threw herself into work. She helped prepare the baby's room. She went out riding with Solmir. She managed the household staff so Lena could rest. She had Radak teach her how to understand the family's finances.

Radak had gone on a spree when Lena first accepted his proposal, buying back the things Tvertko's family had sold to pay their debts. Not all of it had found its way back into daily use. Some of it had been tucked up in the attic crawl space to be dealt with later, but later had never come. There were books, and flatware, and linens, and trunks of old dresses long out of fashion. Yeva decided to sort through it all, keeping what still held meaning for them, and giving away the rest.

The hour was late on a chilly, windy night when Yeva crept into the attic storage space to sort through the dust-covered piles of belongings. She'd found that if she wore herself out, it was easier to go back to sleep after dismissing one of the Beast's nightmares, so she was awake long past the time the rest of the house had gone to sleep. She was rummaging through the trunks of clothes when she found a dusty roll of burlap tucked behind one of the chests. She tugged it free, choking on the dust and trying to stifle her coughs.

She unwrapped the cloth and discovered that it was concealing her father's bow.

It rested unstrung in her hands, feeling heavier than she remembered, and unfamiliar. And yet as she closed her eyes and curled her fingers around the grip, she found that her hands remembered its shape well, and found the touch of its smooth wood to be a comfort.

Beauty.

A shiver ran down Yeva's spine. The word had come to her mind so abruptly, and in the Beast's voice, that for an instant she thought he was behind her and speaking her name aloud.

Startled, her hands let go of the bow. Before it hit the ground, Yeva opened her eyes and found herself standing in a snowy wood. It was the clearing where the Beast had first laid his trap for her, and he lay with his back to her where he'd been before, side rising and falling with each breath, the snow around him churned up and trampled.

Yeva shivered, for she was wearing only a thin wool dress, and the snow was soaking through her stockings. "Beast?" The breathing caught and halted, and Yeva knew he'd heard her. "Beast, did you call for me?"

He didn't answer, and Yeva crept closer. The familiar sense that all this had happened before kept tingling at the back of her mind, along with alarm. *It's a trap,* her memory told her. *He's hunting you. Run away.*

But she knew the Beast now. And he knew her. She knew he wouldn't harm her. She reached out until she could bury her hand up to the wrist in his fur, the soft gray fur that smelled like spices.

The instant she touched him, the Beast leaped. He whirled, snarling with rage and bloodlust, and his eyes locked on Yeva. She scrambled back but then stopped herself, fighting the instinct to flee. "Beast, it's me!" she cried. "It's Beauty. You know me."

There was no response, not the tiniest flicker of recognition in the red, empty eyes. He took a step closer, his body moving like that of a predator stalking its prey. His lips curled back to bare his teeth in a wet, slavering growl.

Beauty felt a sudden stab of fear. This was not her Beast. This . . . this was a monster.

The Beast's muscles bunched, rippling under his long coat as he crouched. He launched himself and Yeva screamed, clasping her arms over her head and dropping into the snow.

Her knees struck wood and her eyes flew open. She was in the attic again. A heartbeat later, the bow she'd dropped clattered to the floor. Her stockings were dry, and though her body shivered with the memory of cold, she found she had no gooseflesh, no reddened fingers, nothing to suggest she'd left the warmth of the attic at all.

Her breath came like a sob as she staggered to her feet. The attic had no windows, only a vent at either end of the house to allow the air to circulate in summer. Yeva stumbled to one of the vents and tore the shutters loose, too rattled to work the clasp. The night air poured in, wrapping Yeva in cold and leaving her shivering in her autumn dress. Her nose tingled with the bite of frost, the first frost.

It was only after she'd been standing there for some time that her eyes adjusted to the darkness outside, and she saw that it had begun to snow.

Yeva threw the necessities she'd chosen all those weeks ago into her pack, hands trembling with urgency. Doe-Eyes jumped down from the foot of Yeva's bed, where she'd been waiting hopefully for her mistress, pretending to sleep while listening as she moved from room to room. More than ever, Yeva could read the dog's heart in her movements, and Yeva paused to grasp at Doe-Eyes's chin. "Yes," she whispered. "We're going." Doe-Eyes gave a sideways prance and then stuck her nose into the pack, smelling dried meat.

Yeva considered leaving a note for her sisters, but told herself she couldn't waste those few precious moments. In truth, she had no idea what to write. That she'd had a vision of the Beast, showing him as the monster they feared him to be, and for that reason she had to return? That finding him and breaking his curse was what she'd been born for, what she'd been yearning for all her life? That she'd never feel content here, in the home full of people who loved her?

No. Better to slip out now. They would wake to discover her room empty, and Lena would run to the attic where she'd hidden their father's bow. She'd find it missing, and see that Doe-Eyes was missing too, and she'd know Yeva was gone.

She put on her old leather leggings that Asenka had made for her at the hunting cabin, and then two woolen dresses overtop, and then her cloak for warmth. She strung the bow, bracing it across her leg and trying not to flinch at how her muscles shook at the effort. She strapped her supplies to her back and slipped the bow over one shoulder.

Yeva paused, bracing against the inside of the door as she stared down the entry hall into the sitting room. She could see her father there, in the claw-footed stuffed chair by the hearth that still bore the worn indentation he'd made over so many long years of sitting in the same spot. She could see him doubled over, his head in his hands. She heard his voice the night he learned of his caravan's fate, the voice that had become so sad, so broken. "Oh, Beauty."

She closed her eyes, groped for the latch at her back, and then slipped out into the night.

TWENTY-FOUR

THOUGH YEVA NEVER WOULD have been able to pinpoint the location of the Beast's valley on a map, nor describe to someone how they might find it, her heart knew exactly where to take her. She thought about renting a horse in one of the villages she passed after dawn, but decided against it. She'd found her way out of the valley on foot, and some part of her, the part that knew the rules of fairy tales like she knew down from up, was certain that she must be on foot to find her way back.

Doe-Eyes, too, seemed to know the way. For all she'd been wary, even frightened, of the Beast at first, she'd grown accustomed to living near a predator, and Yeva had the strangest feeling that the dog was excited to be returning. Though Doe-Eyes had spent every evening with Yeva's family stretched out in front of the fire with her head upside down and beaming in the heat of the coals, there was a spark to her now, a sort of life that had been missing in town.

With every step, Yeva felt lighter. Each league she closed

between her and the Beast made his pull all the stronger, as if she were a needle drawn to a lodestone. Her heart had grown so used to hating him that she couldn't make sense of how her feelings for him had changed, but she knew that just now, in this instant, this crossroads of her life, she was meant to find him. She could not tell what would come after, but she hadn't felt such certainty since the very first time she'd held her own bow in her hands.

She would find him. She would free him.

The snow that had sent her out into the night stopped later that first day, and the pale autumn sun was enough to melt it on the roads. But once she left the road for the forest, the snow lay beneath the trees in cool white swaths that marked out intricate patterns of shadow where the sun never penetrated the branches above. Each one seemed to point onward, north, illuminating her path.

Her sleep, when she paused in the pitch-blackness of night long enough to get some rest, was dreamless. The days flew as though the magic was pulling her onward, summoning her home.

The air shifted when she reached the river where it passed out of the southern border of the Beast's valley. She stopped at the water's edge, gazing down the glittering expanse. The river glittered in the afternoon sun, burbling against the rocks a few paces from her boots, and Doe-Eyes pranced over to lap at it noisily. Here the water was lively and dancing swiftly through its carven course, but a league upstream Yeva could see that it was frozen. The deep winter that froze time itself in the Beast's valley hadn't changed.

Yeva ran, throwing wisdom and endurance to the wind in her haste. Doe-Eyes let out an uncharacteristic, joyous bark and sprinted after her, falling into step at her side and breathing noisily. The air once again singed her lungs with cold.

The castle burst into view, looking as it had always looked, nestled in a cradle of ice and snow where it straddled the river that flowed beneath it. The sound of Yeva's pounding footfalls changed as she hit the stone of the bridge, which she'd once crossed so gingerly. She went first to the den, veering from the castle doors and sliding in her haste down the trodden path to the cave. Despite the violence of her nightmares, she felt no fear—she knew that if the Beast could see her, if he could only know she'd come back for him, the wolf would release him.

The den was empty. Gnawed bones littered the shadowy recesses of the cave, and she could smell him, but his scent was faint and seemed fainter with every breath. Yeva took a step back and looked down, and saw that her tracks were fresh and new but that they were the only ones that had broken the crust of an old snow. No one else had come this way in weeks.

Yeva whirled and made for the castle doors. One of them stood slightly ajar, as if in invitation. She hurried across the dusty marble of the great hall, past the room full of shattered windows, and into the one with the blue velvet divan and the table with books propping it up and tapestries covering the high windows to keep out the drafts.

It was dark and cold, and empty. Her heart ached at the sight of the hearth, which had always been burning bright or glowing with hot coals—she'd never realized how often the Beast must have laid the fire for her until now. She'd taken that warmth for granted, as though the fire had simply lit itself for her each day by magic.

Her legs refused to run anymore, and the ache in her heart began to spread. For the first time an icy trickle of fear lifted the hairs at the back of her neck.

Where is the Beast?

She moved back out into the great hall. Doe-Eyes, panting from the headlong flight through the valley, took one look at the stairs and dropped onto her belly before them. She cast Yeva a baleful look, and Yeva told her to stay before heading up the wide curving stair.

The library was empty, and the master bedroom too—but she'd expected that. It was the tower room she sought, the tower room where she knew she'd find the Beast. She pulled back the tapestry to find the secret door unlocked.

You may come here any time you wish, the Beast had told her. But Yeva's memory of his offer could not quite touch the rising fear in her heart that she refused to look at directly.

She climbed the steps two at a time, calling breathlessly, "Beast? Beast, it's me. Your Beauty." There was no reply, and Yeva imagined him so shocked that she'd return that he could not speak.

But when she burst through the second door at the top of the spiral stair the tower room was empty. The fire in the hearth was unlit, and when Yeva drew nearer and put her hand out to the ashes, she found them ice cold. The carpet crumbled and stank under her feet, and she saw that nothing had been cleaned, dried blood still staining the floor.

The Beast was gone.

Yeva could not think, could not move. She had been so certain she was meant to return, so certain that her whole life had been steering her toward this place, this time, this task. She knew that in it she would find everything she'd ever wanted, everything she'd ever imagined she could be. Instead she'd found an empty castle, as cold and dark as the winter in the valley surrounding it.

Yeva stood in the center of the room, shivering, her eyes seeking anything that might ease the blow.

The knife she'd used to slash the Beast's throat still lay on the floor where she'd dropped it. The smear of blood her leggings had made as she scrambled from him still streaked the stones by the wall. The book whose pages had been spattered by . . .

But wait, where was the book?

Yeva frowned, scanning the room again. That night was so intimately carved into her memory that she could see in her mind's eye exactly where the book had been: by the daybed, lying open as though the Beast had been reading it. She set her bow down and crossed to the far side of the tower room, where she crouched low and saw the faint outline of a rectangle where the book had lain, shielding the ground beneath it from the Beast's blood.

The Beast had moved it.

She summoned up that night once more, ignoring the sting of guilt in order to compare the memory to the room where she stood now. There, on the table by the window, illuminated by the pale winter sun slipping through the cracked shutters, lay the volume she sought.

It was closed. She picked it up and found a guinea fowl's feather between its pages like a bookmark, and she let it fall open there.

The handwriting inside was cramped and slanted, not penned by a scribe like most of the other books. Yeva could not read it. She flipped back a few pages and the writing changed, and then changed again, written by many different people. Past the page the Beast had marked, the vellum was blank. Yeva leafed back to the start and a series of numbers, more easily read than the cramped writing, leaped out at her. They were dates.

The book was a history. And as the occasional word emerged from the tangle of ancient lettering—*land, kingdom, tithe, heir, drought*—she realized it was the history of the family who'd once lived here and the land they'd ruled.

Yeva hurriedly flipped back to the spot marked with the feather. The language was so archaic that she could barely understand any of it, but she saw enough to know that the writer was describing a royal family. A king, his queen, his three sons, princes all. The feather marked the last entry in the book, with nothing to tell of what had happened to this land all those centuries ago, nor the family that had ruled it.

It was the name of the youngest prince that drew Yeva's gaze, but a speck of the Beast's blood had landed on it, making it difficult to read. She leaned close to the page, holding it under a shaft of sunlight.

Eoven, she read.

You may call me Ivan, the Beast had told her once, after she'd told him the story of the Firebird.

Eoven. Ivan.

With trembling fingers, Yeva picked up the feather that had marked the page with the prince's name. She'd thought it a feather from a guinea fowl, but it was stiffer than that, a tail feather from a bird far better suited to flight. She blew on it, dislodging decades or centuries of dust and grime, and ran a shaking fingertip along its spine to knit the disheveled barbs together. She reached out to hold the feather in the light.

The instant the sunlight touched it the feather seemed to burst into flame. Yeva gasped and almost dropped it, but her fingers felt no heat. She tilted the feather this way and that, watching as the sunlight caught and danced, turning the dull browns into fiery red, gold, and orange. Like the leaves in her dream of kissing Solmir, of kissing the man the Beast had once been, the leaves that had turned into a rain of feathers.

The Beast, before vanishing to wherever he'd gone, had left this book here for her to find. And though he could not tell her the origins of his curse, he could leave her clues to discover it herself. Yeva drew the feather close and heard, very softly, so softly she didn't dare breathe for fear she would drown out the sound, the tiniest pulse of music as it brushed her skin.

Her Beast was Prince Ivan. And the quarry he needed her to hunt in order to break his curse was the Firebird, the creature from her father's stories that Yeva had always loved the most.

To save him, she would have to kill the thing she'd longed for all her life.

Yeva picked up her bow.

TWENTY-FIVE

YEVA LET THE MUSIC of the wood wash over her. At first she didn't try to understand it or separate its pattern into individual threads of song. She stood in the center of the clearing, with snowflakes drifting around her like dust motes in a sunbeam, and listened.

When a familiar rhythm asserted itself, tugging her northward, she opened her eyes again and turned in the direction of the song and followed it. Doe-Eyes trotted next to her. The song was elusive, moving this way and that, and Yeva's instincts urged her to move more carefully, to stalk her prey as she'd learned to do. But she was not a hunter today—at least, not the kind of hunter she'd been before.

"Lamya," she said softly, when she sensed the song she'd been tracking was coming from all around her now. "Lamya, I need your help."

There was no reply, but the rhythm of the song changed, like a heartbeat quickening.

Yeva tried again, licking her lips. "Do you remember me? My name is Yeva. I've seen you here, and you've seen me."

Again there was no response, and Yeva's heart tightened. Without the help of one of the strange creatures that lived in this place, she'd have no idea where to start, no clue as to where to find the Firebird in the wood that stretched on forever to the north, to the edge of the world.

"It's for the Beast," Yeva burst out, voice ringing loud in the cold air. "It's for Eoven."

A gust of air nearly knocked her from her feet, the sound of massive wings shattering the quiet and blinding her with snow flung up by the wind. When Yeva had wiped the melting snow from her eyes there was nothing there—but then Lamya emerged from behind a birchling far too slender to have concealed her. She wore nothing but her long, black hair, which fell over her shoulders. "For Eoven?" she asked, her voice velvet.

"He told me he asked you to help him once before."

"He wanted to die," Lamya said dreamily, moving through the snow without stirring a flake, her bare feet perfect and white and showing not a hint of cold. "I have helped many that way."

"He said you couldn't kill him."

Lamya's black eyes swung round to meet Yeva's, and Yeva had to fight the need to shiver with all her might. "The Beast cannot be killed."

"I know," Yeva said, trying not to show her impatience. "I need to—"

"But Eoven can die," Lamya went on as though Yeva had not spoken.

Yeva froze, chilled as though she were as naked as Lamya. "What do you mean?"

"The world of men," Lamya murmured, "is so strange." She

rubbed her body against a rough-barked tree with a little sigh of pleasure. A normal woman would have been left scratched and bleeding, but Lamya's skin only shone all the brighter. When she continued moving, inscribing a wide, lazy circle around the clearing, Yeva saw a glimmer of scales left behind on the tree's bark.

Lamya continued. "For you all things have one nature. Winter is cold. Death is a tragedy. But even in the world of men, this is not true. Your warmest memories are of winter, and the times spent near hearth and home. For the sick and the old death can be a gift. And yet you insist on seeing only the faces of things. I am a woman. I am a dragon. I am these things all the time, and I am never one but not the other."

Yeva's impatience grew. She couldn't afford to alienate Lamya, but the urgency in her heart made it almost impossible to stand and listen. "Please. Tell me what this has to do with Eoven. I've had dreams that he's lost himself, that the animal within him has taken over, and I need to—I need to know that he's all right."

"The Beast was a man and a wolf," Lamya said. "As I am a woman and a dragon. But the day I saw you with him in the wood, he was no longer those things. He was a man only. The face of him still spoke of the wolf, but his nature—the truth of him—was Eoven and not the Beast. You did that to him."

Yeva blinked. "How can that be? He was the Beast when I first came upon him in the woods. He was cursed long before I was even born."

"The Firebird made him a being of two natures," Lamya went on. "You changed him into two beings grappling for a single heart."

A little trickle of horror shivered down the back of Yeva's neck. "You're saying I . . . I caused the wolf to take over?"

"You let the man take over," Lamya corrected her, "and give his heart to you." She lifted a languorous hand and combed her fingers through the long length of her hair so that it fell slowly, carving out the shape of a dragon's wing in the air. "Now, without it, Eoven has no more strength to exist alongside the wolf."

Yeva's eyes burned. She slipped her hand into the pocket at her waist so she could curl her fingers around the feather there. "It was the Firebird that cursed him. And it's the Firebird that can free him. I must find it."

Lamya paused, surprise halting her sinuous movements for the first time since she appeared. "The Firebird?" she echoed. "No one has seen her for many years."

"You must have some idea where to find her," Yeva pleaded, desperation rising. "If I'm the one who did this to the Beast then it's all the more important that I fix it."

Lamya's brows drew together, and her eyes caught Yeva's. All at once their blackness called to Yeva, becoming not an empty abyss but the warmth of a soft, velvet bed. Yeva wanted nothing more than to stagger to Lamya's side and drown in those eyes. "I can help you," Lamya whispered, and her lips were as soft as her eyes. "I can free you from the pain in your heart. Winter does not have to be cold. I can show you heat. . . ."

Yeva found herself aching, found the sharp edges of her thoughts fraying. She was so tired, after all—tired of fairy tales and magic and empty castles, tired of wanting so intensely that she didn't know what she wanted.

Perhaps Lamya could be what she wanted. It would be so easy. . . .

"The Firebird, Lamya." Yeva held up the feather in her hand, her face flushed despite the cold. "Please."

Lamya's lashes fell, and as soon as her gaze left Yeva's, the spell vanished like smoke. "North," she said softly. "I have never seen the Firebird and I have wandered here since the first time the sun ever rose." Her soft voice held a deep sorrow, a longing that touched Yeva so deeply her eyes stung with tears. Yeva was not the only one for whom the Firebird was a symbol of wanting. "You will not find her here. Go north into the next valley, and the one beyond. What you seek can only be north."

Now that Lamya's heat had left her Yeva's body ached with sudden cold. She wrapped her cloak more tightly about her body. She discovered that Doe-Eyes was some distance behind her, belly low to the ground and ears back, her large round eyes fixed fearfully on the dragon-woman. Yeva backed up until she felt her dog's warmth press against her calves.

"Thank you, Lamya," she whispered. Then she ran.

Yeva had barely traveled a few leagues into the next valley before her exhaustion began to catch up with her. She'd slept so little in her haste to return to the Beast, her body now ached, and her eyes burned and itched in the dry, icy air.

She touched the feather in her pocket again. A fortifying warmth began at her fingertips and trickled slowly up her arm, spreading through her body and letting her blink away the exhaustion weighing her down. She could not be sure whether the feather's warmth was magic, or if it was hope that surged through her, urging her to push aside her desire to rest.

When she passed for the second time a gnarled tree, blackened by a strike of lightning, Yeva realized she was walking in circles. The innate sense of direction that had guided her this far had left her, and when she stopped, confused, Doe-Eyes halted too. The dog cocked her head, puzzled by her mistress's sudden lack of direction, then turned and trotted off through the trees.

Yeva called out for her, but for the first time since she'd been a puppy, Doe-Eyes didn't come running at the sound of her voice. Letting out a weary oath, Yeva dragged herself after her pup.

She broke out through a dense, icy thicket and found herself at the river's edge, the same river that passed through the Beast's valley below. Doe-Eyes was drinking from a hole in the ice, lapping at the water greedily. The sun briefly broke through the thick gray clouds and its glare on the river ice jolted Yeva from her weary confusion. Her eyes traveled upriver, and she saw that its course led through a pass between the mountains surrounding the valley she was in. The sun beamed down on Yeva's right cheek before vanishing behind the clouds again, and Yeva realized that the river flowed north to south.

"Thank you, Doe-Eyes," Yeva whispered. She'd found her road north.

Yeva discovered as she walked that she no longer had to listen for the magic of the wood—in fact, she began to feel deafened by it. Though the forest was silent, lacking even the little noises of a hibernating wilderness, her ears rang with music. When darkness fell she made a little camp, and huddled close to the fire with Doe-Eyes sharing her warmth under her cloak.

The magic swelled, and when Yeva looked up, she saw the song for the first time with her eyes. The clouds had cleared, and the sky was dancing. Ribbons of pale green and peach shimmered above her, robbing her of breath until her very heart seemed to beat in time with the magic. She leaned back against a tree so she could fall asleep looking up, and the dancing sky grew brighter and brighter until it burned red and gold and spread wings of flame and sang the Firebird's song.

Yeva woke with a longing in her heart so strong that she leaped to her feet and kept moving north without banking the fire or packing up her belongings. She left behind her food, her flint and tinder, the goose fat she'd been using to protect her lips and cheeks from the icy chapping of the wind. All she brought was what she'd fallen asleep holding: the feather in her pocket, the book of fairy tales tucked inside her cloak, and the bow in her hands with a single arrow to its string.

The sun was high and pale in the vast crystal-blue sky when a flash of brilliant rust red made Yeva skid to a halt. It had been days since she'd last seen even a set of tracks that wasn't hers, much less an animal to leave them. And now a fox appeared ahead of her, sitting primly in the snow with its tail wrapped around its haunches.

"Borovoi?" she asked, her voice hoarse from disuse.

The fox grinned at her, showing a row of pointy little teeth, and inclined its angular head. "That's one question spent."

Yeva drew a breath to retort, but paused, and instead inspected the little fox. Almost as she'd seen the ribbons of magic dancing overhead, she could see in the fox's face the grizzled, mossy beard, the hollow cheeks etched in bark, the ancient eyes of the leshy spirit she'd glimpsed that first day alone in the wood, before she met the rusalka. "You tried to kill me."

"I gave you what you asked for," said Borovoi the fox, the leshy. "I do not lie. Ask what you will."

Yeva could not take her eyes from the creature, caught by its dual nature, the eyes of the ancient forest spirit in the frame of its sharp-cheeked fox face. "I came here to . . ." But the song of magic and the roaring in her ears made it hard to concentrate. Yeva swallowed. "I seek the Firebird."

Borovoi grinned again. "Don't we all?"

"I must find it," Yeva said, throwing all her feeling behind her voice. "It's the key to everything I've ever wanted."

The fox's head tilted the other way. "What will you do if you find it?"

Yeva stared at the fox, exhaustion and confusion and magic tangling her mind so that she couldn't think straight. "I . . . I just want it. It is my destiny."

"The Beast can never find the Firebird himself, you know." The fox lifted one paw and chewed a bit of ice from between its toes. "The bird must come to him. That is why he believed he needed a hunter—someone to trap the Firebird and bring it to him."

Yeva stared at the fox. "The Beast?" she asked slowly, stupidly, her mind full of dancing ribbons of red and gold and a song she'd first heard one winter when she was five years old, sitting by a window and listening to her father read her a story.

"Has her song gotten to you already?" the fox asked, sounding surprised. "I would have thought you'd last longer."

"The Beast," Yeva echoed again. Somewhere in the back of her mind, the word *beast* meant something to her beyond bears and boars and other dangers of the wood her memory conjured. Her hand crept into her pocket by itself, and her fingers touched the soft, worn barbs of a feather. "The Beast!" she cried, remembering. "Yes. I need to find the Firebird for the Beast."

"Go north," said the fox.

"I've *been* going north," Yeva protested, aware that at any moment her exhaustion would catch up with her and she'd be able to travel no farther. "I've been going north for years."

"That's because the Firebird is always north of you," the fox replied. "No matter how far you go."

Yeva stumbled on through the forest, and only by reaching out and finding Doe-Eyes's warm fur with her fingers could she remind herself that she was real, that this was real, that it was no tale from the book tucked close by her breast.

There would be a third, she knew. First Lamya the dragon-woman, then Borovoi the leshy, and now there would be one more. In stories there was always a third sign, a third test, a third bit of wisdom to urge the hero onward. Three wishes, three princes, three feathers, three hearts, three . . .

But Yeva walked, and walked, and found only the next valley, and the one beyond, and the one beyond, and the river she followed grew narrower and narrower until it was nothing more than a stream. She staggered up hills and climbed rock faces and eventually found herself beside a frozen waterfall that emerged like a crystalline blossom from a hidden spring in the rocks. The river's source. The end of her north road.

She saw pale green and peach reflected in the waterfall's frozen folds, and when she blinked and looked harder, she saw red-gold and fire.

She stepped out onto the frozen river, ignoring how it cracked and groaned under her weight. Dimly the sound made her think of some half-lost memory, another time she stepped onto ice that had not held her, but she could not quite remember what it was. Doe-Eyes stood on the bank and watched, and though she whined and cried and paced this way and that, it seemed she could not follow her mistress. And so Yeva walked on alone until she reached the waterfall.

The ice moved, the frozen sheets curling and parting like Lamya's hair, like falling snow before the wind, like autumn leaves from the peony tree. The curtains of ice opened for her like the massive doors of a castle she once knew, revealing that behind the waterfall lay a hidden cave. Yeva would have hesitated to go inside, but the cave was unlike any she'd ever seen, for the inside of the cave was brighter than the daylight where Yeva stood, as though it contained its own tiny sun.

Yeva stepped inside, and the moment her boots touched the cave's stone floor, the ice folded back into place behind her. She could not be afraid, however—in fact, she barely noticed she'd been sealed inside at all.

For before her, asleep with its wings wrapped round its body like a cloak, was the Firebird.

TWENTY-SIX

YEVA FELL TO HER knees. The sound of her body hitting the stone floor woke the Firebird, who lifted its golden head and looked at her. It looked at her like nothing in her life had ever looked at her—it looked at all of her, every inch of her heart, every shadow that had ever darkened her soul, every wrong thing she'd ever said or done or felt. It looked at her and bowed its head.

"Welcome, Beauty," it sang.

Yeva was crying, and not from grief or even joy, but simply because she was too full to contain herself. "I have been looking for you," she said.

"I know." The Firebird unwrapped its wings and stretched them, and Yeva saw they were like a falcon's wings, wide and broad and made for soaring, and their tips brushed each end of the cave though Yeva could have lain down across it many times over.

"I've been looking for you my whole life." But even as Yeva said it, something tiny and quiet stirred deep inside her. Something that, for the first time since she'd picked up the feather in the tower room of the castle, shook her certainty.

"Everyone is," the Firebird said. "But most stop searching. Most tell themselves they have found me in their mates, in their children, in their fields and in their gods."

Yeva's eyes blurred. "The fox," she whispered, trying to sort out memory from dreams, reality from story. "The fox told me you were always north of me, that you'd always be north of me."

"The fox has never found me," the Firebird said. "And he is jealous."

"What are you?" Yeva felt the Firebird's song in that hollow space in her heart, the space that had always known she wanted more than what her mundane life could offer her. "Desire?"

The Firebird spread its wings again, throwing back its head and showing its fiery, breathtaking plumage in a display that dazzled Yeva's half-blinded eyes. "I am the goal. The reward at the end of the quest. The end of the story."

Yeva put her hand into her pocket and touched the feather. Only then did she see that one of the Firebird's tail feathers was missing, and she started. "Eoven," she breathed, struggling to remember. "I'm here for Eoven."

"Who is Eoven?" the Firebird asked.

"I . . ." Yeva stared, bewitched, into the Firebird's knowing eyes. "I don't remember."

"I am what you seek," the Firebird said. "I am the conclusion of your journey. All you've ever wanted. Magic. The music of the forest. Forever. You are home, Beauty."

Yeva's eyes had begun to close, the Firebird's sweet voice warming parts of her she'd long ago forgotten. But her name, the word *beauty*, it rang in her thoughts and her eyes flew open. For a moment she saw not the Firebird, nor its crystal cave or the sky ribbons dancing at the edges of her vision, but a pair of gold eyes, and the rumble of a warm voice, and the feel of a blue velvet divan beneath her cheek.

She saw her Beast, and felt the lonely weight of his gaze, and heard the soft sound of his paws by her door, and smelled spices and wind and, just a little, the smell of wet dog—she remembered.

"You are not real," Yeva said, gasping. "It's as Lamya said. Nothing is in itself only one thing. You can't be all I've ever wanted because I've never wanted only one thing."

The Firebird's eyes narrowed, then softened. They held such acceptance, such knowledge of her. "I am everything," it said.

Yeva forced her hands to tighten, intending to drive her own fingernails into her palms to jolt herself from the Firebird's spell. Instead she found one of her hands was full, and when she looked down she remembered she was still holding her father's bow.

"You're right," Yeva whispered. "You are everything I want. Because you are what will save my Beast. You are the third test."

She raised the bow and fitted the arrow to the string and drew in one motion, so practiced and swift from her months of training with the Beast that it happened all in the quiet between one heartbeat and the next. The Firebird's chest swelled, its wings still outstretched as if daring her to shoot, as if certain she could not.

Yeva's fingers trembled.

I will call you Beauty, said the Beast. *For that is what you are.*

She loosened her fingers and let the arrow fly.

fire

snow

beauty

TWENTY-SEVEN

THE FIREBIRD'S LIGHT WENT out the instant the arrow would have struck it, and Yeva found herself in darkness so complete and solid that she cried out, dropping to the ground so she'd have something to touch, something to tell her she was alive and real. She groped around ahead of her, expecting to touch blood and feathers and the still-warm carcass of the creature, but all she found was a single feather it had left behind, like the one the Beast had left for her to find.

It glimmered at the touch of her fingers, just enough for her to make out the outlines of the cave. The ice curtain had sealed her in, and this time when she approached it, it did not part. It was as solid and as cold as stone. Her arrow had struck the far wall and sunk halfway up its haft into the rock. She couldn't pull it free, and without the sharp edge of the arrowhead, she had nothing with which to chip at the ice sealing the cave's entrance.

Fear surged through her like a winter wind, and like a winter wind, it left her teeth chattering. She was cold, colder than she'd ever been in her life, as though she'd been exposed for weeks but was only noticing it now. Her stomach ached with hunger, and she couldn't remember the last time she'd eaten. She felt dizzy, weak, lost in the dark.

I'm alone, she thought. Her father had taught her that she should never try to comfort herself by lying about her situation. *No heat, no food, and no way out.* She wedged herself in between ice and stone, trying to trap what little body heat she had left, instincts still fighting for survival despite what her senses told her: that she would die here in this cave of ice and darkness. Yeva couldn't help but cry, and it was only some time later, when they began to freeze against her cheeks, that her tears ceased.

If only the Beast were here, Yeva thought, her numb heart warming just enough to ache. *I would tell him I don't care that he's the Beast. I would tell him the Firebird doesn't matter, that he doesn't need to be cured. I would tell him my choice, that I would stay with him forever, and teach him how to find Eoven again, and keep him safe for as long as I live.*

She'd been so sure she was destined to save him that she'd left him to fade away.

The only warmth she could feel came from the feather clutched in her hands, and she lifted it up so she could see its pale light. A lick of flame danced along its edge and then whispered out, too tiny to generate any lasting heat, but Yeva could not stop staring at the afterimages before her eyes. The cave was empty, but with a jolt, Yeva remembered the bow in her hands and the book nestled against her breast.

She had fire. She had wood. And she had kindling.

Her hands began to work before her thoughts had caught up, before she could think twice, before she could stop herself. Who was she without stories, without the promise of the wood she hunted in and the gift her father had given her, to see the quiet, hidden tales the forest held? What was she without the restless wanting that drove her?

She ripped the pages from the book of fairy tales without hesitation, then tore them into smaller pieces. She took her father's bow and wedged one end into a fissure in the stone wall, and then heaved with all her might, crying again even before the great splintering crack rent the silence of the cave.

She set the torn fairy tales and the pieces of her father's bow at the foot of the ice wall, and then picked up the Firebird's feather. She held it in her cupped palms, feeling its light bathe her face one more time. Then she settled it down in the nest of kindling and wood, and let it burn.

Yeva dozed, huddled close to the tiny fire, waking now and then to blow on a failing coal here or tuck a splinter of her father's bow back into the flames there. The fire's heat was melting the ice, but slowly, far too slowly. Yeva wiped at the trickles of frigid water with the edge of her cloak so the moisture wouldn't swamp the fire, and rocked, and waited, and hoped.

She could not be sure how much time had passed when a change woke her with an urgent sense of dread. She automatically leaned for the fire to check it, and found it had dwindled to little more than a few faint coals, coated with thick white ash. She grabbed for the book of stories but all its pages were gone now, and the fire was too low and cold to burn the leather binding.

Yeva staggered to her feet and slammed her shoulder into the ice curtain with all her weight behind it, straining to hear some groan or crack or sign that her fire had thinned the door of her prison even a little—but even her imagination heard nothing. Stifling a sob of panic, she began ripping strips from the bottom of her cloak, finding the driest sections to add to the fire.

No, her thoughts screamed, as she tried again to budge the ice, throwing every ounce of strength she had left against the unyielding wall until her body ached with bruises. *The story doesn't end this way.*

But if her experience with the Firebird had taught her anything, it was that even here, at the edge of the world, life wasn't a story. If she died here no one would tell about it. She'd be one more soul lost to the wilderness, and the Beast would be left forever to run through the trees and hunt and feed without ever looking up, without ever seeing the dancing sky. Yeva slammed against the wall one more time and then stayed there, the side of her face against the wet, too-slowly-melting ice, its cold so shocking that it made her gasp.

And then, with her ear against the ice, she heard a sound. At first she thought it was the ice settling, but when it came a second time, and more loudly, she recognized with a new jolt of terror the roar of a wild beast.

The wall beneath her cheek shuddered, and Yeva lurched back. A chunk of ice fell from the other side of the wall, casting dim, pale-blue light into the cave. The creature roared again, and suddenly Yeva's heart filled. She knew that voice, would know it anywhere, whether it was whispering her name or roaring in fury.

"Beast!" she cried, renewing her efforts and slamming into the wall again—this time her efforts rewarded her with the faintest of splintering sounds. "I'm here!"

There came a great screeching as the Beast raked his claws down the wall outside, then another shudder as his whole body weight came crashing in against the wall. Yeva staggered back, sense reasserting itself and reminding her that he outweighed her many times over, and that trying to help him break down the barrier would most likely end with her crushed under an avalanche of shattered ice.

The growls and roars grew louder as the Beast carved away more and more of the wall. Beauty could see his shape behind the ice, silhouetted by the sun. It took only moments for the entire frozen curtain to fall in a shower of crystal fragments. The Beast burst into the cave in a brilliant glare of sun, blinding Yeva and making her throw up both arms to shield her eyes.

"Beast," she gasped, struggling for breath through her relief. "How did you find me? How did you know to look?"

But when there was no reply, Yeva lowered her arms and squinted through the sudden glare and saw the hulking shape of the Beast circling, head low, each step meticulous and calculating. His lips were drawn back in a snarl, and when she met his red, red gaze she saw no hint of the man she'd come to save.

She took a hesitant step toward him, and the creature's entire body tensed, the muscles in his shoulders bunching, his haunches readying to attack. Yeva froze, hand half outstretched, her mind going blank. She had no weapons anymore. Every bit of gear she'd packed, she'd left behind in a magic-induced haze.

Except . . . the age-worn feather the Beast had left for her was still in her pocket.

She started to reach for it, but the monster stalking her saw the movement and let out a snarl that rattled her very bones. Yeva had only an instant before he leaped at her, and she thrust her hand into her pocket and drew out the feather as she threw herself backward, shielding herself with both hands, instinctively, waiting to feel the Beast's crushing weight, the rending of her body with his claws, the cruel snap of his jaws.

They never came.

When she managed to open her eyes, Yeva saw the Beast looming over her, still snarling, panting with bloodlust—but his focus had narrowed to the feather clutched in her fingers. Compared to the soft, gleaming thing she'd used to start her fire, this feather was dull and dirty and bedraggled, battered by the centuries until it was barely recognizable. But the Beast stared at it, snorting steam into the frigid air, muscles trembling as if he were being held back by invisible bonds.

Yeva scrambled back, lifting the feather like a talisman, heart pounding painfully and fear leaving her mouth bitter and dry. But as the Beast moved to take a step after her, she found her voice and blurted the first words that came to her lips.

"Let me tell you a story!" she cried out. The Beast froze, though his gaze never flickered. Yeva had to draw three breaths before she found her voice again. "I will tell you a fairy tale."

BEAST

Story. Lie. Words. Meaningless. Empty.

She smells of something more than fear and blood. She smells like sky.

We snort and flex our claws until they grind on the stone but she holds us. We could devour her in one leap but she huddles there in her torn clothing and she holds us like no creature ever could.

She is magic. And we will wait for her spell to falter.

TWENTY-EIGHT

"ONCE," YEVA BEGAN, HER voice shaking, her whole body shaking, "there was a man. A king. With three sons." She couldn't push aside the fear that made her want to run for the mouth of the cave, to lunge for freedom. So she closed her eyes instead, and tried with all her might to fool her body into believing she was back in the Beast's valley, in a cell below his castle, speaking to someone on the other side of a locked door— her invisible ally, her friend, the man called Ivan.

"The elder sons begged him to name an heir, each of them wanting the power and wealth they knew would make them content. But the youngest son was different." Yeva's voice steadied a little. "He didn't want his father's throne, had never wanted the life spelled out for him by his birth. What he wanted, he couldn't name. All he knew was that he *wanted*, and that he'd never truly be home, never truly content, until he found all that he longed for.

"His father, the king, had a beautiful garden with a beautiful orchard that was his pride and joy, but every night an invisible thief had been stealing the golden apples from his most prized tree. He gathered his three sons and told them that whichever prince could catch the thief would be named heir. The elder sons were so eager to catch the thief that they fought and grappled with each other all night and missed the thief entirely. It was the youngest prince who, despite having little interest in his father's throne, caught a glimpse of the bandit.

"He came to his father in the morning and told him he'd seen the Firebird, the most elusive of all magic things, stealing the king's golden apples. The king sent his sons out into the world to find the creature, and though the young prince couldn't care less about the throne, the moment he'd seen the Firebird he knew it was all he'd ever wanted."

Yeva's voice, dry with fear and tight with cold, caught in her throat. She heard the Beast draw breath, and for a terrified heartbeat she thought he might leap—but instead he let out a long, low growl.

"Speak." His snarl was barely a voice at all, but there was a word in it, and it made Yeva open her eyes.

The Beast was crouched low, and stared at her with a red gaze that pinned her to the spot, like a serpent staring down a mouse it intends to devour.

Yeva shivered. "Th-the young prince set out to find the Firebird but before long a great gray wolf came out of the forest and demanded the prince's horse. The prince begged him not to eat his horse, but the wolf could not restrain his hunger, and soon had devoured the horse whole. But when the prince explained he sought the Firebird, the wolf took pity on him and offered to carry him to the next kingdom, whose king had boasted of owning the Firebird as a curiosity.

"The prince explained to this king that he needed to bring

the Firebird back to his father, and the king told him that he would give him the Firebird if Ivan would travel to the next kingdom and bring him the thing *he* most coveted, a horse with a golden mane. So the young prince went back to the wolf, who agreed to carry him to the next kingdom and the next king.

"The prince told his story again, and again the king took pity on him and said he'd give Ivan the horse with the golden mane if the prince would go into the next kingdom and bring back Yelena, the most beautiful maiden in the world, with whom the king had fallen madly in love. So the young prince and the wolf traveled on to the next kingdom, and there they found Yelena the Beautiful locked away in a high tower."

Yeva had left the original story, the one her father had read to her from the book she'd turned to ash, behind her. She knew she couldn't possibly guess the truth of Eoven's life, or how he had come to be cursed, or even what had driven him to seek the Firebird. But she'd seen the longing in her own heart reflected in his, in the loneliness of his castle and in the hope on every page of the storybooks he'd kept safe in the tower room all these long centuries.

The truth of his life was that it was Yeva's life, too. And there was a reason she'd always loved and hated the story of Ivan and the Wolf, and the Firebird that sent them out into the world. She'd just never known it until she met the Firebird herself.

The prince's curse wasn't arrogance or cruelty, as it was so often in fairy tales. His curse was wanting, always wanting. And so was Yeva's.

"The young prince went to the king of that land and asked him to release Yelena, but this king was older than the others, and he'd seen more of the world, and he warned Ivan to stay away. He said that no matter how much the young prince wanted Yelena, the satisfaction of desires sated was short and pale compared to the dream of wanting.

"The prince ignored his warning and went back to the gray wolf, who turned himself into a rope stair so that the prince could climb the high tower and take Yelena for himself. They returned to the king who'd asked for her, but when they reached his castle the young prince looked at Yelena and decided that he wanted her for himself, because love would make him happy, and he begged the wolf for his help. The wolf took Yelena's form and the young prince brought him to the king, who was overjoyed to have his heart's desire at least. He gladly gave the prince the horse with the golden mane. Once the young prince was beyond the kingdom's borders, the wolf escaped the castle and ran back to meet him and carry him to the king who'd asked Ivan for the horse.

"But when they reached the castle gates and Ivan looked at the horse with the golden mane, with Yelena on its back and a beautiful golden bridle draped with silk over its neck, he realized he didn't want to part with it, because freedom would make him happy. He begged the wolf to help him again, and the wolf turned itself into the spitting image of the horse with the golden mane. The king was so filled with happiness to have the horse with the golden mane that he told Ivan to go into his menagerie and take the Firebird. He warned the prince, however, not to take the solid-gold cage that housed the Firebird. But when the prince went into the menagerie and saw the Firebird, he saw the cage as well, and he thought that if he could take the cage too, he would have wealth, love, and freedom, and he would finally be happy.

"But as soon as the young prince touched the cage, its golden door opened and the Firebird sprang free. Ivan leaped to capture it, but he was able to catch only a single feather from its tail before it was gone, vanished forever into the north.

"When the wolf escaped and rejoined the young prince, he found him sitting at a crossroads with his head in his hands. The wolf asked him how he could be so unhappy, when he had the love of the most beautiful woman in the world, and the freedom of the swiftest horse in the world, and a golden cage worth enough to buy him any luxuries he could wish for."

Yeva thought of her home, her sisters, her friends Galina and Solmir—she even thought of the Beast's castle, and the books there she hadn't had time to read, and how beautiful the river would have been to walk along in spring. *If only I could break the Beast's spell*, she thought bitterly, *then I could be happy.*

"The prince confessed," Yeva went on, "that the last king had been right, that the dream was what he'd longed for, and he'd never be happy until he found the Firebird and everything he'd ever wanted. None of the things he'd found along the way would ever make him happy."

Her voice petered out, for there the story should have brought the prince home triumphant, to marry Yelena and inherit his father's kingdom and use the golden cage to establish a stable full of mounts sired by the horse with the golden mane, which would be so prized that they'd bring his kingdom a century of prosperity. But there the fairy tale ended, and Yeva lifted her face to find the Beast still watching her. The force of his stare had eased, though, and now that she'd fallen silent, he was starting to stir where he lay against the stone and rumble with discontent deep in his throat.

"How does this story end?" the Beast growled.

Yeva swallowed hard, clutching the old feather in her hand. "I don't know," she whispered. "The wolf and the young prince were cursed to stay together for the rest of their endless lives so that neither could ever be truly content. And only if the Firebird, the one thing the young prince had always wanted more than anything in this world, came back to him on its own, would his curse be broken."

The Beast's claws flexed, and as Yeva watched his face, the gray brows drew in a fraction and he dropped his gaze in confusion. "How do you know this story?"

Yeva's breath caught. "Because it's my story too," she whispered. "Because I thought I wouldn't be happy until I left town to live in the wood, and then I thought I wouldn't be happy until I could hunt every day, and then I thought I wouldn't be happy until I avenged my father's death. Because I spent a year in an old castle with the young prince and the gray wolf and I thought I couldn't be happy until I killed them both, and when I did, I wept harder than I ever have in my life. Because I thought I couldn't be happy until I went home, and then I thought I couldn't be happy until I came back."

The Beast's features flickered, and Yeva's heart began to pound, because there in the red, senseless, animal depths, she thought she saw the faintest glimmer of gold. Greatly daring, she crept forward, her every sense on alert for the slightest sign the Beast's animal nature might take over and cause him to strike.

"Because I thought the reason I'd always felt so restless was because I was meant for magic," Yeva said softly. "That if I could fix the story, that if I rescued the young prince and the gray wolf and I found the Firebird and I held in my hands everything I'd ever wanted, I would live happily ever after."

"How does your story end?" asked the Beast, his voice easing back toward the velvet bass Yeva had come to know so well.

Yeva gazed back at him, all her answers gone. A thousand

fairy tales flashed through her memory, full of quests and dreams and wishes and rewards. But the path ahead of her was blank, as empty as the leather binding of the book of stories she'd brought with her.

"I don't know," she whispered. "I think maybe it doesn't end." She inched forward again and lifted a hand, but the Beast didn't pull away, and he didn't snap at her. Her fingers crept into the soft fur at his chest, and his warmth banished the numbness of the cold. She felt the beating of his heart beneath her hand, and below that, the pulse of the magic binding man and wolf that sang as strongly as ever. Her eyes filled. "I'm so sorry."

The Beast's chest rose and fell under her hand in a sigh. "For what?"

"I was so close," Yeva replied. "The Firebird was here. I almost had it, but I was . . . slow. I could have saved you, and I failed." She lurched forward until she could lean against him, burying her face in his shoulder and feeling his warmth spread through her, chasing away the bone-deep chill the Firebird's cave had left her with. He smelled as he always did, and the familiar scent of wind and spice swelled inside her and she knew she had the answer to the Beast's question. She knew how her story ended.

In a rush, she blurted, "I would give up a thousand happy endings just to go back with you to your valley, and live as we did. I'd give up every fairy tale I've ever known just to hear you say my name again."

The Beast's warmth wrapped around her and the wild song of him swelled, and she could hear the ice curtain melting and dripping and saw in her mind's eye the crystal droplets falling like autumn leaves.

Then a voice whispered, "Beauty," and the warmth tightened, and she felt lips touch her temple, her cheek, the line of her jaw. She realized there were arms around her, and she broke away, gasping. Tears blurred her vision so that when she looked at the Beast she saw only a shimmer, the same shimmer he had when he saw her smile, or unlocked his room full of books, or lit her a lantern to keep the dark at bay. She blinked and blinked and finally her eyes cleared, and before her was a face, a human face. She'd seen it only once before, and a thousand times in her dreams.

"But," Yeva said, "how? I failed. I didn't bring you the Firebird."

The Beast knelt before her, seemingly unaware of the icemelt soaking into his clothes, which were of a fashion Yeva had never seen, from a time so long ago it predated even the oldest paintings and tapestries.

"Yeva," said the Beast, and though there wasn't a hint of a snarl in his voice, it still rumbled, still echoed in her heart and her bones, still warmed her from within. "We were both wrong."

He reached out and took her hands, folding them between both of his and drawing them up so he could press them against his chest, where the same heartbeat sounded, the same magic that called to her, only it wasn't magic, for the man before her was real, more real than the ice or the cave or the ancient feather, which she'd dropped somewhere in the slush, and forgotten.

"Don't you see?" the Beast went on, pulling her close so that she could breathe his scent, feel his hair brush her skin as he pressed his forehead to hers. "You are what I want most in all this world, and you came back to me. Yeva . . . *you* are the Firebird."

Yeva felt dizzy, confused not by the strangeness of this man she couldn't know, but by the fact that he wasn't strange at all. His touch was as familiar to her, and as certain, as the curve of a bow fitting in her palm. "This is a dream," she whispered. "Magic. A fairy tale."

The Beast smiled, and for the first time Yeva saw that he had a dimple, a little crease in his perfect face that made him imperfect, and that his nose was a little crooked, and the gold eyes were more hazel than gold. "Yes," he agreed. "And it's real."

A wolf and a man. A woman and a dragon. Hunter and hunted. Nothing in this world has only one nature.

The Beast's eyes fell to her lips and he bent his head, but there his movements faltered a little. The sudden uncertainty in the tilt of his mouth toward hers was so completely, so utterly human that Yeva felt she might laugh, or cry, or both. So instead, she leaned forward and kissed him, and he let go of her hands so he could wrap his arms around her and pull her body in against his. He was warm and solid and real, and Yeva felt as insubstantial as smoke that might drift away like the ashes of her bow and her stories.

She gave up trying to understand and just kissed him, there in the Firebird's cave. And though Yeva knew she would always long for tomorrow, and for what lay in the next valley, and for what colors she would see in the sky in the years to come, the kiss was, for that single instant, everything she wanted.

EOVEN

It is strange, to be whole. To know every thought and want is from my own heart. That every memory and instinct is mine.

Because I do remember another life. And not the life of the wolf, not the hunt nor the kill, nor the endless hunger. I remember a life before that was good, but not the one I wanted. I remember feeling as though nothing and no one in this world could ever understand the way I wanted, that pang that rings deeper than flesh and bone.

My longing for something else, beyond, into magic and dreams and the things everyone else seemed to leave behind as children. For something I knew I could never truly find.

It's the wanting that brought me here, to

her. To another soul as empty as mine, and yet not empty at all, because it's so full of everything I thought only I ever felt. Her soul against mine feels like music, like a heartbeat, like magic.

Like beauty.

EPILOGUE

EVENTUALLY YEVA WOULD BRING Eoven to the town where she grew up. She would tell her family as best she could what had happened, and they would not understand, but they would welcome Eoven anyway because of the way he looked at Yeva. They'd stay there for a long time together, and Eoven would tell Lena's daughter stories, and teach Asenka's twins to hunt when they were old enough. They'd stay sometimes at the baron's household, and sometimes in Yeva's old room in Radak and Lena's house, and sometimes in a little cottage at the edge of town with a garden and a peony tree and shelves full of books.

Her family would ask them eventually when they intended to be wed, and Yeva and Eoven would look at each other and realize that it hadn't occurred to either of them. Perhaps someday they would marry, and perhaps they would tell *their* children stories and teach them to hunt, and perhaps they'd live at the edge of town and add room after room onto the little cottage.

Or perhaps they would live in the forest, and never speak to another soul again but the trees and the beasts, and they'd tell their stories only to each other.

Or perhaps they'd journey to the far eastern sea and strike out for the edge of the world, where there were dragons, and women with hair like wings, and birds that caught fire when the golden sun hit them just so.

Perhaps they would do all these things.

But before any of it, Beauty and the Beast walked together back along the river leading from the Firebird's cave, with Doe-Eyes trotting at their side. They traveled through each mountain pass and saw that winter was fading away with every step, and when they arrived once again in the Beast's valley they found spring had come and that the windows in the tower room looked out over a meadow filled with wildflowers that bloomed in every shade of red and gold and brilliant fire orange.

And from somewhere past the mountains that separated the Beast's valley from those beyond, behind them, always to the north, the Firebird's song drifted in the air, and called to them, and waited.

A NOTE FROM THE AUTHOR

I dedicated this book to myself.

I've been writing Hunted since I was a child. In my head, in my dreams, in every retelling of Beauty and the Beast that I could consume. In gazing out the window on long car trips, in traveling the world, in those indescribable moments of completeness after reading a particularly beautiful book.

I wrote the beginning of this manuscript at the start of my career, as I waited to find out if my first book would catch a literary agent's attention. (It did. Thank you, Josh Adams.) When that first book became a trilogy, *Hunted* was put on a shelf to gather dust.

It stayed there for five years while I wrote my other books and navigated the new, unknown waters of being an author. It's an awesome job, but it can be all-consuming. It's easy to start drowning without realizing what's happening.

Fortunately, along came Kristen Pettit. My editor's whip-smart advice, along with my agent's encouragement, convinced me to dust off *Hunted* and really look at it again, and that's when I realized that I'd left Yeva in limbo—much like I'd left myself. Neither of us was finished yet.

Though I've never lived with a cursed Beast in medieval Russia, this is my most autobiographical novel. Yeva's dissatisfaction with her life was mine; her guilt over her restlessness, her tendency to pour herself into a single focus to the exclusion of everything else, her inability to fit into the world, her confusion about what she wanted and why she felt incomplete—all the things I'd carried with me the last five years.

So, to quote a favorite musical, I wrote my way out.

I'm blessed with an amazing network of friends, family, and fellow writers who gave me the courage—and, occasionally, the figurative kick in the butt—to keep going.

I owe an unpayable debt (for so, so many reasons) to my best friend and soul sister, Amie, who was this book's first champion and who remains its biggest fan. I'm also forever grateful for my family, who've always encouraged me to tell stories, and my extended family of neighbors and friends, who were among my first fans. I can't express how much support I got from my early readers, especially Cait, who's been asking for this story since we were in high school together, and Stephanie, who has helped me immeasurably as a friend, confidante, and fellow writer. I also must thank everyone who helped me research this book, especially Erin, whose expertise in Slavic folklore was invaluable, and Grimm, who, when I wanted to interview him about archery, put a bow into my hands instead and introduced me to a lifelong passion. And to everyone at HarperTeen, I am so happy and grateful to be a member of your team.

It's hard to admit that despite this network of support, it's difficult to let go of this book and send it out into the world. This book is me, and I've kept it to myself for a long time out of fear. But stories change you, if you let them, and *Hunted* has changed me.

So while I dedicated this book to myself, it's also dedicated to you. Male or female, young or old, if you're reading this book, then you're also that child reading by flashlight and dreaming of other worlds. Don't be scared of her, that inner Beauty, or her dreams. Let her out. She's you, and she's me, and she's magic.

There's no such thing as living happily ever after—there's only living. We make the choice to do it happily.

You are the Firebird. And above everything else, I'm most grateful for you.

**Follow Meagan Spooner to Sherwood Forest
in her next breathtaking retelling**

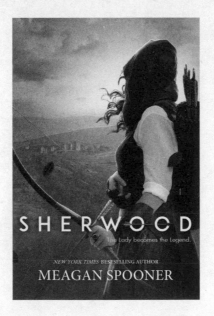

PROLOGUE

He wakes to the sounds of steel and fire, and the distant
wailing of a Saracen woman. His sword is in his hand before he's on his
feet. He'd been dreaming of rain on leaves, of the sound and feel of a wet
day in Sherwood. When he lurches out of his tent in the English-occupied
part of the city, the heat hits him full in the face, dazzling him as he tries
to escape the lingering memory of green and damp and earth. Sand stings
his eyes as a riderless horse gallops past, panicked, a long red line across
its flanks spilling a crimson curtain down its hide.

Before he can begin to tell friend from foe, a blade swings out of the
red-hot midnight toward his face. His sword hand lifts to deflect the blow
automatically, his shoulder taking the brunt of the impact. It's the battle
that brings him back to himself, banishing the last hints of his dream of
home—the frantic staccato of panting and grunting and steel scraping
bone and arrows whistling past. A second or two more and his opponent falls, screaming and trying to hold himself together with both hands
across his stomach.

There's no time to dispatch the Saracen. Robin is forced to leave the man there and fend off another blow from another assailant, knocking him back with an elbow to the stomach.

He is surrounded by the enemy. There are far too few English blades around him. He catches sight of a familiar man, recognizable more for his style of battle than anything else. By now they are all so burned by the sun and rubbed raw by wind that at first glance they seem no different from the infidels they're fighting. In the dark they might as well have been fighting amongst themselves.

"Where is the King?" shouts Robin, his voice breaking.

The other man screams a reply, but over the sounds of battle Robin cannot hear. The other man's sword sticks in his opponent's rib cage, and he's forced to plant a boot against the man's chest to pull it free. He gestures with his sword, then turns to reengage.

Robin sees a crowd in the distance, at the edge of the safe part of the city. Or what had been the safe part—the enemy has penetrated their defenses in the night, bypassing the fortifications. They must have killed the sentries in silence. The distant commotion is a cluster of a dozen English soldiers using a narrow alley to hold off a horde of Saracens one hundred strong. They're making for the edge of the city, guarding something.

The King.

Something thuds into Robin's shoulder, sending him off balance, and he whirls, searching for the blade he knows is coming. There is no one there. It's then that he feels the fiery lance of pain racing down his biceps and he gasps, sword dangling uselessly at his side. He cranes his neck and sees the fletching sprouting from his shoulder. He reaches up, bracing himself as he curls his fingers around the long arrow shaft buried in the muscle there. He breathes in, out, and in again, and then snaps the shaft off with a deft twist.

Robin sways to one side, dizzy, concentrating on the spots that swarm his vision for the space of a breath. Then he passes his sword to his left hand and slings his bow over his shoulder with the wounded arm, and gets moving.

He heads for a set of stone steps leading up to one of the roofs, hoping for a better vantage point. It's the route the women take in the mornings when they bring up their laundry to dry in the sun, and Robin clears the draped fabrics away with a swipe of his sword as he sprints up the steps. The city is lost. He can see it in the way the others are fighting, in the way most of the soldiers have gathered around to ensure the King's safe retreat through the postern gate. But there is too much distance to travel to reach safety. Too many enemies, and not enough blades.

He reaches the rooftop, but before he can scan the city, a shadow darts from a corner across his path. With a roar he raises his sword, momentum already bringing it down before his eyes focus on the figure running past. A child. A girl, which he knows only because of the way her head is covered. She cannot be more than twelve, and for a burning moment her huge black eyes meet his and she freezes. His sword won't stop. His left hand is too clumsy, too weak to divert it.

He throws himself to the side with a cry, his sword striking stone. The tip shatters and the sword leaps from his hand, skidding away. He can hear the girl screaming, speaking too quickly for him to understand any of the few words of Arabic he's learned. He looks up and sees her scrambling away from him to press her back against the half wall surrounding the rooftop. She's unharmed.

Robin pushes himself back up on his left hand, then staggers to the edge of the rooftop. He can still see the men defending the King. There are fewer attackers now, but there are fewer allies as well. Robin reaches for his bow.

Drawing it is an agony, and he can feel the wounded muscle tearing around the arrowhead still lodged in his shoulder. But his aim is true, and from this height he can reach the front line. An attacker goes down, replaced by another behind him. Robin looses another arrow and another man falls.

He sucks in air through his nose, the hot dust scorching his lungs. He can feel the weakness coming, can feel blood pouring past his armpit, down his rib cage. His aim is faltering. But he can see the King now, his crowned helmet gleaming in the light of a blazing fire engulfing one of the gatehouses. They are on the edge of the city. There are horses waiting—they need only to make it another few paces to the gates, which stand open.

Robin draws his bow again. One of the King's defenders goes down, and the firelight glints off a curved blade as its wielder races at the King. Robin draws in a long breath, willing his shaking arm to steady, begging his muscles to hold for one more shot, one last arrow.

Out of the corner of his eye: movement. The glint of light on a blade, the whisper of a soft sole against the sandstone. Robin could turn, could loose his arrow into the man creeping up behind him. His muscles quiver, and with a snarl of pain and focus, Robin narrows his eyes and lets the arrow fly. It courses straight and true through the air, inscribing a gentle arc down, down onto the battlefield, and buries itself in the brain of the King's attacker. Robin takes a breath—the King is away, galloping into the desert.

And then a blade crunches into Robin's side and he's knocked down against the stone with the force of the blow. He cannot move, cannot feel anything below his rib cage—there is no pain. Robin's eyes move slowly, lazily, sweeping across the rooftop. He sees the girl, pressed back into the corner as far as she can, everything covered except her eyes. They fix on his, wide and black. She is silent now.

"Marian," Robin whispers to her. "Don't be afraid."

There are voices above him, but he does not hear them. Instead he can hear rain, a gentle patter against broad green leaves. The smell of wet earth rises all around him, and the world is wrapped in fog. From beneath the padded armor under his mail, he withdraws a chain; on the end of it is a small gold ring set with a bloodred stone. He curls his fist around it, enclosing the little ring in the shelter of his fingers to shield it from the world.

"Marian, I'm sorry."

ONE

"MY LADY." THE VOICE was urgent. "My Lady, please—
please wake up."

Marian swam up out of a dreamless sleep, her mind groggy
and confused. It was dark, but as her eyes adjusted, the light of
a candle came into view. Behind it she could see a familiar face,
drawn and frightened.

"Elena," she croaked, dragging herself upright. "What is it?"

Her maid swallowed, the candlelight bobbing and swaying with the trembling of her hand. "It's my brother, my Lady.
They've got him, they've arrested him and they're going to kill
him at dawn. Please, my Lady, I don't know what to do."

Marian was on her feet before she could think, reaching for
yesterday's dress hanging over her changing screen. She threw it
on over her shift, ignoring the trailing laces at its back. "Where
is my cloak?" she demanded, quick and curt.

"Here, my Lady." Elena was shaking, terrified, but still competent. She thrust the cloak at Marian and then stepped back.

"What are you going to do?"

"I'm going to stop them." She wasn't thinking, just acting. She didn't know what Elena's brother had been accused of or who had arrested him. But Elena's family was from Locksley—Robin was the one who'd suggested Elena for a lady's maid and companion when Marian's mother died. *And I won't let Robin come home to find his people being slaughtered on his own lands.*

Marian flew down the stairs and into the courtyard, where a few torches had lit the way for her. Midge had Jonquille ready and was holding her by the reins. No sign of her father awake yet, for which she was grateful—she didn't have time to argue about whether she should or shouldn't go. Several servants were standing around in their nightclothes, candles transforming their drawn faces into waxy masks. A lad stood by the stables doubled over, red-faced and gasping. She recognized him as the son of one of the farmers from beyond Robin's manor house—he must have run all the way from Locksley town to bring Elena the news. At a dead sprint it was an hour's journey on foot.

Marian ignored them all and bunched her skirts up around her thighs, mounting the dappled mare and taking the reins from Midge. He hadn't bothered to use Jonquille's sidesaddle—this wasn't going to be some genteel day trip through the forest. *Thank you, Midge.*

Jonquille had picked up on her mistress's urgency, and as soon as Marian let her grip on the reins loosen, the mare leaped into a run. The glow of the torches in her manor courtyard fell away behind her, and she was left to race through the darkness.

Edwinstowe was quiet—her father's lands were small, and the town at their center even smaller, and his people all farmers. They'd stir soon, to feed and water their animals and work the land, but they'd sleep until sunrise.

Marian leaned to the side and cut through the finger of the forest that stretched across Edwinstowe lands, aiming for the King's Road. Branches whipped past, and she dropped her head, burying her face in Jonquille's mane. Jonquille knew the way. Locksley was her home, too.

The sound of Jonquille's hooves striking the earth changed, and Marian lifted her head. They were on the road. Not long now. Marian raised her eyes to the glimpses of sky she could see overhead as the branches passed. A terrible lightness painted the sky to the east the color of bloody ink.

"Hurry, love," Marian whispered, leaning low across her horse's neck, trying to lessen the resistance of her body in the wind.

The road forked. The road to the right would take her into the heart of Sherwood, while the road to the left passed through a hedgerow and then on to Locksley town, and beyond it, Locksley Manor. Jonquille knew which way to go without being told, and together they burst through the undergrowth bordering the fields with a gust of honeysuckle and heather on the wind. The landscape was awash in blue-gray light, the cold harbinger of the dawn.

There were torches burning in the center of town. Marian aimed Jonquille at the light, not bothering to slow her down. Men in chain mail stood in a semicircle around the town center, and a figure in dark gray armor and a black tabard stood at the head of the crowd. The Sheriff's men. Beyond them the townsfolk watched, pale-faced and silent.

In the center of the firelight was a young man on his knees in the stocks, a hood of rough-spun canvas over his head and tied around his neck. The soldier nearest him held an ax.

Jonquille broke into the crowd, people scattering left and

right and hens fleeing in a startled wave. Marian threw herself off the horse before the mare came to a full halt—all the better for no one to have time to see her with her skirts hiked up above her knees.

"I demand to know what's going on," she gasped, gripping Jonquille's reins more to support her shaking legs than to control the horse.

The man in the tabard was staring, and with a jolt, Marian recognized him. His eyes raked her over, from her wild hair to her muddy, day-old dress. "My Lady Marian," he said quietly, inclining his torso. "Good morning. Are you all right? You seem . . . distressed."

"Good morning, Sir Guy." Marian smoothed down her hair, abruptly aware that she wasn't wearing the modest veil she ought to have donned. "This man. What is his crime?"

Guy of Gisborne pulled off his horsehair helmet and over his hair. Scars marked the right side of his face, ugly welts of purple that traveled down and vanished under his high collar. "He has been accused and convicted of highway robbery and poaching, my Lady. This is no place for you—allow my men to escort you back to Edwinstowe Manor and I will visit you when I have finished here."

He was already turning and gesturing to the two men on the end, and Marian stepped forward swiftly. "Sir Guy," she said firmly, "I know this man. He is the brother of my own maid. There has been a mistake. Who have you been sent to arrest?"

Gisborne strode over to the young man in the stocks, his stiff-legged gait giving the sound of his steps an uneven quality. He ripped the hood away, ignoring the grunt of pain that emerged when the ties caught against his captive's jaw. "You are William Scarlet, are you not?"

Marian was unprepared for the shock of hearing his name. There'd been no mistake. Gisborne *had* been sent for Elena's brother. Will lifted his head, and Marian's heart sank. He'd been badly beaten, and his eyes were swollen shut. He turned his face toward her, but Marian couldn't tell if he could actually see anything through the bloody ruin of his face.

He didn't answer Gisborne, but spat a mouthful of blood and saliva into the dirt at his feet. Gisborne stepped back, glancing down in distaste.

"You see, my Lady," said Gisborne, "he has no respect for the laws of this land."

Marian wanted to shout at Will—his disregard for Gisborne's authority wasn't going to make her job any easier. But she calmed her thoughts, imagining Robin standing there instead, imagining how he'd handle this situation. *If he were here, this situation wouldn't exist.* She inhaled sharply. "And so you are to execute him? There is no room for leniency? What evidence do you have?"

"My Lady," Gisborne replied patiently, "please leave this to me. These matters are too upsetting for someone of your gentle upbringing."

"Sir Guy." Marian took another step forward. If nothing else, they wouldn't behead Will while she was standing near enough to be spattered by his blood. "Please. I am begging you to spare this man's life."

Gisborne gazed back at her, expressionless. The moment stretched, and then abruptly he turned away and signaled to the man with the ax. "Unlock him."

"Oh, Sir Guy—thank you, I will not forget your mercy." Marian moved forward as the executioner dropped his ax and unlocked the stocks. Elena's brother staggered to his feet.

"We will only take his hand." With a cold, metallic scrape, Gisborne drew his sword. He still carried the sword he'd worn in the Holy Land, as a soldier in the King's army, before he managed to get injured enough to be sent home to England.

Marian's heart froze. Before she could think, she was running forward, putting herself between Gisborne and Will Scarlet. She took Will's arm, lending him her support. They were almost of a height, and he was battered enough that he leaned heavily against her.

"Sir Guy!" she barked, summoning every ounce of command she could. "I demand that you release this man into *my* custody, pending a fair trial. He will be punished, but on *my* terms."

Gisborne lowered his sword, but his grip stayed firm. He was backing down only in deference to her presence, and Marian knew that the second she moved, Gisborne would exact his punishment.

"By what right do you lay claim to this man's fate?" Gisborne asked.

"He is from Locksley town, has lived here his whole life. He cannot have traveled far—the crimes will have been committed on Locksley lands. Though the new laws place these crimes under the Sheriff's jurisdiction, traditionally he must concede to a lord's right to try his own men." Marian tried to keep her voice from shaking. She knew it was improper for a landowner's daughter to have studied such things, but she'd learned some from Robin when they were children, and then from her father, who had never tried to convince her she didn't need to know about the law.

Gisborne frowned, but to Marian's relief, his face bore none of the shock that most gentlemen would display at a lady's familiarity with matters of jurisprudence. "Lady Marian—"

"I will be Lady Locksley," she continued, speaking over him and pitching her voice to carry, "the day Robin returns from the Holy War. In his absence, I demand the right to preserve the spirit of his governance over these lands."

Gisborne was silent for a long moment, watching her. The tip of his sword dropped, resting against the ground. Beside her, Will lifted his head again, and this time Marian could see the flash of his eyes set deep in the puffy skin around them. His breath caught, but he didn't speak.

"Then no one has told you," Gisborne murmured.

"Told me what?"

Before Gisborne could speak, Will jerked forward, shoving Marian hard toward Gisborne. She wasn't ready for his strength—was his unsteadiness as he leaned on her an act?—and she would've gone sprawling in the dirt were it not for Gisborne's quick reflexes, grabbing at her shoulders and hauling her up.

Marian twisted in his grasp to see Will sprinting through the fields, making for the line of trees marking the edge of Sherwood Forest.

Gisborne stopped long enough to make sure Marian's feet were under her, then jerked his head toward his men. "Shoot him," he ordered calmly, then reached for Marian's hand. "Are you unharmed?"

"No—stop!" Marian lunged for the nearest man, the quickest one to draw his bow. She banged into his shoulder hard enough to send pain shooting down her own arm, but more importantly sending his arrow corkscrewing harmlessly into the thatch of a nearby house. "He is *Robin's man*, do you understand?"

She could feel control slipping away. Something was wrong. The townspeople weren't even looking at Will as he disappeared into the trees, safe under their cover. They were watching her. They were silent.

Gisborne muttered something tense and cold under his breath, his eyes on the trees. "Stand down," he blurted finally, striding a few steps away and then turning. "Lady Marian," he said tensely, struggling with his temper. "That man is an outlaw, and there is no telling what crimes he will be willing to commit against the innocent now to stay alive."

"He's Robin's man," Marian repeated through clenched teeth, resisting the urge to massage the shoulder that had banged into the armored bowman.

Gisborne sucked a breath in through his nose, then snapped, "Robin is *dead*."

Marian's brow furrowed, her mind slowing to a halt. The world grew strangely hot and dry, a roaring like wind rising in her ears. "What?"

Gisborne rubbed one gloved hand over his mouth, regret bringing a hint of color to his features. "I am sorry, my Lady. I did not intend to—but it is true. Robin of Locksley is dead, he died three months ago in Jerusalem. We have only just had word of the latest casualties of note."

It's not true. Lies, plots against Locksley lands. The Sheriff's planning to take over, control the taxes, drive these lands into dust to line his coffers.

But she could not speak any of the words. She could only stare at Gisborne, taking in the details of his face as though they'd provide some relief, some hint that he was speaking false. The deep scar on his jaw and neck, suddenly different now, no longer the mark of a traitor—now she could not help but imagine such scars on her Robin. Except that his wounds would never heal, never scar over. She knew Gisborne could tell she was staring at his disfigurement, but she could not look away.

But he just gazed at her, a surprising sympathy in the grim set of his mouth. "I was going to come to you after I dealt with William Scarlet of Locksley town. As Robin is the last in his line, the Sheriff has appointed me to take over the governance and ownership of his lands."

Gisborne reached out for Marian's hand, but she pulled away with a jerk, stumbling backward. "No," she said finally. "No. Robin cannot die."

He paused, taking a careful step forward, approaching her like a man would approach a skittish horse. A detached part of Marian's mind wanted to laugh at his antics, scoffing at the idea that she was some fragile lady about to shatter.

I am the Lady Marian. I am a free woman and I am loved by Robin of Locksley. I don't shatter for someone like Guy of Gisborne.

This time when Gisborne reached out, he managed to take gentle custody of Marian's hand, turning it over so he could drop something small and cold into her palm. "Nevertheless, it is true."

Brow still furrowed, Marian looked down at her palm. The sun had risen while they debated Will's fate, and she could see the object clearly.

It was Robin's mother's ring. Tiny, understated, a simple band of braided gold set with a single tear-shaped ruby. Marian knew it well. She'd worn it every day after he gave it to her, until the day Robin left for the Holy Land wearing it on a chain around his neck.

"I am sorry, my Lady." Gisborne was still cradling her hand in his.

Read all of Meagan Spooner's romantic retellings of your favorite fairy tales.

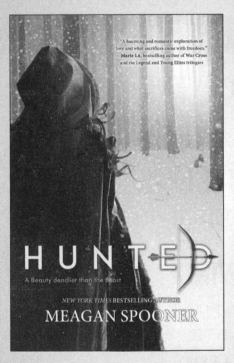

"A haunting and romantic exploration of love and what sacrifices come with freedom."
—Marie Lu, bestselling author of War Cross and the Legend and Young Elites trilogies

HUNTED
A Beauty deadlier than the Beast
NEW YORK TIMES BESTSELLING AUTHOR
MEAGAN SPOONER

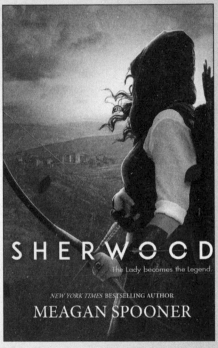

SHERWOOD
The Lady becomes the Legend.
NEW YORK TIMES BESTSELLING AUTHOR
MEAGAN SPOONER

★ Praise for *Hunted*: "Spooner creates a detailed world populated by complex characters. An elegant, classic, and vivid fairy tale."
—Kirkus Reviews (starred review)

An Imprint of HarperCollins*Publishers*

www.epicreads.com